Carrying on the Anatomical Studies

Left to right: Thorstein Veblen, Joseph Schumpeter, John Maynard Keynes, and Alfred Marshall.

The Economic Problem

ROBERT L. HEILBRONER

LESTER C. THUROW

Fifth edition

PRENTICE-HALL, INC. Englewood Cliffs, N.J. 07670

Library of Congress Cataloging in Publication Data

HEILBRONER, ROBERT L.
　The economic problem.

　Includes index.
　　1. Economics.　I. Thurow, Lester C., joint
author.　II. Title.
HB171.5.H39 1978　　330.9'04　　77-22555
　ISBN 0-13-233338-4

THE ECONOMIC PROBLEM, 5th edition
Robert L. Heilbroner and Lester C. Thurow

Cover design by Felix Cooper, from a photograph supplied by Mobil Oil Corporation.

10 9 8 7 6 5 4 3 2 1

Prentice-Hall International, Inc., *London*
Prentice-Hall of Australia Pty. Limited, *Sydney*
Prentice-Hall of Canada, Ltd., *Toronto*
Prentice-Hall of India Private Limited, *New Delhi*
Prentice-Hall of Japan, Inc., *Tokyo*
Prentice-Hall of Southeast Asia Pte. Ltd., *Singapore*
Whitehall Books Limited, *Wellington, New Zealand*

To the instructor

How can you best use *The Economic Problem?* We would like to think by reading it from cover to cover, but we recognize that constraints of time, and differences among interests of instructors or abilities of students, make that an unlikely outcome. Most users of the text will adapt it to their purposes, will stress some parts or chapters or supplements and pass over others. We have tried to make our text as flexible and adaptable as possible, and the purpose of this brief word is to indicate to the instructor our own suggestions for different uses of the book.

"An extra word about" some issue is appended to most, although not all, chapters. These supplements serve a number of purposes. Some are historical. Some are factual. A few are analytic. Many are policy-oriented. In the last category we sometimes deliberately argue a case, rather than stand aloof from the issue. Disagreement, from instructors or students, is welcome. Our hope is that these "Extra words" will spark lively discussions or even formal debates, as a relief from the steady march of pedagogy.

Now let us run over the main sections, indicating the chapters that seem essential, those that can be most conveniently omitted, or those that have some feature worth drawing to your attention.

PART 1 *Economic realities*

We have been impressed (and depressed) by how little economic students, even at graduate level, know about the basic contours and features of the economic landscape. The three chapters of the initial section of the test are therefore designed to draw a rough but reasonably accurate map of our major institutional realities, to suggest the dominant currents of change in those institutions, and to open for examination the major problem areas of the system.

Instructors who want to cover a good deal of analytic material will probably not have time to teach these chapters. We hope, nonetheless, that they will be useful for background reading.

PART 2 *Economic reasoning*

Chapters 7 and 8 ("The market mechanism" and "Tools of economic analysis") seem to us indispensable: they introduce the basic analytical concepts and vocabulary of economics. Chapter 9 ("Some basic economic problems") is probably the most expendable chapter of this unit, if time is short.

PART 3 *Microeconomics—the anatomy of a market system*

First a word to those who want to begin with macroeconomics. There is no reason why you cannot. The macro section was written before the micro section, to be sure that it would stand on its own feet.

Chapters 10 through 15 of the micro section follow the established tradition. We have relegated to our "Extra words" some material, such as "The optimal allocation of individual income" (following Chap. 11) that struck us as less than vital, and we have added a lot of "Extra words" designed to provoke class discussion.

Chapters 16 through 21 are less conventional. Chapter 16 has been completely reworked to bring in public goods, imperfect information, and externalities, under a general rubric of "Where the market mechanism fails." It probably requires special teaching attention. Chapters 17, 18, and 19 take up the theory and facts of income distribution. Here we cover marginal productivity theory, in a manner that tries to mix straightforward exposition with a carefully balanced criticism.

The truly new chapters in this section are Chapters 20 and 21. They introduce to the microeconomic curriculum the problem of the receipts and expenditures of government, usually covered only in a macro course. As you will see, we approach the subject partly from an institutional and partly from an analytic perspective. These should be interesting chapters to teach and discuss with students. (We guarantee that the section on sunk costs (p. 314) will provoke lots of heated dissent!)

PART 4 *Prosperity and recession—the economics of the macro system*

Even more than in our previous edition, we have tried to bring macroeconomics within the overall supply and demand approach to economic analysis. It's important, therefore, that students begin with a firm grasp of Chapter 7, where the market mechanism is first explained.

The sequence of topics in the first chapters (22–31) builds steadily toward Chapter 32, where the determination of GNP is the focus. The exposition has been simplified (the aggregate production function has disappeared), and the fundamentals of the supply-demand approach are as clear as we can make them.

Two basic chapters on money follow; then three more chapters in which inflation, unemployment, and various aspects of growth are examined. Obviously, the last three chapters are the least essential for learning about macroeconomics, but they are certainly the most interesting with respect to applying what has been learned. If time is short for teaching, we suggest they be used as required reading.

PART 5 *The rest of the world*   Not all introductory courses cover international economics, but a textbook would fail in its purposes if it did not present the essentials of this subject. Chapter 38, "Gains from trade," is probably the most useful single chapter of this section, if there is time for only one. Chapters 39 and 40 on foreign exchange are likely to be the most difficult. Some instructors may wish to assign Chapter 41 on the multinational corporation as supplementary reading, in view of the widespread interest in this subject. And the vast problems of underdevelopment and Plan vs. Market provide a "philosophical" conclusion to the text that we hope can be useful as assigned reading.

PART 6 *Quantitative methods*   The longish Chapter 44 is a very brief introduction to some central ideas of statistics and economics. We imagine that few users of our text will cover this chapter systematically, but it can be referred to when words like *correlation* come up in class.

Workbook and reader   We recognize that not all users of the text will want to use the companion volume, the combined student workbook and guide, but we should like to point out that the second book offers a reexposition of certain points that often present difficulties, a detailed set of "do-it-yourself" exercises, and a battery of true-false and multiple choice questions (and answers), as well as a number of readings. In addition there are major tests for each section of the text, answers for which will be found in the *Instructor's Manual,* along with additional test material.

Chapter-by-chapter analysis   In the "Guide to Chapters and Extra Words" we have established three categories: Basic, More advanced, and Institutional. The chapters designated as basic seem to us obligatory for an introductory course. The more advanced chapters can be omitted or assigned as supplementary reading. The institutional chapters are those for which the student needs least assistance with regard to the formal problems of economics. You will see that we have included a few chapters under more than one heading.

The "Extra words" have also been divided into the same three categories. Only one is designated as basic, a brief exposition of the elements of business organization. Every student should know the essential features of a proprietorship, partnership, and a corporation. A number of "Extra words" are classified as more advanced and can be easily omitted. The remaining "Extra words" are designated as institutional. We have put an asterisk next to those that seem to us best suited for class discussion or argument.

A GUIDE TO CHAPTERS

MORE ADVANCED **Institutional**

1 What this book is all about

Part 1 ECONOMIC REALITIES

2 Economic institutions—a bird's-eye view
   □ Business organization
3 The trend of things
   □ The rise of the market economy
4 Some major economic problems
   □ Capitalism

Part 2 ECONOMIC REASONING

5 The way of science
   □ Paradigms
6 Economic science
   □ The economic problem
7 The market mechanism
   □ The constraint of time
8 Tools of economic analysis
   □ Economic causation
9 Some basic economic problems

Part 3 MICROECONOMICS—THE ANATOMY OF A MARKET SYSTEM

10 Introduction to the microeconomy
   □ Private markets and public "markets"
11 Prices and allocation
   □ The optimal allocation of individual income
12 The market in movement
   □ Helping the farmer
13 Operating a competitive firm
14 The competitive firm in action
   □ R & D in competitive industries
15 The real world of imperfect competition
   □ Antitrust
16 Where the market mechanism fails
   □ The city
17 Distribution of income in theory
   □ Corporate saving
18 Distribution of income in fact
   □ Union rates and minimum wages
19 Changing the distribution of income
   □ The problem of equity
20 Economics of taxation
   □ Taxing wealth
21 Economics of public expenditure
   □ The military subsector

□ Extra words. *Those particularly useful for class discussion.

AND EXTRA WORDS

	Institutional	MORE ADVANCED
Part 4 PROSPERITY AND RECESSION—THE ECONOMICS OF THE MACRO SYSTEM		
22 Wealth and output		
□Public vs. private goods and services		□
23 Gross national product		
□Social indicators		□
24 Supply of output		
□ The U.S. standard of living	□	
25 Demand for output		
□Input-output analysis		□
26 Saving and investment		
□Raising the savings rate		□
27 Consumption demand		
□Aid in cash or kind	□*	
28 Investment demand		
□A capital shortage		□*
29 Motivation of investment		
□The elusive investment function		□
30 Government demand		
□State and local finances	□*	
31 Deficit spending		
□The New York City debt crisis	□*	
32 The determination of GNP		
□National income and product accounts		□
33 Money		
□Independence of the Fed	□*	
34 Money and the macro system		
□Monetarism		□
35 The problem of inflation		
□Incomes policy and indexing		□*
36 The problem of unemployment		●
□Government as employer of last resort	□*	
37 Problems of economic growth		●
□National economic planning	□*	
Part 5 THE REST OF THE WORLD		
38 Gains from trade		
□Trade adjustment assistance	□	
39 Mechanism of international transactions		●
40 The international monetary problem		●
41 The multinational corporation	●	
□Controlling the multinationals		□*
42 The underdeveloped world	●	
□Underdevelopment	□	
43 From market to planning	●	
Part 6 QUANTITATIVE METHODS		
44 An introduction to statistics and econometrics		●

Contents

1 WHAT THIS BOOK IS ALL ABOUT, 1

Myster of money   Language of economics   The "difficulty" of economics   Organizing the subject   Economic realities, Part 1   From fact to theory   From theory to practice   The rest of the world   Economic measurements   How should you study economics?   Vocabulary   Diagrams   Key ideas   Questions   Extra words about various subjects   Abstraction

1 Economic realities

2 ECONOMIC INSTITUTIONS—
A BIRD'S EYE VIEW, 8

Politics and economics   Economic individualism   Individual self-interest   Private property   Means of production   Property rights   The case against private property   The case for property   Limits of property   The market mechanism   The flow of productive activity   Factors of production   Distribution   Complexity of the market   Structural elements   Business   Small business   Big business   The industrial sector   Big employers   Households   The work force   Participation   Occupations   Incomes   Distribution of income   The poor   The working class   The rich and near-rich   Middle class   Wealth   Middle-class wealth   Millionaires   Government   Government as buyer   Kinds of public output   Focus   An extra word about business organization

3 THE TREND OF THINGS, 29

The process of growth   Total output   The trend of GNP   Correcting for inflation   Per capita growth   Basic importance of growth   Sources of growth   Productivity   Changes in distribution   Changes in real incomes   Changes in shares   The elimination of poverty?   A theory of riches   Trends in business   Rise of big business   Sales vs. assets   Explaining the trend to business size   A continuing trend to bigness?   From small to large government   Rise of the public sector   Behind the trends   Government intervention   Behind the rise in government   Focus   An extra word about the rise of the market economy

4 SOME MAJOR ECONOMIC PROBLEMS, 48

Inflation   Inflation in retrospect   Recent inflationary experience   Causes of inflation   The shift to services   Increasing power in the marketplace   Expansionist influence of governments   Effects of affluence   A last word   Unemployment   Recessions and unemployment   Impact of recession   Unemployment vs. inflation   Curing unemployment   Big business   A conservative view   The corporation as social arbiter   Dissolution of monopoly   Regulation   Nationalization   Other possibilities   Power: the unresolved problem   Running out of growth   Exponential growth and resources   Resource availability   The technological factor   The heat problem   Doomsday?   Global inequality   Stationary capitalism?   A spaceship economy   Focus   An extra word about capitalism

2 Economic reasoning

5 THE WAY OF SCIENCE, 71

Scientific thinking   Reasoning and method   Scientific theories   Natural science and social science   Social science   The method of social science   Economics as a social science   Focus   An extra word about paradigms

6 ECONOMIC SCIENCE, 81

Economic society   Basic hypotheses   Hypotheses about behavior   Insatiable wants-in-general   Satiable wants-in-particular   Rationality   The economist's view of man   Hypotheses about constraints   Constraints of nature   Constraints and costs   Social constraints   Budget   Basic hypotheses   Economics as a social science   Focus   An extra word about the economic problem

7 THE MARKET MECHANISM, 92

Prices and behavior   Demand   Budgets   Diminishing marginal utility   Demand curves   The puzzle of bread and diamonds   Supply   Supply and demand   Individual and collective supply and demand   Balancing supply and demand   Emergence of the equilibrium price   The market clears   Characteristics of equilibrium prices   Does "demand equal supply"?   The role of competition   Two necessary aspects of competition   Maximizing is subject to constraints   Focus   An extra word about the constraint of time

8 TOOLS OF ECONOMIC ANALYSIS, 105

1. *Ceteris paribus*, 105   2. Functional relationships   3. Identities   4. Schedules   5. Graphs   6. Equations   Economic techniques reviewed   Economic fallacies   Focus   An extra word about economic causation

9 SOME BASIC ECONOMIC PROBLEMS, 116

Problems of data   Economic facts   Aggregation problems   Problems of concepts   Abstraction   Importance of institutions   Tautologies   Problems of prediction   The problem of behavior   Imperfect knowledge   The problem of expectations   Increasing indeterminacy   Is economic theory useful?   Conceptual clarity   Ordinary applicability   Goal-oriented economics   Policy and behavior   The question of goals   Focus

3 Microeconomics—the anatomy of a market system

10 INTRODUCTION TO THE MICROECONOMY, 128

Micro- and macroeconomics   Need for two approaches   The circular flow   The two markets   Production and distribution   Focus   An extra word about private markets and public "markets"

11 PRICES AND ALLOCATION, 134

Rationing   How the market rations   Reservation prices   Maximizing consumers' and producers' surpluses   Price vs. nonprice rationing   Market problems   Shortages   Surpluses   Focus   An extra word about the optimal allocation of individual income

12 THE MARKET IN MOVEMENT, 146

Shifts in demand and supply   Shifts in curves vs. shifts along curves   Price changes   Long and short run   Elasticity   Arc and point elasticity   Elasticities, expenditures, and receipts   Behind elasticities of demand: substitution   Marginal utility again   Necessities and elasticity   The importance of substitutes   Behavior and nature, again   Complements   The case of vanishing resources   Limits to market adjustment   Focus   An extra word about helping the farmer

13 OPERATING A COMPETITIVE FIRM, 167

The rational, maximizing, competitive firm   Economics of the firm   Entrepreneurship   Economic profit   The entrepreneur at work   The problem of scale   The factor mix   Law of variable proportions   Productivity curve: increasing returns   Marginal productivity   Diminishing returns   Average and marginal productivity   Total, average, and marginal product   The law reviewed   Marginal revenue and marginal cost   Marginal revenue product   Total costs and total revenues   Choice among factors   Bidding for factors   Factor pricing   Equimarginal returns   Remuneration of factors   Focus

14 THE COMPETITIVE FIRM IN ACTION, 182

Fixed and variable costs   Unit costs   Fixed and variable costs per unit   Total cost per unit   The cost profile   Average and marginal costs   From cost to revenue   From supply to demand   Between two horizontal curves   Average and marginal revenue   Marginal revenue and marginal cost   Firm and market supply curves   Profits   Working out an example   Entry and exit   Minimizing losses   Long-run equilibrium   Profits and equilibrium   Economic rents   Sources of economic rents   Long run and short run   Economies of scale   Increasing or decreasing long-run costs   Focus   An extra word about R & D in competitive industries

15 THE REAL WORLD OF IMPERFECT COMPETITION, 201

Pure competition defined   Competition in the real world   Monopoly   Motives and markets   Price takers vs. price searchers   "Pure" monopolies   Limits of monopoly   Cost curves for the monopolist   Selling costs   From cost to revenue   Monopoly revenues   Equilibrium for the monopoly   Monopoly vs. competitive prices   Regulating monopolies   Problems of regulation   Oligopoly   Oligopoly cost and demand   The fight for market shares   The "kinked" demand curve   Collusion and price leadership   Excess capacity and price wars   The drive for growth   Growth within markets   MNCs and conglomerates   Assets vs. sales   Monopolistic competition   Equilibrium in monopolistic competition   Cost of market imperfection   Consumer sovereignty   Effect of advertising   Is product differentiation a good thing?   Monopoly and inefficiency   Business and power   Focus   An extra word about antitrust

16 WHERE THE MARKET MECHANISM FAILS, 223

Expectations   Perverse reactions   Cobwebs   Lumpy investment   The problem of information   Transactions costs   Remedying market failures   Public goods   Characteristics of public goods   Free riding   Voting instead of buying   Privatizing public goods?   Externalities   Pollution   "Bads" escape the market   Marginal private and social costs   Social and private marginal costs and benefits   Controlling externalities   Regulation   Costs of regulation   Gains from regulation   Is regulation useful?   Taxation   Antipollution taxes vs. regulations   Subsidies   Are subsidies useful?   Externalities in review   Market strengths and weaknesses   Focus   An extra word about the city

17 DISTRIBUTION OF INCOME IN THEORY, 242

The pure model   Factors and factor services   Direct demand for factors   Derived demand   The supply curve of factors   Labor   The backward-bending curve   Individual vs. collective supply   Psychic income   Mobility of labor   Capital   And savings   The supply curve of savings   Allocating savings   Land   Land vs. space   Rents and incomes   Land rent   Economic or quasi rent   Rents and prices   Economic rents and allocation   Economic rents and incomes   Capitalization   Capitalization and economic rents   Market price for factors   The marginal productivity theory of distribution   No exploitation   Prices and productivities   Marginal productivity and "justice"   Focus   An extra word about corporate saving

18 DISTRIBUTION OF INCOME IN FACT, 259

Rich and poor   Poverty   Low wages   Riches   Property   Instant wealth   Capitalization   The middle strata   Some basic problems   Market imperfections   Ignorance and luck   Time lags   Monopolies   Rents and discrimination   Discrimination against blacks   Discrimination against women   Wage contours   Reference groups   Teamwork and group productivity   Internal labor markets   Uses of marginal productivity theory   Marginal productivity and justice, again   The problem of the starting point   Focus   An extra word about union rates and minimum wages

19 CHANGING THE DISTRIBUTION OF INCOME, 274

1. Changing productivities 2. Intervening on the demand side of the market 3. Taxes and transfers Impact of taxes Effectiveness of transfers Negative Income Tax Work incentives The problem of costs The political issue In review Value judgments in economics Equity vs. efficiency Pareto optimality Economics of exchange Efficiency as a value: more is better Individual preferences Efficiency and policy The dilemma of values Test of social values Focus An extra word about the problem of equity

20 ECONOMICS OF TAXATION, 289

Revenue Federal vs. state and local revenue sources Tax systems Incidence of taxation The case of a sales tax Effects of elasticity Impact on factors Complexity of incidence Regressivity of sales taxes Personal income taxes Progressivity of income taxes Effect of deductions Tax expenditures Vertical effect Loss of progressivity Corporate income taxes Tax integration? Social Security taxes Property taxes Space vs. land Property taxes and wealth Total incidence A proportional system Tax equity Horizontal equity again Is tax reform possible? Focus An extra word about taxing wealth

21 ECONOMICS OF PUBLIC EXPENDITURE, 305

Microeconomic approach Types and kinds of expenditure Where markets do and do not apply Difficulties of local financing Rising state and local responsibilities Grants-in-aid Voting The budgetary process Establishing the level of expenditure The asymmetry of spending and taxing Rational government expenditure Marginal utilities Cost-benefit analysis Overall usefulness Microeconomic methods Cost effectiveness Opportunity costs and budgeting Zero-based budgeting The irrelevance of sunk costs Expenditure incidence The role of judgment The market in a final retrospect Focus An extra word about the military subsector

4 Prosperity and recession—the economics of the macro system

22 WEALTH AND OUTPUT, 322

The macro perspective Output Following the flow of output Intermediate goods Final goods: consumption A second final good: investment Gross and net investment Consumption and investment Wealth Kinds of wealth Capital Wealth and claims Real wealth vs. financial wealth Wealth and output Focus An extra word about public vs. private goods and services

23 GROSS NATIONAL PRODUCT, 333

Final goods Types of final goods Four streams of final output Stocks and flows GNP as a measure GNP and economic welfare Focus An extra word about social indicators

24 SUPPLY OF OUTPUT, 343

Historical record Production-possibility curve Efficiency frontier Importance of the frontiers Law of increasing cost Shifting frontiers outward The supply of growth Labor input and production Participation in the labor force Monetization of work Hours of work Labor productivity Sources of labor productivity Changing sources of growth What we do not know about long-run growth Focus An extra word about the U.S. standard of living

25 DEMAND FOR OUTPUT, 361

Output and demand An economic model Cost and output Costs and incomes Factor costs and national income Factor costs and household incomes Costs of materials Tax costs Indirect vs. direct taxes Taxes as cost Depreciation Replacement expenditure Another view of costs and incomes The three streams of expenditure The completed circuit of demand Crucial role of expenditures The closed circuit From GNP to GNI Incomes and expenditures GNP as a sum of costs and a sum of expenditures Two ways of measuring GNP GNP and GNI NNP and national income The circular flow The great puzzle Focus An extra word about input-output analysis

26 SAVING AND INVESTMENT, 380

The meaning of saving Gross vs. net saving The demand gap The dilemma of saving The offset to savings Increasing expenditure Claims Public and private claims Completed act of offsetting savings Intersectoral offsets Real and money saving Savers and investors Transfer payments and profits Transfers Transfer payments and taxes Profits and demand Saving, investment, and growth Focus An extra word about raising the savings rate

27 CONSUMPTION DEMAND, 396

The household sector Subcomponents of consumption Consumption and GNP Saving in historic perspective Long-run savings behavior The consumption-income relationship Propensity to consume Average propensity to consume Marginal propensity to consume A scatter diagram In simple mathematics A generalized consumption function Individual vs. aggregate consumption Age Passivity of consumption Focus An extra word about aid in cash or kind

28 INVESTMENT DEMAND, 412

Investment: real and financial The investment sector in profile Categories of investment Investment in historic perspective Importance of investment The multiplier Snowball effect Continuing impact of respending Marginal propensity to save Basic multiplier formula Leakages The downward multiplier Focus An extra word about a capital shortage

29   MOTIVATION OF INVESTMENT, 429

Utility vs. profit   Expectations   Induced and autonomous investment   The acceleration principle   Autonomous investment   The determinants of investment   Interest costs Discounting the future   Interest rates and investment   The export sector   Impact of foreign trade   The export multiplier Focus   An extra word about the elusive investment function

30   GOVERNMENT DEMAND, 443

Government in the expenditure flow   Purchases vs. transfers Government sector in historical perspective   The main tasks of government   Economics of the public sector   Fiscal policy Taxes, expenditures, and GNP   Automatic stabilizers   Demand management   Full employment budgets   Time lags   Tax cuts vs. expenditures   Fiscal drag   Grants-in-aid vs. revenue sharing   Responsibility of public demand   Focus   An extra word about state and local finances

31   DEFICIT SPENDING, 461

Deficits and losses   Debts and assets   Real corporate debts Total business debts   Government deficits   Sales vs. taxes The national debt   Internal and external debts   Problems of a national debt   Perpetual public debts   Real burdens   Indirect effects   The public sector again in perspective   Public and private assets   Focus   An extra word about the New York City debt crisis

32   THE DETERMINATION OF GNP, 474

Supply and demand in macro   Short-run fixed supply   Demand curve for GNP   Short-run supply curve   Equilibrium   The circular flow   The demand gap   Movement to equilibrium Movement of equilibrium   The expansion process   Another view of equilibrium   Saving and investment   Interplay of saving and investment   Injections vs. leakages   Intended and unintended S and I   Ex post and ex ante   The paradox of thrift The multiplier   Slope of the leakage curve   A last look at equilibrium   Equilibrium and full employment   Focus   An extra word about national income and product accounts

33   MONEY, 492

The supply of money   Currency   Bookkeeping money   Federal reserve system   The banks' bank   Fractional reserves   Loans and investments   Inside the banking system   Assets and liabilities   T accounts   Excess reserves   Making a loan   The loan is spent   Expanding the money supply   Expansion of the money supply   Limits on the expansion   Why banks must work together   Overlending   Investments and interest   Yields Controlling the money supply   Role of the Federal Reserve Monetary control mechanisms   Asymmetric control   Sticky prices   Paper money and gold   The gold cover   Gold and money   Money and belief   Focus   An extra word about independence of the Fed

34   MONEY AND THE MACRO SYSTEM, 516

The quantity theory of money   Quantity equation   Assumptions of the quantity theory   Testing the quantity theory   Changes in V Changes in T Output and prices   Prices and employment Full employment vs. underemployment   Inflation and public finance   Money and expenditure   Interest rates and the transactions demand for money   Financial demand   Liquidity preference   Demand curve for money   Changing the supply of money   Determination of interest rates   Money and expenditure   The process in diagram   Monetarism   Modern quantity theory   The art of money management   Shifting liquidity preferences   Credit crunches   Monetary and fiscal policy   Focus   An extra word about monetarism

35   THE PROBLEM OF INFLATION, 533

The ABC of the inflationary process   Supply and demand once again   Supply and demand curves   Changes in total demand The supply constraint: bottlenecks   Demand pull vs. cost push The Phillips curve   The trade-off dilemma   Economic costs of unemployment   The unemployment option   Economic costs of inflation   Inflation and income   A zero sum game   Winners and losers   Fixed-income receivers   Labor and capital   No changes in recent years   Why is inflation such a problem? Inflation vs. unemployment again   The XYZ of inflation   The elusive Phillips curve   The quantity theory   The problem of expectations   Controlling inflation   Wage and price controls The recession approach   Stop-go   Inflation as a way of life Global inflation   Focus   An extra word about incomes policy and indexing

36   THE PROBLEM OF UNEMPLOYMENT, 551

The meaning of unemployment   The elastic labor force Participation rates   Severity of unemployment   Impact of unemployment   An analysis of unemployment   Easing the cost of unemployment   Causes and cures   Level of demand   Full employment growth   Technological unemployment Technology and the demand for labor   Incomes vs. employment   New demands   Employment and investment Industry-building inventions   Automation and employment Other causes of unemployment   Structural unemployment Employer of last resort   Frictional unemployment   Capitalism and unemployment   "Reserve Army of the Unemployed"   U.S. vs. European performance   Focus   An extra word about government as employer of last resort

37   PROBLEMS OF ECONOMIC GROWTH, 568

The business cycle   Short vs. long run   Cycles   Reference cycles   Causes of cycles   The multiplier accelerator cycle Boom and bust   Contraction and recovery   Government-caused cycles   Curbing the business cycle   Long-run stable growth Potential vs. actual growth   Demand vs. capacity Marginal capital-output ratio   Income vs. output   Balanced growth in theory   Balanced growth in fact   Policy for balanced growth   Necessity for adequate growth   The dangers of growth Growth and national planning   Plan or market?   Planning and freedom   A last word   Focus   An extra word about national economic planning

5   The rest of the world

38   GAINS FROM TRADE, 585

The bias of nationalism   Source of the difficulty   Gains from trade   Gains from specialization   Unequal advantages   Trade-off relationships   Comparative advantage   Opportunity cost   Exchange ratios   The role of prices   The case for free trade   Classical argument for free trade   The case for tariffs   Mobility   Transition costs   Full employment   National self-sufficiency   Infant industries   Producers' welfare   The basic argument   Frictional problems   Trade and welfare   Focus   An extra word about trade adjustment assistance

39   MECHANISM OF INTERNATIONAL TRANSACTIONS, 604

Foreign money   Mechanism of exchange: imports   Exports   Foreign exchange   Exchange rates   Buying and selling money   Equilibrium prices   Appreciation and depreciation of exchange rates   Balance of payments   Disaggregating the balance of payments   Items in the U.S. balance of payments   Two partial balances   Items on capital account   Summing up the accounts   The "balance"   Fixed exchange rates   Central banks   How central banks work   Importance of liquidity   Why fixed rates?   Focus

40   THE INTERNATIONAL MONETARY PROBLEM, 617

The pre-1972 crisis   Deterioration of trade   The fall on current account   Travel and transportation   Military expenditures   Investment income   Trends on capital account   Short-term trends   The gold drain   The gold rush of 1967–68   Curing the balance of payments deficit   The great monetary muddle   The crisis of August 1971   Painful options   The fight to hold fixed rates   Recent events   Dirty floating   Intervention of central banks   The OPEC crisis   A workable system?   Focus

41   THE MULTINATIONAL CORPORATION, 632

What is a multinational corporation?   International direct investment   "The American Challenge"   The international challenge   Emergence of multinational production   Motives for overseas production   Economics of multinational production   Problems for policy makers   Tax problems   Complications in the balance of payments   Political economics of multinational enterprise   Creating pan-national enterprises   National prerogatives   Host and hostage   Multinationals and world order   Unresolved questions   An unwritten ending   Focus   An extra word about controlling the multinationals

42   THE UNDERDEVELOPED WORLD, 646

Background to underdevelopment   Conditions of backwardness   Social inertia   Further problems: population growth   The population outlook   Nineteenth-century imperialism   Imperialism today   The engineering of development   Building capital from saved labor   Saving output   Problem of equipment   Foreign trade   Terms of trade   Third and fourth worlds   Private foreign investment   The crucial avenue of aid   Economic possibilities for growth   The critical balance   The economic outlook   Social and political problems   Collectivism and underdevelopment   Political implications   Social stresses   The ecological problem   Focus   An extra word about underdevelopment

43   FROM MARKET TO PLANNING, 670

Stages of economic development   Inception of growth   Present vs. past   Planning and its problems   Soviet planning   Success indicators   Profit as a success indicator   The market as a planning tool   Market socialism   Market vs. plan   Economics in mid-development   Private aims, public goals   High consumption economies   Public goods   Income distribution   Externalities   Malfunctions   The rise of planning   A convergence of systems?   Common problems   Convergence and history   Focus

6   Quantitative methods

44   AN INTRODUCTION TO STATISTICS AND ECONOMETRICS, 686

What this chapter is about   I. Some initial cautions   Quality vs. quantity   Patterns of movement   The problem of definitions   Updating series   Mountains out of molehills   Visual deceptions   Perspectives on data   Uses of statistics   II. Distributions and averages   Means   Medians   Another caution: choice of units   Means and medians   A simple illustration   Skewness   Modes   Which average to use?   III. Price indexes   Building a price index   Weights   New goods   New functions   Applying the indexes   Changing the base   Splicing   IV. Sampling   The logic of sampling   Sample size   Bias   Correcting for biases   V. Econometrics.   The use of functions   Functional relationships   Coefficients   VI. Correlations and regression   Analysis of relationships   Correlation and scatter diagrams   Regression   Least squares   Correlation coefficient   Multiple correlation   VII. Correlation and causation   What can correlation tell us?   VIII. Forecasting   Exogenous and endogenous variables   Performance   Limits of prediction   Focus

INDEX, 716

What this book is all about

Most students begin a first course in economics with mixed feelings. On the one hand, everyone knows that economics is terribly important. On the other hand, everyone has the uneasy feeling that it is terribly difficult. It may reassure you to learn that you are not alone in this frame of mind. Every year, national pollsters report that the public lists economic problems, such as inflation or unemployment or taxes, high on its agenda of worries. But every year the pollsters also discover that the economics and business pages of newspapers and magazines are those that are *least* read. It seems that we all worry about economic matters, but we all throw up our hands at the idea of trying to understand what worries us.

Why does economics have this curious mystique? Three reasons suggest themselves. The first is that economics is inextricably involved with money, and money is certainly perplexing.

Mystery of money

Why is a piece of paper "worth" anything at all? What do banks do with the money we put into them? Why isn't there enough money to go around at some times, "too much" money at others— to repeat the baffling opinions we hear.

1

Money is surely one reason for the economic mystique. But the problem with money is not its inherent complexity. It is that we all use money, talk about money, worry about money, without ever having been educated about it. One purpose of learning economics is to repair that serious omission in our knowledge.

Language of economics

A second reason why economics is generally regarded with unease is that it speaks in a tongue we don't quite understand. "Prices are up because of rising demand," says the TV commentator, and we nod our heads. But exactly what is "demand?" What makes it "rise"? What are those other words that the news commentators use with such assurance—gross national product, consumption, investment? What do they really mean? Because we do not "speak" economics, we wonder whether or not we are being bamboozled; and when we ourselves use the words of economics, we often know that we are partly bluffing.

Therefore another purpose of this book is to introduce you to the language of economics. Like all disciplines, it has a fair number of specialized terms, but economics is certainly not any more difficult to speak or to understand than any of a dozen familiar subjects. By the end of the course you should speak it pretty fluently.

The "difficulty" of economics

Last, there is the matter of the mystique itself, the reputation for difficulty that economics has acquired. It may come as a surprise to learn that there was a time when economics was reputed to be a rather easy subject, especially suited to the education of proper young ladies (this was in the 1830s). Later—indeed, up to the Great Crash of 1929—economics was still widely regarded as little more than common sense, instantly comprehensible by all right-thinking persons, especially if they thought along Solid Business Principles.

The aura of mystery that clings to economics today is mainly a product of the past generation or so, when economics itself came into national prominence. The aura is undoubtedly mixed up with the increased use of government powers in the economy, especially the use of spending and taxing to affect the level of national well-being. Here *is* something to be learned that is different from Solid Business Principles. But as you will discover, it is still nothing but logical thought, although applied from a national perspective, rather than from that of an individual enterprise.

Thus if there is one overriding aim of our book it is to demystify economics. Of course this does not mean that we can give you answers to all the problems of the economy. We don't know them. But we hope that when you finish the book, you will never again throw up your hands at the idea of thinking about economic problems. Once and for all, that should have lost its terrors.

Organizing the Subject

How are we going to study economics? We have planned this book to be as flexible as possible, for the lengths of courses and the interests of instructors differ. It may help orient you if we explain the basic layout.

Our book is organized into parts on economic realities, economic reasoning (or theorizing), micro- and macroeconomics, international problems, and statistics and econometrics.

Economic realities, Part 1

Our first three chapters give a bird's-eye perspective on the American economy—its size and shape, its great historical trends and tendencies, its immediately pressing problems. You can't begin to learn "economics" until you are roughly familiar with the things about which economics is concerned. Even if your instructor skips this next section and plunges right into Part 2, we suggest that you take an hour or so to read over "Economic Realities."

From fact to theory

After the tour of realities, we turn to a very different subject—the manner in which economists reason. There is, as you will quickly see, a special, *theoretical*, way of considering economic problems. By this, we mean that economists do not examine each problem by itself, contenting themselves with a careful description of what they see. Rather, economists try to examine problems to discover their underlying characteristics, much as a doctor examines a patient to discover "disease."

The doctor uses the word "disease" because the medical profession has *theories* about how the human organism works—generalized explanation that enable a physician to go beyond mere description into diagnosis and treatment. In much the same way, economists have theories about how the economy works—generalized explanations that allow them to go beyond description to diagnosis and "treatment" by policy prescriptions.

As we will rapidly discover, economists know much less about the economy than doctors know about the body, so that economic theory is a great deal less reliable than medical theory. As in medicine, there are diseases in economics for which no cure is known.

Nevertheless, we can make some important theoretical statements about economic events—statements on which we base both our diagnoses and our suggested cures for economic ills.

From theory to practice

Part 2 is a first guide to economic theorizing. But the main purpose of our study lies ahead, in Parts 3 and 4, microeconomics and macroeconomics. It doesn't matter which part you study first; both are equally important. The purpose of each is to extend your vocabulary and the application of economic reasoning to problems that have been allocated to that particular branch.

What are the two branches? In microeconomics you will study a set of problems ranging from agricultural prices to monopolies, and from urban decay to industrial pollution—problems whose common denominator is that we approach them from the perspective of the "micro" decision makers of the economy, mainly households or business enterprises or individual government agencies. In macroecoeconomics the focus will be on a different group of problems—mainly inflation, unemployment, and economic growth. These problems emerge also from the actions of individual decision makers, but we study them from the perspective of the economy as a whole.

The rest of the world

There is a terrible parochialism, or narrowness, that affects most of us in studying an economy as vast and powerful as our own. We think that it stops at our national borders. It does not, of course. The American economy is closely tied into the world economy, as we discovered with a shock when the Arab oil embargo created long lines at the gas pumps in the fall of 1973. In addition, theories and prescriptions of economics apply just as much to international economic dealings as they do to intranational (or internal) relationships.

Therefore in Part 5 we explore the world of international trade, international finance, international corporations, and international economic trends. Possibly you may not have time for this section in your course. We hope that you will find time to skim over the chapters when you have time to do so.

Economic measurements   Last, we have a special section on quantitative methods—economic statistics and "econometrics." Long before you reach those pages, you will see that economics could not exist without the measurement of economic magnitudes, and that we can't go very far unless we understand the nature of some of these basic measurements. Therefore, Part 6 explains ideas such as "averages" and "correlations" and "sampling." It will give you an intuitive grasp, although not a technical mastery, of these useful terms. The section is especially worth perusing if you have not had much math.

How Should You Study Economics?

Vocabulary   We have already stressed the importance of acquiring a new economic vocabulary. To become economists, you will have to learn at least a dozen words and phrases that have meanings somewhat different from those of everyday usage: *capital, investment, demand,* for example. You will have to master another dozen phrases that come awkwardly to the tongue (and sometimes not at all to the mind): *marginal propensity to consume* is a good example.

In economics, as in French, some people acquire new words and phrases easily, some do not; and in economics, as in French, until you can say things correctly, you are apt to say them very wrongly. So when the text says *gross private domestic investment* those are the words to be learned, not just any combination of three of them because they seem to mean the same thing. Fortunately, the necessary economic vocabulary has far fewer words than French has, and the long and awkward phrases get shorter and easier as you say them a few times.

Diagrams   Associated with learning the vocabulary of economics is learning how to draw a few diagrams. Diagrams are an immensely powerful way of presenting many economic ideas. Far from complicating things, they simplify them enormously. A supply and demand diagram makes things immediately clear in a way that a dozen pages could not.

So you must learn to draw a few diagrams. There is a great temptation to do so hastily, without thinking about the problem that the diagram is trying to make clear. A little care in labeling your axes (how else can anyone know what the diagram is about?) or in making lines tangent where they are supposed to touch, or cross where they are supposed to intersect, will not only make the difference between a poor grade and a better one, but will demonstrate that you truly understand the matter being illustrated.

Key ideas   Studying a vast subject requires organization. This means putting first things first and keeping details and secondary material in the background. To help you do so we have placed key words and concepts at the end of chapters. When you review, ask yourself if you understand the main ideas that they telegraph. If you do not, turn back to the pages on which they are discussed. Page numbers follow each word or concept, for easy reference.

We've tried to simplify the task of learning by putting a highly abbreviated and *goal-oriented* "Focus" at the end of each chapter. This summary does not necessarily embrace all the words or ideas of each chapter; instead, it will try to give you objectives as you review the material. It is an effort to highlight the point of each chapter.

Questions

To help in organizing the subject, take time to answer all the questions at the ends of chapters. We have tried to make them few and central. If your instructor assigns the Student Guide that accompanies this text, do those problems too. There is no substitute for working out an example or for jotting down three reasons for this or four reasons for that. Learning is a process about which we know very little, but we do know that the physical and intellectual act of writing (or mumbling to yourself) is much more effective than *merely* "thinking." Practice, as they say, makes perfect. You might reflect on the story of the sailor on a sinking ship. When asked if he knew how to swim, he answered, "Well, I understand the theory of it. . . ."

Extra words about various subjects

Economics has to be learned by arguing about it. Therefore after most chapters you will find a few additional pages—sometimes to add to your historical, statis-

tical, or analytic knowledge, more often to open for your consideration problems of public policy that are related to the issues we have studied. The policy issues are often controversial. We hope you will worry about them—not just read them. They are there to open debate, not close it.

Abstraction

The idea of arguing brings us to our last word of counsel. Economics, as we have been at pains to say, is really not a hard language to learn. The key words and concepts are not too many or too demanding; the diagrams are no more difficult than those of elementary geometry. It is economic *thinking* that is hard, in a way that may have something to do with the aura of mystery we are out to dispel.

The hardness is not the sheer mental ability that is required. The reason lies, rather, in a special attribute of economic thought. *This is its abstract character.* Abstractness does not mean an indifference to the problems of the real world. Economics is about things as real as being without work. Nevertheless, as economists, we do not study unemployment to learn firsthand about the miseries and sufferings that joblessness inflicts. We study unemployment to understand the causes of this malfunction of the economic system. Similarly, we do not study monopoly to fulminate against the profiteering of greedy capitalists, or labor unions to deplore the abuse of power by labor leaders, or government spending to declaim against politicians. We study these matters to shed light on their mechanisms, their reasons for being, their consequences.

There is nothing unusual in this abstract, analytic approach. All disciplines necessarily abstract from the immediate realities of their subject matters so that they may make broader generalizations or theories. What makes abstraction so difficult in economics is that the problems of the discipline are things that bother and affect us deeply in our lives. It is difficult, even unnatural, to suppress our feelings of approval or anger when we study the operations of the economic system and the main actors in it. The necessary act of abstraction thus becomes mixed up with feelings of economic concern or even partisanship. Yet, unless we make an effort to think analytically and abstractly in a detached way, we can be no more than slaves to our unexamined emotions. Someone who *knows* that corporations or labor unions or governments are "good" or "bad" does not have to study economics, for the subject has nothing to teach such a person.

You must, therefore, make an effort to put aside your natural partisanships and prejudices, as best you can, while you study the problems of economics from its abstract, detached, analytic perspective. After you are done, your feelings will assuredly come back to you. No one has ever lost a sense of social outrage or social justice by taking a course in economics. But many students have changed or modified their preconceived judgments, in one way or another. There is no escape, after all, from living in the world as economic citizens. But there is the option of living in it as intelligent and effective citizens. That is the prize we hope you carry away from this course.

ECONOMIC REALITIES

PART

1

Economic institutions— A bird's-eye view

We can't begin to study economics without knowing something about the economy. But what is "the economy"? When we turn to the economics section of *Time* or *Newsweek* or pick up a business magazine, a jumble of things meets the eye: stock market ups and downs, reports on company fortunes and mishaps, accounts of incomprehensible "fluctuations in the exchange market," columns by business pundits, stories about unemployment or inflation.

How much of this is relevant? How are we to make our way through this barrage of reporting to something that we can identify as "the economy"?

Politics and economics

It may help us if we think about how we organize our impressions of another aspect of society: the government. Suppose that you were asked to give a quick basic description of the American political system. You would surely not begin with a recital of the latest political goings-on, culled from the news magazines and the newspapers. Instead, you would start by describing the basic *premise* on which our governmental system is built, the principle of democracy.

2

8

Next you would explain how our democratic beliefs are translated into action by the *mechanisms* of voting, regular elections, and the like. Thereafter you would probably add a description of the main *institutional structures* of our system: the three branches of government, the division among federal, state, and local authority, and so on. Only then would you be ready to talk about the issues of daily political life.

We need to follow the same approach to gain a first overall comprehension of the American economy. We must begin by clearly understanding the basic *premise* on which the economic system is built. Then we must learn the *mechanisms* through which the premise is set into operation. After that, we can examine the main *institutional structures*.

Economic Individualism

What is the basic economic premise, the counterpart to the principle of democracy? The answer bears a resemblance to the foundation of a democratic government. In depicting our political system, we start from various assumptions about the inviolable political rights of individuals. In describing the economic system, we also start from assumptions about the primary rights of individuals, assumptions that we can label *economic individualism.*

Individual self-interest   The idea of economic individualism has complex ramifications, but its core meaning is simple enough. It is that each individual has the right to promote his or her self-interest by every lawful means.

This may seem like such a self-evident assumption that is is hardly worth emphasizing. But if we examine the scroll of history or look over the organization of economic societies today, we find that nothing like this premise is discoverable in most of the economies of the past or present. The idea of an economic *right* of self-interest has been missing not only from most of history, but even today is not to be found in many parts of the world. In ancient Greece and Rome, in medieval Europe, in Asian peasant societies, in China or the USSR, the idea of economic individualism would have been, or would be, regarded as abhorrent. In these societies, the claims of a larger community—a village, a clan or tribe, a political party or a nation-state—are automatically presumed to come first. The "right" of individuals to promote their own interests is admitted only to the extent that it does not interfere with the interests of the larger group.

Of course, even in our own society, self-interest is not an absolute right. No one can do exactly as he or she wishes in business, government, or private life. Partly through law, partly through custom, the self-seeking actions of individuals are constantly being restrained or denied. Yet, if we look for a basic principle underlying the flux of economic life—a principle comparable to that which underlies political life—we find it in the assumption that individuals have a right to economic "freedom," and that this freedom is not to be curtailed without serious consideration. On this premise is raised the complicated system we call *capitalism*, the system whose workings are the central focus of economics.

Private property   The significance of this fundamental premise becomes evident when we look for a moment at the idea of *private property,* an idea that we know is deeply bound up with capitalism. Private property takes on a special meaning in a society built on economic individualism, a meaning very different from the concept of simple ownership, the kind of ownership that makes you exclaim "That's mine!" when someone takes your hat. All societies recognize the right of individuals to the possession of some personal goods. Even animals have a kind of tacit recognition of "private property" in their nests or lairs or kills.

But under economic individualism, private property is extended in another direction, the direction of the production of wealth, in addition to the enjoyment or consumption of it. In a system of economic individualism, people own their own labor, which is regarded as private property that they may legally dispose of as they desire.

This may also seem the most natural thing in the world; but like economic individualism, it is not. Slaves and serfs, journeymen and apprentices under the feudal guild system, workers in some socialist countries are not legally free to offer or withhold their labor or to bargain over its price. Private property in labor is a distinctive characteristic of a capitalist system.

Means of production

The right to own one's own labor is an essential aspect of economic individualism, and perhaps we are surprised to find that it is by no means a universally recognized right. But there is an even more vital extension of the idea of private property under capitalism. This is the right of individuals to own the means of production, the instruments and agencies by which production itself is carried out. Not just clothes or homes, but fac-

tories and machines, warehouses, railroads, land and even knowledge (as in the case of a patent) can be privately owned under capitalism. Indeed, one of the most striking differences between capitalism and other systems, such as socialism, is that this right of personal ownership of the means of production is missing or severely curtailed in the latter.

Property rights

Extending personal ownership to include ownership of the means of production carries with it a prime consequence in a capitalist economy. It is that the goods or services produced by the help of machines, factories, land, etc., belong to the owners of the means of production. Cars rolling off a General Motors assembly line do not belong to the men and women who made them, the engineers who designed them, or to the managers who supervised their production. They belong to the company that owns the land and machines and sheds in which they were built. (In turn, the company belongs to the stockholders.)

So, too, the wheat coming from a farm does not necessarily belong to the man who planted or harvested it. Usually it belongs in part to the man who owns the farm, who may or may not be the planter and harvester.

The case against private property

Is this a fair arrangement? Socialists say that it is not, and that the automobiles or wheat ought to belong to the workers or to the people-at-large, not to the capitalists who own the factory or the landlord who owns the farm. Of course machines make men productive. But socialists argue that the machines and land would be useless without man's labor, and that there is no reason to remunerate their *owners* simply because they have been given the legal right to possess these powerful instruments of output. In addition, they protest that the ownership of the means of production is concentrated in the hands of a minority and that most wealth (as we shall see on pp. 21–22) is owned by a tiny fraction of society.

The case for property

Defenders of capitalism claim that private property has advantages that outweigh these arguments. They admit that wealth, including the ownership of the means of production, is highly concentrated, but they stress the flexibility of a system in which owners of property, in search of profits, vie with one another for the consumer's patronage. They contrast this dynamic quality of capitalist economies with the bureaucracy that has been the characteristic feature of most systems in which the means of production are owned by the state rather than by individuals. Further, the supporters of capitalism believe that the concept of property, especially the property in one's own labor, is an indispensable precondition for a society of political liberty.

The pros and cons of capitalism and socialism are a profound issue of our time, and one to which we will return. (See "An extra word," p. 66.) Here we wish to do no more than identify the "rights" of property as a fundamental attribute of the system we are trying to understand.

Limits of property

One last word about private property. Capitalism is not an economic system in which only private property exists. There is also a great deal of public property. In the United States, for example, the public school system, the roads, 40 percent of all the land are owned by various arms of government. In other capitalist nations, the extent of public property includes such economic enterprises as airlines, utilities, and automobile works, which are almost entirely privately owned in the U.S.

Moreover, *the rights of private property are constantly being reshaped by law.* What people can and cannot do with their property is defined by statute, not by some absolute right. Because you own your own home does not mean that you can use it to manufacture explosives or to give all-night parties that annoy your neighbors. Because you own a company does not mean that you can make whatever product you please without regard to existing laws, or that you can refuse to allow your workers to join a union, or that you can make false statements about the goods you turn out.

Thus the meaning of property is complex, a matter for lawyers rather than for economists. But the rights of private property in giving property owners a legal claim on output are nonetheless central to our system.

The Market Mechanism

Economic individualism, with its associated rights of private property, is the fundamental premise on which our economic system rests, but it is not the mechanism that sets it into motion. For that we must look to the market system, the flux of activity that knits the individuals of the economy into an operating whole, in much the manner that the mechanism of voting gives cohesion and force to the fundamental political principle of democratic equality.

What is the market mechanism? It is a vast, continuing web of transactions that reaches into nearly every corner of the economy. It is the buying and selling we see as we walk through stores or read about in newspaper stories of business "deals." It is the process of exchange continuously carried on as salesmen, purchasing agents, workers, landlords, and capitalists offer their privately-owned goods or services for sale or seek to buy the privately-owned goods or services of someone else.

The flow of productive activity

We are all familiar with this ubiquitous market system in which every one of us has participated as a buyer and most of us

---

GOODS AND SERVICES

What is a good? What is a service? It is very easy to answer the first question; not so easy to answer the second.

A *good* is any object that we can legally possess. In a slave society, a slave is a good. In our kind of society, goods range from ordinary objects of daily use, which we call consumers' or *consumption goods,* to objects used in production, such as machines or raw materials or factories themselves, all of which we call *capital goods.* Actually, the same good can be either a consumption good or a capital good, depending on whether we use it for our personal enjoyment or in the process of production: oil is a consumption good in a home, a capital good in a factory.

Services are enjoyments or useful activities that we buy without purchasing the object that gives rise to them. Movies are a service, since we buy the right to enter the theater, not the theater and the projection equipment. Factory labor, education, legal advice, fire protection, haircuts are all services. About a third of all our expenditures for personal use (consumption) are services, as we will see in a later chapter.

The difficulty lies in the fact that *all* economic wealth is ultimately reducible to services. Even the food we literally consume is useful because it yields the services of nutrition. Clothes gives us the services of warmth and adornment. Machines and land are valuable to us only because they give rise to a flow of useful services—physical and chemical effects—that enter into production. In other words, all economic activity finally consists in the production and utilization of services. The term *goods* refers to the strictly legal or institutional fact that we privately own some service-yielding objects but not others.

have participated as a seller (of our own working capacities). What we are not used to thinking about is the market as a *mechanism*. Yet, in fact, the continuous transacting of business does not take place in a random, unstructured way. On the contrary, if we look at it from a sufficient distance, the flux of transactions can be seen to "flow" in a regular direction.

Figure 2-1 shows us this flow in schematic form. Let us first look at the black arrows that go clockwise from households to business, and then from business to households. These arrows represent the movement of actual services or products from one place to another.

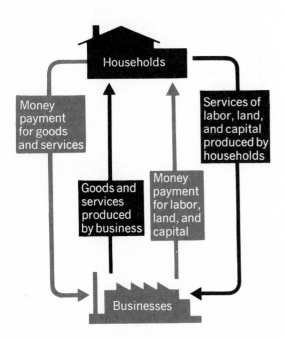

FIG. 2 · 1   The basic market mechanism

Starting from households, these services consist of the skills and energies of labor (and the physical services of capital goods or land) that householders produce and make available to business. Thereafter, as the black arrows show, the products that business has made from these services of labor and resources move back to the households, where they will be consumed.

Thus we can see that the market mechanism organizes the indispensable economic activity of production. The market mechanism is a great circular motion of economic activity converting labor, land, and capital into commodities that will renew and sustain the owners of these resources.

Factors of production

This is probably a good place to learn a necessary term of economic vocabulary. We call the services of labor, land, and capital the *factors of production.*

The term is usually employed to designate the actual physical outputs of labor services or the services of machines or land. Note, however, that the payment for these services goes to the owner of the labor, land, or capital. Thus, workers (including management) are paid wages (or salaries) for their work; landlords are paid rent for their land; and capitalists are paid interest for the use of their capital. Thus the words *factors of production* have historical and social as well as purely technical significance. A factor or production is not just a productive service; it is a productive service *offered for sale*. One can, perhaps, speak of "factors of production" in China or the USSR, but these words have a meaning different from their meaning in a capitalist economy. (See "An extra word" at the end of Chapter 3 for more of this.)

Distribution

We have seen how the market mechanism moves real services and goods "clockwise" around the economy. But we have yet to take note of another circular flow going in the opposite direction. This is the flow of money payments, also an intrinsic part of the transaction web. With every individual market transaction, goods or services move in one direction, and money moves in the other.

Our red arrows in Fig. 2-1 show us this second circular flow of payments going opposite to the flow of real activity. With every household purchase of a business product, money moves from the hands of householders to the hands of business. And with every purchase of the services of the factors of production, money moves from business into the owners of these factors—wages and salaries going to labor, rent to landowners, profit or interest to owners of capital resources. *Thus we can see that in addition to organizing production, the market mechanism also organizes the distribution or sharing-out of incomes.*

Complexity of the market

Of course, Fig. 2-1 does not depict the entire market mechanism. It has omitted a vital flow of goods

and services from one business to another, matched by a return flow of payments from business to business. No less vital, government has been left out, both as a buyer of goods and services and as a producer of outputs of its own, thereby linking the government with households and business. Figure 2-2 shows these complicated interlocks.

We will be returning many times to the market mechanism, for it plays a major role in the workings of a capitalist system. We should note here, however, that, as in the case of private property, the mechanism is far from simple. By no means all of the economic world is knit together by buying and selling. Parts of production and parts of distribution are organized along the lines of custom and tradition or command. Think, for example, of how religious or military activity is carried out, or how household income is divided up among the members of the family.

Moreover, the kinds of buying and

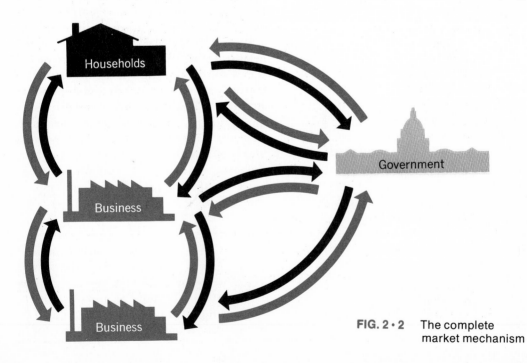

FIG. 2·2   The complete market mechanism

selling that we find in the economy vary greatly. The arrows that depict the sale of a factor of production represent very different realities if they represent a migrant farm worker selling his labor to a packing company, or a Wall Street lawyer selling his services to a client. So, too, the nature of the buying and selling that establishes interactions of steel companies and automobile firms is obviously not like that which governs the trading among sidewalk hucksters and their suppliers.

All these problems of market structure will assume their rightful places as we get deeper into the study of microeconomics. Nonetheless, in this first view of the economy as a whole, we are eager to put the market mechanism in the center of the picture, for it is certainly the most important organizing force in our economic life. That is why many economists speak of capitalism itself as a market system.

Structural Elements

Our identification of private property and a market system has done more than give us an initial sense of what we mean by The Economy. It has also begun to identify the main structural elements that we find in the economic system, elements compara-

ble to Congress or the Executive Branch. In this first fly-over of the economy we next want to gain a better impression of these dominant institutional features.

Business Of course we know where to start. Business enterprise is the very heart of an economic system of private property and market relationships. Let us begin, then, by a look at the world in business.

The first thing we notice is the enormous number of business enterprises—about 13 million in all. If we divide them into proprietorships (businesses owned by a single person), partnerships, and corporations, the world of business is classified in Table 2 · 1.

Small business Just looking at Table 2 · 1 makes one conclusion immediately clear: *there are at least two worlds of business.* One of them is the world of small business. It embraces nearly all proprietorships and partnerships as well as a very large percentage of corporations. Here are the vast bulk of the firms we find in the yellow pages of the phone book, the great preponderance of the country's farms, myriad mom-and-pop stores, restaurants, motels, movie houses, dry cleaners, druggists, retailers—in short, perhaps 95 percent of all the business firms in the nation.

Table 2 · 1 Dimensions of business, 1972

	Total number of firms (000s omitted)	Total sales (billions)	Average sale per firm
Proprietorships	10,173	$ 276	$ 27,131
Partnerships	992	104	104,839
Corporations	1,812	2,007	1,107,616

Small business is the part of the business world with which we are all most familiar. We understand how a hardware store operates, whereas we have only vague ideas about how General Motors operates. But the world of small business warrants our attentions for two other reasons.

First, small business is the employer of a substantial fraction—about a third—of the nation's labor force. Second, the world of small business is the source of much "middle-class" opinion. Of the 13 million small businesses in the country, three quarters have sales (not profits) of less than $50,000 a year. These are tiny enterprises, but they certainly give a small business point of view to at least 10 million households, one out of every seven households.

We should know something about what life is like in this world, and indeed, a considerable amount of economics is concerned with the problems of operating a small business. Later, in Chapters 13 and 14, when we reach microeconomics, we will study how small business fits into the economic picture.

Big business   We have already glimpsed another business world, mainly to be found in the corporate enterprises of the nation. Compare the average size of the sales of corporations (Table 2 • 1) with those of proprietorships and partnerships. But even these figures hide the extraordinary difference between very big business and small business. Within the world of corporations, for example, 89 percent do less than $1 million worth of business a year. But the 11 percent that do more than $1 million worth of sales a year take in 87 percent of the receipts of all corporations.

Thus, counterposed to a world of very numerous small businesses, there is the world of much less numerous big businesses. How large a world is it? Suppose we count as a big business any corporation with assets worth more than $250 million. There are roughly 1,000 such businesses in America. Half of them are in finance, mainly insurance and banking. A quarter are in manufacturing. The rest are to be found in transportation, utilities, communication, trade. Just to get an idea of scale, the largest enterprise in the nation is AT&T, with assets of $80 billion and sales of $29 billion in 1975. The largest *industrial* firm was Exxon, with assets of $33 billion and sales of $45 billion. These two firms together probably commanded as much wealth (assets) as all the 10 million proprietorships of the nation.

16

The industrial sector

Big business is to be found in all sectors; but its special place is the industrial sector, in which manufacturing plays the predominant role.

Table 2·2   Industrial sector, 1975

	$ billion
Total sales of all 436,000 industrial firms	$1083
Total sales of the 500 biggest industrial corporations	865

The figures in Table 2·2 show once again the twofold division of the business world. If we subtract the 500 biggest industrial corporations and their sales from the total of all manufacturing firms and their sales, we see that 435,500 industrial firms sold $218 billion worth of output—about a fifth of the total. The top 500 firms—one-tenth of one percent of the total number—accounted for almost 80 percent of all sales. *Indeed, if we take only the biggest 100 firms, we find that they are the source of almost half the sales of the entire industrial sector.*

Big employers

Big business obviously dominates many areas of the marketplace. Is big business also a big employer? That varies from one field to another. In manufacturing, the top 500 firms employ about 75 percent of all persons in manufacturing. In transportation and public utilities, about half the work force is hired by a giant utility or airline or railway (most of the rest work for small trucking firms). In finance, insurance, and real estate, the top 150 companies employ about 30 percent of the persons working in that area. In retail trade, the top 50 companies hire about 21 percent of the total.

In all, about a third of the nation's work force is employed by a firm that we would call a "big business."* To put it differently, 800 leading firms in manufacturing, transportation, utilities, finance, and retailing employ roughly as many persons as the remaining 13 million proprietorships, partnerships and smaller corporations.

*There is no official designation of a "big" business. We have used the *Fortune* magazine list of the top 500 industrial firms plus their list of the top 50 firms in banking, insurance, finance, transportation, utilities, and retailing.

A PARADE OF BUSINESS FIRMS

We shall have a good deal to investigate in later chapters about the world of big business. But it might be useful to end this initial survey with a dramatization of the problem. Suppose that we lined up our roughly 13 million businesses in order of size, starting with the smallest, along an imaginary road from San Francisco to New York. There will be 4,000 businesses to the mile, or a little less than one per foot. Suppose further that we planted a flag for each business. The height of the flagpole represents the volume of sales: each $10,000 in sales is shown by one foot of pole.

The line of flagpoles is a very interesting sight. From San Francisco to about Reno, Nevada, it is almost unnoticeable, a row of poles about a foot high. From Reno eastward the poles increase in height until, near Columbus, Ohio—about four-fifths of the way across the nation—flags fly about 10 feet in the air, symbolizing $100,000 in sales. Looking backward from Columbus, we can see that 10 million out of 12 million firms have sales of less than that amount.

But as we approach the eastern terminus, the poles suddenly begin to mount. There are about 300,000 firms in the country with sales over $500,000. These corporations occupy the last 75 miles of the 3,000-mile road. There are 200,000 firms with sales of over $1 million. They occupy the last 50 miles of the road, with poles at least 100 feet high. Then there are 1,000 firms with sales of $50,000,000 or more. They take up the last quarter-mile before the city limits, flags flying at skyscraper heights, 500 feet up.

But this is still not the climax. At the very gates of New York, on the last 100 feet of the last mile, we find the 100 largest industrial firms. They have sales of at least $1.5 billion, so that their flags are literally miles high, in the clouds. Along the last 10 feet of the road, there are the ten largest companies. Their sales are roughly $10 billion and up: their flags fly 120 miles in the air, literally in the stratosphere.

Households

Business is not the only institutional feature we need to inspect in this introduction to the economy. In our look at the market mechanism, we caught a glimpse of another focus of economic activity: the households that constitute factors of production. These households also receive incomes paid to the factors of production. To size them up quickly, look at Table 2·3.

Table 2·3　Household characteristics, 1976

	Millions
Total population	215
Number of households	72
Families	56
One-person households	16
Individuals in work force	99

The work force　　Our table shows us an interesting fact about the household "sector." There are more individual workers than there are households. This means that a "typical" household must have more than one member in the labor market.

But what is a "typical" household? The answer is not easy to give because there are many kinds of households: young or elderly households with only one individual in them; young married households without children; families with young children; families with offspring who are no longer young.

Economists look at the relation between households and work in terms of a *participation rate,* showing the percentage of various groups who are working or looking for work. In the formal language of the statistician, they are "in the labor market." Table 2·4 shows how considerable is the variation of these rates.

Table 2·4　Participation rates, 1976

	Percent of group in labor market
Males, 20 years and older	81
Females, 20 years and older	47
Both sexes, 16–19	55
Males, 65 and older	22
Females, 65 and older	8

Participation　　The table shows us some unexpected things about our work force. It is still made up mainly of men. Thus *sex is still a decisive element in determining the characteristics of the labor force,* although we will see in our next chapter that this has changed significantly and will probably change still further in the years to come. *Age is also a powerful determinant of participation.*

Occupations　　What sort of work does our labor force perform? Table 2·5 gives us a quick answer.

Table 2·5　Occupational distribution of the labor force, 1976

	Percent
Professional	15
Managerial	11
Sales	6
Clerical	18
Craftsmen	13
Operatives	15
Nonfarm laborers	5
Service workers	14
Farm workers	3

Later we will be looking more carefully into problems of occupations. Here we might note in passing that "white-collar" jobs—professional, managerial, sales, and clerical—include almost half the working force. Here is another strong root of the American "middle-class" mentality.

Incomes

Households interest us not only because they are the source of our labor power, but also because they are the focus of our income and our wealth. Much of the buying that powers the economic machine is cycled through the household, where purchasing power is collected as wages, salaries, dividends, interest, and rents, to be pumped out again as a flow of spending for consumers' goods. Consumer buying, as we will see later, is a strong force in the momentum of our economy, although we should emphasize right away that household buying is not the only force. Business and government are also buyers in their own right and strong influences in maintaining the flow of purchasing power.

Distribution of income

If we focus on households at this stage of our inquiry, it is because their function as buyers leads us naturally to inquire into the distribution of purchasing power among families. This is a subject about which many people are very sensitive. A persistent stress on *political* equality leads us to ignore or play down the facts of economic inequality. We even lack adequate statistics about wealth, largely because of an unwillingness to pay official recognition to this aspect of our economic realities.

There are many ways of describing income distribution. We will use a method that will divide the country into five equal layers, like a great cake. The layers will help us give dollars-and-cents definitions of what we usually have in mind when we speak of the poor, the working class, the middle class, and so on. As we will see, the amounts are not at all what most of us imagine.

The poor

We begin with the bottom layer, the poor. By our definition, this will include all the households in the bottom 20 percent of the nation. From data gathered by the Census Bureau, we know that the highest income of a family in this bottom slice of the five-layered cake was $6,500 in 1974. By coincidence, this corresponds almost exactly to the income computed by

POVERTY

What characteristics distinguish poor families? Old age is one: almost a third of the low income group consists of retirees. Curiously, youth is also characteristic. A household (married or single) headed by someone under age 25 is much more likely to be a low income family than one headed by an older person. Color counts. About 9 percent of the white population is poor; about one third of the black population. Sex enters the picture. Households headed by a female are twice as likely to be poor as one headed by a male. Schooling is an attribute. Almost half of all poor families have only grade school educations. Occupation is another: one fourth of all the nation's farmers are poor.

Many of the characteristics overlap: poor families are often old and black and poorly educated. No one characteristic is decisive in "making" a family poor. The poor are not poor just because they have no education, but often have no education because they have come from poor households themselves.

the Bureau of Labor Statistics as representing a level of "near-poverty" for a family of four persons.

The box headed "Poverty" shows some of the characteristics of poor families, but there are two additional facts about poverty that we should note.

First, not all families who are counted as poor in any given census remain poor in the next census. About one-seventh of all poor households are young people, just starting their careers. Some of these low-income beginners will escape from poverty. In addition, about a third of the members of the poverty class are older people. Many of these were not poor in an earlier, more productive stage of their economic lives. At the same time, this also means that some families that are not poor when a census is taken will fall into poverty at a later stage of their lives. The moral of this is that poverty is not entirely static. At any moment, some families are escaping from poverty, some entering it. What counts, of course, is whether the net movement is in or out.

A second characteristic also deserves to be noted. Sixty percent of the families below the poverty line have at least one wage earner in the labor force. Thus their poverty reflects inadequate earnings. A considerable amount of poverty, in other words, reflects the fact that some jobs do not pay enough to lift a jobholder above the low-income level. In some regions, certain jobs are so low-paying that even two jobholders in a family (especially if one works only seasonally) will not suffice to bring the family out of poverty. This is often the case, for example, with migrant farm workers, or with immigrants who must seek employment in the least desirable jobs.

The working class

We usually define the working class in terms of certain occupations. We call a factory operative— but not a sales clerk—working class, even though the factory employee may make more than a sales clerk.

For our purposes, however, we will just take the next two layers of the income cake and call them working class. This will include the 40 percent of the population that is above the poor. We choose this method to find out how large an income a family can make and still remain in the working class, as we have defined it. The answer is just under $15,000. To put it differently, 40 percent of the families in the country earn more than $6,500 but less than $15,000 a year.

The rich and near-rich

With the bottom three-fifths of the nation tagged—one-fifth poor, two-fifths working class—we are ready to look into the income levels of upper echelons.

First the rich. Where do riches begin? A realistic answer is probably around $100,000 a year, the magic six-figure income that goes with major corporate responsibility. There are probably fewer than 200,000 such rich families in America. They are literally the icing on the cake.

But under the truly rich is a considerably larger group that we will call the upper class. This is the top 5 percent of the nation, its doctors, airline pilots, managers, lawyers—even some economists. Some 2,750,000 families are in this top 5 percent.

How much income does it take to get there? In 1974 a family made it into the upper class with an income of $32,000. These numbers have a certain shock value. It takes more money to be rich, but less to be upper class, than we ordinarily think.

Middle class

This leaves us with the middle class—the class to which we all think we belong. By our method of cutting the cake, the middle class includes 35 percent of the nation—everyone above the $15,000 top working-class income and below the $32,000 upper-class income. In 1975 an average white married couple, both working, earned about $17,250—just enough to enter middle class economic territory. No wonder that a middle-class feeling pervades American society, regardless of the occupation or social milieu from which families come.

Wealth

It is obvious that there are great extremes of income distribution in the United States. Paul Samuelson, perhaps the nation's most famous economist, has made the observation that if we built an income pyramid out of children's blocks, with each layer representing $1,000 of income, the peak would be far higher than the Eiffel Tower; but most of us would be within a yard of the ground.

Even more striking than the inequality of income, however, is the inequality of wealth.

Table 2·6   Distribution of wealth, 1969

Percent of total population		Percent of total wealth
Lowest	25.0	0.0
Next	32.0	6.6
Next	24.0	17.2
Top	19.0	76.2
Top	0.5	25.8

A PARADE OF INCOMES

Suppose that like our parade of flags across the nation, representing the sales of business firms, we lined up the population in order of its income. Assume the height of the middle family to be 6 feet, representing a median income of $13,000 in 1975. This will be our height, as observers. What would our parade look like?*

It would begin with a few families *below* the ground, for there are some households with negative incomes; that is, they report losses for the year. Mainly these are families with business losses, and their negative incomes are not matched by general poverty. Following close on their heels comes a long line of grotesque dwarfs who comprise about one-fifth of all families, people less than 2 feet tall. Some are shorter than 1 foot.

Only after the parade is half over do we reach people whose faces are at our level. Then come the giants. When we reach the last 5 percent of the parade—incomes around $30,000—people are 18 feet tall. At the end of the parade, people tower 600 to 6,000 feet into the air—100 to 1,000 times taller than the middle height. A billionaire who earns 5 percent on his wealth has an income of $50 million. There are only 2 billionaires in the country.

*See the brilliant description of an "income parade" by Jan Pen, *Income Distribution*, trans. Trevor S. Preston (New York: Praeger, 1971), pp. 48–59.

As Table 2 • 6 shows, the bottom quarter of American households—roughly the group we have called the poor—*had no wealth at all*. The group that we have designated the working class had little more, by way of wealth, than the value of its cars and houses and perhaps a small savings account.*

Middle-class wealth

Recent figures tell us something additional about the distribution of wealth. In 1972 there were just under 13 million households with a net worth of $60,000 or more. This is approximately as many households as we would find in the top fifth of the nation—all the middle class plus the upper class and the rich. Of those 13 million wealth holders, 5 million had estates of less than $100,000—say the value of a house, and a modest insurance policy—and another 5 million had estates worth between $100,000 and $200,000, a sum that probably represents savings accounts, life insurance, some real estate, and perhaps a few stocks and bonds. This is certainly affluence, although not on a princely scale.

Next we find approximately 2 million families with estates ranging from $200,-000 to $500,000. This number dovetails more or less with the number of families in the top 5 percent. This is certainly a class of the well-to-do. But compared with what is to follow, it is not yet the class of the rich. In 1972 there were an estimated 425,000 families with assets worth half a million to a million, and just under 225,000 households with estates of $1 million or more. These last households are what we call millionaires.

*Remember that you own only that part of a house or car that you have paid for. Someone else owns the rest.

Millionaires

How much wealth do millionaires own in all? The total value of all 13 million households with assets of $60,000 or more was $2.2 trillion in 1972. The value of the assets held by the richest million persons was estimated to be about three-quarters of a trillion dollars. Other estimates have placed the ownership of half to three-quarters of all corporation stocks and bonds and of all real estate, in the hands of millionaire families.

We ought to know more than we do about the distribution of wealth among households, for here is where the ownership of land and capital is located. All that we can say is that the ownership of these elements of private property is tremendously concentrated. Although some property income goes into the hands of the upper 60 percent of the population—as interest on savings accounts or dividends on stocks held in pension funds or gains in the cash value of insurance policies—these sources of income are insignificant compared with income from work. Most property income is channeled to the small percentage of families that own the bulk of the private assets of the nation.

Government

We have almost completed our first overview of the economy; but there remains one last institution with which we must gain a first acquaintance: the government.

How shall we begin to size up such a vast and complex institution? Let us begin by thinking about production. We do not ordinarily think of the government as a producer of goods and services, for under capitalism most production is carried out by private business firms. Yet a substantial fraction of our total output is directly produced by government employees, and an even larger fraction of our incomes is received from government agencies, as Table 2 • 7 shows.

Table 2 • 7   Size of government sector, 1975

	Percent of total
Output produced by government	12
Personal incomes paid by government	30
Employment by government	22
Output purchased by government	22

Government as buyer

The table shows us that the government as a whole employs about one-fifth of our work force and consumes about one-fifth of our output. A large portion of the output purchased by government is actually made by private business and then ultimately bought by government. Armaments are a good example. Built in private factories, for the most part, arms count as public "output" only because government is the final buyer of the missile or plane.

The amount of output *directly* produced by government is much less than that bought by it. But it is a very important *kind* of output as Table 2 • 8 shows.

Kinds of public output

Table 2 • 8 makes two points that we would be wise to remember. The first is that *the word "government" in economics does not mean just the federal government.* As we will see, the federal government plays a crucial role when it comes to efforts to change the course of economic events, but from the point of

Table 2 • 8   Kinds of direct public output, as shown by public employment, 1972

	Federal	State	Local
	(number of employees) in thousands		
National defense	3,561	—	—
Postal service	666	—	—
Education	20	1,260	4,367
Highways	5	291	315
Health	217	570	549
Police	34	63	484
Fire protection	—	—	276
Sanitation	—	—	195
Resources and recreation	228	159	209
Financial administration	101	98	153
Other	109	535	1,325
Total	**2,795**	**2,937**	**7,872**

view of government as a major economic institution—an employer of labor and a source of direct production—state and local governments surpass the federal!

Second, the variety of outputs reminds us that government is not just a dead weight on the economy, as so many tend to think. Anyone who has ever gone to a public school, been treated in a public hospital, traveled on a public road, or flown in a plane guided by a public beacon system has been the recipient of government "production" and knows how vital public output can be. Even those who emphasize the maddening bureaucracy and inefficiency that can come from government activity (although government has no monopoly on either) should reflect that the system of private enterprise itself depends on the invisible output of law enforcement on which this economy, like all economies, rests.

Focus

We don't want you to memorize a lot of facts in this fact-filled chapter. Here is where abstraction shows its usefulness in reducing a complex reality to a manageable set of basic ideas. We suggest that you study the chapter to learn three main ideas:

1. The way we can describe an economic system in terms of premises, mechanisms, and institutions.
2. The key premise of economic individualism and its effect on the idea of private property.
3. The idea of a market system as a mechanism for organizing production and distribution. (There will be lots more on this as we move along.)

What should you do with the arrays of facts? It will help if you think about the way in which they can be generalized to highlight these salient features of our economy:

Business and labor unions: "two worlds" in terms of size.

The household: a source of labor, a recipient of incomes with which it buys goods and services.

Income and wealth: its unequal division.

Government's many roles: producer, buyer of output, employer.

QUESTIONS

1. What would you identify as the main premises, mechanisms and structural features of India or Russia?

2. Reproduce the flows of the market mechanism in a diagram.

3. What is a "factor of production"? In a slave society, would slaves be a factor of production?

4. Would it be possible to have a private property economy without private ownership of land and capital? And while you are thinking about that, would it be possible to have an economy in which the state owned all land and capital but permitted private property in labor?

5. Do you think that the acts of production and distribution of income are intrinsically interlinked in our system, or do you think that the distribution of incomes is quite separate from the production of goods?

6. How would you explain the fact that big business has made so much less headway in farming or retailing than in industrial production?

7. Do the facts of income and wealth distribution surprise you? Please you? Shock you? With what arguments would you defend the existing distribution? An argument based on fairness and equity? On efficiency? On natural differences among men?

8. When we say that government is "too big" in this country, do we mean government as producer, employer, or payer of incomes? Is it possible to argue that government is too *small* a producer, employer, or income payer?

24

Business organization

Business is a central institution in our economic system, and all of us ought to know something about how business, especially the corporation, is legally organized. Although corporations are the dominant form of business property, too few people are well informed about them. Here is a brief introduction to the main forms of business organization.

PROPRIETORSHIPS

A proprietorship is the simplest kind of business organization. Usually it can be set up without any legal fuss at all, simply by opening a place of business. Sometimes one has to register or get a license, for instance, to open a liquor store or to set up practice as a physician or lawyer. But proprietorships are the easiest to understand of all forms of business.

They are, also, as we have seen, the most widespread form (see Table 2 • 1). Why are not all businesses proprietorships? The answer lies in certain problems that proprietorships have.

1. *A proprietorship has difficulty growing because its ability to borrow money is limited to the amount of credit that its owner proprietor can raise.* Only a very rich man can borrow very much.
2. A proprietor is personally liable for all losses that his business may incur (he also gets all its profits). A rich man is not likely to open a proprietary business, because if an unexpected loss is incurred—if his business is sued by an irate customer and it loses the case—*the proprietor must pay from his own funds any obligations that the business cannot pay from its funds.* In fact, there is really no division between the property of the owner and that of the business.
3. *When a proprietor dies, the business comes to an end.* All debts must be paid, and a new business established to take over the old. This is hard on the spouse of the proprietor, the employees, and the creditors.

PARTNERSHIPS

Partnerships remedy many of these difficulties. Basically, a partnership is a combination of proprietors who have agreed, usually by legal formalities, to share a certain proportion of the profits and the losses of their business. The fact that there are now several people associated in the business obviously makes it easier to raise additional capital. Very large businesses have been partnerships, at least until recent days.

Nonetheless there are still problems for partnerships.

1. *Partners are together responsible for all the losses or debts of the business.* Jointly they have, like proprietors, "unlimited" liability, although some partners may have limited liability.
2. *The death of each partner requires the business to be legally reconstituted.* When a partner of a firm dies, the firm usually has to undergo a reorganization. This is expensive and bothersome and often creates frictions.

CORPORATIONS

The corporation, as we have seen, is the most powerful although not the most prevalent form of business organization. Let us be sure that we understand exactly what a corporation is.

1. *A corporation is a legal entity created by the state.* Unlike a proprietorship or a partnership, all corporations must apply to their states for a charter allowing them to carry on business. The charter specifies in general terms the kinds of business they will carry on and the general financial structures they will have. Charters cost money, which is one reason that all proprietorships are not corporations. Another reason is that corporations pay income taxes on "their" income, before it goes to stockholders.

2. *Once a corporation is chartered, it exists as a "person"*; that is, the corporation itself—not the individuals who own it or work for it—can bring suit, be sued, or own property. This has an immediate advantage. It is that the liability of an owner of a corporation is limited to the money he has put into the corporation. If the corporation is sued for more funds than the business possesses, the corporation will declare bankruptcy, and there is no recourse to the private funds of the persons who own it.

3. *Because the corporation is a "person" it does not go out of business when its owners die.* The corporation is "immortal." It goes on until it fails as a business organization or voluntarily goes out of business, or until its charter is revoked by the state.

CORPORATE ORGANIZATION

Clearly, the corporation has substantial advantages over proprietorships and partnerships. But how does it run? Who owns it?

A corporation is owned by the individuals who buy shares in it. Suppose that a corporation is granted a charter to carry on a business in retail trade. The charter also specifies how many shares of stock this business enterprise is allowed to issue. For example, a corporation may be formed with the right to issue 100,000 shares. If these shares are sold to individuals at a price of $10 each, the original shareholders (also called stockholders) will have put $1 million into the corporation. In return each will receive stock certificates indicating how many shares that person has bought.

These stock certificates are somewhat like a partnership agreement, although there are noteworthy differences. If you buy 1,000 shares in our imaginary corporation, you will own one percent of the corporation. You will have the right to receive one percent of all income that it pays out as dividends on its stock. You will also be entitled to cast 1,000 votes—one vote per share—at the meetings of shareholders that all corporations must hold. In this way, a shareholder is very much like a junior partner who was given a one percent interest in a business.

ADVANTAGES OF SHARE OWNERSHIP

But here are the critical differences between corporations and partnerships.

1. *As we have already said, a stockholder is not personally liable for any debts that the corporation cannot pay.* If the company goes bankrupt, the share-

holder will lose his investment of $10,000 (1,000 shares @ $10) but cannot be sued for any further money. *Liability is thereby limited to the amount the shareholder has invested.*

2. Unlike partnership shares, which are usually very difficult to sell, corporation shares are generally easy to sell, if one owns the stock of a company that is listed (bought and sold) on one of the nation's several stock markets. (The shares of a very small corporation are not, of course, so easy to sell, although they are less difficult to dispose of than a partnership.) Moreover, a stockholder may sell shares to anyone, at any price. If our imaginary corporation prospers, its shares may sell for $20 each. A stockholder is perfectly free to sell any number of shares at that price. As we have just mentioned, marketplaces for stocks and bonds have developed along with the corporation, to facilitate such sales of stock. The most important of these markets, the New York Stock Exchange, was organized in 1817. Today over 20 billion shares a year are bought and sold on the stock exchange. Thus with the corporation comes the advantage of a much greater "liquidity" of personal wealth—that is, greater ease of turning assets into cash.

3. Shares of stock entitle the stockholder to the dividends that the directors of the corporation (see below) may decide to pay out for each share. But a shareholder is not entitled to any fixed amount of profit. If the corporation prospers, the directors may vote to pay a large dividend. But they are under no obligation to do so. They may wish to use the earnings of the corporation for other purposes, such as the purchase of new equipment or land. If the corporation suffers losses, ordinarily the directors will vote to pay no dividend or only a small one to be paid from past earnings. Thus as an owner of ordinary "common" stock, the stockholder must take the risk of having his dividends rise or fall.

4. Corporations are also allowed to issue bonds, as well as stock. A bond is different from a share of stock in two ways. First, a bond has a *stated value* printed on its face, whereas a share of stock does not. A $1,000 bond issued by a corporation is a certificate for a debt of $1,000. The bondholder is not a sharer in the profits of the company but a creditor of the corporation—someone to whom the corporation is in debt for $1,000. In case of corporate bankruptcy, the claims of bondholders take precedence over those of shareowners.

   Second, a bond also states on its face the *amount of income* it will pay to bondholders. A $1,000 bond may declare that it will pay $80 a year as interest. Unlike dividends, this interest payment will not rise if the corporation makes money, nor will it fall if it does not. Thus there is no element of profit-sharing in bonds, as there is in stocks.

   There is a compensation for this, however. The risk of owning a bond is usually less than that of owning a stock. A bond is a legal obligation of the corporation, which *must* pay interest, and which *must* buy back the bond itself when a fixed term of years has expired and the bond becomes "due." If it fails to meet either of these obligations, the courts will declare the firm bankrupt, and all its assets will be turned over to the bondholders to satisfy their debts. If the firm's assets are not enough to repay the bondholders, they will suffer a degree of loss; but the shareholders will lose *all* of their equity, for a share of stock has no such obligations attached to it and never becomes "due." No shareholder can sue a corporation if it fails to pay a dividend.

OWNERSHIP AND CONTROL

One last matter is also of significance in discussing the organization of the corporation. The new mode of structuring enterprise has made possible a development of great importance: the separation of ownership and control.

As we have seen, stockholders are the actual owners of a corporation, but it is obviously impossible for large numbers of stockholders to meet regularly and run a company. AT&T has well over 1,000,000 stockholders. Where could they meet? How could they possibly decide what the company should do?

All corporations, small or large, therefore, are run by boards of directors (who may or may not own stock in the company), and who are elected by the stockholders. At regular intervals, all stockholders are asked to elect or reelect members of the board, each casting as many votes as the number of shares that stockholder owns. In turn, the board of directors appoints the "management"—main officials of the corporation; for example, its president and vice-presidents. Management hires the rest of the employees. As the number of shareowners grows, it is not surprising that power drifts into the hands of the management. (The extent to which managers can operate independently of, or even contrary to, the interests of stockholders is one of the hotly debated questions in economics.)

STOCK EXCHANGES

We have mentioned stock exchanges as the organized markets in which shares are traded. An important thing to realize is that buying a share of stock does not put money into a corporation, unless the stock is newly issued by the company.

Most of the shares bought and sold on the stock exchanges are old shares, issued years ago. When you buy a share of General Motors, the money you pay does *not* go to General Motors. It goes to the individual who sold you the shares. If you own shares in a company that produces cigarettes, and you want to get out of this business because you disapprove of smoking, you sell your shares. *But doing so does not take any money out of the cigarette business.* It simply transfers your shares to another person who will pay you for your stock certificates.

Does it then make no difference to a cigarette company whether you buy its shares or not? Not quite. Corporations like to have their shares "well regarded" by the public, because from time to time they *do* issue new shares, and they want an eager market for these shares. So, too, if their shares are in general disfavor, they will sell for lower prices, and at a lower price a company is easier to "take over" than at a higher price.* Finally, managers usually own shares in their own companies. As the shares go up, they become richer. So companies are far from indifferent to the fate of their shares. Nonetheless we should clearly understand that we do not put money "into" businesses when we buy their outstanding shares.

---

*A "take-over" is a concerted effort, usually by a small group of individuals who own a considerable amount of the company's stock, to round up enough proxies (votes) to oust an incumbent management and to install a management of its own. Take-overs are dramatic when they occur. They are not frequent, but they happen often enough so that corporations keep an eye out for "raiding" interests. If the price of their stock falls, it is often an invitation to be taken over, simply because it is cheaper to buy the votes (shares) when their price is depressed.

The trend of things

After our first view of the structure of things, we need another orienting approach. This one is still intended to give us an initial perspective on the economic scene, but unlike our first chapter, it will not be an overflight to identify the main features of the economic system. Instead we must imagine a kind of speeded-up camera view of the economic system over time, a view that will show us the *changes* in institutions that we have identified as central to our system.

The Process of Growth

Suppose that we had such an imaginary camera, and trained it on the U.S. economy over the last 75 years or so. What would be the most striking changes that would meet our eye?

There is no doubt about the first impression: it would be a sense of growth. Everything would be getting larger. Business firms would be growing in size. Labor unions would be bigger. There would be many more households, and each household would be richer. Government would be much larger. And underlying all of this, the extent of the market system itself—the great circular flow of inputs and outputs—would be steadily increasing in size.

Growth is not, of course, the only thing we would notice. Businesses are different as well as bigger when we compare 1975 and 1900: there are far more corporations now than in the old days, far more "diversified" businesses, fewer family firms. Households are different because more women work outside the home. Labor unions today are no longer mainly craft unions, limited to one occupation. Government is not only bigger but has a different philosophy.

Total output Nonetheless, it is growth that first commands our attention. The camera vision of the economy gives us a picture that keeps widening. It *has* to widen to encompass the increase in the sheer mass of output. Hence the first institution whose growth we must examine is that of the market system itself.

More specifically, we must trace the tremendous growth in our total output. The technical name for this flow of output is gross national product (GNP), a term we will use many times in the future and which we will later define more carefully. Here we only note that it is the dollar value of our annual flow of final output.

FIG. 3·1 Value of GNP, 1900–1975, current prices

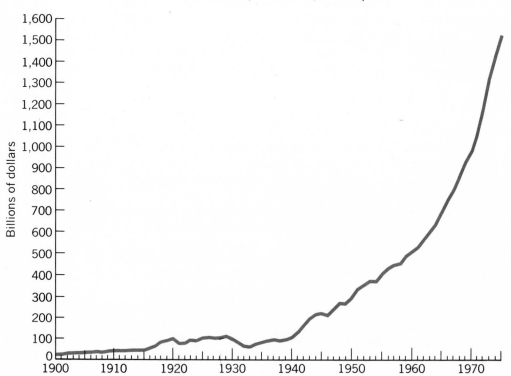

VOLUME AND VALUE

You should be warned that there is no entirely satisfactory way of wringing price increases out of the hodgepodge of goods and services called GNP, because different items in this collection of goods rise or fall in price in different degrees. There is always a certain element of arbitrariness in correcting GNP for price changes. Different methods, each perfectly defensible, will yield somewhat different measures of "corrected" GNP.

Isn't there some way of getting around the problem of dollar values when we compare GNPs? One way is to measure actual physical volumes. When certain kinds of outputs, such as foodstuffs, bulk very large in GNP, as they do in India or China, we sometimes measure growth just by adding up the tonnages of food production.

The problem, of course, is that the composition of these tonnages may change—more wheat one year, more rice another—which gets us into another comparison problem. And then such a measure ignores entirely the outputs of nonagricultural goods. (We meet the same problem if we try to measure growth by tonnages of freight, metal production, etc.)

A more defensible way might be to consider GNP as a sum total of labor time, the embodiment of so many million hours of work. Even this does not get us around the measurement and comparison problem, for we use different kinds of labor as time goes on. Therefore, we have to make the difficult assumption that all kinds of labor, skilled and unskilled, trained and untrained, can be "reduced" to multiples of one "basic" kind. That basic labor, in turn, would have to boil down to some constant unit of "effort." But does the unit of "effort"—of human energy—remain constant over time?

In the end, the task of measuring an aggregate of different things can never be solved to our complete satisfaction. Any concept of GNP always has an element of unmeasureableness about it. Growth is a concept that we constantly use, but that remains tantalizingly beyond precise definition.

The trend of GNP

Figure 3.1 gives us a graphic representation of this increase in yearly output.

Correcting for inflation

As we can see, the dollar value of all output from 1900 to 1975 has grown by a factor of almost 100. But perhaps a cautionary thought will have already struck you. If we measure the growth of output by comparing the dollar value of production over time, what seems to be growth in actual economic activity may be no more than a rise in prices. If the economy in 1975 produced no more actual tons of grain than the economy in 1900, but if grain prices today were double those of 1900, our GNP figures would show "growth" where there was really nothing but inflation.

To arrive at a measure of real growth, we have to correct for changes in prices. How we do so is a matter that you can study in our chapter on quantitative methods (pp. 695ff.). Essentially, we take one year as a *base* and use the prices of that year to evaluate output in all succeeding years.

Here is an elementary example. Suppose that our grain economy produces 1 million tons in 1900 and 2 million tons in 1975, but wheat sells for $1 in 1900 and $2 in 1975. Our GNP in the current prices of 1900 and 1975 is $1 million for 1900 and $4 million 75 years later. But if we evaluate the GNP using only the 1900 prices (i.e., $1 per bushel), our GNP is reduced to $2 million in 1975. This constant dollar GNP is often referred to as the real GNP, while the current dollar GNP is called the nominal GNP. We can use the prices of any year as the "base." The important thing is that all outputs must be evaluated with only one set of prices.

Figure 3.2 shows us the much reduced growth of output when output is measured in 1958 dollars.

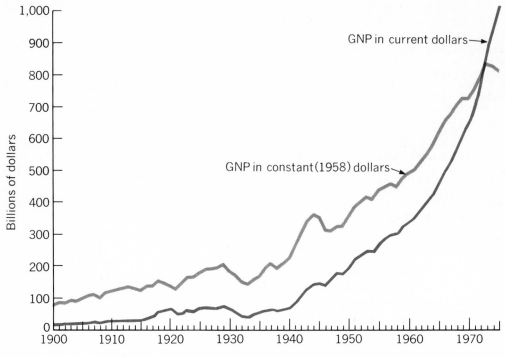

FIG. 3 · 2   GNP in constant (1958) and current dollars

Per capita growth

As we can see, growth in real (or constant dollar) terms is much less dramatic than growth in current dollars that make no allowance for rising prices. Nonetheless, the value of 1975 output, compared to that of 1900, with price changes eliminated as best we can, still shows a growth factor of eight.

But there still remains one last adjustment to be made. The growth of output is a massive assemblage of goods and services to be distributed among the nation's households, and the number of those households has increased. In 1900, United States population was 76 million; in 1975 it was 214 million. **To bring our constant GNP down to life size, we have to divide it by population, to get GNP per person, or per capita.**

THE DIFFERENCE THAT GROWTH RATES MAKE

The normal range in growth rates for capitalist economies does not seem to be very great. How much difference does it make, after all, if output grows at 1.7 or 2.7 percent?

The answer is: an amazing difference. This is because growth is an *exponential* phenomenon involving a percentage rate of growth on a steadily rising base. At 1.7 percent, per-capita real income will double in about 40 years. At 2.7 percent, it will double in 26 years.

Recently, Professor Kenneth Boulding pointed out that before World War II no country sustained more than 2.3 percent per-capita growth of GNP. Since World War II, Japan has achieved a per-capita growth rate of 8 percent. Boulding writes: "The difference between 2.3 and 8 percent may be dramatically illustrated by pointing out that [at 2.3 percent] children are twice as rich as their parents—i.e., per capita income approximately doubles every generation—while at 8 percent per annum, children are six times as rich as their parents."

Basic importance of growth

As Fig. 3.3 shows, between 1913 and 1972 real per capita growth ranged between 1.7 and 2.0 percent per year. That may not seem very much, but growth rates compound, like interest in a bank. A rate of 1.8 percent was enough to give the average citizen in 1975 six times as large a volume of goods and services as the average citizen got in 1900. Whether or not average happiness multiplied six times is another question. We will look into the relation between GNP and personal well-being in Chapter 23 and again in Chapter 37.

Sources of growth

How do we explain this long upward trend? Here we can give only a brief summary of the causes that we will study more systematically in macroeconomics (Part 4). Essentially, we grew for two reasons:

1. **The quantity of "inputs" going into the economic process increased.**

In 1900 our labor force was 27 million. In 1975 it was 95 million. Obviously, larger inputs of labor produce larger outputs of goods and services. (Whether they may even produce *proportionally* larger outputs is another question that we will investigate later.)

Our inputs of capital increased as well. In 1900 the total horsepower energy delivered by "prime movers"—engines of all kinds, work animals, ships, trains, etc.—was 65 million horsepower. In 1975 it was 25 *billion.*

Land in use also increased. In 1900, there were 839 million acres of land used for farming purposes, and over 1,000 million acres for nonfarm purposes such as grazing. By 1975, land in farms had increased to over 1,000 million acres, and land in nonfarm use had also increased: we had reclaimed "virgin land" and made it economically productive.

2. **The quality of inputs improved.**

The population working in 1975 was not only more numerous than in 1900, it was better trained and better schooled.

FIG. 3·3   Real GNP per capita (1958 dollars)

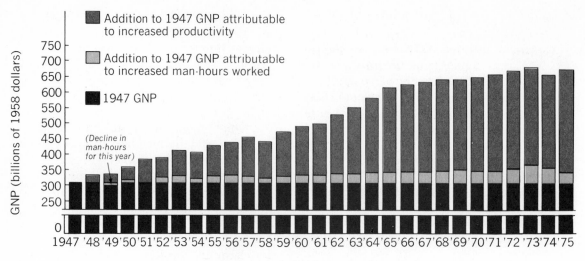

FIG. 3 · 4   Source of GNP increases, 1947–1975

The best overall gauge of this is the amount of education stored up in the work force. In 1900, when only 6.4 percent of the working population had gone beyond grade school, there were 223 million man-years of schooling embodied in the population. In 1975, when over two-thirds of the population had finished high school, the stock of education embodied in the population had grown to 991 million man-years.

The quality of capital has also increased, along with its quantity. As an indication of the importance of the changing quality of capital, consider the contribution made to our output by the availability of surfaced roads. In 1900 there were about 150,000 miles of such roads. In 1975, there were almost 4 million miles. That is an increase in the "quantity" of roads of over 25 times. But that increase does not begin to measure the difference in the transport capability of the two road systems, one of them gravelled, narrow, built for traffic that averaged 10 to 20 miles per hour; the other, concrete or asphalt, multilane, fast-paced.

Productivity   There are still other sources of growth, such as shifts in occupations and efficiencies of large-scale operation, but the main ones are the increase in the quantity and the quality of inputs. Of the two, improvements in the quality of inputs—in human skills, in improved designs of capital equipment—have been far more important than mere increases in quantity. **Better skills and technology enable the labor force to increase its productivity, the amount of goods and services it can turn out in a given time.** Figure 3.4 shows how this increase in productivity has overweighed the increase in sheer man-hours during the last 25 years.

Changes in Distribution

We have seen how striking was the increase in output in the twentieth century, but what happened to the division of this output among the various classes of society? Have the rich gotten richer and the poor poorer? Has the trend been in the direction of greater equality?

Changes in real incomes The question is not easy to answer. Remember, we are interested in the changes in shares going to different groups, not just in absolute amounts. There has certainly been a tremendous change in the dollar amounts that we have used to define different social classes, as Fig. 3.5 shows.

Changes in shares The figures show that growth has helped boost all income classes, but has the *proportion* of income going to the various classes also changed? That is not what we find. Figure 3.6 shows that sharing-out of incomes among social groups has been remarkably steady.

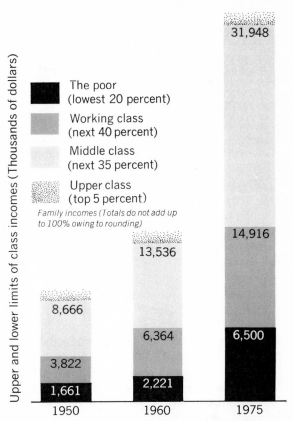

FIG. 3·5 Changes in dollar limits of social classes

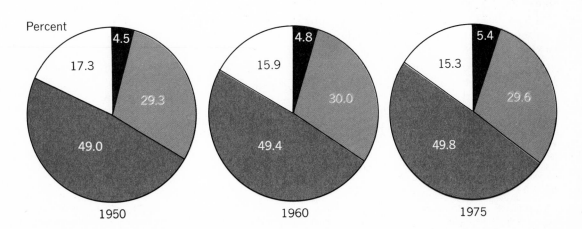

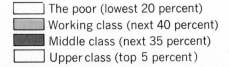

FIG. 3·6 Families' shares of total income

Thus the distribution of total income among those at the top, in the middle, and on the bottom has not shifted very much. The poor have a little larger share of the income cake; the well-to-do, a little smaller. Only if we go back to the 1920s do we see a marked change. In those days, the share of the top 5 percent was perhaps twice as large as it is today. In addition, various social programs, such as Medicare or state-supported higher education, have probably raised the real income of the poorest 20 percent somewhat more than Fig. 3.6 shows.*

*A more detailed study of changes in income distribution would have to take into account some facts that are not included in the figures above. For technical reasons, the Census Bureau does not include most forms of capital income (such as capital gains on stocks or real estate) in its computation of incomes. If it did, the share of the top 1 percent would be doubled. The Census Bureau also does not fully take into account cash and noncash payments to the poor, such as food stamps or welfare aid. This would add to the share of the poor. In other words, the Census figures are mainly derived from earnings, not returns on capital or "transfers" that may benefit high- or low-income groups. It is extremely difficult to net out the effects of all these flows of money. The result is probably more favorable to lower income groups, but it is not possible to say by exactly how much. In all likelihood, the net change is not very great.

The elimination of poverty?

Does this mean that poverty is being eliminated from the United States? Without a question the number of persons below the designated "low income level" has been dropping, both absolutely and relative to the larger population, even though the threshold of a poverty income has been steadily adjusted upward to allow for inflation. We can see this gradual shrinkage in Table 3·1, where we should note the reversal of the trend in the 1975 recession.

Table 3·1 Persons below low income level

	1959	1965	1969	1975
All persons (millions)	39.5	33.2	24.1	25.9
Percent of population	22.4	17.3	12.1	12.3

These figures do not tell us, however, whether poverty simply melts away as a result of overall growth or whether we eliminate certain kinds of poverty (eg., poverty from low wages), while leaving other kinds relatively untouched. During the past 20 years, the conditions of life in the slums of many big cities have worsened. This makes it difficult to say that we have less of a poverty problem in the nation as a whole. Possibly we have a greater one!

We will return to the question of poverty in Chapter 19, where we will examine what economic theory has to say on the matter. (Meanwhile, someone interested in the subject might look at the box on page 36 for a somewhat more systematic profile of the poor than we have heretofore had.

A *theory of riches*

Meanwhile, what of the other end of the spectrum? Is there an explanation of great wealth and its persistence, despite inheritance and other laws that would seem to make it difficult to hold on to?

One explanation is simply that the rich are lucky. Luck seems to have a great deal to do with the selection of the new individuals who appear at the extreme end of our income and wealth distribution. If we examine the composition of the list of wealthiest citizens provided by *Fortune* magazine, we find that it breaks into two groups. The first consists of individuals who have inherited money from the past. Their grandparents or great grandparents were lucky; and they have preserved their inherited luck by diversifying their holdings among many companies, which greatly adds to their chances of staying rich.

But the second group consists of individuals who have become wealthy without inheritance. In 1973 *Fortune* listed 39 individuals who had made from $50 million to $700 million in the previous *five years* without inheriting wealth or having been previously on *Fortune's* list of the wealthiest. Were the winners smarter or shrewder than everyone else?

A test of special abilities is to ask someone to repeat a performance. How many who have made a great fortune in one activity or investment managed to go on to earn another great fortune on another activity or investment? The answer is none. If the *Fortune* list is examined, it is impossible to identify anyone whose personal fortune had two or more upward leaps. The typical pattern is for a man to make a great fortune and then to settle down and earn the market rate of return on his existing portfolio.* The implication is that the main cause of vast wealth is simply luck.

Trends in Business

We have examined the main trends in personal income. Now let us turn to business. Here one change immediately strikes the eye. **There is a marked decline of the independent, small business—with its self-employed worker—as a main form of enterprise.**

In 1900 there were about 8 million independent enterprises, including 5.7 million farms. By 1975, as we saw in our last chapter, the number of proprietorships had grown to over 10 million, a figure that included some 2.8 million farms. Meanwhile, the labor force itself more than tripled. Thus as a percentage of all persons working, the proportion of self-employed has fallen from about 30 percent in 1900 to under 10 percent.

*Lester Thurow, *Generating Inequality* (New York: Basic Books, 1975), p. 153.

Just to get an idea of scale, the 100th largest industrial corporation in 1975 ranked by sales was Carnation Corporation. Its sales that year were just over $2 billion. It was not the 100th largest in terms of assets, which just topped $1 billion. The 100th biggest firm in assets was Merck, with $1.5 billion. Its sales were also $1.5 billion.

Thus it makes a difference whether we rank companies in size by sales or assets. At the very top of the heap, 8 of the first 10 firms in sales are also among the top 10 in assets, but this coincidence is no longer true once we get part way down the list. Examples: Esmark was 35th in sales, 110th in assets; Greyhound 41st in sales, 114th in assets; Burroughs 55th in assets, 124th in sales.

Which is more important, sales or assets? Sales measure the dominance of a company within its field; assets measure its overall financial strength.

Actually both sales and assets measure size, but what counts in the marketplace is profitability. Here the correct measure is the net rate of return: the rate of profit earned per dollar of capital. The average big business earns twice to three times the return of the average small business, but really spectacular rates of return are usually found in smaller businesses on their way to stardom.

Last rule of thumb: To make it into the top 500 companies, your sales have to be about $250 million; your assets $30 million.

Rise of big business

With the decline of the self-employed worker has come the rise of the giant firm. Back in 1900, the giant corporation was just arriving on the scene. In 1901 financier J. P. Morgan created the first billion-dollar company when he formed the United States Steel Corporation out of a dozen smaller enterprises. In that year, the total capitalization of all corporations valued at more than $1 million was only $5 billion. By 1904 it was $20 billion. In 1972 it was over $3 trillion.

It hardly comes as a surprise that the main trend of the past 75 years has been the emergence of big business. More interesting is the question of whether big business is continuing to grow. This is a more difficult question to answer, for it depends on what we mean by "growth."

Certainly the place of the biggest companies within the world of corporations has been rising, at least during the years up to the early 1970s, as Table 3 · 2 shows.

Table 3 · 2 shows the share of corporate assets held by the top 100 or 200 companies. As we can see, the top 100 companies in the 1970s held approximately as large a share of total corporate wealth as the top 200 companies in 1948.

Sales vs. assets

This growing concentration of assets in the hands of the mightiest corporations is not the same thing, however, as a growing predominance of those companies *in each marketplace*. The share of the biggest companies in various markets has tended to remain about the same—up in a few industries, down in others. This is a matter we will look into much more carefully in Chapter 15, but it is important to have the general conclusion now. **Over the last quarter-century, concentration of business has continued to increase if we measure assets, not if we measure sales.**

Explaining the trend to business size

Can we explain the long-term trend toward the concentration of business assets, as we did the trend toward growth in GNP? By and large, economists would stress three main reasons for the appearance of giant enterprise.

Table 3 · 2 Largest manufacturing corporations' share of assets (percent)

	1948	1960	1970	1973
100 largest corporations	40.2	46.4	48.5	47.6
200 largest corporations	48.2	56.3	60.4	56.9

1. Advances in technology have made possible the mass production of goods or services at falling costs.

The rise of big business is very much a creature of technology, for bigness has been the consequence of methods of manufacture that enabled companies to achieve large volumes of output. Without the steam engine, the lathe, the railroad, it is difficult to imagine a really big business.

But technology went on to do more than make large-scale production possible. Typically it also brought an economic effect that we call *economies of scale*. That is, technology not only enlarged, it also cheapened the process of production. Costs per unit fell as output rose. The process is perfectly exemplified in the huge reduction of cost in producing automobiles on an assembly line rather than one car at a time (see box).

Economies of scale provided further powerful impetus toward a growth in size. The firm that pioneered in the introduction of mass production technology usually secured a competitive selling advantage over its competitors, enabling it to grow in size and thereby to increase its advantage still further. These cost-reducing advantages were important causes of the initial emergence of giant companies in many industries. Similarly, the absence of such technologies explains why corporate giants did not emerge in all fields.

2. Concentration is also a result of corporate mergers.

Ever since J. P. Morgan assembled U.S. Steel, mergers have been a major source of corporate growth. At the very end of the nineteenth century there was the first great merger "wave," out of which came the first huge companies, including U.S. Steel. In 1890 most industries were competitive, without a single company dominating the field. By 1904 one or two giant firms, usually created by mergers, had arisen to control at least half the output in 78 different industries.

Again, between 1951 and 1960 one-fifth of the top 1,000 corporations disap-

MASS PRODUCTION IN ACTION

Allan Nevins has described what mass production techniques looked like in the early Ford assembly lines

Just how were the main assembly lines and lines of component production and supply kept in harmony? For the chassis alone, from 1,000 to 4,000 pieces of each component had to be furnished each day at just the right point and right minute; a single failure, and the whole mechanism would come to a jarring standstill. . . . Superintendents had to know every hour just how many components were being produced and how many were in stock. Whenever danger of shortage appeared, the shortage chaser—a familiar figure in all automobile factories—flung himself into the breach. Counters and checkers reported to him. Verifying in person any ominous news, he mobilized the foreman concerned to repair deficiencies. Three times a day he made typed reports in manifold to the factory clearing-house, at the same time chalking on blackboards in the clearing-house office a statement of results in each factory-production department and each assembling department.[1]

Such systematizing in itself resulted in astonishing increases in productivity. With each operation analyzed and subdivided into its simplest components, with a steady stream of work passing before stationary men, with a relentless but manageable pace of work, the total time required to assemble a car dropped astonishingly. Within a single year, the time required to assemble a motor fell from 600 minutes to 226 minutes; to build a chassis, from 12 hours and 28 minutes to 1 hour and 33 minutes. A stopwatch man was told to observe a 3-minute assembly in which men assembled rods and pistons, a simple operation. The job was divided into three jobs, and half the men turned out the same output as before.

As the example of the assembly line illustrates, the technology behind economies of scale often reduced the act of labor to robot-like movements. A brilliant account of this fragmentation of work will be found in Harry Braverman's *Labor and Monopoly Capital* (New York: Monthly Review Press, 1974).

[1] *Ford, the Times, the Man, the Company* (New York: Scribner's, 1954), 1,507

peared—not because they failed, but because they were bought up by other corporations. In all, mergers have accounted for about two-fifths of the increase in concentration between 1950 and 1970; internal growth accounts for the rest.

3. Depressions or recessions plunge many smaller firms into bankruptcy and make it possible for larger, more financially secure firms to buy them up very cheaply.

Certainly the process of concentration is abetted by economic distress. When industries are threatened, the weak producers go under; the stronger ones emerge relatively stronger than before. Consider, for example, that three once prominent American automobile producers succumbed to the mild recessions of the 1950s and 1960s and to the pressure of foreign competition: Studebaker, Packard, Kaiser Motors.

A continuing trend to bigness?

Has the trend to big business leveled off? Some recent statistics imply that the pace of concentration may have slowed during the last few years; other figures suggest not. Certainly the underlying forces of concentration—technical advances, mergers, business cycles—are still very much with us; "big business" remains a major economic problem. We will return to it in our next chapter.

From Small to Large Government

We pass now to the last great trend of the economy, a trend whose end result has been the emergence of that large government apparatus we noted in our previous chapter.

Rise of the public sector

There are three quite different ways of measuring the rise of the public sector. The first is to examine the proportion of GNP that government directly produces or purchases. This might be regarded as a rough indication of the degree to which we have become a "statist" economy.

A second way is to inquire into the extent to which the government reallocates incomes by taxing some persons and giving others "transfers payments" such as Social Security benefits or welfare or unemployment insurance. This might be regarded as an index of the degree to which we have become a welfare state.

Last is the extent to which government interferes in the working of the economy by regulating various aspects of economic life or by exercising its economic powers in other ways. This, by far the most difficult to measure exactly, might be thought of as an indication of the extent to which we have moved in the direction of a guided or controlled capitalism.

Behind the trends

Figure 3.7 shows the first two measurements: public purchases and income reallocation. Let us begin by examining the trend of production or purchases. As we can see, a steadily rising fraction of GNP is produced or bought by government. Today about a fifth of all output is produced to fill government demand. What the graph does not show, however, is that increased state and local buying, even more than federal buying, causes the rise.

Federal purchases have increased mainly with our growing role in world affairs. In 1900, total U.S. military purchases came to $300 million; in 1975, to $84 billion. But nonfederal purchasing—for education, roads, police, and similar functions—accounts for the major portion of total government buying. In 1975 the states and localities bought $215 billion worth of GNP; the federal government (including defense) bought only $124 billion.

Second, we notice the rapid rise in the amount of GNP reallocated by government. Here is where the expansion of the federal sector has played the leading role. In 1929, only .9 percent of GNP was redistributed by government. In 1975, transfer payments amounted to 11 percent of GNP, and the great bulk of this originated with the federal government. If we add both the goods produced or purchased by the federal government and the various transfer payments it has made, a total of $375 billion passed through its hands, or about 25 percent of GNP.

Government intervention

What reasons lay behind this swelling volume of government buying or spending? Let us defer the answer until we examine the last indication of the growing presence of govern-

FIG. 3·7   All government buying or spending

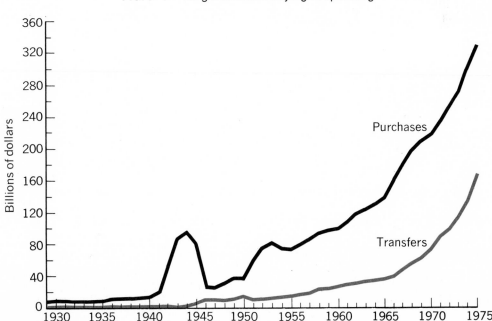

ment, the widening role of government as a supervisor or regulator of the economy.

Because of its varied nature, and because the importance of government intervention is not always shown by the amount of money that an agency spends or the number personnel it employs, this is a trend that defies easy quantification or graphic representation. Much of the spending that we have noted, for example, is carried out through established departments of the executive branch of government, especially Health, Education, and Welfare, from which Social Security checks flow, and the Defense Department, source of military spending.

But we ought to have at least some indication, however impressionistic and incomplete, of the widening reach of government concern within various areas of the economic system. The following list gives us some inkling of the variety and importance of these functions:

Function

Civil Aeronautics Board	Regulates air routes and fares
Environmental Protection Agency	Administers antipollution legislation
Federal Reserve Board	Regulates supply of money
Federal Communications Commission	Assigns airwave frequencies to stations
Federal Trade Commission	Polices business activities in restraint of trade
Interstate Commerce Commission	Regulates rail, canal, and truck industry
National Labor Relations Board	Supervises election of unions
National Science Foundation	Supports scientific research
Tariff Commission	Holds hearings for relief of tariff
Office of Economic Opportunity	Oversees employment practices

Behind the rise in government

How shall we account for all these trends of government: more buying, more transfer payments, more regulation and intervention? Among the many causes are these developments:

•The growing size of business has evoked a need for government supervision. As business firms have increased in size, private decisions have become fraught with social consequences. It is impossible for a big company to make an important decision that does not have widespread repercussions. Building or not building a plant may spell prosperity or decline for a town, even a state. Cut-throat competition can spell ruin for an industry. Polluting a river can ruin a region. Much government effort, at the local and state as well as federal level, represents attempts to prevent big business from creating social or economic problems, or to cope with problems it has created.

•Technology brings a need for public supervision. An impressive amount of government effort goes into the regulation of problem-creating technologies. Examples: the network of state and local highway and police authorities that deal with the automobile; the panoply of agencies designed to cope with airplanes, television and radio, atomic energy, new drugs, and weaponry. As long as technology increases its power to affect our social and natural environment, it is likely that public supervision will also increase.

•Urbanization brings a need for government. City life has its appeals, but it also has its perils. Men and women cannot live in crowded quarters without police, public health, traffic, sanitation, and educational facilities far more complex than those needed in a rural setting. Government is, and always has been, concentrated in cities. As a nation urbanizes, it requires more government.

•Increases in scale bring a need for government. Industrialization knits an economy together into a kind of vast, interlocked machinery. An unindustrialized, localized economy is like a pile of sand: if you poke a finger into one side of it, some businesses and individuals will be affected, but those on the other side of the pile will remain undisturbed. The growing scale and specialization of industrial operations unifies the sandpile. You poke one side of it, and the entire pile shakes. Problems can no longer be localized. The difficulties of the economy grow in extent: there is a need for a national, not a local, energy program, for national transportation, urban and educational programs. Government—largely federal government—is the principal means by which such problems are handled.

•Economic malfunction has brought government intervention. Fifty or seventy-five years ago, the prevailing attitude toward the economy was a kind of awed respect. People felt that the economy was best left alone, that it was fruitless as well as ill-advised to try to change its normal workings. That attitude changed once and for all with the advent of the Great Depression. In the ensuing collapse, the role of government greatly enlarged, to restore the economy to working order. The trauma of the Depression and the determination to prevent its recurrence were a watershed in the trend of government spending and government intervention.

•A new philosophy of "entitlement" has replaced the older one of "rugged individualism." Largely, but not wholly as a consequence of the experience of the Depression, a profound change has been registered in public attitudes toward the appropriate role of government. We no longer live in a society in which old-age retirement, medical expenses, and income during periods of unemployment are felt to be properly the responsibility of the individuals concerned. For better or worse, these and similar responsibilities have been gradually assumed by governments in all capitalist nations. In fact, the United States is a laggard in these matters compared with many European capitalist states. Here lie crucial reasons for the swelling volume of state, local, and federal production and purchase that have steadily enlarged the place of government within the economy.

No doubt there are other causes that could be added to this list. But the overall conclusion is already evident. In modern capitalism, government is a major factor in the economic system. How well it fulfills its functions and to what extent it realizes the hopes that have been thrust upon it are themes that will constantly occupy us as we continue with our studies.

FOCUS

As before, we don't want you to stuff yourself with a lot of facts and figures that will soon be out of date and that you will quickly forget. Instead, concentrate on some central ideas about four major *trends* in:

Growth

How do we measure growth?
What are its two main sources?

Distribution

What is the trend in dollar incomes for all classes?
What is the basic pattern in income shares?
Why can we explain the trend in growth better than the trends in distribution?

Business

Why has big business gotten bigger?

Government

What are the main reasons for the growth of federal, state, and local spending?
Are these the same reasons as those that explain the increase in government functions?

In reviewing this chapter, think about reasons for the big changes we have noted. How many of these trends do you think will continue?

QUESTIONS

1. Can you think of a theory of poverty that would match the "luck" theory of Instant Riches?

2. Here are some raw data:

	GNP (current $billions)	Price index	Population (millions)
1965	$ 688	100	194
1970	982	123	204
1975	1,498	170	214

What is real GNP per capita in 1970 and 1975 in 1965 dollars? In 1975 dollars? (Hint: you will need a new price index with 1975=100.)

3. If there were no change whatsoever in technology, do you think that a larger quantity of labor might result in GNP growing faster or slower than the sheer increase of man-hour input? Hint: Can people organize their activities better as their numbers change? Does this continue indefinitely?

4. Do you think it might be possible to construct a theory to explain why the pretax, pretransfer shares of income are so "fixed"? Could there be a kind of pecking order in society? Could different income groups establish economic "distances" that satisfy them? Would they then strive only to retain, not to increase, those differences?

5. Can you imagine an invention that would result in rapid concentration in a very unconcentrated industry, say the restaurant business? Or the laundry business? Can you imagine an invention that could radically deconcentrate an industry? How might a watch-sized CB radio affect AT&T? What invention could do the same for Exxon? U.S. Steel?

6. What forces do you think might bring about a concentration in labor unions; that is, the growth of a few dominant unions?

7. Do you think that the rise of government within the economy is "socialistic"? "Capitalistic"? What would you mean by either term?

44

The rise of the market economy

Our chapter on trends neglected the biggest trend of all, the long movement that brought the basic institution of capitalism and the market system into being. Here, in capsule form, is a review of that historic process.

PREMARKET SOCIETIES

We tend to think that markets are the normal form of social organization, that they have always existed. In a manner of speaking, they have. Men traded with one another at least as far back as the last Ice Age: the mammoth-hunters of the Russian steppes obtained shells from the Mediterranean region, as did the hunters of the central valleys of France. In fact, on the moors of Pomerania in northeastern Germany, archeologists have come across an oaken box with the remains of its original leather shoulder strap. In it were a dagger, a sickle head, and a needle, all of Bronze Age manufacture. According to the conjectures of experts, this was very likely the sample kit of a prototype of the traveling salesman, an itinerant representative who collected orders for the specialized production of his community.

Thus it seems as if we could discover evidences of a market organization of society deep in the past. But these surprising notes of modernity must be interpreted with caution. If markets, buying and selling—even highly organized trading bodies—were well-nigh ubiquitous features of ancient Greece or Rome or of feudalism, they should not be confused with the presence of a market *society*. Trade has existed as an important adjunct to society from earliest times, but the fundamental tasks of production or distribution were largely divorced from the market process. Over most of mankind's history, markets were *not* the means used by men to solve the economic problem.

The reason for this is easy to grasp. In the marketplaces of antiquity, men traded goods or bought and sold services. *But they did not buy or sell land, labor, or capital (the "factors of production") that entered into the production of these goods and services.* Nor, for that matter, did they entrust the distribution of the output of those factors of production mainly to the marketplace. Production and distribution were largely organized by the **rules of tradition**—rules of custom and habit sanctified by long usage—or by the **imperatives of command**—the orders handed down by rulers. Both these are age-old methods of arranging economic affairs. Certainly production and distribution were not organized by a network of trade and exchange in which human labor or the use of land or capital were directed by the invisible push and pull of market forces.

LABOR, LAND, CAPITAL

Then how did pre-modern society combine its factors of production? The answer comes as something of a shock: *there were no factors of production.* Of course, labor has always existed, for men have always had to expend effort to remain alive; land has always played its essential role as the great source of sustenance, together with the sea; and capital is as old as the first hunting implements or digging sticks.

Yet, *labor, land, or capital were never considered to be commodities for sale.* Labor was performed as part of the social duties of a peasant cultivator, a serf, or a slave, but in none of these roles was the laborer *paid* for his work. The peasant or serf raised his crop, handed over to the landlord his often onerous rent—usually by surrendering a portion of the actual crop—and kept body and soul together with what was left. The slave was the property of his owner, given his subsistence but certainly not remunerated by anything resembling a wage. Here and there, labor was performed in exchange for money—the work of skilled artisans, jewelers, armorers, and the like—but probably something like 70 to 80 percent of all the productive activity that sustained economic life in the pre-market economy was totally unconnected with anything that resembled a "market."

The same was true for land and capital. Land was the basis of power and status, perhaps the most important form of wealth, but it was rarely, and only under great duress, bought and sold. A medieval lord would no more have thought of selling a portion of his ancestral estates to a neighboring lord than the governor of Connecticut would think of selling off a few counties to the governor of Rhode Island. Capital, too, was an agency of the productive process for which nothing like a market existed. A few merchants dealt in gold and silver, and the owner of a ship might sell his capital equipment to another. But the idea that one's productive property was an "asset," worth a certain price and producing a certain income, was as foreign to premarket society as the idea, today, that shares of common stock should never be sold, but handed down like family heirlooms.

THE ECONOMIC REVOLUTION

How did wageless labor, unrentable land, and private treasures become "factors of production"; that is, abstract commodities to be bought and sold like so many yards of cloth or bushels of wheat? The answer is that a vast revolution undermined the world of tradition and command and brought into being the market relationships of the modern world. Beginning roughly in the sixteenth century—although with roots that can be traced much further back—a gradual process of change tore apart the bonds and customs of the medieval world and ushered in the market society we know.

We cannot trace that long, tortuous, and often bloody revolution here. In part it was brought about by the expulsion of English peasants from their lands through the "enclosure" of common grazing lands. This enclosure took place to make private pasturage for the lord's sheep, whose wool had become a profitable commodity. As late as 1820, the Duchess of Sutherland evicted 15,000 tenants from 794,000 acres, replacing them with 131,000 sheep. The tenants, deprived of their traditional access to the fields, drifted into the towns, where they were forced to sell their services as a factor of production: *labor.*

In France, the creation of factors of production bore painfully on land. From the eleventh century on, as goods began to flow into medieval Europe, lords of feudal manors began to convert the work "dues" owed by their serfs into cash payments, a trickle of copper coins. When prices began to rise in sixteenth-century Europe, especially as gold from the New World flowed in, the lords found themselves in a terrible squeeze. Like everything in feudal life, once the dues were set, they were fixed and unchangeable. But the prices of merchandise were not fixed. Although more and more of the serfs' obligations were changed from "kind" to cash, prices kept rising so fast that the feudal lords found it impossible to meet their bills.

Hence we begin to find a new economic individual, the *impoverished* aristocrat. In the year 1530 in the Gévaudan region of France, 121 lords had an income of 21,400 livres, but one of them had 5,000 livres of the sum, another 2,000, and the rest averaged 121 livres each. Meanwhile, the richest town merchants had incomes up to 65,000 livres. Thus the balance of power turned against the landed aristocracy, reducing some to shabby gentility. Meanwhile, the upstart merchants lost no time in acquiring lands that they soon came to regard not as ancestral estates but as potential capital.

EMERGENCE OF THE FACTORS OF PRODUCTION

This brief glance at economic history should bring us to realize that the factors of production, without which a market society could not exist, are not eternal attributes of a natural order. *They are the creations of a process of historic change,* a change that divorced "labor" from social life. Labor became an abstract quantity of effort offered for sale to bidders for labor power. Land became mere real estate, wholly separated from its ancient prerogatives of status and power. Not least, the idea of "capital" dawned upon a society. Wealth had, of course, always been known, but it was *particular* wealth—a gold cup, a chest of jewels, a ship. Now wealth lost its form and shape to become an abstract sum of value whose all-important consideration was only its "yield."

BACK TO THE PRESENT

We dip briefly into history to help us locate ourselves in the present. The private property that is inseparable from the factors of production, the market mechanism that binds the factors into a great circle of production and distribution—all this is the creation of relatively modern history. Economics itself is a modern creation, for there was little to puzzle out about it before the web of transactions took over the guidance of society from its age-old patterns of tradition or command. Indeed, the first truly modern economist, still a towering figure in economic thought, was Adam Smith (1723–1790), whose great book *The Wealth of Nations* appeared in the very year of the American Revolution. Economics, as we know it, is not much older than our nation, and our nation is not much older than the capitalist system itself.

Some major economic problems

We have begun to acquaint ourselves with that bewildering place called *the economy,* and we are almost ready to take up the formal business of economics itself. But we need one last overview before we settle down to the business of economics itself. Everyone studies economics, at least in part, to learn something about the economic problems that beset us. Let us therefore look at some of these problems, so that we can have them at the back of our minds when we begin our more formal studies. We will deal with four big issues, in part because they are surely on your mind, in part because it is possible to discuss them broadly without using any more actual economic knowledge than we already possess.

Inflation

4

There is no question where to begin. For the last decade, the pollsters tell us, the problem that has headed the list of worries of the public has been inflation. What should we know about this central concern?

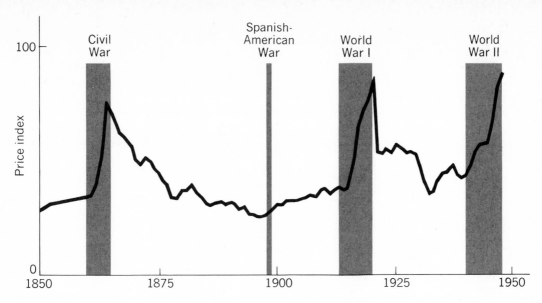

FIG. 4·1   Inflation in perspective

Inflation in retrospect

Inflation is both a very old problem and a very new one. If we look back over history, we discover many inflationary periods. Diocletian tried (in vain) to curb a Roman inflation in the fourth century A.D. Between 1150 and 1325, the cost of living in medieval Europe rose fourfold. Between 1520 and 1650, prices doubled and quadrupled, largely as a result of gold pouring into Europe from the newly opened mines of the New World. In the years following the Civil War, the South experienced a ferocious inflation. Finally, during World War I, prices in the United States rose 100 percent.

Let us focus closer on the U.S. experience up to 1950 (Fig. 4.-1). Two things should be noted about this chart. First, major wars are regularly accompanied by inflation. The reasons are obvious enough. War greatly increases the volume of public expenditure, but governments do not curb private spending by an equal amount through taxation. Invariably, wars are financed largely by borrowing; and the total amount of spending, public and private, rises rapidly. Meanwhile, the amount of goods available to households is cut back to make room for war production. The result is the classic description of inflation: *too much money chasing too few goods.*

Second, U.S. inflations have always been relatively short-lived in the past. Notice that prices fell during the long period 1866 to 1900, and again from 1925 to 1933. The hundred-year trend, although generally tilted upward, is marked with long valleys as well as sharp peaks.

Recent inflationary experience

Now examine Fig. 4.-2, which shows the record of U.S. price changes since 1950. Once again we notice that the outbreak of war has brought price rises, albeit relatively small ones. But in a vital way, contemporary experience differs from that of the past. Peaks of inflationary rises have not been followed by long, gradual declines. Instead, inflation seems to have become a chronic element in the economic situation. Only in late 1975 did the rate of inflation begin to abate substantially, al-

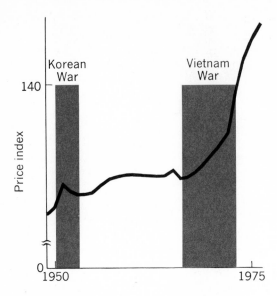

FIG. 4·2 Wholesale prices since 1950

though it did not come to a halt. The slowdown was achieved only by the application of economic policies that resulted in severe economic hardship for many.

Causes of inflation

What causes inflations? Many things. We know that we are likely to suffer from inflation if our banking system creates too much money (we will study that in Chapter 34). The trouble is, we don't know exactly how much money is "too much."

We also know that inflation always results when the spending of households and businesses and governments presses against the limits of our capacity to produce goods and services—the "money-chasing-goods" problem. Here, the trouble is that inflation sometimes begins *before* we've reached operating "capacity."

We know that price rises can be brought on by accidents of nature such as massive crop failures or by political actions such as an oil embargo. But we also know that inflation can occur without these accidents.

Finally, we know that inflation will break out if wages or other payments to factors of production are raised more rapidly than productivity, so that costs per unit of output are pushed up. But we don't know why inflation happens even when costs don't seem to be "pushing"— indeed, when wages in many areas are lagging behind the cost of living.

We will not be able to inquire more deeply into these causes of inflation until we have learned something more about the way our economy works. Yet we already know enough to enable us to follow a few general arguments about its origins.

The shift to services

One fact that we notice in all industrialized nations is the movement of an ever larger fraction of their work forces into the service industries. In the U.S., as we have seen, almost 70 percent of the labor force works in offices, shops, classrooms, municipal and state and federal buildings, producing the "services" that are ever more in demand in a highly urbanized, high-consumption society.

WAGES AND COSTS

It isn't higher wages that make prices rise, but higher wages per unit of output. Suppose a factory pays $1 million a year in wages and makes 1 million units of clothing. Wage cost *per unit* is $1. Now suppose that wages go up 25 percent *but productivity rises 50 percent.* Wage cost is now $1.25 million. Output is 1.5 million units. Wage cost per unit is $1,250,000 ÷ 1,500,000 = $0.83. *Wage costs per unit have actually fallen.*

Could this happen? Yes, if higher wages cause workers to work harder, or simply if technology has improved and boosted output.

Professor William Baumol has suggested that *this shift to services may have important inflationary implications.* Productivity in many areas of the service sector probably lags behind productivity in most industrial tasks. (We say "probably" because service productivity is often bafflingly difficult to measure.) But wages in the service sector tend to be drawn up toward the levels established in the great industrial enterprises. Thus wages in many service businesses or government agencies may rise faster than output, pushing up prices. Between 1967 and 1975, when the consumer price index rose by 61 percent, the price index of services rose by 67 percent, whereas that of manufactured goods rose by only 50 percent.

Increasing power in the marketplace

We have already noted that one of the most striking differences between modern inflations and those of the past is that in former days, inflationary peaks were followed by long deflationary periods when prices fell. Why did they fall? One reason is that it was not unusual, in the nineteenth and early twentieth centuries, for large companies to announce across-the-board wage cuts when times were bad. In addition, prices declined as a result of technological advances and as the consequence of sporadic "price wars" that would break out among industrial competitors.

Most of that seems a part of the past beyond recall. Technology continues to lower costs, but this has been offset by a "ratchet tendency" shown by wages and prices since World War II. **A ratchet tendency means that prices and wages go up, but they rarely or never come down.** This characteristic is probably due to the increasing presence of concentrated big industry, to stronger trade unions, and to a business climate in which wage cuts and price wars are no longer regarded as legitimate economic policies. These changes have undoubtedly added to our inflationary propensities.

Expansionist influence of governments

A third change, equally visible throughout the Western world and Japan, *is the much larger role played by the public sector in generating demand.* This does not mean that government spending by itself is inherently inflationary. As we will learn, *any* kind of spending can send prices up, once we reach an area of reasonably full employment. Rather, the presence of large government sectors and the knowledge that governments are dedicated to policies of economic growth help bring about inflation by influencing *private* expenditures in an inflation-producing way.

In the old days, when governments were minor contributors to GNP, and when large-scale government policies against recession were unknown, the public expected bad times as well as good and behaved accordingly. At the first sign of an economic storm, sails were furled. Businesses cut back on expansion programs; people meekly accepted wage cuts; consumers gave up "luxuries." As a consequence, private spending of all kinds dwindled, lessening the pressure on prices.

That has also changed. **Corporations, labor leaders, and the public now expect governments to prevent recessions.** Accordingly, they no longer trim their sails at the first sight of trouble on the horizon. The willingness to maintain private spending serves to set a floor under the economy, adding to the ratchet-like movement of incomes and prices.

Effects of affluence

A last suggestion is closely related to the previous ones. *The staying power of labor is now vastly strengthened compared with its prewar days.* Only a generation ago, a strike was essentially limited by the meager savings of working families or the pittance of support that unions could offer. There was no unemployment compensation, no welfare, no large union treasury. Today, strikes are backed by very substantial staying power, and both corporations and municipalities know it. Thus there is a tendency to settle for higher wages than would be granted if the employer felt that by waiting a few weeks he could enforce a better bargain.

Add to that a change that affluence makes in the expectations of the public. Strikes of teachers, transportation workers, sanitation workers, and others who were formerly resigned to low wages have added impetus to the inflationary surge of industrial nations. A policeman in New York City in 1920 did not think that he had a "right" to earn as much as a worker in the Ford plant in Detroit. A policeman today sees no reason why he should not. In an affluent society, where personal aspirations are encouraged and the constraints of poverty are lessened, the established "pecking order" of an old-fashioned society gives way to a free-for-all, in which each group tries to exploit its economic strength to the hilt. This may be good for the group concerned and may lead to a more equitable distribution of income, but it also lends its momentum to the forces that push our society toward a seemingly unstoppable inflation.

A last word

It is clear that the causes of inflation are many and deep-seated. Inflation is not an economic tendency that we are likely to be able to reverse or even to control with mild policies. Most economists today expect a chronic, endemic inflation at annual rates of between 3 to 8 percent a year as the "price" of running a reasonably fast-moving, reasonably fully-employed economy. Later, in Chapter 35 we will explore some of the possibilities for slowing inflation, but it is a bitter truth that no one today expects to see the process come to a halt.

Unemployment

Ask American citizens what is their *second* most worrisome economic problem, and you will likely get agreement that it is unemployment. Unlike inflation, however, unemployment has not been high on the public's complaints for ten years. This is because large-scale unemployment is a fairly recent problem, the consequence of the economic recession of 1973–1975.

Recessions and unemployment

Because unemployment and recession are so closely linked, we had better begin by asking: what is a recession? The answer is very simple. A recession is a drop in the gross national product that lasts for at least 6 months. The word *depression* is used to refer to a severe drop in GNP, but there is no generally accepted definition of when a recession becomes a depression. People generally call a downturn a recession if their neighbor is unemployed, but a depression if they are unemployed.

Although recessions always bring unemployment, we can suffer from unemployment even without recession, if our growth is too slow. Each year our productivity increases by about 3 percent and our labor force by about 1 percent (on the

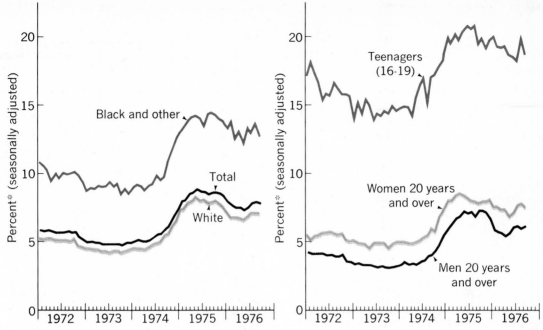

Unemployment as percent of civilian labor force in group specified.
Source: Department of Labor

FIG. 4 · 3   Impact of recession on employment

average). This means that each year we have the ability to turn out about 4 percent more goods. *Unless our GNP grows by at least that rate, we will not be able to keep up with our rising productivity capacity. The consequence is that there will be un-sold goods and workers who are let go or not rehired.*

Impact of recession

Let us trace exactly what happens when GNP falls or lags. The pace of business activity slows down. There is less demand for consumer goods and services, less demand for plant and equipment and other business items. Some businesses fire people, other businesses hire fewer new workers. Because our labor force is steadily growing as our population swells, even a small decrease in the willingness to take on new workers spells a sharp rise in unemployment for certain groups, such as young people.

When a recession really deepens, as in 1975, it is not just the young who cannot find work, but experienced workers find themselves thrown out of work, as Fig. 4.3 shows.

Unemployment vs. inflation

Unemployment is a problem that has to be judged differently from the way we judge inflation. Rising prices affect everyone, although some kinds of wage earners or profit-receivers gain while others lose. Unemployment, however, is a sharply focused economic ill. As we can also see from Fig. 4.3, some groups, such as teenagers or blacks, bear the brunt of unemployment much more painfully than others.

Meanwhile, within the ranks of the unemployed, suffering is also concentrated. When we state that 8 percent of the (white) labor force is unemployed, this does not mean that every white worker is laid off for 8 percent of the year. It means that some workers are unemployed for long periods. In mid-1975, for example, 15 percent of all the 7.8 million jobless had been without work for over *half a year.* Many of them had exhausted all unemployment insurance and had to go on welfare. Another 15 percent of the unemployed had been without work for more than 15 weeks. Another 30 percent had experienced unemployment for more than 5 weeks.

Curing unemployment

How can unemployment be cured? That, too will have to await a fuller discussion of economics, but we can anticipate the main points.

1. To cure unemployment, we must raise GNP. Additions to GNP may come from increased consumer outlays, increased business outlays, or increased government outlays.

2. In remedying unemployment, an increase in spending may lead to a faster inflation. The issue, therefore, is to determine how much inflation the public will bear in order to eliminate excess unemployment. We have seen that unemployment affects some individuals or families much more harshly than inflation affects any family. Yet, the general feeling of the public is that inflation is a more serious economic ailment than unemployment! The reason is clear. Most people feel hurt by inflation, even if they aren't. Only a small minority of people feel the full brunt of recession.

3. Some groups will experience high unemployment, even if we have a high level of GNP. Men and women who do not

THE GREAT DEPRESSION

The Great Depression was probably the most dangerous economic episode in American life. GNP fell precipitously from $104 billion in 1929 to $56 billion in 1933. Unemployment rose from 1.5 million to 12.8 million: one person in every four in the labor force was out of work. Residential construction fell by 90 percent; nine million savings accounts were lost as banks closed their doors. Eighty-five thousand businesses failed. Wages fell to 5 cents an hour in sawmills, 6 cents in brick and tile manufacturing, 7½ cents in general contracting. As the stock market crashed, $30 billion in financial assets vanished. By 1932 nearly one in five of all Detroit schoolchildren was officially registered as seriously undernourished.

What caused the Great Depression? To this day we do not have a wholly convincing account. In part it was the consequence of a general decline in business expansion: investment expenditures fell by 88 percent from 1929 to 1933. But underlying this collapse were a number of contributory factors. Farm incomes had been steadily falling for years. The distribution of income was worsening, with profits booming at the same time that wage income was basically unchanged. Compounding and aggravating these weaknesses in the economy was a devastating collapse in credit. Whole structures of companies, pyramided one atop the other, fell like so many houses of cards when the stock market fell. And to worsen matters still further, the monetary authorities pursued policies of "prudence" and "caution" that unwittingly weakened the economy still further.

Can another Great Depression devastate the economy? Most economists would doubt it. Most bank accounts are today insured by the Federal Deposit Insurance Corporation, so that the wholesale wiping out of household assets would not happen again. The stock market, although still subject to wide swings, is unlikely to drag households or businesses into insolvency, because stocks can no longer be bought on the thin "margins" (partial payments) characteristic of the 1930s. Most important of all, the sheer size of government expenditure today makes a total collapse almost impossible. Moreover, if a severe depression were to begin, government would pursue policies of expansion either unknown or unthinkable in those days of laissez-faire economics. We will be studying all these matters later.

THE GHETTO SKILL MIX

A sad example of the lack of fit between the skills demanded by employers and those possessed by the labor force is to be found in the ghetto, where typically the labor force is badly undertrained. A study by the First National City Bank explored this situation in New York City.

As we can see, in only one category—unskilled service—was the prospective demand for labor roughly in line with the skills available. This meant a reasonable employment prospect for maids, restaurant workers, bellhops, and the like—among the lowest-paid occupations in the nation.

As for the common laborer, who comprised over half the "skill pool" of the New York ghetto, his outlook was bleak indeed—less than one percent of new jobs would open in that area. Conversely, for the widest job market in the city—the white-collar trades that offer two-thirds of the new jobs— the ghetto could offer only one-seventh of its residents as adequately trained. These extreme disproportions still apply to the situation in New York and many other slum-ridden cities. If these figures have any meaning, it is that ghetto poverty is here to stay, short of a herculean effort to rescue the trapped ghetto resident.

	Occupational distribution of ghetto unemployed, 1968	Estimated job openings, 1965– 1975
White collar	13.6%	65.7%
Craftsmen	2.8	7.4
Operatives	14.7	7.7
Unskilled personal service	16.6	18.6
Laborers	52.3	0.6

have the right skills or training will not be able to fill existing jobs. Members of groups who are discriminated against or people with undesired characteristics (such as teenagers who quit jobs casually) will have trouble finding work. To cure this "structural" unemployment requires special programs. We will discuss some of them in Chapter 36.

4. A big issue for the future is how much the government should do about unemployment. Should the government become an "employer of last resort," offering guaranteed work to all who seek work? Should the government impose price controls in order to curb inflation, while spending more? We will come back to these issues many times.

Big Business

Almost from our first look at the economy, the tremendous size of the modern giant corporation has caught our eye. It is hardly surprising that the giant corporation has been bothering society for almost a hundred years. Massive agglomerations of private business power exist. (So do massive agglomerations of union power.) The question is what to do about it? Here are some of the answers.

A conservative view The first suggestion is most prominently associated with the name of Nobel laureate Milton Friedman. Professor Friedman is a philosophic conservative whose response to the question of what a corporation should do to discharge its social responsibility is very simple: make money.

The function of a business organization in society, argues Friedman, is to serve as an efficient agent of production, not as a locus of social improvement. It serves that productive function best by striving after profit—conforming, while doing so, to the basic rules and legal norms of society. It is not up to business to "do good"; it is up to government to prevent it from doing bad.

Moreover, says Friedman, as soon as a businessman tries to apply any rules other than moneymaking, he takes into his own hands powers that rightfully belong to others, such as political authorities. Friedman would even forbid corporations to give money to charities or universities. Their business, their responsibility to society, he insists, is *production*. Let the dividend-receivers give away the money the corporations pay them, but do not let corporations become the active social welfare agencies of society.

The corporation as social arbiter

Friedman's position has a number of weaknesses, especially in its assumption that stockholders' claims to corporate profits are more valid than are the claims of a corporation's management and workers. This view dismisses the fact that management and workers have done more to create those profits than stockholders have done.

It is interesting to note that few corporate heads espouse Friedman's position. They take the view that the corporation, by virtue of its immense size and strength, has power thrust upon it, whether it wishes to have it or not. The solution to this problem, as these men see it, is for corporate executives to act "professionally" in using this power, doing their best to judge fairly among the claims of the many groups to whom they are responsible: labor, stockholders, customers, and the public at large.

There is no doubt that many top corporate executives think of themselves as the referees among contending groups, and no doubt many of them use caution and forethought in exercising the power of decision. But the weaknesses of this argument are also not difficult to see. There are no criteria for "qualifying" as a responsible corporate executive (see box, p. 59). Nor is there any clear guideline, even for the most scrupulous executive, defining the correct manner in which to exercise responsibility. Should an executive's concern for the prevention of pollution take precedence over concern for turning in a good profit statement at the end of the year? Or for giving wage increases? Or for

reducing the price of the product? Is the company's contribution to charity or education supposed to represent the executive's preferences or those of customers or workers? Has Xerox a right to help the cause of public broadcasting; the makers of firearms to help support the National Rifle Association?

These questions begin to indicate the complexity of the issue of "social responsibility" and the problems implicit in allowing important *social* decisions to be made by private individuals who are not publicly accountable for their actions.

Dissolution of monopoly

A third approach to the problem of responsibility takes yet another tack. *It suggests that the power of big business be curbed by dividing large corporations into several much smaller units.* A number of studies have shown that the largest *plant* size needed for industrial efficiency is far smaller (in terms of financial assets) than the giant firms typical of the *Fortune* list of the top 500 industrial corporations (or for that matter of the next 500). Hence a number of economists have suggested that a very strict application of antitrust legislation should be applied, not only to prohibit mergers but to separate a huge enterprise such as General Motors into its natural constituent units: a Buick Company, an Oldsmobile Company, a Chevrolet Company, and so on.

One major problem stands in the way of this frontal attack on corporate power. It is that size leads to good effects as well as bad ones. As John Kenneth Galbraith has wittily remarked, "The showpieces [of the economy] are, with rare exceptions, the industries which are dominated by a handful of large firms. The foreign visitor, brought to the United States . . . visits the same firms as do the attorneys of the Department of Justice in their search for monopoly."

The other side of that coin is that small competitive industry is typically beset by low research and development programs, antilabor practices, and a general absence of the kinds of amenities that we associate with "big business." As we shall later see, in some cases more competition might actually do more harm than good.

Regulation

Regulation has been a long-standing American response to the problem of corporate power. Regulation has sought to influence or prohibit corporate actions in many fields: pricing, advertising, designing products, dealing with unions or minority groups, and still other areas. Given the variety of ways in which corporations are regulated, it is hardly surprising that the effectiveness of the regulatory process is very uneven. Yet we can discern two general attributes that affect most regulatory agencies.

First, economic events tend to change faster than the regulations governing them. City building codes that were perfectly appropriate when adopted become obsolete and then retard the use of new techniques and materials that would be more efficient and just as safe. Why are not regulations kept abreast of events?

Partly because the political process is simply slower than the economic process, partly because any regulation soon creates its own defenders. Vested interests, formed around existing codes, fight to prevent changes in the regulations. The plumber who installs the copper pipes required by law might not be the plumber who would install the plastic pipes if they were allowed.

Second, regulatory commissions often take on the view of the very industry they are supposed to regulate, because they must turn to that industry for the expertise to staff their own agencies. Thus it is common for a regulatory body to become the captive of its own ward. The Interstate Commerce Commission, established in 1887 to regulate the railroads, is a prime example of this reversal of roles. When the ICC was established, the railroads were a monopoly that badly needed public supervision. Autos and trucks had not yet come into existence, so that there were few alternative means of bulk transportation in many areas.

By the end of the first quarter of the twentieth century, however, the railway industry was no longer without effective substitutes. Cars, trucks, buses, planes, pipelines—all provided effective competition. At this point, the ICC became interested in protecting the railroads

---

A REGULATION HORROR STORY

An example of how the ICC protects its "clients" against competition was turned up by the Senate Select Committee on Small Business. It concerned a small trucking firm that wished to extend trucking service to two Alabama towns not directly served by any large carrier. After 4½ years of proceedings, the ICC granted the applicant limited approval to serve one of the towns but not the other. In its report, the commission stated that these towns had "only limited transportation needs" and that additional service was therefore not warranted.

In effect, the commission *prevented* the second town from enjoying trucking service.

In similar actions, the ICC has limited competition by preventing private truckers from choosing new routes that would greatly shorten trucking hauls, forbidding trucks that carried goods one way to pick up goods for a return load, and limiting the products that certain carriers might legally haul. The commission has ruled that a live chicken is an "agricultural commodity" but a dead chicken is not; that nuts in the shell qualify as agricultural goods but not shelled nuts. These regulations follow from a law that states that motor vehicles carrying agricultural commodities are exempt from ICC regulation. It was therefore in the "interest" of the ICC to define an agricultural commodity as narrowly as possible, to broaden its area of control and minimize the competition that would otherwise arise.

against competition, rather than in curbing abuses. One by one, these alternative modes of transport fell under its aegis (or under that of other regulatory agencies), and quasi-monopoly prices were set, as little "empires" were established for each form of transportation.

Nationalization

Then why not nationalize the large firms? The thought comes as rank heresy to a nation that has been accustomed to equating nationalization with socialism. *Yet Germany, France, England, Sweden, Italy, and a host of other capitalist nations have nationalized industries ranging from oil refineries to airlines, from automobile production to the output of coal and electricity.* Hence, Professor Galbraith has suggested that we should nationalize corporations charged with the public interest, such as the giant armaments producers who are wholly dependent on the Pentagon, in order to bring such firms under public control.

But would nationalization achieve its purpose of assuring social responsibility? In 1971, the Pentagon arranged special contracts and "loans" to save Lockheed Aircraft, one of its "ward" companies, from bankruptcy, the fate of an ordinary inefficient firm. Outright nationalization would only cement this union of political and economic power, by making Lockheed a part of the Pentagon and thus making it even more difficult to put pressure on it to perform efficiently.

Or take the Tennessee Valley Authority, perhaps the most famous American public enterprise. It is being sued for the environmental devastation it has wrought by its strip-mining operations. So, too, the Atomic Energy Commission, which operates "nationalized" plants, has been severely criticized for its careless supervision of radioactive processes.

The problem is that nationalization not only removes the affected enterprise entirely from the pressures of the market, but almost inevitably brings it under the political shelter of the government, further removing the venture from any effective criticism.

Other possibilities

All these difficulties make it clear that the problem of social responsibility will not be easy to solve (or for that matter, even to *define*), no matter what step we choose, from Professor Friedman's laissez faire to Galbraith's nationalization. For each of these problems with the corporation, we could easily construct counterparts that have to do with the control over labor unions or over the government itself.

What, then, is to be done? A number of other lines of action suggest themselves. One is the widening of the legal *responsibility* of the corporation to include areas of activity for which it now has little or no accountability. Environmental damage is one of these. Consumer protection is another.

A second step would be a widening of *public accountability through disclosure*, the so-called fishbowl method of regulation. Corporations could be required to report to public agencies to make known corporate expenditures for pollution control, political lobbying, and so on. Corporate tax returns could be opened to public scrutiny. Unions and corporations both could be required to make public disclosure of their race practices, with regard to hiring or admission, advancement, and rates of pay.

Still another course of action would be to appoint *public members* to boards of directors of large companies or to executive organs of large unions and to charge these members with protecting the consumers'

PORTRAIT OF A CHIEF EXECUTIVE

A capsule profile of the chief executives of the biggest 500 industrial corporations

Family's Economic Status

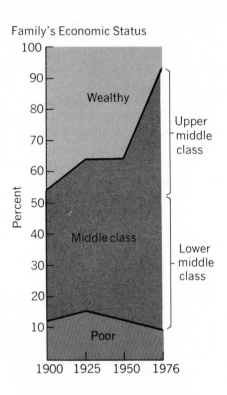

Father's occupation

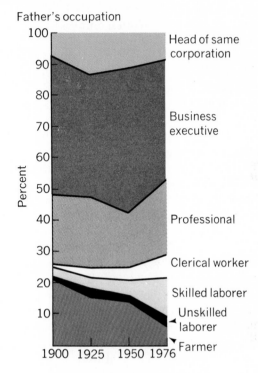

Highest Educational Level Attained

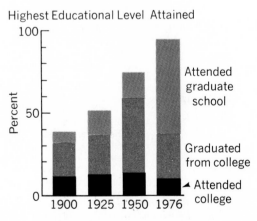

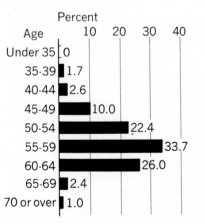

Reprinted by special permission from the May 1976 issue of Fortune Magazine; © 1976 by Time Inc.

interest and with reporting behavior that seemed contrary to the public interest. Worker-members of boards of directors might also serve such a useful purpose (there are such members in Germany and a movement toward "workers' co-determination" in a number of other European nations).

Finally, there is the corrective action of dedicated private individuals such as Ralph Nader, who rose to fame on his exposé of the safety practices of the auto industry, and who has since turned his guns on pollution, other irresponsibilities of big business, and on poor performance in the federal bureaucracy. *Such public pressure is necessarily sporadic and usually short-lived, but it has been a powerful source of social change.*

Power: the unresolved problem

It would be a mistake to conclude this recital with the implication that corporate (or union or government) power can be easily brought under control through a few legal remedies or by the power of public opinion. Certainly, many abuses can be curbed, and much better levels of social performance achieved.

Yet mass organizations seem an inescapable concomitant of our age of high technology and increasing social interdependence. Here we should note that, depending on our interests, we stress different aspects of this universal phenomenon. To some, who fear the continued growth of very large-scale business, the most significant aspect is that we have not managed to control business power. To others, concerned over the emergence of large labor unions, it is labor power that most dangerously eludes effective control. And to still others who are most worried by the growth of big government, it is the growth of public power that is the main problem.

Thus the question of economic power remains, at best, only partially resolved. As A. A. Berle has written: "Some of these corporations can be thought of only in somewhat the same way we have heretofore thought of nations." Unlike nations, however, their power has not been rationalized in law, fully tested in practice, or well defined in philosophy. Unquestionably, the political and social influence and the economic power of the great centers of production pose problems with which capitalism—indeed, all industrialized societies—will have to cope for many years to come.

THE EXPONENTIAL FACTS OF LIFE

Exponential growth is a startling phenomenon. It is illustrated in the famous parable about the farmer who has a lily pond in which there is a single lily that doubles its size each day. After a year, the pond is completely covered. How long did it take for the pond to be *half* covered? The answer is—364 days. In the last day the doubling lily will completely fill the pond.

Exponential examples such as these must always be used with great care. Their mathematical logic does not take into account the feedback mechanisms that inhibit explosive behavior of exponential series. Long before the lily covered half the pond it would probably have used up the nutrient matter in the pond and ceased growing. Long before the horrendous projections of exponential population growth, in which human beings will stand on one another's shoulders in a few centuries, feedbacks would have slowed down or halted or reversed population trends. Exponential trends show the *potential* growth of variables, but this potential is rarely realized.

One last point. There is a convenient way of figuring how long it takes for any quantity to double, if we know its exponential growth rate. *It is to divide the growth rate into the number 70.* Thus if population is growing at 2 percent a year, it will double in 35 years ($70 \div 2$). If the growth rate rises to 3 percent, the doubling time drops to 23+ years ($70 \div 3$).

Running Out of Growth

One last problem remains for our consideration. We have seen that growth has been the great central trend of American capitalism; indeed, of all capitalist systems. As we have already mentioned, a necessity to continue growth is a prime requirement if we are to maintain a high level of employment. Now we must face the fact that growth is a destructive as well as constructive process and that sooner or later, perhaps within a generation, growth may have to taper off substantially or even come to a halt.

Exponential growth and resources

Why do we face such an unprecedented challenge? The reason is that growth of the kind that has carried forward both capitalism and industrial socialism is a process that converts the raw materials of the planet into commodities that men use for their consumption or for further production. Thus along with growth has come a steady rise in the volume of raw materials that man has extracted from the planet and an even more rapid increase in the energy he has harnessed, both for the extraction and the processing of those raw materials.

What is alarming is that the rate of use of resources rises with frightening rapidity because growth is an exponential process. Today, global industrial output is rising about 7 percent a year, thereby doubling every 10 years. If we project this rate of growth for another 50 years, the rate of use of resources would double 5 times (assuming that today's technology of industrial production is essentially unchanged). Thus 50 years hence we would need 32 times as much material input as we need today. A century hence, when output would have doubled 10 times, we

would need over 1,000 times the present volume of output, and this gargantuan volume of extraction would still be relentlessly doubling.

Resource availability

Does this mean that we will run out of resources? Table 4.1 shows a 1972 estimate of the number of years that then known and estimated future resources would supply us at present growth rates.

Table 4·1   Global resource availability

	Years of global resource availability at present growth rates (1972)	
Resource	If present resources stocks are used	If resource stocks are quintupled
Aluminum	31	55
Coal	111	150
Copper	21	48
Iron	93	173
Lead	21	64
Manganese	46	94
Natural gas	22	49
Petroleum	20	50
Silver	13	42
Tin	15	61
Tungsten	28	72

Source: Meadows, *et al., The Limits to Growth* (Washington, D.C.: Potomac Associates, 1972).

At first glance, the figures are sobering, to say the least. Yet we must be careful before we take them at face value. Resources are not so "fixed" as the table shows, for these reserves include only those deposits of minerals that are available with today's technology. They do not include minerals that exist in levels of concentration that are not "economic"; that is, too costly to utilize with existing techniques. But techniques change, and with them, the volume of "economic" resources. Consider the fact that taconite, the main source of iron today, was not even considered a resource in the days when the high-grade ores of the Mesabi Range provided most of our ore.

Some economic resources, such as oil, may be exhausted within a relatively short time. In general, however, resources exist in vast quantities, especially if we consider the gigantic amounts of minerals locked into the earth's crust or present in "trace amounts" in its seas. Given the technology and the energy, we could literally "mine the seas and melt the rocks" to provide ourselves with "unlimited" resources.

The technological factor   *We are therefore essentially engaged in a race between technology and the exponentially rising demands for raw materials.* Technology enters this race in many different ways. It may enable us to recycle existing wastes, so that we do not need to extract as much new material. It may enable us to get more usable resources from a given quantity of raw material. It may open up new modes of production that enable us to shift production techniques away from materials that are becoming scarce (and therefore expensive) to those that remain abundant and therefore cheap. It gives us new sources of energy that enable us to use materials that are now too "low-grade" for economic production.

A primary question in estimating the "limits" to growth is therefore the rate at which we will develop the appropriate technology. Unfortunately, the link between research and development and economically usable technology is not clearly understood. We do not really know whether we will find an appropriate technology to run a vast private automobile fleet in the year 2000 or whether we will be able to turn out enough high quality steel to support global industrialization 50 years hence. More important, we do not know if a technology that permitted us to "mine the seas and melt the rocks" will be perfected or whether such a technology would be compatible with other ecological and environmental considerations.

The heat problem   Mention of the environment opens a last problem of great importance. To extract resources on the scale required to sustain industrial growth on its present path will require the application of tremendous amounts of energy. Production of this energy, if it uses the combustion of conventional fuels or nuclear power (including fusion power) is associated with the generation of heat. This man-made heat may be our most serious long-run environmental barrier. A number of scientists have expressed concern that the massing of industrial processes is already capable of throwing off so much heat that it can alter the climate patterns of the world in disastrous ways. They fear that at today's growth rates, the continued exponential generation of man-made heat would, in a matter of about a century, approach the danger zone. Man-made heat would then be generated in such quantities that it would begin to warm up the atmosphere—a process that would be fatal if allowed to go on unchecked for another century or so.

Doomsday?   Projections such as these can give rise to Doomsday attitudes, beliefs that we are racing hell-bent on an unalterable disaster course. This is not what economists who are concerned about the growth problem have in mind. A terrible resource shortage or a climatic disaster is possible, but by no means inevitable. Sources of energy such as solar power generators or wind machines can utilize the existing heat and energy in the atmosphere to provide us with substantial amounts of power that do not pour man-made heat into the air. Moreover, if we begin to encroach seriously on our resource base, we can expect resource prices to rise, thereby providing an incentive to conserve raw materials. Further, a shift toward "safer" consumption, such as human services, opens an avenue for nonpolluting, nonresource-using growth.

For all these and still other reasons, a Doomsday attitude is not warranted. The frightening picture of a world running out of resources or fatally overloading its environment is a projection of what would happen if growth continued at its present rate, unabated and uncontrolled, but the very dangers we have cited make such a fatally self-destructive course highly improbable.

That is not, however, an end to our analysis. The worry about growth is not that it will lead the world into a catastrophe. It is simply that our present kind of industrial growth must slow down. We cannot yet give a very clear timetable for when it must slow down or by how much or in exactly what industries and fields, but few would deny that safe industrial expansion will be more and more difficult to achieve in the coming decades. Significantly, a number of industrial countries have already officially adopted growth policies that are less than the maximum possible rate.

Global inequality

Two problems must be squarely faced if we contemplate the consequences of limiting growth. The first problem has to do with the unequal distribution of income (and resources) among the nations of the world. As we shall see in Chapter 42, standards of living in underdeveloped nations today are far below even the poorest levels in advanced countries. Thus the prospect of an enforced slowdown in the rate of industrial output raises the specter of *an international struggle for resources* as the poor countries attempt to build modern industrial structures and as developed nations continue along their present course.

The question of an impending slowdown for industrial growth therefore poses a major economic problem for international relations. How are the remaining easily available resources of the world to be shared? As the advanced nations continue to build up their industrial systems, will they leave the underdeveloped regions on a permanently lower level of well-being? Will the poorer countries, many of which already have (or will have) The Bomb, acquiesce in such a two-class world?

Stationary capitalism?

Second, we must ask whether a very low rate of industrial growth is compatible with capitalism.

Economists from Adam Smith through Karl Marx down to the present day have pointed out that such a "stationary state" would pose very great difficulties for a capitalist system. As we have seen, even a slowing of growth can set into motion a downward spiral of incomes and employment. A permanent slowdown might plunge capitalism into severe depression.

Moreover, the end of growth would mean that the struggle among various social groups for higher incomes for themselves would take place in a fixed or even shrinking economic system. There would no longer be more available for all. One group's gain could only come at another's loss. Whether capitalism can make that adjustment—or whether industrial socialism can make it better—are questions that our analysis raises but cannot answer.

A spaceship economy

What is certain, is that *all* industrial systems, socialist as well as capitalist, will eventually have to change their attitudes toward growth. In the long run there is no alternative to viewing the earth itself as a spaceship (in economist Kenneth Boulding's phrase) to whose ultimately finite carrying capacity its passengers must adjust their ways. From this point of view, production itself suddenly appears as a "throughput," beginning with the raw material of the environment and ending with the converted material of the production process, which is returned to the environment by way of emissions, residuals, and so on. In managing this throughput, the task of producers is not to maximize "growth," but to do as little damage to the environment as possible during the inescapable process of transformation by which man lives. If growth enters man's calculations in this period of rationally controlled production,

it can be only insofar as he can extract more and more "utility" from less and less material input; that is, as he learns to economize on the use of the environment by recycling his wastes and by avoiding the disturbance of delicate ecological systems.

Such a spaceship economy is still some distance off, although by no means so far away that our children or grandchildren may not encounter its problems. Much depends on the rate at which the Third World grows in population and productivity and on the technological means of lessening pollution in the advanced countries. Not least, a true spaceship earth would require a feeling of international amity sufficiently great so that the industrialized peoples of the world would willingly acquiesce in global production ceilings that penalized them much more severely than their poorer sister nations.

These longer perspectives begin to make us aware of the complexity of the problem of growth. Growth is desperately needed by a world that is, in most nations, still desperately poor. Yet, growth is already beginning to threaten a world that is running out of "environment." If growth inevitably brings environmental danger, we shall be faced with a cruel choice indeed. Today we have only begun to recognize the problems of pollution-generating growth, and we are engaged in devising remedies for these problems on a national basis. Ahead lies the much more formidable problem of a world in which growth may encounter ecological barriers on a worldwide scale, bringing the need for new political and economic arrangements for which we have no precedent. The true Age of Spaceship Earth is still some distance in the future, but for the first time the passengers on the craft are aware of its limitations.

FOCUS

Our purpose in bringing you face-to-face with the biggest problems in economics is clearly not to give you "answers" to them. There are no answers in the sense of widely agreed-upon policies on inflation, unemployment, control of big business (or big labor or big government), and long-term growth. Instead, we would like to leave you with these conclusions to reflect on.

Inflation. Coping with inflation is a problem of very great perplexity that we will have to postpone until we know more about such things as how money "works." Perhaps you can already anticipate that the great debate will hinge on what kinds of measures the government should take: tax measures, money measures, or outright controls.

Unemployment. This is the cruelest problem of the economy, although we must remember that the general public thinks that inflation is worse. Try to remember that unemployment responds to GNP. The trick is to find a middle ground between spending that creates inflation and spending that creates employment.

Don't forget about "structural" unemployment, caused by a misfit between skills and jobs, discrimination, or employee characteristics.

Big business. There are pros and cons for many arguments about how to make big business more responsible:

- leaving business alone
- relying on managerial ethics
- breaking up big firms
- regulating firms
- nationalizing firms

No approach is entirely satisfactory, nor are some other suggestions we mention at the end.

Conclusion. Controlling large-scale organizations of any kind is a major problem deeply rooted in all industrial economies, capitalist or socialist.

Growth. Above all, remember the exponential character of growth and the indefinite meaning of a *resource.*

Technology will determine how long growth will continue, both with regard to the resources it uses and the environmental damage it creates.

Sooner or later growth will have to slow down. With a slowing down we can expect serious tensions between rich and poor nations and between rich and poor groups within nations.

The struggle to attain a Spaceship Earth psychology or government will be painful and protracted.

QUESTIONS

No questions this time. This is a chapter to reflect on, no so much one to "master" in terms of answers. The big questions are spelled out in the "Focus" above. Answers lie in being more questioning about our usual answers.

Capitalism

We have raised many big problems but remained silent on the biggest one of all. Surely some of you have asked whether the root problem is not the economic system itself: capitalism. Here is an effort to open a discussion on that profoundly serious but extremely elusive query.

WHAT IS CAPITALISM?

We had better begin with definitions. If we are now to ask whether America's troubles are due to capitalism, we should know what we mean by that crucial word.

It is surprisingly difficult to find a succinct definition of capitalism. All shades of opinion, however, from right to left, would agree that its essential characteristics are these:

1. The legal right to private ownership of the means of production.

Under capitalism, as we noted in Chapter 2, the productive equipment of society is owned by a minority of individuals (capitalists) who have the right to use this property for private gain.

2. The market determination of distribution.

Capitalism relies primarily on the market system, not only to allocate its resources among various uses but also to establish the levels of income (such as wages, rents, profits) of different social classes.

WHAT IS SOCIALISM?

As we might expect, socialism is something of a mirror image of capitalism. "In its primary usage," writes Paul M. Sweezy, a leading Socialist theoretician, "the term 'socialism' means a social system which is differentiated from other social systems by the character of its property relations. . . . Capitalism recognizes a relatively unrestricted right of private ownership in the means of production, while socialism denies this right and reserves such ownership to public bodies."[1]

Thus Sweezy, like most Socialists, makes the crucial distinction between capitalism and socialism the question of *property ownership*—to which most Socialists would also add that socialism, unlike capitalism, depends primarily on *planning,* rather than on the market, both for its overall allocation of resources and for its distribution of income. Underlying these differences in conceptions of property, or in market vs. planning, we can also see a profound rift between societies that are based on economic individualism and those that are not (see 45–47).

IDEAL TYPES VS. REAL CASES

These definitions are what the sociologist Max Weber called "ideal types." They are meant to summarize and abstract out of the enormous variety of actual institutions and historical experiences those essential elements that make up a pure model of the

---

[1]Paul M. Sweezy, *Socialism* (New York: McGraw-Hill, 1948), p. 3.

institution or activity in which we are interested. The emphasis on public vs. private property, on market vs. planned distribution, or on economic individualism vs. economic community-mindedness, serves to sharpen our conception of the "irreducible" elements of capitalism and socialism that are to be discovered behind their many variations in actual history.

No sooner do we create these ideal types than we find ourselves in something of a quandary. The question arises: what practical function do these models of capitalism and socialism serve? If one asks a dedicated humanitarian Socialist if socialism is better than capitalism, he will unhesitatingly tell you that it is because he believes in the superiority of public over private ownership or prefers planning over the market or group rather than individual economic rights.

The same humanitarian Socialist, however, recoils in horror at the repressiveness of Russia and looks with approval on the humaneness of (capitalist) Denmark. How does he reconcile this contradiction? By telling you that Russia is not "really" socialist but only a grim travesty of socialism, and that Denmark is not "really" capitalist but a modified socialist version of capitalism. Yet, unquestionably, the Soviet Union has public ownership of property, a thorough-going system of planning, and group "rights." Denmark has private ownership of property, a general market determination of incomes and outputs, and a great deal of economic individualism.

The point of this disconcerting confrontation is clear. It is that the elements that all agree are decisive in defining capitalism and socialism as "ideal types" do not necessarily tell us very much about the societies that display those characteristic elements. As a matter of fact, thinking about the differences among capitalist nations—compare Sweden and the Union of South Africa—or among socialist countries—contrast Russia and China—we begin to wonder if the words *capitalism* and *socialism* mean anything at all.

CAPITALISM AND SOCIALISM AS ECONOMIC SYSTEMS

The terms *do* mean something, although, as we shall see, there are crucial areas of life to which they add little if any understanding. In other areas they add a good deal, and it is to these that we now direct our attention.

The first such area is that of economics proper. *Capitalism and socialism as ideal types identify for us a series of economic problems that we find among all members of each type.*

What are these problems? For capitalism, we have but to refer to the chapter we have just completed. Whether we look to Japan or Sweden, the Union of South Africa or the United States, we see inflation and unemployment, a struggle to restrain big business (or labor), worries about growth.

Can we find problems common to socialism? To a certain extent our comparison is muddied by the fact that so many socialist systems are still in (or only very recently out of) a period of backwardness. Hence we do not really have "mature" socialisms to compare with mature capitalisms.

Nonetheless, there seems to be a set of common economic problems built into socialism in much the same fashion as the problems that are intrinsically part of the capitalist mechanism. As we would expect, these are problems of public ownership and planning—in particular, the problem of controlling unwieldy state bureaucracies and avoiding inefficient production and distribution directives. Indeed, one of the most brilliant Socialist economic theoreticians, the late Oskar Lange, wrote presciently in 1938: *"The real danger of socialism is that of the bureaucratization of economic life. . . ."*[2]

PROBLEMS AND SOLUTIONS

Our discussion suggests that the ideal types of "capitalism" and "socialism" *are* useful because they indicate different kinds of problems that the two systems tend to generate. Now let us ask an extremely important question that our findings pose. Granted that capitalism and socialism have common problems, *does this mean that they all find similar solutions to these problems?*

To ask the question is to answer it. Obviously, different capitalisms respond to their economic and social and political problems in very different ways, as do different socialisms. Take capitalism as an example. Two well-known Marxist critics of capitalism have written that genuine planning or resolute action to provide housing would be impossible in America because "such planning and such action . . . will never be undertaken by a government run by and for the rich, as every capitalist government is and must be."[3] They have obviously concentrated on the lack of an effective social sector in the U.S., and overlooked the planning and housing undertaken by Norway, Sweden, Denmark, New Zealand, Netherlands, and other governments presumably run by and for the rich, since they are certainly countries where private ownership of the means of production prevails.

Nor does it follow that because all capitalist systems suffer from economic instability, all will therefore have the same degree of unemployment. During the 1970s when unemployment here reached levels over 8 percent, in West Germany unemployment never rose over two percent of the labor force. In New Zealand it was considerably less than that.

This same variety of responses can be found in socialist economies. Oskar Lange's diagnosis of bureaucracy has proved true within all socialisms, but some have responded with a reliance on market socialism (Yugoslavia or pre-invasion Czechoslovakia). In others, efforts have been made to solve the problem with better computer planning (U.S.S.R.). Still others have searched for "moral incentives" (Cuba or China).

CAPITALISM ABROAD

All this has an obvious relevance to the central issue with which we began this chapter. We can see now that whereas many of the problems that beset America undoubtedly have their roots in our capitalist institutions, the fact that we often cope with them inadequately is not a matter that can be blamed solely on capitalism as such.

[2]Oskar Lange and Fred M. Taylor, *On the Economic Theory of Socialism* (New York: McGraw-Hill, 1956), p. 109.
[3]Paul Sweezy and Paul Baran, *Monopoly Capital* (New York: *Monthly Review Press,* 1966), p. 300.

Take, for example, the question of social neglect that is so dismaying an aspect of American life. If we compare the United States with Norway in terms of various indicators of social well-being, there is no doubt that we show up poorly. Infant mortality in the United States is a full 50 percent higher than it is in Norway. Norway spends a higher proportion of its GNP on education than we do, and did so even when it had a smaller GNP per capita than we have. Norway has more hospital beds per thousand population than we have. It allocates a larger proportion of its GNP to social security expenditures than does the United States. Its cities are essentially free of all slums. Poverty as a result of social neglect has been virtually eliminated in Norway. Yet, by the criteria of property ownership or the market distribution of income or the presence of economic individualism, Norway is unquestionably a "capitalist" society.

The same superior social performance can be found in other European capitalist nations. Denmark, Sweden, Netherlands, Austria, West Germany, England, and still other nations have managed to cope with, or to get rid of, many aspects of social life that plague the United States.

CAPITALISM OR AMERICAN CAPITALISM

All this has chastening, as well as encouraging, implications. It is that much of what troubles America seems to be related to factors that, however much exacerbated by our economic system, cannot be uniquely attributed to capitalism as such. The poor level of social services in America, the powerful role played by the military, the "rat-race" tempo of American big-city life, the extent of our slums, the callous treatment of criminals, the obsession with "communism," and other unlovely aspects of our social system are not predominant in many other capitalist systems.

The problem, in other words, resides as much in those elements of our society that are American as in those that are capitalist. To put it differently, the significant question for us is to understand why capitalism here has not achieved a number of possibilities realized by capitalism elsewhere. Unless we understand and correct these failures, a change of economic systems in this country might produce only an *American* socialism that would manifest many of the very failings of American capitalism.

ECONOMIC
REASONING

PART
2

The way of science

Preliminary reconnaissance of that *terra incognita* called The Economy has made us ready to plunge into economics proper. Or almost ready. For the discipline we call economics consists of applying the methods of economic reasoning to the complex problems of the real world. Before we can do that, we have to know what economic reasoning is about.

Scientific Thinking

Is there any special way of reasoning or thinking in economics? The answer is that economists try to think as scientists. We say "try," because there are important differences between the ways of thinking used in chemistry and physics and those used in economics, but let that pass for the moment. **The point is that economists regard economics as a scientific endeavor and try to reason in scientific ways.**

That leads, of course, to the questions, what is scientific reasoning, and what is special about it?

5

71

Scientific reasoning has these characteristics:

1. **Its basic concern is with facts.**

Scientists collect facts, arrange facts, argue about facts, and try to explain facts. To a scientist, a fact is an item of experience that another scientist can be expected to detect in the same way. Scientists avoid collecting, arranging, arguing about, or trying to explain things that are not identifiable in this public way. Religious revelations, for example, are not part of a scientist's concern. Neither are mystic or aesthetic states of mind. These are very significant aspects of life, but they cannot be observed and measured in the explicit and exact way that facts can be.

2. **Scientific reasoning tries to explain facts in terms of laws.**

The objective of science is not merely to collect facts, but to explain them. By "explain," a scientist usually means that he or she tries to find "laws" at work in the world of facts. By laws, a scientist means regular and repeatable patterns of events or relationships among events. Stones fall, and scientists conjecture that there is a law about falling objects. Living things die, and scientists conjecture that there are laws about vital processes. Balloons expand when they heat up, and scientists look for laws about the properties of gases.

Laws are not definitive explanations of how the universe works. Human understanding permits no such godlike understanding. Laws are only well-established *hypotheses*—tentative generalizations that seem to fit the facts, although they can never be assumed to be absolutely true. Thus, the law of gravitation is a generalization that masses attract each other in a certain way. One of the laws of living matter is that life requires sustenance—unlike rocks, which do not need to be fed. The law of gases says that molecules move faster when energy (heat) is applied to them. Since we have not observed every situation and every fact in the universe, we cannot say that our laws and hypotheses are absolutely true. Tomorrow an apple might fall up! We might find a living organism that doesn't require food, or we might discover molecules moving faster when they are put in a freezer. But insofar as we have been able to judge, certain generalizations about the natural universe seem to be true. We call these generalizations *laws*.

Hypotheses thus describe the relationships of facts in ways that emphasize regularities we can observe. For all their inherently tentative character, hypotheses are the most powerful intellectual tools we have for introducing order into the confusion of the universe.

3. **Scientific reasoning uses laws to predict.**

The purpose of establishing laws is to enable us to explain the past course of events and to predict their future course. Because we have the law of gravity, we predict that the next stone we will drop will fall at a certain speed. Because we have a hypothesis about the chemistry of life, we predict that a certain intake of calories is required to keep a being alive. Because we hypothesize about gas, we predict an explosion—a very fast expansion—if we apply a flame to gasoline vapor.

Prediction is among the most formidable intellectual powers that mankind possesses, our secret of our mastery over nature. It derives, we can see, from our ability to place new facts into categories whose regularities we have already explained by hypotheses. We assume the new facts will behave like the previous ones, and we hope that the hypothesis will continue to be descriptive. If it is not, our hypothesis will have to be changed, because the facts, obviously, cannot be.

4. Scientific reasoning is value free.

Finally, we should note that scientific reasoning deliberately tries to exclude an aspect of thinking that is often the dominant element in nonscientific thought. This is the element of personal likes and dislikes, of moral judgments, that we call values. Many, perhaps most of life's most precious achievements involve values. Art, justice, government are unthinkable without considerations of value. But these are not fields of science.

When science examines its facts or searches for explanatory hypotheses or predicts, it does not accept some facts because they are considered "good" and reject others because they are considered "bad." Science does not categorize facts by preference of the observer. It does not shape hypotheses that accord with the scientists' political or religious beliefs. Nor does science conceal unwelcome predictions or announce untrue results. It behaves toward its research object with complete impartiality and disinterest.

At least this is what science claims to do. Scientists are fallible, like all humankind. Social scientists, moreover, are placed in an unusual position when they seek to be value free. Nonetheless, objectivity is the aim of scientific reasoning.

Reasoning and method

We have not yet gone into the scientific method, the way scientists work. Their method is to experiment and to reason about the outcome of experiments. It is a method that has three critical requirements:

1. Experiments must be performed in ways that can be repeated and reconfirmed—or disproved—by other scientists. The reason that palmistry is not a science is that the "experiments" of one gypsy do not yield the same results as the experiments of another. Rather, each gypsy has secrets. A scientific experiment conducted in secret ways is not a bona fide experiment at all.

2. Scientific experiments must be run in ways that permit them to fail. The very essence of an experiment is that it may not confirm the expected hypothesis. An experiment that could not produce negative results would not be a true scientific procedure. We will see later that this requirement has particular relevance for social scientists.

3. Scientific experiments and scientific fact-gathering have to allow for disturbing influences from the outside. Experiments to test the law of gravity must allow for the resistance of air. The scientist makes allowances for impurities in his experiment; and as we shall see, so must the social scientist.

Scientific theories

Last, the question of theory. What do we mean by a theory of gravitation or a theory of evolution? We mean little more than a hypothesis of considerable explanatory power. Some hypotheses are capable of being generalized to cover *many kinds* of events, and we often upgrade their titles from hypotheses to theories. Thus the hypothesis of gravitation becomes the theory of gravitation.

Another way of saying much the same thing is that theories are hypotheses that have stood the test of time, having been subjected to frequent tests and having passed all of them. That is not to say, of course, that theories cannot fail. Science is littered with discarded theories, the victims of disconcerting facts.

Natural Science and Social Science

This detour through the ways and means of scientific reasoning and scientific method brings us closer to the problem of economic reasoning, but there is still an intervening step to be taken. Economic reasoning, as we have said, prides itself on its resemblance to scientific reasoning. But economics is not concerned with the factual aspects of the universe that attract the attention of physicists, astronomers, chemists, and the like. Economics and its sister disciplines (sociology and politics) are concerned with society. The economist's universe is the social universe, in which individuals and groups are the focuses of attention.

Social science   Thus, economics is a social science. How does a social science compare with a natural science?

1. Social science, like natural science, is concerned with facts. However, these are not the facts of nature, but the facts of society. Economics does not study the laws of metallurgy, although it is very interested in the facts of steel-making, which vary from one society to another. It does not study the laws of psychology, but it is extremely concerned with the ways in which people behave.

Thus social science mainly observes certain kinds of facts having to do with the way mankind organizes its activities, produces and distributes goods and services, forms governments, creates family or kinship units.

2. Social science tries to explain social facts by laws that rest on tentative hypotheses, in exactly the same way that natural science tries to explain its facts. The main objectives of a social scientist are to observe human events and to discern patterns of regularity among them, just as a natural scientist might observe the planets to divine their laws of movement. For reasons that we will touch on immediately, the formulation of laws (or theories) is a great deal more difficult for a social scientist than for a natural scientist, but the objective is the same.

3. Social science tries to predict.

A social scientist hopes to use hypotheses to predict social action, just as a natural scientist uses natural laws to predict natural events. Suppose that a social scientist observes that wars have always taken place when famines have broken out. That leads to the hypothesis that famine is the cause of war. When a climatologist predicts a famine next year, the social scientist predicts war.

Can social scientists predict events with the same degree of success that natural scientists can? They cannot, and we must understand the reason why this is so.

Social scientists are dealing with people, and people have a unique attribute: conscious will. Natural scientists make their predictions about molecules, planets, bacteria, and other objects that do not have conscious purpose. The actions that the social scientist observes do not happen because men and women interact as do molecules or planets or bacteria. Actions that social science observes are shot through with intentions, desires, hopes, and fears. Events that take place under the social scientist's microscope occur because the objects of his scrutiny want to achieve some ends and to avoid others.

This conscious willing element confronts the social scientist with an element of potential disturbance that cannot happen in the natural world. Planets have no choice about continuing their heavenly trajectories. Bacteria multiply whether they will or not. But humans do not *necessarily* behave in given ways. Famines may have provoked wars from time immemorial, but the next famine may cause an outbreak of altruism. Perhaps it will trigger the social adoption of passive mystical states, the furthest thing from war. Stranger things have happened. Thus, social prediction is immensely complicated because the objects of social science may change their ways of thinking about, or reacting to, events. We will return to this crucial point in Chapter 9, when we discuss some of the basic difficulties of economic theory.

4. Social science also tries to be value free.

Social science shares with natural science a commitment to honesty about its results, openness about its methods. It has much more difficulty than natural science has, however, in adhering to the ideal of a value-free inquiry. An experiment or hypothesis of natural science normally is concerned with little that is moral or value laden. Social science, on the other hand, reasons about a society of which the reasoner is usually a member. Thus, social science inquiry, starting with the initial selection of "the facts" or with the designation of "crucial" relations, is apt to be powerfully influenced by the social scientist's own stake in society.

Very few social scientists are indifferent to the outcome of their research. It is not a matter of indifference to them if the world works this way or that. *Almost all social scientists are interested in changing the world, not merely in observing it.* They want to probe into the causes of crime or bad government or war or economic difficulty, in order to correct these ills. They examine the innermost workings of society to bring hidden relationships

into the open as part of a program to alter society, perhaps in a radical way. Or they may conduct research that they hope will justify the status quo. To maintain a value-free posture is very difficult when a social scientist's own moral and material future may be affected by what he discovers.

We can begin to see why it is very difficult for social science to duplicate exactly the reasoning of natural science. Nor is there any reason why it should. Social science is about society, where the very essence of life is wish and motive and purpose. Unless we think that men and women are as inert as grains of sand, there is no cause to think that their behavior can be described in the way we describe the behavior of simpler things. Indeed, what is astonishing is how much of society, not how little, lends itself to scientific reasoning, with its hypotheses and laws.

The method of social science We have seen that natural science relies on experiments to confirm or disprove its hypotheses. But social science can rely on experiments rarely, because of two situations.

1. Humans seldom permit themselves to be made the objects of experiment. Occasionally we use humans as "laboratory data," for example when we test new medicines on volunteers. But here we are really testing the validity of a hypothesis about the medicine, not about the people. It is possible to run controlled experiments, usually in universities, about the ways in which opinions are formed or in which group pressures can change the perceptions of a subject. In recent years there have been a number of economic experiments, such as testing welfare systems to determine their impacts on work behavior.

But social experiments are difficult to mount on a large scale. There is no way of "seeing" if our nation would be better off with a parliamentary system. There is no way of "trying out" a policy of large scale monetary reform. Such experiments in social and economic affairs become part of life. They cannot be isolated from history or quickly changed if unsuccessful.

2. Experiments and observations are hard to keep free of outside influences. Imagine that some economist established a hypothesis that inflation was the result of lowering the interest rate. How would we test it? Suppose we *did* lower the interest rate, and prices rose. Does that experiment confirm the hypothesis? Unfortunately, it does not. First, we would have to be certain that the lower rate was the *only* new element in the economic situation. There might have been crop failures. Perhaps the government changed its tax policy, or the President may have said something that changed businessmen's attitudes. Any of these events, rather than the reduction in interest rates, may have caused prices to rise.

Are there ways of allowing for such external disturbances? We shall see that there *are* methods that economists use, methods exactly like those of natural scientists. These methods often involve a sophisticated use of statistics (see "An extra word" at the end of Chapter 8). But we can also see that it is much harder to allow for the effect of economic or social impurities than for physical or chemical ones. A larger residue of uncertainty always remains in economic predictions than in predictions about the natural world.

Economics as a social science

This short introduction to economic reasoning has set the stage for an examination of economics proper. Economics is obviously about the social universe, not the natural universe. It searches out facts, especially social facts, relevant to its concerns. It tries to formulate generalizations or hypotheses from these facts (we shall discuss a number of important economic laws). By looking at new facts in the light of hypotheses or theories, economics tries to predict how events may turn out. Understandably, its predictions suffer from difficulties of a universe full of changeable wills and tremendous "impurities."

How can we pursue a scientific study of economics in the face of all these difficulties is the great challenge of our subject.

FOCUS

This is a short but idea-packed chapter. Let us try to straighten out the main things to keep in mind.

• Differences between natural science and social science. One main difference has to do with the word *behavior*. How does the meaning of the word *behavior* differ when we speak of the behavior of an atomic particle or the behavior of a household?

• Purity of experiments. Can we eliminate all the impurities that get into laboratory experiments (dirt in test tubes, air in vacuums, dust on balances)? Can we even imagine how to eliminate all the corresponding extraneous influences in social experiments?

• Main components of scientific reasoning: facts; hypotheses or theories; predictions. Can you explain how a scientist goes about proposing a scientific law?

● Scientific method. Without the experimental, value-free method, scientific reasoning would be of limited value. To what degree can we apply the methods of science—including value freedom—to society? If we did *not* try to apply such methods, how else could we explain society?

WORDS AND CONCEPTS YOU SHOULD KNOW

Starting with this chapter, a section like this one follows each "Focus." The purpose of the "Focus" is to review the main ideas of the chapter and to help you establish principal learning objectives for yourself. But as we said in our first chapter, one of the stumbling blocks in mastering any new discipline is acquiring its special vocabulary. This section is designed to aid you in doing that.

The Words or Concepts you will find below are part of the working vocabulary of an economist. Take a moment to think about each of them, even if they have been covered in your "Focus." Most of the Words or Concepts have precise definitions that you should be able to state in a sentence or two. If you can frame a good definition in your mind, move on. If not, turn back to the page or pages indicated and refresh your memory. You might make a check mark opposite terms that you could not define clearly, to help you review later on.

Hypotheses, 72
Laws, 72–73
Scientific theories, 73

Experimental method, 73
Value-free, 73, 75

QUESTIONS

1. Does all scientific reasoning involve prediction? Suppose that you were engaged in classifying moon rocks never before seen by man. Would that be "scientific" work? Why or why not? Would it involve facts and hypotheses? If you found a workable system of classification, would this imply a prediction about moon rocks that you had not yet looked at?

2. If science is supposed to be value free, can a scientist have strong moral beliefs? What do we mean by "value-free" scientific work?

3. Does the experimental method always work? Suppose you test a coin to see if it is fairly balanced. You count the number of times it comes up heads or tails. Suppose that it comes up heads 1,000 consecutive times. That would certainly make you suspicious, but does it *prove* the coin is unbalanced? Does this mean that the experimental method is wrong or that not all hypotheses can be tested by experiment?

4. Suppose that a social scientist is convinced that women are inferior to men in intelligence. Would he be within the bounds of value freedom if he eagerly propounded this theory to all who would listen? Suppose he considers blacks, instead of women, intellectually inferior to other races? Suppose his theory is that blacks are superior to whites, or women to men? Do you feel equally comfortable with your answers to all these variations of one question?

Paradigms

How does science advance? The prevailing view used to be that it grew by accretion, gradually adding new knowledge and better established hypotheses while shedding error and disproved hypotheses. That view has now been seriously challenged by the influential book, *The Structure of Scientific Revolutions,* by Thomas Kuhn, published in 1962.

Kuhn's view is that the growth of science is not a continuous, seamless extension of knowledge. Rather, science grows in discontinuous leaps, in which one prevailing paradigm is displaced by another. *A paradigm is a set of premises, views, rules, conventions, and beliefs that form the kinds of questions that a science asks.* For example, the Ptolemaic paradigm, with its view of the earth as the center of the universe, was replaced by the Copernican paradigm, which based its questions on the premise that the planets revolve around the sun. In cosmology the Newtonian paradigm was displaced by the Einsteinian, in biology the "Biblical" paradigm by the Darwinian.

Paradigms change, says Kuhn, when the puzzles encountered by scientists become more and more difficult to answer within the existing set of ground rules. Then, usually in a short space of time, a new view of things comes to the fore, explaining the puzzles of the earlier paradigm and reorienting the questions for scientists who will work within the new rules.

PRECLASSICAL AND CLASSICAL ECONOMICS

Kuhn's short, provocative book is worth reading by anyone interested in science or social science. The question it raises for us is whether economics also has "paradigms." The answer seems to be both yes and no.

First the yes answer. We can easily separate the history of economic thought into paradigm-like divisions that resemble the bounded inquiries of science. One of the first such paradigms was the economics of the medieval schoolmen, who argued and worried about the moral problems raised by the emerging market process. For example, one of their main concerns was whether lending money at interest (usury) was in fact a sin (in the early Middle Ages it had been considered a *mortal* sin); and they endlessly discussed the criteria for the "just" prices at which commodities should sell.

That view of the economic world was displaced by the Classical economists, whose most brilliant achievements were expressed in the works of Adam Smith

(1723–1790) and David Ricardo (1772–1823). The Classical economists had no interest whatever in "just" prices or in the sinfulness of usury. For them the great question was *how to understand, not evaluate, economic processes, in particular the accumulation and distribution of national wealth.* Smith, in particular, wrote an extraordinary exposition of how the members of society, although engaged in a search for their individual betterment, were nonetheless guided by an "invisible hand" (the market) to expand the wealth of nations. Ricardo wrote with equal force about the course of national economic growth, arguing that a growing population, pressing against limited fertile acreage, would drive up crop prices and divert the wealth of the country into the hands of the landlords.

MARGINALIST ECONOMICS

The Classical "paradigm" concerned large issues of national growth and dealt boldly with the fate of social classes. Then, around the 1870s, a new angle of vision abruptly displaced the older one. The new view had numerous European originators, perhaps preeminent among them Stanley W. Jevons and Leon Walras. As a group they are referred to as the Marginalists, for *they turned the focus of economic inquiry away from growth and class conflict into a study of the interactions of individuals.*

The new paradigm explained many things that the older Classical one did not, above all the finer workings of the price system. But just as the Classical paradigm had dropped all interest in the just prices of the medievalists, so the Marginalists paid little attention to the questions of growth and class fortune that had so preoccupied the Classicists.

KEYNESIAN ECONOMICS

Inherent in the Marginalist view of the world, with its extreme emphasis on interacting individuals rather than on classes, was a "micro" approach to economic problems. The next radical shift in views came from the work of John Maynard Keynes (1883–1946), whose perception of the economic system brought into focus a new "macro" perspective on *total* income, *total* employment, *total* output. The most striking result of Keynes's shift from a micro to a macro perspective was his discovery that an economy that worked well at the micro level did not necessarily work well at the marco level. From the perspective of the Marginalists, there had been no recognition of the problem of mass unemployment or a continuing depression. Indeed, such an economic state of affairs could hardly be envisioned with their concepts.

PARADIGMS OR NOT?

Hence we can certainly discern sharp changes in the views and visions of economics. The very definition of the economic problem itself alters as we go from the medieval schoolmen to the Keynesians.

Why, then, should we not call this a series of paradigmatic shifts, similar to those in science? *The main reason is that the new economic "paradigms" do not explain the questions of the older views they displace. Unlike the new paradigms of natural science, which embrace the problems of their predecessors, the shifts in economics are characterized by the fact that they ignore or dismiss the very questions that disturbed their predecessors.* Classical economists, as we have said, forgot about economic justice; Marginalist economists, about growth or classes, Keynesian economists, about the inner working of the market.

Hence the shifts in economics are not quite like those in science, although the concept of a change of perspectives, bringing new problems into view, is as applicable to one as to the other. We can relate these shifts in perspective to the changing backdrop of social organization. Each paradigm of economic thought reflects to some degree the historical characteristics and problems of its time. This reflection of social issues and problems in economic thought differs, too, from the nature of scientific paradigms. Change in social structures generally plays a small role in causing one scientific perspective to replace another.

What paradigm rules economics today? A mixture of Marginalist and Keynesian thought lies behind most contemporary micro- and macroeconomics. A Marxian view, a paradigm in itself (see box, p. 120), underlies much of the radical critique of our time. Perhaps it is fair to say that no paradigm is firmly ensconced today. We live in a period in which much of the conventional wisdom of the past has been tried and found wanting. Economics is in a state of self-scrutiny, dissatisfied with its established paradigms, not yet ready to formulate a new one. Indeed, perhaps the search for such a new paradigm, a perspective that will highlight new elements of reality and suggest new modes of analysis, is the most pressing economic task of our time.

Economic
science

How is it possible to think "scientifically" about the massive facts, trends and problems that we have encountered in our first chapters? That is the challenge to which we must now address ourselves. We must consider how to think about economic reality, not as mere observers, but as social scientists.

Economic society   Let us begin with a reflection on the subject matter of economics itself. What it is that we are trying to reason about as economists? Certainly it is not the economic attributes of *all* societies. Our first chapters focus on the United States not merely because we are naturally interested in the economic aspects of our own country, but also because the United States is a kind of society that lends itself to economic analysis. Economic reasoning, we should note at the outset, applies most cogently to societies that are built on the foundations of economic individualism. These are market societies, capitalisms.

Equally to be noted, economic reasoning will not try to come to grips with all of society. Our earlier survey paid no attention to vast areas of social life that we call

6

sociological or political, much less religious or artistic. Economics is concerned with the facts that bear on only one aspect of our social life: our efforts to produce and to distribute wealth. Boom and bust, inflation and depression, poverty and riches, growth or no growth—all can be described in terms of the production of wealth and its distribution.

Basic hypotheses   Our task, then, is to find some way of explaining production and distribution in scientific terms. Therefore, economists observe the *human* universe, just as natural scientists observe the universe, in search of data and orderly relationships that may permit them to construct hypotheses. What do economists see, when they scrutinize the world of economic activity? Two attributes of a market society attract their attention:

1. Individuals in such a society seem to display regular behavior patterns when they participate in economic activities as buyers and sellers, householders or businesspeople. They behave in acquisitive, money-searching, cost-minimizing ways.
2. A series of obstacles is seen to stand between the acquisitive drive of marketers and their realization of economic gain. Some are obstacles of nature: it is difficult to wrest wealth from the earth and to fashion it into the articles we want. Some are obstacles of social institutions: laws and customs of many kinds inhibit marketers from pursuing their gains exactly as they might wish.

Thus an extraordinary conclusion begins to dawn. A great deal of the activity of a market society can be explained as the outcome of two interacting forces. One is the force of behavior—a force that we have described in terms of the acquisitive behavior of men and women in a market society. The other is the counterforce of nature or of social institutions—a series of obstacles that holds back or channels or directs the acquisitive drive. This suggests the daring scientific task that economics sets for itself. It is to explain the events of economic reality—even to predict some of the events of future economic reality—by reasoning based on fundamental hypotheses about acquisitive behavior and its obstacles.

Hypotheses About Behavior

Obviously we must investigate these hypotheses with a great deal of care. Let us start with the economist's assumption about behavior. We can sum it up in a sentence: *man is a maximizer.*

What does that hypothesis mean? Essentially, it means that people in market societies seek to gain as much pleasureable wealth from their economic activity as they can. We call this pleasureable wealth "utility." Thus we hypothesize that men and women are utility-maximizers.

Note that we define utility as *pleasurable* wealth. Economists do not argue that people try to accumulate the largest amount of wealth possible, regardless of its pleasures. We all know that after a certain point, wealth-producing work brings fatigue or even pain. Therefore we assume that as people work to maximize their wealth, they take into account the pains (or disutilities) of achieving it. Later we will look into this maximizing assumption critically, but it will help us if we begin by trying to understand it sympathetically. It is plausible that most of us do seek wealth and that we balance its pleasures against the nuisances and difficulties of achieving it.

Insatiable wants-in-general

Economics not only assumes that men and women are maximizers, but it also has a hypothesis about why they behave so acquisitively. The hypothesis is that peoples' wants are insatiable; that human desires for utility can never be filled.

Are our wants, in fact, insatiable? Does human nature keep us on a treadmill of striving that can never bring us to a point of contentment? As with maximizing, there is a prima facie plausibility about the assumption. For if we include among our aims leisure as well as goods, more time to enjoy ourselves as well as more income to be enjoyed, it seems true enough that something very much like insatiability afflicts most people. At least this seems true in societies that encourage striving for status and success and that set high value on consumption and recreation.

Perhaps in different kinds of society, that chronic dissatisfaction would disappear. In today's market society, it is probably an accurate enough general description of our state of mind. We *are* driven to acquire goods, to gain higher income, to increase our enjoyment of leisure. Surveys regularly show that men and women at all economic levels express a desire for more income (usually about 10 percent more than they actually have), and *this drive for more does not seem to diminish as we move up the economic scale.* If it did, we would be hard put to explain why people who are generally in the upper echelons of the distribution of wealth and income work just as hard as, or even harder than, those on the lower rungs of the economic ladder.

Satiable wants-in-particular

There is, however, a very important qualification to the assumption that wants are insatiable for all wealth, including leisure. The qualification is that economists assume that human wants for particular kinds of wealth, including leisure, are indeed capable of being satiated. This idea of the satiability of particular wants will play a key role in our next chapter, when we shall see how we can derive the concept of demand and demand "curves" from our hypotheses concerning behavior.

Rationality

A set of beliefs about human wants thus lies behind the economist's hypothesis that man is a maximizing creature. Equally important is an assumption about the way that individuals think and act as they go about striving to fulfill their insatiable wants-in-general or their satiable wants-in-particular. This assumption is that man is a *rational* maximizer. By this economists mean that people in a market milieu stop to consider the various courses of action open to them and to calculate in some fashion the means that will best suit their maximizing aims. There may be two different ways of producing a good. As rational maximizers, people will choose the method that will yield them the good for the smallest effort or cost.

This concept of rational maximizing does not mean that human beings may not wish, on some occasions, to go to more trouble than necessary. After all, people could worship God in very simple buildings or out-of-doors, but they go to extraordinary lengths to erect magnificent churches and decorate them with sculpture and paintings. It is meaningless to apply the word *rational* to pursuits such as these, which may have vast importance for society.

But when people are engaged in producing the goods and services of ordinary life, seeking to achieve the largest possible incomes or the most satisfaction-yielding patterns of consumption, the economist assumes that they *will* stop to think about the differing ways of attaining a given end and will then choose the way that is least costly.

The economist's view of man Of course, economists do not believe that men and women are solely rational, acquisitive creatures. They are fully aware that a hundred motivations impel people: aesthetic, political, religious. If they concentrate on the rational and acquisitive elements in people, it is because they believe these to be decisive for economic behavior; that is, for the explanation of our productive and distributive activities.

Economic theory is therefore a study of the effects of one aspect of human beings as it motivates them to undertake their worldly activities. Very often, as economists well know, other attributes will override or blunt the acquisitive, maximizing orientation. To the extent that this is so, economic theory loses its clarity or may even suggest outcomes different from those that we find in fact. But economists think that rational maximizing—the calculated pursuit of pleasurable wealth—is universal and strong enough to serve as a good working hypothesis on which to build their complicated theories. To put it differently, economists do *not* think that political or religious or other such motives regularly overwhelm maximizing behavior. If that were so, economic theory would be of little avail.

Hypotheses About Constraints

So far, we have traced the basic assumptions of economic reasoning about behavior. What about obstacles? As we have seen, people do not maximize in a vacuum or, to speak in more economic terms, in a world where all goods are free, available effortlessly in infinite amounts. Instead, people exert their maximizing efforts in a world where nature and social institutions "oppose" those efforts. Goods and services are not free but must be won by working with the scarce elements of the physical world. Land, resources, man-made artifacts inherited from past generations are not boundlessly abundant. Laws and social organizations constantly impede our maximizing impulses. *We call all these natural and social obstacles constraints.*

Constraints of nature As we shall see, there are many kinds of constraints. Among the most interesting and important are the constraints imposed by nature—the obstacles that nature places in our way when we try to maximize production. As economists, we distinguish three general tendencies in the ways that nature constraints our productive efforts, and we express these tendencies in three "laws" of production. We shall learn these three laws again, later on. They are here for you to meet, not yet to master.

1. The law of diminishing returns.

Why can we not grow all the world's

food in a flowerpot? The question makes us think about a property of nature that is of utmost importance for economics. *As we add more and more of one kind of input (seed, in this case) to a fixed quantity of other inputs (the soil in the flowerpot), the amount of additional output will, after a time, diminish.* It may even fall to zero.

The idea of this basic constraint is easy to grasp. Note that it is a constraint imposed by nature, not by human behavior. Our productive powers depend in large part on our skills and technology. Maybe someday a miracle seed *will* enable us to feed the world from a flowerpot. Even then, we would expect that additional inputs of seed would eventually yield diminishing returns of food. This constraint has to do with the germinative properties of seeds and soil, not with our behavior as producers.

2. The law of increasing cost.

A second aspect of the constraining tendencies of nature resembles the law of diminishing returns but is differently caused. In the phenomenon of diminishing returns we watch what happens to the output of a product as we add more and more of *one kind* of input, holding the others constant. *In the law of increasing cost we watch what happens to the output of a product as we combine more and more of all kinds of inputs to make that product. Once again we eventually experience a decreasing increment of output as we increase inputs.*

Suppose we have a community that divides its land, labor, and capital between two occupations: dairy farming and grain raising. If the community should decide to use all of its inputs to produce milk, all land, labor, and capital formerly used for grain must be assigned to the production of milk. At first the result may be very favorable. But unless there is no difference between one piece of land and another,

between the skills of dairy and grain farmers, or between the equipment used for producing milk and grain, productivity is bound to fail. As we move from using resources best suited to milk production to those least suited to it, the amount of additional milk resulting from our efforts will decrease. Finally we will be forced to take ill-suited land (such as deserts), untrained labor, and inappropriate capital and put them to work producing milk, where their yield will be very low. As a result, the successive increments of milk output will decline as we concentrate more and more of all our resources and efforts on this one output alone. This, too, is the consequence of nature's characteristics, not ours.

3. Returns to scale.

A third attribute to nature that enters into economic analysis is somewhat different from the previous two. It sets nature in the role of an efficiency engineer as well as a constrainer. This attribute is called *scale* or *returns to scale. It refers to a simple but profound fact about production; namely, that size matters.*

In a small garage, can we produce automobiles as cheaply as we can produce them in a large assembly plant? Obviously not. Certain aspects of automobile making cannot be efficiently reduced in size or scale. We cannot produce a car efficiently in a garage, because there would be no way to arrange a flow of production through such a small area. We cannot produce steel cheaply by the pound, because the equipment that it takes to make steel cannot today be miniaturized.

Most products or processes exhibit these so-called *economies of scale.* The attainment of a certain size enables us to use more efficient technologies or to attain a finer subdivision of labor than would be possible with a smaller size. Eventually, as the scale of production becomes very large, costs per unit may again increase because of the sheer difficulties of running a huge operation.

Notice that economies of scale result from technology, which is a product of human effort. Strictly speaking, the laws of scale reflect the limitations of human capacity as well as the stubborn facts of physics and chemistry. What is significant is that the constraints imposed by scale can be calculated and described much like those of nature.

Constraints and costs

All these properties of nature set the stage for maximizing behavior. People seek wealth through the production and exchange of goods and services, but they do not maximize in a world where goods can be limitlessly and effortlessly obtained. Nature offers us its services easily or reluctantly, depending on whether we are trying to maximize output by adding more and more of one kind of input (when we encounter diminishing returns); or whether we are trying to increase the output of one good or service at the expense of others (when the law of increasing cost comes into play); or whether we are seeking to organize our production in accordance with the technological characteristics of the agencies of production (economies of scale).

Thus constraints will play a basic role in establishing costs or supplies. We shall return to these considerations in our next chapter, where we encounter a *supply curve,* the counterpart of the demand curve, about which we first heard a few pages back.

Social constraints

Perhaps we can already see the makings of a powerful analytic device in the interplay of maximizing drives and constraining influences. Before we move on, however, it is necessary to recognize that nature is not the only constraint on the maximizing force of behavior.

Society's constraints on our behavior are just as effective as nature's. The *law* is a major constraining factor on our acquisitive propensities. *Competition* also limits freedom of action, preventing us from charging as much as we would like for goods or services. The banking system, labor unions, the legal underpinnings of private property are all institutions that operate like the constraints of nature in curbing the unhampered exercise of our maximizing impulse. We shall spend a lot of time later investigating how these constraints affect individual behavior.

Budget

Last, there is the constraint of our available resources, our budget. Like technology, this is partly a constraint imposed by nature, partly one that is the consequence of man. Different societies enjoy different settings in nature—rich or poor soils, cold or warm climates, easily available or scarce mineral deposits. These gifts of nature help establish the limits of our productive activities, our national budget of annual output.

But of course nature does not establish our budget constraints by itself. Technology and social organizations determine our economic budget of capabilities along with nature. Some societies make much better use of their natural resources than others do. No less to the point, social institutions fix our individual budgets within society. Even in the poorest society there is usually enough for a few individuals to indulge their maximizing propensities to the hilt—if society will allow them to gather or keep a disproportionate share of the nation's wealth. Thus budgetary considerations continually impinge on the maximizing drives of individuals, as well as nations.

Basic Hypotheses

Let us briefly review the basic propositions in this first look into economic analysis. They can be summed up very simply.

Because economics generalizes about human behavior and the behavior of nature, it can theorize about, and predict, the operations of a market society. If we were not able to make such generalizations, if we could not begin with the plausible hypothesis that people are maximizers and that nature (and social institutions) constrain their behavior in clearly defined ways, we could not hazard the simplest predictive statement about economic society. We could not explain why a store that wants to sell more goods marks its prices down rather than up or why copper costs will probably rise if we try to double copper production in a short period of time.

Economics as a social science Perhaps these simple generalizations about behavior and nature do not seem to be an impressive foundation for a social science. Ask yourself, though, whether we can match these economic generalizations when we think in political or sociological terms. Are there political or social laws of behavior that we can count on with the same degree of certainty we find in laws of economics? Are there constraints of nature, comparable to the laws of production, discoverable in the political and social areas of life? There are not. That is why we are so much less able to predict political or sociological events than to predict economic events.

Although economic prediction has sharp limitations, its underlying structure of behavioral and natural laws gives it unique strength. Its capabilities we must now explore. The place to begin must be obvious from our look into economic reality and our first acquaintance with supply and demand. It is the market mechanism.

FOCUS Here is the chapter in which we watch the emergence of economics as a social science. The chapter covers a number of technical aspects (like diminishing returns) to be discussed again later. Don't try to learn them yet. Instead, concentrate on these main ideas.

- Economic science is concerned with the production of wealth and its distribution.

- From their observations of production and distribution, economists hypothesize that: 1) people behave like rational maximizers of pleasurable wealth and 2) nature and institutions serve as constraints on people's activity.

- In market societies, people have insatiable desires for pleasurable wealth, although not insatiable desires for any one thing.

- When we describe nature as a constrainer, we generalize about the resistances to our maximizing impulse. Later, under the laws of supply and demand, we shall combine our generalizations about maximizing and restraining.

- *The capacity of economics to predict the outcome of the economic process depends on the presence of these laws of behavior and nature.* If there were no such laws, economics could not make the simplest prediction. Although these laws are far from perfect, their presence gives economics a unique analytical capability.

WORDS AND CONCEPTS YOU SHOULD KNOW

Maximizing, 82
Constraints, 84–86
Economic man, 84
Rationality, 83
Insatiable wants, 83

Satiable wants, 83
Three laws of production, 84–85 (These will
   be studied in detail later.)
Social vs. natural constraints, 86

QUESTIONS

1. Do you feel like a maximizer? Are you content with your income? If you are not, do you expect that some day you will be satisfied?

2. Do you act rationally when you spend money? Do you consciously try to weigh the various advantages of buying this instead of that and to spend your money for the item that will give you the greatest pleasure? Consciously or not, do you generally act as a rational maximizer?

3. How valid do you think the laws of behavior are? If they are *not* valid, why does economic society function and not collapse? If they *are* valid, why can't economists predict more accurately?

4. In what way is competition an institution? Are people naturally competitive? Would there be competition in a society that denied spatial or social mobility to labor, as under feudalism?

5. Can you think of any laws that describe political activity comparable to economic maximizing or natural constraints? Is there a law of political power? Are there constraints of national size? Might it be possible to devise an economics of politics?

Additonal questions to ponder

6. Suppose that you had a very large flowerpot and extraordinary chemicals and seeds. Could you conceivably grow all the world's food in it? Why would you still get diminishing returns?

7. Consider the law of increasing cost in a society that ordinarily devoted half its efforts to farming, half to hunting. What would be the effect of increasing the output of farm products? Of game?

8. Describe the economies of scale that might be anticipated if you were opening a department store. What economies might be expected as the store grew larger? Do you think you would eventually reach a ceiling on these economies?

The economic problem

Underneath the problems of inflation or monopoly or money, an economist sees a process at work, one that he must understand before he can turn his attention to the issues of the day, no matter how pressing. That process is society's basic *mechanism for survival,* a mechanism for accomplishing the complicated tasks of production and distribution that are necessary for its own continuity.

The economist sees something else, something that at first seems quite astonishing. *Looking not only over the diversity of contemporary societies, but back over the sweep of history, he sees that man has succeeded in solving the production and distribution problems in but three ways.* That is, within the enormous diversity of social institutions that guide and shape the economic process, the economist divines three overarching *types* of systems that separately or in combination enable humankind to meet its economic challenge. These three great systems can be called economies run by *Tradition,* economies run by *Command,* or by the *Market.* We have spoken briefly of Tradition and Command, and at greater length about the Market. But we have not yet put all three systems into a historic context.

TRADITION

Perhaps the oldest and, until recent years, by far the most prevalent way of solving the economic challenge has been by tradition. It has been a mode of social organization in which both production and distribution were based on procedures devised in the distant past, rigidified by a long process of trial and error, and maintained by heavy sanctions of law, custom, and belief.

Societies based on tradition solve the economic problem very manageably. But we must note one very important consequence of the mechanism of tradition. *Its solution to the problems of production and distribution is a static one. A society that follows the path of tradition in its regulation of economic affairs does so at the expense of large-scale rapid social and economic change.*

The economy of a Bedouin tribe or a Burmese village, for example, has not changed essentially over the past hundred or even thousand years. The bulk of the peoples living in tradition-bound societies repeat, in the daily patterns of their economic life, much of the routine that characterized them in the distant past. Such societies may rise and fall, wax and wane; but external events—war, climate, political adventures and misadventures—are mainly responsible for their changing fortunes. Internal, self-generated economic change is but a small factor in the history of most tradition-bound states. *Tradition solves the economic problem, but it does so at the cost of economic progress.*

COMMAND

A second manner of solving the problem of economic continuity also displays an ancient lineage. This is the method of imposed authority, of economic command. The orders of an economic commander-in-chief organize the system here, rather than the changelessness of tradition.

Authoritarian economic organization is widely found in history. We discover it in ancient Egypt and in the despotisms of medieval and classical China, which produced, among other things, the colossal Great Wall. It is evident in the slave labor by which many of the great public works of ancient Rome were built, or for that matter, in any slave economy, including that of pre-Civil War U.S.A. We find it today in the dictates of the communist economic authorities. In less drastic form we find it also in our own society; for example, in the form of taxes; that is, in the preemption of part of our income by the public authorities for public purposes.

Quite aside from its obvious use in meeting emergencies, command has a further advantage in solving the economic problem. Unlike tradition, the exercise of command has no inherent effect of slowing down economic change. *Indeed, the exercise of command is the most powerful instrument society has for enforcing economic change.* Command in modern China or Russia has effected radical alterations in systems of production and distribution. Even in our own society, it is sometimes necessary for economic authority to intervene in the normal flow of economic life, to speed up or bring about change.

THE MARKET

There is a third solution to the economic problem, a third way of maintaining socially viable patterns of production and distribution. This is the *market organization of society.* In truly remarkable fashion, with minimum recourse either to tradition or command, market organization allows society to insure its own provisioning. Because we live in a market-run society, we are apt to take for granted the puzzling—indeed, almost paradoxical—nature of the market solution to the economic problem.

Assume for a moment that we could act as economic advisers to a society that had not yet decided on its mode of economic organization. We could imagine the leaders of such a nation saying, "We have always experienced a highly tradition-bound way of life. Our men hunt and cultivate the fields and perform their tasks as they are brought up to do by the force of example and the instruction of their elders. We know, too, something of what can be done by economic command. We are prepared, if necessary, to sign an edict making it compulsory for many of our men to work on community projects for our national development. Tell us, is there any other way we can organize our society so that it will function successfully—or better yet, more successfully?"

Suppose we answered, "Yes, there is another way. Organize your society along the lines of a market economy."

"Very well," say the leaders. "What do we then tell people to do? How do we assign them to their various tasks?"

"That's the very point," we would answer. "In a market economy, no one is assigned to any task. In fact, the main idea of a market society is that each person is allowed to decide for himself what to do."

There is consternation among the leaders. "You mean there is no assignment of some men to mining and others to cattle raising? No manner of designating some for transportation and others for weaving? You leave this to people to decide for themselves? What happens if they do not decide correctly? What happens if no one volunteers to go into the mines, or if no one offers himself as a railway engineer?"

"You may rest assured," we tell the leaders, "none of that will happen. In a market society, all the jobs will be filled because it will be to people's advantage to fill them."

Our respondents accept this with uncertain expressions. "Now look," one of them finally says, "let us suppose that we take your advice and allow our people to do as they please. Let's talk about something specific, like cloth production. Just how do we fix the right level of cloth output in this 'market society' of yours?"

"You don't," we reply.

"We don't! Then how do we know there will be enough cloth produced?"

"There will be," we tell him. "The market will see to that."

"Then how do we know there won't be *too much* cloth produced?" he asks triumphantly.

"Ah, but the market will see to that too!"

"Then what is this market that will do these wonderful things? Who runs it?"

"Oh, nobody runs the market," we answer. "It runs itself. In fact there really isn't any such *thing* as 'the market.' It's just a word we use to describe the way people behave."

"But I thought people behave the way they want to?"

"So they do," we say. "But never fear. They will want to behave the way you want them to behave."

"I am afraid," says the chief of the delegation, "that we are wasting our time. We thought you had in mind a serious proposal. What you suggest is inconceivable. Good day, sir."

ECONOMICS AND THE MARKET SYSTEM

Economics, as we commonly conceive it, and as we shall study it in much of this book, is primarily concerned with these very market problems. Societies that rely primarily on tradition to solve their economic problems are of less interest to the professional economist than to the cultural anthropologist or the sociologist. Societies that solve their economic problems primarily by the exercise of command present interesting economic questions, some of which we will address later in this book, for command plays a leading role in our form of mixed public and private economy.

But it is a society that solves its economic problems by the market process that presents an aspect especially interesting to the economist. We are such a society, and many (although not all) of the problems we encounter in America today have to do with the workings or misworkings of the market system. We will gain our first inside view of its mechanisms in our next chapter.

The market mechanism

Our quick look at the economy has given us a general understanding of the market system. The next step in understanding the fundamental concepts of economics is to learn much more about that system.

What impresses us first when we study the market as a solution to the economic problem? The striking fact is that the market uses only one means of persuasion to induce people to engage in production or to undertake the tasks of distribution. It is neither time-honored tradition nor the edict of any authority that tells the members of a market society what to do. *It is price.*

Prices and behavior

Thus the first attribute of a market system that we must examine is how prices take the place of tradition or command to become the guide to economic behavior.

The answer lies in maximization. Through prices, acquisitive individuals learn what course of action will maximize their incomes or minimize their expenditures. This means that in the word *price* we include prices of labor or capital or land prices that we call wages, profits, interest, or rent. Of course, within the category of prices we also include those ordinary prices that we pay for the goods and services we consume and the materials we purchase in order to build a home or to operate a store or factory. In each case, the only way that we can tell how to maximize our receipts and minimize our costs is by "reading" the signals of price that the market gives us.*

Therefore, if we are to understand how the market works as a mechanism—that is, how it acts as a guide to the solution of the economic problem—we must first understand how the market sets prices. When we say the market, we mean the activity of buying and selling, or in more precise economic language, *demand and supply.* Let us discover how demand and supply interact to establish prices.

Demand

When you enter the market for goods and services (almost every time you walk along a shopping street), two factors determine whether or not you will actually become a buyer and not just a window-shopper. The first factor is your taste for the good. It is your taste that determines in large degree whether a good offers you pleasure or utility, and how much. The windows of shops are crammed with things you could afford to buy but which you simply do not wish to own, because they do not offer you sufficient utility. Perhaps if some of these were cheaper, you might wish to own them; but some goods you would not want even if they were free. For such goods, for which your tastes are too weak to motivate you, your demand is zero. *Thus taste determines your willingness to buy.*

*In the real world, reading prices can be very complicated, for it involves not only how much we know about the market, but how much we *think* we know about it. Here we simplify matters and assume, to begin with, that we all have perfect knowledge.

On the other hand, taste is by no means the only component of demand. Shop windows are also full of goods that you might very much like to own but cannot afford to buy. Your demand for Rolls Royces is also apt to be zero. *In other words, demand also hinges on your ability to buy—on your possession of sufficient wealth or income as well as on your taste.* If demand did not hinge on ability as well as willingness to buy, the poor, whose wants are always very large, would constitute a great source of demand.

Budgets

Note that your demand for goods depends on your willingness and ability to buy goods or services *at their going price.* From this it follows that the amounts of goods you demand will change as their prices change, just as it also follows that the amounts you will demand change as your wealth or income changes. There is no difficulty understanding why changing prices should change our ability to buy: our wealth simply stretches further or less far. **In economic language, our budget constraint is loosened when prices fall and tightened when they rise.**

Diminishing marginal utility

Why should our *willingness* to buy be related to price? The answer returns us again to the behavioral hypotheses of our last chapter. People are maximizing creatures, but they do not want ever more of the *same* commodity. On the contrary, as we saw, economists take as a plausible generalization that additional increments of the same good or service, within some stated period of time, will yield smaller and smaller increments of pleasure. These increments of pleasure are called *marginal utility,* and the general tendency of

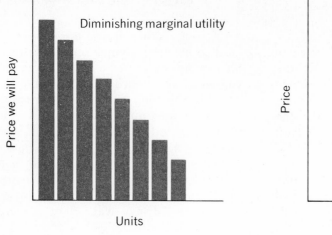
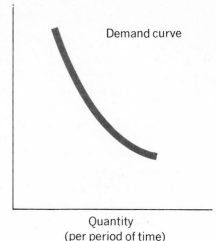

FIG. 7·1   Diminishing marginal utility and a demand curve

marginal utility to diminish is called the *law of diminishing marginal utility.* Remember: diminishing marginal utility refers strictly to behavior and not to nature. The units of goods we continue to buy are not smaller—only the pleasure associated with each additional unit.

Demand curves   In the bar chart on the left of Fig. 7·1, we show the ever-smaller amounts of money we are willing to pay for additional units of some good or service, simply because each additional unit gives us less utility than its predecessor. In the graph on the right, we

have drawn a *demand curve* to generalize this basic relationship between the quantity of a good we are interested in acquiring and the price we are willing to pay for it.

Figure 7·1 deserves a careful look. Note that each *additional* unit affords us less utility, so we are not willing to pay as much for the next unit as for the one we just bought. This does not mean that the *total utility* we derive from 3 or 4 units is less than that derived from the first. Far from it. It is the *addition* to our utility from the last unit that is much lower than the *addition* of the first or second.

Does diminishing marginal utility really determine how much we buy? The idea seems far removed from common sense, but is it? Suppose we decide to buy a cake of fancy soap. In commonsense language, we'll do so only "if it's not too expensive." In the language of the economist this means we'll only do so *if the utilities we expect from the soap are greater than the utilities we derive from the money we have to spend to get the soap.*

If we buy one or two cakes, doesn't this demonstrate that the pleasure of the soap is greater than the pleasure of holding onto the money or spending it for something

UTILITIES AND DEMAND

Price of soap = marginal utility of the money it costs

else? In that case, why don't we buy a year's supply of the soap? The commonsense answer is that we don't want *that much* soap. It would be a nuisance. We wouldn't use it all for months and months, etc. *In the language of the economist, the utilities of the cakes of soap after the first few would be less than the utilities of the money they would cost.*

In the accompanying diagram we show these diminishing marginal utilities of successive cakes. The price of soap represents the utility of the money we have to pay. As you can see, if soap costs *OA,* we'll buy three cakes; no more.

The puzzle of bread and diamonds

The notion of diminishing marginal utility also clears up another puzzle of economic life. This is why we are willing to pay so little for bread, which is a necessity for life, and so much for diamonds, which are not. The answer is that we have so much bread that the marginal utility of any loaf we are thinking of buying is very little, whereas we have so few diamonds that each carat has a very high marginal utility. If we were locked inside Tiffany's over a long holiday, the prices we would pay for bread and diamonds, after a few days, would be very different from those we would have paid when we entered.

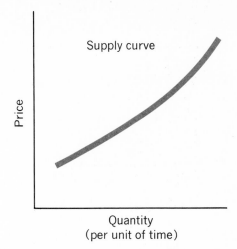

FIG. 7·2   The short-run supply curve

Supply

What about the supply side? Here, too, willingness and ability enter into the seller's actions. As we would expect, they bring about reactions different from those in the case of demand.

At high prices, sellers are much more *willing* to supply goods and services because they will take in more money. They will also be much more easily *able* to offer more goods because higher prices will enable less efficient suppliers to enter the market, or will cover the higher costs of production that may result from increasing their outputs.

Therefore, we depict supply curves as rising in the short run. These rising curves present a contrast to the falling curves of demanders: sellers eagerly respond to high prices; buyers respond negatively. Figure 7·2 shows such a typical supply curve.

Supply and demand

The idea that buyers welcome low prices and sellers welcome high prices is hardly apt to come as a surprise. What is surprising is that the meaning of words *supply* and *demand* differs from the one we ordinarily carry about in our heads. It is very important to understand that when we speak of demand as economists, we do not refer to a single purchase at a given price. **Demand in its proper economic sense refers to the various quantities of goods or services that we are willing and able to buy at different prices at a given time.** That relationship is shown by our demand curve.

The same relationship between price and quantity enters into the word *supply.* When we say *supply,* we do not mean the amount a seller puts on the market at a given price. We mean the various amounts offered at different prices. Thus our supply curves, like our demand curves, portray the relationship between willingness and ability to enter into transactions at different prices.

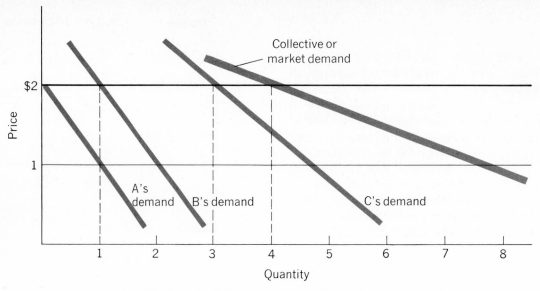

FIG. 7·3   Individual and market demand curves

Individual and collective supply and demand

We must add one last word before we investigate the market at work. Thus far we have considered only the factors that make an *individual* more willing and able to buy as prices fall or less willing and able to sell. Generally when we speak of supply and demand we refer to markets composed of *many* suppliers and demanders. That gives us an additional reason for relating

price and behavior. If we assume that most individuals have somewhat different willingnesses and abilities to buy, because their incomes and their tastes are different, or they have unequal willingnesses or abilities to sell, then we can see that *a change in price will bring into the market new buyers or sellers:* As price falls, it will tempt or permit one person after another to buy, thereby adding to the quantity of the good that will be purchased at that price. Conversely, as prices rise, the number of

FIG. 7·4   Individual and market supply curves

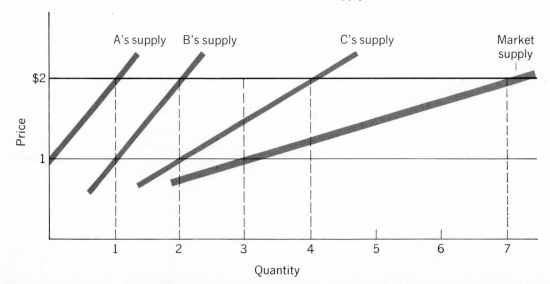

sellers drawn into the market will increase, and the quantity of goods they offer will rise accordingly.

We can see this graphically in Fig. 7·3. Here we show three individuals' demand curves. At the going market price of $2, A is either not willing or not able to buy any of the commodity. B is both willing and able to buy 1 unit. C buys 3 units. If we add up their demands, we get a *collective or market demand curve*. At the indicated market price of $2, the quantity demanded is 4 units. What would it be (approximately) for each buyer, and for the group, at a price of $1?

The same, of course, applies to supply. In Fig. 7·4 we show individual supply curves and a collective or market supply curve that is 7 units at $2 market supply. What would total supply be at a price of $1? What would seller A's supply be at $1?

Balancing supply and demand

We are now ready to see how the market mechanism works. Undoubtedly you have already grasped the crucial point on which the mechanism depends. *This is the opposing behavior that a change in prices brings about for buyers and sellers. Rising prices will be matched by an increase in the willingness and ability of sellers to offer goods, but in a decrease in the willingness and ability of buyers to take goods.*

It is through these opposing reactions that the market mechanism works. Let us examine the process in an imaginary market for shoes in a small city. In Table 7·1 we show the price-quantity relationships of buyers and of sellers: how many thousand pairs will be offered for sale or sought for purchase at a range of prices from $50 to $5. We call such an array of price-quality relationships a *schedule* of supply and demand.

Table 7·1 Demand and supply schedules

Price	Quantity demanded (1,000 prs.)	Quantity supplied (1,000 prs.)
$50	1	125
$45	5	90
$40	10	70
$35	20	50
$30	25	35
$25	30	30
$20	40	20
$15	50	10
$10	75	5
$ 5	100	0

As before, the schedules tell us that buyers and sellers react differently to prices. At high prices, buyers are either not willing or unable to purchase more than small quantities of shoes, whereas sellers would be only too willing and able to flood the city with them. At very low prices, the quantity of shoes demanded would be very great, but few shoe manufacturers would be willing or able to gratify buyers at such low prices.

If we now look at *both* schedules at *each* price level, we discover an interesting thing. *There is one price*—$25 in our example—*at which the quantity demanded is exactly the same as the quantity supplied.* At every other price, either one schedule or the other is larger, but at $25 the amounts in both columns are the same: 30,000 pairs of shoes. We call this balancing price the *equilibrium price.* We shall soon see that it *is* the price that emerges spontaneously in an actual market where supply and demand contend.*

---

*Of course we have made up our schedules so that the quantities demanded and supplied would be equal at $25. The price that actually brought about such a balancing of supply and demand might be some odd number such as $24.98.

Emergence of the Equilibrium Price

How do we know that an equilibrium price will be brought about by the interaction of supply and demand? The process is one of the most important in all of economics, so we should understand it very clearly.

Suppose in our example above that for some reason or other the shoe retailers put a price tag on their shoes not of $25 but of $45. What would happen? Our schedules show us that at this price shoe manufacturers will be pouring out shoes at the rate of 90,000 pairs a year, whereas customers would be buying them at the rate of only 5,000 pairs a year. Shortly, the shoe factories would be bulging with unsold merchandise. It is plain what the outcome of this situation must be. In order to realize some revenue, shoe manufacturers will begin to unload their stocks at lower prices. *They do so because this is the rational course for competitive maximizers to pursue.*

As they reduce the price, the situation will begin to improve. At $40, demand picks up from 5,000 pairs to 10,000, while at the same time the slightly lower price discourages some producers, so that output falls from 90,000 pairs to 70,000. Shoe manufacturers are still turning out more shoes than the market can absorb at the going prices, although the difference between the quantities supplied and the quantities demanded is smaller than it was before.

Let us suppose that the competitive pressure continues to reduce prices so that shoes soon sell at $30. Now a much more satisfactory state of affairs exists. Producers will be turning out 35,000 pairs of shoes. Consumers will be buying them at a rate of 25,000 a year. Still there is an imbalance. Some shoes will still be piling up, unsold, at the factory. Prices will therefore continue to fall, eventually to $25. At this point, the quantity of shoes supplied by the manufacturers—30,000 pairs—is exactly that demanded by customers. There is no longer a surplus of unsold shoes hanging over the market and acting to press prices down.

The market clears

Now let us quickly trace the interplay of supply and demand from the other direction. Suppose that prices were originally $5. Our schedules tell us that customers would be standing in line at the shoe stores, but producers would be largely shut down, unwilling or unable to make shoes at those prices. We can easily imagine that customers, many of whom would gladly pay more than $5, let it be known that they would welcome a supply of shoes at $10 or even more. They, too, are trying to maximize their utilities. If enough customers bid $10, a trickle of shoe output begins. Nevertheless, the quantity of shoes demanded at $10 far exceeds the available supply. Customers snap up the few pairs around and tell shoe stores they would gladly pay $20 a pair. Prices rise accordingly. Now we are getting closer to a balance of quantities offered and bid for. At $20 there will be a demand for 40,000 pairs of shoes, and output will have risen to 20,000 pairs. Still the pressure of unsatisfied demand raises prices further. Finally a price of $25 is tried. Now, once again, the quantities supplied and demanded are exactly in balance. There is no further pressure from unsatisfied customers to force the price up further, because at $25 no customer who can afford the going price will remain unsatisfied. The market "clears."

Characteristics of equilibrium prices Thus we can see how *the interaction of supply and demand brings about the establishment of a price at which both suppliers and demanders are willing and able to sell or buy the same quantity of goods.* We can visualize the equilibrating process more easily if we now transfer our supply and demand schedules to graph paper. Figure 7•5 is the representation of the shoe market we have been dealing with.

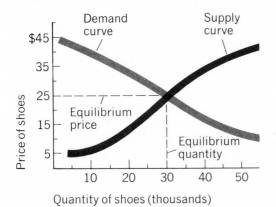

FIG. 7•5 Determination of an equilibrium price

The graph shows us at a glance the situation we have analyzed in detail. At the price of $25, the quantities demanded and supplied are equal: 30,000 pairs of shoes. The graph also shows more vividly than the schedules why this is an *equilibrium* price.

Suppose that the price were temporarily lifted above $25. If you will draw a horizontal pencil line from any point on the vertical axis above the $25 mark to represent this price, you will find that it intersects the demand curve before it reaches the supply curve. In other words, *the quantity demanded is less than the quantity supplied at any price above the equilibrium price, and the excess of the*

quantity supplied means that there will be a downward pressure on prices, back toward the equilibrium point.

The situation is exactly reversed if prices should fall below the equilibrium point. Now the quantity demanded is greater than that supplied, and the pressure of buyers will push the price up to the equilibrium point.

Thus equilibrium prices have two important characteristics:

1. They are the prices that will spontaneously establish themselves through the free play of the forces of supply and demand.
2. Once established, they will persist unless the forces of supply and demand themselves change.

Does "demand equal supply"? There is one last thing carefully to be noted about equilibrium prices. They are the prices that bring about an equality in the *quantities demanded* and the *quantities supplied.* They are not the prices that bring about an equality of "supply and demand." Probably the most common beginning mistake in economics is to say that supply and demand are equal when prices are in equilibrium. If we remember that both supply and demand mean the *relationships* between quantities and prices, we can see that an equality of supply and demand would mean that the demand schedule and the supply schedule for a commodity were alike, so that the curves would lie one on top of the other. In turn, this would mean that at a price of $50, buyers of shoes would be willing and able to buy the same number of shoes that suppliers would be willing to offer at that price, and the same for buyers at $5. If such were the case, prices would be wholly indeterminate and could race high and low with no tension of opposing interests to bring them to a stable resting place.

Hence we must take care to use the words *supply* or *demand* to refer only to relationships or schedules. When we want to speak of the effect of a particular price on our willingness or ability either to buy or sell, we use the longer phrase *quantity demanded* or *quantity supplied*.

The role of competition

We have seen how stable, lasting prices may spontaneously emerge from the flux of the marketplace, but we have silently passed over a basic condition for the formation of these prices. This is the role played by competition in the operation of the market mechanism.

Competition is often discussed as a somewhat unpleasant attribute of economic man. Now, however, we can see that it is an attribute that is indispensable if we are to have socially acceptable outcomes for a market process.

Competition is the regulator that "supervises" the orderly working of the market. But economic competition (unlike the competition for prizes outside economic life) is not a single contest. It is a *continuing process*. It monitors a race that no one ever wins, a race where all must go on endlessly trying to stay in front, to avoid the economic penalties of falling behind.

Moreover, unlike the contests of ordinary life, economic *competition involves not just a single struggle among rivals, but two struggles*. One is between the two sides of the markets; the other is among the marketers on each side. The competitive marketplace is not only where the clash of interest between buyer and seller is worked out by the opposition of supply and demand, but also where buyers contend against buyers and sellers against sellers.

Two necessary aspects of competition

It is this double aspect of the competitive process that accounts for its usefulness. A market in which buyers and sellers had no conflict of interest would not be competitive, for prices could then be arranged at some level convenient for both sides, instead of representing a compromise between the divergent interests of the two. Conversely, a market that was no more than a place where opposing forces contended would be only a tug of war, a bargaining contest with an unpredictable outcome, unless we knew the respective strengths and cunning of the two sides.

Competition drives buyers and sellers to a meeting point because each side of the price contest is also contesting against itself. Vying takes place not merely *between* those who want high prices and those who want low ones. On each side of this divide, vying takes place *among* marketers whose self-interest urges them to meet the demands of the other side. If some unsatisfied shoe buyers, although preferring low prices to high ones, did not want shoes enough to offer a little higher price than the prevailing one, and if some unsatisfied sellers, although hoping for high prices, were not driven by self-interest to offer a price a little below that of their rivals, the price would not move to that balancing point where the two sides arrived at the best possible settlement.

Thus, whereas buyers as a group want low prices, each individual buyer has to pay as high a price as he can to get "into" the market. Whereas sellers as a group want high prices, each individual seller has to trim his prices if he is to be able to "meet" the competition.

Maximizing is subject to constraints

Does the extraordinary market mechanism bear a relation to the general notion of maximizing and constraints? Indeed it does. Both buyers and sellers are driven by maximizing impulses and constrained by forces of nature and social institutions, as well as by their limited incomes or wealth.

Buyers and sellers both are *willing* to respond to price signals because they wish to maximize their incomes or utilities. Neither can maximize at will. Buyers are constrained by their budgets, and sellers are constrained by their costs. Thus the *ability* of buyers or sellers to respond to price signals is limited by obstacles of budgets or cost.

In addition, buyers and sellers are both constrained by the operation of the market. A seller might like to sell his goods above the market price, and a buyer might like to buy goods below the market price; but the presence of competitors means that a seller who quotes a price above the market will be unable to find a buyer, and a buyer who makes a bid below the market will be unable to find a seller.

Thus the market mechanism is a very important example of what economists call "maximizing subject to constraints." Furthermore, we can see that it is the very interaction of the maximizing drives and the constraining obstacles that leads the market to the establishment of equilibrium prices. We can also see that if we could know these maximizing forces and constraints beforehand, we would know the supply and demand curves of a market and could actually predict what its equilibrium price would be! In actual fact, our knowledge falls far short of such omniscience, but the imaginary example nonetheless begins to open up for us the analytical possibilities of economics.

FOCUS   **What are you supposed to gain from this chapter? Above all, an understanding of how a market works. Here are questions you should be able to answer.**

- **Why do price changes signal different things to buyers and sellers?**
- **Why is it necessary to specify both willingness and ability in talking about supply and demand schedules?**
- **Why is marginal, not total, utility so important in determining our demand schedules?**
- **Why is the meaning of the word "demand" not the same as "quantity demanded"? (Ditto for "supply" and "quantity supplied.")**
- **Why does an equilibrium price "clear" a market?**

• Why is competition a double battle—between buyers and sellers, and among buyers themselves and sellers themselves? Why do we need both battles to have a working market system?

In the end, there is also one exercise everyone should do. Insert reasonable numbers in the table for question 1, and graph them on the axes below your table.

WORDS AND CONCEPTS YOU SHOULD KNOW

Demand, 93
Total vs. marginal utility, 93
Diminishing marginal utility, 93
Demand curves, 94

Supply, 95
Equilibrium price, 97–99
Clearing the market, 98
Two aspects of competition, 100–101

SUPPLY AND DEMAND FOR BOOKS

Price of books	Quantity demanded	Quantity supplied
$10		
9		
8		
7		
6		
5		
4		
3		
2		
1		

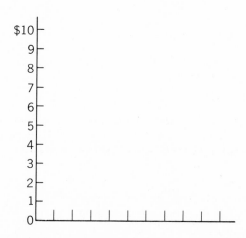

QUESTIONS

1. Fill in reasonable numbers for quantities demanded and supplied and graph your answers. What is the equilibrium price of books in your example?

2. Choose some arbitrary price above equilibrium. How will maximizing behavior lead this higher price back to the equilibrium price? Be sure to describe the contest that will take place among sellers and among buyers.

3. Now go through the same exercise with a price lower than the equilibrium. Once again, trace the return of the price to equilibrium.

4. Subtract the quantities in your supply schedule from those in your demand schedule. There will be a plus or minus difference at all prices except one. Why is that? Does that help explain why equilibrium prices clear markets?

5. Why are so many necessities of life, such as salt, so cheap, since they are indispensable?

6. Whatever quantity is sold must, by definition, be bought. Then why do we not say that the market will clear at any price? (Hint: look again at question 2.)

The constraint of time

We normally think of consumers as subject to the economic consequences imposed by their limited material resources (including, of course, money). Yet there is a more formidable constraint imposed by time. In fact, the pressures imposed by a scarcity of time are in some ways much more intractable than those imposed by a scarcity of means.

The time constraint takes two forms. In the first place, there is the basic constraint imposed by longevity itself. This is a constraint over which we have little control and about which we do not even have much information. We know how rich we are, but we do not know how long we will live. Yet one of our objectives as maximizers is to spread our energies and enjoyments efficiently over our hoped-for lifetime. We all speak of our years of "maximum earning power," although none of us can be sure that we will live out those years; and we are all aware of the futility of postponing consumption too long. As rational maximizers, we have to try to spend our incomes during those years when our capacity for enjoyment is greatest.

A second time constraint has to do with the allocation of time within the consumption process. We are all forced to spend some time shopping; that is, acquiring consumption goods. The more time spent shopping, the better informed we will be, but at the expense of time left for consuming. In addition, when choosing which goods to buy, one consideration, besides price, is time. *Will we have time to use these goods?* Why don't we all buy violins, multivolume sets of books, elaborate hobby kits? Because we haven't got the time to use them or to learn to use them or to enjoy them.

Hence we are continually saving time, in order to make time for the act of consuming. In fact, as our wealth increases and we own more and more material goods, the value of extra time increases proportionally. The marginal utility of goods goes down; that of time goes up. *Hence we begin to spend our income to loosen our time constraint.* We fly when we could go more cheaply by train or car. We buy gadgets to save household time. We eat out more, not only because it is enjoyable, but because it saves the time needed for cooking. We buy (or rent) expensive golf carts so that we can maximize our golf-playing time by cutting down on course-walking time.

Time was not always so valuable. When goods were scarcer, the time constraint was not so acutely felt. People used to travel slowly and visit one another for weeks. Men in business dined at leisure and came home for a midday nap. As Steffan Linder says in his amusing and keen book, *The Harried Leisure Class,* no one does that any more; not so much because they haven't the money, but they haven't the time.

Can we find something to loosen the time constraint, as additional money loosens the income constraint? One great change in the past was the invention of artificial light, making it possible to do many things at night that were formerly limited to daylight hours. It seems difficult to imagine an invention that would equal that. Perhaps pills will allow us to pack in as much sleep in four hours as we now get in eight. Perhaps better access to information will save shopping time; although if you are someone who enjoys shopping, the process of browsing and looking around is not an invasion of your consumption, it is part of it.

Economists cannot do much about the time constraint, because, as we have said, our capacity to loosen it is very limited. We can only predict that as we get materially richer, we will get temporally poorer by comparison. More and more of our material budgets will be used to save time.

Tools of economic analysis

Having had a glimpse at the basic assumptions of economic theory and a longer look at the market mechanism, we can advance toward a full-fledged exploration of micro and macro analysis. At this point along the way, we need to learn something more about the working techniques of economic analysis itself.

This chapter will give us a series of concepts that we shall use in thinking clearly about economics. Some of the concepts seem very simple but are more subtle than they appear at first. Others look demanding at first, even though they are actually very simple. There are six of these intellectual tools. Try to master them, for we will be using them continuously from here on.

1. Ceteris paribus

The first concept is one that we met in our view of the scientific method. It is the need to eliminate "impurities" from our experiments and observations.

In economics, this search for "pure" facts or hypotheses takes the form of an attempt to "hold other things constant" while we observe the particular economic relationships we are interested in.

This assumption of holding "other

things equal" is called by its Latin name, **ceteris paribus.** It is extremely easy to apply in theory and extremely difficult to apply in practice. In our examination of the demand curve, for example, we assume that the *income* and *tastes* of the person (or of the collection of persons) are unchanged while we examine the influence of price on the quantities of shoes they are willing and able to buy. The reason is obvious. If we allowed their incomes or tastes to change, both their willingness *and* their ability would also change. If prices doubled but a fad for shoes developed, or if prices tripled but income quadrupled, we would not find that "demand" decreased as prices rose.

Ceteris paribus is applied every time we speak of supply and demand, and on many other occasions as well. Since we know that in reality prices, tastes, incomes, population size, technology, moods, and many other elements of society are continually changing, we can see why this is a heroic assumption. It is one that is almost impossible to trace in actual life or to correct for, fully, by special statistical techniques.

Yet we can also see that unless we apply ceteris paribus, *at least in our minds, we cannot isolate the particular interactions and causal sequences that we want to investigate.* The economic world then becomes a vast Chinese puzzle. Every piece interlocks with every other, and no one can tell what the effect of any one thing is on any other. If economics is to be useful, it must be able to tell us something about the effect of changing *only* price or *only* income or *only* taste or any *one* of a number of other things. We can do so only by assuming that other things are "equal" and by holding them unchanged in our minds while we perform the intellectual experiment in whose outcome we are interested.

2. *Functional relationships*

Economics, it is already very clear, is about relationships—relationships of mankind and nature, and relationships of individuals to one another. The laws of diminishing marginal utility or diminishing returns or supply and demand are all statements of those relationships, which we can use to explain or predict economic matters.

We call these relationships that portray the effect of one thing on another *functional relationships.* Functional relationships may relate the effect of price on the quantities offered or bought, or the effect of successive inputs of the same factor on outputs of a given product, or the effect of population growth on economic growth, or whatever.

One important point: functional relationships are not "logical" relationships of the kind we find in geometry or arithmetic, such as the square of the hypotenuse of a right triangle being equal to the sum of the squares of the other two sides, or the number 6 being the product of 2 times 3 or 3 times 2. Functional relationships cannot be discovered by deductive reasoning. They are descriptions of real events that we can discover only by empirical investigation. We then search for ways of expressing these relationships in graphs or mathematical terms. In economics, the technique used for discovering these relationships is called *econometrics.* You can get a first taste of this subject, if you wish, in Chapter 44.

3. *Identities*

Before going on, we must clarify an important distinction between functional relationships and another kind of relationship called an *identity.* We need this distinction because both relationships use the word *equals,* although the word has different meanings in the two cases.

A few pages ahead we shall meet the expression

$$Q_d = f(P)$$

which we read "Quantity demanded (Q_d) *equals* $f(P)$" or "*is* a function of price $[f(P)]$." This refers to the kind of relationship we have been talking about. We shall also find another kind of "equals," typified by the statement $P \equiv S$ or purchases equals sales. $P \equiv S$ is *not* a functional relationship, because purchases do not "depend" on sales. They are *the same thing* as sales, viewed from the vantage point of the buyer instead of the seller. P and S are identities: Q and P are not. The identity sign is $\equiv$.

Identities are true by definition. They cannot be "proved" true or false, because there is nothing to be proved. On the other hand, when we say that the quantity purchased will depend on price, there is a great deal to be proved. Empirical investigation may disclose that the suggested relationship is not true. It may show that a relationship exists but that the nature of the relationship is not always the same. Identities are changeless as well as true. They are logical statements that require no investigations of human action. The signs $\equiv$ and = do not mean the same things.

Sometimes identities and behavioral equations are written in the same manner with an equal sign (=). Technically, identities should be written with an identity sign ($\equiv$). Unfortunately, the sign also reads "equals." Since it is important to know the difference between definitions, which do not need proof, and hypotheses, which *always* need demonstration or proof we shall carefully differentiate between the equal sign (=) and the identity sign ($\equiv$). Whenever you see an equal sign, you know that a behavioral relationship is being hypothesized. When you see the identity sign, you will know that a definition is being offered, not a statement about behavior.

Identities, being definitions, deserve our attention because they are the way we establish a precise working language. Learning this language, with its special vocabulary, is essential to being able to speak economics accurately.

4. Schedules

We are familiar with the next item in our kit of intellectual tools. It is one of the techniques used to establish functional relationships: the technique of drawing up *schedules* or lists of the different values of elements.

We met such schedules in Chapter 7, in our lists of the quantities of shoes supplied or demanded at various prices. Schedules are thus the empirical or

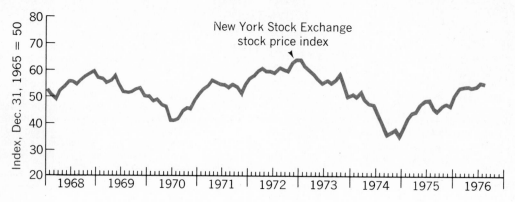

FIG. 8·1   Stock market prices

hypothetical data whose functional interconnection we wish to investigate. In our next chapter we shall look into some of the problems of drawing up such schedules in real life. We must understand, though, that we use them in economic analysis as "examples" of the raw material of behavior scrutinized by economic theory.

5. Graphs

The depiction of functional relationships through schedules is simple enough, but economists usually prefer to represent these relationships by graphs or equations. This is so because schedules show the relationship only between *specific* quantities and prices or specific data of any kind. Graphs and equations show the *generalized* relationship, the relationship that covers all quantities and prices or all values of any two things we are interested in.

The simplest and most intuitively obvious method of showing a functional relationship in its general form is through a graph. Everyone is familiar with graphs of one kind or another, but not all graphs show functional relationships. A graph of stock prices over time, as in Fig. 8·1, shows us the level of prices in different periods. It does not show a behavioral con-

nection between a date and a price. Such a graph merely describes and summarizes history. No one would maintain that such and such a date *caused* stock market prices to take such and such a level.

On the other hand, a graph that related the price of a stock and the quantities that we are willing and able to buy *at that price, ceteris paribus,* is indeed a graphic depiction of a functional relation. If we look at the hypothetical graph below, we

FIG. 8·2   Price/quantity relationship of a hypothetical stock

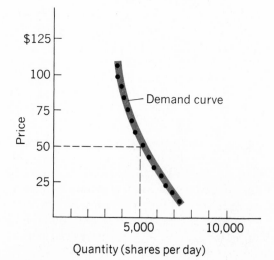

can note the dots that show us the particular price/quantity relationships. Now we can tell the quantity that would be demanded at any price, simply by going up the "price" axis, over to the demand curve, and down to the "quantity" axis. In Fig. 8·2, for example, at a price of $50 the quantity demanded is 5,000 shares per day.*

6. Equations   A third way of representing functional relationships is often used for its simplicity and brevity. *Equations are very convenient means of expressing functional relationships, since they allow us to consider the impact of more than one factor at a time.* A typical equation for demand might look like this:

$$Q_d = f(P)$$

Most of us are familiar with equations but may have forgotten their vocabulary. There are three terms in the equation above: Q_d, f, and P. Each has a name. We are interested in seeing how our quantity

demanded (Q_d) is affected by changes in prices (P). In other words, our "demand" is dependent on changes in price. Therefore the term Q_d is called the *dependent variable:* "variable" because it changes; "dependent" because it is the result of changes in P. As we would imagine, the name for P is the *independent variable*.

Now for the term f. The definition of f is simply "function" or "function of," so that we read $Q_d = f(P)$ as "quantity demanded is a function of price." If we knew that the quantity demanded was a function of both price *and* income (Y) we would write $Q_d = f(P, Y)$. Such equations tell us what independent variables affect what dependent variables, but they do not tell us *how* Q_d changes with changes in P or Y.

The "how" depends on our actual analysis of actual market behavior. Let us take a very simple case for illustrative purposes. Suppose that a survey of consumer purchasing intentions tells us that consumers would take 100 units of a product if its price were zero—that is, if it were given away free—and that they would buy one-half unit less each time the price went up by $1. The demand equation would then be:

$$Q_d = 100 - .5(P)$$

*Technically we would need a schedule of survey results showing the quantities demanded for every conceivable price in order to draw a graph. In fact, we obtain results for a variety of prices and assume that the relationship between the unmeasured points is like that of the measured points. The process of sketching in unmeasured points is called *interpolation*.

Thus, if price were \$10, buyers would take $100 - .5 \times 10$, or 95 units.*

We should stop to note one important property of ordinary price/quantity demand or supply functions. It is that they have opposite "signs." A normal demand function is negative, showing that quantities demanded *fall* as prices rise. A supply function is usually positive, showing that quantities supplied *rise* as prices rise. A survey of producers might tell us that the quantity supplied would go up by 2 units for every \$1 increase in price, or

$$Q_s = 2 (P)$$

Note that the sign of the function 2 is positive, whereas the sign of the demand function was negative, $-.5$.

Economic techniques reviewed

The basic assumptions that economics makes regarding economic society can be summed up in two sets of general propositions or laws—laws about behavior and laws about production. What we have

*Suppose we wanted an equation that would measure the effect on quantity demanded of both price and income (see box). Such an equation might be:

$$Q_d = 100 - .5 (P) + .1 (Y)$$

where Y = income

In this equation the quantity demanded goes *up* by 100 units whenever incomes rise by \$1,000. As before, it goes *down* by ½ unit as prices rise by \$1. If incomes were \$2,000 and P were \$10, the quantity demanded would be $(100 - .5 \times 10 + .1 \times 2,000) = 295$ units.

been learning in this chapter are the *techniques* of economic analysis—the ways in which economics uses its basic premises.

These techniques, as we have seen, revolve around the central idea of functional relationships. Because behavior or production is sufficiently "regular," functions enable us to explain or predict economic activity. Their relationships are presented in the form of graphs or equations derived from the underlying schedules of data.

As we have seen, the ability to establish functional relationships depends critically on the *ceteris paribus* assumption. Unless we hold other things equal, either by econometric means or simply in our heads, we cannot isolate the effect of one variable on another.

Economic fallacies

No chapter on the mode of economic thought would be complete without reference to economic fallacies. Actually there is no special class of fallacies that are called economic. The mistakes we find in economic thought are only examples of a larger class of mistaken ways of thinking that we call fallacies. But they are serious enough to justify a warning in general and some attention to one fallacy in particular.

The general warning can do no more than ask us to be on guard against the sloppy thinking that can make fools of us in any area. It is easy to fall into errors of false syllogisms,* of trying to prove an argument *post hoc, ergo propter hoc* ("after the fact, therefore the cause of the fact"). An example would be "proving" that government spending must be inflationary by pointing out that the government spent large sums during periods when inflation was present, ignoring other factors that may have been at work.

The gallery of such mistaken conclusions is all too large in all fields. One fallacy that has a special relevance to economics is called the *fallacy of composition.* Suppose we had an island community in which all farmers sold their produce to one another. Suppose further that one farmer was able to get rich by cheating: selling his produce at the same price as everyone else, but putting fewer

*See the questions at the end of this chapter.

vegetables into his bushel baskets. Does it not follow that all farmers could get rich if all cheated?

We can see that there is a fallacy here. Where does it arise? In the first example, when our cheating farmer got rich, we ignored a small side effect of his action. The side effect was that a loss in real income was inflicted on the community. To ignore that side effect was proper so long as our focus of attention was what happened to the one farmer. When we broaden our inquiry to the entire community, the loss of income becomes a consideration. Everyone loses as much by being shortchanged as he gains by shortchanging. The side effects have become central effects. What was true for one turns out not to be true for all. Later on, in macroeconomics, we will find a very important example of exactly such a fallacy when we encounter what is called the Paradox of Thrift.

FOCUS This is a chapter about the techniques of economic analysis, not about the basic assumptions underlying economic theory. We should become familiar with a few ideas, or tools.

Ceteris paribus: the assumption that everything other than the two variables whose relationship is being investigated is "kept equal." *Without ceteris paribus we cannot discern functional relationships.*

Functional relationships: relationships that show that *x* "depends" on *y*, lying at the very center of economic analysis. They are not logical or deductive relationships but relationships that we discover by *empirical investigation.*

Identities: purely definitional, therefore *not subject to proof or to empirical investigation.* Such definitions can, however, be very important.

Functional relationships use three techniques:

  schedules, or lists of data

  graphs, or visual presentations

  equations

We should learn the meaning of three equational terms: the *independent variable,* the "causative" element that interests us; the *dependent variable,* the element whose behavior is affected by the independent variable; and the *function,* a mathematical statement of the relation between the two. We should learn to read the sentence $x = f(y)$ as "x is a function of y." Here, x is the dependent variable; y is the independent variable.

We must learn to be on guard against *economic fallacies,* especially against the *fallacy of composition.*

WORDS AND CONCEPTS YOU SHOULD KNOW

Ceteris paribus, 105–6
Functional relationships, 106
Two kinds of variables, 109
Identities, 106–7

Equalities, 107
Schedules, 107–8
Graphs, 107–8

QUESTIONS

1. Suppose you would acquire 52 books a year if books were free, but that your acquisitions would drop by 5 books for every dollar that you had to pay. Can you write a demand function for books?

2. Can you write a hypothetical function that might relate your demand for food and the price of food, assuming ceteris paribus?

3. "The quantity of food bought equals the quantity sold." Is this statement a functional relationship? If not, why not? Is it an identity?

4. Here is a schedule of supply and demand:

Price	Units supplied	Units demanded
$1	0	50
2	5	40
3	10	30
4	20	25
5	30	20
6	50	10

Does the schedule show an equilibrium price? Can you draw a graph and approximate the equilibrium price? What is it?

5. How do we read aloud the following?

$C = f(Y)$ where C = consumption and Y = income.

Which is the independent variable? The dependent?

6. Which of the following statements is a fallacy?

All X is Y
Z is Y
Therefore Z is X

All X is Y
Z is X
Therefore Z is Y

Try substituting classes of objects for the X's and Y, and individual objects for the Z's. Example: All planets (X's) are heavenly bodies (Y). The sun (Z) is a heavenly body (Y). Therefore the sun (Z) is a planet (X). Clearly, a false syllogism. Since the sun is a heavenly body, however, Z is Y.

Other fallacies:
If I can move to the head of the line, all individuals can move to the head of the line.

If I can save more by spending less, all individuals should be able to save more by spending less. (Hint: if all spend less, what will happen to our incomes?)

The fact that Lenin called inflation a major weapon that could destroy the bourgeoisie indicates that inflations are part of the Communist strategy for the overthrow of capitalism.

Economic causation

Economists depend more and more on sophisticated techniques of statistical analysis, wedded to economic theory, called econometrics, and we devote Chapter 44 to explaining some of the basic ideas of econometrics. There you will learn something about how functional relationships are expressed as "correlations." If the word is strange to you, look at pp. 704ff now.

Here we would like to make you aware of a special problem. If two variables move together, or are correlated, does that mean that one is the *cause* of the other? Few problems are so vexing, so deep, and so slippery.

CORRELATIONS

When we say that there is a high correlation between two variables—let us say cigarette smoking and heart disease—do we mean that cigarette smoking *causes* heart disease?

The question has no simple answer. All sorts of disputes rage over the degree of "causation" that can be attributed to correlations. Econometrics cannot solve these disputes, because the word "cause"—as anyone knows who has ever looked into a book on philosophy—is a perplexing and elusive one. Econometrics can, however, shed a strong light on some of the pitfalls associated with the word. In particular, it makes us very cautious about declaring that such and such an event is the cause of another, simply because there is a high degree of correlation between them.

Here are a few examples to think about.

1. **Wrong-way causation.** It is a statistical fact that there is a positive correlation between the number of babies born in various cities of northwestern Europe and the number of storks' nests in those cities. Is this evidence that storks really do bring babies? The answer is that we are using a correlation to establish a causal connection in the wrong way. The true line of causation lies in the opposite direction. Cities that have more children tend to have more houses, which offer storks more chimneys to build their nests in!

2. **Spurious causation.** Suppose there was a positive correlation all during the 1970s between the cost of living in Paris and the numbers of Americans visiting there. Does that imply that American visitors are the cause of price increases in that city?

Here at least there is little danger of getting the causal links back to front. Few people would argue that more Americans visit Paris *because* its prices are going up. It would be equally difficult to argue that American tourists are the cause of rising Parisian prices, simply because the total amount of American spending is small in relation to the total amount of expenditure in Paris (with the exception of a few tourist traps).

The answer, then, is that the correlation is spurious in terms of causality, although it is real in terms of sheer statistics. The true explanation for the correlation is that the rising numbers of American visitors and the rising costs of living in Paris are both aspects of a worldwide expansion in incomes and prices. Neither is the "cause" of the other. Both are the results of more fundamental, broader-ranging phenomena.

Another example relates to the high correlation between education and income. Is this evidence that education *causes* the educated person to earn more money? Here the case is complex. In part, the correlation is also spurious. People coming from high-income families tend to be given more education than those from low-income families. They also tend to go into higher-paying careers because of their advantageous background. Therefore they are both more schooled and better paid just because they come from wealthy families. The schooling itself is not a cause of their incomes. Yet it is *also* true that studies of siblings show that more education does increase lifetime earnings! Thus education adds something to a person's income, although not as much as we might think if we disregarded the person's initial place on the scale of wealth.

3. The problem of ceteris paribus. Finally, we must consider again the now familiar problem of *ceteris paribus,* the necessity of other things being equal. Suppose we correlate prices and sales, in order to test the hypothesis that lower prices "cause" us to increase the quantities we buy. Now suppose that the correlation turns out to be very poor. Does that disprove the hypothesis? Not necessarily. First we have to find out what happened to income during this period. We also have to find out what, if anything, happened to our tastes. We might also have to consider changes in the prices of other, competitive goods.

As we know, this problem affects all scientific tests, not just those of economics. Scientists cannot test the law of gravitation unless "other things" are equal, such as an absence of air that would cause a feather to fall much more slowly than Galileo predicted. The trouble with the social sciences is that the "other things" are often more difficult to spot—or just to think of—than they are in the laboratory. For example, what are we to make of the fact that there is a positive correlation between shoe sizes and mathematical ability among school children? The answer, once we think about it, is that we have not held "other things" equal in one very important respect—the age of the school children. Of course older children, with bigger feet, will be able to do more arithmetic than little children. Hence the first thing to do is to see if there is a correlation between shoe sizes of children of *equal ages* and mathematical ability. Children of equal ages will also have different shoe sizes, but the correlation with problem-solving ability is hardly likely to be there.

WHAT CAN CORRELATION TELL US?

These (and still other) pitfalls make econometricians extremely cautious about using correlations to "prove" causal hypotheses. *Even the closest correlation may not show in which direction the causal influences are working.*

So, too, *the interconnectedness of the economic process often causes many series of data to move together.* In inflationary periods, for example, most prices tend to rise, or in depression many indexes tend to fall, without establishing that any of these series was directly responsible for a movement in another particular series.

Finally, econometricians are constantly on the lookout for factors that have not been held constant during a correlation, so that *ceteris paribus conditions were not in fact maintained.*

Is there an answer to such puzzling problems of correlation and causation? There is a partial answer. We cannot claim that a correlation is proof that a causal relationship exists. But every valid hypothesis—economic or other—*must* show a high and "significant" correlation coefficient between "cause" and "effect," provided that we are reasonably certain that our statistical test has rigorously excluded spurious correlations and unsuspected "other things."

This exclusion is often very difficult, sometimes impossible to achieve with real data. A physicist can hold "other things equal" in his laboratory, but the world will not stand still just so an economist can test his theories. *The net result is that correlations are a more powerful device for* disproving *hypotheses than for proving them.* All we can say on the positive side is that a causal relationship is likely to exist (or at least has not been shown *not* to exist) when we can demonstrate a strong correlation backed by solid reasoning.

All this has a moral. Because economists deal with quantifiable data, correlation analysis is one of the essential tools in the economist's kit. All the "laws" of economics, from supply and demand to the various relationships of macroeconomics, are constantly being subjected to highly sophisticated econometric tests, *because these are the only objective methods we have for establishing whether variable X is causally associated with variable Y.* Thus we constantly use correlations to buttress—not to prove—our belief in economic relationships. Conversely, when careful correlation analysis fails to show high coefficients, there is good reason to look very skeptically at our economic hypotheses.

Hence, correlation is an indispensable part of economic science. That is not the same thing as saying that it *is* economic science. Behind the tools of econometrics lies the process of *economic reasoning*—that is, the attempt to explain why people behave in certain ways on the marketplace, or how the hard realities of the economic process shape and constrain the ongoing economic process.

Some basic economic problems

Economics is by no means a "finished" discipline. Unlike geometry or chemistry, its relations or facts are not logically beyond question or empirically secure. Rather, like all the social sciences, economics is built on foundations that we *know* to be unfinished, inadequate, perhaps even wrong.

Thus economics is constantly in the process of self-examination, and the analytical explanations it offers are constantly in need of reevaluation. This is the case partly because the society that economics examines is changing, and partly because our understanding of that society is also changing. Therefore part of learning economics is learning what we do not know, becoming aware of our ignorance as well as of our knowledge. Learning what economists don't know and are trying to find out may make the subject a little disturbing to the student who would like economics served up like the multiplication table, but at least it promises that the subject matter will not be as boring as the multiplication table.

Nothing is "harder" than data; nothing is "softer." The experienced economic statistician learns to look for certain pitfalls when he tries to collect facts about the economic world. Here are some of them.

1. UNSEASONED DATA

If you examine many figures, even from the most official statistical sources, you will discover that they change from one edition to the next. In the 1975 edition of the *U.S. Statistical Abstract,* the figure for U.S. gross national product in 1969 is $930.3 billion. In the edition published in 1972, the 1969 figures were $929.3 billion. What accounts for the change? Largely the fact that many data take considerable time to collect. Most current data are revised, sometimes substantially, in a matter of a few years. Moral: do not rashly base your findings on small numerical differences that may disappear when all the data have been collected.

2. DEFINITIONS

The Statistical Abstract (1975) shows that 24.2 million households were below official poverty levels in 1974. Does this tell us how many *families* were below this level? No, it does not. A household is not necessarily a family (it can be one person). Actually, in 1974 only about 19.4 million families were below the poverty line. Moral: carefully read all table headings and footnotes in your research material.

3. STATISTICAL DECEPTIONS

The endless figures on rising thefts, assaults, etc., attesting to the existence of crime waves may be correct; but before we can show that a crime wave exists, we would have to know other circumstances. Was there a population increase (normally bringing a larger *number* of crimes but not necessarily a larger proportion of crime *per capita*)? Did crime reporting methods change (affecting the number of crimes we *know about,* but not necessarily the number that really occurred)? What about seemingly unconnected things such as changes in prices (causing more thefts to involve sums that made them, by law, major rather than minor offenses)? Moral: use caution first, last, and always in dealing with data.*

*There is more on this problem in Chapter 44, "Introduction to Statistics and Econometrics."

Problems of Data

Economic facts   Economics, as we know, tries to generalize about the results that emerge as people engage in the acts of production and distribution. How does it gain its knowledge about these results? The answer, obviously, is from *economic data,* the collection of facts about economic activity.

The question here is how accurate are our data on production and distribution? The answer, unhappily, is that we know much less than the smooth curves of our diagrams indicate.

There are many reasons why our knowledge is limited. One reason is that it is almost impossible to carry out experiments that will result in the actual "shapes" of curves such as diminishing returns or supply and demand or even changes in scale. The difficulty arises in part because society cannot be tinkered with to establish functional relationships in a laboratory-like manner.

Limitations are due also to ceteris paribus, rearing its ugly head. It is very difficult to isolate the facts we seek from the raw data of experience. Even if we seek a simple schedule of automobile prices, we encounter vexing problems. Do prices reflect discounts that dealers may give? Do they take into account trade-ins? Have we eliminated price changes due to changes in the style or quality of cars? The raw data of automobile prices, like all raw data, come to us in a fashion that is often misleading if we are to use them, unexamined, to prove a case.

Aggregation problems   A second difficulty with data has to do with the problem of *aggregation.* Suppose that we want to know about the output of steel, perhaps in order to establish functional relationships between steel output and inputs of labor or capital. If we go out into the market-place, we discover a curious fact: there is no such thing as "steel." There are steel bars and steel sheets, steel ingots and structural beams, but "steel" as such is a nonexistent commodity. (Even ingots vary in the quality of steel they contain.)

Aggregates make it difficult to establish functional relationships, because we are caught in the problem of comparing apples and pears. Data that indicate a rising output of "steel" may conceal the fact that the kinds or qualities of steel products are changing, so that the figure for "total output" may lead us to conclusions that a finer analysis would not support. If products such as steel or wheat or coal are actually aggregates, how much more deceptive are data such as "clothing" or "food" or that largest aggregate of all, gross national product!

What can we do in the face of this difficulty? In part we can "correct" for the distortions of aggregates by the use of econometric techniques. But to a large degree we are left with a problem that is insoluble. Some degree of aggregation is present in nearly all economic data. Therefore some degree of deception is inherent in all economic data. There is no escape from this dilemma of economic statistics. Without the use of data, we cannot reason about economic phenomena. The inherent problems of data, however, teach us to be cautious and careful in jumping to conclusions on the basis of "facts" that may turn out to be a great deal less solid than they appear.

Problems of Concepts

Abstraction   Problems with data lead to a further, inherent problem in economic reasoning: the *level of abstraction* necessary for carrying on our investigations.

Like all sciences, economics struggles with the hopeless complexity of real life by *abstracting* crucial aspects of complex processes. It is only by abstraction that we arrive at concepts such as that of economic man, whose living counterpart is not to be discovered in real life, although some of his attributes are certainly discernible.

Abstraction is both the central strength and one of the most vulnerable weaknesses of economics. Economic "reality" is at least as complex as the newspapers, which are themselves drastic simplifications of the real events of economic life. Still, unless we abstract from the confusion of newspaper events we cannot even begin to describe the basic functional relationships that are among the main objectives of economic inquiry. Think of trying to construct a supply and demand diagram from the financial pages! Thus it is wrong to think of abstraction as a defect of economics. Abstraction is an indispensable prerequisite of all scientific thinking.

What is the weakness of abstraction, then? It lies in the fact that there is no single valid "level" of abstraction, no absolutely sure rule that will focus our attention on the invisible forces we wish to uncover. In abstracting from the richness of life to arrive at the concept of economic man, for example, we ignore impulses and feelings that lead people away from maximizing. If we are incorrect in ignoring those other forces, which may make men and women behave in illogical ways or may make generosity and compassion central constituents of behavior, we may end up with an abstraction that leads to unsubstantiated economic conclusions.

Indeed, the errors that economics makes—and they are many—are rarely the result of a faulty train of reasoning. Almost always they stem from mistaken premises, ill-founded initial assumptions about behavior or possibly about nature. These mistakes, in turn, are often traceable to abstractions that fail to do justice to important attributes of behavior or the physical world. *If economic reasoning starts from the wrong place or the wrong premises, it must almost of necessity end up with the wrong conclusions.*

Importance of institutions

In the inescapable process of abstraction, an element of error involves the weight that we assign institutions. To take an example that is central to our inquiry, we study the economy as if it were a market system. Is it? The market certainly describes very well the organization of economic life in many areas, as in the determination of prices for used cars or perhaps (although somewhat less well) prices and outputs of new cars.

Does it also describe a process that is tacitly taken for granted, even though it is fundamental to the operation of the automotive markets—the decision to build highways or mass transit? Take other areas. Does the market mechanism explain how resources are allocated to peace or war, space medicine or home medicine, public housing or private homes?

Few economists would claim that these basic decisions can be explained by economic analysis. Yet they are determinative for our society. *Do we then misrepresent the basic problem of our social system when we examine it as a market mechanism and not as a power mechanism with markets playing an effective but subordinate role?*

There is no clear answer to this problem, but the examples we have given should add a cautionary note to our use of economic analysis. By setting the level of abstraction so high that institutional realities drop out of focus, crucial aspects of contemporary society can be easily removed from the picture. On the other hand, if we change the focus to highlight institutional problems, we tend to end up with a newspaper account of economic life without any discernible patterns or tendencies.

The aim of economics, and of all social science, is to discover a middle level of abstraction, where the dominant facts are clearly present and where large movements are also discernible. This is an objective that is a great deal easier to specify on paper than to attain in fact.

Tautologies

A related difficulty of economic theory is that some of its underlying concepts are *tautologies.* Tautologies are statements that cannot be proven false because there is no empirical or operational way to examine them.

Tautologies play a large part in economic thought. Take, for example, our conception of economic man. We have said that his aim is to maximize his pleasureable wealth, or his utilities. Now this is a very elusive statement. If we had said that his aim was to maximize his *money income*, we might put the statement to the test of observation. We might discover that it was untrue. A businessman, for example, may refuse to cheat, although cheating might make his money income larger.

When we say that individuals seek to maximize their *utilities*, however, we are dealing with a concept that defies empirical testing. No matter what a person does—cheating or not cheating, working hard or not working hard, seeking a million dollars or leading a life of ease—we can always claim that he or she is maximizing his or her utilities, and there is no way of disproving the contention.

Take the central idea of equilibrium. Is equilibrium a tautology? We know that markets bring about equilibrium prices at which quantities supplied and demanded are equal. But how do we know, looking at the real world, whether or not a price is an equilibrium price?

The question requires that we return to our distinction between behavioral equations and identities. When we look at the actual world, we see markets in which purchases equal sales at all sorts of prices. Because purchases *always* equal sales, how do we know whether a *particular* level of purchases-and-sales represents the level that corresponds to an equilibrium level? The answer is that we don't. The notion of an equilibrium price presupposes that we know the schedules of demand and supply. If we do not know these schedules, we cannot tell whether a given price is in fact an equilibrium price—and certainly the fact that purchases ≡ sales is no such indication.

Since we do not know these schedules in the great majority of cases, it is very difficult to say whether a given price is or is not an equilibrium price. Indeed, if we had some system of ascertaining the elusive supply and demand schedules, we would probably find that most prices were *not* in equilibrium. They should be in the process of moving *toward* equilibrium, but it is possible that they are moving away. Even when they are moving toward equilibrium, they seldom reach it, because the equilibrium point itself is constantly changing as *ceteris paribus* conditions change—tastes or incomes or the prices of other goods.

Problems of Prediction

Basic to economic reasoning is its power of prediction. Indeed, what is so remarkable about the market mechanism is that it works in predictable ways. That is why we can say that if prices rise, *ceteris paribus*, quantities demanded will fall. If prices fall, *ceteris paribus*, the quantity supplied will fall.

The problem of behavior   No other social science has this seemingly simple but enormously valuable predictive capacity. That is, no other social science can lean with confidence on functional relationships of the kind that underpin economics.

With just how much confidence can economics lean on those relationships? The answer is disconcerting. The actual

120

predictive record of economics is spotty, even poor. In critical areas such as the prediction of national income, the batting average is far from good. Thus despite the clarity of our schedules, graphs, and equations, the predictive power of economics is a great deal more impressive in theory than in fact. Why?

Imperfect knowledge

The first reason for inadequacy is probably self-evident from our foregoing discussion. An ability to predict the outcome of the market process hinges on our foreknowledge of the shapes and positions of supply and demand curves, or the functions we can insert into equations of supply and demand.

It can hardly come as a surprise that this foreknowledge is both small and shaky. We know very little about the actual willingness and ability of masses of individuals to buy and sell various goods. We do not have very good information about the costs of production of a great many commodities. Worse, unless we possess complete knowledge, we cannot act as the rational maximizers we are supposed to be. How would a businessman or businesswoman maximize profits without knowing the price of every possible alternative source of supply or the state of the marketplace in every nook and corner of the world?

In fact, of course, neither can hope to encompass all the knowledge that would enable him or her to make a perfect calculation of the most profitable course. As for consumers, they do not begin to have the encyclopedic knowledge that would enable them to behave as our market model supposes. Moreover, the *costs of ascertaining the knowledge* that would enable one to maximize may be so great that we can never become more than pale approximations of the economic creature we are supposed to be. How much time can we spend comparison shopping? How many catalogs must one consult before buying a chair?

Information is particularly scanty when we concern ourselves with the future. Buyers and sellers often have no inkling of what the future will bring, and no way of finding out. Think of the effect of weather on crops. The task of acting as a rational maximizer in this situation requires that one have a mathematician's knowledge of probabilities. *In fact, the difficulties of being a rational maximizer are so great that we act on hunches, guesses, rumor, and faith.*

The problem of expectations

Still another even more vexing problem is that we often cannot depend on economic theory as a predictive tool. It is unreliable because basic supply and demand functions are capable of bewildering, totally unforeseeable shifts—not just in their numerical values but in their *signs*.

Take the normal case of a downward sloping demand curve. The curve shows us that the quantities we demand will increase as prices fall and decrease as prices rise. In the main, that is no doubt true. Now assume that prices rise and that buyers interpret this rise as indicative of a further rise in the future. Suppose the prices of machine tools go up and that the general talk is that they will be going higher, perhaps because of an impending wage settlement that will send up costs. Buyers may well rush in to buy *more* machine tools at their higher price, hoping to get their needs filled before things get worse.

The same "perverse" reaction can affect the sign of the supply function. Ordinarily, lower prices will result in fewer goods being offered for sale; higher prices, in more. Again, suppose that suppliers interpret a price fall as indicative of a worse fall coming. Rumors of a coming depression or of vast imports in transit might create such a frame of mind. In that case, suppliers will react to lower prices by trying to sell *more* at the lowered price, before prices go lower still. Conversely, if prices are going up and are expected to go still higher, sellers will not increase their offerings but will hold back, waiting for still better opportunities.

Thus the "signal" of higher or lower prices does not always result in the behavior that is described by any given supply or demand function. Behavior depends on the state of mind, the expectations of buyers and sellers. Ordinarily we have no way of knowing this state of mind. Moreover, expectations can change overnight. That is another reason why prediction is much more difficult in fact than in our initial presentation.

It is instructive in this regard to compare the problems of economic prediction with those of meteorology. Both have some obvious difficulties in common, mainly the enormous mass of data needed for accurate prediction. Unfortunately, economics has one problem that weather forecasting does not. The weather forecaster does not have to contend with winds or clouds changing their minds. Economists, on the other hand, must deal with not only the often unmanageable (or unknown) data of economic weather, but also with intentions, expectations, moods, and feelings. To put it differently, the economist is concerned with data that "behave" in a meaning of that word that never troubles the natural scientist.

Increasing indeterminacy   There is a last, but telling reason why prediction is difficult, and why the reliability of economic rea-

soning may suffer accordingly. This reason has to do with the increasing indeterminacy of behavior in an affluent economic setting.*

Here it may help us to go back to the tautology of "maximizing utilities." Suppose we suggested that maximizing be defined in a more testable way, such as the effort to gain as much income or profit as possible (within normal moral and legal limits) or to spend as little money as possible for the purchase of goods of a given kind. Now imagine that we were to go to a poor country—say England in Charles Dickens' day—to see if we could verify this hypothesis about behavior. It seems plausible that we would find that market activities roughly approximated what we would expect. Workers and capitalists both, in that setting, were more or less forced to strive after every last penny. Most consumers were forced to squeeze every sixpence when they went shopping.

When we turn to behavior in our own much more affluent society, however, the hypothesis of maximization is much less likely to be valid. We can by no means be sure, for instance, that we will always choose a higher paying over a lower paying job. Just because we are better off than members of a poor society, we can weigh aspects other than the differential in pay.

So, too, we do not always buy the cheapest item available to us. We may feel that its very cheapness means that it may not be as good as a competitive item, even though the two are really equally good. How else would we explain consumers' preferences for brand-name aspirin over nonbrand-name, although most consumers have heard that all aspirin is chemically the same?

Nor is maximization a concept that gives us much predictive insight into the

*This is a position originally put forth by Adolph Lowe in *On Economic Knowledge* (1965, 1970).

behavior of big firms. When we speak of a small profit-maximizing firm, we can foretell fairly well what measures its manager will have to take, as we will see when we study the competitive firm in Chapters 11 and 12. Such clearcut predictive capability becomes increasingly fuzzy when we examine the behavior of large firms that are not maximizing in order to survive from day to day, but to grow over the long term.

Ford and General Motors, for example, may choose very different strategies, according to their different interpretations of the outlook for coming years. One company may embark on a program of heavy capital investment. The other may retrench, preparing for an expected recession. Yet officials of both companies would declare that they were seeking to maximize their firm's sales or profits or asset values over the period in question. Thus, *maximization* becomes a word that loses its clear predictive content once we leave the world of Dickensian behavior and small factories and enter the world of affluence and giant firms.

Is Economic Theory Useful?

In the face of all this criticism, how do we justify economics? What is left of our fundamental elements? What good is a study of the market mechanism?

Conceptual clarity There are three answers to these searching questions. First, *economics gives us a set of concepts to cope with the flux of economic reality.* The kind of puzzle we posed in our box,

"Supply and Demand, Again," on page 100 is the sort of tangled thinking that we are rescued from by the ideas of supply and demand and equilibrium prices, even though we have great difficulty in finding real-world counterparts to these ideas.

This situation is not unique to economics. Physics deals with ideas like "force" or "matter," although it has great difficulty in giving empirical meaning to these terms. As in physics, the ideas of economics must be judged by their *usefulness*, not necessarily by their representation of unambiguous "things."

Ordinary applicability Second, if we except periods of rapid change or shifting expectations, *economic theory provides a roughly accurate guide to the outcomes that we can expect from changes in the market.* After all, it is still true that the managers of the A&P, when they wish to increase their sales, do not advertise that their prices are *higher* than their competitors'! So, too, the many "predictable" outcomes of economc investigation give us confidence that people do maximize a great deal of the time. In this chapter we have stressed the shortcomings and inadequacies of economic theory, but it might be well to redress the balance somewhat by being grateful for what we have.

This underlying reliability is strengthened because it is much easier to predict and explain *average* behavior than *individual* behavior. Many individuals act in ways that do not accord with the assumptions of economic theory, but to a great extent these "abnormal" actions are mutually offsetting. One person may invest in the stock market because his horoscope says to do so, rather than because he has rationally calculated how to maximize his gains; but he is apt to be cancelled by another who will not invest in the market because *her* horoscope tells her *not* to.

In the aggregate, our market decisions should be sufficiently linked to the stimuli of economics to enable us to make generalizations about *average* economic behavior, without consulting the stars. Our predictional system breaks down only when large numbers of people behave "irrationally" in those recurrent moods or epidemic-like shifts in expectations that sweep over us.

Goal-oriented economics

Third, *economic theory can be useful as an instrument to help us gain desired goals. That is, we can use the theory of the market mechanism to tell us what kind of behavior or what sorts of expectations we will require for a smoothly functioning economic system.*

We can develop economic theories that tell us, for example, how the economy should be run to increase its output over a given period of time. This goal-oriented (or normative) capability is a unique characteristic of economics. We cannot use political theory or sociological theory in a normative way, because we cannot develop clear-cut, quantifiable relationships in these fields as we can in economics.

Goals will not be achieved, however, just because we can state them. Suppose that we want to achieve a certain rate of growth. To reach that goal, we need policy measures to change the course of events in the desired direction.

Policy and behavior

What policy measures? *The answer depends on whether or not we assume that we know what economic behavior will be.* If we feel confident in our ability to predict the future

course of business spending, based on maximizing, for example, we may content ourselves with lowering the rate of interest at which business can borrow money. In the face of a national emergency, however, we may not feel justified in trusting to such a simple view of business maximizing. Or suppose that we are unsure whether maximizing business people will spend more or less, because we are not sure of their expectations.

In that case, we would want to use our knowledge of economics in a different manner, employing it to specify the kind of behavior that is required to reach a policy objective. If we need more business spending, we may wish to add many incentives besides those of cheaper money—subsidies or tax incentives, for example. The economist may prescribe public alternatives to business spending as a "backup" measure. The point is that behavior, the critical link in prediction, becomes a prime policy concern for the goal-oriented economic policy maker, rather than a matter taken as "given."

The question of goals

Of course, the question of goals raises large issues. Who is to choose the goals? What does economics have to do with these crucial social decisons?

The answer is both simple and difficult. The simple answer is that economists have no special qualification at all with respect to the choice of society's goals. At best they may know something about institutional barriers that can get in the way of attaining certain goals, or the conflicts and difficulties implicit in reaching two seemingly compatible goals at once, or the possible range of alternative courses that society might follow to attain its objectives.

About the rightness or wrongness of

the goals themselves, economists have no more right to speak with authority than have other informed members of society. Whether or not we should grow fast or slow, seek income equality or inequality, break up or protect labor unions or big business, pursue an active energy policy or trust to the natural workings of science—all are matters about which the economist is only one voice and one vote among many. Only after the goals have been chosen do the economist's skills come into play.

Who then chooses the goals? The electorate and its chosen leaders, of course. The difficult part of the answer concerns the ability of democratic electorates to select their leaders and destinations wisely. This is no different in the case of economic destinations than it is for political or social ones. Choosing wise economic policies is a process that is not fundamentally dissimilar from choosing wise laws. Whether or not democratic societies will govern their economic affairs as well (or as badly) as their political or social affairs is a question that history has not yet determined. It is our hope that a goal-oriented use of economics will help us succeed in that aspect of our historic task.

FOCUS Here is a chapter to be thought about carefully, for it calls into question the very foundations on which we base our attempt to reason scientifically about economics. Two basic kinds of problems weaken economic theory:

1. The difficulty of ascertaining economic data. Many of the most important economic data are aggregates—and aggregates, we discover, are statistical hornets' nests. There is no escaping them, but we must expect to be stung.

A second problem associated with data is to decide which data are relevant. *This is really the problem of determining the appropriate level of abstraction from which to approach a problem.* If the level is too high—too "theoretical"—the most important institutional data may drop out. If it is too low—too "empirical"—we may have only masses of facts and no organizing vision. There is no "solution" to this basic problem, but we should be aware of it, so we can guard against a level of abstraction that is either too high or too low.

2. The reliability of basic theory. Here we meet two more kinds of difficulties. *First, many theoretical concepts turn out to be tautologies—untestable conceptions.* Hence they can never be falsified. We can never know, for instance, if our theory that individuals maximize pleasurable wealth, or utilities, is a useful description or a fiction.

Second, *we must recognize that the behavioral assumptions of economics are open to considerable doubt.* For one thing, changed expectations will turn behavior 180° in its tracks. For another, in a world of affluent households and giant firms, the idea of what we mean by "maximizing" loses its sharpness, either for a consumer or a business firm.

Is this a wholesale condemnation of economics? We could hardly expect it to be so, given that we are writing a textbook on the subject. The conventional explanations and predictions of economics are still reasonably reliable for ordinary activity. They serve to classify our thinking in many areas. And most important of all, even if *economic theory cannot be used for exact prediction, it can be used to help us attain goals. We can use economics to specify how we should behave to achieve desired outcomes.* This does not make the economist superhuman or specially qualified to establish goals for society. But an economist's skills may help society achieve its goals.

WORDS AND CONCEPTS YOU SHOULD KNOW

Data, 117
Aggregation problems, 117–18
Level of abstraction, 118–19

Tautology, 119–20
Expectations and prediction, 121–22
Three uses of theory, 123–24

QUESTIONS

1. If you were asked to compile an index for the price of shoes, how would you go about doing so? (HINT: look into Chapter 44 to see the process of "weighting" averages.) Would any index that you constructed be wholly accurate if the "mix" of shoe styles changed?

2. Make a list of various levels of abstraction. What is "the real world?" What is a workable level of abstraction—the newspapers? Which newspapers? What about magazines? Books? Theories? Do you think such a systematic ladder of abstractions can be made? Do you think we can deal with the world without abstractions? How do we know if our abstractions are correct?

3. How much research would you have to do to act as a utility-maximizing consumer if you want to buy a car? Some clothes? A TV? Potatoes? Do you think there is some relationship between our degree of imperfection of knowledge and the role we play in the economic system; i.e., consumer or producer? Is the *kind of market* pertinent?

4. Do you think that power is an institution? Is it an abstraction? Can we deal with power theoretically? (There are no answers to these questions, but they should be thought about.)

5. Describe the effect of a *change in expectations* on your rational maximizing behavior as a trader in stocks. Show how your buying and selling behavior would both be altered.

6. Can you give an operational meaning to "maximum income-seeking" for a small businessman in a country like India? Can you make the same predictive statement for, say, the actions that A.T.&T. is likely to take? What accounts for the difference? Do you think consumer behavior should be more predictable in India than in the United States? Why?

7. Can you think of a test that *might* show whether a price was at equilibrium? Suppose that inventories were piling up. Would that be suggestive of the fact that prices were higher or lower than equilibrium? Might such a pile-up arise from reasons other than a price that was different from equilibrium—for instance, the expectations of businesspeople?

8. What is the difference between predicting and prescribing? If you prescribed a certain kind of economic behavior as a means to an end, is that a value-free use of economics? What kinds of actions or pronouncements might restore "perverse" markets to normal operaton?

9. Which of the following are tautologies: (1) Everything always turns out for the best in the long run. (2) People always act in their own self-interest. (3) The effort to maximize incomes always results in economic success. (HINT: to which of these statements could you apply some kind of empirical test?)

MICROECONOMICS—
the ANATOMY
of a MARKET
SYSTEM

PART

3

Introduction to the microeconomy

Having completed our preparatory work, we are ready to venture into the territory of microeconomics. Actually, we know a good deal about that territory from our first two sections. We glimpsed the essential problem of microeconomics when we discovered the market mechanism as a central institution of our society. In Part Two, we learned about how the market works and about the concepts we use to analyze its operation.

Now we are going to fortify our comprehension by going more carefully into the dynamics of the system. We still have much to find out about demand and a lot to learn about supply—in particular, how firms operate in a market setting. A little further along we will be investigating the special problems raised by the existence of giant firms. The vital question of the distribution of income, perhaps the most "politically" significant task of the market, must be looked into with special care. All of that in good time.

10

Micro- and macro-economics

The way to begin is with a careful look at the overall field itself.

What is microeconomics, as contrasted with macroeconomics? Why do we study it separately, instead of joining the two in a unified study of the operation of the economy as a whole?

The answer, as we already know, is that we study economics from two perspectives because we need two different approaches to the economic world, to understand two different kinds of problems in that world. Both micro- and macroeconomics are relevant for the study of how we produce and how we distribute wealth. The difference is that one approach emphasizes the *total* production or distribution of the system, while the other approaches them from the point of view of individual decision makers, such as firms or individuals.

Although we need two approaches to illumine the movement of the economy as a whole and the currents within the economy, we will constantly be using the *same* concepts, such as supply and demand or the laws of production, in both inquiries. Our two-perspective approach reflects the fact that the problems characteristic of micro- or macro- economics become blurred when we use the point of view of one to examine the other.

Take the problem of inflation. Obviously, inflation has to do with the relation between the total demand for goods and the total supply of goods. Inflation has often been described as "too much money chasing too few goods." This problem lends itself naturally to an analysis that begins with an aggregative approach to demand, such as that implicit in *national* income, or an aggregative conception of supply, suggested by gross *national* output. If we begin from the other end of the scale, where we concentrate on the production of particular goods or the demands of particular individuals or groups of individuals, it is very hard to grasp the problem of inflation. To put it differently, mi-

croeconomics will help us understand why prices rise in, say, the market for beef or wheat, cars or houses, but it is less helpful in explaining why prices rise in *all* markets simultaneously.

Need for two approaches Economists thus use two lenses to study the economy: one to see the actions and interactions of its individual participants; one to see the economy in a bigger scale. *Neither perspective by itself is sufficient.* A view through the macro lens does not tell us much about the process of allocating resources to various uses or distributing income within an economic society. Macroeconomics, as we shall see, is interested in the size of total output. It throws almost no analytical light on whether that output consists of Cadillacs or Chevrolets, of bread or cake. So, too, macroeconomics is interested in the size of total incomes. It does not explain why income is divided in such unequal shares.

At the same time, microeconomics by itself is also inadequate. It tells us a great deal about Chevrolets and Cadillacs, bread and cake, but it does not tell us whether total income and output will be large or small. Yet there is clearly some relation between the proportions of Cadillacs to Chevrolets or cake to bread and the level of wealth that a society enjoys. Thus we cannot fully analyze the motives of microeconomic behavior without taking into account the macroeconomic setting for that behavior.

The circular flow Looking through the microeconomic lens, we must set that lens at the proper focal length to highlight the activities we want to investigate.

What are those activities? Essentially, they are the microeconomy *as a system.*

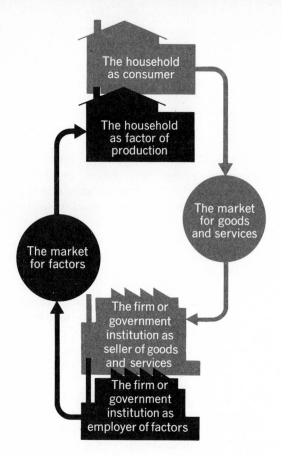

FIG. 10·1 Circular flow in microview

That is, they are the real goings-on in the economic world—men and women shopping, working, offering their services or their assets—*seen as parts of an integrated whole,* a great chain of activities linked into one network.

This is a perspective that we have already examined (Chap. 2). Figure 10·1 reminds us of the essential circularity of the market flow of purchasing power. (We omit for the moment the flow of goods and services traveling in the opposite direction.) As the arrows show, purchasing power travels into a great loop from households to firms and government agencies, then back from firms and agencies into households.

We are already familiar with this general system. Notice that in our representation of the flow we now divide the marketplace into two main kinds of markets—a market for goods and services and a market for factors. In the market for goods and services, buyers and sellers are meeting in immense numbers of submarkets. Prices of the enormous range of commodities produced by the system are being formed by their encounters. In the market for factors, the services of land, labor, and capital are being bought and sold in innumerable other encounters whose outcome will be the wages and rents and interest that reward the factors of production.

The two markets   Our model gives us a further clarification. *Households and firms (including government units) both participate in each of the two basic markets, but on different "sides" of each market.* In the market for goods, the household is a buyer. In the market for factors, the household is a seller, as its members offer their services for hire. In the market for goods, the firm is a seller. In the market for factors, the firm buys. Thus we can redraw our model of the circular flow with supply and demand curves that show the twofold participation of each of the basic participants in the two markets.

In Fig. 10·2 we can see that the household is the source of the demand curve in the market for goods. Then it is the source of the supply curve in the market for factors. The firm shapes the supply curve in the goods market, and the demand curve in the factor market.

Thus, far from being a chaos of buying and selling, the market system is a "seamless web"—a network of transactions with demand on one market reflected in supply in another, and supply in one market reflected in demand on another. This circular flow—this linkage of demand and

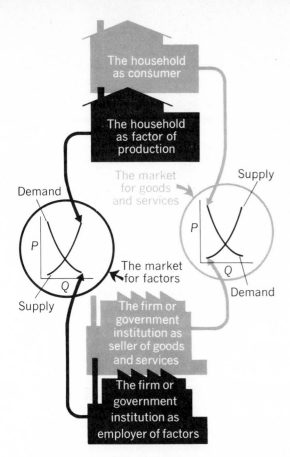

FIG. 10·2 Demand and supply curve in the circular flow

self; that is, with the production and distribution of goods and services. The market for goods is clearly the central locus where the production decisions of society will be determined. The market for factors is the place where distribution of incomes will take place.

The two main institutions, households and firms (including government units), also locate key *decision-making points.* Within the household there will be crucial determinations of taste or of the willingness to buy. We have identified these determinations as major elements in demand. Within the firm there will occur technical decisions that greatly affect supply. We are already generally acquainted with some of the laws of production that will affect those decisions.

Like many models, ours operates at a very high level of abstraction. It lumps together the richest investor and the poorest laborer in the market for factors. It jumbles the sale of caviar and hospital care into one undifferentiated market for goods and services. Nevertheless, this abstract conception begins to untangle the flux of market activities in the world around us. It even clarifies our task in the chapters ahead. We must study the two different markets and the two different institutions, one at a time, to find out the actions and motivations characteristic of each. We begin in our next chapter by taking a searching look at households and their demand for goods and services.

supply—will be one of the main keys to understanding how the economy works as a whole.

Production and distribution   Last, our model gives us a way of connecting the market mechanism with the economic problem it-

The basic difference is that microeconomics begins its analysis from the vantage point of individual firms or households, rather than from that of the aggregate activities of all firms or households. Thus microeconomics begins by looking into the ways that typical householders or firms spend their money or make their economic decisions, and does not "add up" all these decisions into macro aggregates. Macro begins just the other way, with the total spending of the economy, and does not much inquire into the individual activities taking place within this aggregate. As a result, microeconomics is not much concerned about how big GNP is, and macroeconomics is unconcerned about what GNP consists of.

Actually, macro and micro fade into each other, as we see in dealing with the market mechanism as a system. After all, the micro system comprises the entire economy and is certainly a macro idea. But from our micro perspective we do not inquire into the volume of total purchasing power, but rather look into the interaction of firms and households in the markets for where purchasing power is generated and spent.

The best way to review this chapter is to reproduce Figure 10 · 2 on page 131. This will make you familiar with the role that households and firms (always including government institutions) play in each of the two basic kinds of markets. If you can draw this diagram correctly, you clearly understand the main idea of the chapter.

WORDS AND CONCEPTS YOU SHOULD KNOW

All through this book, "Focus" sections will help you establish the main learning targets for each lesson. But you will also need to pay special attention to the new items of vocabulary that keep emerging. In these Words and Concepts sections, vocabulary items are singled out for your attention. Even if you have already paid heed to them in your "Focus," take a moment to frame a good working definition in your mind. If you have trouble, you'll find page references to refresh your memory.

Macroeconomics, 129   Microeconomics, 129   Circular flow, 129–30   Two markets, 130–31

QUESTIONS

1. Do you think there is an analog to micro- and macroeconomics in other social sciences? Take politics. What is micropolitics? What is macropolitics? (How about voting behavior versus revolution?)

2. Which of the following pairs do you think would best be analyzed by a microeconomic approach; inflation or high prices of meat; national unemployment or black unemployment; automobile output or small-car output; the total supply of housing or the supply of cooperatives? What is characteristic of your choices? Can you add examples?

3. What is the difference between the market for goods and for factors? Can a household be a buyer in the market for factors? (Suppose it hires a maid!) Can it be a seller in the market for goods? (Suppose it sells vegetables on its front porch?) *Is a household then really a firm?*

4. What is the interaction between the market for goods and services and the market for factors?

Private markets and public "markets"

In our analysis of the circular flow we skipped a little hastily over the difference between two flows of income and output. One flow comes from the interplay of households and private firms. The other comes from the interplay of households and government agencies. Let us look into a few of the differences.

1. In the private part of the economy incomes are very different, depending on individual skills, inheritance, luck, and so forth. In the public part of the system we all have the same "income"—one vote.

2. In the private part of the system we spend as much or as little of our incomes as we wish in each market. In the public part we spend all or nothing. We use all of our vote for one side (or person) or the other, or we do not vote at all.

3. In the public section of the system, we buy goods and services, just as we do in the private section. Education, defense, and justice are public goods and services, but we buy them in a curious, indirect manner. First, we use our equal incomes (votes) to support or oppose politicians who promise to institute or diminish the public goods we want. We vote for (or against) defense-minded or education-minded representatives. We cannot, however, actually buy the public output we want unless 51 percent of the public also spends its votes the same way. There is no way of buying *some* public education or *some* defense or *some* justice just for ourselves. It is all or none, quite unlike the situation in the private portion of the system.

4. Furthermore, having voted for a public good, we have not yet determined the outcome of the public process. Pressure groups can influence the expenditures that our representatives make. Much also depends on the kinds of taxes that the government chooses. Taxes inevitably favor some groups over others. Here again, the decision of the majority is imposed on all of us. There is no legal way of not paying taxes, even though you voted against them in the first place.

5. Yet, although taxes are an involuntary expenditure for each individual, they are voluntary from the point of view of society as a whole. We could, after all, vote to have no education, no defense. And although private expenditures are voluntary in one sense—if we don't like a good, we just don't buy it—in another sense they are more compulsory than public goods. It is possible to get a "free ride" on public goods, for example, by enjoying the nation's public output even though you may pay no taxes whatsoever. There is almost no way of enjoying private output without spending your own income.

We will have many occasions, as we go on, to look into the problems created by these two kinds of income, especially in Chapter 16. Perhaps you can see that there are moral dilemmas connected with the highly egalitarian distribution of "voting income," just as there are with the highly unequal distribution of money income.

Prices and allocation

How prices are formed in the market system should now be less of a mystery. Although we cannot look very fully into supply curves until we probe the operations of the firm, we understand in general that prices in the marketplace for goods reflect the interplay of the demand schedules of consumers and the supply schedules of producers. In our next chapter, changes in demand will affect prices, and various characteristics of demand will exert different influences on the price structure.

Before we turn to the dynamics of supply and demand, let us use the price mechanism to shed more light on the problems of microeconomics. Our understanding of that price mechanism reveals how the market system solves the problems of allocation. In particular, it clears up the puzzle of how the market system *rations* goods among all claimants and uses for the good.

11

Rationing   In one form or another, rationing— or the allocation of goods among claimants—is a disagreeable but inescapable task that every economic system must carry out; for in all societies, the prevailing reality of life has been the inadequacy of output to fill the wants and needs of the

134

people. In traditional economies, rationing is performed by a general adherence to rigidly established rules. Whether by caste or class or family position or whatever, these rules determine the rights of various individuals to share in the economic product. In command societies, the division of the social product is carried out in a more explicitly directed fashion, as the governing authorities determine the rights of various groups or persons to share in the fruits of society.

A market society, as we know, minimizes the heavy hand of tradition or the authoritative one of command. It cannot escape some system of rationing, though, to prevent what would otherwise be an impossibly destructuve struggle among its citizens. This critical allocative task is also accomplished by the price mechanism. **One of the prime functions of a market is to determine who shall be allowed to acquire goods and who shall not.**

How the market rations Imagine a market with ten buyers, each willing and able to buy one unit of a commodity, but each having a different maximum price that is agreeable to him. Imagine ten suppliers, each also willing and able to put one unit of supply on the market, again each at a different price. Such a market might look like Table 11 • 1.

Remember that the maximum prices may differ because different people have different desires for the commodity or be-

cause they have different incomes. The person who is willing to pay the highest prices may not desire the commodity the most. He or she may simply have the most income and be willing and able to pay more for everything.

As we can see, the equilibrium price will lie at $6, for at this price there will be five suppliers of one unit each and five purchasers of one each. Now let us make a graph and let each bar stand for one person. The height of the bar tells us the maximum each person will be willing to pay for the unit of the commodity or the minimum he or she would sell it for. If we line up our marketers in order of their demand and supply capabilities, our market will look like Fig. 11 • 1 (p. 136).

What we have drawn is in fact nothing but a standard supply-and-demand diagram. But look what it shows us. All the buyers who can afford and are willing to pay the equilibrium price (or more) will get the goods they want. All those who cannot will not. So, too, all the sellers who are willing and able to supply the commodity at its equilibrium price or less will be able to consummate sales. All those who cannot will not.

Thus the market, in establishing an equilibrium price, has in effect allocated the goods among some buyers and withheld it from others. It has permitted some sellers to do business and denied that privilege to others. In our case in Chapter 7 anyone who could pay $25 or more got a pair of shoes. Those who could not pay

Table 11 • 1

Price	$11	$10	$9	$8	$7	$6	$5	$4	$3	$2	$1
Number willing and able, at above price, to											
buy one unit	0	1	2	3	4	5	6	7	8	9	10
sell one unit	10	9	8	7	6	5	4	3	2	1	0

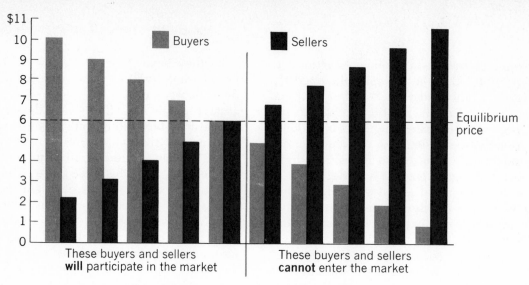

Buyers   Sellers

Equilibrium price

These buyers and sellers **will** participate in the market

These buyers and sellers **cannot** enter the market

FIG. 11·1   How the market rations

that much were unable to get shoes. All producers who could turn out shoes for $25 or less were able to do business, and those who could not meet that price were unable to make any sales at all.

Note that the market is in this way a means of excluding certain people from economic activity; namely, customers with too little money or with too weak desires or suppliers unwilling or unable to operate at a certain price.

Reservation prices

Now take another look at Fig. 11 · 1. Let us use the term *reservation price* for the *maximum amount* that a buyer is willing and able to spend for a unit of a good. The first consumer on the left has a reservation price of $10. The last one on the right has a reservation price of $1. Reservation prices are also the *minimum amounts* that sellers demand. The first seller on the left has a reservation price of $2; the last one on the right has one of $11.

Now look at the difference between these reservation prices and the actual market price. The consumer on the left, who would have been willing to pay $10 for the commodity, gets it for only $6; he or

she has a *consumer's surplus* of $4. The first seller on the left, who would have been willing to sell at $2 and who actually sells at $6, has a *producer's surplus* of $4. Notice also that every consumer who can afford to buy gets some consumer's surplus, except for the marginal (last) consumer, who is forced to pay full reservation price. The same is true for sellers. All get producers' surpluses, except for the marginal seller who can just meet the market clearing price of $6.

Maximizing consumers' and producers' surpluses

Now we can see two things the market has accomplished, in addition to rationing the good and establishing an equilibrium price for it. First, *it has rationed the good to those consumers who get the largest consumer surplus from it.* As we can see from our diagram, those consumers to whom the good is not worth $6 are not given any of the good. Only those whose estimation of the good is equal to or above its market price will get it.

There is a warning that we must quickly and forcefully interject here. Although our market maximizes consumers surpluses, we cannot say that it establishes the "best" allocation of goods, because the ability to buy the good varies according to the income of each consumer. With a different initial distribution of income, a different line-up of consumers with different reservation prices would almost certainly occur. Hence consumers' surplus is maximized, *given the initial distribution of income.* This is not to say that the initial distribution is a good one. In Chapter 19 we will come back to the crucial question of what that initial distribution might be.

Second, note that *the market has also maximized producers' surpluses,* because those producers who enjoy a surplus are those whose costs are below $6. The market, therefore, permits only the most efficient sellers or producers to supply goods. It thereby serves as an agency for assuring the *efficiency* of production, since it caters to sellers who are able to provide the good with the least cost, which usually means the smallest use of society's resources.

Price vs. Nonprice Rationing

The rationing system of the market is both its triumph and its trouble. At the outset of our book we briefly surveyed the problems of nonmarket control mechanisms. In the case of tradition, we remember, the problem is the profound inertia that comes from a static arrangement of economic duties and rewards. In command economies, the problem lies in the difficulty of administering a system without resort to bureaucratic inefficiency on the one hand or dictatorial intervention on the other.

Against these very grave difficulties of other systems, the price system has two great advantages: (1) *it is highly dynamic,* and (2) *it is self-enforcing.* That is, on the one hand it provides an easy avenue for change to enter the system; on the other, it permits economic activity to take place without anyone overseeing the system.

The second (self-enforcing) attribute of the market is especially useful with regard to the rationing function. In place of ration tickets with their almost inevitable black markets or cumbersome inspectorates or queues of customers trying to be first in line, *the price system operates without any kind of visible administration apparatus or side effect.* The energies that must go into planning or the frictions that come out of it are alike rendered unnecessary by the self-policing market mechanism.

Market problems

On the other hand, the system has the defects of its virtues. If it is efficient and dynamic, it is also devoid of values. It recognizes no priorities of claim to the goods and services of society except those of wealth and income. Those with income and wealth receive the goods and services that the economy produces; those without income and wealth receive nothing.

If all shared alike or all incomes were distributed in accordance with some universally approved principle, this neutrality of the market would be perfectly acceptable, for then each would enter the market on equal terms. At least they would enter with advantages and disadvantages that bore the stamp of social approval. But when inheritance still perpetuates large fortunes made in the past, and unemployment or old age can bring extreme deprivation, the rationing results of the market often affront our sense of morality.

Therefore every market society interferes to some extent with the "natural" outcome of the price rationing system. In times of emergency, it issues special permits that take precedence over money and thereby prevents the richer members of society from buying up all the supplies of scarce and costly items. In depressed areas, it may distribute basic food or clothing to those who have no money to buy them. To an ever-increasing extent it uses its taxes and transfer payments to redistribute the ration tickets of money in accordance with the prevailing sense of justice.

Shortages

Our view of the price system as a rationing mechanism helps to clarify the meaning of two words we often hear as a result of intervention into the market-rationing process: *shortage* and *surplus*.

What do we mean when we say there is a *shortage* of housing for low-income groups? The everyday meaning is that people with low incomes cannot find enough housing. Yet in every market there are always some buyers who are unsatisfied. We have previously noted, for instance, that in our shoe market, all buyers who could not or would not pay $25 had to go without shoes. Does this mean there was a shoe "shortage"?

Certainly no one uses that word to describe the outcome of a normal market, even though there are always buyers and sellers who are excluded from that market because they cannot meet the going price. Then what does a "shortage" mean? We can see now that shortage usually refers to a situation in which some nonmarket agency, such as the government, fixes the price below the equilibrium price.

Figure 11·2 shows us such a situation. Note that at the price established by the government, the quantity demanded is much greater than the quantity supplied. If this were a free market, the price would soon rise to the equilibrium point, and we would hear no more about a shortage. So long as the price is fixed at the ceiling, this equilibrating process cannot take place. Thus the quantity demanded will remain larger than the quantity supplied, and some buyers will go unsatisfied *even though they are willing and able to pay the current price.*

This bears directly on the problem of price controls. The problem with such controls is that they tend to fix prices that are below the level that would be established in a free (inflationary) market. As a result, some buyers who would ordi-

RATIONING BABIES

Because the market is such an efficient distributive mechanism, it has been proposed as a means to achieve Zero Population Growth, assuming that this were the declared national policy. Since a sizeable minority (probably about 15 percent) of all families voluntarily choose to have no children or only one, a country can achieve ZPG even if some families have more than two children. The question is how to decide which families should be allowed to have the extra children? Professor Kenneth Boulding has ventured an answer that leans heavily on the market mechanism. He proposes that each girl and boy at adolescence be given 110 green stamps, of which 100 are required if a woman is to have a legal child. (The penalty for having an illegal child would be very severe, possibly even sterilization.) Unwanted or surplus stamps would then be sold in a market organized for that purpose. It can be seen that the total number of stamps would permit the population as a whole to have 2.2 children per family—the ZPG rate. The market would therefore serve to ration the extra stamps, making them available to those with higher incomes or a greater desire for chilrdren. "As an incidental benefit," writes Boulding, tongue in cheek, "the rich will have loads of children and become poor, and the poor have few children and become rich."

When this scheme was first published, it provoked a storm of criticism. Commenting on its reception, Boulding observes: "This modest and humane proposal, so much more humane than that of Swift, who proposed that we eat the surplus babies, has been received with so many cries of anguish and horror that it illustrates the extraordinary difficulty of applying rational principles to processes involving human generation."[*]

*Kenneth E. Boulding, *Economics as a Science* (New York: McGraw-Hill, 1970), p. 39.

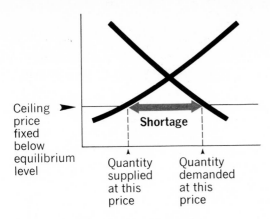

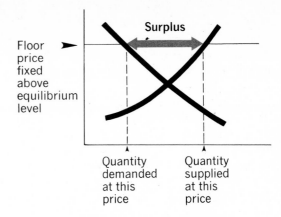

FIG. 11·2   Shortages

FIG. 11·3   Surpluses

narily have been priced out of the market remain *in* the market, although there are not enough goods offered to satisfy their demands. The result tends to be queues in stores to buy things before they are gone, under-the-counter deals to get on a preferred list, or black or gray markets selling goods illegally at higher prices than are officially sanctioned.

Surpluses

The opposite takes place with a surplus. In Fig. 11·3, we see a price floor fixed above the equilibrium price. That happens when the government supports a crop above its free market price.

In this situation, the quantity supplied is greater than that demanded (note that we should *not* say that "supply" is greater than "demand"). In a free market, the price would fall until the two quantities were equal. If the government continues to support the commodity, then the quantity bought by private industries will not be as large as the quantity offered by farmers. Unsold amounts will be a "surplus," bought by government.

Thus the words *shortage* and *surplus* mean situations in which there are sellers and buyers who are willing and able to enter the market at the going price but who remain active and unsatisfied because the price mechanism has not eliminated them. This is very different from a free market where there are unsatisfied buyers

and sellers *who cannot meet the going price* and who are therefore not taken into account. Poor people, who have no demand for fresh caviar at $60 per pound, do not complain of a caviar shortage. If the price of fresh caviar were set by government decree at $1 a pound, there would soon be a colossal "shortage."

What about the situation with low cost housing? Essentially what we mean when we talk of a shortage of inexpensive housing is that we view the outcome of this particular market situation with noneconomic eyes and pronounce the result distasteful. By the standards of the market, the poor who cannot afford to buy housing are simply buyers at the extreme lower right end of the demand curve. Their elimination from the market for housing is only one more example of the rationing process that takes place in *every* market. When we single out certain goods or services (such as a doctors' care or higher education) as being in "short supply," we imply that we do not approve of the price mechanism as the appropriate means of allocating scarce resources in these particular instances. Our disapproval does not imply that the market is not as efficient a distributor as ever. What we do not like is the outcome of the market rationing process. The underlying distribution (or maldistribution) of income clashes with other standards of the public interest that we value more highly than efficiency.

RATIONING WITHOUT TEARS

Although we now understand that the price system is a rationing system, when we say "rationing" we usually mean a system of coupons or publicly determined priorities. If there were a permanent shortage of gasoline—meaning that at going prices, the quantity of gas sought would be larger than the quantity offered—we might ration by allowing each car owner an equal amount or by assuring that certain vehicles, such as ambulances, always had first crack at supplies.

No sooner do we begin to think about rationing by coupon or by priority than we begin to see the complexity of the problem. Clearly, the purpose of rationing is to prevent rich people from riding about in Cadillacs while poor people can't afford the gas to ride to work in their Volkswagens.

Imagine that you were in charge of nonprice rationing. Suppose that the number of gallons of gas expected to be available were 100 billion. Would you now determine the basic ration by dividing this number by the population, giving each person an equal allotment? That would enormously benefit a family with one car and many children, and penalize a single person who might desperately depend on his car. And what would a family do if it got its coupons but did not own a car? Would you perhaps ration supplies per car owner, rather than per person? Here, of course, the trouble is that you would be giving the same allotment to all car owners, without knowing their respective needs. Some owners, such as Hertz and Avis, would be desperate for supplies. Other owners, who hardly used their cars, would not need all their coupons.

Might these very difficulties prompt you to follow a scheme that resembles Boulding's proposal for rationing babies? Suppose you issued to each adult a book of coupons entitling him to his basic allotment of gallons, and *you allowed individuals to buy or sell these coupons!* To be sure, rich citizens would now be in a position to buy up coupon books, but poor citizens would not have to sell their books. If they needed their basic allotment, they would keep their coupons. If they did not need their allotment, they could supplement their income by selling it.

The point of such a plan is to use the market as a means by which individuals can determine their own economic activities according to their marginal utilities, and to combine that use with the overall fairness that a market may not attain. The ration books would insure a basically democratic sharing of one part of the national wealth, but they would permit individuals to maximize their surpluses in a way that rationing alone would not.

FOCUS This short and simple chapter is one of the most important in this entire section, for the idea of the market as a rationing system—a means of determining who will and who will not be permitted to share in the output of society or to sell his own output to society—is absolutely fundamental to an understanding of our form of economic society.

The "technical" aspects of the chapter are sufficiently self-evident, so that we need not review them here. The only point that may require some reflection is the meaning of *shortage* and *surplus;* but once you have mastered the rationing idea, there should be no difficulty in understanding what each term means.

Rather, if there is a matter to be mulled over, it is the question of the rationale of the market system. Why should price and income be permitted to decide the division of society's wealth? We can all think of cases in which deserving persons are excluded from enjoying their "fair share" of the world's goods because they cannot afford the going price (or what is the same thing, because they do not have enough income). If we did not all feel that the price allocation mechanism were not faulty to some degree, we would simply allow those without incomes to suffer the consequences—whether malnutrition or starvation. Because we do not feel this way, all market systems have supplementary rationing systems, such as welfare payments, charities, and the like.

But if the market system is not morally defensible when pressed to extremes, why do we acquiesce in it as the best allocation device short of these extremes? The answer lies in the extraordinary difficulties of devising an alternative to the market system, especially for a society that sets high store on the quantity and variety of commodities that it produces. Reread the box above, in which we describe the difficulties of gasoline rationing, and think about how you would arrange the equitable division of goods (or income) without a market to rely on. Incidentally, the problems you will encounter are very much like those in our preceding "Extra word," when we compared private markets and public "markets."

One last point. There is an aspect of the allocation process that applies to one individual who seeks to distribute his or her income most efficiently for personal consumption (maximizing one's own consumer's surplus), in addition to the problem of many individuals that we take up in our chapter. We have put this piece of economic analysis in the "Extra word" that follows, and we recommend it to those students who enjoy the application of "pure" economic theory to everyday life.

WORDS AND CONCEPTS YOU SHOULD KNOW

Allocation, 134–35
Rationing, 134–36
Reservation prices, 136
Consumers' and producers' surpluses, 136–37

Shortages and surpluses, 138–39
Equilibrium (once again), 135
Equalizing marginal utilities, 143–45*

*See "An extra word" at the end of this chapter.

QUESTIONS

1. Why is rationing an inescapable problem in our economic society? Is it inescapable in all societies? Traditional ones? How is it solved there?

2. Explain how the market rations a commodity like automobiles. What other means of allocating autos could we devise? What are the advantages and disadvantages of a market rationing process?

3. Under what circumstances is the market not regarded as a satisfactory rationing mechanism?

4. If income distribution were determined by majority vote, do you think there would ever be a public demand for nonmarket rationing?

5. What do we mean when we say there is a shortage of low-cost housing? Is there a shortage of high-cost housing?

6. Do you have reservation prices for, say, gasoline? What would be your reservation price for 10 gallons per month? Twenty? One hundred? Is this the same as your demand curve for gas?

7. If your reservation price for a certain movie that would be shown only once in your neighborhood were $5 and the admission price were $2, what would be your consumer's surplus? Does that mean you would see the movie twice?
HINT: Your reservation price for the second showing would probably be a lot lower than for the first.

8. Explain how a market maximizes consumer surpluses. How does income distribution enter into this picture? Does income distribution enter into the determination of producers' surpluses?

9. How can total consumer surplus be so much larger for a commodity such as water than for one such as wine? Why do we pay attention to the relation only at the margin, and not to total consumer surplus?

Optimal allocation of individual income

There is another way in which a market allows us to allocate income efficiently. We have shown how a market maximizes consumers' surpluses in a market composed of different individuals with different reservation prices (or differing marginal utilities) competing for one good. Now let us see how the market mechanism also maximizes the consumer's surplus (or total utilities) of one person who shops in many markets for many goods.

An intuitive example may help us begin. Suppose that you had to spend your weekly income each Monday, but that you had to make up your shopping list, once and for all, before leaving your house. If you had enough price catalogs, that would not be impossible to do, although you might debate the merits of this item versus that one. *Suppose you had to make up the list without knowing what prices were!*

Two problems would present themselves. First, you would not know how many goods you could buy, *in toto,* because you would not know whether your income would suffice to buy a few goods or many. Second, you would have no way of "ranking" the priority of your purchases. Knowing the prices of bread and cake, you can decide how much you want to spend on each. Not knowing these prices, how could you make a rational decision whether to buy many units of bread and no cake or fifty-fifty or some other combination?

You might think, perhaps, that a "rational" man would buy bread first, then cake. But suppose after he had made his irrevocable decision he found that bread was very expensive and cake very cheap. He might then regret having decided to buy so much bread and dearly wish he had chosen cake instead.

This seemingly trivial example contains more than may at first meet the eye, for it shows us how the existence of prices enables us to behave as rational maximizers in disposing of our incomes. Therefore let us pursue our line of reasoning a little further.

In Fig. 11 · 4 we show our reservation prices for three commodities. In each case,

FIG. 11 · 4   Allocating income

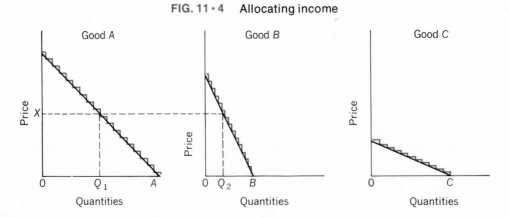

our reservation price for another unit of the same good diminishes because the good gives us less marginal utility. At the same time, as the diagram makes clear, the schedule of reservation prices is very different for each good. Good A is very important to us, so our initial reservation price is very high; Good B less so; Good C still less. (We have drawn our reservation prices in steplike fashion and overlaid a generalized schedule of reservation prices, which is, of course, our familiar demand curve.)*

MARGINS VS. TOTALS

The question we want to elucidate is this: *how much of each good will we buy to get the largest possible satisfaction from our income?*

Suppose we had an unlimited income. This is the same thing as supposing that the goods were free, that their prices were zero. How much of Goods A, B, and C would we then acquire? An unlimited amount? Certainly not. As our diagram shows, we don't want unlimited quantities of A, B, and C. Beyond a certain point, their marginal utilities are negative. They are nuisances. We could even have negative reservation prices: we would pay someone to take the stuff away. Thus, with no budget constraint we consume quantities $OA + OB + OC$.

Now notice something interesting about this unlimited consumption. The three demand curves reflect differing marginal utilities of the three goods. Looking at these curves, we see that the *total* utility we get from A will be greater than that we get from B or C, and that the *total* utility of B will be greater than that of C. Why then don't we take more of A and B, since their total utility is so large? The answer, also apparent from the graph, is that after we have acquired quantity OA of Good A *we don't get any further utility from it.* The same is true of B after we have OB of it, and of course of C, after OC.

This begins to clarify a very important point. To get the maximum amount of enjoyment from our income—even from an *unlimited* income—we need pay no attention to the total utilities we get from various commodities. Their marginal utilities are all we need to know. We will reach a maximum of satisfaction from our total expenditure when we get as much utility from the marginal unit of one good as from another. *Indeed, the rule for maximizing our total satisfaction is to acquire goods until their marginal utilities per dollar of expenditure are equal.*

THE EQUIMARGINAL RULE

This equimarginal rule has many applications in economics, for it has an astonishing property. It means that we don't have to stop to compare totals when we maximize values. *We need compare only margins.* Later we will see that this applies to entrepreneurs trying to maximize total revenues and to minimize total costs. They too will need to look at only marginal costs and incomes. For ourselves as consumers, it means that we do not have to try to compare whether we get more "total" satisfaction out of bread or out of cake. All we have to do is worry about whether we want one more loaf of bread or one more piece of cake. If we buy whichever we want more of at the moment, we will automatically be maximizing our total well-being. When we equally desire another unit of each, we have spent our income as efficiently as possible.

*Remember that each of these schedules of reservation prices depends on our initial income. With a different income, we might have a different set of desires for the three goods.

So far, we have imagined that we had no budget constraint. Of course we do have such constraints. Our incomes are limited, and prices are not zero. Then how does the equimarginal principal apply?

If you will turn back to Fig. 11 • 4 you will see an X on the price axis of Good A. If you draw a line parallel to the quantity axis all the way across the diagram, we can imagine that this is the price of Goods A, B, and C. We picture them having the same price: e.g., $5 for a basket of fruit (Good A), a necktie (Good B), a movie ticket (Good C). (We could draw different prices for each good, but that would only complicate the diagram without changing the principle.)

Now how much of A, B, and C do we buy? If you will drop a line from the point where price intersects the demand curve, you will see that we buy (approximately) OQ_1 of Good A, and OQ_2 of Good B. We buy none of Good C. Why? Because the price is higher than our top reservation price. We don't want to go to the movies at $5, given our budget constraint.

Now look at Goods A and B. You obviously have much more consumer surplus from A than from B. Why then, don't you buy more of A and less of B? The answer is that you are getting as much satisfaction *at the margin* for Good A as for Good B. If you bought another unit of Good A, and one less unit of Good B, you would be giving up more consumer's surplus than you would be getting. *Thus budget constraints limit the amount of goods we can buy, but we still maximize our well-being by seeking equal marginal utilities from those we buy.*

EQUALIZING MARGINAL UTILITIES

Now let us take one last step. We have just seen that we maximize our personal well-being by equalizing the marginal utilities of goods, not their total utilities. *We can then see that we will spend our income optimally when we get the same satisfaction from a dollar spent on each good.* If the marginal utility of a dollar's worth of bread is equal to that of a dollar's worth of cake, we have obviously achieved our aim.

When we speak of "a dollar's worth" of bread, we are speaking of its price. Therefore we can set up a formula that will describe the way we allocate our incomes to maximize our satisfactions.

$$\frac{\text{Marginal Utility of Good A}}{\text{Price of Good A}} = \frac{\text{Marginal Utility of Good B}}{\text{Price of Good B}}$$

or in more abstract terms:

$$\frac{MU_1}{P_1} = \frac{MU_2}{P_2} = \frac{MU_n}{P_n}$$

where *MU* stands for the marginal utilities of Goods 1, 2 . . . *n*, and *P* stands for their respective prices.

Here is the equimarginal principle at work. We are maximizing our well-being by equating the *marginal* utilities of different goods in proportion to their prices, so that each dollar of expenditure for each good gives us the same enjoyment. We may still get a much larger amount of enjoyment from one kind of good than from another, but we will only decrease our total welfare if we lose sight of the equimarginal principle.

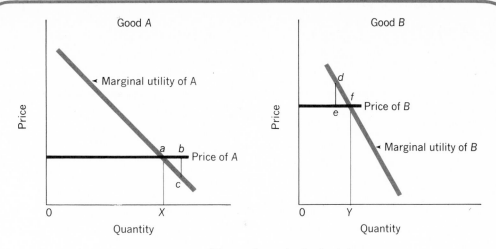

FIG. 11 · 5   The equimarginal principle

For one last demonstration of this, examine Fig. 11 • 5. It shows us two goods, A and B. A is very cheap and gives us much total pleasure. B is dearer and provides less total satisfaction but more marginal satisfaction per unit. At their respective prices, we buy *OX* of Good A and *OY* of Good B. Should we buy more A and less B? If we did, we would incur the consumer's loss (negative surplus) shown by triangle *abc* and forego the potential consumer's surplus shown by triangle *def.* We are obviously best off when we follow the equimarginal rule.

A TAUTOLOGY?

Do we *really* use prices to maximize our consumers' surpluses? Do we really follow the equimarginal principle when we push a grocery cart through the supermarket aisles?

In point of fact, we are faced here with a tautology, a statement that cannot be demonstrated empirically. We cannot measure marginal utilities, so we cannot divide them by prices to see if equalization is occurring. Therefore, there is really no way of proving that we follow the marginal rule, nor any way of teaching us how to do so. Nonetheless, we get a certain intellectual insight in discovering that we tend to be rational maximizers, dutifully trying to follow the equimarginal rule.

Who would deny that we experience something that the words *consumer surplus* describe very well? Who has not gone to buy something that he expected to pay $10 for, found it on sale, and felt at firsthand the pleasures of that little triangle *def?** Who has not bought something on impulse "because it was cheap" and later regretted it— a clear case of *abc?* However imperfectly, it seems that we do try to spend our limited incomes so that we will get about as much pleasure from the last dollar spent for food as for clothes or entertainment or whatever. Indeed, when we go to spend our incomes, what other guide can we use than the marginal utilities that we will get from this versus that, compared with their prices?

Thus the idea of maximizing our individual well-being by using prices to allocate our incomes according to the equimarginal principle seems plausible. Although it remains a tautology, the hypothesis is a fruitful one, and economics has built on it a powerful theory of how we behave as consumers and why.

*In this case, we expected to buy *OY* of Good B at a price *d*, rather than *e*.

The market in movement

Equilibrium prices, emerging from the wholly unsupervised interaction of competing buyers and sellers, are now a part of our understanding. These prices, once formed, silently and efficiently perform the necessary social task of allocating goods among buyers and sellers. Yet our analysis is still too static to resemble the actual play of the marketplace, for one of the attributes of an equilibrium price, we remember, is its lasting quality, its persistence. Things are different in the real world around us, where prices are often in movement. How can we introduce this element of change into our analysis of microeconomic relations?

The answer is that the word equilibrium *does not imply changelessness. Equilibrium prices last only as long as the forces that produce them do not change. To put it differently, if we want to explain why any price changes, we must always look for changes in the forces of supply and demand that produced the price in the first place.*

12

146

Shifts in Demand and Supply

What makes supply and demand change? If we recall the definition of those words, we are asking: What might change our willingness or ability to buy or sell something at any given price? Having asked the question, it is not difficult to answer it. If our incomes rise or fall, that will clearly alter our *ability* to buy. Similarly, a change in the prices of other commodities will alter our real income and thus our ability to buy. When food goes up, we go to the movies less often. Finally, a change in tastes will change our *willingness* to buy.

On the seller's side things are a bit more complicated. If we are owners of the factors of production (labor, land, or capital), changes in incomes or tastes will also change our ability and willingness to offer these factors on the market. If we are making decisions for firms, changes in *cost* will be the main determinant. We shall study these changes when we turn to the firm in later chapters.

Shifts in curves vs. shifts along curves   Thus changes in tastes or prices or in income or wealth will shift our whole demand schedule. The same changes, plus any change in costs, will shift our whole supply schedule.

Note that this is very different from a change in the quantity we buy or sell when *prices* change. In the first case, as our willingness and ability to buy or sell is increased or diminished, *the whole demand and supply schedule (or curve) shifts bodily.* In the second place, when our basic willingness and ability is unchanged, but prices change, our schedule (or curve) is unchanged, but *we move back or forth along it.*

Here are the two cases to be studied carefully in Fig. 12·1 (p. 148). Note that when our demand schedule shifts, we buy a *different amount at the same price.* If our willingness and ability to buy is enhanced, we will buy a larger amount; if they are diminished, a smaller amount. Similarly, the quantity a seller will offer will vary as his willingness and ability are altered. Thus demand and supply curves can shift about, rightward and leftward, up and down, as the economic circumstances they represent change. In reality, these schedules are continuously in change, since tastes and incomes and attitudes and technical capabilities (which affect costs and therefore sellers' actions) are also continuously in flux.

Price changes   How do changes in supply and demand affect prices? We have already seen the underlying process at work for shoes. Changes in supply or demand will alter the *quantities* that will be sought or offered on the market at a given price. An increase in demand, for instance, will raise the quantity sought. Since there are not enough goods offered to match this quantity, prices will be bid up by unsatisfied buyers to a new level. At that level, quantities offered and sought will again balance. Similarly, if supply shifts, there will be too much or too little put on the market in relation to the existing quantity of demand, and competition among sellers will push prices up or down to a new level at which quantities sought and offered again clear.

In Fig. 12·2, we show what happens to the equilibrium price in two cases: first, when demand increases (perhaps owing to a sudden craze for the good in question): second, when demand decreases (when the craze is over). Quite obviously, a rise in demand, other things being equal, will

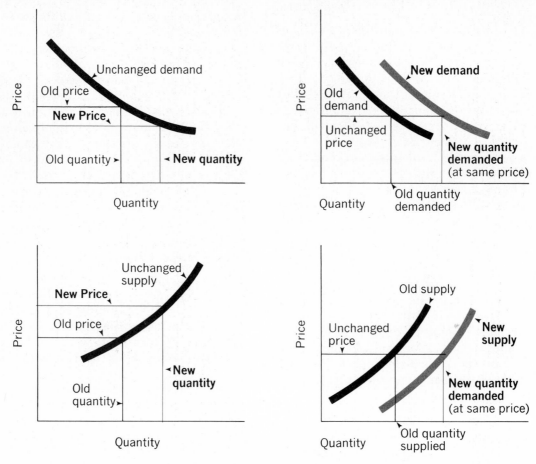

A change in price alone changes the QUANTITY we demand or supply

Unchanged demand

Price

Old price

New Price

Old quantity ► ◄ New quantity

Quantity

Unchanged supply

New Price

Old price

◄ New quantity

Old quantity ►

Price

Quantity

A change in our willingness or ability changes our whole DEMAND SCHEDULE

New demand

Old demand

Unchanged price

New quantity demanded (at same price)

Old quantity demanded

Price

Quantity

Old supply

Unchanged price

New supply

New quantity demanded (at same price)

Old quantity supplied

Price

Quantity

FIG. 12 · 1   Changes in quantities demanded or supplied
vs. changes in demand or supply

FIG. 12 · 2   Shifts in demand change equilibrium prices

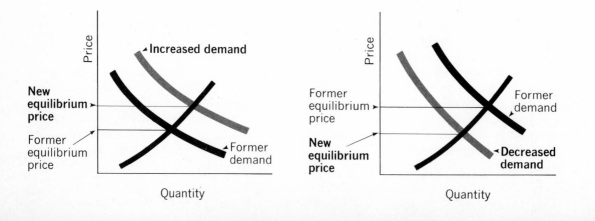

Price

◄ Increased demand

New equilibrium price

Former equilibrium price

◄ Former demand

Quantity

Price

Former equilibrium ► price

New equilibrium price

Former demand

◄ Decreased demand

Quantity

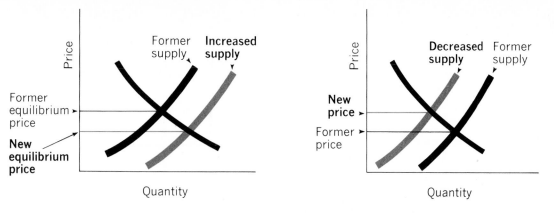

FIG. 12·3   Shifts in supply change equilibrium prices

cause prices to rise; a fall will cause them to fall.

We can depict the same process from the supply side. In Fig. 12·3, we show the impact on price of a sudden rise in supply and the impact of a fall. Again the diagram makes clear what is intuitively obvious: an increased supply (given an unchanging demand) leads to lower prices; a decreased supply to higher prices.

And if supply and demand *both* change? Then the result will be higher or lower prices, depending on the shapes and new positions of the two curves; that is, depending on the relative changes in the willingness and ability of both sides. Figure 12·4 shows a few possibilities, where S and D are the original supply and demand curves, and S' and D' the new curves.

FIG. 12·4   How shifts in both supply and demand affect prices

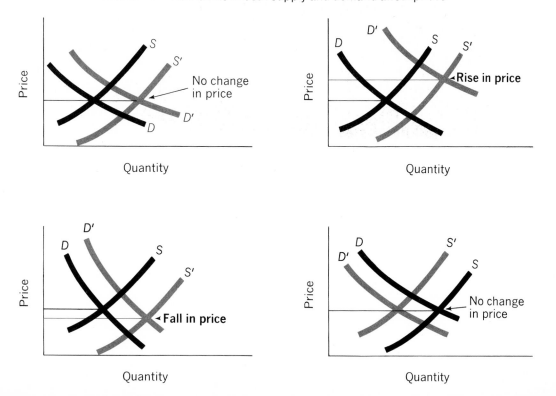

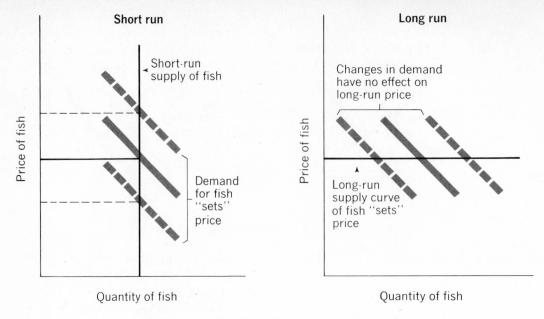

FIG. 12·5 Short- and long-run supply curves

Long and short run

There is one point we should add to conclude our discussion of supply and demand. Students often wonder which "really" sets the price—supply or demand. Alfred Marshall, the great late-nineteenth-century economist, gave the right answer: *both do*, just as both blades of a scissors do the cutting.

Yet, whereas prices are always determined by the intersection of supply and demand schedules, we can differentiate between the *short run*, when demand tends to be the more dynamic force, and the *long run*, when supply is the more important force. In Fig. 12·5 we see (on the left) short-run fixed supply, as in the instance of fishermen bringing a catch to a dock. Since the size of the catch cannot be changed, the supply curve is fixed in place, and the demand curve is the only possible dynamic influence. Broken lines show that changes in demand alone will set the price.

Now let us shift to the long run and draw a horizontal supply curve representing the average cost of production of fish

(and thus the supply price of fish) in the long run. Fluctuations in demand now have no effect on price, whereas a change in fishing costs that would raise or lower the supply curve would immediately affect the price.

In all cases, do not forget, *both* demand and supply enter into the formation of price. In the short run, as a rule, changes in demand are more likely to affect changes in prices, whereas in the long run, changes in supply are apt to be the predominant cause of changes in price.

Elasticity

We have seen how shifts in demand or supply affect price, but *how much* do they affect price? Suppose, for example, that demand schedules have increased by 10 percent. Do we know how large an effect this change will have on price?

These questions lead us to a still deeper scrutiny of the nature of supply and

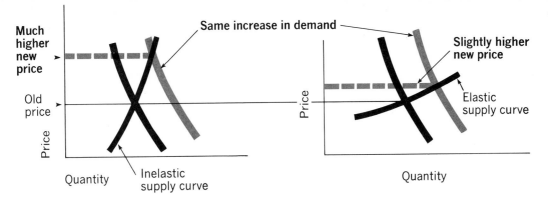

FIG. 12·6   How elasticity of supply curve affects price

demand, by way of a new concept called *elasticity* or, more properly, *price elasticity*. Elasticities describe the shapes of supply and demand curves and thereby tell us a good deal about whether a given change in demand or supply will have a small or large effect on price. Figure 12·6 illustrates the case with two supply curves. Our diagrams show two commodities selling at the same equilibrium prices and facing identical demand schedules. Note, however, that the two commodities have very different supply curves. In both cases, demand now increases by the same amount. Notice how much greater is the price increase for the good with the inelastic (steep) supply curve.

Similarly, the price change that would be associated with a change in supply will be greater for a commodity with an inelastic demand curve than for one with an elastic (gently sloping) demand curve.

Figure 12·7 shows two identical supply curves matched against very different demand curves. Notice how the commodity with inelastic demand suffers a much greater fall in price.

Elasticities are powerful factors in explaining price movements, because the word *elasticity* refers to our sensitivity of response to price changes. An elastic demand (or supply) means that changes in price strongly affect buyers' or sellers' willingness or ability to buy or sell. When schedules are inelastic, the effect of price is small. **In more precise terms, an elastic demand (or supply) is one in which a given percentage change in prices brings about a larger percentage change in the quantity demanded (or supplied).** An inelastic schedule or curve is one in which the response in the quantities we are willing and able to buy or sell is proportionally less than the change in price.

FIG. 12·7   How elasticity of demand curve affects price

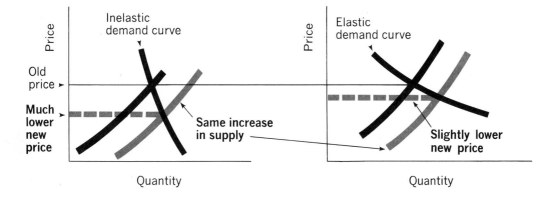

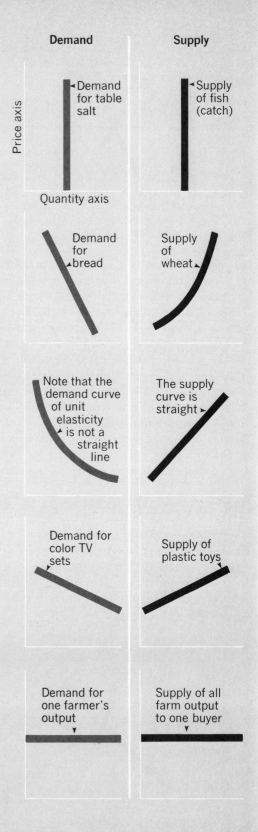

FIG. 12·8 A family of supply and demand curves

TOTALLY INELASTIC DEMAND OR SUPPLY. The quantity offered or sought is unchanged despite a change in price. Examples: Within normal price ranges there is probably no change at all in the quantity of table salt bought. Similarly, a fisherman landing a catch of fish will have to sell it all at any price within reason.

INELASTIC DEMAND OR SUPPLY. Quantity offered or sought changes proportionately less than price. Examples: We probably do not buy twice as much bread if the price of bread drops to half. On the supply side, the price of wheat may double, but farmers are unable (at least for a long time) to offer twice as much wheat for sale.

UNIT ELASTICITY. This is a special case in which quantities demanded or supplied respond in exact proportion to price changes. (Note the shape of the demand curve, a rectangular hyperbola.) Examples: Many goods may fit this description, but it is impossible flatly to state that any one good does so.

ELASTIC DEMAND OR SUPPLY. Price changes induce proportionally larger changes in quantity. Examples: Many luxury goods increase dramatically in sales volume when their price is lowered. On the other side, elastic supply usually affects items that are easy to produce, so that a small price rise induces a rush for expanded output.

TOTALLY ELASTIC DEMAND OR SUPPLY. The quantity supplied or demanded at the going price is "infinite." Examples: This seemingly odd case turns out to be of great importance in describing the market outlook of the typical small competitive firm. Merely as a hint: For an individual farmer, the demand curve for his output at the going price looks horizontal because he can sell all the grain he can possibly grow at that price. A grain dealer can also buy all he wants at that price.

152

We should notice that we can use another term—*income elasticity*—to describe how our willingness or ability to buy or sell responds to a change in *income,* rather than price. With many commodities, income elasticities of both demand and supply are more significant than price elasticities in actual economic life.

The idea of income elasticity is exactly the same as price elasticity. Sales of an income-elastic good or service rise proportionately *faster* than income. Sales of an income-inelastic commodity rise *less than propor-*

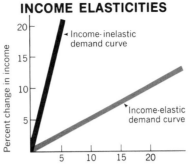

INCOME ELASTICITIES

tionately with income. These relationships are graphed in the accompanying figure.

Do not be fooled into thinking that these are supply curves because they slope upwards. "Income" demand curves show a functional relation different from that of "price" demand curves. In the curves shown, we assume that prices are unchanged, otherwise we would not have *ceteris paribus.*

As an exercise, try drawing an income-elastic and an income-inelastic supply curve.

It helps if we see what elasticities of different kinds look like. Figure 12·8 is a family of supply and demand curves that illustrates the range of buying and selling responses associated with a change in prices.

Arc and point elasticity

A loud warning must be sounded while you are looking at the family of curves in Fig. 12·8. *It is that the elasticity of most demand curves changes from point to point!* Actually there are only three normally shaped curves whose elasticity does not change: (1) totally inelastic (vertical) curves; (2) totally elastic (horizontal) curves; and (3) curves of unitary elasticity of demand or supply. Note in Fig. 12·9 that a fall in price of 50 percent, from $10 to $5, brings an increase in demand of 100 percent, from 1 unit to 2. But a second fall of 50 percent, from $5 to $2.50 would clearly not result in another 100 percent increase in purchases. As we go down the curve, the proportionate response of quantity to price steadily diminishes. Our curve becomes less and less elastic.

What, then, do we mean by "elastic" or "inelastic" demand, when elasticity changes as we move up or down the curve? There are two answers:

1. We can measure the elasticity of a given

schedule or a *portion of the curve;* for example, the portion that lies between the price of $10 and $5 or any other two points. The answer gives us the "average" elasticity for that part of the curve, and for that part only. We call this *arc elasticity.*

2. We can also measure (by using the calculus) the elasticity at any point on the curve. This is *"point elasticity,"* and this measure of elasticity will change

FIG. 12·9   Tricky calibrations II

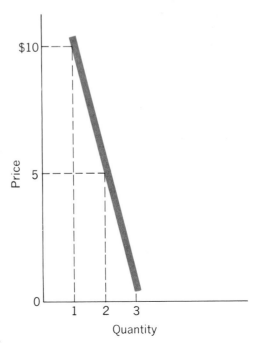

from point to point. In theoretical economics, we often use point elasticity for accuracy. In practical economics we usually use arc elasticity, because we are interested in large-scale effects.

Elasticities, expenditures, and receipts

Elasticities not only affect the determination of market prices, they also have a very great effect on the fortunes of buyers and sellers in the marketplace. That is, it makes a great deal of difference to a buyer whether the supply curve of a commodity he wants is elastic or not, for that will affect very drastically the amount he will have to spend on that particular commodity if its price changes. It makes an equal amount of difference to a seller whether the demand curve for his output is elastic or not, for that will determine what happens to his total revenues as prices change.

Here is an instance in point. Table 12·1 shows three demand schedules: elastic, inelastic, and of unit elasticity. Let us see how these three differently constituted schedules would affect the fortunes of a seller who had to cater to the demand represented by each.

Table 12·1 Demand schedules for three goods

| | QUANTITIES DEMANDED | | |
Price	Inelastic demand	Unit elasticity	Elastic demand
$10	100	100	100
9	101	111 1/9	120
8	102	125	150
7	103	143	200
6	104	166 2/5	300
5	105	200	450
4	106	250	650
3	107	333 1/3	900
2	108	500	1,400
1	109	1,000	3,000

MORE ON ELASTICITIES

For rough and ready purposes, we speak of steeply sloping demand or supply curves as *inelastic* and of gradually sloping ones as *elastic*.

As economic analysts, we should note that all sloping demand curves can be divided into elastic and inelastic portions. Take the curve below.

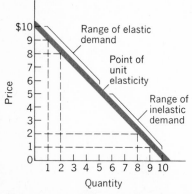

Price / Quantity

$10, 9, 8, 7, 6, 5, 4, 3, 2, 1, 0

Range of elastic demand

Point of unit elasticity

Range of inelastic demand

1 2 3 4 5 6 7 8 9 10

We show that above the point of unitary elasticity it is an elastic demand curve; below the unitary point, an in-

elastic one. You should prove this by figuring out the elasticity for, say, a fall in price from $9 to $8; and again from $2 to $1.

If you have made these calculations, you should be able to see why the following formula is used for elasticity:

$$n = -\frac{\Delta Q/Q}{\Delta P/P}$$

In this formula, *n* stands for "elasticity"; ΔP for the *change* in price and ΔQ for the change in quantity. Thus the formula shows us the *percentage* change in quantity, in relation to a *percentage* change in price. (The Greek letter Δ, *delta*, stands for "change in." Note that we use the initials *P* and *Q* as denominations in our formula.)

Why does the formula have a minus sign in front of it? The reason is

that a *decrease* in price is associated with an *increase* in quantity demanded. Dividing the positive quantity change by the negative price change will give us a "minus" answer. For convenience, we therefore put a minus sign in front of the equation, to make the answers positive instead of negative numbers. Any number larger than 1 therefore stands for an elastic price response; any number less than 1, for an inelastic price response. For example, an elasticity coefficient of -2 means that a 1 percent price rise would cause a 2 percent decrease in quantity demanded.

Final note. Elasticity works just as well going up as coming down. We have used illustrations showing the change in *Q* associated with a fall in price. The same principles and the same formula apply to a rise in price and a fall in quantity. Try working your previous examples "backward." Notice that you get slightly different elasticities, because the proportionate change from, e.g., $9 to $8 is not the same as that from $8 to $9!

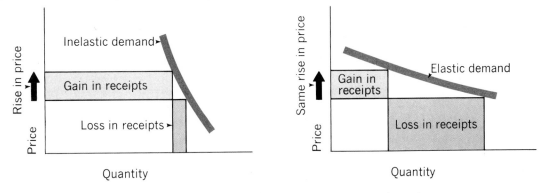

FIG. 12·10   How elasticities affect receipts when prices change

Notice that a very interesting result follows from these different schedules. The amounts spent (price times quantity) are in Table 12·2. The total amount spent for each commodity (and thus the total amount received by a firm) will be very different over the indicated range of prices.

To a seller of goods, it makes a lot of difference whether or not the demand he faces is elastic. *If demand is elastic and he cuts his price, he will take in more revenue.* If his demand is inelastic and he cuts his price, he will take in *less* revenue.

Conversely, a business that raises its price will be lucky if the demand for its product is inelastic, for then receipts will actually increase. Compare the fortunes of the two businesses depicted in Fig. 12·10. Note that by blocking in the change in price times the change in quantity, we can show the change in receipts. (Because we have ignored changes in costs, we cannot show changes in profits.)

Our figure shows something else. If we reverse the direction of the price change, our businesses' fortunes take a sharp change. A demand curve that is elastic spells bad news for a business that seeks to raise prices, but the same demand curve brings good fortune to one that intends to cut prices. Just the opposite is the case with an elastic demand curve: now the condition of demand is favorable

for a price rise, since the seller will hold most sales even at the higher price; but inelastic demand is bad for one who cuts prices, since it will gain few additional customers (or the old ones will increase their purchases only slightly) when prices fall.

Table 12·2   Total expenditures (or receipts)

Price	Goods with demand schedules that are		
	Inelastic	Unit elastic	Elastic
$10	1,000	1,000	1,000
9	909	1,000	1,080
8	816	1,000	1,200
7	717	1,000	1,400
6	612	1,000	1,800
5	525	1,000	2,250
4	424	1,000	2,600
3	321	1,000	2,700
2	216	1,000	2,800
1	109	1,000	3,000

Obviously, what all business people would like to have is a demand for their product that was inelastic in an upward direction and elastic at lower than existing prices, so that they stood to gain whether they raised or lowered prices. As we shall see when we study pricing under oligopoly, just the opposite is apt to be the case.

Behind Elasticities of Demand: Substitution

Because elasticities are so important in accounting for the behavior of prices, we must press our investigation further. However, we must leave the supply side of elasticity to be studied when we look into the behavior of factors and firms. Here we will ask why are demand curves shaped the way they are? Why is our price (or income) sensitivity for some commodities so great and for others so slight?

If we think of a good or service for which our demand might be very inelastic—say eyeglasses (assuming we need them)—and compare it with another for which our demand is apt to be highly elastic—say, a trip to Europe—the difference is not difficult to grasp. One thing is a necessity; the other is a luxury, but what do we mean by *necessity* and *luxury*?

One attribute of a necessity is that it is not easily replaced by a substitute. If we need eyeglasses, we will spend a great deal of money, if we must, to acquire a pair. Hence such a necessity has a very inelastic demand curve.

Marginal utility again

Necessities are never absolute in the sense that nothing can be substituted for the commodity in question. High enough prices will drive buyers to *some* substitute, however imperfect.* Just when will the buyer be driven to the "next-best thing"? As we know, economists say that the decision will be made by a comparison of the marginal utility derived from a dollar's worth of the high-priced item with that derived from the lower-priced substitute. As the price of champagne goes up and up, there comes a point when we would rather spend our next dollar for a substantial amount of beer, rather than for a sip of champagne.

Necessities and elasticity

We have seen that necessities have inelastic demand curves, so that we stick to them as prices rise. What about when they fall? Won't we rush to buy necessities, just because they *are* necessities? Won't that make their demand curves elastic?

Surprisingly, the answer is that we do not rush to buy necessities when their prices fall. Why? The answer is that necessities are the things we buy *first*, just because they are necessities. Having bought what we needed before the fall in price, we are not tempted to buy much more, if any more, after the fall. Bread, as we commented before, is a great deal more valuable for life than diamonds are: but we ordinarily have enough bread, so that the marginal utility of another loaf is no greater than that of an equivalent expenditure on any other good. Thus, as the price of bread drops, the quantity we seek expands only slightly. So, too, with eyeglasses.

Compare the case with a luxury, such as a trip to Europe. There are many substitutes for such a trip: trips out West, trips South, or some other kind of vacation. As a result, if the price of a European trip goes up, we are easily persuaded to switch to some alternative plan. Conversely, when the price of a European trip gets cheaper, we are quick to substitute *it* for other

---

*What *would* be the substitute for eyeglasses? For a very nearsighted person, the demand for one pair of glasses would be absolutely inelastic over a considerable price range. But when glasses got to be, say $500 a pair, substitutes would begin to appear. At those prices, one could hire someone to guide him around or to read aloud. Admittedly this is less satisfactory than having glasses; but if the choice is between spending a very large amount on glasses and on personal help, the latter might seem preferable. Of course, there are some goods without any substitutes—air, for example. Such goods are "free goods," because no one owns them. If a good such as air could be owned, it would have to be subject to stringent public control, to prevent its owners from exacting a horrendous price for it.

possible vacation alternatives, and our demand accordingly displays its elastic properties.

Do not make the mistake, however, of thinking that elasticity is purely a function of whether items are "expensive" or not. Studies have shown that the demand for subway transportation in New York City is price-elastic, which hardly means that riding in the subways is the prerogative of millionaires. The point, rather, is that the demand for subway rides is closely affected by the comparative prices of substitutes—bus fares and taxis. Thus *it is the ease or difficulty of substitution that always lies behind the various elasticities of demand schedules.*

The importance of substitutes

Time also plays an important role in shaping our demand curves. Suppose, for example, that the price of orange juice suddenly soared, owing to a crop failure. Would the demand for orange juice be elastic or inelastic?

In the short run, it would generally be more inelastic than in the longer run. Lovers of orange juice would likely be willing to pay a higher price for their favorite juice because (they would believe) there was really no other juice quite as good. As weeks went by, they might be tempted to try other breakfast juices, and no doubt some of these experiments would

"take." Substitutes would be found, after all.

The point is that it takes time and information for patterns of demand to change. Thus demand curves generally become more elastic as time goes on, and the range of discovered substitutes becomes larger.

Because substitutes form a vast chain of alternatives for buyers, changes in the prices of substitutes change the positions of demand curves. Here is a new idea to be thought about carefully. Our existing demand curve for bread or diamonds has the shape (elasticity) it does because substitutes exist at various prices. When the prices of those substitutes *change*, the original commodity suddenly looks "cheaper" or "more expensive." If the price of subway rides rises from 50 cents to 65 cents, while the price of taxi rides remains the same, we will be tempted to switch part of our transportation from subways to taxis. If subway rides went to $1, there would be a mass exodus to taxis. Thus we should add changes in the prices of substitutes to changes in taste and in income when we consider the possible causes of a shift in demand. If the price of a substitute commodity rises, the demand for the original commodity will rise. As the price of substitutes falls, demand for the original commodity will fall. This may, of course, bring changes in the price of the original commodity.

THE SEARCH FOR SUBSTITUTES

The search for substitutes is a complicated process that can lead to equally complicated supply-and-demand reactions. Just after a taxi strike in New York City, when fares went up 50 percent, people switched to substitutes (they rode buses, subways, or walked), and the taxi business suffered severely. Then after the shock of the increase wore off, business revived. People got used to higher fares; that is, they discovered that the marginal utility of a high-priced taxi ride was still greater than the marginal utility of the money they saved by using other transportation, plus the marginal utility of the time they wasted or the business they lost because they weren't taking taxis. In other words, the substitutes weren't satisfactory. Gradually, people began taking more cab rides, and taxi receipts were higher than before the fare hike. The quantity of taxi service consumed was down somewhat, but not by as much as the original drop. In this case, demand proved to be more *inelastic* over time than it was in the very short run.

Behavior and nature, again

There is a last point we should make before we leave the subject of substitution. We have seen that the substitutability of one product for another is the underlying cause of elasticity. Indeed, more and more we are led to see "products" themselves as bundles of utilities surrounded with other competing bundles that offer a whole range of alternatives for a buyer's satisfaction.

What is it that ultimately determines how close the substitutes come to the commodity in question? As with all questions in economics that are pursued to the end, the answer lies in two aspects of reality before which economic inquiry comes to a halt. One of these is human behavior, with its tastes and drives and wants. One person's substitute will not be another's.

The other ultimate basing point is the technical and physical nature of the world that forces certain constraints upon us. Cotton may be a substitute for wool because they both have the properties of fibers, but diamonds are not a substitute for the same end-use, because they lack the requisite physical properties. Diamonds, as finery, may be a substitute for clothes made out of cotton; but until we learn how to spin diamonds, they will not be a substitute for the cloth itself.

Complements

In addition to substitution, there is another connection between commodities. This is the relationship of *complementarity*. Complementarity means that some commodities are technically linked, so that you cannot very well use one without using the other, even though they are sold separately. Automobiles and gasoline are examples of such complementary goods, as are cameras and film.

Here is another instance of change in the price of one good actually affecting the position of the demand curve for the other. If the price of film goes up, it becomes more expensive to operate cameras. Hence the demand for cameras is apt to drop. Note that the price of cameras has not changed in the first instance. Rather, when the price of the complementary good, the film, goes up, the whole demand curve for cameras shifts to the left. Thereafter, the price of cameras is apt to fall, too.

The case of vanishing resources

One last application of the ideas of this chapter should bring home the importance of substitutes and elasticities. The application has to do with a problem that we discussed in Chapter 4: the danger of running out of resources, such as oil.

Suppose we do run out of oil. Does that mean that one day the gas pumps go dry and the economy comes to a screeching halt? Price analysis allows us to see that this is not the way a depleting resource exerts its effect. As oil reserves get scarcer, the cost of producing oil rises, shifting supply curves leftward. Meanwhile, as the demand for oil continues to grow, demand curves shift to the right.

The result is, of course, a rise in the price of gasoline (or of any other scarce resource). At higher prices we will consume less, partly through personal economies, partly because there will be strong incentives to redesign automobiles to use less gas. In the 1950s, no auto maker stressed fuel economies in his advertising; now all do. As a result, as Fig. 12·11 shows, our demand curve for gas—the price we are able and willing to pay—may be rising, even though the amount we actually purchase is diminishing. Note that Q_1 is less than Q_0.

How high can the price of gasoline go? The answer, of course, depends on the availability of substitutes. This in turn

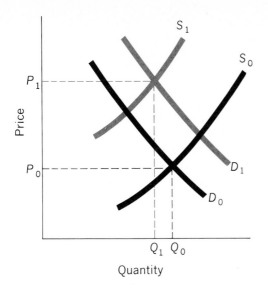

FIG. 12·11   A resource "squeeze"

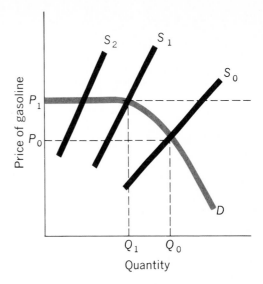

FIG. 12·12   Effect of very high prices

hinges on the urgency to find substitutes. At 40¢ a gallon there may be "no alternative" to gasoline. At $4.00 per gallon there will be a tremendous incentive to find alternatives: public transportation, bicycles, electric vehicles, and the like. Indeed, at very high prices, gasoline-driven vehicles are likely to become as rare as electric vehicles (once fairly popular) are today. To put it differently: at very high prices, the demand curve for gas will become increasingly elastic, as Fig. 12·12 shows. After we reach price P_1 further decreases in supply have no further effect on price but simply result in decreased use.

As price rises from P_0 to P_1, we may, for a time, be acutely aware of a "shortage" of gas. Once consumption shrinks to Q_1 we are likely to have adjusted to other energy sources (including our own feet) and may be almost unaware of the further contraction of consumption if the supply curve continues its leftward shift.

Limits to market adjustment   Does this mean that the price mechanism can effectively ward off the dangers of resource exhaustion? Not entirely. The price mechanism will

signal when supplies begin to run short, thereby encouraging the use of other resources. It is possible, however, that alternative resources will be much less efficient, unless a great deal of research and development goes into them.

For example, many modes of energy could replace that of oil on which we still depend so heavily. As of today, however, each alternate mode presents dangers or limitations. Coal cannot power our cars. Nuclear fuels give rise to dangerous wastes. Solar energy is not yet an economical substitute for fossil fuels. It may be that all these handicaps can be overcome. But it will take years of research and development to bring these alternatives into effective use. By the time the market signals are unmistakable, it may be too late to achieve a smooth transition from one energy base to another. This is equally true for the more or less simultaneous exhaustion of many kinds of minerals, which are now substitutes for one another and for which no good substitutes now exist as a group.

The central question is thus a matter of technology; and beyond technology, of social adaptability. The market can forewarn us of resource squeezes. It can steer the economy in the direction of resource "safety." It can greatly cushion the impact of resource exhaustion. But in itself the market cannot guarantee that technology will discover or perfect the substitutes we need to maintain given economic activities. Further, if those activities have to be curtailed or given up, the market is no guarantor that our social institutions will accommodate themselves readily to the demands placed upon them.

FOCUS This chapter is called "The Market in Movement," and its central idea is how prices change. This idea leads us to an examination of shifts in demand and supply curves, and to a clear distinction between the meaning of a change in the quantity demanded or supplied, in which we move along a given curve, and a shift in demand or supply in which the curve itself changes.

This central concept and the graphic treatment of shifting supply and demand curves will be one of our main tools in the micro and macro sections of this book. Now is the time to learn how to use it. Go through the questions with great care, especially questions 3, 4, 5, and 6.

The second principal idea is that of elasticity. Question 4 is crucial here. If you really want to be sure that you have mastered elasticity, work out an example in which price goes from $10 to $1 by one-dollar steps and quantities go from 1 unit to 10 units, by even steps. *Then show that the elasticity will be different at each price change.* This difference is, of course, due to variation in the proportional changes. Look at the box on page 154 if you are in doubt.

Behind the techniques is a central idea: substitution. Substitution, it has been said, is the law of economic life, the key to everything. It is certainly the key to elasticity. Think about the kinds of substitutes that exist even for the most "necessary" items. What are substitutes for water? For bread? For cotton cloth? Surprisingly, there are many. It is not so easy to find commodities (like the eyeglasses in our chapter) for which substitutes are really hard to find. You might make up a list; and while you are at it, a list of "tied" commodities that have complementary characteristics. Then test your final comprehension of our chapter by completing this sentence: When the price of Good A falls, the prices of substitutes will _____ (rise/fall), and the price of complements will _____ (rise/fall). Work out your answer from the text, pp. 157–58.

The question of global resource adequacy is a much-debated one on which opinions differ. You might glance back at Chapter 4 (p. 61), in view of what you have learned about substitutes, and try to think through the problem in large-scale terms. Certainly there are substitutes for, say, copper. Are there substitutes for copper and tin and silver, taken together? For all ten leading minerals? The answer hinges, of course, on technology (can we "mine the seas, melt the rocks"?) and on social adaptability. If we can't mine the seas, etc., how can we adapt our society to a changed economic environment?

WORDS AND CONCEPTS YOU SHOULD KNOW

Equilibrium again, 146
Shifts in demand or supply curves, 147–49
Elasticity, 150–51
Elastic and inelastic S and D curves, 152
Elasticity and receipts, 154–55
Substitutes, 156–57
Necessities, 156–57
Complements, 158

QUESTIONS

1. What changes in your economic condition would increase your demand for clothes? Draw a diagram to illustrate such a change. Show on it whether you would buy more or less clothes at the prices you formerly paid. If you wanted to buy the same quantity as before, would you be willing and able to pay prices different from those you paid earlier?

2. Suppose that you are a seller of costume jewelry. What changes in your economic condition would decrease your supply curve? Suppose that costs dropped. If demand were unchanged, what would happen to the price in a competitive market?

3. Draw the following: an elastic demand curve and an inelastic supply curve; an inelastic demand curve and an elastic supply curve; a demand curve of infinite elasticity and a totally inelastic supply curve. Now give examples of commodities that each one of these curves might represent. Caution: remember that elasticities change in most curves.

4. Show on a diagram why elasticity has so much effect in determining price changes. (Refer back to the diagrams on p. 155 to be sure that you are right.)

5. Draw a diagram that shows what we mean by an increase in the quantity supplied; another diagram to show what is meant by an increase in supply. Now do the same for a decrease in quantity supplied and in supply. (Warning: it is very easy to get these wrong. Check yourself by seeing if the decreased supply curve shows the seller offering less goods at the same prices.) Now do the same exercise for demand.

6. Show on a diagram (or with figures) why you would rather be the seller of a good for which demand was elastic, if you were in a market with falling prices. Suppose prices were rising—would you still be glad about the elasticity of demand?

7. How does substitution affect elasticity? If there are many substitutes for a product, is demand for it elastic or inelastic? Why?

8. If you were a legislator choosing a product on which to levy an excise tax, would you choose a necessity or a luxury? Which would yield the larger revenue? Show how your answer hinges on the different elasticities of "luxuries" and "necessities."

9. By and large, are luxuries apt to enjoy elastic or inelastic demands? Has this anything to do with their price? Can high-priced goods have inelastic demands?

10. Why is demand more apt to become elastic over time?

11. The price of pipe tobacco rises. What is apt to be the effect on the demand for pipes? On the demand for cigars?

Helping the farmer

Traditionally, farming has been a trouble-ridden occupation. All through the 1920s, the farmer was the "sick man" of the American economy. Each year saw more farmers going into tenantry, until by 1929 four out of ten farmers in the nation were no longer independent operators. Each year the farmer seemed to fall further behind the city dweller in terms of relative well-being. In 1910 the income per worker on the farm had been not quite 40 percent of the nonfarm worker. By 1930, it was just under 30 percent.

Part of this trouble on the farm, without question, stemmed from the difficult heritage of the past. Beset now by drought, now by the exploitation of powerful railroad and storage combines, now by his own penchant for land speculation, the farmer was proverbially an ailing member of the economy. In addition, the American farmers had been traditionally careless of the earth, indifferent to the technology of agriculture. Looking at the average individual farmer, one would have said that he was poor because he was unproductive. Between 1910 and 1920, for instance, while nonfarm output per worker rose by nearly 20 percent, output per farm worker actually fell. Between 1920 and 1930, farm productivity improved somewhat, but not nearly so fast as productivity off the farm. For the great majority of the nation's agricultural producers, the trouble appeared to be that they could not grow or raise enough to make a decent living.

If we had looked at farming as a whole, however, a very different answer would have suggested itself. Suppose that farm productivity *had* kept pace with that of the nation. Would farm income as a whole have risen? The answer is disconcerting. The *demand* for farm products was quite unlike that for manufactured products generally. In the manufacturing sector, when productivity rose and costs accordingly fell, the cheaper prices of manufactured goods attracted vast new markets, as with the Ford car. Not so with farm products, however. When food prices fell, people did not tend to increase their actual consumption very greatly. Increases in over-all farm output resulted in much lower prices but not in larger cash receipts for the farmer. Faced with an *inelastic demand,* a flood of output only leaves sellers *worse* off than before, as we saw in our last chapter.

That is very much what happened during the 1920s. From 1915 to 1920, the farmer prospered because World War I greatly increased the demand for his product. Prices for farm output rose, and his cash receipts rose as well; in fact, they more than doubled.

Following the war, when European farms resumed production, American farmers' crops simply glutted the market. Although prices fell precipitously (40 percent in the single year 1920–21), the purchases of farm products did not respond in anything like equal measure. As a result, the cash receipts of the farmer toppled almost as fast as prices. In turn, an ailing farm sector contributed to a general economic weakness that would culminate in the Great Depression.

THE NEW DEAL

At its core, the trouble with the farm sector was that the market mechanism did not yield a satisfactory result for farmers. Two causes were evident. One was the inelastic demand for food. The second was the inability of a vast, highly competitive industry like agriculture to limit its own output, so that it would not constantly "break the market" every time a bumper crop was harvested.

This chronic condition of agriculture was one of the first problems attended to by Franklin Roosevelt's New Deal administration. The New Deal could not alter the first cause, the inelasticity of demand, for that arose from the nature of the consumer's desire for food. It could change the condition of supply, which hurled itself, selfdestructively, against an unyielding demand. One of the earliest pieces of New Deal legislation—the Agricultural Adjustment Act—sought to establish machinery to be used by farmers, as a group, to accomplish what they could not do as competitive individuals: curtail output.

The curtailment was sought by offering payments to farmers who agreed to cut back their acreage or in other ways hold down their output. In the first year of the act, there was no time to cut back acreage, so that every fourth row of growing cotton had to be plowed under, and 6 million pigs were slaughtered. In a nation hungry and ill-clad, such a spectacle of waste aroused sardonic and bitter comment. Yet, if the program reflected an appalling inability of a society to handle its distribution problem, its attack on overproduction was not without results. In both 1934 and 1935 more than 30 million acres were taken out of production in return for government payments of $1.1 billion. Farm prices rose as a result. Wheat, having slumped to 38¢ a bushel in 1932, rose to $1.02 in 1936. Cotton doubled in price, hog prices tripled, and the net income of the American farmer climbed from the fearful low of $2.5 billion in 1932 to $5 billion in 1936.

SUPPORT PRICES

Later the New Deal sought to raise farm incomes by establishing *support prices* at which the government would, if necessary, buy farm output. Because the New Deal sought to raise incomes, not to stabilize production, these prices were set at a level *higher* than equilibrium market prices. Given these support prices, farmers could confidently plan their future production, since they knew their output would be bought. But because prices were above equilibrium levels, they chose to grow more than the consumer was willing to consume at the support price. In other words, surpluses emerged, as in Fig. 12 · 13 on the next page.

At support price P_1 consumers want to buy quantity Q_1. Farmers, however, produce quantity Q_2. The difference has to be bought and stored by the government. In 1960, government warehouses bulged with unsold crops worth $6 billion.

To avoid these surpluses, the government limited the acreage that farmers could plant if they wanted to qualify for support payments. In this way, as Fig. 12 · 14 shows, they hoped to push back the supply curve so that the market generated an equilibrium at quantity Q_1.

The strategy might have worked, were it not for the extraordinary increase in agricultural productivity, resulting from new technologies. Between 1940 and the late 1960s, harvested acreage declined by 15 percent, but the yield per acre increased by

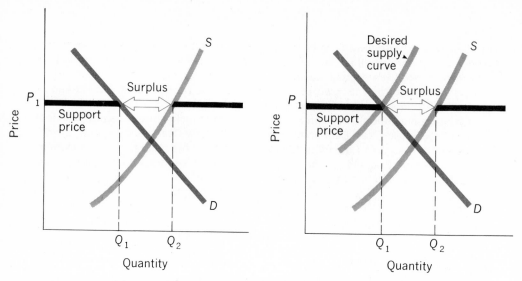

FIG. 12·13   Price-support surplus   FIG. 12·14   The effort to limit supply

over *70 percent.* The result was a flood of output. Huge quantities had to be purchased and stored by the government. Only the massive distribution of these supplies to the underdeveloped lands during the late 1960s prevented the surplus problem from becoming a permanent national embarrassment.

INCOME SUPPORT

To avoid these unwanted and politically unwelcome effects, the Nixon administration in 1973 finally adopted a plan that had been proposed almost a quarter-century earlier by Charles Brannan, Secretary of Agriculture under President Truman. The so-called Brannan Plan supports farm *incomes,* not prices. A "target price" is established by law for various crops, but this target price does not apply to the actual selling prices of the crops. The free play of forces on the market allows prices to reach whatever levels supply and demand dictate.

The farmer is fully protected, nonetheless. If actual market prices are below target prices, the government will send a farmer a check for the difference that results from selling his crop below the target level. (Moreover, there is a limit of $20,000 per farmer in these support income payments, whereas there was no limit under previous plans that sent enormous sums to some very large farm operators). Two results follow:

1. When production is high and prices fall, consumers get the benefit of cheaper food prices, although as taxpayers they will still have to give up a certain amount of income to be transferred to farmers.
2. Because target prices are fairly high, farmers can plan with assurance for high outputs, without worrying about "breaking the market." In an era of world food shortages and high domestic food prices, this helps assure a high level of farm output.

CONTROLS IN A COMPETITIVE INDUSTRY

Now let's suppose that as a result of various circumstances, food prices take a sharp upward turn. The government decides that to control the rate of inflation it is going to freeze all retail food prices.

If all prices were at or above their equilibrium when controls were imposed and if these equilibrium levels were not changing, price freezes would have no immediate impact, since they would be the same prices that the market would have sooner or later set. Let us assume that this is not the case and that the controls are going to hold some prices below their equilibrium level, as in Fig. 12·15.

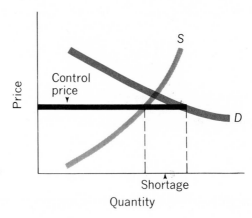

FIG. 12·15   Price controls

PROBLEMS OF PRICE CONTROLS

As we have seen, whenever prices are held below their equilibrium level, shortages will occur; that is, people will want to buy more of the commodity than suppliers are willing to supply. Since price is not being used to ration the existing supplies, some other technique must be found. The only alternatives are to distribute goods and services on a first-come first-served basis or to establish formal rationing. Note that if the government control procedures break down and black markets are established, *we are right back to rationing by prices.* The only difference is that in the black market, prices are illegal. Purchasers or sellers at these illegal prices can be thrown in jail.

If formal rationing is used, governments seek to reduce the demand curve for the commodity by insisting that you must have both money *and* ration coupons to buy a pound of beefsteak. By limiting the amount of beef covered by ration coupons to the known supply of beef, it becomes possible to push the demand curve back to the point where it just crosses the supply curve at the desired price. The problem with this procedure is that the farmer now has no incentive to expand his production. The only way he will produce more is if he is able to get a higher price. Thus the controls that reduce the price of food retard the expansion of the food supply.

Suppose, instead, that we ration on a first-come, first-served basis. Now the problem is the opportunity cost of shopping time. The price of purchasing a good is now the money you must pay plus the time you must wait in line to get what you want.

For most people, beefsteak that sells for 50¢ per pound but requires a 2-hour wait in line is not cheap beefsteak.

Now let's assume that the farmer has the option of selling his production to foreigners as well as to Americans. A freeze on retail prices is not a freeze on prices on the farm. Foreign buyers can therefore offer farmers more than American retailers can. Accordingly, farmers sell their crops to foreign buyers. This not only leads to greater U.S. shortages, but it can also create other problems. After the freeze is established, suppose soybean prices rise because of foreign demand. With higher soybean prices, U.S. chicken growers may find that chickens sell below the cost of feeding them. If this occurs, they will stop raising chickens and further aggravate the shortage of meat. Another possibility is that producers may simply hang onto their production, waiting for the freeze to be lifted. If cattle are withheld from the market, for example, shortages are once again exacerbated.

As a result, there are a host of adverse consequences stemming from the effort to control the increase in retail food prices. If retail controls are to be effective in holding prices below their equilibrium levels, they require formal rationing as a complement to price ceilings, plus some nonprice effort to increase the supply of foodstuffs. Eliminating acreage controls would be one nonprice action to increase production in the face of a price freeze.

THE FARM PICTURE IN PERSPECTIVE

As any agricultural economist can tell you, the farmer leads anything but a serene life. He must make difficult guesses about the course of prices years into the future. Prices take large swings, seldom settle into stable patterns, and may not be a very good guide to the future.

Efforts to correct these difficulties have not been marked by great success. The original price support program was costly, inefficient, and not always equitable. The new income-support program hopes to avoid many of these problems, but it may be expensive if market prices fall and target prices are set too high, under political pressure.

Yet, in all this, it is important to gain a sense of long-term perspective. We have seen that the farmer, unable to control economic swings, has traditionally been their victim. What we have tried to do, in the last four decades, is to intervene in the market process, to make it yield results more in accord with our conceptions of social justice. Despite all the difficulties we have discussed, the results are far from unimpressive. Agriculture, as an income-producing activity has benefited substantially—especially for the million-odd successful farmers who produce 90 percent of our marketed farm products. Between 1940 and 1964, farm operator families enjoying the use of electricity increased from 33 percent to more than 95 percent; telephones increased from 25 percent to 76 percent; refrigerators from 15 percent to more than 90 percent. In the West, Midwest, and Northeast, the independent farm operator is today, as he never was, at a close parity with the urban middle class in living standards. In the South, traditionally a laggard area, farm incomes are rising faster than the national average. The important lesson is that it is possible to intervene in the market process to bring about desired social ends, although as our chapter has made abundantly clear, the process of intervention is far from simple and full of unexpected pitfalls.

Operating a competitive firm

Most of us have firsthand knowledge of the household, whose role is crucial in determining the demand for goods. We know a lot less about the firm, whose function is to supply us with goods. In this chapter, we enter the factory gates of a competitive firm, to find out what goes on inside.

The rational, maximizing, competitive firm

Note *competitive* firm. We will leave the operation of the giant corporation until later. There are several good reasons for this initial limitation of our investigation.

First, the kind of small, highly competitive firm we shall describe exists as an important reality on the business scene, and we must understand how such firms do in fact survive and what role they play. Second, even the biggest and most monopolistic firms bear certain family resemblances to small competitive ones, so that our study will lay the groundwork for a later analysis of very big business. Third, until we have grasped how the market mechanism works with small competitive firms, we will not be in a position to understand and to measure the difference that

13

167

large firms and imperfect competition add to the system.

In addition to limiting our scrutiny to markets made up of small, competitive firms, we shall add two assumptions about the behavior of these firms—one assumption realistic, one perhaps not. The unrealistic assumption is that our firm acts *intelligently and rationally* in the pursuit of its goals. Since the world is littered with bankruptcies that result from mistaken calculations and foolish decisions, this assumption may strain our credulity, but at least it will do no violence to understanding the *principles* of the market system. We recall learning about this assumption of rationality in Chapter 6.

As we also remember from that chapter, we shall assume that our firm is motivated by a desire to *maximize its profits*. Later, when we study the operations of very large firms, we shall have to ask whether this second assumption makes much sense in their case. Here, when we deal with the "atomistic" competition of small firms, the assumption stands up very well because, as we shall see, *it is only by trying to maximize short-term profits that small firms manage to survive at all*. This gives to microtheory both a positive and a normative function. It tells us how small firms usually do behave, and thereby enables us to make predictions about the way the market system works. It also serves as a goal-oriented description of how small business firms *should* conduct their affairs if they hope to survive.

Economics of the Firm

The first person we encounter inside the factory gates is an economic personage we have not previously studied. It is the boss of the works, the organizer of the firm, the *entrepreneur*.

Entrepreneurship

An entrepreneur is not necessarily a capitalist; that is, the person who has supplied capital to the business. The entrepreneur may act as the risker of capital, but so may a bank. The capitalist may be a group of people who have lent money to the business but never visited the premises. An entrepreneur provides a service that is essentially different from that of putting up capital. His or her contribution is *organizational*. Indeed, some economists have suggested that it is proper to think of four factors of production: labor, land, capital, and enterpreneurship, instead of the traditional first three alone.

Economic profit

As a "fourth" factor of production, the entrepreneur is paid a wage, *the wage of management*. It can, of course, be very high, since entrepreneurship is a valuable skill, the skill of maximizing a firm's *economic profit*.

This is not the profit of everyday usage. In ordinary usage we call "profit" any sum left over after a firm has paid its wages and salaries, rents, costs of materials, taxes, etc. Included in that ordinary profit is an amount that an economist excludes from his definition of a true economic profit. This is the interest that is owed to the capitalist for the use of his or her capital. In other words, if a firm has a plant and equipment worth $1 million and makes a profit of $50,000, an economist, before declaring the $50,000 to be a true economic profit, would first ask whether the firm had taken into account the interest owing to it on this capital. If interest rates were 5 percent, and no such allowance had been made (and it usually is not the ordinary accounting practice when the firm owns its own capital), an economist would say that no real economic profits were earned.

Economic profit, in other words, refers to the residual—if there is one. Indeed, our analysis shows us how an entrepreneur tries to create economic profits after appropriately remunerating all the factors, including capitalists, and how the operation of the market constantly tends to make this economic profit disappear, despite the best entrepreneurial efforts. (That will become clear in our next chapter, rather than in this one.)

One last point. Who gets the residual? It goes to the owner of the business, who is legally entitled to any profits it enjoys. That owner, as we have said, may or may not be the enterpreneur. In a cooperatively owned factory it might be the work force. Usually it is a proprietor, a group of partners, or shareholders. In all cases, this residual economic profit is over and above any recompense for the services these factors supply, including the service of making capital available.

The entrepreneur at work

To earn the wages of management, the enterpreneur

- *buys factors in the factor market*
- *combines factors in the enterprise, to produce output as inexpensively as possible*
- *sells the finished product in the goods market*

These three tasks may be enormously complicated in real life. Buying factors in the factor market is likely to entail bargaining with unions, establishing credit connections with banks, and arranging complex real estate deals. Producing output for the goods market will surely need technical skills, including those of a designer to make the output of one entrepreneur distinguishable from that of another. Selling goods and services will require the special skills of advertising personnel and a sales force.

As a result, enterpreneurship is often revealed by the ability of one firm to gain an edge over another in hiring labor and talented designers, obtaining credit or land, and devising selling techniques. In the competitive firm whose factory we are visiting, however, none of these real-life situations will be presumed to exist. The entrepreneur will be hiring labor, capital, and land on terms exactly equal with his competitors. Moreover, being such a small part of the industry, this entrepreneur cannot influence the markets for factors or goods, whatever he or she does. We shall assume, furthermore, that the plant produces some product that cannot be differentiated from that of competitors. A farmer's wheat, a metal manufacturer's nails or screws, the stampings of a small plastics factory are examples of these kinds of goods. Last, because output is exactly the same as that of competitors, the entrepreneur will have no use for the wiles of advertising or elaborate selling costs. What good would it do for a farmer to advertise "Buy wheat!"?

In subsequent chapters, we shall look more carefully into these conditions of atomistic competition, as well as into the problems of enterpreneurship in situations to which these special conditions do not apply. Here, the very severity of the setting for our competitive firm highlights the essential economic function of entrepreneurship. If we think of the entrepreneur buying factors of production, turning out a product that is indistinguishable from competing products, then selling it in a situation of absolute equality, only one task remains. *He must buy the right amounts of factors' services and combine these efficiently, in order to produce output as cheaply as possible.*

The problem of scale

When we now enter the factory, we begin to understand the economic problem that the enterpreneur faces. Around us we see machines, people, space. Why are they combined in the proportions that we find? Why did the entrepreneur hire this many workers, that much floor space, so much capital?

The answer lies partly in engineering and partly in economics. We will learn about these matters bit by bit in this chapter and the next one, so that you should not expect an instant answer. A good place to begin is with a fact of technology or engineering called *indivisibility*. It is an aspect of something we first discussed in Chapter 6; namely, that *size matters*. In this case it matters because with each factor there is a certain *minimum scale* that must be attained if we are to generate production at less than very high costs.

From one industry to another, this minimum size changes, largely because of technical or engineering considerations. Suppose that we were considering opening a bookstore. A bookstore may be very small, but it must occupy *some* space. It must stock a reasonable number of books and employ at least one person to sell them. If we were in agriculture, we would need a farm of at least a certain area, depending on our crop, and a basic amount of capital in the form of buildings, equipment, fertilizer, seed. If we were in manufacturing, there would be a minimum size of plant or machinery essential for our operation. If we were in a mass-production business, such as steel, the smallest efficient plant might run into an investment of millions of dollars and a work force of thousands; but that would take us well out of the world of atomistic competition to which we are still devoting our attention.

In other words, the first decision about hiring factors involves the physical (or engineering) fact that there is a certain amount of each factor that we must hire for technical reasons. This is what we mean by minimum scale. If problems of scale did not exist, we could produce television sets as efficiently in a garage as in a vast plant or raise cattle as cheaply in our back yard as on a range.

The factor mix

Indivisibilities of land, labor, or (mostly) capital help explain the initial decisions that an entrepreneur must make. There is a certain critical size or scale necessary to produce at all, although this size differs from one activity to another. Capital must be available to buy the factors needed to operate at that scale, or the business couldn't be started at all.

Suppose our entrepreneur has enough capital to start up operations, and suppose further that he hires the smallest possible amount of labor, land, and capital. Is there any reason to believe that this is the *combination* of factors that will enable him to produce as cheaply as possible? The question brings us to the next problem of entrepreneurship—*deciding what mix of factors will be most profitable*. How does an entrepreneur decide how much labor, how much land, how much capital to hire?

Law of Variable Proportions

As we shall see, this is by no means a simple question to answer, for many considerations bear on the decision to hire a factor or not. One extremely important fact, to which we must now pay close attention, does lie at the center of any businessman's calculations. This is the changing physical productivity that results from combining different amounts of one factor with fixed amounts of the others. Here the entrepreneur encounters the laws of production that we first encountered in Chapter 6.

Productivity curve: increasing returns

Let us begin with a case that is very simple to imagine. Suppose we have a farmer who has a farm of 100 acres, a certain amount of equipment, and no labor at all. Now let us observe what happens as he hires one man, then a second man of the same abilities, then a third, and so on. Obviously, the output of the farm will grow. What we want to find out, however, is whether it will grow in some clearly defined pattern that we can attribute to the changing amounts of the factor that is being added.

What would such a curve of productivity look like? Assume that one man, working the 100 acres alone as best he can, produces 1,000 bushels of grain. A second man, helping the first, should be enormously valuable, because the two men can begin to specialize and divide the work, each doing the jobs he is better at and saving the time formerly wasted by moving from one job to the next. As a consequence of this division of labor, output may jump to 3,000 bushels.

Marginal productivity

Since the *difference* in output is 2,000 bushels, we speak of the *marginal productivity* of labor, when two men are working, as 2,000 bushels. Note that we should not (although in carelessness we sometimes do) speak of the marginal productivity of the *second* man. Alone, his efforts are no more productive than those of the first man; if we fired the first man, worker number 2 would produce

only 1,000 bushels. What makes the difference is the jump in the combined productivity of the *two* men, once specialization can be introduced. Hence we should speak of the changing marginal productivity of *labor*, not of the individual.

It is not difficult to imagine an increasing specialization taking place with the third, fourth, and fifth man, so that the addition of another unit of labor input in each case brings about an output larger than was realized by the average of all the previous men. Remember that this does not mean the successive factor units themselves are more productive. **It means that as we add units of one factor, the total mix of these units plus the fixed amounts of other factors, forms an increasingly efficient technical combination.***

We call the range of factor inputs, over which average productivity rises, a range of *increasing average returns*. It is, of course, a stage of production that is highly favorable for the producer. Every time he adds a factor, efficiency rises. (As a result, as we shall see in our next chapter, costs per unit of output fall.) The rate of increase will not be the same, for the initial large marginal leaps in productivity will give way to smaller ones. But the overall trend of productivity, whether we measure it by looking at *total* output or at *average* output per man, will still be up. All this keeps on happening, of course, because the factor we are adding has not yet reached its point of maximum technical efficiency with the given amount of other factors.

---

*With each additional man, the proportions of land, labor, and capital are altered, so that the change in the level of output should rightfully be ascribed to new levels of efficiency resulting from the interaction of *all three factors*. But since labor is the factor whose input we are varying, it has become customary to call the change in output the result of a change in "labor productivity." If we were altering land or capital alone, we would call the change the result of changes in their productivities, even though, as with labor, the real cause is the changing efficiency of *all* factors in different mixes.

Diminishing returns

At a certain point, the farmer notices a disconcerting phenomenon. Marginal output no longer rises when he adds another man. Total output will still be rising, but a quick calculation reveals that the last man on the team has added less to output than his predecessor.

What has happened is that we have overshot the point of maximum technical efficiency for the factor we are adding. Labor is now beginning to "crowd" land or equipment. Opportunities for further specialization have become nonexistent. We call this condition of falling marginal performance a condition of decreasing or diminishing returns. As the words suggest, we are getting back less and less as we add the critical factor—not only from the "marginal" man, but from the combined labor of all men.

If we now go on adding labor, we will soon reach a point at which the contribution of the marginal man will be so small that average output per man will also fall. Now, of course, costs will be rising per unit. If we went on foolishly adding more and more men, eventually the addition of another worker would add nothing to total output. In fact, the next worker might so disrupt the factor mix that *total* output would actually fall and we would be in a condition of negative returns.

Average and marginal productivity

This changing profile of physical productivity is one of the most important generalizations that economics makes about the real world. It will help us to think it through if we now study the relationships of marginal and average productivity and of total output in Table 13 · 1.

Total, average, and marginal product

All three columns are integrally related to one another, and it is important to understand the exact nature of their relationships.

1. The column for total output is related to the column for marginal output, because the rise in total output results from the successive marginal increments. For instance, the reason total output goes from 7,800 bushels with 4 men to 9,800 with 5 men is that the marginal output associated with the fifth man is 2,000 bushels. Thus, if we know the schedule of total outputs, we can always figure the schedule of marginal outputs simply by observing how much total output rises with each additional unit of factor input.

2. It stands to reason, therefore, that if we know the schedule of marginal outputs, it is simple to figure total output: we just add up the marginal increments.

Table 13 · 1

Number of men	Total output	Marginal productivity (change in output)		Average productivity (total output ÷ no. of men)	
1	1,000	1,000 ⎫	Increasing	1,000 ⎫	
2	3,000	2,000 ⎬	marginal	1,500 ⎪	Increasing
3	5,500	2,500 ⎭	productivity	1,833 ⎬	average
4	7,800	2,300 ⎫		1,950 ⎪	productivity
5	9,800	2,000 ⎪	Decreasing	1,960 ⎭	
6	11,600	1,800 ⎬	marginal	1,930 ⎫	Decreasing
7	13,100	1,500 ⎪	productivity	1,871 ⎬	average
8	14,300	1,200 ⎭		1,790 ⎭	productivity

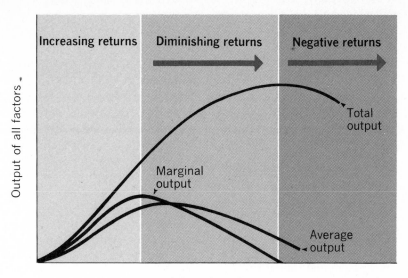

FIG. 13 · 1   The law of variable proportions

3. Finally, the meaning of average productivity is also apparent. It is simply total output divided by the number of men (or of any factor unit in which we are interested).

One thing must be carefully studied in this example. Note that marginal productivity begins to diminish with the fourth man, who adds only 2,300 bushels to output, and not 2,500 as did his predecessor. Average productivity, however, rises until we hire the sixth man, because the fifth man, although producing less than the fourth, is still more productive than the average output of all four men. **Thus marginal productivity can be falling while average productivity is still rising.**

The three curves in Fig. 13 · 1 all show the same phenomenon, only in a graphic way. The top curve shows us that as we add men to our farm, output at first rises very rapidly, then slowly, then actually declines. This is the curve we met in Chapter 3. The marginal productivity curve shows us *why* this is happening to total output. As we add men, the contribution they can make to output changes markedly. At first each man adds so much

that average output grows rapidly. Thereafter marginal output falls, although average output still rises. Finally, each man adds so little that he actually pulls down the average that obtained before his hiring. The average curve, as we have just indicated, merely sums up the overall output in an arithmetical way by showing us what the average person contributes to it.

Put into the form of a generalization, we can say that *as we add successive units of one factor to fixed amounts of others, the marginal output of the units of the variable factor will at first rise and then decline. We call this the law of variable proportions or the law of diminishing returns, or we can simply talk about it as the physical productivity curve.*

The law reviewed   The generalizations of the law of variable proportions constitute one of the key insights that microeconomics gives us into the workings of the real world. Let us be certain that we understand exactly what the law says and implies.

1. The law of variable proportions describes what happens to physical productivity when we add units of one factor and *hold the others constant.* As we added labor in the example above, we did not also add land or capital. Had we done so, there would have been no way of ascribing changes in output to the addition of one factor rather than the other.

2. The law applies to adding *any* factor to fixed quantities of the others. Suppose that we had started with a fixed amount of labor and capital and had added successive acres of land.

   The first acre would not have been very productive, for we would have had to squeeze too much labor and capital into its area. The second acre would have permitted a better utilization of all three factors, and so *its* marginal productivity would have been much higher. But in time the addition of successive units of land would pass the point of optimum mix, until another acre would add so little yield that the average production of all acres would be pulled down. The same pattern of increase, diminution, and final decrease would of course attend the addition of doses of capital—say successive bags of fertilizer or additional tractors—to a fixed amount of land and labor.

3. Unlike many other "laws" in economics, the law of variable proportions has nothing to do with behavior. The actions of people on the marketplace or the impulses or restraints of utility and disutility play no role in diminishing returns. Essentially, the law expresses a constraint imposed by the laws of nature. If there were no such constraint, we could indeed grow all the world's food on a single acre or even in a flowerpot, simply by adding more and more labor and capital.

Marginal Revenue and Marginal Cost

Now we must get back to our point of interest: the firm seeking to hire factors to its own best advantage. Is a knowledge of factor productivity all a businessperson needs? To revert to our first illustration, suppose we knew that one person being considered for our bookstore has a productivity of (i.e., could sell) 5 books a day. Would that alone tell us to hire that person?

The question answers itself. Before we can hire the clerk or any other factor, we have to know two other things: (1) *what the unit of the factor will cost,* and (2) *how much revenue our firm will get as a result of hiring that unit of the factor.*

If the price of a salesperson is $7,500 and we think she will sell 20 books a day at an average markup of $2 per book, then if she works for 250 days she will bring in revenues of $10,000 (20 × $2 × 250). Obviously, it will pay to hire her. On the other hand, if her productivity were less— if she sold only 12 books per day—then the revenues from hiring her would only be $6,000 (12 × $2 × 250), or $1,000 less than her wage. She would be a dead loss.

Marginal revenue product

Here we can add a simple term to our vocabulary. We call the marginal revenue we get from adding a unit of a factor its *marginal revenue product.* It is simply the *physical* increase in output from the additional factor, multiplied by the price at which we sell that output.

The hiring rule is then very simple. If the marginal revenue product of a factor is greater than its cost, hire it. If it isn't, don't. (Furthermore, it will raise our profit if we fire any factors whose marginal revenue products are less than their cost.)

Let us see how this actually works in practice. In the next schedules we go back to the farm, this time armed with two new pieces of information. We now know that labor costs $4,500 per man and that a bushel of wheat sells for $2.50. (Later we

Here is a good place to review the different constraints of nature that we first encountered in Chapter 6. We are now familiar with the law of diminishing returns. The key element in this law is the effect on productivity of adding *one factor only, while holding the others constant.*

The law of increasing cost differs in an important regard. It describes the effect on output of adding *all factors,* not just one. Suppose we wanted to increase the national production of wheat and began to take land, labor, and capital from other uses and put them into wheat farming. At first we might encounter no change in produc-

tivity per combined "unit" of land + labor + capital (say, per hundred men, hundred acres, and $10,000 worth of equipment). But soon we would be forced to use factors that were less and less appropriate to wheat output. Imagine trying to grow wheat in Nevada, using casino croupiers as workers and hotel limousines hitched to plows! *The law of increasing cost therefore refers to the decline in output that results from using factors that are not specialized in the output*

of the good in question. In the law of diminishing returns this problem of specialization does not enter: all our units of added factor input are presumed to be homogenous.

Last, we have constraints having to do with scale. We discuss the problem in our next chapter. As we shall see, its constraints have to do with technological considerations that make operations more efficient over a certain size. Changes in scale are one way we avoid diminishing returns, which presuppose that the scale of an operation is fixed because the input of the two complementary factors does not change.

will look into *how* we know these things, but here we can take them for granted.) Our farm schedule of marginal costs and marginal revenue products therefore looks like Table 13 • 2.

What does our table tell us? Our first man seems to be very unprofitable, for he costs us $4,500 and brings in only $2,500. We suspect, however, that he is so unprofitable because he is trying to spread his one unit of labor over the whole farm. The addition of a second man confirms our suspicions. He also costs us $4,500, but brings in $5,000. (Remember it is not the second man himself who does so, but the two men working together who give rise to an increase in revenues of that amount.) The third and fourth and fifth men also

show profits, when we compare their marginal revenue products to their marginal costs, but when we reach the sixth man, the law of diminishing returns brings its decisive force to bear. The sixth man is unable to increase the revenues of the team by more than $4,500, which is just his hire. It is not worthwhile to engage him.

Total costs and total revenues Are we certain that hiring 5 men will really maximize the profits of the farm? We can find out by adding up our *total* costs and our *total* revenues and figuring our profit at each level of operation. Table 13 • 3 does just that.

Table 13 • 2

Number of men	Marginal cost per man @ $4,500	Marginal physical output per man (from Table 13 • 1)	Marginal revenue product per man (output × $2.50)	Marginal profit or loss
1	$4,500	1,000	$2,500	−2,000
2	4,500	2,000	5,000	500
3	4,500	2,500	6,250	1,750
4	4,500	2,300	5,750	1,250
5	4,500	2,000	5,000	500
6	4,500	1,800	4,500	0
7	4,500	1,500	3,750	−750
8	4,500	1,200	3,000	−1,500

Table 13 · 3

Number of men	Total cost of men	Total revenue	Profit (total revenue less total cost)
1	$ 4,500	$ 2,500	−$2,000
2	9,000	7,500	− 1,500
3	13,500	13,750	250
4	18,000	19,500	1,500
5	22,500	24,500	2,000
6	27,000	29,000	2,000
7	31,500	32,750	1,250
8	36,000	35,750	− 250

We are really fooling ourselves when we "check" on our former calculations about marginal changes by looking at the totals; for just as with marginal and total output, the totals are themselves nothing but the sum of the marginal changes! As long as each man brings *some* addition to revenue, large or small (that is, so long as marginal revenue is larger than marginal cost when that man is hired), then the total of all revenues must be growing larger too. When we add up the marginal contributions, we measure each different-sized contribution. We should not consider it surprising that the whole is the sum of what we put into it.

As Table 13 · 3 shows, our best profit comes with the hiring of 5 men. The addition of a sixth does us no good. A seventh lowers our net income—not because of his lack of skill or effort, but because with 7 men the mix of labor and the fixed amounts of other factors is no longer so efficient as before. An eighth involves us in an actual loss.

We can also see now how neatly the physical productivity curve ties together marginal cost and marginal revenue product, for three things would entice us to hire the sixth or even the seventh man.

1. **A fall in cost.** If wages dropped to any figure under $4,500, our sixth man will immediately pay his way. By how much would

they have to drop to make it worthwhile to hire the seventh man? Marginal revenue product when 7 men are working is only $3,750. The wage level would have to drop below that point to bring a profit from 7 men.

2. **A rise in the price of output.** If the demand for grain increased, and the price of grain went to $3, our calculations would change again. Now the sixth man is certainly profitable: adding him now brings a marginal revenue product of 1,800 bushels × $3, or $5,400, far above his wage. Is the seventh man profitable at his wage of $4,500? His physical productivity is 1,500 bushels. At $3 per bushel he is not quite worth hiring. At $3.01 he would be.

3. **An increase in productivity.** If a change in skills or techniques raises the physical output of each man, this will also change the margin of profitable factor use. Any small increase will lead to the employment of the sixth man.

Choice among factors   We have talked, so far, as if an entrepreneur had only one "scarce" factor and as if the only task were to decide how much of that factor to add. But that is not quite the problem faced by business people. They have to decide not only *whether* to add to output at all, but *which* factor to hire in order to do so.

How does a businessperson make such a choice? How would we choose between adding a salesclerk or inventory to our bookstore, or how would the farmer decide between hiring labor or spending the same sum on capital or land? Suppose the farmer has already hired 4 men and has also rented a certain amount of land and used a certain amount of capital. Now when he thinks about expanding output, he needs to know not only how much the addition of another man will yield him, but *what the alternatives are.*

They might look like this.

1. He can hire a fifth worker for $4,500, who will, as we know, bring about an increase of 2,000 bushels in production.

2. He could spend the same amount on land, renting an acre that would increase his output by, let us say, 2,100 bushels.

3. For the same outlay he could engage the services of a tractor that would add 2,200 bushels a year to his output.

The next step is easy. The entrepreneur compares *the cost* of hiring a unit of each factor with the *marginal revenue product* of the factor. Thus, in the example above:

Factor	Marginal physical product	Selling price of goods	Marginal revenue product
Labor	2,000 bu.	$2.50	$5,000
Land	2,100 bu.	2.50	5,250
Capital	2,200 bu.	2.50	5,500

Now, comparing marginal revenue products and cost:

Factor	Marginal revenue product	Cost	Profit
Labor	$5,000	$4,500	$ 500
Land	5,250	4,500	750
Capital	5,500	4,500	1,000

Obviously, the tractor is the best buy, dollar for dollar, and the entrepreneur should spend money on tractors, as long as the relative prices and productivities of the factors are unchanged.*

Bidding for factors

Will factor prices remain unchanged? We have not yet inquired into the factor market, where wages, rents, and interest are priced; but to an entrepreneur in a competitive firm, that process doesn't matter. Prices "exist" for

land, labor, and capital, and there is no alternative to accepting them.

Nonetheless, we can now see how an entrepreneur's reactions to the prices of factors can affect those prices. You will remember we assumed, at the outset of our discussion, that the entrepreneur—farmer or manufacturer—was able to bid for additional factors without thereby affecting their prices.

This assumption followed from the premise of atomistic firms from which we started. The amount of land or labor or capital that such a small firm can add to its operations is so insignificant a portion of the total supply of that factor that the individual firm's demand does not affect the price of the factor appreciably, if at all. If 10,000 young women are looking for sales work in New York City, the addition of a few salespeople in any single business will not change the going price for salespeople at all. Neither will a small farmer's demand, by itself, alter the rent of land, nor will one firm's demand for capital change the rate of interest.

Therefore, for *one small firm, the supply curve of any factor looks like a horizontal line.* It is infinitely elastic, because a firm can engage all of the factor it requires at the going price without affecting the price of that factor at all.

This is not the case when many small firms all begin to demand the same factor. If all stores are looking for sales help, the salaries of salespeople will rise. If many farmers seek land or capital, rentals or interest (or the prices of capital goods) will go up. As a result, each firm will find that the going price for the factor in general demand has a mysterious tendency to rise, as Fig. 13 • 2 shows.*

---

*Ideally, an economist would wish to compare the marginal productivities of much smaller amounts of these three factors: i.e., an hour's worth of labor or a very small parcel of land or a day's use of a tractor. We have dealt in big chunks because factors often do come in indivisible units, and because this is the way the problem usually looks in the business world.

*The diagram does not emphasize a very important difference in *scale*. One inch along the horizontal axis of the industry diagram on the left may represent 100,000 units. The same inch along the firm's horizontal axis would then stand for only a few units.

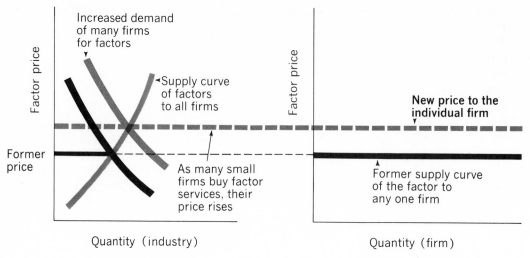

FIG. 13·2   Supply curve to all firms vs. supply curve to one firm

Supply and demand set the prices of factors, just as they do when consumers buy goods, only now the demand is exercised by a cluster of firms or an industry. The individual firm has no impact on the market and no choice but to accept its price as given.

Factor pricing   We can now finish the first part of our analysis. We remember that in our last example it was profitable for farmers to buy tractors, rather than land or labor. Now we must suppose that many farmers, finding themselves in the same situation, all bid for tractors. The result, of course, is that tractor prices will rise. The consequence of this, plainly, is that tractors become less profitable to the farmer, compared with land or labor, than they were originally. Suppose that the price of tractor hire goes up to $5,000, so that for an outlay of $4,500 a farmer can now afford a tractor only 4 days out of the week instead of 5 (or if he buys a tractor, he has to get a smaller model). Since the expenditure of $4,500 will now buy fewer tractor inputs, the tractor's addition to output will also

decrease. Let us imagine that tractor output falls by almost one-fifth with the cut in tractor hours. Then $4,500 of expenditure will bring an increase in output of 1,800 bushels instead of 2,200. At $2.50 per bushel, the marginal revenue from using a tractor now amounts to only $4,500. There is no net profit in using tractors at all!

Equimarginal returns   Actually things will work out in less dramatic fashion than this. As tractor prices rise (and as the marginal productivity of tractors falls, owing to their more intensive use), the profit advantage between tractors and land will narrow. At a certain point, land will be just as attractive to farmers as tractors. Thereafter, since both land and tractors are still better buys than labor, the price of *both* land and tractors will continue to rise. Again as a result, the profit difference between them and labor will narrow until the same profit will be derived from an equal expenditure on any of the three fac-

QUESTIONS

1. Suppose that you were about to open a small business—say a drugstore. What do you think would be the factors critical in determining the scale of your operation? Suppose it were a farm? A factory?

2. Once you had started the business, what consideration would be uppermost in your mind when you were deciding how much of the factors to hire? What is the cardinal rule you would have to bear in mind in deciding if a unit of a factor would or would not pay its way?

3. One thing that would affect your decision to hire or not to hire a factor would be the amount of physical increase in output it would yield. What is the generalization we make about the change in output associated with combining more and more of one factor with a fixed combination of others? Is this generalization based on behavior? State the law of variable proportions as carefully as you can.

4. What is meant by marginal productivity? What is its relation to average productivity? Suppose you were considering the increase in your drug sales that would result from adding square feet of space. Draw up a schedule showing that the addition of square footage (in units of 100 sq ft) would at first yield increasing returns (dollars of sales) and then diminishing returns.

5. Suppose that a manufacturer had the following information for a given plant and number of workers:

Number of machines	1	2	3	4	5	6	7	8
Total output (units)	100	250	450	600	710	750	775	780

What would be the marginal productivity of each successive machine? The average productivity from using additional machines? When would diminishing *marginal* productivity set in? Diminishing average productivity?

6. Why must we hold the other factors constant to derive the law of variable proportions?

7. Suppose that each machine in Question 5 cost $1,000 and that each unit of output sold for $10. How many machines would it be most profitable to hire? (Figure out the marginal revenue product and marginal cost for each machine added.)

8. What would be the most profitable number to have if the cost of the machine rose to $1,500? If the price per unit of sales fell to $9?

9. Suppose the manufacturer had the following alternatives. It would be possible to
   • spend $1,000 on a machine that would add 115 units to sales (each unit selling at $10)
   • spend $5,000 to hire a new worker who would increase output by 510 units
   • rent new space for $10,000 that would make possible an increase in output of 1,100 units
   How would one know which was the best factor to hire? Show that the manufacturer would begin by asking what the dollar return would be per dollar of cost for each factor. What is this in the case of the machine? The new worker? The land?

10. If one manufacturer in a competitive market adds to factor inputs, will that affect their price? What happens when all manufacturers bid for the same factor? In the example above, which factor will be bid for? What will happen to its price? To its marginal productivity? Which factor will then become the "best buy"? What will happen to *its* price? What will be the final outcome of the bidding?

The competitive firm in action

Once again let us become imaginary entrepreneurs. Since we are familiar with the firm's calculations in regard to buying factor services, let us extend our knowledge into a full appreciation of what the cost problem looks like to us.

Fixed and variable costs

We know that a firm's total costs must rise as it hires additional factors. Yet, as businesspeople, we can see that our total costs will not rise proportionally as fast as our additional factor costs, because some costs of production will not be affected by an increase in factor input. Real estate taxes, for example, will remain unchanged if we hire one person or 100—so long as we do not acquire additional land. We can assume that the depreciation cost of machinery will not be affected by additions to land or labor. Rent will be unchanged, unless the premises are expanded. The cost of electric light will not vary appreciably despite additions to labor or machinery. Neither will the salary of the president. Thus some costs, determined by legal contract or by usage or by the unchanging use of one factor, do not vary with output. We call these fixed costs.

In sharp contrast with fixed costs is another kind of cost that does vary directly with output. Here are many factor costs,

14

for generally we vary inputs of labor and capital (and sometimes land) every time we seek a new level of production. To increase output almost always requires the payment of more wages and the employment of more capital (if only in the form of inventories or goods in process) and sometimes the rental of more space. *All costs that vary with output are called variable costs.*

Unit costs   This significant division between fixed and variable costs also requires us to shift our view a little within the business enterprise. We have been mainly concerned with calculating the costs of *inputs* in relation to their marginal productivities. Now we must turn around and begin to think about costs in relation to *output*.

In particular, we have to learn to think in terms of *cost per unit of output*. As we have seen, when a manufacturer (or a farmer or a storekeeper) expands output, total costs usually rise because variable costs are going up. Total costs do not rise proportionally as fast as variable costs, because fixed costs are set. Since it is not easy to work with this upward rising curve of total costs, businesspeople and economists usually convert the figures for total cost into *unit costs*. They do this by dividing the total cost by the number of units of goods produced. This results, of course, in a figure for the *average cost per unit of output*. We shall see that this gives us a very useful way of figuring what happens to costs as output expands.

Fixed and variable costs per unit   There is certainly no difficulty in picturing what happens to fixed costs per unit of output as output rises. By definition, they must fall. Suppose a manufacturer has fixed costs (rent, certain indirect taxes, depreciation, and overhead) of $10,000 a

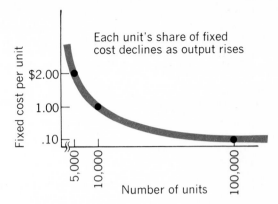

FIG. 14 · 1   Profile of fixed costs per unit

year. If 5,000 units of the product are produced per year, each unit will have to bear $2 of fixed cost as its share. If output rises to 10,000 units, the unit share of fixed costs will shrink to $1. At 100,000 units it would be a dime. Thus a curve of fixed costs per unit of output would look like Fig. 14 · 1.

What about variable costs per unit? Here the situation is more complex, for it depends directly on the analysis of the productivity curve we discussed in our last chapter. Hence, let us first set up a hypothetical schedule of output for our manufacturer (Table 14 · 1). As in the case of our farmer, once again we see the law of variable proportions at work. The total numbers of units produced will rise at first rapidly, then more slowly, with the addition of labor input to the plant.

Table 14 · 1

Number of men	Total output (thousand units)	Marginal product (thousand units)
1	5	5
2	13	8
3	23	10
4	32	9
5	39	7
6	44	5
7	47	3
8	49	2

Table 14 · 2

Number of men	Total variable cost @ $5,000 per man	Total output (units)	Average variable cost per unit of output (cost ÷ output)
1	$ 5,000	5,000	$1.00
2	10,000	13,000	.77
3	15,000	23,000	.65
4	20,000	32,000	.63
5	25,000	39,000	.64
6	30,000	44,000	.68
7	35,000	47,000	.74
8	40,000	49,000	.82

To convert this schedule of physical productivity into a unit cost figure, we must do two things:

1. Calculate total variable cost for each level of output.

2. Then divide the total variable cost by the number of units, to get average variable cost per unit of output.

Table 14 · 2 shows the figures (assuming that the going wage is $5,000).

Notice that average variable costs per unit decline at first and thereafter rise. The reason is by now clear enough. Variable cost increases by a set amount: $5,000 per man—as factors are added. Output, however, obeys the law of variable proportions, increasing rapidly at first and then displaying diminishing returns. It stands to reason, then, that the variable cost *per unit* of output will be falling as long as output is growing faster than costs, and that it will begin to rise as soon as additions to output start to get smaller.

If we graph the typical variable cost curve per unit of output, it will be the dish-shaped or U-shaped profile that Fig. 14 · 2 shows.

Total cost per unit

We can now set up a complete cost schedule for our enterprise by combining fixed and variable costs, as in Table 14 · 3. Notice how marginal costs begin to turn up *before* average costs.

If we graph the last two columns of

FIG. 14 · 2   Profile of changing variable costs per unit

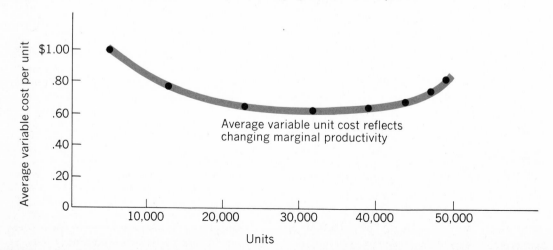

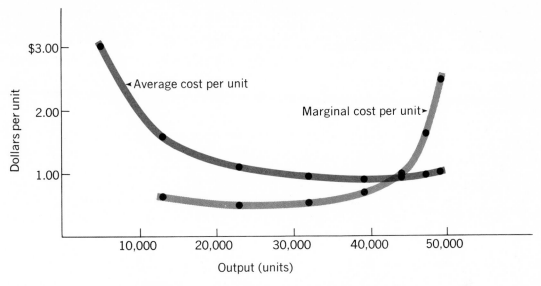

FIG. 14·3   Average and marginal cost per unit

figures—average and marginal cost per unit—we get the very important diagram in Fig. 14 · 3.

The cost profile   We have reached the end of our cost calculations, and it will help to take stock of what we have done. Actually, despite all the figures and diagrams, the procedure has been quite simple.

1. We began by seeing what would happen to our *fixed costs* per unit as we expanded output. Since fixed costs, by their nature, do not increase as production increases, the amount of fixed cost that had to be charged to each unit of output fell sharply as output rose.

2. Next we calculated the *variable costs* that would have to be borne by each unit as output increased. Here the critical process at work was the law of variable proportions. As

Table 14 · 3

Number of men	Total cost ($10,000 fixed cost + $5,000 per man)	Output (units)	COST PER UNIT OF OUTPUT Average (total cost ÷ output)		Marginal (changes in cost ÷ change in output)*	
1	$15,000	5,000	$3.00	Falling avg. cost	$	Falling marginal cost
2	20,000	13,000	1.54		.63	
3	25,000	23,000	1.09		.50	
4	30,000	32,000	.94		.55	
5	35,000	39,000	.90		.71	Rising marginal cost
6	40,000	44,000	.91	Rising avg. cost	1.00	
7	45,000	47,000	.96		1.67	
8	50,000	49,000	1.02		2.50	

*Ideally, we should like to show how marginal cost changes with *each* additional unit of output. Here our data show the change in costs associated with considerable jumps in output as we add each man. Hence we estimate the marginal cost per unit by taking the *change in total costs* and dividing this by the *change in total output.* The result is really an "average" marginal cost, since each individual item costs actually a tiny fraction less, or more, than its predecessor. We have shown the data this way since it is much closer to the way businessmen figure.

the marginal productivity of factors increased, variable cost per unit fell. When the inevitable stage of diminishing returns set in, variable costs per unit had to rise.

3. Adding together fixed and variable costs, we obtained the *total unit cost* of output. Like the variable cost curve, average total unit costs are dish-shaped, reflecting the changing marginal productivity of factors as output grows.

4. Finally, we show the changing *marginal cost per unit*—the increase in total costs divided by the increase in output. As before, it is the changing marginal costs that the entrepreneur actually experiences in altering output. It is the increase at the margin that alters total cost and therefore determines average cost.

Average and marginal costs

Actually, the cost profile that we have worked out would be known by any businessperson who had never studied microeconomics. Whenever a firm starts producing, its average cost per unit of output is very high. A General Motors plant turning out only a few hundred cars a year would have astronomical costs per automobile.

As output increases, unit costs come down steadily, partly because overhead (fixed costs) is now spread over more units, partly because the factors are used at much greater efficiency. Finally, after some point of maximum factor efficiency, average unit costs begin to mount. Even though overhead continues to decline, it is now so small a fraction of cost per unit that its further decline does not count for much, while the rising inefficiency of factors steadily pushes up variable cost per unit. If General Motors tries to jam through more cars than a plant is designed to produce, the cost per auto will again begin to soar.

So much for the *average* cost per unit. By directing our attention to the changes

that occur in total cost and total output every time we alter the number of factors we engage, the *marginal* cost curve per unit simply tells us why all this is happening. In other words, as our plant first moves into high gear, the cars we add to the line (the marginal output) will cost considerably less than the average of all cars processed previously. Later, when diminishing returns begin to work against us, we would expect the added (marginal) cars to be high-cost cars, higher in cost than the average of all cars built so far.

Since the cost of marginal output always "leads" the cost of average output in this way, we can understand an important relationship that all marginal and average cost curves bear to each other. The marginal cost curve always cuts the average cost curve at the lowest point of average cost.

Why? Because as long as the additional cars are cheaper than the average of all cars, their production must be *reducing* average cost; that is, as long as the marginal cost curve is lower than the average cost curve, the average cost curve must be falling. Conversely, as soon as additional output is more expensive than the average for all previous output, that additional production must *raise* average costs. Again (look at the previous diagram), as soon as marginal cost is above average cost, average cost must begin to rise. Hence it follows that the MC (marginal cost) curve must cross the AC (average cost) curve at the minimum point of average cost. This relationship has nothing to do with economics, as such, but with simple logic, as Fig. 14 • 4 may elucidate.*

---

*It follows that the marginal productivity curve always crosses the average productivity curve at its peak. Look at Fig. 13 • 1. As long as marginal productivity is *higher* than average productivity, the average curve must be *rising*. As soon as additional (marginal) output is *less than* the preceding average output, the lower marginal output must *diminish* the average. The relation is exactly that of Fig. 14 • 4, only upside down.

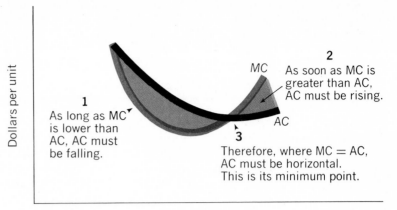

1 As long as MC is lower than AC, AC must be falling.

2 As soon as MC is greater than AC, AC must be rising.

3 Therefore, where MC = AC, AC must be horizontal. This is its minimum point.

MC   AC

Dollars per unit

Quantity

FIG. 14·4
Relation of marginal and average cost per unit

From cost to revenue

The cost profile gives us a clear picture of what happens to unit costs as our firm hires additional factors. But that is only half the information we need for understanding how a firm operates with one foot in the factor market and the other in the market for goods. Now we need a comparable profile of what happens to revenues as the firm sells the output its factors have made for it.

From supply to demand

This brings us over from supply to demand—from dealing with factors who are selling their services, back to householders who are buying goods. What the entrepreneur wants to know is whether "the market" will buy the firm's goods and if so, at just what price it will buy them. In other words, what is the demand curve for this particular output? From that, revenues can easily be figured.

What does the demand curve look like for a small competitive firm? Let us take the case of the manufacturer with whose costs we are now familiar, and assume that the "units" are simple metal stampings selling at the rate of several million each year. The manufacturer knows two things about the market for those stampings:

1. A going price for stampings (say $1.50) is established by the market.

2. The firm can sell all the stampings it can make at the going price without altering that price by so much as a penny. The market will not be affected whether the shop closes down entirely or whether it sells every last stamping it can afford to make at the price the market offers.

Between two horizontal curves

What our manufacturer knows in his bones, we can translate into economics. The price of any commodity is set in the goods market by the interplay of supply and demand. Our firm is one of the many suppliers whose willingness and ability to sell at different prices (largely determined by their costs) makes up the supply curve. The demand curve for the commodity is familiar to us as the expression of the consumers' willingness and ability to buy.

Now we can also see that as far as the output of any *one* small firm is concerned, the demand for *its* output is a horizontal line—that there is an "infinite" willingness to buy its product, provided it can be supplied at the going price. The output of any one seller, in other words, is too small to affect the equilibrium price for the market as a whole. Why, then, cannot an ambitious firm make an "infinite" profit by expanding its sales to match demand? The shape of its cost curve gives the answer. As factor productivity declines, marginal costs soon rise above selling price.

Thus the competitive firm operates between two horizontal curves. On the supply side it faces a perfectly elastic supply of factors, meaning that it can hire all the factors it wishes without changing prices an iota in the factor market. On the demand side it also faces a perfectly elastic curve, meaning that it can sell as much as it can produce without any perceptible price effect here, either. As a result, the firm is squeezed between two forces that it is powerless to change. It must therefore devote all its energies to those parts of the market process that are in its control: the efficient combining of factors to minimize its costs and the selection of the most profitable scale and line of output.

Average and marginal revenue

Facing a known demand curve, the manufacturer can now calculate his revenues. The firm will take in an amount determined by its total unit output multiplied by the price of each unit. And since, with a horizontal demand curve, the price of each unit will be exactly the same price as the previous one, the marginal revenue of each unit sold—that is, the additional amount it will bring it—will be unchanged no matter how much is sold by the firm. If the selling price is $1.50, then the marginal revenue per unit will be $1.50. As a result, average revenue per unit will also be $1.50. The schedules of revenue will look like Table 14 • 4. We can see that a graph of the average and marginal costs curves for this (or any) small, highly competitive firm would be horizontal, as in Fig. 14 • 5.

Table 14 • 4

Output (units)	Price per unit	Marginal revenue per unit	Total revenue	Average revenue per unit
5,000	$1.50	$1.50	$ 7,500	$1.50
10,000	1.50	1.50	15,000	1.50
20,000	1.50	1.50	30,000	1.50
40,000	1.50	1.50	60,000	1.50

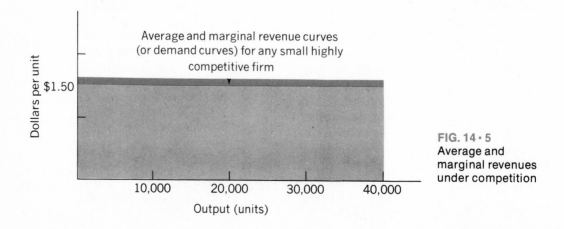

FIG. 14 • 5
Average and marginal revenues under competition

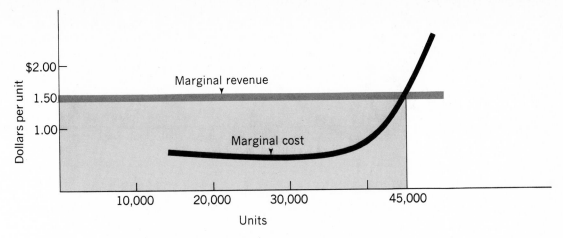

FIG. 14·6   The point of optimum output

Marginal revenue and marginal cost

Now we have all the information we want. We have a cost profile that tells us what happens to unit costs as we hire or fire factors. We have a revenue profile that tells us what happens to unit revenues as we do the same. It remains only to put the two together to discover just how much output the firm should make to maximize its profits.

We can do this very simply by superimposing the revenue diagram on top of the cost diagram. The point where the marginal revenue and the marginal cost curves meet should indicate exactly what the most profitable output will be. As we can see in Fig. 14·6, it is just about at 45,000 units.

Why is this the point of best possible output? Because another unit of output—as we can see by looking at the two curves—will cost more than it brings in, while a unit less of output would deprive us of the additional net revenue that another unit of output could bring.

Firm and market supply curves

Our discussion of the relation between the marginal cost and marginal revenue curves leads to a further insight. The marginal cost curve is the

firm's supply curve. Suppose price rises from P_1 to P_2 in Fig. 14·7. As far as the firm is concerned, it does not matter where its average cost is. What counts is whether additional production will be profitable. Further, it will be profitable only if the marginal cost of that additional production does not exceed marginal revenue.

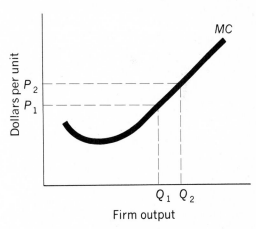

FIG. 14·7   The firm's supply curve

Therefore, when price rises, the firm's output increases from Q_1 to Q_2, a point determined by the intersection of the MC curve and the new price.

It follows that the supply curve of a competitive industry is the horizontal summation of the marginal cost curves of its firms, just as the market demand for

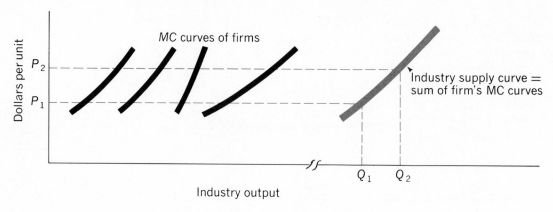

FIG. 14 · 8   The industry's supply curve

goods is the summation of the demands of individuals. We show such a market supply curve in Fig. 14 · 8, for simplicity's sake drawing only the rising portion of the *MC* curves.

The point we must bear in mind is more than just a geometrical demonstration. It is that marginal costs, not average costs, determine most production decisions. When prices rise or fall, the change in quantity will reflect the ease or difficulty of adding to, or diminishing, production, as that ease or difficulty is reflected in the shape of its *MC* schedule.

Profits

Now let us return to the firm producing the quantity of stampings that just equates marginal cost and marginal revenue. What

is the total amount of economic profit at the firm's best level of output? This is very difficult to tell from diagrams that show only marginal costs and marginal revenues. As we have just seen, these curves tell us how large *output* will be. But we must add another curve to enable us quickly to see what the *profit* will be at each level of output.

This is our familiar average cost curve. Average costs, we know, are nothing but total costs reduced to a per-unit basis. Average revenues are also on a per-unit basis. Hence, if we compare the average unit revenue and cost curves at any point, they will tell us at a glance what total revenues and costs look like at that point.

Figure 14 · 9 reveals what our situation is at the point of optimum output.

FIG. 14 · 9   The firm in equilibrium with profits

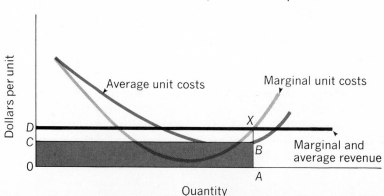

(This time we generalize the diagram rather than putting it into the specific terms of our illustrative firm.)

The diagram shows several things. First, as before, it indicates our most profitable output as the amount *OA* − the output indicated by the point *X*, where the marginal revenue and marginal cost curves meet. **Remember:** We use marginal costs and marginal revenues to determine the point of optimum output.

Second, it shows us that at output *OA*, our *average cost* is *OC* (= *AB*) and our *average revenue* is *OD* (= *AX*), the same as our marginal revenue, since the demand curve for the firm is horizontal. Our profit on the *average* unit of output must therefore be *CD* (= *BX*), the difference between average costs and average revenues at this point. The *total* profit is therefore the rectangle *CDXB*, which is the average profit per unit (*CD*) times the number of units. **Remember again: we use average costs and average revenues to calculate profits.**

Working out an example

We can translate this in terms of our firm. At the point where *MC* = *MR*, it is making about 45,000 stampings, as Fig. 14 • 6 shows, at an average cost that we will estimate at 92¢ per unit. (Table 14 • 3 does not show us the exact cost at 45,000 units, but we will assume it is 1¢ more than the 91¢ cost of making 44,000 units). Since the selling price is $1.50, we are now taking in a total of $1.50 × 45,000 units, or $67,500, while our total cost is 92¢ × 45,000 units or $41,400. Our profit is the difference between total revenues and total costs, or $26,100.

Note that at an output of 44,000 units our revenues would have been $1.50 × 44,000 or $66,000, and our total costs 91¢ × 44,000 or $40,040, with the result that our profit would have been slightly smaller

($25,960). If we sold a larger quantity, 46,000 units, at a cost of, say, 94¢ per unit, our revenues would have come to $69,000 and our costs to $43,240, with a profit of the difference, or $25,760, also less than the $26,100 we made at an output of 45,000 units. Thus, given our cost figures and our selling price, an output of 45,000 is the optimal level for our firm. It gives us the maximum economic profit obtainable.

However satisfactory from the point of view of the firm, this is not yet a satisfactory stopping point from the point of view of the system as a whole. If our firm is typical of the metal stamping industry, then small firms throughout this line of business are making profits comparable to ours. In other lines of endeavor, though, numerous businesses do not make $26,100 in economic profit. *Hence entrepreneurs in these lines will now begin to move into our profitable industry.*

Entry and exit

Perhaps we can anticipate what will now happen. Our firm is going to experience the same "mysterious" change in prices that we have already witnessed in the factor market, when many firms altered their demands for land or labor or capital, and the prices of these factor services changed accordingly. Only this time, it is the price of goods, not of factors, that will change, for the influx of entrepreneurs from other areas will move the industry supply curve to the right and thereby reduce the going price. As the going price falls, our own business will be powerless to stop a fall in the price for its goods. We can see the process in Fig. 14 • 10, on the following page.

How long will this influx of firms continue? Suppose that it continues until price falls *below* the average cost curve of our representative firm. Now its position looks like Fig. 14 • 11. Output will still be

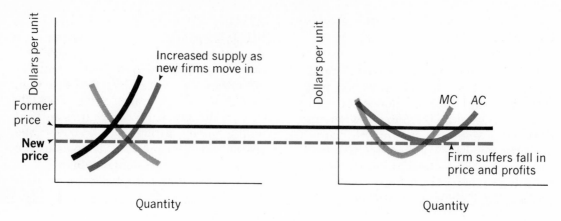

FIG. 14 · 10   The industry in adjustment to profits

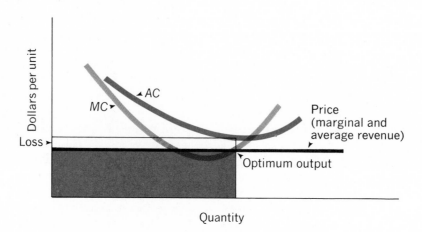

FIG. 14 · 11   The firm suffering a loss

FIG. 14 · 12   Industry adjustment to losses

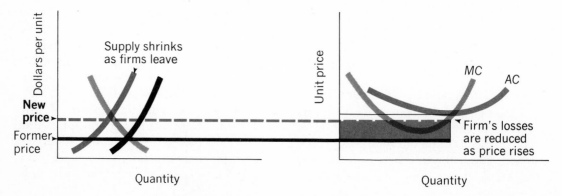

set where $MC = MR$ (it always is), but now the average cost curve is above the average revenue curve at this point. The unavoidable result is a loss for the firm, as the diagram shows.

What will happen? Clearly, we need a reverse adjustment process—an exodus of firms into greener pastures, so that the supply curve for our industry can move to the left, bringing higher prices for all producers. This may not be a rapid process. Eventually, the withdrawal of producers should bring about the necessary adjustment shown in Fig. 14 · 12.

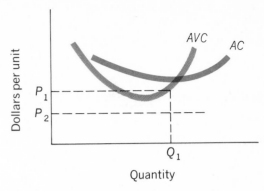

FIG. 14 · 13   Adjusting to losses

Minimizing losses

The process of minimizing losses (which is as close as an unfortunate entrepreneur can get to maximizing profits) is worth a careful look because it again illustrates the importance of marginal, rather than average, costs. Figure 14 · 13 reproduces the relevant aspects of our previous diagram, showing a firm whose selling price is below average cost. It produces quantity Q_1, where $MC = P_1$, and it clearly suffers losses because AC is higher than price.

Why does the firm not quit entirely? The answer is that a decision to quit would bring larger losses, not smaller ones, because fixed costs—depreciation, interest, certain taxes, etc.—must be paid even if production is cut to zero. Therefore, as long as price is as high as minimum average variable cost, a firm will continue to produce, although on a reduced scale, since each unit of output contributes something over and above variable cost to fixed cost.

Only if price falls below average variable cost (P_2 in Fig. 14 · 13) will the firm quit entirely. Now production does not even cover the direct variable costs to which it gives rise, much less contribute

anything to fixed cost. Therefore zero production is the way to minimize losses.

How long can a firm go on incurring losses? The answer depends on how rapidly it can terminate its fixed costs, such as getting rid of its buildings, machinery, etc., or how long it can incur losses without going bankrupt. The firm may limp along for an extended period, continuing to add production to the market and thereby delaying the leftward shift of the industry's supply curve.

Long-run equilibrium

Sooner or later, whether through the entry of new firms or the gradual withdrawal or disappearance of old ones, we reach a point of equilibrium both for the firm and the industry. It looks like Fig. 14 · 14, on the next page.

Note that this position of equilibrium has two characteristics.

1. Marginal cost equals marginal revenue, so there is no incentive for the individual entrepreneur to alter his own output.

2. Average cost equals average revenue (or price), so there is no incentive for firms to enter or leave the industry.

Thus we can state the condition for the equilibrium resting point of our firm and industry as being a four-way equality:

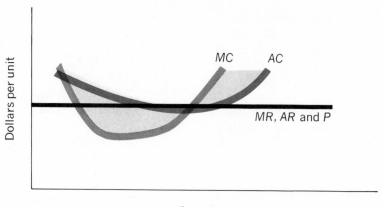

FIG. 14 • 14   The marginal firm in equilibrium with no profit

$$MC = MR = AC = P$$

| Marginal cost | = | Marginal revenue | = | Average cost | = | Price (average revenue) |

Profits and equilibrium

We have reached an equilibrium both for the firm and for the industry. It is certainly an uncomfortable one for ourselves as typical manufacturers; for in the final resting point of the firm, it is clear that *profits have been totally eliminated.* Is this a realistic assumption?

The question forces us again to confront the slippery question of what "profits" are. By definition, they are not returns to factors, for these payments have already been made by the firm—including all payments made to capitalists and entrepreneurs for the full value of their contribution to output.

To put it differently, we do not include in the term *profit* any revenues the firm *must* have to stay in business. An accountant, examining the books of a marginal firm in an industry, might find that there was a bookkeeping profit. An economist, looking at these revenues, would not call this sum a true *economic profit* if it were necessary to maintain the firm (or its entrepreneur) in operation. We

should note as well that profits are usually figured as a return on the capital invested in a firm, not as a return on each unit sold. It is simpler for our purposes, however (and it does no violence to the argument) to talk of profits in relation to output (= sales) rather than as a return on investment.

What are economic profits, then? There have been numerous attempts to define them as the return for risk or for innovation, and so on. However we describe them, we are driven to the conclusion that in a "perfect" competitive market, the forces of competition would indeed press toward zero the returns of the *marginal* firms in all industries, so that the cost and revenue profile of the last firms able to remain alive in each industry would look like our diagram.

Economic rents

Note, however, that these are marginal firms. Here is a clue to how profits can exist even in a highly competitive situation. In Fig. 14 • 15 we show the supply curve of an industry broken into the individual supply curves of its constituent firms. Some of these firms, for reasons that we will discuss below, will be lower-cost producers than others. When the industry equilibrium price is finally established, they will be the beneficiaries of the difference between the going price, which reduces the profits of the *marginal* firm to zero, and the lower unit costs attributable to their superior efficiency. Industry equilibrium leaves them in the enviable position of the firm shown in Figure 14 · 9.

These intramarginal profits are called economic rents or sometimes quasi rents or just plain rents. They are exactly the same thing as producers' surplus. More important, they are the only true economic profits that we find in competitive industries.

Sources of economic rents   Where do these economic rents arise? From several sources. One source may be personnel. Workers hired at the same wage are not always equally productive. A superior manager will recruit or organize a superior work force and gain rents as a result. Another source can be location. Not all prices adjust quickly to changed conditions. A retail store may enjoy a movement of population into its area. The value of its location increases, but its actual rental payments may not rise until a new lease is signed. An economic rent results. Third, just plain luck or the uncertainties of the business world constantly create positive or negative quasi rents. An entrepreneur goes into a business having calculated costs and revenues, then finds that costs have fallen or revenues risen, for reasons that could not be anticipated. Positive or negative economic rents—profits or losses—will ensue. Uncertainty is, in fact as well as in proverb, fundamental to life and a major source of the good or bad fortune that besets the best-laid plans of entrepreneurs.

Thus, economic profits enter the competitive world from changes in the economic setting, from random runs of good and bad luck, from unequal distributions of talent or resources. As a general rule, these sources of rent are ephemeral, and the normal, profit-seeking movement of the industry will erode and eventually erase them. Badly run firms will go out of business or hire a better manager. Badly located firms will pick up and move. Contracts will come to an end and be renegotiated to remove quasi rents. Movements of the marketplace that create positive rents one year will create negative ones the next. Luck evens out. Thus in the long run, we can expect a tendency in a competitive market to eliminate existing economic rents, although new ones may be created as conditions change.

FIG. 14 · 15   Economic rents

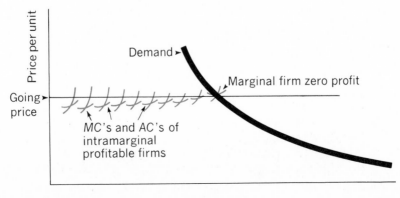

Long Run and Short Run

We have seen how the market makes it necessary for firms to produce goods at the lowest points along their average unit cost curves and to sell those goods at prices that will yield no profit to the least efficient firm in the industry. Yet there is one last adjustment process to consider. In all our investigations into the firm's operations, we have hitherto taken for granted that the *scale of output* would remain unchanged. As a result, all of our adjustments have involved us in moving back and forth along a cost curve that was basically set in place by one or more limiting factors.

This may be accurate enough in the short run, when most firms are circumscribed by a given size of plant, but it certainly does not describe the long run. For in the long run, all costs are variable. A firm can usually enlarge its scale of plant; and as the scale increases, it is often possible to realize additional savings in cost, as a result of still finer specialization of the production process. If our expanding firm confines its growth to a single plant, the cost curves of these successive scales of output are apt to look like Fig. 14 • 16.

Economies of scale   The decision to move from a plant of a given scale to the next largest size is a complex one. If we imagine a firm choosing among a very large number of "blueprints," we could picture its long-run average cost profile in

FIG. 14 • 16   Long-run cost curve

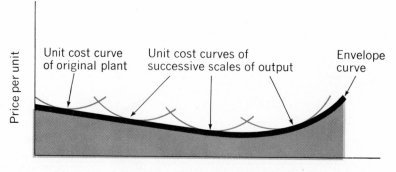

Price per unit

Unit cost curve of original plant

Unit cost curves of successive scales of output

Envelope curve

Quantity

terms of the envelope curve we have indicated in Fig. 14·16. We have explained that this long-run average unit cost curve (or envelope curve) initially slopes downward, owing to *economies of scale.*

Our diagram shows, however, that economies of scale do not go on forever. At some point—again determined by technology—the limits of efficient plant operation are reached. A sprawling enterprise begins to stretch too thin the coordinating powers of management. *Diseconomies of scale* enter, and the long-run unit cost curve again begins to mount.

Note, however, that these long-run cost curves apply to individual *plants.* What about a firm that pushes each plant to its optimum size and then adds a new plant, or a firm that diversifies its efforts among many different kinds of businesses, like the conglomerates? Does it also face a long-run, upward sloping cost curve, owing perhaps to eventual diseconomies of management? We really do not know the answer. To hazard an unsubstantiated guess, it may well be that the new technology of information retrieval has so increased the efficiency of management that the economically effective size of multiplants or diversified plants is today extremely large. For all practical purposes, the long-run cost curve is probably horizontal or perhaps even falling.

Increasing or decreasing long-run costs

There is still, however, another situation that can alter our firm's long-run costs. Together with all of its competitors it may be subject to *increasing or decreasing costs for the industry as a whole.*

The sources of these changes in cost do not lie within the firm, in the relative efficiency of various factor mixes. Rather, they are changes thrust upon the firm, for better or worse, by the interaction of the growing industry of which it is a part and the economy as a whole. A new industry, by its very expansion may bring into being satellite firms that provide some of its necessary inputs; and as the main new industry grows, the satellites also expand and thereby realize economies of scale that will benefit the main industry itself. The automobile industry was surely an instance of such long-run falling costs (for a long period, at least) resulting from the economies of scale enjoyed by makers of tires, batteries, and other equipment. In turn, the rise of low-cost trucking brought other such "external" economies to many other industries.

Industries may also experience long-run rising costs if their expansion pushes them up against factor scarcity of a stubbornly inelastic kind. Extractive industries may be forced to use progressively less-accessible mineral deposits, or agricultural industries may be forced to use progressively less-fertile or less-conveniently-located land. Such industries would experience a gradual rise in unit costs as their output increased.

Are most industries the beneficiaries of decreasing cost or the victims of increasing cost? Empirical studies seem to suggest that save for youthful, growing industries, and for the special case of extractive ones, most industries enjoy a middle position of roughly constant long-run unit costs, at least over a considerable period of time.

Focus   Just as in our previous chapter, the best way to master the ideas of this one is to work out some examples. Taking the time to answer the questions from 1 to 11 will show you whether you have grasped the central points of the chapter. In fact, we don't know any way to learn the very important relations of fixed and variable costs, or total costs and revenues, other than taking the time to work the examples through. The ideas are not hard, but the calculations are laborious, and it is easy to make mistakes in them.

Here is where graphing helps. You should be able to draw an accurate graph showing that an *MC* curve cuts an *AC* curve at its lowest point, and you should be able to explain why. (See discussion under the head "Average and marginal costs.") You should be able to draw an accurate graphic representation of a firm in equilibrium that also makes profits, and you should be able to do the same for a firm incurring losses and a firm that is just breaking even. There is a tendency to draw lines carelessly—not touching where they should touch, crossing at the wrong places, etc. That carelessness often means that you do not really understand why the lines touch or cross as they do. In addition, your carelessness will prevent your instructor from seeing that you understand. So graph slowly and accurately.

The most important *idea* here is that of intramarginal profits, or quasi rents, or producers' surplus. The words all mean the same thing: true economic profit, or profit that cannot be explained as the return to capital or land. When we study monopolies, we will see that their profits can easily be explained by the "scarcity" that monopoly creates. In a competitive industry, by definition no such scarcity can exist. There cannot be "monopoly" profits in the marginal firms. Indeed, the only way that economic profits can find their way into a competitive industry is from intramarginal advantages. These may not last indefinitely; in fact, there is a tendency for such profits to be eroded by the natural movement of firms and factors. But for a time they can exist, giving rise to profits within an industry that is profitless at the margin.

WORDS AND CONCEPTS YOU SHOULD KNOW

Unit costs, 183
Fixed vs. variable cost, 182–83
Average vs. marginal costs per unit, 186
Average vs. marginal revenue per unit, 188
U-shaped total unit cost curve, 185–86
MC=AC=MR=P, 194

Entry and exit, 191, 193
Economic (or quasi) rents, 194–95
Intramarginal profits, 194–95
Economies of scale, 196–97
Increasing or decreasing long-run unit costs, 197

QUESTIONS

1. If you were a retail grocer, what kinds of costs would be fixed for you? If you were a manufacturer who owned a large computer, would its maintenance be a fixed cost? If you *rented* the computer, would it be?

2. Assume that your fixed costs are $500 a week and that your output can vary from 100 to 1,000 units, given the scale of your enterprise. Graph what happens to fixed costs per unit.

3. Assume that your plant hires 6 workers successively, and that output changes as follows:

Number of workers	1	2	3	4	5	6
Total units of output per week	100	300	550	700	750	800

What is the marginal product of each worker? If each worker costs you $100 per week, what is the variable cost per unit as you add personnel?

4. If you add fixed costs of $500 per week to the variable cost you have just ascertained, what is the average cost per unit? What is the marginal cost per unit? (Remember, this is figured by dividing the *change in total cost by the change in total output.*)

5. Graph the curve of average total unit costs and marginal unit costs. Why does the marginal unit cost curve cross the average unit cost curve at its lowest point?

6. What does average revenue mean and what is its relation to price? What is meant by marginal revenue? Why is marginal revenue the same as average revenue for a competitive firm?

7. Explain carefully why a competitive firm operates between two horizontal curves, one on the demand side and one on the factor supply side.

8. Suppose (in the example above) you sell the output of your firm at $1.35 per unit. Draw in such a marginal revenue curve. Now very carefully indicate where the *MR* and *MC* curves meet. Show on the diagram the output corresponding to this point. What is the approximate average cost at this output? Is there a profit here? Indicate by letters the rectangle that shows the profit per unit of output and the number of units.

9. What will be the result, in a competitive industry, of such a profit? Draw a diagram showing how an influx of firms can change the ruling market price. Will it be higher or lower?

10. Draw a diagram showing how price could drop below the lowest point on the average total unit cost curve, and indicate the loss the firm would suffer. Explain, by means of a diagram, why a manufacturer may remain in business even though the firm cannot sell its output for the full cost of producing it. What will determine whether or not it is worth its while to quit entirely?

11. Carefully draw a diagram showing the equilibrium position for the firm. Explain how *MR* and *MC* are all the firm is concerned with. How do *AR* and *AC* enter the picture? Why do *MR* and *MC*, by themselves, fail to give an equilibrium price in a competitive industry?

12. Suppose that you are a druggist and you know that the least efficient druggist in town makes virtually no profit at all. Assuming that you both sell in the same market, at the same prices, and that you hire factors at the same prices also, what causes could bring about a profit to your enterprise? What would you expect to be the trend of these profits?

13. Would you expect economies of scale from greatly enlarging your drugstore? Why or why not?

14. Do you think as the entire drugstore business expands it enjoys external economies or suffers from external diseconomies? How about the goldmining business?

R & D in competitive industries

Competitive industries face a problem of great consequence: a relative lack of research and development in their fields. Worse, they face the problem because they *are* competitive. It does not pay most firms to invest in R&D, because every discovery will be quickly made available to all others. Even patent rights do not overcome this difficulty. Patents are seldom effective in preventing others from using a similar process or making a similar product. It is virtually impossible to surround a new invention with so many patents that competition is effectively ruled out, and it is very expensive to try to do so. Moreover, even if it were possible for a competitive firm to assure itself of all rewards from a patent, does this make sense from the social point of view? Such a patent would create a monopoly, displacing competition.

The problem of R&D is pertinent because we use the model of a competitive industry as a benchmark of efficiency. Yet, an industry that cannot generate research will not be efficient over time, even though it may avoid waste at some time. Inefficiency is probable because the firm cannot generate technical advances that are at the heart of economic growth. When we think of low-productivity, "backward" industries, we name highly competitive ones: cotton textiles, coal mining, service industries such as hotels, restaurants, barbershops.

Is there a solution to this problem? There is food for thought in considering the case of the industry with the highest rate of productivity growth since World War II. This is agriculture, the very epitome of a competitive industry! How did farming give rise to such vast advances, when no farmer—for the reasons that we have cited—could invest in significant R&D expenditures? The answer is that agriculture was the beneficiary of R&D carried out for it by two other sectors.

One of these was the big makers of farm equipment, where extensive research and development greatly improved the machines used on the farm. Even more helpful was the R&D carried out by the government. The federal government sponsors a substantial volume of agricultural research in the nation's land grant schools of agriculture. Here new seeds, new processes and products have been developed and tested, then disseminated by agricultural experiment stations and agricultural extension agents to the nation's farmers. In fact, this is a socially financed R&D program, in which the taxpayer foots the bill, then reaps the benefits through improved products. None of the gains become "monopoly" profits, as they would if the R&D resulted in privately owned, effectively defended patents.

Can the agriculture R&D system be extended to other competitive industries? Perhaps. The Bureau of Mines already works to improve general productivity, as it does to improve general safety. Big industries are clearly interested in developing machines to sell to laggard competitive businesses. Today we see fancy computerized cash registers on the counters of small grocery stores, centralized billing systems for small retail establishments, revolving clothes racks for dry cleaners. Moreover, in many of the high-competition industries a few big producers have emerged who *do* carry on R&D. Even if their R&D cannot be patented, it cannot be duplicated by the competition because it requires too much capital.

So competitive industries are not static. Nonetheless, the degree of innovation and technical change that competitive industries exhibit differs markedly from the rapid pace of change in more concentrated, big-business sectors. As we see in our next "Extra word," this backwardness constitutes a major argument against applying antitrust laws to break monopolistic industries into competitive ones.

The real world of imperfect competition

Now we must ask a question that has surely occurred to the reader. Does the world really behave as microtheory has portrayed it? Do firms really equate marginal costs and revenues or balance the advantages of one factor versus another with the fine precision that our model has indicated?

We already know one condition that must be fulfilled if firms are to behave as we have pictured them. This is the condition of "pure" competition, the environment we take for granted during our theoretical microeconomic investigations. Now is the time to look carefully into exactly what the term means.

Pure competition defined

In general, when economists use the term *pure competition*, they imply three necessary attributes of the market situation:

1. Large numbers of marketers

Unless there are numerous buyers and sellers facing one another across the market and jostling one another on each side of it, the competitive process will not fully work itself out. When the number of marketers is few (whether as buyers or sellers), the vying among them that gives

15

201

competition its resistless force is apt to be muted or even lacking entirely. As the extreme case of this we have outright *collusion* (a few buyers or sellers agree to bid at only one low price or to offer at only one high price). Even when collusion is absent, fewness of buyers or sellers will lead, as we shall see in our next chapter, to results that are considerably at variance with those of the competitive process we have assumed.

How many buyers or sellers does it take to make a fully competitive market? There is no clear-cut answer. The critical number is reached when no firm, by varying its scale of output, is able to affect the price of the factors it buys or the product it sells. We have pictured this condition in terms of the horizontal factor supply and market demand curves that present the purely competitive firm with the unalterable data of factor and goods prices to which it must accommodate itself. **Thus under conditions of pure competition, the only thing the firm can control is its scale of output and the mix of factors it uses. All prices are beyond its power to influence.**

2. Ease of entry into, and exit from, industries

A second prerequisite for so-called pure competition is a condition that we have already relied upon frequently in discussing the operation of the market. **This is the ability of firms and factors to move freely and easily from one industry to another in search of the highest possible return.** Only in this way can supply and demand schedules move rightward and leftward, bringing about the needed adjustments of quantities and prices.

We have seen as well that this is by no means an easy set of conditions to achieve. With firms, as previously with factors, it rules out all legal barriers to interindustry

movement, such as restrictive patents. Beyond this it implies that if the initial scale of manufacture is very large, industry cannot be considered as meeting the requirements for pure competition. In automobile or steel manufacturing, for example, the minimum size of plant entails an investment of millions of dollars. The degree of competitive pressure from "outside" entrepreneurs, therefore, is obviously much less than in the stationery store business, where a newcomer can enter for an investment of a few thousand dollars.

Ease of exit is a no less necessary and equally demanding requirement. The competitive process will not shift about supply curves if some producers cannot withdraw their investments in land or capital and move them to alternative uses. Yet, as we have seen, this inability to move out can indeed retard adjustments of supply, particularly in industries with large fixed investments that are highly "specific" in their use. Such industries may go on producing even if they cannot cover their full costs, as long as their revenues bring in enough to nibble away at fixed expenses (see p. 193). Thus the problems of securing easy entry and exit further restrict the environment of pure competition to industries requiring no large or technically specific investments.

3. Nondifferentiated goods

Even these strict conditions still do not define the state of competition we have implicitly assumed. It is possible for a market to consist of many small buyers and sellers, each operating with relatively simple equipment. Yet these firms may not compete fully against one another. This is the case when each firm sells a product that is *differentiated* (or distinguishable) from that of its competitors. If there is a difference, however slight, between one firm's product and another's, the demand curve for the product of each will be sloping rather than horizontal, even if the slope is very small. As a result, product differentiation will enable a seller to hold onto *some* trade even if the product's price is a trifle higher than the competitor's; whereas in a purely competitive market where goods and services are indistinguishable from one another, no marketer can depart in the slightest degree from the prevailing price.

In some markets, perfectly anonymous undifferentiated commodities are sold. In the market for grain or for coal, no seller can ask even a penny more than the going price for his product. In the great bulk of retail and wholesale markets, however, such totally undifferentiated products are the exception rather than the rule.

Why must commodities be exactly alike for a state of pure competition to exist? **The answer is that only identical commodities compete solely on the basis of price.** Much of what we call "competition" in the impure markets of the real world consists in differentiating products through style, design, services, etc., so that they will *not* have to compete just on price. We shall look into this very common case of "imperfect competition" later in this chapter. But we must rule it out as a permissible form of competition to bring about the exact results of our market analysis thus far. The essential rule for a purely competitive market is that the word "competition" must mean *price competition only.*

Competition in the real world   Obviously, pure competition is an extremely demanding state of affairs. It requires numerous small firms selling identical products in a highly mobile and fluid environment. Hence the search for perfect examples of pure competition is apt to end with very few cases. Why, then, do we spend so much time analyzing it?

The answer is twofold. In part it lies in the fact that as much as 40 or 50 percent of the output of the nation comes from sectors that *resemble*—even though they do not exactly qualify for—pure competition. The service trades, the wholesale markets, much retailing, some raw material production are near enough to being "pure" in their competitive structures, so that we can apply the reasoning of price theory very closely in understanding the market results we see in those industries.

The second reason is that even in those sectors or industries where pure competition obviously does not apply, the mechanism of the competitive firm will still be applicable. Supply and demand, factor productivities, marginal revenue and marginal cost will continue to be the prevailing guidelines. Hence we must understand the basic workings of the small firm, because most of them will still apply. Unless we know to what results these workings lead us in the ideal environment of pure competition, we will hardly be in a position to know what a difference monopoly or oligopoly makes to the workings of the market system.

Monopoly

Monopoly (and nowadays oligopoly) are bad words to most people, just as competition is a good word, although not everyone can specify exactly what is good or bad about them. Often we get the impression that the aims of the monopolist are evil and grasping, while those of the competitor are wholesome and altruistic. Therefore, the essential difference between a world of pure competition and one of very impure competition is one of motives and drives— of well-meaning competitors and ill-intentioned monopolists.

Motives and markets

The truth is that exactly the same motives drive the monopoly and the competitive firm. Both seek to maximize their profits. Indeed, the competitive firm, faced with the necessity of watching costs and revenues in order to survive, is apt to be, if anything, more pennypinching and more intensely profit-oriented than the monopolist who (as we shall see) can afford to take a less hungry attitude toward profits. The lesson to be learned—and to remember—is that motives have nothing to do with the problem of less-than-pure competition. **The difference between a monopoly, an oligopoly, and a situation of pure competition is entirely one of market structure; that is, of the number of firms, ease of entry or exit, and the degree of differentiation among their goods.**

Price takers vs. price searchers

We have noted a very precise distinction between the competitive situation (numerous firms, undifferentiated goods) and markets with few sellers or highly differentiated goods. In the competitive case, as we have seen, each firm caters to so small a section of the market that the demand curve for its product is, for all intents and purposes, horizontal. By way of contrast, in a monopolistic or oligopolistic market structure there are so few firms that each one faces a downward sloping demand curve. Each monopoly firm, in fact, faces the demand curve of its own industry. That means that each firm, by varying its output, can affect the price of its product.

Another way of describing this difference is to call purely competitive firms, who have no control over their price, *price-takers* and to label monopolies or oligopolies or any firm that can affect the price of its product, *price-searchers*.

"Pure" monopolies

By examining the economic problems faced by a "pure" monopoly, let us see how such a price-searcher operates. Why do we place the word "pure" in quotes? Because monopoly is not as easy to define as one might think. Essentially, the word means that there is only *one* seller of a particular good or service. The trouble comes in defining the "particular" good or service. In a sense, any seller of a differentiated good is a monopolist, for no one else dispenses *quite* the same utilities as he does. Each shoe-shine boy has his "own" customers, some of whom would probably continue to patronize his stand even if he charged slightly more than his competition.

Thus at one end of the difficulty is the fact that there is an element of monopoly

---

How do we recognize a monopoly? Because of the problem of substitutes, there is no very clear sign, except in a few cases such as the "natural" monopolies. Usually when we speak of monopolies we mean (a) very large businesses with (b) much higher than competitive profits and (c) relatively little direct product competition. Not many firms satisfy all three conditions. Exxon or GM is a monopoly by criteria a and b, but not by c; Polaroid by b and c but not a. Note, furthermore, that even small businesses can be monopolies, as "the

HOW MONOPOLISTIC IS A MONOPOLY?—

only gambling house in town" famed in all Westerns.

An interesting case in point is the telephone company. Most people assume that A.T.&T. is a monopoly, if ever there was one. Yet in fact, although the Bell Telephone system provides 82 percent of all telephone service in the country, there are actually 1800 telephone companies, quite independent of the Bell System.

nesses can be monopolies, as "the

in many seemingly competitive goods, a complication we shall come back to later. At the other end of the problem there are so-called "natural" monopolies, where economies of scale lead to one seller supplying the whole market, such as a local utility company. Yet even here there are substitutes. If power rates become exhorbitant, we *could* switch from electric light to candlelight. Hence, before we can draw conclusions from the mere fact that a company provides the "only" service of its kind, we need to know how easy or difficult it would be to find substitutes, however imperfect, for its output.

Limits of monopoly

Evidently the problem of defining a "pure" monopoly is not easily resolved. Let us, however, agree to call the local power company a monopoly, because no one else sells gas and electricity to the community. In Fig. 15·1 we show what the demand curve of such a monopoly looks like.

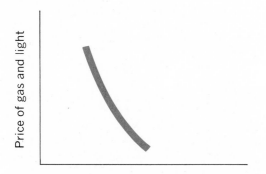

FIG. 15·1   Demand curve for a monopoly

One point is immediately clear. **The monopolistic firm faces the same kind of demand curve that the competitive industry faces.** That is so because both cater to *all* the demand for that particular product. A corollary follows. The demand

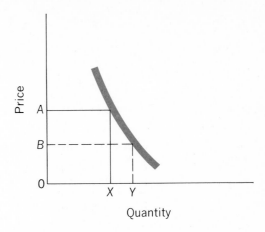

FIG. 15·2   Demand curve as a constraint on the monopolist

curve itself imposes a fundamental limitation of the monopolist's power to control the market. Suppose a monopoly is selling quantity *OX* at price *OA* as shown in Fig. 15·2. The firm would prefer to sell quantity *OY* at price *OA*, but there is no way of forcing the market to take a larger quantity of its product—unless it lowers the price to *OB.**

The situation is very similar (on the seller's side) to a *union*. A union can raise the price of labor, since it controls the supply of labor, but it cannot force employers to hire more labor than they want. Hence the question "Can unions raise wages?" must be answered "Yes," insofar as those who continue to be hired are concerned. But until we know the elasticity of the demand for labor, we cannot say if unions can raise the total amount of labor's revenues.

*What would be the *most* profitable course for a monopolist to follow? It would be to act as a "discriminating" monopolist, selling output at *varying* prices, depending on how much each buyer was willing and able to pay. (One could imagine a discriminating monopolist doling out the product this way at an auction). In fact, it amounts to a transfer of *all* consumers' surplus to the producer! Why are not monopolists discriminating pricers? (1) In some industries it is illegal. (2) It is extremely difficult to carry out. This is because buyers can trade among themselves, setting up a "secondhand" market that will compete with the monopolist. Nevertheless, discriminatory pricing is not uncommon in certain fields: antiques, used cars, pawnshops—and perhaps some professional fees.

We will study this question again in Chapter 19.

There is one thing a monopoly can do, however, that neither a union nor a purely competitive firm can. A monopoly can advertise and thereby seek to move to the right, or change the slope of, the demand curve for its product. Advertising does not "pay" in a purely competitive firm selling undifferentiated goods, for such a firm has no way of being sure that *its* goods—and not a competitor's—will benefit. But advertising *can* be profitable for a monopoly that will get all the demand it can conjure up. We can think of advertising as an attempt to sell larger quantities of a good or service without reducing prices, by shifting the demand curve itself. Figure 15·3 shows us this important effect, and we will talk about it further in a moment.

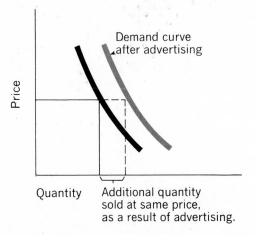

Demand curve after advertising

Price

Quantity   Additional quantity sold at same price, as a result of advertising.

FIG. 15·3   Advertising and demand

Cost curves for the monopolist

We have seen in what way the shape of the demand curves faced by monopolists differ from those faced by competitive firms. Are cost curves similarly different?

In general, they are not. We can take the cost profile of a monopoly as being essentially like that of a competitive firm. The monopoly, like the competitive firm, buys factors and exerts no control over their prices. A.T.&T. does not affect the level of wages or the price of land or capital by its decisions to expand production or not.* The monopolist, like the competitive entrepreneur, experiences the effects of changing productivity as he hires additional factors and, again like the competitive firm, shops for the best buy in the factor markets. Thus the same U-shaped average cost curve and the same more steeply sloped marginal cost curve will describe the cost changes experienced by a monopolist quite as well as those of a competitive firm.

Selling costs

There is, however, one item of cost for a monopolist (or as we shall later see, for any seller in an imperfectly competitive market) that does not arise in a milieu of pure competition. This is the need to incur *selling cost*, in an effort to affect the position or the shape of the demand curve. Advertising, a sales and service force, or the cost of product design are all important elements in the total cost picture of many businesses that sell differentiated products.

Selling costs are a prime concern in the *strategy* of firms. But they do not change the basic configuration of *MR* and *MC* curves, nor the imperative rule that the road to profit maximization is to bring *MC* equal to *MR*.

---

*There is a special situation with only one *buyer*—a "monopsony." A large employer who is the only substantial buyer of labor in a small town may be a monopsonist, whose decisions to hire labor or land or capital *will* affect their prices. For the monopsonist, the marginal cost curve is affected not only by the changing productivity of a factor but by its rising price, as more and more of the factor is hired. Because this is a situation infrequently found in the marketplace, we shall not analyze it further here. The principles involved are in no way different from those of monopoly.

From Cost to Revenue

Monopoly revenues   It is when we come to the revenue side of the picture that we meet the critical distinction of monopoly. Unlike a competitive firm, *a monopoly has a marginal revenue curve that is different from its average revenue curve.* The difference arises because each time a monopoly sells more output, it must reduce the price, not on just the last unit sold, but on *all* units, whereas a competitive firm sells its larger output at the same price. Therefore, as the monopoly's sales increase, its *marginal* revenues will fall.

A table may make this clear. Let us suppose we have a monopoly that is faced with an average revenue or price schedule as in Table 15·1.

Table 15·1

Quantity sold	Price	Total revenue	Marginal revenue
1	$20	$20	$20
2	19	38	18
3	18	54	16
4	17	68	14
5	16	80	12
6	15	90	10

The graph of such a marginal revenue curve looks like Fig. 15·4. Note that at an output of 6 units, AR (price) = $15; MR = $10.

What determines the shape of the marginal revenue curve? Obviously, the change in quantity demanded that will be brought about by a drop in price. In turn, this reflects—as we remember from our discussion in Chapter 12—the elasticity of demand which, in turn, hinges on our tastes and the availability of substitutes.

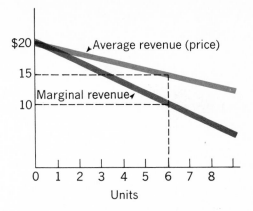

FIG. 15·4   Average and marginal revenue for a monopolist

Note especially that the MR curve lies below the AR curve because the monopolist must lower prices on *all* units sold, not on just the marginal unit. Thus each additional item "drags down" the revenue of all output.*

Equilibrium for the monopoly   The next step is obvious. We must superimpose the cost and the revenue profiles to determine the equilibrium position for the monopolist. We can see it in Fig. 15·5.

What will be the equilibrium position? The monopoly seeking to maximize profit is guided by exactly the same rule as the competitive firm: it adds factors so long as the marginal revenue they bring in is greater than their marginal cost. Hence we look for the intersection of the MC and MR curves on Fig. 15·5 to discover its optimum output, as the graph shows.

And what will the profit be? As before, profit reflects the spread of *average* cost and *average* revenue. The intersection of the MC and MR curves determines what

*A discriminating monopolist, who sells output at *different* prices, will work down the demand curve, selling each unit at a lower price but not lowering the price of earlier units. In this special case, price and marginal revenue will be identical. (See footnote, p. 205.)

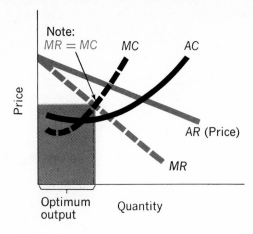

FIG. 15·5 Equilibrium for the monopolist

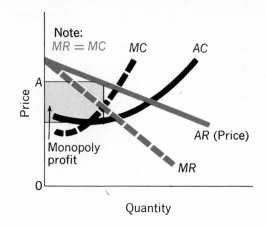

FIG. 15·6 Monopoly profit

our output will be. Knowing that, we can tell what our average cost and price (or average revenue) will be. Hence we can easily block in the profit of the enterprise. We do this in Fig. 15·6.

Monopoly vs. competitive prices

What is the difference between this price and that of a purely competitive market? We remember the formula for the equilibrium price of such a market: $MC = MR = AC = $ Price. In the monopoly situation, MC still equals MR (this is always the profit-maximizing guide), but price certainly does not equal AC. Whereas the competitive firm is forced to price its goods at the lowest point on its cost curve, the monopolist will sell at a price above cost. Then, too, there is no pressure from "outside" forcing the monopoly to reduce costs. Hence its entire cost curve may well lie above that of a competitive industry producing the same product. It is interesting to note that when hard pressed, some big auto firms (not even monopolies) have reduced overhead expenses by as much as a third. But most of the time, monopolies are not hard pressed.

If this were the case in a competitive market, we know what the remedy would be. An influx of firms would move the sup-

ply curve to the right. As a result, prices would fall until excess profits had been wiped out. **But in a monopoly situation, by the very definition of a monopoly, there is no entry into the market.** Hence the monopoly is able to restrict its output to the amount that will bring in the high profit it enjoys.

Regulating monopolies

Most "natural" monopolies, such as the utility companies, are regulated by public authorities. By imposing price ceilings on these monopolies, the regulating commissions seek to approximate the results of a competitive environment. As Fig. 15·7 shows, its MR will be

FIG. 15·7 Regulation of monopoly

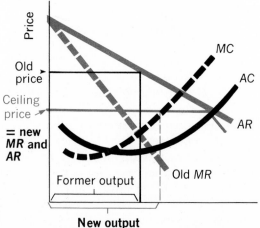

horizontal along the price ceiling, just like that of a competitive firm, and therefore its output will expand beyond the level of an unregulated monopoly.

Problems of regulation
The problem of regulation, however, is not quite so simple as our diagram would make it seem. Two issues in particular deserve to be mentioned.

The first is that most regulating commissions, such as those that set prices of telephone calls or gas and electric or water bills allow the regulated industry to make a "fair" profit on its capital. The hot issues arise when the value of this capital is calculated. Is it the *original* value of the capital invested in the business or the value of that equipment (which may be 10 or 20 years old) *if it had to be replaced today?* When present-day "replacement" prices are as much as 100 percent higher than those of the original equipment, we can see that it makes a huge difference on which base a regulatory commission figures a company's rates.

The second issue is the relation between the regulators and the regulated, an issue we looked into in Chapter 4. There is widespread feeling that regulat-ing agencies have been lax, and more often than not, sympathetic to the interests of the industry rather than its customers. One study has even shown that the presence or absence of regulatory commissions in different states seemed to make no difference at all to the structure of electric utility rates! Thus, the regulation of monopoly takes us rapidly from the relatively well-illumined territory of economics into the more shadowy terrain of politics. Many economists agree that regulation is the best "cure" for the evils of monopoly, but what is the best cure for the evils of regulation?

Oligopoly

Monopoly in its pure form is a rarity, and unregulated monopoly rarer still, Most big corporations operate in a market structure of oligopoly, rather than monopoly. In an oligopolistic market situation, a few sellers divide the bulk of the market, sometimes with a long tail of smaller competitors who share the leftovers.

The automobile industry is a proto-typical oligopoly. In 1972 there were 165 manufacturers of "motor vehicles and car bodies" in the United States, but the four biggest companies shared 93 percent of

---

CONCENTRATION RATIOS: WHAT IS AN INDUSTRY?

Economists generally measure the degree of concentration by comparing the ratio of total sales or total assets of the top 4 or the top 8 companies to the total sales or assets of their industry. But immediately we encounter the difficult problem of defining *industry.* For example, the top 4 companies make 81 percent of a commodity for which there is really no adequate substitute: salt. Yet if we put salt into an industrial classification called "chemical preparations not elsewhere specified," the share of the top 4 companies falls to a paltry 23 percent of the output of that larger group of products.

Take another example. A housewife shopping for salad dressing is a consumer in an "industry" in which the top 4 producers sell 57 percent of the product. If she thinks of herself as a consumer browsing in an industry called "pickles and sauces," the top 4 salad dressing makers' share of output is only 29 percent. So, too, a farmer, looking for a tractor is buying in a "market" in which the top 4 companies make 72 percent of the total output; but if we think of a tractor as belonging to a larger industry called "farm machinery and equipment," the share of the top 4 is only 44 percent.

How *should* we draw lines around industries or products? One way is by measuring how much the sales of product A increase if the price of product B rises. Here is the idea of substitution (p. 156) applied to an important problem of economic policy. We call the measure of interproduct influence *the cross-elasticity of substitution.* If a rise in the price of A leads *many* customers to switch to B, there is at least a prima facie case for drawing the line of the industry to include both. Of course, the argument then arises as to how many consumers it takes to make "many" of them.

the market. The 8 biggest shared 99 percent of the market. There were 136 companies making tires and inner tubes in 1972, but the top 4 firms together shared 73 percent of the business. The top 8 had 90 percent.

Oligopoly cost and demand

What does a typical oligopoly look like, under the lens of price theory? On the cost side, it is much the same as a monopolist, with a dish-shaped cost curve that includes selling expense. There is, however, an essential difference between the demand curve of a monopolist and that of an oligopolist. The demand curve for a monopolist, since it comprises the entire demand for the commodity, has a familiar downward sloping shape. The demand curve for the oligopolist, although also downward slop-ing, does not have the clear-cut position of the monopolist's curve.

On the contrary, the essence of the oligopoly's demand curve is that it is un-certain; moreover, that its position de-pends on what the oligopoly and its com-petitors do. Like the monopoly, the oligopoly is free to raise or lower its price. Unlike the monopoly, the oligopoly does not do so against a "fixed" demand curve. If one oligopoly raises its price, its com-petitors may "meet" competition by rais-ing theirs. Or they may keep their prices unchanged. Or an oligopoly may eschew price raises or cuts and lure business away by altering the product or simply by changing its image in advertising. Each of these responses will have a different im-pact on the demand curves of all its com-petitors.

The fight for market shares

This extreme indeter-minacy brings its ef-fects to bear on the character of oligopolistic competition. It makes price competition the least favored, rather than the standard, mode of competi-tion. Instead of price wars, a fight for shares of the market becomes the normal mode of competition. This is, of course, totally unlike the other market structures we have examined. No competitive firm fights for a share of the market, because its output is insignificant. A monopoly does not worry about its share, because it has the whole market for itself. But a fight for shares is the very heart of the oligopolistic struggle.

Moreover, because each producer tries to be "better" than its main competi-tors in one way or another, the fight usually takes the form of winning cus-tomers to a carefully *differentiated* product. A Ford is made to be distinguish-able from a Chevy; a Chevy from a Chrysler.

In the fight for market shares, price cutting becomes a much feared means of competing. Each oligopolist thinks he is better than the competition at designing or advertising or at serving customers. No one thinks he is better at price cutting. Moreover, each oligopolist fears that a price cut will be met by retaliatory price cuts, leaving market shares more or less unchanged and everyone worse off.

The "kinked" demand curve

Thus we can see that it is not possible to ar-rive at neat models of oligopolistic behavior that predict how big companies will respond. But one among many models of behavior has been worked out and is worth familiarizing outselves with, because it allows us to show graphically why oligopolists do not like to resort to price competition.

Suppose that you were the president of a large company that, along with three other very similar companies, sold roughly 80 percent of a certain commodity. Sup-pose also that a price had been established for your commodity. It yielded you and your competitors a "reasonable" profit, but

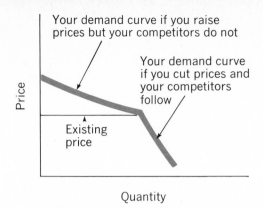

Your demand curve if you raise prices but your competitors do not

Your demand curve if you cut prices and your competitors follow

Existing price

Price

Quantity

FIG. 15·8   Kinked demand curve

you and your fellow officers were trying to increase that profit.

One possibility that would certainly be discussed would be to raise the price of your product and hope that your customers would continue to be loyal to you. Your company economists might point out that their analyses showed a very elastic demand for your product *if you raised your price, but your competitors did not.* That is, at the higher price, many of your "loyal" customers would switch to a competitive brand, so that your revenues would fall sharply and your profits decline.

Suppose, then, you took the other tack and gambled on that very elasticity of demand by cutting your prices. Would not other firms' customers switch to you and thereby raise your revenues and profits? This time your advisors might point out that if you cut your price, your competitors would almost certainly do the same, to prevent you from taking a portion of "their" market. As a result, with prices cut all around, you would probably find demand very much less elastic.

As Fig. 15·8 shows, you are facing a *kinked* demand curve. In this situation, you might well be tempted to sit tight and do nothing, for a very interesting thing happens to the marginal revenue curve that is derived from a kinked demand curve.

In Fig. 15·9 we now get two marginal revenue curves: one applicable to the upper, elastic section of the demand curve; the other applicable to the lower, inelastic section. At the point of the kink, the marginal revenue curve is discontinuous,

GAME THEORY

A competitive firm has no strategy, because it has no options. It is forced to maximize its short-run profits, or it will soon be forced out of business. But the introduction of market imperfections opens the way for numerous strategies.

The problems of strategy have led to the development of game theory, a new approach to economic analysis. Suppose that we have two arch-rival firms who dominate an industry. The board of directors of Firm A meets one day to decide on price policy. The president opens with, "Trustworthy sources I am unable to reveal inform me that if we raise our prices, Firm B, our main competitor, will raise its prices. I calculate that Firm B and ourselves will each boost profits by $10 million as a consequence. Therefore, I recommend that we raise prices immediately."

At this point, the president is interrupted by the company treasurer, who is a graduate of the Harvard Business School. "I must recommend against this proposal on two counts. First, Firm B may well be baiting a trap for us. If we raise our prices, they will *not* raise theirs. We will thereupon lose a vast amount of business to B. I estimate that this will cause us a loss of $10 million, and that Firm B will make a profit of $20 million.

"Second, suppose that firm B *does* raise prices. Then, as profit-maximizing directors, we should certainly not raise ours; for in that case, by keeping our prices low, we will steal away a great deal of business from B, and we will make a profit of $20 million, while they lose $10 million."

"Well reasoned," says the chairman of the board. "It is not only clear that we should not raise prices, but I suggest that we inform Company B—discreetly, of course—that we *will* raise prices, as they suggest, in order to tempt them to do so. That will make our strategy foolproof."

In due course, this information is transmitted to Firm B, where a similar discussion takes place. Firm B resolves to "accept" Firm A's offer, but in fact not to raise prices at all. Result: neither firm raises prices, because neither trusts the other. Instead of each gaining $10 million, which would have been the result of a price rise by both firms, the two firms stand pat and accept the much smaller profits that accrue from *minimizing risk.*

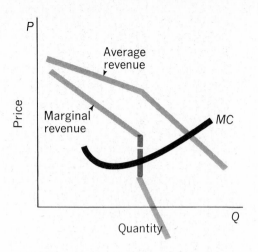

FIG. 15·9   Discontinuous MR curve

dropping vertically from the end of one slope to the beginning of the next. As a result, there is no single point of intersection of the marginal revenue and marginal cost curves. This means that an oligopoly's costs can change considerably before it is forced to alter its optimum volume of output or selling price.

The kinked demand curve helps explain why oligopoly prices are often so unvarying even without collusion among firms. It does not really explain how the existing price is arrived at; for once cost or demand conditions have changed enough to overcome oligopolistic inertia, a new "kink" will again appear around the changed price. The kinked curve thus shows what forces affect *changes* in the oligopolistic situation, rather than how supply and demand originally determine the going price.

Collusion and price leadership   Another way of avoiding price competition has probably already occurred to the reader. It is for the dominant firms to agree not to undersell one another.

Such agreements have existed, undoubtedly do exist, and certainly minimize price cutting. They are, however, illegal under the antitrust laws. When unearthed, they lead to prosecution, fines, and even jail sentences. Therefore, outright collusion is probably only used as a last resort. Moreover, outright collusion is often not necessary because a kind of tacit collusion called *price leadership* can do just as well.

Price leadership exists when one company sets prices for the entire industry. For years, CPC International set the price of corn starch. From time to time, when the market situation seemed to warrant it, CPC would announce a change in price. Immediately thereafter its two or three big competitors and its host of small fry competition would change their prices.

Did CPC confer with its major competitors over lunch before changing its price? Probably not. Its competitors were glad to follow the leader, because all recognized that this was the best way to maximize profits for the industry as a whole.*

Excess capacity and price wars   Price leadership may lead to comfortable price relations within an industry, and it is a very common mode of pricing in oligopolistic markets. From time to time, however, the system breaks down. As long as business is good, firms gladly abide by a "live and let live" philosophy that permits competition to focus on the relatively safe means of product differentiation.

When business is poor, price leadership is not always accepted. This difference is generated by the fact that

---

*How are price leaders "chosen"? The situation varies from one industry to another. Sometimes it is the biggest firm; sometimes the most aggressive. Sometimes leadership shifts around. There is no fixed pattern.

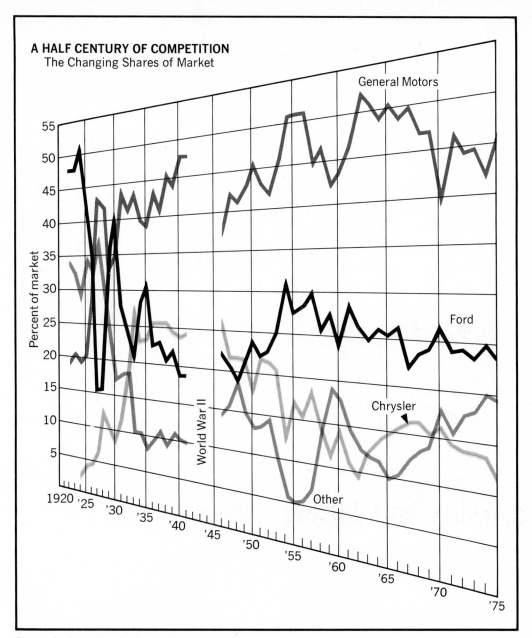

A HALF CENTURY OF COMPETITION
The Changing Shares of Market

Percent of market

General Motors

Ford

Chrysler

Other

World War II

1920 '25 '30 '35 '40 '45 '50 '55 '60 '65 '70 '75

55
50
45
40
35
30
25
20
15
10
5

Source: Joe Argenziano for *Fortune* Magazine.

Fortune magazine writes: During the last half century, the auto industry has reached a few crucial turning points that affected the fortunes of competitors for many years. In the 1920s, Alfred Sloan of General Motors wrested the lead from Henry Ford. Then, when car production resumed after World War II, Henry Ford II restored his company to a strong No. 2 position. The "other category" now includes mainly imports plus American Motors, which holds less than 5 percent of the market. The chart is based on R. L. Polk & Company's compilation of new-car registration figures.

prices above the equilibrium for a competitive market lead to a condition known as *excess capacity*. Each seller within the industry is tempted to enlarge his production capacity to the size that the "administered" price indicates. The result, as Fig. 15·10 shows, is excess capacity; that is, the ability to supply more output (Q_1) than the market will take at that price (Q_2). In desperation, the rivals turn to price cutting, and "price wars" are apt to break out until stability is once more achieved.

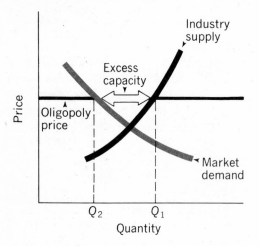

FIG. 15·10   Excess capacity

The drive for growth

We have concentrated on the tactics of competition among oligopolies, but we must not leave this form of industrial market structure without paying heed to a central aspect of oilgopolistic life. This aspect is the drive for growth that characterizes virtually all oligopolistic firms.

To be sure, all firms in a market system seek to grow. But small competitive firms are hampered in their efforts because their rising marginal cost curves do not permit a single plant or business to

expand very far. Monopolies, as we have seen, are few; and their growth, by definition, is limited to expansion of their industries. The growth situation is very different for an oligopoly. To begin with, because an oligopoly is a large firm, it normally has many plants and therefore tends to enjoy economies of scale or long-run unit cost curves that are horizontal rather than upward-climbing. Thus there is no cost impediment to growth, at least not for a long time.

Second, the typical oligopolist is not as highly concentrated as the auto or tire manufacturers. The share of the industry served by the top 4 companies is frequently less than 50 percent, and the biggest single company often serves only about a quarter or less of the business. *Thus the field for expansion is very great, and the drive to widen one's share correspondingly powerful.* Growth may be the dream of the small business in a competitive industry, but it is the stuff of daily life for the oligopolist.

Growth within markets

How is growth achieved? Usually by plowing back profits into more capital equipment or by buying up the ready-made plant and equipment of smaller companies in the field. It is virtually impossible to expand sales without an increase in capital assets, and therefore we find all successful oligopolies steadily building up the value of their capital.

For a considerable period a successful oligopoly can increase its share of the market in this way. But at a certain point, further growth within the market becomes difficult. The cost of gaining additional business rises, as indifferent customers are wooed and others customers remain loyal to competitive brands. Or a specter of an antitrust suit may loom because a company threatens, by virtue of its growth, to "monopolize" a market.

MNCs and conglomerates

Two responses are open to the successful oligopoly. First, it may transfer its fight for market shares from a national to an international basis. This is the basic thrust behind the growth of the multinational corporations (MNCs), to which we devote all of Chapter 41.

Or the oligopolist may decide to become a conglomerate; that is, to acquire capital in other industries. By diversifying its sales, it not only escapes the eye of the Justice Department antitrust lawyers, but it also avoids putting all its eggs in one basket.

Assets vs. sales

The rise of the conglomerate helps explain a curious and seemingly contradictory state of affairs that we noticed in Chapter 3. There we saw that the share of total assets coming under the control of giant companies—virtually all of them oligopolists—had risen dramatically, so that the top 100 industrial companies in 1970 owned about 50 percent of all the assets of all manufacturing companies, about the same share as the top 200 companies had owned in 1948. We also noted that the concentration of sales did not parallel that of assets. Actually, a study of the nation's markets shows no overall drift toward a more highly concentrated pattern *within* markets.

Now we can understand the dynamics of this phenomenon. The concentration of assets is partly explained by the continued growth of some companies within their industries, and by the very rapid rise of conglomerates, often through mergers. We recall from Chapter 3 that between 1951 and 1960 one-fifth of the biggest companies

disappeared, absorbed within the remaining four-fifths! At the same time, the thrust overseas and the diversification of growth have allowed oligopolies to grow without causing marked changes in their dominance within their own industries.

Monopolistic Competition

We will return to the world of oligopolies in our next chapter, but we must first continue our survey of competition in the real world. For oligopoly, although perhaps the most significant departure from the ideal of pure competition, is not the most common departure. Once we pass from the manufacturing to the retail or service sectors where competition is still intense and characterized by numerous small units, we encounter a new kind of market situation, equally strange to the pages of a text on pure competition. This is a situation in which there are many firms, with relatively easy entrance and exit, but where *each firm sells a product slightly differentiated from that of every other.* Here is the world of the average store or the small competitive manufacturer of a brand-name product—indeed, of all sellers who can identify their products for the public and who must face the competition of many other makers of similar but not exactly identical products.

Economists call this market situation tinged by monopoly imperfect competition or monopolistic competition. How does it differ from pure competition? Once again, there is no difference on the cost side. That is the same for both a perfectly competitive and an imperfectly competitive firm, except for the presence of selling costs in imperfect competition. The difference, again, comes in the nature of the demand curve.

We recall that the special attribute of the demand curve facing a firm in a purely competitive situation is its horizontal character. By way of contrast, *in a market of imperfect competition, the demand curve facing each seller slopes gently downward* because one seller's good or service is not exactly like that of competitors, and because the seller therefore has some ability to raise price without losing all his business.

Equilibrium in monopolistic competition

What is the equilibrium position of such an imperfectly competitive firm—say a dress manufacturer? In Fig. 15 • 11 on the left, an imperfect competitor is obviously making substantial profits. Note that the firm's best position where $MR = MC$ is *exactly* like that of any firm, monopolies included.

But our firm is not a monopolist, and its profits are therefore not immune to erasure by entry into its field. In Fig. 15 • 11 we show the same firm after *other entrepreneurs have moved into the industry* (with additional, similar, although not identical, products) and thereby have taken away some of our firm's market and *moved its demand curve to the left.*

Note that our final position for the marginal dress firm has no more profit than that of a purely competitive seller because $AC = AR$. On the other hand, because its demand curve slopes, the equilibrium point cannot be at the lowest point on the average cost curve, nor will output have reached optimum size. (Of course, intramarginal firms can be more profitable than the marginal case we have graphed.)

This outcome clearly dissipates economic well-being. The fact that firms are forced to operate to the left of the optimums on their cost curves means that *they have not been able to combine factors to yield their greatest efficiency.* This failure penalizes factors, once when they are paid too little because their potential marginal productivity has not been reached, and again as consumers when they are forced to pay too much for products that have not been produced at lowest possible cost. In addition, wastage is incurred because the attempt to differentiate products leads in many instances to too many small units; for example, four gas stations at one intersection.

Inefficient though it may be, *mo-*

FIG. 15 • 11   Monopolistic competition

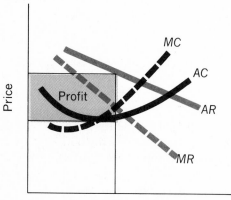

Before other firms enter

Quantity

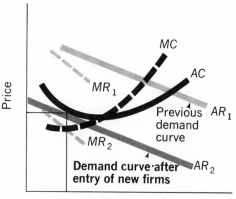

After other firms enter

Quantity

nopolistic competition yields no profit for the marginal firm in an industry. The entrepreneur therefore feels fully as hard-pressed as would the producer of an undif-ferentiated commodity. The difference is that a monopolistic competitive business-person has the possibility of *further dif-ferentiating* a product, hoping thereby to tilt the demand curve in a more inelastic position. In turn, this might permit a slight price rise, to squeeze out a tiny "pure mo-nopoly" profit. The result is that mo-nopolistic competition fosters a tremen-dous variety of goods—the ladies garment industry being a prime example.

Cost of Market Imperfection

It is time to take stock of our review of market imperfection in its many forms, from monopoly through monopolistic com-petition. What does the overall imperfec-tion of the market mean to the consumer?

Consumer sovereignty In theory, the answer is very clear. In a purely competitive market, the consumer is king. Indeed, the rationale of such a market is often described as *consumer sovereignty*.

The term means two things. First, in a purely competitive market *the consumer determines the allocation of resources by virtue of his or her demand.* Second, *the consumer enjoys goods that are sold as cheaply and produced as abundantly as possible.* As we have seen, in a purely competitive market there exist no profits (except transitory intramarginal rents). Each firm is producing the goods that consumers want, in the largest quantity and at the lowest cost possible, given its cost curves.

In an imperfectly competitive market the consumer loses much of this sovereignty. Firms have *strategies*, includ-ing the strategy of influencing consumer demand. Profits are not competed away, so consumers' surplus is transferred to producers. Output is not maximized but is reduced by whatever amount results from higher-than-competitive prices.

Effect of advertising No one contests these general conclusions. How great are they, however, in actuality? Here the problem becomes muddier.

Take the question of consumer de-mand. In 1867 we spent an estimated $50 million to persuade consumers to buy products. In 1900 advertising expendi-tures were $500 million. In 1971 they were $21 *billion*—roughly two-thirds as much as we spend on primary and secondary education. Indeed, advertising expendi-tures can be considered as a vast campaign to educate individuals to be good consumers.

To what extent does advertising in-fringe on consumer sovereignty? The question is perplexing. For one thing, it is no longer possible to think of consumers as having "natural" tastes, once we go be-yond a subsistence economy. For that reason, much advertising has a genuine in-formational purpose. People do have to made aware that it is possible (and imaginable) for, say, a factory worker to take a vacation by airplane rather than in the family car.

Moreover, numerous efforts to create tastes have failed. In the mid-1950s the Ford Motor Company poured a quarter of a billion dollars into a new car, the Edsel, and performed prodigies of advertising to make the American public like it. The public did not, and the car had to be dis-continued. So, too, consumers spontaneously decided to buy small sports cars, beginning in the 1950s; and after valiant efforts to turn the tide, the major American manufacturers capitulated and admitted that the American car buyers *did* want small cars.

Yet, it is obvious that all advertising is not informational and that consumers' tastes are manipulated to a considerable (although not clearly measureable) degree. We are mainly creatures of brand preference as a result of advertising exposure, not because we have sampled all the choices and made up our minds. It is difficult to contemplate the battles of aspirins, soaps (up to 10 percent of the price of soap is selling expense), cars, and cigarettes, without recognizing that much of this represents a waste of resources, including the very scarce resource of talent largely devoted to annulling the talent in a different advertising agency.

Is product differentiation a good thing?

Product differentiation is also an ambiguous case. Few would deny that the proliferation of "models" is often carried to the point of absurdity—and more important, to the point of substantial economic waste.

Yet, as with advertising, the question is where to draw the line. Where product differentiation results in variations in the actual product, and not merely in its "image," one must ask whether an affluent society should aim to produce the largest possible quantity of a standardized product at the least possible cost or to offer an array of differing products that please our palates, admittedly at somewhat higher costs. Few consumers in a rich society would prefer an inexpensive uniform to more expensive, individualized clothes. From this point of view, even the wasteful parade of car styles has a certain rationale.

Thus, as with advertising, *some* production differentiation plays a useful and utility-increasing function. The question is how much? It is difficult to form a purely objective judgment, for even if the amount of "useless" product differentiation is relatively small, its impact on the public taste may be disproportionately large. The problem is perhaps particularly acute insofar as much of our "taste" for style seems to be the product of the deliberate advertising efforts of manufacturers. No doubt there is a real aesthetic pleasure in variety, although one doubts that it would take the form of a yearning for "this year's model" without a good deal of external stimulation. Product differentiation thus becomes in part an effort to maximize the public's utilities. It is also in part an effort to create those "utilities" in order to maximize the producers' profits.

Monopoly and inefficiency

What about the second main attribute of consumer sovereignty—the ability to buy goods as cheaply as possible? To what extent does oligopoly introduce inefficiency into the system or transfer consumers' surplus to producers?

Once again the evidence in fact is murkier than in theory. For one thing, we tend to leap to the conclusion that a competitive firm, which has managed to combine its factors as profitably as possible, has also reached the frontiers of technological efficiency. Is this really so? Suppose that the competitive firm cannot afford the equipment that might lead to economies of large-scale production. Suppose it cannot afford large expenditure on research and development. Suppose that its workers suffer from low morale and therefore do not produce as much as they might.

These are not wild suppositions. There is good evidence that many large firms are more efficient, in terms of productivity per man-hour, than small firms, although of course some large, monopolistic firms tolerate highly inefficient practices simply because of the lack of competition. Big businesses generate higher rates of technical progress than small, competitive firms, and may well "justify" their short-run monopoly profits by long-run technical progress.*

Once again, however, we must consider the other side. Profits in monopolistic industries as a whole are 50 to 100 percent higher than those in competitive industries. In certain fields, such as prescription medicines, there is evidence that consumers are sometimes badly exploited. Brand name aspirins, for example, sell for up to three times the cost of unbranded versions of the same product. Certain medicines, such as antibiotics and the like, have enjoyed enormous profits— which is to say, have forced consumers to pay far more than they would have had to pay were the rate of profit a "competitive" one.

To turn the coin over once more, a further complication is introduced by virtue of the fact that oligopolies have often, although not always, provided more agreeable working conditions, more handsome offices, and safer plants than have small competitive firms. Thus some of the loss of consumers' surplus is regained in the form of lessened disutilities of work.

Needless to say, this is not solely the result of a kindlier attitude on the part of big producers but reflects their sheltered position against the harsh pressures of competition. Nonetheless, the gains in work conditions and morale are real and must be counted in the balance.

Business and power

Thus the economic balance sheet is by no means simple to draw up. The advantages are not all on one side, the disadvantages on the other. Although we take the model of pure competition as a baseline for efficiency and economic "virtue," we find in fact that the world is more complicated than that.

There is, however, one final consideration. It concerns power. Economists do not speak much about power because in the competitive situation which is taken as the norm, power disappears. At the core of the idea of consumers' sovereignty is the idea that the firm does not have power, that business cannot impose its will either on those it hires or on those it serves.

Clearly this is not true in the real world of imperfect competition. That is why the issue of how to control power becomes of increasing consequence—not just in the sphere of government, where it has always been a central concern of philosophers and political thinkers, but in the private spheres of business and labor. In Chapter 4 we reviewed some of the responses that economists have offered to this deep-rooted and recalcitrant question. None of them seems to resolve the issue very satisfactorily, a fact that may reflect the limited capacity of mankind to cope with its highly technical, bureaucratic organizations of production in any society, socialist or capitalist. We will think about this again in Chapter 43.

---

*The evidence is not clear that leading technical advances *arise* mainly in the laboratories of big business. The solo inventor, tinkerer, and inspired genius continue to make significant contributions. (See Jewkes, Sawers, and Stillerman, *The Sources of Invention* (1960) for a fascinating discussion of this.) Wherever they originate, however, technical advances are usually put into the economic mainstream through big companies that buy the rights to these inventions. Small companies simply cannot afford to do so.

Focus   This chapter is full of technical material that will require some practice to master, but you should not lose sight of its real purpose. This is to move from the refined theory of pure competition to the real world of imperfect competition—the world of monopolies, oligopolies, and smaller, "monopolistically" competitive firms. The question that should be foremost in your mind is: what difference does this make?

We can begin at the end of the chapter, where we come to our conclusions. They are not simple. We have to understand the difference between a world of perfect consumer sovereignty and the real world, in which power resides in business (and labor) organizations but in which there are benefits as well as costs from advertising, product differentiation, and technical change. We should also see that the world of consumer sovereignty rests on the preconditions of a world of pure competition. Look back at pp. 201–2 to review these prerequisites. Are they possible? Are they desirable?

Thus there cannot be a simplistic summing-up of the costs of imperfect competition, because the assumptions of pure competition are not wholly plausible. That is why it is so difficult to resolve the thorny problems of monopoly and oligopoly. Someone remarked that only economists really like competition. Do you think this is a justified remark? Is there nothing to be said for competition? How much competition should there be? How can competition be defined? These are among the principal questions in economics and among the most elusive.

Now for the technical matters. These largely involve learning how to draw the equilibrium positions of monopolies and firms in markets in which monopolistic competition prevails. Questions 3–5 and 10 will be useful exercises here. More difficult is mastery of the idea of oligopolistic competition. Despite the kinked demand curve diagram, we have no way of reducing the complexity of this kind of competition to the clarity of a diagram. It will help if you review the box on p. 211. This will make clear how complicated the strategies of competition can be in a world in which oligopolists know that their individual actions will affect those of their competitors.

Last and noteworthy is the matter of corporate growth. You will be repaid for the minute or two it takes to reread pp. 37–40 in Chapter 3, in the light of what you know about the growth potential of oligopolies (p. 214). This is the expansion process that powers the capitalist world, and you should understand it clearly.

WORDS AND CONCEPTS YOU SHOULD KNOW

Three conditions for pure competition, 201–2
Price takers vs. price searchers, 204
Monopoly, 203–5
Monopoly equilibrium, 207–8
Oligopoly, 209–14
Concentration ratios, 209
"Kinked" demand curve, 210–11
Price leadership, 212

Excess capacity, 212–13
Market shares, 214
Conglomerates, 215
Monopolistic competition, 215–17
Monopolistic competition equilibrium, 216
Consumer sovereignty, 217
Pros and cons of differentiation and advertising, 217–18

QUESTIONS

1. In what way, if any, do the motives of a monopolist differ from those of a perfect competitor? In what way does the time span of their decision making differ? Can this affect the monopolist's behavior (as contrasted to his or her motivation)?

2. How would you define a monopoly? Are monopolies necessarily large? What constraints does a demand curve put on the behavior of a monopoly?

3. Suppose that you were the only seller of a certain kind of machinery in the nation. Suppose further that you discovered that your demand curve looked like this:

Price	$100	$90	$80	$70
Quantity of machines sold		1	2	3	4

What is the average revenue at each price? What is the marginal revenue at each price? Draw a diagram showing the marginal and average revenues.

4. Now superimpose on this diagram a hypothetical cost profile for your business. Where is the point of equilibrium for the monopolist? Is this the same, in terms of MC and MR, as the point for the competitive firm? Now show the equilibrium output and price.

5. Does the equilibrium output of the monopolist yield a profit? What are the relevant costs for figuring profit, average costs per unit, or marginal costs? Show on your diagram the difference between average cost and selling price.

6. Why will a monopolist's selling price not be pushed to the lowest point on the cost curve?

7. What is the difference between monopoly and oligopoly? Between oligopoly and pure competition? Between pure competition and monopolistic (or imperfect) competition? Between the latter and oligopoly? Can these differences be expressed in demand curves?

8. What is a differentiated commodity? Give examples. Draw the demand curve for a farmer selling wheat and that for a toy manufacturer selling a special kind of doll. What will happen if the doll manufacturer makes a large profit? What will the dollmaker's final point of equilibrium look like if there are many competitors?

9. Can you explain why growth is so important in the world of oligopoly? Discuss the differences in both cost and demand, in comparison to pure competitive industries and monopolies. Could a monopoly grow faster than its industry without becoming either a multinational corporation or a conglomerate?

10. Compare on two diagrams the equilibrium of the purely competitive firm and of the imperfectly competitive one. Show, by a dotted line, what the demand curve would look like for the imperfectly competitive firm if its product differentiation were removed. Where would its output now be located? What would be its selling price? Would the consumer gain from this?

11. Make a list of the main institutional changes you can think of that would be needed if we were to institute a system of perfect competition.

12. Is excess capacity possible in a truly competitive industry? A monopoly? Why in an oligopoly?

Antitrust

Only a few decades ago, there was virtually unanimous agreement among economists that a strict application of antitrust laws was one of the most effective remedies for the problems of oligopoly. Today this zeal is on the wane, although, as we shall see, it is much too early to write finis to antitrust prosecutions designed to break big companies into little ones.

Why has the zeal for antitrust declined? There are a number of reasons. One is that economists have come to recognize that an industry with one or two giant firms and a tail of small firms does not operate very differently—if at all—than does an industry with five or six leading members. Whether concentration ratios give the top four firms 30 percent or 60 percent of an industry does not seem to affect their oligopolistic decision making. Product differentiation continues. The struggle for market shares goes on. Price leadership persists. Even the breakup of the aluminum industry from a near-monopoly under the domination of Alcoa to an industry in which four firms have big shares of the market does not appear to have changed aluminum prices or aluminum pricing policies.

Economists have also begun to pay more attention to a matter we have stressed several times in our text. This is the fact that industries dominated by big firms have the ability to create technical advances. Competitive firms, as we have seen, may be more efficent at any moment, selling their output at lower prices, but over time, many competitive industries have remained technologically static, whereas the oligopolistic industries—with some exceptions—have been innovators.

A third consideration is the tremendous time lag involved in major antitrust cases. A big antitrust case may go on for twenty or thirty years before it is finally resolved. One may ask whether the eventual savings are worth the huge legal costs.

Moreover, many antitrust actions seem to make little economic sense. For example, antitrust laws prohibit the merger of two firms whose combined assets would be less than those of the industry leader, but the courts do nothing to break up the leader itself. This situation exists because antitrust is against "combination" on principle, but not against bigness, as such. Yet the price policies of one big business often restrain trade as much as if two former competitors were combined.

Thus a great deal of the missionary zeal has ebbed from the antitrust cause. Large cases are still brought. Suits are pending against IBM and AT&T, but it is no longer clear what the economic benefits of these suits will be, even if successful.

Defenders of antitrust legislation do not seriously question the above views. It is not really imaginable that General Motors, for example, will ever be broken into a thousand firms, each with a capitalization of $40 million, even though GM is big enough to yield that many pieces. In all likelihood, trust busting GM would result in the formation of three or four giant firms, each worth $10 billion or so and each still possessing enormous market power.

But the defenders of antitrust do not want to give up the implicit threat that antitrust prosecution carries. The ghost of Senator Sherman, the sponsor of the original antitrust legislation, sits on the board of directors of all large firms, according to George Stigler, an eminent economist. There the ghost exercises a cautionary influence against actions that might be taken if there were no threat of antitrust action. Threat of an antitrust suit may well stay the hand of General Motors from price policies that could force Chrysler, maybe even Ford, to the wall. The ghost thereby serves to prevent the rise of supergiant firms whose political and social power might be considered inimical to our democracy, if not injurious to our economy.

Where the market mechanism fails

The outcome of the market process in the world of real competition has shown itself to be different from that of the powerless world of pure competition, once elements of power intruded. Even when power elements, such as monopolies or oligopolies, are entirely absent, the real world often has problems serious enough to cause the market mechanism to break down or to give poor economic results.

Expectations

One such instance of misfunction results from an aspect of market behavior that we briefly noted in Chapter 9 (p. 121–22). This is the role played by expectations—anticipations about the future—in shaping our rational responses as buyers or sellers.

Let us quickly review how expectations work. Suppose that buyers of a commodity discover that its price is rising. If they expect that this rise in price will be short-lived or even if they think that the new higher price will persist for a fairly long time, they will behave the way textbooks say they should. In the face of higher prices, quantities demanded will

16

decline. A new equilibrium price will be established, and that will be that. The market will have performed its task.

Perverse reactions

Now suppose that the rise in prices sets off expectations that prices will rise still more. This is a very common experience in inflationary times, when the mounting prices of goods lead us to believe that prices will be still higher tomorrow, not that they will be lower or remain at their new levels. *In this case of inflationary expectations, we do not behave as normal demanders. Instead of curtailing our willingness to buy, the rise in prices spurs it on. Better to buy more today than wait till tomorrow when prices will be higher still. Thus, expectations can induce perverse reactions in the marketplace.* Of course, the same kinds of perverse reactions can affect the supply curves of sellers. Ordinarily, a rise in prices brings about an increase in the quantities offered. Not, however, if expectations point in the direction of still higher prices. Then sellers will hold back, causing the supply curve to shift leftward.

The result, as we can see in Fig. 16·1, is that prices can move violently upward and that the movement of prices can continue to feed upon itself, because demand and supply curves (D_1, D_2, D_3 and S_1, S_2, S_3) are themselves being shifted by the very fact that prices have changed. In deflationary times, the same process can work in reverse.

Such perverse price movements can lead to very dangerous consequences. They play a major role in the cumulative, self-sustaining processes of inflation or collapse. They can cause commodity prices to shoot to dizzying heights or plummet to the depths. At their worst, perverse behavior threatens to make an entire economy go out of control, as in the

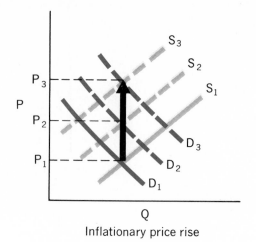

Inflationary price rise

FIG. 16·1   A self-feeding price rise

case of hyperinflations or panics. At best, they disrupt smooth, orderly markets and bring shocks and dislocations to the economy.

Cobwebs

One kind of market failure associated with expectations is peculiarly tied into agricultural products. Take Christmas trees as an example.

In Fig. 16·2 we show the supply and demand curves for Christmas trees and imagine that the quantity supplied is initially indicated by point *A* on the quantity axis.

FIG. 16·2   The cobweb

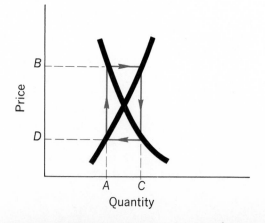

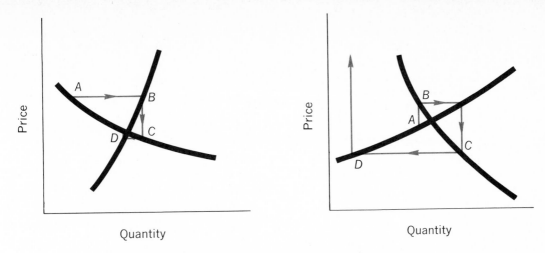

FIG. 16·3   Stabilizing and explosive cobwebs

We can see that quantity A will sell at price B. Figuring that this will be *next year's* price, tree growers now plant the amount they are willing and able to offer at price B—quantity C. Alas, when the harvest comes, it is found that quantity C will fetch only price D. Now the process goes into reverse. Growers will figure that next year's price will be D, and they plant amount A, since at price D the quantity they wish to supply is no more than that. Thereupon, next harvest time, the price goes back to B, and around we go. If the supply and demand schedules were differently sloped, we could have a so-called *cobweb* that converged toward equilibrium, as we show on the left of Fig. 16·3; and we could have one that "exploded" as we see in the diagram on the right.

Lumpy investment   Cobwebs are peculiar to agriculture because there is such a long wait between production decisions and sales results. But expectations can play an equally disruptive role in industry, especially where expansion takes place through big, expensive "units" of investment. Steel, railroads, oil refineries, chemical plants—indeed, most of the major industry processes fit into this category of "lumpy" investment.

Suppose that we have an oligopoly with five leading firms, and that the industry as a whole is experiencing a gradual increase in demand. Because existing supply is inadequate to demand, prices will be slowly rising. The actual increase in demand may be no more than could be supplied by one additional plant; but because each oligopolist expects to capture the lion's share of the new market, very likely more than one firm, possibly all of them, will be tempted into building a plant.

The result is market failure. If more than one firm builds, the industry will have excess capacity, with consequent losses. If no one builds, the market will not meet the growing demand, and economic rents will be earned. If only one firm responds, a new equilibrium will be reached, but at the probable cost of dividing the market less equally and rendering the industry less competitive.

The problem of information   Cobwebs as well as "lumpy" investment are, in part, the consequence of obdurate facts: economic processes take time, and certain production methods require large sums of capital. Both cases also illustrate another attribute of all economic systems: *the need for accurate information* (see Chap. 9, p. 117).

Without correct information, marketers cannot make correct decisions, except by luck. If buyers and sellers *knew* what future prices would be, we would not have perverse, inflationary (or deflationary) reactions. Instead, prices would immediately rise or fall to their proper equilibrium levels, and they would stay there until forces in the market place changed.

Typically, marketers do not have adequate information. Consumers guide themselves by hearsay, by casual information picked up by random sampling, or by their susceptibility to advertising. Who has time to investigate which brand of toothpaste is really best or even tastes best? Even professional buyers, such as industrial purchasing agents, cannot know every price of every product, including all substitutes.

The lack of information can be remedied, at least up to a point; but the remedy costs money or its equivalent—time. Few of us have the resources or patience to do a complete research job on every item we buy. Would it even be rational to do so? **Thus a certain amount of ignorance always remains in all markets, causing prices and quantities to differ from what they would be if we had complete information. These differences can be very great,** as anyone knows who has ever discovered, with sinking heart, that he or she paid "much too much" for a given article or sold it for "much too little."

Transactions costs

The cost of amassing information is actually part of a still broader category of market problems that we call *transactions costs*. Many markets do not reach their "correct" targets, not only because the marketers are uninformed, but because even when they are informed, they cannot take advantage of the market mechanism.

A laboratory assistant making $5 an hour in one city may hear of a job at $6 an hour in another. She should move there, not only for her sake but so that society can allocate its resources most efficiently. The cost of moving may be so great, however, that she decides she cannot afford to move, even though she would earn back the cost in a year or two. So, too, a business executive who cannot "afford" to take a better paying job because he would lose his pension rights, or an employer who cannot afford to hire a productive older worker because he will be stuck with his pension costs—these are all instances of failures in the market process caused by transactions costs. Needless to say, they can be expensive failures.

Remedying market failures

Can these kinds of market failures be corrected? Some can, some cannot. The problem of lumpy investment, for example, seems to have no remedy short of interfering in the market and allowing oligopolists to designate one firm as the builder (or giving that power to the government). Cobwebs can be greatly reduced if farmers are given forecasts on which to base their plantings—assuming that the forecasts will be correct.

Transactions costs can be greatly lessened in many cases by arranging for low-cost government loans to workers who seek to relocate, or by making pensions more flexible or less expensive for employers who hire older workers. Ignorance can be reduced by the simple expedient of providing more information through truth-in-advertising legislation, through consumer protection agencies, or simply through better economic reporting services.

We should recognize, however, that there is a residue of arbitrariness even in the best intentioned remedies. Take the matter of consumer information. We "inform" the consumer, through labels on cigarette packages, that smoking is dangerous, but we do not prohibit the advertising of cigarettes. We spread "market information" by having the incomprehensible contents of medications printed on their containers, but we allow the consumer to be misinformed through advertising that claims superiority of one kind of aspirin over another.

Why? There is no clear rationale in these cases. Essentially we are trying to repair omissions in the market system—injecting information, so that consumers can make better choices—without becoming paternalistic. Perhaps we think it is better to allow the consumer to make some mistakes than to allow the government to make them for him.

On the other hand, we should clearly recognize that the consequences of the market failures we have discussed can be very serious. *Moreover, there is no remedy for any of these failings "within" the market.* Unlike market power, the destabilizing effects of inflationary or panicky expectations, cobwebs, lumpy investments, sheer ignorance, or transactions costs cannot be removed by restructuring the market. These all arise from conditions over which the market has no control: time, technology, ignorance. The only way to mitigate them is to use a nonmarket mechanism, such as government or a public interest group, to provide what the market lacks, be it plausible forecasts, controls, guidance, or other helps. The results of such interference may leave a great deal to be desired, but we must not lose sight of the reason why we turn to them in the first place.

Public Goods

We have been describing instances in which the market functions poorly in guiding the private economy to an efficient use of its resources. Now we must turn to an area where the market does not work at all. This is in the provision of a class of indispensable outputs we call public goods.

Characteristics of public goods What is a public good? Defense is a perfect example of such a good. So is the national weather service, or the provision of lighthouses off rocky coasts. Perhaps you can see that such goods have these curious attributes:

1. **The consumption of a public good by one individual does not interfere with its consumption by another.** A lighthouse is as effective for ten boats as for one. A weather service is as useful for 100 million TV viewers as for 100. By way of contrast, private goods cannot be consumed in the same way. Food, clothing, or doctors' services that I use cannot also be consumed by you.

2. **No one can be excluded from the use of a public good.** I can deny you the use of my car. There is no way of denying you the use of "my" national defense system.

3. **Most important of all, public goods can be provided only by collective decisions.** My private consumption depends on my individual decision to spend or not spend my income. But there is no way that I can, by myself, buy defense, weather services, or a lighthouse service.* We must

---

*Not even if I were immensely rich or an absolute monarch? In that case we would not have a market system, but a command economy catering to one person. Then indeed there would be no distinction between public and private goods.

not only agree to buy the public good or services, but agree *how much* to buy!

Not all public goods are entirely "pure." Highways, education, the law courts, or sanitation services are not so universally available as lighthouses or defense. The amount of education, road space, court time, or garbage services that I consume does affect the amount left over for you. It is possible to exclude some citizens from schools or roads. But even these less perfect examples share in the third basic attribute of public goods. They must all be produced by collective decisions, usually by the voting system of the community.

Free riding

Because of their characteristics, all public goods share a common difficulty. *Their provision cannot be entrusted to the decision making mechanism of the market.*

In the use of ordinary goods, each person can consume only as much as that person buys. Here the market works very well. In the use of public goods, each person will not buy an amount that he or she really wants, because each can enjoy the goods that someone else buys. Do not forget that there is no way of excluding others from the use of a pure public good (or from most not-so-pure ones). Therefore each of us would try to get a "free ride" if we attempted to use the market to determine the level of output.

An example may help. Lighthouse service is a pure public good. Why couldn't we make it a private good, selling the light to users? The answer is that no boatowner would be willing to pay what the light is actually worth to him. Why should he? So long as someone else builds a lighthouse, the boatowner can enjoy its services "free!"

Voting instead of buying

How do we then determine the level of provision of such goods? By eschewing the useless market mechanism and availing ourselves of another means of decision making: voting. We vote for the amount of public goods we want; and because voting is a curious mechanism (see "An extra word" in Chapter 10), sometimes we oversupply ourselves with these goods, and sometimes we undersupply ourselves. We swim in defense, starve in prison reform, because defense has "friends in Congress;" prisons do not.

Is there a remedy for the problem? Some economists have suggested that we should try to bring as many public goods as possible into the market system, by getting rid of their "public" characteristics. We could charge admission to the city's parks, so that we could produce only as much park service as people were willing to buy. We could charge tolls on all roads, even streets, and limit the building or repair of highways to the amount of private demand for road services. We might limit the use of law courts to those who would hire the judge and jury, or ask the police to interfere on behalf of only those citizens who wore a badge attesting to their contribution to the police wage fund.

Privatizing public goods?

Such a "privatization" of public goods might indeed bring the level of their production up, or down, to the amount that we would consume if they were strictly private goods, like cars or movie tickets. The problems are twofold. First, there are innumerable technical difficulties in making many public goods into private ones. Imagine the problems in charging a toll for each city street!

Second, and more arresting, the idea offends our sense of justice. Suppose that we could convert defense into a private good. The defense system would then defend only those who bought its services. Presumably the more you bought, the better you would be defended. Few believers in democracy would like to see our national defense converted into a bastion for the rich. Nor would we remove from public use the law courts, the schools, the police, and so on.

There are valid arguments and clever techniques for returning *some* public goods into the market's fold. The main point to keep in mind is that it is impossible to make all goods private; and for the ones that should remain public, the market cannot be used to establish a desirable level of output. Here the market mechanism must give way to a political method of making economic decisions.

Externalities

This last instance of market failure opens the way for an examination of a final broad area of difficulty, closely connected with the attributes of public goods. It is the problem of allowing for the "externalities" of production; that is, for the effects of the output of private goods and services on persons other than those who are directly buying or selling or using the goods in question.

Pollution   Externalities bring us to one of the most vexing and sometimes dangerous problems in our economic system—controlling pollution.

What is pollution, from an economic point of view? It is the production of wastes, dirt, noise, congestion and other things that we do not want. Although we don't think of smoke, smog, traffic din, and traffic jams as part of society's "production," these facts of economic life are certainly the consequence of producing things we do want. Smoke is part of the output process that also gives us steel or cement. Smog arises from the production of industrial energy and heat, among other things. Traffic is a by-product of transportation. In current jargon, economists call these unwanted by-products "bads" to stress their relation to things we call "goods."

"Bads" escape the market   Why do externalities exist? The basic answer is technological: we do not know how to produce goods "cleanly;" i.e., without wastes and noxious by-products such as smoke. The economic answer calls our attention to another aspect of the problem. Externalities refer to the fact that the output of "bads" does not pass through the market system. A factory may produce smoke, etc., without having to pay anyone for producing these harmful goods. So, too, certain inputs used by firms—air, water, even space in an esthetic rather than economic sense—are available without charge, so that there is no constraint to urge a firm to use air or water sparingly or to build a handsome rather than an ugly factory or building.*

In other words, pollution exists because it is the cheapest way to do many things, some having to do with producing goods, some with consuming them. It is

---

*Some externalities are not "bads," but "goods." A new office building may increase the property value of a neighborhood. Here is a positive externality. The benefit gained by others results from the new building but is not paid to the owners of that building. Such externalities give some private goods the partial attributes of public goods.

cheaper to litter than to buy waste cans (and less trouble, too); cheaper to pour wastes into a river than to clean them up. That is, it is cheaper for the individual or the firm, but it may not be cheaper for the community. A firm may dump its wastes "for free" into a river, but people living downstream from the firm will suffer the costs of having to cope with polluted water.

Marginal private and social costs

The point is so fundamental it is worth elaborating. In back of the conception of the marketplace as an *efficient* allocator of goods and incomes is a silent assumption. It is that all the inputs going into the process are owned by some individual and that all the outputs are bought by some person or firm or agency. Presumably, then, the price at which commodities are offered will include all the costs that are incurred in the process. Presumably also, the price that will be offered will reflect all the prospective benefits accruing to the buyer. In other words, prices established in the marketplace are supposed to take into account *all* the disutilities involved in the process of production, such as fatigue or unpleasantness of work, and *all* the utilities ultimately gained by the final consumer of those goods.

What the problem of pollution has brought home is that the market is not a means for effectively registering a great many of these costs and benefits. The examples of the damage wrought by smoke that is not charged against the factory or of a neighborhood nuisance such as a bar or a hideous advertising sign are instances of economic activities in which *private costs are less than social costs*. These "social" costs are, of course, private costs incurred by other people. Contrariwise, when a person spends money to educate himself, he benefits not only himself but also the community, partly because he becomes a more productive citizen and partly because he presumably becomes a more responsible one. Thus the *social benefits* of some expenditures may be greater than their *private benefits*.

Social and private marginal costs and benefits

Suppose that the social and private gains and losses do not coincide. How does that reflect on the efficiency of the market process?

The answer is very plain. If we are interested ultimately in maximizing everyone's well-being, we want the price system to act as a guide to firms and factors and consumers, urging them to buy more or produce more of socially useful goods and to make or buy fewer socially dele-terious ones. We want an economy that produces more goods and less "bads." But under a pricing system that takes no account of the externalities wrought by consumption and production, the economy will produce too many bads and too few goods. Because no charge for smoke is levied on the factory owner, there is no economic incentive to economize on smoke, perhaps by switching to more expensive but less smoky fuel.

In more technical language, the marginal private cost of some goods, with negative externalities, is less than their marginal social cost. Sometimes the process works in reverse, and the marginal social benefit or gain from an economic act is less than the private benefit. Education is such a good. A personal dollar spent on education is worth more to the community than the "dollar's worth" of education to the person. Education benefits the whole community, not just the individual. It is just because its marginal social benefit is greater than its marginal private benefit that we have public education or loans to college students.

There is an important final principle here. The market is an instrument for bringing marginal *private* costs and benefits together. It cannot handle marginal *social* costs and benefits. This is because, as we have seen, social costs and benefits are "external" to the market. They escape the registration of the price system. Only public intervention of some kind can bring social costs under control or can increase social benefits.

Controlling Externalities

How can we bring the process of pollution under social control? Basically, we can attack the problem in three ways. We can

1. Regulate the activity that creates it
2. Tax the activity that creates it
3. Subsidize the polluter, to stop (or lessen) his activity

Regulation

Faced with the ugly view of smoke belching from a factory chimney, sludge pouring from a mill into a lake, automobiles choking a city, or persons being injured by contaminants, most ecologically concerned persons cry for regulation: "Pass a law to forbid smoky chimneys or sulfurous coal. Pass a law to make mills dispose of their wastes elsewhere or purify them. Pass a law against automobiles in the central city."

What are the economic effects of regulation? Essentially the idea behind passing laws is to internalize a previous externality. That is, a regulation seeks to impose a cost on an activity that was previously "free" for the individual or firm, although not free, as we have seen, for society. This means that individuals or firms must stop the polluting activity entirely or bear the cost of whatever penalty is imposed by law, or else find ways of carrying out their activities without giving rise to pollution.

Costs of regulation

Let us take the case of a firm that pollutes the environment as a joint product of producing goods or services. Suppose a regulation is passed, enjoining that firm to install antipollution devices—smoke scrubbers or waste-treatment facilities. Who bears this cost?

The answer seems obvious at first look: the firm must bear it. In fact it would, in the form of reduced profits, if it were a monopoly or an oligopoly prevented from raising prices (say by price ceilings).

If the firm is competitive or if it does pass its higher costs along in higher selling prices, we arrive at a different answer. Examine Fig. 16·4. Our firm's original marginal cost (or supply) curve is S_1. The need to install new antipollution equipment raises it by an amount ac to S_2. Now a little economic analysis will show us that the cost is in fact borne by three groups, not just by the firm. First, the firm will bear some of the cost because at the higher price, it will sell less output. How much less depends on the elasticity of demand for its product. But unless demand is totally inelastic (a vertical line), its sales and income must contract.

Two other groups also bear part of the cost. One group is the factors of production. Fewer factors will be employed because output has fallen. Their loss of income is therefore also a part of the economic cost of antipollution regulation. Last, of course, is the consumer. Prices will rise from P_1 to P_2. Note that the rise in price bc is less than the full rise in costs ab so that the consumer will not bear all the costs (unless, once again, we have vertical demand curves).

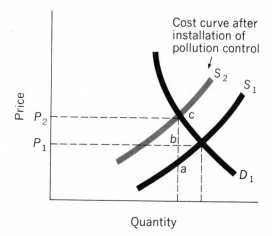

FIG. 16·4 Effects of regulation

Gains from regulation

Offsetting all these costs is the fact that each of these three groups and the general public now have a better environment. There is no reason, however, why each of these three groups, singly or collectively, should think that *its* benefit outweighs *its* costs. Most of the benefit is likely to go to the general public, rather than to the individuals actually involved in the production or consumption of the polluting good or service.

Thus a regulation forcing car manufacturers to make cleaner engines will cost the manufacturers some lost sales, will cost the consumer added expense for a car, and will cost lost income for whatever land, labor, and capital is no longer employed at higher production costs. As part of "the public," all three groups will benefit from cleaner air, but each is likely to feel its specific loss more keenly than its general gain.

Is regulation useful?

So, too, regulations are good or bad, mainly depending on their ease of enforcement. Compare the effectiveness of speed limits, which attempt to lessen the externality of accidents, and of regulations against littering. It is difficult enough to enforce speed laws, but it is almost impossible to enforce antilittering laws. On the other hand, regulation of the disposal of radioactive wastes is simpler to enforce because the polluters are few and easily supervised.

This in turn is largely a matter of cost. If we were prepared to have traffic policemen posted on every mile of highway or every city block, regulation could be just as effective for speed violations or littering as for radioactive disposal. Obviously the cost would be horrendous, and so would most people's reaction to being overpoliced.

Taxation

A second way to cope with pollution is to tax it. When a government decides to tax pollution (often called effluent charges), it is essentially creating a price system for disposal processes. If an individual company found that it could clean up its own pollutants more cheaply than paying the tax, it would do so, thereby avoiding the tax. If the company could not clean up its own pollutants more cheaply than the tax cost (which is often the case because of economies of scale in pollution control), it would pay the necessary tax and look to the state to clean up the environment.*

The effluent charge looks like, but is not, a license to pollute. It is a license that allows you to give some of your pollutants to the state *for a price.*

As a result of effluent charges, an activity that was formerly costless is no longer so. Thus, in terms of their economic impacts, these charges are just like government regulations. In fact, they are a type of government regulation. They raise the supply curve for the good in question, with all of the corresponding ramifications. The difference is that each producer can decide for himself whether it pays to install clean-up equipment and not pay the tax or to pollute and pay whatever tax costs are imposed.

Antipollution taxes vs. regulations

Which is better, regulation or taxation? As we have seen, regulation affects all polluters alike, and this is both its strength and its weakness. Taxation enables each polluter to determine for himself what course of action is best. Some polluters will achieve low pollution targets more cheaply by installing anti-pollution equipment, thereby avoiding taxes on their effluents, while other polluters will find it more profitable to pay the tax.

Here practical considerations are likely to be all-important. For example, taxation on effluents discharged into streams is likely to be more practical than taxation on smoke coming from chimneys. The state can install a sewage treatment plant, but it cannot clean up air that is

---

*Ideally, the tax would be set high enough so that the city or state would have enough tax revenue to install the devices for cleaning up whatever pollution remains.

contaminated by producers who find it cheaper to pay a pollution tax than to install smoke-suppressing equipment. Moreover, to be effective, a pollution tax should vary with the amount of pollution—a paper mill or a utility plant paying more taxes if it increases its output of waste or smoke. One of the problems with taxation is that of installing monitoring equipment. It is difficult to make accurate measurements of pollution or to allow for differences in environmental harm caused by the same amount of smoke coming from two factories located in different areas.

Subsidies

The third way of dealing with pollution is to *subsidize polluters to stop polluting;* that is, the government pays polluters to install the necessary equipment to clean up their effluents.

As we might expect, subsidies have impacts quite different from those of regulation or taxation. Because the government pays the costs of the antipollution equipment, the private firm incurs no costs. Its supply curves do not shift. No fewer factors are employed. Prices to the consumer remain unchanged. One curious effect is that the total amount of resources devoted to pollution control will therefore be larger under subsidy than under taxation or regulation. The reason is obvious: there will be no reduction in output, as in the case of the other two techniques.

Are subsidies useful?

Economists typically object to subsidies because they camouflage the true economic costs of producing goods and services cleanly. When regulations or taxes increase the price of paper or steel, the individual or firm becomes aware that the environment is not free and that there may be heavy costs in producing goods in a way that will not damage the environment. The increased

price will lead him to demand less of these goods. But when he gets clean environment through the allocation of a portion of his taxes, he has no "price signal" to show him the cost of pollution associated with particular commodities.

Nevertheless, there are cases when subsidies may be the easiest way to avoid pollution. For example, it might be more effective to pay homeowners to turn in old cans and bottles than to try to regulate their garbage disposal habits or to tax them for each bottle or can thrown away. Subsidies may therefore sometimes be expedient means of achieving a desired end, even if they may not be the most desirable means from other points of view.

Externalities in review

Externalities are one of the most widespread instances of failure in the market, but they differ markedly from the problem of public goods. The difference is that it is possible to allow the market system itself to handle the otherwise hidden costs of pollution by using the various techniques we have examined.

Therefore, in offsetting externalities in the production of private goods, we avoid some of the arbitrariness that troubles us in the provision of public goods. We can internalize the costs of pollution in a way that we cannot "privatize" the costs or benefits of pure public goods.

Nonetheless, we must keep in mind the theme of this chapter. It is that a market system has weak spots or ineffective areas peculiar to its institutional nature. *Its inability to put a price on external effects or to give a producer the rewards of producing external benefits means that the system, left to itself, will work poorly or even dangerously. The remedy requires political intervention of one kind or another—regulation, taxation, or sub-*

sidy—for there is no recourse other than political action when the self-regulating economic mechanism fails.

Market strengths and weaknesses   This is not a conclusion that should be interpreted as a kind of general plea for more government. Many economists who severely criticize the market want less government—certainly less bureaucratic, nonparticipatory, nondemocratic government. The point, however, is to recognize that the existence and causes of market malfunction make some government intervention inescapable. We can then seek to use government power to repair individual market failures in order to strengthen the operation of the system as a whole.

After so much criticism of the market system, perhaps it is well to conclude by recalling its strengths. Basically they are two. First, the market encourages individuals to exert energies, skills, ambition, and risk-taking in the economic pursuits of life. This activity gives to market systems a high degree of flexibility, vitality, inventiveness, changefulness. For all their failures (see the "Extra word" to follow) the market economies have displayed astonishing growth, and the source of that growth lies ultimately in the activities of their marketers.

Second, the system minimizes the need for government supervision, although it cannot dispense with it, for reasons we now understand. It would be a mistake to suppose that every instance of government intervention is an abridgment of freedom, or that every area of market activity is an exemplar of liberty. The truth is that government and market are equally capable of promoting liberty or giving rise to oppression. Nonetheless, in a world in which the concentration of government power has been one of the greatest scourges of mankind, there is clearly something to be said for the existence of a mechanism capable of handling the basic economic tasks of society with but a minimal dependence on political authority.

FOCUS   This chapter covers so many kinds of problems and touches on so many subjects that the first thing to do is to stress the red thread that runs through our discussion. It is the thread of the limits of market usefulness. This is different from the imperfections of a market in which giant corporations pose problems of oligopolistic competition. Here we examine the inability of a "perfect" market to cope with certain aspects of real economic life.

What are those aspects? The chapter separates the limits of the market into various categories. There is the problem of expectations and information. There is the problem of lengthy and lumpy production processes. There are transactions costs. These are a group of problems whose roots lie in the difficulties of technology, human foresight, temporal duration.

Next is a group of problems discussed under the heading of public goods. The trouble with public goods is that there is no effective way of making them private. (Review their properties on page 227.) Therefore, we cannot produce them by allowing each person to buy as much as he or she wishes. This is because each person benefits from everyone else's use of a public good, and is therefore too tempted to buy as little as possible for himself or herself. There is no way of using the market to provide these goods. We are forced into voting as the social mechanism of allocation. Another look at the "Extra word" to Chapter 10 will remind you of the problems of allocation by voting.

Of course you should be familiar with the question of externalities and the main remedies for pollution. Carefully study questions 5, 6, and 7. Last is the general problem of market vs. government. A look at the self-destructive tendencies of market pressures in cities (in the "Extra word" ahead) puts the problem in clear view. Is there any way of offsetting or preventing market processes that cause damage, except to use the countervailing force of government? That is a question that emerges again and again in our chapter. Hence we must remind ourselves that markets cannot be judged purely by their failings. The balance between government and market, between centralized and decentralized decision making, between markets that work and those that do not is a crucial issue of our age.

WORDS AND CONCEPTS YOU SHOULD KNOW

Expectations, 223–24
Perverse market behavior, 224
Cobwebs, 224–25
Transactions costs, 226
Public goods, 227–29
Free riding, 228
Externalities, 229–31

Three ways to control externalities, 231–34
Economic "bads," 229
Marginal social vs. private cost, 230
Pros and cons of regulation, taxation, and subsidies, 231–34
Internalizing externalities, 232–33
Market strengths, 235

QUESTIONS

1. As a seller who seeks to maximize, would you increase or decrease your market offerings if prices rise and you expect them to remain at their new high level? Suppose you expect them to fall? To rise still further?

2. Can you imagine an industrial process that might result in a cobweb? Why or why not? Hint: Suppose that farming became hydroponic, therefore much less dependent on the seasons. Would the cobweb persist?

3. Is there any solution to the problem of lumpy investment other than collusion or government intervention? What do you think is the best way around this situation?

4. Explain the mechanism of a "free ride." Are there any free rides in private goods? How about window displays? Skywriting? What kinds of public goods do you think should be made "private"? The national parks? Public schools? Public beaches? Public hospitals? In each case, why or why not?

5. Can you think of an externality imposed by a producer on a consumer? (That's easy.) Of one imposed by a producer on another producer? (How about the effect on work efficiency caused by the noise of erecting a building?) Of an externality imposed by a consumer on another consumer? Of one imposed by consumers on producers?

6. Explain carefully why a perfectly competitive market will turn out an assortment of goods in which the sum of the private costs and benefits imposed by, or enjoyed from, those goods will be different from the sum of the social costs and benefits associated with those goods.

7. What do you think would be the best way to control the following externalities: (1) a smoke-producing utility company, (2) roadside littering, (3) overfishing in a stream, (4) noise from a jetport, (5) radiation hazards in a hospital, (6) billboards, (7) pornography, (8) overcutting forests, (9) noise from diesel trucks and motorcycles. In each case, discuss the relative merits of taxation, subsidy, or outright regulation.

The city

Our survey of market problems has touched on many kinds of difficulties: prices that "run away" because of expectations, transactions that are too costly to consummate, areas of production that a market system can't handle, dangers and annoyances that are inflicted because of external side effects.

There is still another malfunction of the economic system. Its causes are partly (not wholly) the peculiar effects of market processes. The problem to which we refer is the slum, the deteriorated urban environment. Why do slums arise? What can economic analysis tell us about their causes, their remedies?

CAUSES FOR SLUMS: CITY FINANCES

Slums are not purely economic in their origin. The best proof of that is to visit a capitalist nation such as Sweden or Denmark or Holland or Austria, where you will seek in vain for slums. In all of their cities there are certain kinds of typical urban problems—congestion, air pollution, and the like—and in most of them you will find some fine residential areas and some working-class areas. But slums of the kind that we find in the United States are not to be found everywhere.

Why do we have such a slum problem? The main reasons are two. One is that slums reflect the inability of city administrations to provide adequate police, well-maintained parks, enough sanitation services, and the like in all quarters of the city. This in turn is largely a consequence of the American tax system, which loads upon municipalities and states costs that are borne in other nations by their central governments. American cities are poor because they are expected to pay all or a large part of the costs of welfare, local public hospitals, schools, and other services. Most cities cannot maintain a high quality of urban environment because they are strapped for funds and unable to raise local property or sales taxes—their main sources of revenue—for fear of driving out the businesses and prosperous middle class whom they wish to attract. Chapter 21 deals further with this problem.

RACIAL DISCRIMINATION

The second reason is the racial segregation and prejudice that still afflicts American society. Because blacks and other minorities are excluded from many residential areas, they tend to cluster in ethnic neighborhoods. Because the residents of these neighborhoods are mainly members of minorities whose incomes are low (for reasons that we will investigate in Chapter 17), the neighborhood is rundown. Unemployment is much higher here than elsewhere in the city, especially among teenagers. Job openings are few, and many jobs are dead-end. Discouragement and apathy and the prevailing dependence on welfare lead young slum dwellers to seek the excitement of the streets rather than the boredom of the life of a delivery boy.

Thus social and political factors predominate in the appearance of slums. Nonetheless, economic analysis also sheds some light on the problems of urban decay.

ECONOMIC SEGREGATION

Before World War II, most of the population of any large metropolitan area lived in the central city. There was no choice, since one had to live in the central city if one were to work in the city. With the development of commuter transportation, particularly the automobile, our large metropolitan areas have become a maze of suburbs, each with its own local government surrounding a central city. People have been liberated from having to live close to their place of work.

Where *do* they want to live? Obviously, in the place that has the most pleasant environment. That environment is created by two basic forces. Part is purchased privately in the form of a home and yard. Part is purchased *collectively* in the form of good schools, parks, clean streets, police and fire protection.

The privately purchased portion of the environment is not an economic problem. People simply purchase what they can afford. (If it is a social problem, it is because of income distribution, which we will study in the coming chapters.) The collectively purchased part, however, presents a different series of questions. Since local governments basically depend upon property taxes, the amount that individuals have to pay as a share of the necessary collective expenditures depends not only upon the value of *their* homes, but also upon the value of the homes around them.

Imagine purchasing a certain amount of collective environment—schools, police, etc.—that costs $2,000 per year per person. *The amount that you personally are going to have to pay depends largely upon the value of your neighbors' houses.* The more expensive their houses, the less taxes you have to pay. Conversely, the less expensive their houses, the more you will have to pay. As a result, you will want to live in a neighborhood with homes at least as expensive as yours, and you will want to keep out all homes that are less expensive than yours. If you allow cheaper homes to be built, your costs will go up, since the number of people in the community will rise, but their tax payments will not go up equivalently. They will be paying less than the average tax.

ECONOMICS OF ZONING

If residents of a town restrict homebuilding to houses that cost more than the average existing homes, their own taxes will fall. If residents allow less-than-average cost homes to be built, their taxes will rise. As a result, zoning rules are used to maintain a minimum standard for housing in each area.

This process leads to a condition of economic segregation, because the central city and its suburbs have people of very different income levels and very different per-capita tax bases. In poor suburbs it becomes expensive to buy good schools, because the effective property tax rate would have to be very high. Conversely, in rich suburbs it becomes cheap to buy good schools because the effective property tax rate can be very low. As a result, poor neighborhoods buy fewer schools than rich neighborhoods, even if their desires for schools are exactly the same.*

*Recent Supreme Court decisions have challenged the constitutionality of these unequal taxes' bases and may bring about a more equitable distribution of educational expenditure.

As a result of economic segregation, we also find wide disparities in the distribution of public services. The poor man with a poor private environment has a poor public environment, not because *he* is poor but because he lives with other poor people. If we think of governmental expenditures as being one of the prime means of providing equal opportunity through good education, recreational, and cultural facilities, then we see that *local governments are unable to fulfill this role because of the economic segregation that has occurred.*

THE NEIGHBORHOOD EFFECT

Let's return to the central city. There, another economic process exacerbates the pull of economically homogeneous suburbs. The value of a home depends partly upon the condition of the home itself and partly upon the condition of the neighborhood. The *same* house in different areas can bring very different prices. A poor neighborhood can bring the value of a good house down by as much as 60 to 70 percent.

The value of your home therefore depends mostly upon the actions of others. What your neighbors do to maintain their homes and what the city does to provide public services will dominate the price at which you can sell your house. *As a result, you have a rational economic incentive to undermaintain your home.* To do so cuts your costs and has little impact on the price of your home, as long as the *other* homes are well maintained and good public services are provided. If other homes are not maintained or public services are bad, good maintenance on your home will be wasted. It will not show up in the price you can get for your home.

As a result, economic incentives lead to neighborhood deterioration once anything happens to disrupt the stable character of the neighborhood. Movement to the suburbs starts; stability is broken. The quality of public services may start to deteriorate as high income and high tax paying citizens move out. This tempts the economic man in all of us to quit maintaining our property and move to the suburbs to get the quality housing and public services we want. If we yield to this temptation, we make the collective problem worse and accelerate the process.

Once again we have each individual acting in his own economic self-interest, with results that may *not* be socially optimal and once again there is no market correction for the situation. No one is being *economically* irrational. The only solution is therefore to change the structure of the market. Metropolitan-wide tax raising authorities would be one solution, since they could establish uniform tax rates that would make it impossible to lower your own tax bill by moving into areas without poor people (and hopefully with people wealthier than you).

COMMUTER TRANSPORTATION

In most cities, where about 70 percent of us live, the possibility of living long distances from one's place of work did not exist until the automobile became an instrument of mass transportation. Curiously, however, as transportation has become more efficient, there is no evidence that there has been any reduction in the average commuting time. What has happened is that the average commuter now lives many more miles away from his work than he previously did. Therefore the urban transportation system exists not as an instrument to cut commuting times but as a means to allow us to live farther away from our jobs and to purchase the housing we want in the neighborhood that we like. In all probability, further improvements in urban transportation will have the same effect. This is not to say that improved transportation would be worthless. Being able to purchase a desired house with desired neighbors may be of great value to a person.

In the two decades after World War II, the automobile was overwhelmingly the preferred instrument of mass transportation. Immense investments were made in cars and roads. Since the late 1960s, however, it has become difficult, if not impossible, to improve further the efficiency of the automobile transportation system in most urban areas. Pollution is one reason. Most urban areas are reaching a critical point where the air is barely able to digest the automobile fumes emitted. The volume of cars must be curtailed, or the characteristics of the automobile engine must be modified. Regulation, taxes, subsidies, or all three can be used to correct this situation.

LAND UTILIZATION

Land utilization problems present another problem. Automobiles are such a land intensive (land-using) method of transportation, that they require great quantities of land to move a limited number of people. Only 1.1 persons occupy the average commuter car. This land-intensive aspect of auto use comes into conflict with a stubborn fact—the limited land area in central cities. The question is where to find land to locate roads to allow more people to enter the city or to move around in it. We soon begin to reach the point where the only solution is to tear down the city to build roads. Alas, this also destroys the city as a place where one can find jobs.

MASS TRANSPORTATION

The "obvious" solution to this congeries of problems is more mass transportation. But the existence of the automobile makes it difficult, if not impossible, to finance and utilize other types of urban mass transit. The automobile has great private advantages. No alternative mode of transportation allows you to walk out the front door and find your mode of transportation waiting for you. Busses and trains will never be quite as convenient. Bicycles cannot give you the same air-conditioned, poshly tailored, private compartment with your own radio and tape deck. Most public transportation systems require many people to transfer from one vehicle to another. This takes time and is inconvenient.

The peculiar character of automobile cost curves also makes it difficult for public transportation to compete with the automobile. The automobile has high average costs, but very low marginal costs. Volkswagen used to advertise "three pennies a mile." That was the marginal cost. But according to *Consumer's Report,* a New Yorker paid almost $2,000 per year in depreciation, insurance, taxes, etc., to *own* a car, before he ever drove a mile. That enters the average cost but was not included in the 3¢ per mile.

PUBLIC VS. PRIVATE TRANSPORTATION COSTS

Thus the *average* cost per auto commuter trip may be several dollars, although the marginal cost may be just a few pennies. Unfortunately, the commuter, judging whether public transportation is cheaper than private transportation, will compare not the average costs of his or her automobile with the public transit fare, but the marginal costs. Public transit, however, if it is to be self-financed must charge enough to cover its average costs. These average costs can be well below the average costs of the automobile but still well above the auto's marginal costs. *As a result, public transit can attract automobile riders only if it charges a fare that is below the auto's marginal costs. This means running a huge deficit in the transit authority.* The public's enjoyment of the automobile being what it is, even a free public transportation system might not attract the desired number of riders.*

Any deficit must be picked up by the taxpayers, a group that may not benefit at all. Certainly the central city taxpayers will not benefit from a transit system that extends far into the suburbs. Yet they may be called upon to pay the deficit caused by distant commuters. Taxpayers do not want to pay the bill for something they do not use, and there is no way to charge the commuter a price that will cover costs.

As a result, the economic system leads to incentives that encourage automobile driving, despite attendant problems of pollution and congestion, and make it difficult to change that mode of transportation. Public opinion polls illustrate the problem. Many automobile commuters are in favor of building an urban transportation system—not because they would use it, but because they think that *others* might use it, enabling them to ride their autos along uncongested streets. This attitude can be seen 'n a "scientific sample" taken from the Los Angeles *Times* Reader Panel. People were asked, "If by some miracle a rapid transit system were in effect tomorrow, would you ride to work on it?" In response, 50 percent said they "wouldn't, definitely, flatly." Another 10.8 percent said they probably would not; 2.6 percent said they probably would. Only 4.7 percent said they definitely would. On the other hand, an overwhelming number (86.6 percent) said that they believed that Los Angeles needed a new rapid transit system!

Public transportation is therefore viable only if the public is willing to take steps to curtail its own utilization of the automobile. Its willingness to do so will perhaps depend upon the seriousness of the health hazard created by automobile pollutants or by the mounting problems of an energy crisis.

Once again, *collective decision making, through political processes, is the only way to solve a problem that the market mechanism cannot solve.* Whether the political process can convince people that their long-term state of well-being would be improved by setting aside their immediate individual preferences is a possibility that remains to be seen. It need hardly be said that it is one of the most important decisions the next decade will bring.

---

*Alternatively, the marginal cost of auto travel could be raised by heavy tolls. This is hardly likely to be popular solution.

Distribution
of income
in theory

With this chapter we enter what is perhaps the most important major area of microeconomics. Having explored in some detail the dynamics of the demand for goods and the calculations of firms—both competitive and monopolistic—in the provision of goods, we have left unexamined a crucial area of the economy. This is the market for factors, where wages, rent, and interest are determined.

This area is crucial for two reasons. First, it leads us to complete the analysis of the circular flow, which has provided the basic pattern of our analysis. When we have understood the factor market we will have knit together the household and the firm in their second major interaction—this time with the household acting as supplier rather than demander, and with the firm providing demand rather than supply.

Second, our analysis is crucial because it takes us to the consideration of a problem of major political and social importance: the *distribution of income*, the main theme in this and the next two chapters.

17

The pure model   We have seen that product markets do not always work exactly as the "pure" competitive model would predict. So, too, we shall discover that factor markets depart from the competitive ideal. Big unions, for example, have some of the same effects as big business, and other imperfections lead to problems in factor pricing that are the counterparts of similar problems in product markets.

Nevertheless, as with the market for goods and services, we need the model of a pure competitive system, both to gain insight into the dynamics of the actual world and to provide a benchmark to measure its departures from the norm. Therefore in this chapter we shall hold our skepticism in check and examine the forces that bear on the distribution of income in a "perfect" competitive world. That will enable us to move into the imperfect world of reality in our chapter to come.

Factors and factor services

We must begin with a simple but distinguishing fact that separates the market for factors from that for goods. When we buy or sell goods, we take possession of, or deliver, an actual commodity. **But when we speak of buying or selling factors, we mean only that we are buying or selling a stream of services that a factor produces.** When we buy or sell "labor," we do not buy or sell the human being who produces that labor—only the value of his work efforts. So, too, when we buy or sell "capital," we are not purchasing or selling a sum of money or a capital asset. We are hiring or offering the use of that money or equipment. Land, too, enters the market for factors as an agency of production whose services we rent but need not actually purchase as so much real estate.

Obviously we can buy land as real estate, and we can buy capital goods and various forms of capital, such as stocks and bonds. (We cannot buy human labor as an entity, because slavery is illegal. In former times one *could* buy labor outright.) It stands to reason, then, that there should be a relationship between the price of factors, considered as assets (actual capital goods or real estate) and the price of the stream of services that factors produce: the *interest* earned on capital, the *rent* of land. There is such a relationship which we will study later under the heading of "capitalization." Here we must recognize that the market for factors is not a market in which the assets are sold, but in which the productive services—the earnings—of these assets are priced.

As in every market, these prices will be determined by the interplay of supply and demand. Therefore to study the factor market we must first look into the forces that determine the demand for factors, and then into the forces that determine their supply.

Direct demand for factors

Who buys factor services? Part of the answer is very simple. A portion of the services of labor, land, and capital is demanded directly by consumers for their own personal enjoyment, exactly as with any good or service. This kind of demand for factors of production takes the guise of the demand for lawyers and barbers and servants or the demand for plots of land for personal dwellings or the demand for cars and washing machines or other personal capital goods or the demand for loans for consumption purposes. To the extent that factors are demanded directly for these utility-yielding purposes, there is nothing in analyzing the demand for them that differs from the demand curves we have previously studied.

Derived demand

Most factors of production do not earn their incomes by selling their services directly to final consumers. They sell them, instead, to firms. In turn, firms want the services of these factors not for the firm's personal enjoyment, but to put them to profitable use.

Thus we speak of the firm's demand for factors as *derived demand*. Its demand is derived from the consumers' demand for the output the firm makes. We recall that each firm will hire labor (or any other factor) until the factor's marginal revenue product (its physical product multiplied by the selling price of the product) just equals what it costs the firm to hire that factor. Marginal revenue product curves can then be derived by plotting the marginal revenue product (marginal output × selling price of output) for each successive unit of the factor.

We see this in Fig. 17·1, where the derived demand for a factor leads Firm 1 to employ quantity *OA*. Derived demand of Firm 2 results in the hire of *OB*, and the summed demand of both firms gives us a market demand of *OC*.

This however leaves us with the question of factor price only half explained. We understand the elements that enter into the demand curve for the factor. But we cannot understand how the price of the factor is established until we know something about the supply curves in the

factor market. That is the missing element we need to complete the full chain of the circular flow.

The Supply Curve of Factors

What do we know about the willingness and ability of the owners of land, capital, and labor to offer their services on the marketplace at varying prices for these services?

Labor   By far the most important supply curve in the factor market is that of labor—meaning, let us remember, labor of all grades, from the least skilled workman to the most highly trained scientist or the most effective entrepreneur.

As Fig. 17·2 shows, the supply curve for the labor of most individuals has a curious shape. Up to wage level *OA*, we have no trouble explaining things. Economists assume that labor involves *disutility*. Moreover, just as we assume that increasing amounts of a utility-yielding good give us diminishing marginal utility, so we assume that increasing amounts of labor involve *increasing marginal disutility*.

FIG. 17·1   Derived demand for factors

FIG. 17·2   The backward-bending supply curve of labor

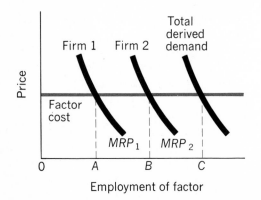

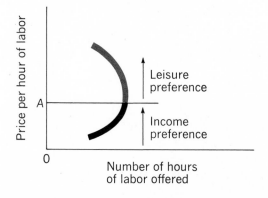

Therefore the curve rises up to level *OA* because we will not be willing to work longer hours (i.e., to offer a larger quantity of labor services within a given time period), unless we are paid more per hour.

The backward-bending curve

How then do we explain the "backward-bending" portion of the rising curve above wage level *OA*? The answer lies in adding to the rising marginal disutility of labor the falling marginal utility of *income* itself, on the assumption that an extra dollar of income to a person who is making $10,000 is worth less than the utility of an additional dollar when that person was making only $5,000. Above a certain income level leisure is preferable to more income.

Together, these two forces explain very clearly why the supply curve of labor bends backward above a certain level. Take a designer who has been tempted to work 70 hours a week by wage raises that have finally reached $7 an hour. Now suppose that wages go up another 10 percent. It is possible of course, that the marginal utility of the additional income may outweigh the marginal disutility of these long hours, so that the designer stays on the job or works even longer hours. If, however, his or her marginal utility of income has reached a low enough point and his or her marginal disutility of work a high enough point, the raise may bring a new possibility: the designer may work *fewer* hours and enjoy the same (or a somewhat higher) income as well as additional leisure. For example, as pay goes up 10 percent the designer may reduce his or her workweek by 5 percent.

Backward-bending supply curves help explain the long secular trend toward reducing the workweek. Over the last century, weekly hours have decreased by about 40 percent. Although many factors have converged to bring about this result, one of them is certainly the desire of individual men and women to give up the marginal utility of potential income for that of increased leisure.

Individual vs. collective supply

A cautionary note is useful here. We can speak with some degree of confidence about the backward bending supply curve of individual labor, especially when labor is paid by the hour or by the piece. But we must distinguish the supply curve of the individual from that of the labor force as a whole. As the price of labor rises, some persons will be tempted to enter the labor market because the opportunity cost of remaining "leisured" is now too great. This accounts for the entrance of many housewives into the market as the price for part-time office work goes up. Later we will study this problem of the "participation rates" of the population when we look into the macroeconomic problem of employment. **Here it is necessary to understand that the collective supply curve of labor is probably upward sloping rather than backward bending.** (It would be backward bending if wages rose so high that married women, for example, dropped out of the labor force as their husbands' earnings rose, but that does not seem to be the case.)

Psychic income

The supply curve of labor is further complicated because work brings not only disutilities but positive enjoyments. Jobs bring friendships, relieve boredom, may lead to power or prestige. Many people derive deep satisfactions from their work and would not change jobs even if they could improve their incomes by doing so. Indeed, it is very likely that individuals seek to maximize their "psychic incomes" rather than their money incomes, combining the utilities derived from their earnings and the quite separate utilities from their work, and balancing these gains against the disutilities that work also involves.

The difficulty in speaking about psychic incomes is that it involves us in an unmeasurable concept—a tautology. Therefore when we speak about the supply curve of labor, we generally make the assumption that individuals behave roughly as money maximizers, an assumption that has prima facie evidence in the long-run exodus from low-paying to higher-paying occupations and from low-wage regions to high-wage regions.

Mobility of labor   More than a million American families change addresses in a typical year, so that over a decade the normal mobility of the labor force may transport 20 million to 30 million people (including wives and children) from one part of the country to another. Without this potential influx of labor, we would expect wages to shoot up steeply whenever an industry in a particular locality expanded, with the result that further profitable expansion might then become impossible.

We also speak of mobility of labor in a vertical sense, referring to the movement from occupation to occupation. Here the barriers to mobility are not usually geographical but institutional (for instance, trade union restrictions on membership) or social (discrimination against the upward mobility of blacks) or economic (the lack of sufficient income to gain a needed amount of education). Despite these obstacles, occupational mobility is also very impressive from generation to generation, as the astounding changes in the structure of the U.S. labor force have demonstrated (see box at bottom of opposite page).

Here again the upward streaming of the population in response to the inducement of better incomes makes the long-run elasticities of supply of favored professions much greater than they are in the short run. This is a force tending to reduce the differences between income extremes, since the mobility of labor will not only shift the supply curve to the right in the favored occupations (thereby exerting a downward pressure on incomes), but will move the supply curve to the left in those industries it leaves, bringing an upward impetus to incomes. Figure 17·3 shows how this process works.

FIG. 17·3   Effect of labor mobility on relative wages

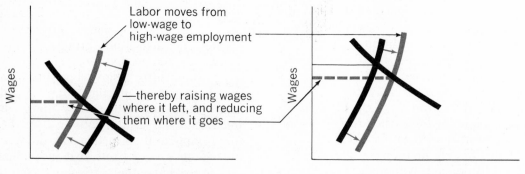

Low-wage employment   High-wage employment

Do people really work less as they get richer, trading leisure for income? The table below shows us what appears to be a steady decline in hours worked per year, for an average employee.

Year	Yearly hours worked
1890	2789
1900	2766
1910	2705
1920	2564
1930	2477
1940	2278
1950	2131
1960	1985
1970	1990

Yet, on second look the table is deceptive. For the "average" employee is an average of the hours

THE PUZZLE OF LABOR DISUTILITY

worked by men and women. As more and more women have entered the labor force, *most of them working part time,* of course the average working hours per employee has dropped. If we look at men and women separately, we find quite another conclusion. Both men and women were working *longer* hours (about 7 percent more) over the last decade, even though their real incomes were up.

Has the individual backward-bending curve changed its time-honored shape? Many answers have been suggested to explain the countertrend to longer hours *and* higher real incomes. One explanation is that leisure is now more expensive

(campers instead of canoes), so that we work more hours to earn a shorter but more expensive vacation. Another explanation is that we work longer hours because the time spent in unpaid work—household chores—has dropped, so that we have more time "available" for paid work. Again, it has been suggested that we work longer hours because we have switched to less "productive" but more enjoyable work, leaving the assembly line for the office.

Which of these answers is correct? *We do not know.* The upward twist in the individual labor supply curve remains an ill-understood fact. It should lead us, however, to be skeptical of claims that Americans are about to perish of boredom. Evidently work is more popular than the textbooks make it out to be.

Capital   What about capital? First, let us be clear what we mean by the supply curve of capital. When an economist talks about the factor of production *capital,* he is not talking about money or stocks and money. It is real plant and equipment to which he refers. At any moment, the total supply of this plant and equipment is fixed. Therefore the supply curve for total capital is a perfectly inelastic, vertical line, as Fig. '17•4 shows.

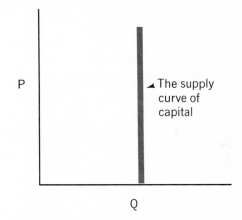

FIG. 17•4   The supply curve of capital

What kinds of work do people do in the United States? The table below gives us a picture of the shifting occupational profile of the nation's work force over the last seventy-odd years, together with projections of the U.S. Department of Labor for 1980.

Note particularly the dramatic change from 1900 to 1975. This striking growth in professional and managerial work, together with the drift from blue- to white-collar jobs, lies behind most discussion of "postindustrial" society as the direction in which we may be headed.

UNITED STATES' WORK PROFILE

	Percent of labor force 1900	1975	1980
Managerial and professional			
Professional and technical workers	4.1	15.0	16.3
Managers, officials, and proprietors (nonfarm)	5.9	10.5	10.0
White-collar			
Clerical workers	3.1	17.3	18.2
Sales workers	4.8	6.4	6.0
Blue-collar			
Skilled workers and foremen	10.3	12.8	12.8
Semiskilled workers	12.8	15.2	16.2
Unskilled workers	12.4	4.9	3.7
Household and other service workers	8.9	13.7	13.8
Farm			
Farmers and farm managers	20.0	1.9 }	2.7
Farm laborers	17.6	1.6 }	

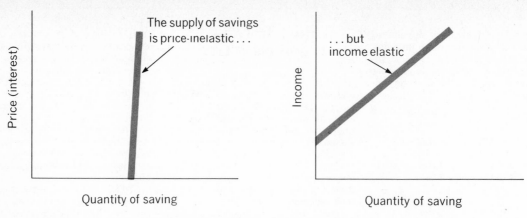

FIG. 17 · 5   The supply curve of savings

And savings

But our stock of capital over time is not fixed. We are constantly using up capital and adding new capital. Additions usually outweigh the wear and tear. *The supply curve of capital refers to these additions, which come from our savings. In turn, savings arise partly from our "propensity" to save out of a changing income, and partly from our willingness to save from a given income.*

The supply curve of savings

Do individuals or businesses supply *more* savings, out of a given income, if interest rates rise? The answer, by and large, seems to be no. Savings are relatively price inelastic, particularly if we are interested in the flow of total saving. Income is much more important than price in determining the supply of saving. When we turn to macroeconomics, the relation between income and savings will turn out to be a central focus of study. Thus we should become familiar with two conceptions of the supply curve of capital: a highly *price-inelastic* supply and a highly *income-elastic* supply. We see these in Fig. 17 · 5.

Allocating savings

At the same time, the allocation of savings is very responsive to price. As savers, we frequently reallocate

the way we dispose of our savings, shifting our "portfolios" among checking accounts, savings accounts, insurance, or stocks and bonds, as the various returns offered by these assets change (or as our assessment of their risk changes). For example, the rise in interest rates in the early 1970s resulted in a tremendous movement from noninterest-bearing checking accounts into interest-bearing savings accounts. Financial institutions also shift real investment funds in response to different rates of return.

Thus, when we picture the supply curve for saving, we should also bear in mind what this curve looks like to any particular demander. From the point of view of an enterprise in the market for capital, savings are highly price elastic; that is, a firm can attract savings by offering a higher return than a competitive enterprise offers. As a result, savers will shift their capital from one enterprise to the other, as in Fig. 17 · 6. This bears an obvious relation to the mobility of labor, and we can indeed speak of it as the *mobility of capital.*

Land

Finally, let us consider the supply curve of land. At any moment, the total supply of land, like capital, is fixed. To a limited extent, there is a counterpart to saving which adds to capital. By applying

248

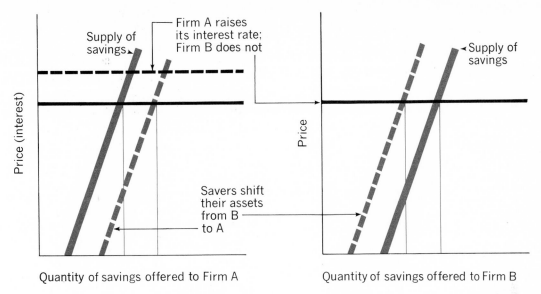

FIG. 17·6   Reallocation of savings

capital and labor we can slowly add to land, by dredging, clearing forests, reclaiming swamps and deserts. Therefore the long-run supply curve for land is slightly price elastic, as Fig. 17·7 shows.

As with capital, however, it is possible to speak of the *mobility of land.* This seems strange, since land is obviously not moveable. Land can, however, be used for very different purposes, depending on the returns to be had from them. If we picture the supply curve of land for, say, shopping centers or orange groves or industrial sites, we can picture an upward sloping curve, just like the supply curve of capital for any one use. Land can be—and constantly is— moved from use to use, as various enterprises bid for it. Thus the supply curve may be very elastic to any one user, even though the overall supply curve to society is very inelastic.

Land vs. space   In addition, we must differentiate land from space. We can create space much more easily than we can create land. Space is essentially a function of the availability of capital and labor, not of land. Every time we put up a high-rise building where there was previously a low one, we have created more space on the same amount of land. As a result, the supply curve for space will be very price-elastic—a higher price for space (rent) bringing more onto the market, as Fig. 17·8 shows. In the long run, space is available in indefinite amounts.

FIG. 17·7   Supply curve for land

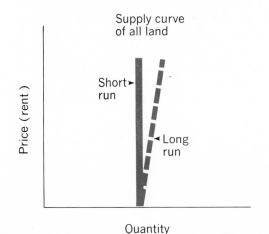

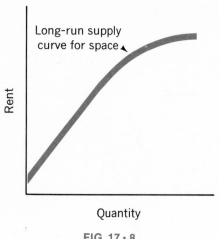

Rent

Long-run supply
curve for space ↗

Quantity

FIG. 17 · 8

Rents and Incomes

The importance of time in bringing about increases in land or space alerts us to a very important reason for the existence of very large incomes (and very large disparities of incomes) in the short run. This is the phenomenon of *economic rent* (also called quasi rent).

We have already discussed this matter on pp. 194–95, where we identified the incomes of intramarginal firms in a competitive industry as consisting of economic rents. Now we want to examine these rents more carefully, for they will help us in analyzing the distribution of income.

Land rent   First let us get rid of some confusing terminology, by distinguishing economic rents (or quasi rents, the same thing) from the earnings of land as a factor of production, which is also called rent. The distinction is clear in thought. It is muddied only because usage has chosen similar words for dissimilar things.

The rent earned by land as a factor of production is the payment we make to its owner for its services to the market. If we cease to pay land rent or pay less rent, the amount of land offered on the market will fall. If we pay more, it will rise. This rent is both a payment made to a factor of production to compensate its owner for its services and an element of cost that must enter into the calculation of selling prices. If a farmer must pay $100 rent to get an additional field, that $100 will clearly be part of the cost of producing a new crop.

Economic or   Economic rents or
quasi rent   quasi rents differ in
                     important ways from
true land rent.

1. Economic rent is not a return earned by the factor, in that the payment has nothing to do with inducing the factor to enter the market.
2. Economic rents are not a cost that helps to determine selling price. They are earnings determined by selling price.
3. Quasi rents apply to all factors, not just to land.

An illustration may clarify the problem. Figure 17·9 shows the supply curve for "first class" office space in New York City. Notice that over a considerable range there is an unchanging price for space. Up to amount OX, you can get all the space you want at rent OA (per square foot). This is real land rent, in the sense of being a necessary payment for a factor service. If there were no rent paid, no space would be forthcoming.

Next, look at the situation after we have used up OX amount of space. We can rent additional space up to OY, but only at rising prices (rents). Perhaps expenditures are needed to induce landlords to upgrade "second-class" space. Each new area that is tempted onto the market at a higher price earns real rent, in that it would not appear unless a higher price were paid. But notice that all the offices previously offered at lower prices are now in a position to ask higher rentals because the price of the marginal unit has increased. Thus here we have a mixture of real rents and economic or quasi rents. The marginal landlord is receiving real rent. All the other (intramarginal) landlords who can now get higher rentals are the beneficiaries of a scarcity price that gives them a bonus over the real rent they originally received. This bonus is economic or quasi rent.

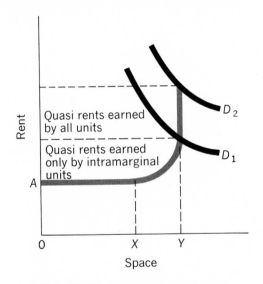

FIG. 17·9   Rents and quasi rents

Finally we reach the point OY, at which there is no more space to be had at any price. Suppose the demand for space continues to rise from D_1 to D_2. The price of office space will rise as well, and *all* landlords will be receiving quasi rents on top of their real rents.

Rents and prices   Here is where we make a clear distinction. True rent is a cost that must be paid to bring land into production. Quasi rent is not such a cost. It is wholly the result of

scarcity and plays no role in determining the real cost to society of producing goods or services. If demand fell from D_2 to D_1, a great deal of quasi rent would disappear, although not a foot of office space would be withdrawn.

Thus true rent helps determine price whereas economic or quasi rent is determined by price. We can see that rent must be paid if office space OX is to appear, but that quasi rent is not a necessary cost of production for space thereafter.

This conclusion, however, applies only to our analysis of costs from a social point of view. From the point of view of the individual producer, the distinction disappears. A renter must pay the landlord whatever it costs to rent space, be it rent or quasi rent. Thus quasi rents enter into the renter's costs and help determine the price that must be asked for his or her goods.

Economic rents and allocation   From the social point of view, economic rent is a waste. If we could eliminate it, say by taxing it away, it would not diminish production at all, only the incomes of the owners of scarce resources. Quasi rents are therefore wholly "unearned" incomes.

Nonetheless, they serve a useful function for society. They allocate a scarce commodity—in this case, office space among various claimants for that commodity. The fact that quasi rents are a "monopoly return" is neither here nor there, so far as their rationing function is concerned. If there were no quasi rents, office space would be leased at prices that failed to equate quantities demanded and supplied. There would be a "shortage" of space, and rationing would take place on some other basis—first come, first served or political influence or having an "in" with the landlord, instead of through the price mechanism.

Economic rents and incomes

Finally, *we must make careful note of the fact that economic rents are not returns limited to land.* Take car rentals. Suppose we can rent all the car transportation we need at the going price. Suddenly there is a jump in demand, and the rentable fleet is too small. Rentals will rise. If no additional cars come onto the market, the fleet owners will simply enjoy economic rents (quasi rents) on their cars.

In the same way, the earnings of actors or authors or of anyone possessing scarce talent or skills are likely to be partly economic rents. An actress might be perfectly happy to offer her services for a good movie role at $50,000, but she may be able to get $100,000 because of her name. The first $50,000, without which she would not work, is her wage. The rest is an economic rent. So, too, a plumber who would be willing to work for standard wages, but who gets double because he is the only plumber in town, earns economic rents. And as we have already seen, economic rent explains a part of business profits, as returns going to intramarginal firms.

Capitalization

Economic rents lead us to the process called *capitalization.* As we have mentioned, buyers of land and capital often have the option of buying the actual real estate or machinery they use, instead of just paying for its sevices. Capitalization is the means by which we place a value on a factor as an asset.

Suppose that an office building makes $100,000 a year in rentals and that we decide to buy the building. How much would it be worth? The answer depends, of course, on the riskiness of the investment. Some buildings, like some machines or bonds or businesses, are safer buys than others. For each class of risk there is a rate of return established by other buyers and sellers of similar assets. Suppose that the rate of return applicable to our building is 10 percent. Then we will capitalize it at $1 million. This is because $1 million at 10 percent gives us a return of $100,000.

We can capitalize any factor (or any business) by dividing its current earnings by the appropriate interest rate. The appropriate interest rate tells us the opportunity cost of our money: how much we could get for it if we bought some other factor or asset of similar risk. Notice that as the interest rate falls, so does the opportunity cost. We have to be content with a smaller return on our money. Thus if we are buying land that rents for $1,000, and the appropriate interest rate is 5 percent, the land will sell for $20,000 ($20,000 × .05 = $1,000). If the interest rate *falls* to 4 percent, the value of the land will *rise* to $25,000.

Capitalization and economic rents

Capitalization is important in determining the asset prices of factors. It is also important because it gets rid of economic rents! Suppose the $100,000 rental income were virtually all quasi rent and that the building were sold for $1 million. The new owners of the building will still be making $100,000 a year, *but it will no longer be an economic rent.* It will be a normal market return on the capital they expended. They will have paid for their quasi rents in the opportunity cost of their capital.

The gainer in the transaction will be the original owner of the building. Perhaps the building cost him very little, and the $1 million sale price came as a great capital gain. He will have capitalized his quasi rents into a large sum of capital; but on the sum, in the future, he can expect to make no more than the normal rate of interest.

Market Price for Factors

We are finally in a position to assemble the pieces of the puzzle. We have traced the forces that give rise to the supply curves of the different factors, and we understand the explanation for the demand curves as well. Hence we understand how factors are priced in the market, which is to say we understand the mechanism for determining *factor incomes*.

Can we generalize about the result? One would think, in the light of all the varieties of supply curves we have discussed, that this would be impossible. If we think about the nature of the demand curve for factors, however, we see that this

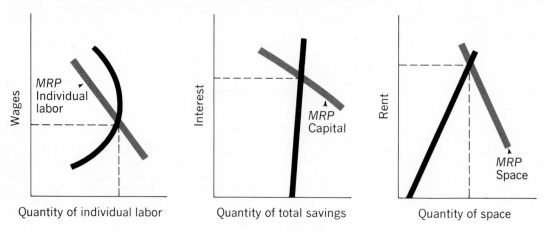

FIG. 17 · 10   Marginal revenue products and earnings

is not so. The shape and position of the supply curve for any factor will determine how much of it appears on the market at any given price. *But whatever the amount of the factor, it will be paid a return equal to the marginal revenue product of that factor.* Remember that the entrepreneur will go on hiring all factors as long as their marginal revenue products are greater than their marginal costs. Thus, whatever the shape or position of the supply curve, the earnings of the factor will always be equal to the marginal revenue it brings to the buyer, as Fig. 17 · 8 shows.

We could draw other curves, showing the collective supply of labor, the supply of savings to a given user, or the total quantity of land, but the conclusion would be the same. In each case, the market rate of wages, interest, and rent would be equal to the marginal revenue product of that factor.

The marginal productivity theory of distribution   We call this generalization about factor prices the *marginal productivity theory of distribution*. What it tells us is very simple. The income of any factor will be de-

termined by the contribution each factor makes to the revenue of the enterprise. Its income will be higher or lower, depending on the willingness and ability of suppliers of factor services to enter the market at different prices; but at all prices, factors will earn amounts equal to the marginal revenue they produce.

No exploitation   Two conclusions follow from this theory. *The first is that there can be no exploitation of any factor.* Each factor will receive an amount exactly equal to the revenue it produces for the firm.* There can be no unpaid labor or unrewarded land or capital. A worker or capitalist or landlord may not be willing to offer his services at going rates of pay, but none can claim that his earnings are less than the revenues he brings into the firm: for as we have seen, every profit-maximizing entrepreneur must keep on hiring factors until their marginal revenue products equal their marginal cost.

Moreover, no factor can claim that some other factor is paid too much. To be

---

*When a factor is bought directly by a consumer, the factor will receive the money value of the marginal utility it produces for the consumer.

sure, some factors will earn quasi rents, a waste from society's point of view, as we have seen. We have also seen that quasi rents are a temporary phenomenon, slowly eliminated by mobility of factors into an area of scarcity. In the long run, the returns to land, capital, and labor will reflect the actual contributions that each makes to output.

$$\frac{\text{Price of Factor A}}{\begin{array}{c}\text{Marginal Productivity}\\ \text{of Factor A}\end{array}} = \frac{\text{Price of Factor B}}{\begin{array}{c}\text{Marginal Productivity}\\ \text{of Factor B}\end{array}}$$

Prices and productivities   The second conclusion follows from the first. *It is that all factors will be paid in proportion to their productivity.*

Suppose that an entrepreneur can hire a unit of Factor A, say an acre of land, which will produce a marginal revenue product of $20, or an extra worker whose marginal revenue product will be $40. We know that the entrepreneur will have to pay $20 to hire the acre of land and cannot pay more than that, and that he or she will have to pay $40 for the worker and cannot pay less than that.

What accounts for the difference between the earnings of a unit of land and a unit of labor? Their marginal revenue products. But these marginal revenue products, we recall, are only the *physical* marginal products of the factors multiplied by the market value of the output to which they contribute. The value of the output must be the same, since land and labor will both be adding to the output of the same commodity. The difference in their marginal *revenue* products is therefore solely the result of the fact that a unit of land creates fewer units of output than a unit of labor.

It follows, therefore, that factor prices must be proportional to their physical productivities, or that:

Marginal productivity and "justice"   This is a very remarkable solution to the problem of distribution. What it says is that in competitive systems, all factors will be rewarded in proportion to their contribution to output. If an acre of land is only half as productive as a unit of labor, it will be paid only half as much. If it is twice as productive, it will be paid double. If skilled labor produces three times as much as unskilled, its wage rate will be three times that of unskilled, and so on. The resulting pattern of income distribution thus seems both "just" and "efficient." It seems just because everyone is getting all the income he or she produces, and because no one is getting any income he or she has not produced. It seems efficient because entrepreneurs will use factors in a way that maximizes their contribution to output, thereby not only giving the factors their largest possible reward but giving society the greatest overall output to be had from them.

Is this conclusion valid? Do the earnings of land, labor, and capital reflect their contributions to output? The question takes us from a consideration of how the factor market works "in theory"—that is, under conditions of perfect competition—to a consideration of how it works in fact. It brings us also to look carefully into the question of whether or not marginal productivity establishes a pattern of rewards that can rest its case on some definition of "justice." We will look into these extremely important questions in our next chapters.

Focus

Marginal productivity theory holds a time-honored place in economic analysis, although as we shall discover in our next chapter, it is open to very serious criticism. Nonetheless, we cannot criticize something we do not understand, and our purpose here is to get a clear picture of what the theory is about.

The upshot of the theory is very simple. It is that all factors in a system of pure competition will be paid the full value of their marginal revenue products. This follows because any entrepreneur who was paying any factor less than the value of its *MRP* could increase his or her income by hiring more of that factor. Since all entrepreneurs would be doing the same thing, the earnings of the factor would rise. If a factor were paid in excess of its *MRP,* it would not be earning its keep. The entrepreneur would let it go.

This analysis has very important social, even moral overtones, which we touch in our last pages and review in our next chapter. If all factors are paid incomes equal to their *MRPs* there can be no exploitation in the system. But let us not linger on this question yet. The analysis of the preceding pages investigates the supply and demand curves that will determine the income for each factor. The demand curves (direct or derived) stem from the value of the output of the factor—a matter we have already learned about. Therefore, the chapter concentrates on the differently shaped supply curves for the factors. Long and short run play important roles here, as well as differing elasticities for the factor supply as a whole or for uses of that factor among competing ends. We seem to end up with a great many supply curves. Actually, these are only graphic representations of how labor services or services of land or capital make many responses to changes in price or income.

You should certainly study the section on economic rents (quasi rents). For one thing, you will want to clarify the difference between real land rent, which we pay to tempt a landholder to offer his land for use, and an economic rent, the source of purely a scarcity gain. Second, you should understand that economic rents are both wasteful and useful. They can be entirely taxed away without changing the supply of factor services. Yet, they also serve to allocate the scarce (expensive) factor economically. Finally, the process of capitalization gets rid of such quasi rents. Because business is constantly "capitalizing" the value of its assets, this is a bit of economics that you should make an effort to master if you want to understand the business world.

WORDS AND CONCEPTS YOU SHOULD KNOW

Factor services, 243
Direct vs. derived demand, 243–44
Backward-bending supply curve of labor, 244–45
Psychic income, 245–46
Supply curve of savings, 248
Land vs. space, 249
Land rent vs. economic rent, 250–51
Capitalization, 252
Quasi rents, 250–52
Marginal productivity theory of distribution, 254–55

QUESTIONS

1. When suburban homeowners buy real estate, what services are they actually buying? When they hire domestic help, what services are they buying? When they borrow money from a bank?

2. What is meant by the *derived* demand for labor? What is its relationship to the marginal revenue product of labor? To clarify your understanding, do the following: (1) run over in your mind the law of diminishing returns (2) be sure you understand how this law affects marginal *physical* productivity; (3) explain how we go from marginal physical product to marginal *revenue* product; and (4) explain how marginal revenue product influences the willingness of the employer to hire a factor.

3. Suppose you had $10,000, that you kept half in cash and invested the rest at 6 percent. If the rate of interest went up to 7 percent, would you be tempted to invest more? Or the same? Or might you think that it would be wise to invest a little less, since your income was now higher? Are there reasonable arguments for all three?

4. If the rent of a piece of land is $500 and the rate of interest is 5 percent, what is the value of the land? Suppose the rate falls to 2½ percent; does the value of the land rise or fall? If the rental increases to $1,000 and interest is unchanged, what happens to the value of the land?

5. What do you think the supply curve of executive labor looks like? Is it backward bending? Would you expect it to be more or less backward bending than the supply curve of common labor? Why?

6. What do you think are the main impediments to factor mobility in the labor market? Location? Education? Discrimination? Wealth? How would you lessen these barriers?

7. Exactly what is rent? How does it differ from quasi rent? Is there any similarity between rent and interest, or rent and wages? What is the role of ownership in rent, profits, *and wages*?

8. What is meant by saying that rent is price determining? What does it mean to say that economic rent is price-determined? Show on a diagram.

9. Explain carefully how factor returns are proportional to their marginal productivities. What conditions would be necessary to make this theoretical conclusion true in the real world?

Corporate saving

In discussing the market for capital, we have been talking as if savers were all individuals. In fact this is not true. Corporations occupy a prominent place among savers. In 1975, corporate savings (depreciation allowances plus after-tax profits) exceeded all the investment in corporate plant and equipment. Corporate saving is therefore basic in creating and allocating investment. As we shall see, this poses problems.

First, however, we need to understand why the corporation saves. There are two reasons. One has to do with the double taxation of corporate income paid out as dividends. Corporate income is taxed once as the earnings of the firm—the rate for most big companies is roughly 50 percent. The income remaining after taxes can then be distributed as dividends and taxed again as part of stockholders' incomes.

Such taxation establishes a strong incentive not to pay large dividends but to hold the earnings in the company; that is, to save them. Saved earnings are untaxed. However, even though the earnings remain in the company, they will add to the value of the stockholder's shares, which should rise in price. These increases in value (capital gains) will not, however, be taxed unless the stockholder sells the security. If he or she does sell, the tax on the capital gains is somewhat less than on income.

A second incentive for corporate saving lies with the manager. By building up a fund of corporate savings, the manager gains access to finance without the need to pass before the judgment of the capital market. Funds come to the manager free, without borrowing and paying interest.

What is the problem with internal financing? It is that corporate saving lowers the efficiency of the capital market. A large fraction of the nation's investment funds escapes the test of the market. Funds can then be allocated for uses that might not be justified if the company had to pay the market rate for its money.

The steel industry, for example, is not generally regarded as very efficient. Its profit ratio has for years been below the national average. Yet steel has been able to pay for new equipment from its own savings. This investment may not have been possible if steel had to compete for savings against more efficient industries.

One often suggested remedy for this badly functioning market is to abolish corporate income tax. Each stockholder would be responsible for paying income tax on his or her share of corporate income, regardless of whether the income had been paid out as dividends or saved within the company. As a result, there would be tremendous pressure from stockholders for a very high rate of payout.

It has also been suggested that we tax the retained earnings (or savings) of a corporation. A corporation that saved would therefore have to pay an extra tax. As you can see, a combination of such a tax plus an integration of corporate and personal taxation would entirely reverse the pressures that now exist for corporate saving. Saving would once again be determined by individual decisions, and companies, like any other borrower, would have to bid for these savings.

The biggest objection to this plan is the fear that individual savers would not save as large a fraction of their incomes as corporations do. As a result, the funds available for national investment and growth might be diminished. Whether this fear is well founded we do not know. Nor can we predict whether the effort to end corporate saving is likely to gain political favor. We do know that the factor market for capital departs in a crucial way from the model of the market that economic theory depicts.

Distribution of income in fact

In the preceding chapter, we entered the factor market. We learned something about the behavioral elements that give us the various supply curves of factors, and we gained a general understanding of how incomes are determined in a market system. Now we want to put our first grasp of the subject to the test of a searching criticism. At the end of the last chapter we reached the conclusion that the prices of factors could be explained by their marginal productivities. Does this mean that we now have the key to understanding the actual distribution of income in our society? Can we explain riches and poverty, high-paid professions and low-paid ones, in terms of marginal productivity?

The quick answer to that question is No. Marginal productivity does not explain the basic facts of income distribution as we find it in the United States. Nonetheless, there is a valuable use for the theory. At the end of our chapter we will come back to the question of how we can use marginal productivity. First, however, let us discuss why it fails to explain income distribution as we find it in reality.

18

Rich and Poor

Chapter 2 made us familiar with the contours of income distribution. Perhaps you recall our discussion of "classes" on pp. 20–21 or the income "parade" in the box on p. 21. How much of this panorama can marginal productivity help us understand?

By and large we can eliminate two ends of the income parade. Marginal productivity theory does not explain the existence or persistence of most poverty, and it does not adequately account for the presence of most very high incomes. Let us begin by seeing why this is the case.

Poverty   We have looked into poverty more than once (pp. 20 and 36), and we are familiar with some of its attributes.

Quickly let us review a few major characteristics of American families who are in poverty in 1975.

- About a third of them are black.
- Over a third are families headed by a female.
- 11 percent of them are over 65 years of age.
- 39 percent live in female-headed households.
- 42 percent are juveniles.
- 9 percent of the family heads are unemployed.

These are not, of course, the only "reasons" for being poor. They are causative factors that figure to some extent in many cases of poverty. *Moreover, these characteristics of poverty have very little to do with marginal productivity.* There is no reason to believe that the marginal productivity of blacks or women condemns so many of them to low income status. (We shall discuss that question later.) Persons over 65 need not have low marginal productivity. Some of our most prominent artists, statesmen, lawyers, or executives are older than 65. And of course, the marginal productivity of an unemployed person is zero—not because he or she is not "productive," but because he or she has no job.

Low wages   Marginal productivity theory therefore gives us very little insight into the reasons for the low incomes of the bottom fifth of the nation. It sheds light on this bottom bracket only to the extent that its members are employed in very low wage (presumably low productivity) jobs. A considerable number of those in poverty do hold low-wage jobs: 40 percent of "the poor" work. But we shall see that their low pay is better explained by market imperfections than by attributing a kind of "innate" low productivity to the person who holds the job.

Thus poverty is a question that we must examine from perspectives other than that of marginal productivity. Why does the economy not produce full employment? Why does it have regional differences in productivity? Why does discrimination exist? Why is there a "culture of poverty" in the slums, from which it is difficult to break away?

Some of these questions are dealt with in this text. Others go beyond the scope or knowledge of economists. Clearly, when we want to explain most poverty, marginal productivity theory will serve us poorly.

Riches   What about the upper end of the income scale, the top 5 percent of families enjoying incomes over $32,000 or the topmost echelon of millionaires? Can marginal productivity help us explain high incomes?

To some extent perhaps it can. The marginal revenue product—that is, the saleable output—of many skilled professions helps to explain why airplane pilots, surgeons, lawyers, skilled artisans, and TV newscasters have high incomes; but even here, however, is a problem. Some of these high incomes, as we already know, are rents. Pay is high partly because there are many hurdles placed in the way of learning highly-paid trades. Thus, just as in the case of low-wage earners, market imperfections must be taken into account in explaining these extremes of income.

Property

More important, the topmost echelons of income reflect the unequal ownership of property. As we have seen in Chapter 2, the top 2 percent of all families owns 44 percent of all family wealth. Thus almost half of all property income is channeled into their hands. In 1975, this provided $100 billion for the 1.1 million families at the apex of the pyramid.

Can marginal productivity explain this concentration of property incomes? Not very well. Conventional economic theory explains the accumulation of wealth by saving. Undoubtedly some persons do accumulate modest sums by refraining from consumption, but they do not accumulate fortunes. If you start with $100,000—a sum possessed only by a very small fraction of all families—and if you invest the sum at 10 percent, paying a 50 percent tax on your interest, it would take a lifetime (actually 47 years) to pile up $1 million.

Very few millions are put together this way. As we noted in Chapter 3, the goal of riches seems to have two approaches. One of them is the road of inheritance, the source of approximately half of today's fortunes. The other is the road of "instant riches," the main source of new fortunes and in most cases the original source of the old fortunes as well.

Instant wealth

How does someone become rich overnight? As we saw earlier (p. 37), luck is helpful—once, anyway. People who make a fortune in one endeavor rarely go on to make as great a gain in another. Financial institutions, who employ the best expertise available, actually do not fare any better with their investments than the average performance of the stock market.

If luck seems to play a crucial role in selecting the winner, another element establishes the size of the winnings. Suppose that an inventor figures it will cost $1 million to build and equip a plant to make a newly-patented product. The product should sell at a price that will bring a profit of $300,000. A bank puts up the money.

Capitalization   The plant is built and the expected $300,-000 profit is realized. That much is luck. Now comes the instant fortune. To the nation's capital markets, the actual cost of the plant is of no consequence. *What counts is its return and the going rate of return on similar kinds of investments.* If that rate is 10 percent, the inventor's plant is suddenly worth $3 million, for this is the sum that will yield $300,000 at a 10 percent return. The inventor is now worth $2 million, over and above what he owes to the bank. He will have risen to the status of an instant millionaire because the financial markets will have capitalized his earnings into capital gains, not because his marginal productivity—or his saving—has made him rich.

The Middle Strata

Thus we do not look to marginal productivity theory—although we may use other elements of economic analysis—when we seek to explain the presence of very high incomes. Then what about the middle strata, the 85 percent of families who are above the status of "low income" and below that of the top 5 percent? Can marginal productivity help us here?

Table 18 · 1   Mean earnings of males, 1975*

Engineers, salaried	18,159
Sales workers	15,866
Primary and secondary school teachers	19,108
Managers, self-employed	12,997
Clerical workers	12,379
Manufacturing operatives	11,191
Service workers	10,199
Laborers, nonfarm	9,296

*Full-time, year-around.

Some basic problems   Consider Table 18 · 1. Can we say, on the basis of marginal productivity theory, that a salaried engineer who earns $18,000 is twice as "productive" as a laborer who earns $9,000? Or should we say that the engineer is *only* twice as productive as a laborer because the former makes only twice as much? It is hard to make sense of the question, because it is very difficult to figure the marginal revenue products of engineers or laborers. Even if we knew their productivities, it would be difficult to state that earnings in different occupations reflected productivities, because of the many barriers to mobility. We will soon discuss this further.

Meanwhile consider a second problem. If we examine the earnings of supposedly homogeneous groups such as female secretaries or male laborers or doctors or professors, we find that some members of the occupation may earn four or five times as much as another. Few people would claim that a highly-paid secretary is as productive as *five* low-paid secretaries or that similar productivity differences could be found in other occupations.

Still another problem is illogical differentials that persist over time. Women, for example, average only half of what men earn. Blacks average only about 84 percent of whites. Yet black women earn almost 96 percent as much as white women earn, whereas black men earn only 73 percent of the amount that white men earn. Results such as these would be far-fetched in the world of pure competition that marginal productivity theory describes.

Market Imperfections

This last sentence gives us a clue, for it brings us to problems that prevent the market from bringing about the results that theory predicts. Market imperfections play the same role in the factor market that noncompetitive market structures play in the market for goods and services. They result in prices higher or lower than the long-run equilibrium prices that a competitive supply and demand setting would produce. Let us look into some of these imperfections.

Ignorance and luck

Markets often fail to bring about a level of earnings corresponding to relative marginal productivities, because marketers do not have all the relevant information. A skilled mason in Connecticut may not know that there is a brisk demand for masons in Arizona—or even Rhode Island. A high-school graduate looking for her first job may not know that the possibilities for high wages are much greater in printing than in retailing. This is a market imperfection that we have already examined under the heading of *transactions cost.* Here we need only remind ourselves of its presence, as one reason why earnings depart from levels that can be explained by a theory based on rational, informed behavior. Luck and chance play roles in determining the spread of ordinary earnings, just as in the attainment of wealth.

Time lags

Another market imperfection is the problem of time lags. As equilibrium prices for factors change, substantial periods of time may be needed to bring actual earnings into line with long-run equilibrium earnings.

Think about Medicare and Medicaid and the consequent outward shift in the demand for medical care and doctors. Although there is a long-run upward sloping demand curve for doctors, the supply is more or less fixed at the moment. Thus, as Fig. 18·1 shows, when demand shifts from D_0 to D_1, the incomes of doctors (or price of doctors' services) will at first rise from P_1 to P_2, and only gradually fall to P_3. Supposing that it takes 5 to 10 years to train doctors, their earnings will not be at their long-run equilibrium for a 5 to 10 year period. If we add the time necessary to expand medical schools, the lags can

FIG. 18·1 Time lags and earnings

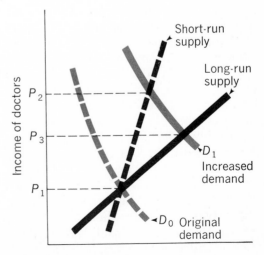

Quantity of doctors

easily be much longer. Moreover, by the time the schools are built, the long-run equilibrium price for medical care probably will have moved again.

The opposite situation arises when demand curves fall. Because it is difficult to move into new occupations as a person grows older, it may take a long period of time for the existing supply of doctors (or teachers or skilled workers) to shrink to the new long-run equilibrium. For substantial periods of time, wages paid to such occupations can therefore be below the long-run equilibrium level.

In both cases, the actual distribution of income accords with the marginal productivity of doctors or whomever. But this is a short-run rather than a long-run measure of their marginal productivity. In one case, doctors will be receiving incomes *above* their *long-run* marginal revenue product. In the other, they will be receiving *less* than their long-run marginal revenue product.

Monopolies

Ignorance and luck and time lags are involuntary market imperfections. More striking are market imperfections introduced by institutions that *deliberately seek to set factor prices above or below equilibrium prices*. This is the case whenever there is an element of monopolization in the factor market; for instance, in a small town where one landowner controls virtually all the real estate or where a single bank controls the availability of local capital. In these cases we would expect the level of rents or interest to be higher than the equilibrium level. In the same way, if one company dominates the labor market, we may find that wages are *below* their equilibrium levels—that labor is paid less than its marginal revenue product because it has nowhere else to look for work.

One of the most important institutions creating factor "monopolies" is the labor union. Essentially, a union tries to establish a floor for wages above the equilibrium rate that the market would establish. In this way, the economic effect of a union is exactly like that of a minimum wage law.

In dealing with monopolies of all kinds in the factor market, we have to distinguish between two questions. The first has to do with the earnings of the factors. No one doubts that factor earnings can be depressed below their competitive equilibrium levels in a one-company town or can be raised above their competitive levels by a powerful union. The more interesting question is the effect of such changes on the total earnings of the factor. Can a union, by raising wages, increase total payrolls, or will the effect of higher wages be to shrink payrolls? Look for this question in "An extra word" at the end of the chapter.

Rents and discrimination

We have already seen how economic rents create unearned incomes. Anything that inhibits the mobility of factors—anything that impedes their movement from lower-paid to higher-paid occupations—creates or perpetuates economic rents and enters into the explanation of income differences. Barriers of race and wealth, of patents and initiation fees, of geography and social custom—all give rise to shelters behind which economic rents flourish. If blacks, for instance, are systematically excluded from managerial positions, the supply of managers will be smaller than otherwise. Existing (white) managers will therefore enjoy economic rents.

The other side of this story is that barriers can constitute sources of *discrimination that lower the earnings of those who are discriminated against.*

Economic discrimination can take many forms. Wage discrimination occurs when two identical people are paid different wages for the same work. Employment discrimination exists when unemployment is concentrated among a preselected group. Occupational discrimination leads to limits on entry into good jobs and a corresponding increase in the supply of labor to less desirable jobs. Human capital discrimination occurs when individuals are not allowed to acquire certain types of human capital, such as education or training. All of these forms of discrimination will lead to lower incomes for the person discriminated against and higher incomes for someone else.

There are essentially two ways in which discrimination can be enforced. The discriminator may have some monopoly power vis-à-vis the discriminatee, either in the form of direct government intervention, such as the South African laws that bar blacks from certain jobs, or be-

cause he controls some complementary factor of production. For example, if whites own all the physical capital or land, blacks must of necessity work for whites.

Alternatively, the discriminator may have a *taste* for discrimination. He may not want to associate with the discriminatee, and he may be willing to take whatever actions are necessary to avoid this association. If he refuses to shop in stores with black saleswomen, then the derived demand for black saleswomen falls, and their market wage falls.

Discrimination against blacks To what extent does discrimination enter into income distribution in the United States? The most obvious instance has to do with blacks. The average black family has an income only 61.5 percent that of the average white family. In virtually every field, black earnings are less than white earnings in the same jobs. In itself, of course, such facts do not prove that wage discrimination exists. An apologist for the differentials in wages could claim that there is a real difference in the marginal productivity of whites and blacks. In that case the question is whether there has been discrimination at a more basic level; for instance, in the access to human capital.

Only a few years ago, it would have been simple to demonstrate that blacks were systematically prevented from acquiring equal skills or gaining access to jobs on equal terms. Their marginal productivity was lower because they were forced into the bottom jobs of society, unable to gain admission into many colleges, kept out of high-wage trades, and simply condemned by their own past poverty from accumulating the money needed to buy an education that would allow them to compete.

This picture is now changing in some important respects. As Table 18·2 shows, median incomes of black families are now much closer to those of white families, especially among younger workers. This change is the result of a substantial lowering of barriers against blacks entering many professions and occupations.

Income of black and other nonwhite families with college educations has risen dramatically. In 1961 only 28 percent of these educated families made more than $10,000. In 1970, 67 percent passed the $10,000 mark. Even more striking, in 1961 only 3.4 percent of college-educated nonwhites made over $15,000. In 1970, 48 percent made $15,000 or more. Discrimination against blacks is probably most serious today in low-paying, not high-paying jobs. The color of poverty in many countries, including our own, is still disproportionately black.

Discrimination against women   A second major area of discrimination militates against women. Table 18·3 compares women's pay (on a full-time, year-round basis) to that of men. As the table shows, women typically earn substantially less than men in all occupations. A portion of this differential may stem from women withdrawing from the labor force to have children and to nurture them in their early years, but there is no doubt that these "economic" reasons for pay differentials do not begin to account for the full differences we observe.

Statistics comparing men and women at age 35 show that the average *single* woman will be on her job another 31 years—longer than her male counterpart will work—and the average *married* woman will work another 24 years. Second, the facts show that married women are *less* likely to leave one employer for another than men are (only 8.6 percent of employed women changed employers in a year compared with 11 percent of men). Finally, U.S. Public Health data reveal that on the average, women are absent from work only 5.3 days per year, a fractionally *better* record than men's.

In recent years we have seen a good deal of stirring for equal rights for women, and we get the impression that discrimina-

Table 18·2   Median income of black families as a percentage of median income of white families*

	ALL BLACK FAMILIES	
Husband's age	1959 (57%)	1974 (75%)
Under 35	62%	87%
35–44	60	71
45–54	55	69
55–64	51	66
65 and over	57	69

*Husband-and-wife families only.

Table 18 · 3   Male and female earning differentials, 1975, full-time, full-year workers

Occupation	Women	Men
Professional, management	**10,797**	18,159
Engineers, salaried	**9,749**	18,072
Sales workers	**6,252**	15,866
Craft	**7,866**	12,899
Clerical	**7,790**	12,379
Operatives	**6,490**	11,191
Service workers	**5,328**	10,199
Nonfarm laborers	**7,114**	9,296
Laborers, farm	**n.a.**	8,397

tion against women is disappearing. The statistics do not support this. The proportional gap between male and female earnings of full-time workers has not changed since the 1930s!

Will it change? The Women's Liberation movement has won court battles to establish the right of equal pay for equal work, as well as equal rights to jobs, regardless of sex. Perhaps this will begin to alter our prevailing sexist patterns.

For the United States has been very slow to admit women to a full range of professional and occupational opportunities. Only about 10 percent of our doctors are women, for example, whereas in West Germany 20 percent and in the U.S.S.R., 70 percent, are women. Perhaps even more surprising, in Sweden 70 percent of overhead crane operators are women, an occupation virtually unknown to women in the U.S.[1] These surprising percentages at both ends of the "social" scale leave little doubt that women *could* earn a great deal more than they do, if the barriers of discrimination were removed.

Wage contours   Another distributional problem arises because people have strong feelings about

[1]The Conference Board, *Record*, Feb. 1971, p. 10.

how much they are "entitled" to. In our competitive model, each person is a rational income maximizer, out for himself. At no time does any supplier of labor look at the wages of *other* laborers, except to determine whether or not he is being paid the competitive rate of return.

Yet, real people do not focus narrowly on their own wages but look around them at the entire wage structure. A policeman looks at firemen's wages, at truckers', perhaps even at schoolteachers' incomes. This interest in other incomes has different labels. Psychologists might call it envy; sociologists might call it relative deprivation; economists have labeled it *wage contours*.

In simple competitive economics, what other groups of workers are paid is irrelevant to what you should be paid. It is all a matter of relative marginal productivities. In the real world, groups of workers do look at other groups ("reference groups," in sociologists' terms) to see if they are being paid fairly. Studies in this area reveal that people strongly feel that their economic benefits should be proportional to their costs (i.e., their efforts, hardships, and the like). and that *equals should be treated equally*. Since there are various types of "costs" in different situations, and different rewards (income, esteem, status, power), the problem of defining "equals" immediately arises. To what group of people do you compare yourself, to determine whether you are being treated relatively "equally" and "proportionally"?

Reference groups   Reference groups seem to be both stable and restricted— people look at groups that are economically close to themselves. This helps explain why very large inequalities in the distribution of economic rewards seem to cause relatively little dissatisfaction, whereas small inequalities can raise a great commotion. A policeman does not "expect" to make as much as a movie actor—Hollywood is not his reference group. He does expect to make as much as, or more than, a sanitation worker, perhaps as much as a teacher. Changes in the pay of his reference groups therefore bring immediate changes in his estimation of the fairness of his own pay.

As a result of these comparisons, wage contours lead groups strongly to resist changes in relative wage rates. Even the person benefitting from a change in relative wages may feel that it is unfair that she receive more than someone else. She does not think that she is putting out more effort. Consequently, labor economists have discovered that wage rates among many groups move together, almost independently of movements in the supply and demand curves in each occupation.

Teamwork and group productivity Reference groups influence the distribution of income in another way. This is because much output requires *teamwork*, and the productivity of any individual worker can be substantially affected by the morale of the group to which he or she belongs. A team that is generally content with its pay and conditions of work will far outproduce a team that is discontent. Higher team productivity is of course reflected in higher productivity of all its members. (The squabbles of baseball teams are well publicized examples of the bickering and discontent that affects productivity in many occupations.)

Thus it is probably more realistic to think that workers are paid in proportion to their team productivity than in accordance with the individual's productivity, which often cannot even be measured. Those who work in high-productivity teams make more money than those in low productivity teams, even though their individual skills may be identical. This, too, accounts for much of the variance we find among people with similar skills.

Internal Labor Markets

Let us notice one final imperfection in the labor market, an imperfection we call the "internal" labor market.

Up to this point we have been talking as if most workers acquired their skills before entering the labor market—say, at school—and then auctioned off their skills to the highest bidder, as if they were so many sacks of grain. In fact, most of the U.S. work force acquires job skills informally, taught by another worker on the job. A presidential commission found that 60 percent of all workers had acquired their skills by on-the-job training. Only 12 percent reported that formal education was the way they had learned their job.

On-the-job training is a very efficient way of training a labor force. It teaches skills that are necessary and does not waste time teaching things that are not. It is cheap because the learner is producing goods and service while he or she is still being taught. But on-the-job training creates major imperfections in the job market. For one thing, it means that there cannot be a supply curve of labor similar to that of individuals who are ready to work *before* they are hired. A worker who is trained on the job does not become part of the labor supply for that job until *after* he is hired. This means it is impossible to speak of his or her marginal productivity until after the worker is hired.

Moreover, on-the-job-training requires "discriminatory" behavior on the part of employers. Older workers will not train younger ones if they feel threatened by their own proteges, who might take away their jobs. Thus employers create "internal" labor markets, with graduated wage steps, carefully regulated "port-of-entry" jobs, and a seniority system that lays off the younger person first, regardless of his or her productivity. Another sizeable portion of the differentials that we find in earnings must be credited to these internal labor markets. Age-in-grade counts for more than marginal productivity in almost all occupations.

Uses of marginal productivity theory

All these difficulties explain why the distribution of income, even in the middle range, cannot be fully explained by marginal productivity theory, and why we must be very careful in assuming that the theory adequately accounts for variations in earnings—riches and poverty aside.

Should we then forget about the theory? Not quite. For just as the pure theory of competition helped to explain movements and tendencies in the real market, even if not real market prices, so marginal productivity can also enlighten us with respect to economic reality. *It tells us how entrepreneurs behave in hiring factors.* It explains the simple but crucial fact that entrepreneurs will not knowingly hire a factor (or a team of factors) that does not "pay its way." Thus the theory of marginal productivity serves as a first approximation to a theory of employment for the firm, even if it does not explain very much about factor incomes. However incomes are determined—by law, power, custom, or the marketplace—entrepreneurs will be guided in hiring factors by their relative profitability, which is to say, by comparing their cost with the marginal revenue product he can hope to obtain from them. As its marginal productivities rise, more of a factor will be hired. As they fall, less of it will be used.

Thus the theory helps elucidate one aspect of economic life. We simply must be careful not to claim that it explains income distribution or that different levels of earnings are "justified" by marginal productivity.

Marginal productivity and justice, again

One last question remains to be considered. Even if the theory of marginal productivity has only limited application to the real world, does it not remain as a kind of goal for a society interested in justice?

You may remember that the theory seemed to establish that in a fully competitive market, the levels of remuneration would be "just" because each factor would be compensated fully for the contribution it made to output. We remember that all factors in a competitive market earned their marginal revenue products. What could be fairer than that?

The question is trickier than you might think. Of course it makes us ask "What is *fair?*" a question we will come back to at the end of the coming chapter. It also seems to imply that there is one, and only one, distribution of income that would qualify as "fair." The impression given by marginal productivity theory is that there is one pattern of wages and rents and interest that would be established once and for all if a perfect market prevailed, but that is not so.

Once again an illustration is the best way to understand the problem. Suppose that we decide through our political system to establish a much more equal distribution of income—perhaps imposing wage floors and taxing high incomes much more steeply than we do. Such a shift would change demand patterns, since poor families have a higher relative demand for food, and rich families have a higher relative demand for luxury goods. Our redistribution of income will therefore shift the demand curve for food to the right and move that for luxuries to the left.

But higher demand curves for food products will lead to higher food prices and to higher incomes for those factors of production specialized in the food industry. Conversely, those factors of production specialized in luxury industries will face a lower demand curve and lose income. Moreover, unspecialized factors of production will also be affected. Let's assume that the food industry is capital-intensive—it uses a lot of capital per unit of output—while the luxury industries are labor-intensive, using little capital per unit of output. Such a shift in demand will therefore mean an increase in the price of capital relative to the price of labor. Not only will people with farming skills become richer relative to those with luxury skills, but all capitalists will become richer relative to all laborers.

The problem of the starting point

Now, both before and after these shifts, we can imagine factors being remunerated according to their marginal revenue products. Both worlds can be in equilibrium. But the distribution of the two worlds will be different—not only regarding those who happen to be in one industry or another, but also regarding the share of income going to capital and to labor!

Thus the marginal productivity theory of distribution can be consistent with many kinds of income distribution, depending on the conditions from which we begin. So, too, the distribution of income can change—still in accord with marginal productivity—depending on changes in "taste" or in technology. These new distributions of income can become more or less unequal, can favor one group or class over another.

Marginal productivity theory therefore essentially takes as a "given" the starting point of the circular flow and ignores exogenous changes that can alter that flow. We are then thrown back on the unanswered questions of how the initial starting point came into being or of how changing tastes or technology enters the system. History or the political process or the ill-understood course of technical development thus become the critical determinants of the income distribution process, even assuming that the market system operates perfectly. Marginal productivity theory could then describe the process of change, but not the starting point or the critical factors at work in altering the circular flow.

Moreover, each such different society could "justify" its different distribution of income by appealing to marginal productivity. This means that ultimately we must choose between alternative income distributions—none justifiable "once and for all"—because each reflects a given set of historical, cultural, and technical forces. There is no escape from making a value judgment at least once, before we agree that the market process should thereafter decide income distribution, whatever that determination may be.

FOCUS

Is marginal productivity theory useable? This is the central question of this chapter. And the final answer to which we arrive is that it is useful as an analytical means of understanding how much of a factor an employer hires, but not very useful in explaining how much income a factor makes. Our supplement on minimum wages and unions is really an application of the theory to employment.

The reason that the theory fails to explain incomes lies mainly in the difference between the real world and the world of pure competition. All the market imperfections that we have studied cause incomes to depart from the levels that marginal productivity theory would impose. Ignorance and luck, time lags, monopolies, rents and discrimination, considerations of justice (wage contours), of reference groups, of teamwork and on the job training—all exert their pressures on incomes, helping to bring about the inequalities, and the lasting differentials, and the anomalies that marginal productivity theory can not adequately explain.

To these familiar problems we add the phenomena of poverty and riches—two aspects of the real world on which simple marginal productivity theory throws very little light. It will help if you go back to Chapter 2, in the light of what you now know, and ask yourself to what degree you think marginal productivity can be used to explain the income levels of the various classes that we described on pp. 19–22.

WORDS AND CONCEPTS YOU SHOULD KNOW

Causes of poverty, 260
Cause of wealth, 260–61
Capitalization and "instant riches," 261–62
Market imperfections, 263–66
Discrimination against blacks, 265–66
Discrimination against women, 266–67

Wage contours, 267
Reference groups, 267–68
Internal labor markets, 268–69
Marginal productivity theory and employment, 269
Marginal productivity theory and "fairness," 269–70

QUESTIONS

1. How much of the differences in occupational earnings shown in Table 18 · 1 do you think can be ascribed to marginal productivity? Can you devise a research program that would enable you to study this with allowance for all market imperfections?

2. Which of the following do you consider to be market imperfections that result in earnings higher than those that would be produced by a free market: (1) certification by state boards before anyone can practice medicine (2) limiting admission to medical school by aptitude examinations, (3) the costs of education, if these can be covered by a long-term loan.

3. Suppose it could be shown that the marginal productivity of blacks in a given occupation was less than that of whites. Would that explain their lower rates of pay? Justify them?

4. A woman patents a gadget that brings her an annual net income of $100,000. The market return for her category of risky products is 20 percent. What is her patent worth? Can you show that the higher the degree of risk, the *less* will be her capitalized gain?

5. Suppose that consumers' tastes shift from expensive wine to cheap beer. How could that alter the distribution of income, assuming that everyone was paid his marginal revenue product?

6. How would you define *exploitation*? How many of the market imperfections that we have discussed could give rise to exploitation as you have defined it?

Union rates and minimum wages

Can unions raise wages? Can the government raise the wages of the poor by imposed minimum wages? Few questions in economics generate such heat. We'll try to throw a little economic light on them, too.

Minimum wages enforced by law and minimum wages enforced by union contract have very similar attributes. Both are equivalent to price supports for agricultural products, in that they establish a price higher than that which the market would establish by itself. If they did not, they would not serve any purpose. Thus in Fig. 18 • 2 we can view the wage line *AB* as established by union or government, for in both cases its effect is to establish a wage "floor" above that set by the intersection of supply and demand.

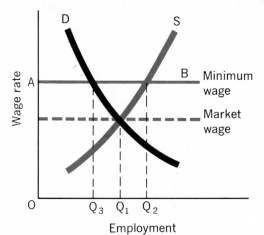

Fig. 18 • 2   Effect of minimum wage laws

The diagram shows that the volume of employment would be Q_1, if there were no union or minimum wage. This is also the amount of labor that workers would offer at that wage. At the new higher wage level *AB,* employers now want to hire only Q_3 worth of labor, while workers are now interested in supplying Q_2 worth of labor services. As we can see, there must be a labor surplus, just as there is an agricultural surplus when farm prices are set above the market equilibrium.

Three effects follow. Some workers will lose their jobs because the new higher minimum wage is above their marginal revenue product (or above what the employer estimates their *MRP* to be). In the diagram, this amount of lost employment is represented by Q_1–Q_3. Here are the delivery boys who are let go when the minimum wage is raised to $2.50 an hour and small grocery stores decide to cut down their help. Here are the elevator operators who are replaced by automatic elevators when a union wage contract finally tips the balance in favor of automation.

Second, some workers—those between O and Q_3—will find their incomes raised. Here are the grocery boys who are kept on at higher pay; the elevator operators who are not fired but have fatter pay envelopes.

Third, there will be a larger number of workers than formerly—those between Q_1 and Q_2—looking for work. Their condition will be neither better nor worse than before the union floor or the minimum wage, for at the previous wage rate these people were not seeking work, nor did they have any income. Nonetheless, their presence in the labor market will be noted in the statistics of unemployment, and it may have social and political consequences.

Is there a net gain or loss in the situation? As you can see, the increase in earnings of the group that is retained can be compared with the loss in income of the group that is fired. There are, however, problems in such a comparison. It is much easier to calculate gains and losses on a diagram than to compute them in real life. This is because everything hinges on the slopes of the two curves. Suppose, for example, that we think that the demand for labor is extremely inelastic. Then even though unemployment rises, no one will lose his or her job. All will remain employed with higher earnings. To make the point clear, we show this case in Fig. 18 · 3, with a totally inelastic demand curve.

On the other hand, suppose that the demand for labor is highly price elastic. Then many workers could lose their jobs, as you can easily see, if you draw a diagram with an elastic curve.

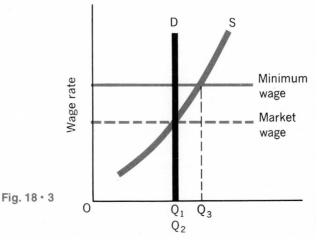

Fig. 18 · 3

What is the shape of the actual demand curve for labor? Studies indicate that it is probably quite inelastic, so that minimum wage laws do not have a severe adverse effect on total employment. Rather, their effect is likely to be heavily concentrated on certain groups, such as teen-agers. The illustration of delivery boys is not an idle one. A high minimum wage may well result in substantial teen-age unemployment in menial jobs. This has led to suggestions that there should be lower minimum wages for adolescents than for adults, a scheme that has been used in Europe but that has so far been opposed by labor unions in this country.

Union wage settlements also have their gains and losses, exactly as do minimum wage laws. Once again the critical factor is the elasticity of the demand for labor. But there is a difference with respect to the impact of union settlements. Minimum wage laws affect only the fringe of workers whose pay is below the minimum. Union settlements typically affect all workers in the industry. The incentive to substitute machines for people or simply to economize on labor is therefore much greater. The economic consequences of a union wage settlement are, accordingly, likely to be more substantial than those of a boost in minimum wages.

Changing the distribution of income

Can we change the distribution of income? Of course we can. Should we? That is a more difficult question. When we speak of deliberately trying to change the distribution of income, our purpose is usually to make it fairer. By *fairer,* we generally mean more equal, although not always. Sometimes we say it is not fair that certain groups, such as school teachers, do not get higher incomes, even though they are already receiving incomes that are above the median for the society. In the discussion that follows, we will largely be concerned with ways of making income distribution "fairer" by making it more equal. At the end of the chapter we will take up the question of the value judgments that lie behind this decision. First let us concern ourselves with ways and means.

If you want to change income distribution, you must choose among four basic ways of going about your task. You may try to change the marginal productivities of individuals and then let them fend for themselves on the market. Or you may try to limit the workings of the market, so that certain people will receive larger or smaller incomes, even if their marginal productivities remain the same. Or you may let marginal productivities and

19

274

markets alone and intervene by the mechanism of taxes and transfers, rearranging the rewards of society according to some principle of equity. Finally, you can introduce some system of rewards wholly different from market-determined rewards. This is surely the boldest and most far-reaching method, but it is one about which economists have very little to say. Accordingly, we will confine ourselves to the first three methods.

1. Changing productivities

Assuming that low marginal productivity is a basic reason—if not the only reason—for low incomes, someone who wants to change income distribution would do well to begin by boosting the marginal productivity of the least skilled and trained. How is that to be done? By and large, by giving *education*, a generalized skill, or *training*, a specialized skill, to those who lack them.

Education and income. A glance at Table 19-1 makes it clear that there is strong functional relationship between education and lifetime earnings.

Table 19·1 Male education and average lifetime earnings

	Lifetime earnings (1975)
Elementary school	
0–7 years	$275,000
8 years	366,000
High school	
1–3 years	448,000
4 years	581,000
College	
1–3 years	629,000
4 years	812,000

We must be careful not to jump to the conclusion that education is the direct cause of these earnings, however. For example, 30 percent of white high-school graduates will end up making more money than the average college graduate, and 20 percent of college graduates will make less than the average high-school graduate. Clearly there is no guarantee that education will pay off for everyone.

There is also a problem of scale. The table shows us that college graduates as a group have higher incomes. This may be because there are fewer of them and they earn scarcity rents. If everyone went to college, the supply and demand situation would be radically different, and the extra earnings of the college group much smaller.

Last there is the problem of circular causation that we have encountered before (see the box, "Perpetuation of Income Differences," in the preceding chapter p. 261). Education may indeed be a factor in increasing lifetime earnings. It is also true that someone coming from a high-income family will receive more education and will probably earn a high income *because of his social station in life*. When we correct for the starting point on the income scale, education still yields a return, but a much smaller one than the figures in Table 19·1 indicate. Probably the cost of a college education gives its recipient a lifetime return of about 7 to 10 percent on that investment, hardly a bonanza.

Investment in human capital. Even if the advantages of education are frequently exaggerated in terms of their strictly economic results, there is no doubt that education is a help toward higher income. For one thing, it teaches general skills such as reading, writing, and math. Equally valuable is its teaching of behavior expected in high-level occupations: how to speak "politely," how to be punctual, how to relate to authority, and other often overlooked attributes of classroom discipline that prepare us for managerial jobs.

How does one measure inequality? How does one determine, between two unequal income distributions, which is more unequal? One widely used way of measuring inequality—or more accurately, of measuring the distribution of any variable, such as income, age, weight, I.Q.—is to use a geometrical device called a Lorenz curve.

We construct a Lorenz curve by drawing a box, as illustrated in the graph. The vertical and horizontal axes, depicting the variables in which we are interested, are measured on a percentage scale. Thus in the diagram, the vertical axis shows percentages of total income from zero to 100, and the horizontal axis shows percentages of all families, from zero to 100.

Next, we rank families in terms of the variable we wish to measure (income in this case), from lowest to highest, and then indicate on the graph the relationship between a given percentage of families and the corresponding percentage of total income. Below, for example, the dots show that in the U.S., in 1972, the first

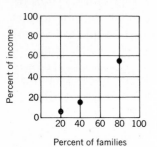

Percent of families

GINI COEFFICIENTS

(lowest income) 20 percent of all families received just over 5 percent of all income, the first 40 percent about 17 percent of all income, and the first 80 percent of families about 58 percent of income. If we fill in enough of these relationships, we get a "curve"—a so-called Lorenz curve—of income distribution.

Now comes the Gini coefficient. What would a perfectly equal distribution of income look like on a Lorenz diagram? It would be a "curve" in which each successive percentage group of similar families enjoyed the same percentage of income: the first 20 percent getting 20 percent of income; the first 40 percent, 40 percent of income; the first 60 percent, 60 percent of income. What would a curve of "perfect equality" look like? It would be a straight line, from one corner to the other.

And how about "perfect" inequality? It would show the last (richest) family getting *all* the income, and the first 99.9 ... percent getting none. We show both these distributions in the chart at bottom right, together with a Lorenz curve that roughly depicts the actual distribution in America today.

Probably you have already seen what the Gini coefficient will measure. It is the ratio between the dashed area outlined by the Lorenz curve and the full area under the 45° line. In the case of perfect equality, the area enclosed by the Lorenz curve is zero, and the

coefficient would also be zero. In the case of "perfect" inequality, the area enclosed by the curve, as shown by the dotted line, is virtually as great as the area under the 45 line, so that the Gini coefficient is 1.0. Thus, the closer to zero, the less the inequality of any given distribution.

In actual fact, the Gini coefficient for the United States in 1970 was slightly less than .40. This is about the same coefficient that we find in most West European countries, and it is probably considerably less than the coefficients of many underdeveloped countries, where the distribution of income is highly bi-modal (see p. 694). Whether or not the "Gini" is rising or falling within the United States (or whether it is rising or falling between groups such as blacks and whites) is a complex problem, about which opinions differ. Probably whatever movements exist are small and slow. The usefulness of the Lorenz curve with its Gini coefficient is that it enables us to speak about these changes in a precise manner and therefore to compare our findings in a way that would not otherwise be possible.

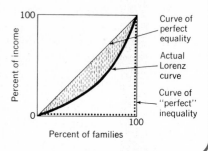

Percent of families

Thus, programs to invest in education can help poorer citizens overcome the handicap of being without the advantages of schooling.

Education is not the only way of lifting marginal productivity. Investments in the health of low-income persons can also increase their earning power. Investments in housing may improve marginal productivity by giving poor persons a "stake" and an incentive to succeed. Investments in programs to overcome barriers to mobility

of all kinds enable persons to put productivities to better use. To use the market mechanism to their advantage, highly skilled workers must have money to move where their talents are in demand. They must know about jobs where their abilities could be best put to use. They must not be barred from certain jobs because of discrimination.

All these investments in human capital, including investment, need not be judged by their contribution to marginal productivity. We may deliberately undertake programs to improve the conditions of the poor because our values incline us in that direction, whether or not an economic calculus would show a net monetary gain. In the end, values are decisive in determining what we should do—and what we actually do—in altering income distribution. There will be more about this at the end of this chapter.

2. Intervening on the demand side of the market

A quite different way of going about the task of changing the income distribution is to intervene on the demand side of the market. The most widespread current intervention is that of minimum wages—whether imposed by law or unions. As we have seen in the "Extra word" at the end of Chapter 18, minimum wages have two impacts. They raise earnings for those who are employed but may cause some other people to lose their jobs. The size of these two groups depends upon the elasticity of demand for labor.

In the last decade there have been two other broad attempts to intervene on the demand side of the labor market. Governments have attempted to alter the demand for workers by antidiscrimination or affirmative action laws and regulations and by subsidizing private on-the-job training.

Antidiscrimination laws apply to every employer. No one can legally deny a person a job or a promotion based upon age, sex, race, or national origin. Affirmative action regulations apply only to firms that do business with government or receive payments from government, but many companies are in this category. Here government requires that the firm, public agency, or university have some plan for altering its distribution of employment in favor of groups that are underemployed relative to their proportion of the population. Usually blacks and women are designated as the groups requiring affirmative action.

Effects of intervention. How successful have these interventions been? In some cases, especially for well-educated members of disadvantaged groups, the programs have undoubtedly yielded substantial gains. For the average black or average woman, the impact has been virtually unnoticeable.

This negative verdict is also true of the effort to change the demand for labor through government subsidies given to employers who agreed to hire disadvantaged workers. Here two difficulties have been encountered. First, the years since 1970 have been plagued with recession. During recessions the new, nonseniority worker is always the first to be laid off. Therefore, the gains from subsidized hiring have been short-lived or have disappeared.

Second, there is the fact that employers normally hire some disadvantaged workers. Thus, if they are subsidized to hire blacks, they may well hire the same black workers they would have hired anyway and apply for a payment for having done so. Economists call such payments a dead-weight loss, and there is considerable suspicion that most of the subsidy payments made in the 1960s and 1970s were in fact dead-weight losses. The attempt to move demand curves by regulation or payment has not been a great success.

3. Taxes and transfers

A third means of altering income distribution is to tax high incomes and to subsidize low ones. Taxes and subsidies (or transfers, as they are called) are used by all governments to redistribute incomes. Let us examine them carefully.

To begin, it is helpful to classify taxes into three types, so far as their effect on income distribution is concerned. We call a tax *progressive* if it takes an increasing proportion of income as income rises, so that a rich person pays a larger fraction of income in taxes than a poor person does. We call a tax *proportional* if it takes an equal fraction of the income of a rich or a poor person; and we call it *regressive* if it takes a larger fraction of a low income than of a high one. Someone who wants to make income more equally distributed will want a progressive tax system. Someone who wants it more unequally distributed will want a regressive system.

Impact of taxes   What kind of a system do we actually have? That is not a question to which a simple answer can be given. For one thing, we have more than one system. Our tax system for income is different from that for wealth. As we shall see in some detail in the next chapter, it is not always possible to know who ultimately pays a tax.

In general, our system of taxing incomes seems to be proportional when we add all of our taxes. Some taxes, such as the federal income tax, are progressive. Others, such as state and local sales taxes, are regressive. The two elements seem to balance out, leaving us with a proportional tax system that does not alter the market distribution of earnings. Taxes lower everyone's income by the same fraction and leave everyone with the same share of income they had before taxes.

If we look at inheritance taxes, the basic instrument for controlling the distribution of wealth, we see a system that looks progressive. Maximum tax rates reach 77 percent. But the loopholes to avoid these progressive taxes are so nu-

AFFIRMATIVE ACTION PROGRAMS

No government program to alter the distribution of earnings has been more controversial than the affirmative action requirements, for affirmative action offends people in a way that antidiscrimination laws do not. People may object violently to the results of antidiscrimination laws or to techniques of compliance, such as busing; but almost no one is willing to argue that an unequal start is a good thing. People may call training programs for the poor inefficient, but no one calls them un-American.

Affirmative action laws make people angry because they seem to be unfair. In order to find qualified members of minority groups, firms or agencies or universities have to pass over fully qualified members of majority groups. Is it fair not to hire a qualified white electrician because affirmative action gives a preference to a black one, or not to hire a young male graduate student as a teacher because a college is short of women instructors?

The fairness issue really comes down to the obligations of one generation to redress the grievances of another. Suppose that discrimination disappeared magically tomorrow. Blacks would still be holding the jobs that were open to them in the discrimination-filled past. If nothing further were done, it would take about 45 years—the time it takes for a generation to pass through the labor market—for the effects of past discrimination to be eliminated. Affirmative action can thus be viewed as an attempt to offset the impact of past injustice.

Does it also create present injustice? Is the white electrician, the male graduate student fairly treated? Most people say no. At the same time, we must try to see the problem from the viewpoint of the whole society as well as from that of the offended person. Is it not possible that a society is becoming more fair, even though some individuals are being treated less fairly? Those persons who suffer from affirmative action today are the victims of our efforts to overcome the unfairness of the past. The problem is therefore whether we can remedy the failures of past generations without inflicting injuries on some members of the present generation.

Ideally there is no reason why not. To raise up a previously dispriviledged person does not require that someone else be put down. But the ideal solution requires an expansive economy where the demand for talent outstrips the supply. In a sluggish environment, the fight for advancement becomes a zero sum game, and my gain becomes possible only at the expense of your loss. This has been the situation during the past ten years of inadequate growth. In such a situation there are bound to be losers. The question is: who will they be?

merous that almost no one pays them. Inheritance tax collections amount to an annual wealth tax of less than 0.2 percent. Obviously, these taxes cannot have much impact on the distribution of wealth.

Effectiveness of transfers

Although taxes do not have much impact on the distribution of income, transfer payments do. If we look at the families in the bottom 20 percent of the population, we find that over 60 percent of their income comes in the form of transfer payments. Without such payments, their share of total income would be less than half of what it is now.

At the same time, existing income transfer programs are not well coordinated. Some poor people receive a lot of benefits; other poor people receive none. Some programs provide benefits for people who, on a lifetime basis, will not be poor. Programs are often locally administered, leading to benefit levels that differ greatly from state to state.

Negative Income Tax

To overcome these problems, Presidents or presidential candidates in both parties have recommended the establishment of a Negative Income Tax. In 1975 the Department of Labor Statistics defined as "poor" an urban family of four having less than $5,500 annual income. Under a Negative Income Tax, we would transfer income to all families having less than that amount. This would have cost about $15 billion, roughly one percent of GNP.

This seems like a simple method of eliminating poverty. It has problems, however. Suppose that we also decided *not* to help people as they rose above the officially defined poverty level, so that we reduced the amount of aid by the amount of any income a poor family earned. Thus,

if a family earned $3,000, it would then get $2,500 in assistance. If it earned $4,000, it would get $1,500. If it earned $5,500, it would get nothing.

This seems equitable, at first look. *Actually, it is the same as a 100 percent tax on all earnings under $5,500.* Why should any family bother to earn any sum less then $5,500 if its welfare is immediately reduced by that amount? Would it not be sensible—rational—to stay on relief, rather than take a low-paying and probably unpleasant job?

Work incentives

Unfortunately, this is the way many welfare programs have been administered in the past. Not surprisingly, they have resulted in strong disincentives to work. Accordingly, economists now propose that assistance programs should have work incentives built into them.

This means we must tax below-poverty earnings at less than 100 percent. To make the arithmetic simple, let's tax at 50 percent—actually a very high tax rate, since it is the top rate currently paid on the highest salaries earned in the United States. If a family earns $1,000, it must then pay $500 in taxes. This now leaves it with an income of $5,500 after taxes ($5,000 in assistance plus $1,000 in earnings, less $500 in taxes).

Note, however, that we are now making transfer payments to people whose pre-tax income is $6,000—*above* our poverty line of $5,500. If we are to avoid taxing away all increases in earned incomes, we shall have to continue to make transfer payments until family earnings reach $10,500. At this point, a family's budget would look like this:

Transfer income	$5,500
Earned income	$10,000
Tax on earnings	− $5,000
Net income	$10,500

The problem of costs

This presents us with two problems. The first is economic. Under the plan we have just examined, a "poor" family earning $10,500 would have an advantage over a family that was not deemed "poor" and that earned the same amount, because the second family would owe taxes on all its $10,500 income and would therefore end up less well off than the income-supported family. To remove this inequity, we would have to pay support allowances to *all* families and remove all taxes on nonpoor families' earnings up to $10,500. Costs would rise from the approximately $15 billion needed to eliminate poverty if we impose a 100 percent tax, to a level between $40 and $50 billion. A sharp increase in income tax rates above $10,500 would be necessary to finance this.

The political issue

The second problem is political. Could we persuade the more fortunate to bear the entire income tax burden? With incomes above $10,500, these families would be neither "in" nor "near" poverty. They would have to recognize the unfairness of programs that lock others into low income brackets with a 100 percent tax on earnings.

There is no economic answer to this question. What is at stake is essentially a political choice between two patterns of income distribution. That choice will be exercised through political programs that will favor one group or another—those at the bottom of the scale or those who are sufficiently affluent to be in the higher taxpaying brackets.

In review

Can we change income distributions? Yes, of course. But not all ways of doing so are equally effective. Efforts to change

marginal productivities have not yet shown marked results, although this does not detract from their worthwhileness on other criteria. Interventions through minimum wages, unions, or government requirements have undoubtedly benefited some groups but cannot be judged to have made a large-scale difference in our national distribution of income. The impact of taxes, as we have seen—and as we shall see in more detail in Chapter 20—has not affected the overall shares. Only income transfers seem to have made a substantial difference to a large group of the population. *In all likelihood, this will be the means by which we can work the* quickest *changes in income shares, although a determined attack on discriminatory barriers might work the largest and longest-lasting effect.*

Value Judgments in Economics

So we can change income distribution, even though the task is by no means easy. But should we? We cannot study the mechanics of the problem without sooner or later coming to grips with the morality, the politics, the philosophy—*the values*—of the problem.

Equity vs. efficiency

Does economics have anything to say about value judgments? Traditionally, economists have been extremely cautious about making one kind of value judgment—that concerning *equity*. By equity, we mean justice: an equitable distribution of income is a just distribution, an inequitable one, an unjust distribution.

Of course this raises the question of what we mean by *just*. Philosophers have argued over the meaning of that word for millennia. Economists have politely bowed out of the discussion. They have refused to say what they thought was just, or else they have taken the position that as economists they had no special claim to knowledge about justice. They have therefore traditionally declared their own preferences to be no more than those of any citizen and have equally carefully tried to keep personal preference out of their economic analyses.

On the other hand, economists have been quick to claim the validity of their analyses regarding *efficiency*. By and large they have distinguished between efficiency and equity, in economic terms, as follows. **Problems of equity involve matters such as the distribution of income.** Here the concept of justice enters, so that the economist has refused to say which of two or more income distributions is better. **Efficiency, on the other hand, involves problems of minimizing input and maximizing output.** Most people claim that a larger output is preferable to a smaller one, or that we want to get as much output as possible for a given input. Therefore economists have freely offered advice about efficiency, without feeling that they were getting involved in value judgments.

mutual condition. Seeing that you are very poor and that I am very rich, he decides that our mutual condition will be improved if some of my possessions are transferred to you.

How could he justify his decision? Essentially he could not, unless he made the value judgment that our more equal new condition was "better" than our former less equal condition. Obviously, he cannot *know* that. Perhaps he is wrong. For all he knows, my increased enjoyment of still more wealth might be greater than your decreased enjoyment of less wealth.

But, said Pareto, suppose that we can arrange matters so that one of us gains *while the other remains exactly as he was before.* Now we no longer have to make dubious calculations. No one has lost; someone has gained. Our second combined position is unambiguously better than the first. Moreover, Pareto added, there is a second way to accomplish the same end. Our social situation may be altered so that you gain and I lose, perhaps by giving you some of my income. But if you can *compensate me for my loss in some other way, so that I declare myself as satisfied as I was before,* once again there has been an unambiguous gain in welfare. We have improved our efficiency in a way that seems quite free of any interjection of values.

Pareto optimality

The clearest example of an efficiency criterion is called Pareto Optimality, named after its inventor, the brilliant Italian sociologist and economist Vilfredo Pareto (1848–1923).

Pareto gave us a definition of efficiency that has an immediate, intuitive appeal. Suppose our society is composed of only you and me, each of us enjoying a certain condition of well-being. Now a third person arrives and appraises our

Economics of exchange

This clever principle is obviously relevant to a market system. Suppose that you have a vast tract of land; I have huge piles of money. If you willingly accept some of my money for your land, and I willingly part with that money in exchange for your land, we should move in the direction of Paretian Optimality. We would not enter into the exchange unless the utility of the money was greater to you than the utility of the land you will sell.

Similarly, I would not offer the money unless your land was worth more to me than the sum I must pay. By voluntary exchange, we will arrive at a redistribution of wealth that will make both of us better off by our own estimation of what we want or that will, at worst, leave one of us just as well off, while the other is better off.

Thus an economy of exchange, in which we can trade goods and services, should lead us in the direction of greater efficiency—more utility for at least one person; less for none. It is not difficult to show that a perfectly competitive system should lead to Pareto Optimality. In such a system, all available output would have been attained, given the original starting point. Eventually no one could further improve his or her lot unless someone else was made less well off.

Efficiency as a value: more is better

Is Pareto's principle correct? Does it establish a criterion for efficiency that is *quite free of all value judgments?* Economists thought so until recent times. We have come to see that underlying the idea of efficiency are two value judgments every bit as arbitrary and personal, every bit as imbued with concepts of justice and ethics, as the ideas of equity.

One of these is the notion that *more is better.* This is a notion that underlies the conception of economic man, to whom we have continually referred in our analysis of maximizing. Yet, we have been careful to describe maximizing as a general description of how people *do* behave, not how they *ought to* behave in some moral sense.

Is more always better? Not necessarily. More may be dangerous, as we have seen when we studied the long-term implications of industrial growth in Chapter 4. Or more may be unpleasant, vulgar, greedy. Or more may be meaningless in terms of utilities. Think of someone who does not want to be richer—let us say a person who has found that the greatest happiness in life comes from divesting himself of his worldly goods, as Jesus or Thoreau preached. Such a person can deliberately follow a course that lessens his possessions—without becoming less satisfied.

Thus the idea that more is better is not a *fact.* It is a *judgment.* It may be an accurate description of human affairs, but it cannot be an accurate prescription for human affairs—at least not without injecting a value judgment into the end we propose.

Individual preferences

The second value judgment on which Paretian efficiency rests is the notion of the *autonomy of our individual preferences.* Central to the Paretian idea is the belief that we make up our own minds, free of any influence: that we know what is best for ourselves.

Do we? The more we study the workings of society, the less convincing becomes the idea of the autonomous individual. We are all creatures of our family training, our group beliefs, our culture. Our "wants" and "needs," our desires and drives are shaped in a social mold from which none of us can wholly escape. We are bombarded by advertising, moved by political exhortations, influenced by philosophic beliefs.

Thus the value judgment hidden in Pareto's assumption about individual choice is that "autonomous" choice would be *better* than social choice. But if, in fact, individuals are never wholly autonomous, then the line between individual and social choice becomes blurred. We can no longer claim that "free choice" is always better than socially imposed choice, because there is an element of social choice even in the "freest" individual decision.

Efficiency and policy

Thus we are skeptical nowadays about claiming that Pareto Optimality is a "value-free" concept. This makes us skeptical, as well, of claims that a society of free exchange will, by its voluntary activities, unerringly move in the direction of increased social well-being. This is all the more true because most actual social changes do not fulfill the Paretian principle that no one should be made worse off (or should be compensated if he is made worse off). Almost all important economic policies deliberately seek to benefit one group *at the expense of another*. Laws that protect labor unions hurt employers. Laws that protect labor unions hurt employers. Laws that protect industries (such as tariffs) harm consumers. Laws that improve the condition of the poor do so at the expense of the rich. We are plunged into a sea of equity judgments every time we make economic policy decisions, even if those decisions aim at efficiency.

The dilemma of values

If economics is inextricably entangled with equity, does that reduce all analysis to a question of sheer preference? You prefer one policy, I another. Who is to say which is better?

To some extent, economics and all social science are forever entangled with just such problems. As an economist, you may take the position that the best distribution of income entrusts one person with virtually all the nations' wealth, while the rest of the people are slaves. Perhaps you will say that this accords with your judgment of what is best. There is no way of "proving" your values wrong, just as there is no way of proving wrong the values of another economist who plumps for a totally equal distribution of income. At best we might be able to analyze the effect of both distributions on output; but even that, as we have seen, is a value judgment, insofar as we declare our preference for one size of income over another?

Can we specify with certainty what a "fair" income distribution would look like? Of course not. Can we specify a distribution of income that would accord with what most people think is "fair?" Here we put the question in such a way that we could test the results, for example by an opinion poll.

If we took such a poll, most persons in the United States would probably agree that existing income is not "fairly" distributed. They consider it unfair that some people are as poor as they are and others are as rich as they are.

Suppose we ask whether the public would approve of an income distribution that had the same "shape" as that for one group in which the more obvious advantages and disadvantages of the real world were minimized. *That group consists of the white adult males who work full-*

TOWARD AN OPERATIONAL DEFINITION OF FAIRNESS

time and full-year. In general, these workers suffer minimally or not at all from the handicaps of race, sex, age, personal deficiencies, or bad economic policies. By examining their earnings rather than their incomes we can eliminate the effects of inherited wealth. Might not such a standard appeal to many people as constituting an "operational" definition of a just income distribution?

Since the poll has never been taken, we cannot answer the question. But we can examine what income distribution would look like under such a dispensation. The results are shown in the table. It is interesting to

note that this standard of fairness, if applied, would reduce the dispersion of income by 40 percent.

Annual earnings ($000s)	Distribution of income in accordance with "fairness" standard	Actual distribution of income, 1970
$ 0–1	1.7%	10.4%
1–2	1.3	8.3
2–3	1.5	6.9
3–4	3.0	6.8
4–5	4.4	6.2
5–6	6.8	6.7
6–7	8.6	7.0
7–8	10.5	7.8
8–10	19.7	13.2
10–15	27.9	17.7
15–20	11.2	6.8
25 & over	3.3	2.3

Test of social values

Yet there is no reason to conclude from this that one economic prescription will be *judged* as good as another, for the policies of economists are subject in real life to a test much more severe than that of the private value judgments of the economist himself. They are tested by the *collective judgments of society.* Some policies will gain the approval and support of large numbers of people. Others will earn their dislike, even their hatred.

Social values are a fact of life as real as supply and demand curves—perhaps even more easily identifiable in real life. Like supply and demand curves, social values can change. But at any time they operate as strong forces within society, rejecting some economic policies, endorsing others. Thus we can hope to improve our feelings of social welfare by advocating policies that accord with social values. We can also, of course, try to change social values so that they will accord with our policies. An economist in favor of slavery will seek to convince people that slavery is best. An egalitarian economist will write tracts advocating his program of equality. In all likelihood, the values of society will change only slowly, paying scant heed to extreme proposals. Our policies will be deemed better or worse, insofar as they succeed in bringing about changes that accord with these slowly changing values.

FOCUS

Here is a chapter that is partly down to earth and partly up in the clouds. Let us start on earth. We are interested here in laying out a general approach to the challenge of income distribution. Silently, of course, the cloudy questions of the back of the chapter obtrude: why should we want to change income distribution? Why not leave it alone? Why not make it less equal?

Assuming that most of us share the presumption in favor of lessening inequality, how can we go about implementing our preferences? This chapter examines the three main means by which we have tried to do so: changing the access to human capital, mainly through education; changing the demand curve for factors by intervention; and taxes and subsidies. (We do not examine a fourth, powerful means, which would be to abandon the market system entirely, in favor of some other way of assigning income to individuals.)

We will not review here the pros and cons of these three methods. By far the most socially significant is that of transfer payments. Therefore we look into the problems of the negative income tax with some care. This is an issue that you should certainly be familiar with.

Thereafter we turn to a set of questions that underlie much of this book. What is the rationale for economic judgments? What is the meaning of "efficiency"? Is it possible to talk about efficiency without smuggling in values? These are the kinds of questions that we often debate hotly among ourselves. Here is a chance to think carefully through the argument.

Some of you will want to go further, into the philosophic presumptions that incline most of us in favor of equality as a general social goal—or at least against inequality as a basic principle. Our "Extra word" takes up the question in some detail.

Can you answer this question: "Is it consistent to favor equality as a general social principle and still to endorse inequality under certain conditions?" If you cannot answer, look into "An extra word" at the end of the chapter.

WORDS AND CONCEPTS YOU SHOULD KNOW

Human capital, 275–76
Gini coefficient, 276
Affirmative action programs, 278
Progressive, proportional, and regressive
   taxes, 278
Negative income tax, 279

Work incentives, 279–80
Equity, 280
Efficiency, 281
Pareto Optimality, 281
Individual preferences, 282

QUESTIONS

1. Do you think the present educational system works to reduce or to maintain the structure of inequality in rewards? How would you suggest changing it, if you wanted less inequality? More?

2. Why is the sales tax regressive? Why do you think a property tax is regressive? (Hint: landlords add the tax to rents. The demand for housing is inelastic. Rents rise. Show this in diagrams.)

3. Suppose that we instituted a family allowance program that insured an annual income of $6,000 per family, and we taxed all earned income at one third. How high a total income could a family earn before its tax payments to the government exceeded the government's payments to it?

4. Which of the following statements are value judgments:
Economic competition produces low prices.
Economic competition produces well-being.
Economic competition produces poor mental health.
Economic competition is inferior to economic cooperation.

5. Individual A has 100 acres, and B has $1000. If I give A $100 from B and B 10 acres from A, can I claim to have increased total well-being? Suppose they exchange voluntarily. Then what?

6. Why is "More is better" a value judgment? Why is it not a simple statement of fact? Can you think of instances in which more is not better?

7. Do you consider yourself an "autonomous" individual? Can you imagine a situation in which you might be better off if your choices were made for you by someone else than by yourself? How about the choices of a child? An uninformed consumer?

The problem of equity

Behind economic equity judgments are two possible starting points. One is the belief, rooted in Greek philosophy, that men are by nature *unequal*. The other is the belief that men are *equal*—a point of view that made its forceful appearance into Western thought in the eighteenth century, with the work of Jean Jacques Rousseau.

EQUALITY AND INEQUALITY

Now this contradiction in starting points is not a disagreement about facts. Of course human beings are not exactly alike. The disagreement is about the nature of the arguments that one must bring to bear to justify social policies. Someone who believes that men are inherently unequal will demand a justification for any policy whose objective is to make men more equal. Since the policy goes against his fundamental assumption, he begins with the need to be "shown" that *some* equality might produce a better society than the existing condition of inequality.

For one who begins from the position of Rousseau, just the opposite is true. Since his premise is that men are equal, he will have to be shown that *some* inequality will produce a better society. Suppose we believe, in accordance with the prevailing value judgments, that a rising level of national output would be a good thing. We would then have to demonstrate that output would be higher if there were *some* inequalities in rewards than if there were none. We might do so by claiming that higher rewards for higher output will tempt people to work harder. We would then have justified our admission of inequality because it was a means to the end of higher output. It also follows that to advocate such a policy we would have to rank our preference for output *above* our preference for equality.

RULES FOR EQUITY

Most Americans—indeed, most people in the modern world—subscribe to the idea that people are equal rather than unequal. This means that there is an underlying bias in favor of equality in their social values. We hear of policies in every nation that seek to diminish the differences between rich and poor. We hear of very few policies that openly advocate greater inequality. Even policies that support greater inequality—for example tax loopholes for millionaires are "justified" in terms of their ultimate effect in raising the incomes of *all,* presumably lessening poverty.

Starting with this bias in favor of equality, we need some understanding of the kinds of exceptions we may make to the general rule. That is, we need to know, and to look carefully into, the arguments in favor of inequality. As we shall see, there are four of them.

1. *We agree that inequality is justified if everyone has a "fair chance" to get ahead.*

Most of us do not object to inequality of outcomes—in fact, we generally favor it—if we are convinced that the race was run under fair conditions, with no one handicapped at the start.

What are fair conditions? That is where the argument becomes complex. Are large inheritances "fair"? Most Americans agree that *some* inheritance is fair but that taxes should prevent the full passage of wealth from generation to generation. What about inheritances of talent? No one is much concerned about this. Inheritances of culture? We are beginning to get exercised over the handicaps that are "inherited" by persons born in the slum or to nonwhite parents.

2. We agree to inequality when it is the outcome of individual preferences.

If the outcome of the economic game results in unequal incomes, we justify these inequalities when they accord with different personal desires. One man works harder than another, so he deserves a larger income. One chooses to enter the law and makes a fortune; the other chooses to enter the ministry and make do with a small income. We acquiesce in these inequalities to the degree that they appear to mirror individual preferences.

3. We abide by inequality when it reflects merit.

Merit is not quite the same as fairness or personal preference. It has to do with our belief in the propriety of higher rewards when they are "justified" by a larger contribution to output. Here is the belief that underpins the idea that factors should be paid their marginal revenue product. We do not object to factors receiving different remunerations in the market, because we can show that each factor contributes a different amount to total output.

This is, of course, only a value judgment. Suppose there are two workers, side by side, on the assembly line. One is young, strong, unmarried and very productive. The other is older, married, has a large family and many expenses—and less productive. Should the first be compensated more highly than the second? We find ourselves in a conflict of values here. Our bias toward equality tells us no. Our exception for merit tells us yes. There is no correct solution for this or any other problem involving value judgments. Once again, social values prevail, sometimes paying the younger person more than the older, sometimes both the same, sometimes the older more.

4. Finally, we agree in violating the spirit of equality when we are convinced that inequality is for the common good.

The common good is often translated into practical terms of gross national product. Thus we may agree to allow unequal rewards because we are convinced (or persuaded) that this inequality will ultimately benefit us all, by raising all incomes as well as the incomes of those who are favored.

Here we are again allowing ourselves to be swayed by the idea that more is better. But it is possible that we can define the common good in other terms that may also justify some inequality. We may establish environmental safety and quality as the highest goals of society and then decide that certain inequalities of rewards are the most expeditious ways of achieving this common good. For instance, we might reward persons who behaved in an environmentally favorable way. We might lower their taxes or subsidize them. The point remains that it *is* the common good that justifies the departure from the value norm of equality.

The difficult question here is to define the common good. There are many conceptions of what such an objective should be. All incorporate value judgments. Even the common good of survival, which might justify giving a larger reward to those who must be entrusted with survival, is a value judgment. Do all societies deserve to survive? Was Nazi Germany justified in seeking survival at all costs?

EQUITY AND ECONOMICS

These general principles do not describe the way we *should* think about inequality. They are an attempt to describe the way we do think about it—the arguments that we commonly hear or raise ourselves, to defend an unequal distribution of goods and services, or of wealth.

Each of these arguments, as we can see, poses its own tangled problems. And there is every reason that they should be tangled, for the distribution of incomes poses the most perplexing of all economic problems to any society. At one extreme, it criticizes all the privileges and inequalities that every society displays, forcing us to explain to ourselves why one man should enjoy an income larger than he can spend, while another suffers from an income too small to permit him to live in decency. At the other extreme, it forces us to examine the complications and contradictions of a society of absolutely equal incomes, where each individual (or family?) received the same amount as every other, regardless of differences in his physical capacities, his life situation, his potential contribution to society.

Both extremes pose economic as well as moral problems. A society of "total inequality" would probably work very poorly—most slave societies have. A society of "complete equality" would also probably work poorly—attempts in early Soviet history to reward all workers alike resulted in a near breakdown in production.

Thus we have to compromise, to find reasons to support income distributions that are neither completely equal or completely unequal. Here is where we lean partly on our actual knowledge of the effects of income distribution on work and output, and partly on our value systems that define allowable exceptions to our basic rule that societies should seek equality as their goal, not inequality. As our values change—and we are now living in a period when values seem to be changing rapidly—we accord different weights to the various arguments by which we traditionally justify unequal incomes.

THE UNAVOIDABLE PROBLEM

Economic equity is complex, confusing, and often disconcerting. It makes us uneasy, not only because it confronts us with the often shaky presumptions we make about equity, but because we recognize that no solution will ever be found that can be demonstrated to be superior to all others. Economic efficiency, as we have been at some pains to show, is also a disguised belief in economic equity of a certain sort. Thus in the end we are thrown back on the moral promptings that are the very foundation of social life, but that are nonetheless the most vulnerable of any of society's institutions.

Yet, however difficult or dismaying, there is no escape from trying to specify what you mean by equity. If you fail to make such an effort, you will only end up with a hodgepodge of feelings about equity, many of them contradictory or unsatisfying. This does not mean that you can work out a scheme of economic equity that will be free of contradictions or uncertainties. But at least you will have understood why certain contradictions are inherent in the problem of equity, and you will be in a position to act with both intelligence and purpose when you are forced—as we are all forced—to decide which economic policies are better and which are worse.

Economics of taxation

All through our text we have been looking at government. During our study of microeconomics we have constantly been concerned with government as a regulator of markets or an intervenor in environmental problems, or a redistributor of incomes. In our macroeconomic section we will be dealing with government as a stabilizer and growth-promoter for the entire economy. But we have not yet had a chance to examine the workings of government as a major economic institution. Where does it get its revenue? How does it allocate its income? What principles regulate its decision making? These are the questions of this chapter and succeeding ones. It need hardly be said that they are among the most important in economics.

Revenue

All governments need revenue. How do they get it? The answer varies significantly, depending on whether we are interested in federal or nonfederal government. Let us therefore begin by

20

looking at Table 20 • 1 showing the major sources of revenue for each:

Table 20 • 1   Sources of revenue, 1975

Source	Federal	State and local
Personal income taxes	42.1%	9.7%
Estate and gift taxes	1.7	0.7
Corporate income taxes	14.9	2.8
Indirect business (sales) taxes	7.8	24.4
Property taxes	—	23.1
Social insurance taxes	32.9	6.6
Federal grants	—	23.2
Charges for services	0.7	11.4
Total dollars (billions)	**$286.5**	**234.3**

Federal vs. state and local revenue sources

How can we summarize this table? A few outstanding differences are:

1. The federal government derives most of its income from three sources: personal income taxes, corporate income taxes, and social insurance (social security) taxes. Sales taxes (such as federal excise taxes on liquor or gasoline) add a small amount, but all the rest is essentially trivial. Note especially the insignificant amount raised by estate taxes, a matter we mentioned in our preceding chapter.

2. State and local governments depend on a different set of revenue sources. Their major sources of income are sales taxes, property taxes, and grants from the federal government, together accounting for 70 percent of their income, in roughly equal shares. (Of course the federal grants in turn come from money raised by the federal government from income and social security taxes; but so far as the states or localities are concerned, it is the federal grants system that is the "original" source.)

Tax systems

There are 38,000 tax-imposing authorities in the nation, apart from the federal government: states, townships, counties, school districts, water districts, transportation authorities, and the like. Therefore, we pay taxes largely according to where we live and the taxing authority we come under.

To discover what an "average" person pays in taxes, we will obviously have to simplify this complex reality. We shall inquire into the manner in which different *kinds* of taxes affect individuals or enterprises; and we will investigate whether these different kinds of taxes are *progressive, proportional* or *regressive*—that is, whether they take an ever larger, an always equal, or an ever smaller percentage of incomes as we move from low to high income brackets.

Incidence of taxation

This question will bring us to a major problem of microeconomics. The problem is the incidence of taxation—who pays a tax, such as an income or sales or property tax?

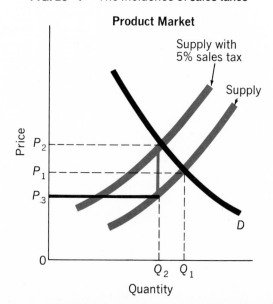

FIG. 20 • 1   The incidence of sales taxes

The question seems nonsensical. Doesn't the person who writes out a check to the government or pays a bill with a tax on it obviously pay the tax? Not necessarily. Let's take the case of a sales tax. If a state levies a tax of 5 percent on some commodity, the cost of the commodity rises by this amount. This is the same thing as an upward shift in its supply curve, as in Fig. 20·1. As a result, the price rises from P_1 to P_2.

The case of a sales tax

Now look carefully at the consequences. First, we see that the price has risen *less* than the sales tax: the price is up from P_1 to P_2; the sales tax has raised costs from P_3 to P_2. Second, you will notice that the producer's income has gone down for two reasons. First, his sales have dropped from Q_1 to Q_2. Second, the revenue that he retains after remitting the tax has also gone down from $P_1 \cdot Q_1$ to $P_3 \cdot Q_2$ the original sales price. As a consequence, his profits have fallen.

Who has now paid the tax? The consumer has paid some—the rise in price from P_1 to P_2, combined with the decrease in his consumption of the good. The producer has paid some—the drop in profits we have just analyzed. But this is not all. Because the producer's income has fallen, his demand for factors has dropped from D_1 to D_2 (see Fig. 20·2). Hence the prices of the factors and the quantities employed will fall. So they, too, bear part of the tax. In Fig. 20·2 factors of production suffer a cut-back in price from L to M and a reduction in quantities employed from X to Y. Hence their incomes will fall from $OL \times OX$ to $OM \times OY$.

As a result, the sales tax will actually be shared by consumers, producers, and factors of production. The point is that the retail storekeeper, who actually makes out the check to the government, or the

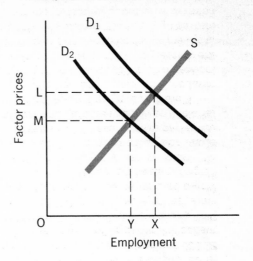

FIG. 20·2   Impact of sales tax on factors

consumer who pays his pennies of sales tax is very likely not the sole bearer of the tax.

Effects of elasticity

How much of the tax will a storekeeper or a consumer bear? That depends on the elasticity of demand for the product. If demand is totally elastic, the storekeeper will mark up items by the amount of the sales tax and will sell as many items as before. In that case, the consumer will pay it all, and the retailer or seller will simply act as the collection agency for the government.

More likely, when a sales tax is imposed, sellers will shave profit margins, to avoid a serious loss of volume. They will mark up price by less than the tax and make up the difference out of profits. Sellers and consumers both will then bear the tax.

In Fig. 20·3, we see what a difference the elasticity of demand makes. In this diagram, a sales tax raises two supply curves by equal amounts, but the amount passed onto the consumer is much greater on the right, where demand is inelastic, than on the left, where it is not.

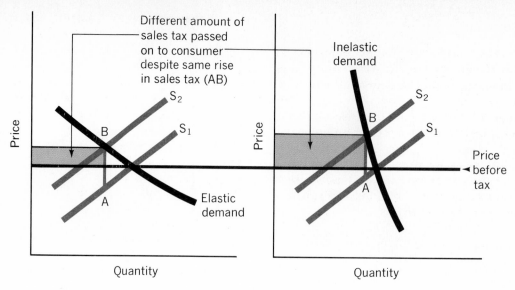

FIG. 20·3   Effect of elasticity on tax incidence for consumers

Impact on factors

The same analysis holds if we move back to the impact of the tax on factor incomes. If retail sales drop because of the sales tax, the retailer will diminish orders to suppliers. Suppliers will reduce production, and their demand for factors will shift to the left.

What happens to factor incomes? We can see the answer in Fig. 20·4, where two producers each cut their demand for factors by an equal amount ($A'B'$). As the diagram shows, the fall in factor prices and quantities depends on the elasticity of factor supply. In the figure on the right, the supply curve is very inelastic. Perhaps there is no place for these factors to go. They will have to accept a large fall in wages or other income. In the case on the left, the drop in factor prices causes factors

FIG. 20·4   Elasticity and incidence of taxes on factors

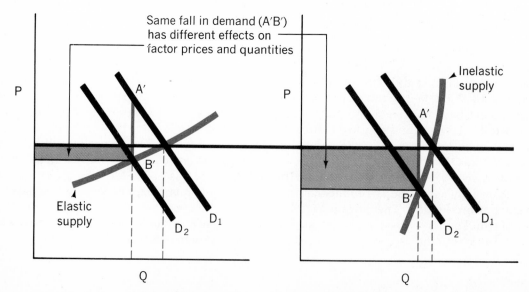

to seek employment elsewhere. Those who remain in the business will suffer a much smaller fall in incomes.

Complexity of incidence

Perhaps we can now see how difficult it is to answer the question of who pays a tax. Even in what seems to be the clear case of a sales tax, we have to know two things to answer the question:

1. How much of the tax is shifted "forward" to the consumer, how much is absorbed by the seller or producer, and how much is shifted backward to the factors of production? That requires a knowledge of elasticities of demand and supply that we often do not possess.

2. To determine how much of a sales tax is paid by any one person, we also have to know the extent to which that individual is a consumer, a producer, or a factor. Think about the impact of a 3¢ tax per pack of cigarettes on a tobacconist who does not smoke but who owns 10 shares of Phillip Morris. Such are the difficulties of coming to clear-cut pronouncements about tax incidence.

Regressivity of sales taxes

Nonetheless, we can venture one generalization. A sales tax on "necessities" is sure to be passed on to the consumer to a much greater extent that one on luxuries. This is because the demand curve for necessities is, by definition, less elastic than the demand curve for luxuries. Most necessities, such as food, bulk larger in the budgets of low-income families than of high-income families. On the average, food costs absorb about 30 percent of an $8,000 family budget, in contrast with just over 20 percent of an $18,000 budget. *Therefore sales taxes on necessities are regressive.* By way of contrast, sales taxes on luxuries may be progressive, if they are levied only on goods bought by upper-class families. A sales tax on yachts will have a very different incidence on rich and poor than a sales tax on gasoline or on retail items in general.

Personal income taxes

What about the incidence of a personal income tax? At one level, this is the simplest tax to discuss in terms of its incidence. If we are taxed on our net incomes, we have only one way of "shifting" the tax. This is to work less, thereby lowering our incomes. In theory, high income tax rates might deter rich people from working. Income taxes lessen the marginal utility of additional work, because they may take away half or more of the money income we derive from it. Therefore they may increase our preference for nonwork—leisure.

Actually, studies indicate that very few highly-paid persons curtail their efforts significantly because of income taxes. Neither the number of hours we work nor the intensity of our work efforts seems to change if taxes increase or decrease. Economists therefore go on the assumption that income taxes are borne directly by the individuals who pay them, and that they do not significantly alter work habits.

Income taxes may, however, change income tax payment habits. When taxes are felt to be high, people find means of avoiding them. Payments in cash go unreported to the government. Time and money are spent in finding legal ways to beat—or cheat—the government. These effects may be very large. Guesses on non-reported income run into the tens of billions, and the search of tax "shelters" and loopholes gives employment to a small army of tax lawyers and accountants. We will go further into this below.

Progressivity of income taxes Income taxes, levied by federal, state, or local (usually municipal) authorities are all progressive in their structure. Without exception, the rate of taxes rises as income rises: the federal income tax, for example, begins at 14 percent and increases to 50 percent at a taxable income level of $44,000 for a married couple. (It goes to 70 percent on property income.)

However, there is a great deal of difference between rates "on paper" and actual income taxes paid by families. This is because we do not pay taxes on our total or gross income, but on our "taxable" incomes. Taxable incomes are our gross incomes less various exemptions and deductions permitted by law. For example, we are allowed to deduct $1,000 for each dependent (including ourselves) in figuring our income tax. We can deduct interest that we pay, which is usually interest on mortgages on our houses. We can deduct all state and local taxes from our federal income tax. We can take off charitable contributions, legitimate business expenses, and a long list of other items.

Effect of deductions Deductions affect the incidence of the income tax structure in two ways. In the first place, they often create "horizontal" inequities. Two families or individuals with identical incomes may pay very different taxes because one can use a deduction and another cannot. For years, owners of oil properties enjoyed a deduction known as a depletion allowance. It enabled them to reduce their taxable income from oil by as much as a third below the actual oil income. Owners of state and local bonds have for years enjoyed the privilege of not paying any federal tax on the interest from these bonds. Thus, two households, side by side

in identical houses, enjoying identical incomes, may pay hugely different taxes.

Tax expenditures These deductions are often called loopholes because they enable a number of wealthy persons to find legal escapes from high taxation. Some loopholes have been written into the law as the result of lobbying efforts to protect or favor particular companies or classes of persons or even individuals.

Most loopholes, however, like all deductions, were originally intended to achieve some public purpose. We are allowed to deduct mortgage interest to encourage home ownership. We can take charities off our gross income to encourage the private support of universities, museums, and other worthy causes. We exempt state and local bonds from federal taxation to help localities finance their operations. Depletion allowances were supposed to encourage oil well drilling. We permit varous business expenses because business insists that it could not operate effectively without such deductions.

These deductions-with-a-purpose are therefore properly regarded as *tax expenditures*. We permit or encourage someone to do something by deliberately exempting specific expenditures from taxation. The question, then, is whether the activities that have been encouraged are worth the loss of revenue required to get them.

That is a difficult question, with more than one answer. The tax exemption of state and local bonds has probably eased their financing problems, but at the cost of creating a special group of non-tax-paying bondholders, most of them in the upper income brackets. Deductions for charity are the mainstay of many institutions, but some of those institutions, such as museums, could also be fully supported directly by government assistance, without giving special benefits to wealthy donors.

Thus the problem is to judge the benefits of tax expenditures against their costs. One cost is simply the total amount of revenue that the federal government has sacrificed for various objectives presumably promoted by tax deductions. In 1975 the amount was over $90 billion. A second cost is the loss of horizontal equity. Because of loopholes, many wealthy people escape taxation entirely. In 1969, there were 761 persons with incomes over $100,000 who paid no federal income taxes at all; 56 with incomes over $1 million also paid not a cent of tax.

Table 20 · 2

Adjusted family income ($000)	Scheduled federal income tax rates	Actual federal income tax rates
0–3	15%	1%
3–5	18	5
5–10	20	7
10–15	24	10
15–20	28	12
20–25	32	14
25–50	39	17
50–75	48	24
75–100	53	27
100–500	61	30
500–1,000	68	33
1,000+	69	34

Vertical effect   The use of deductions and loopholes has a second, "vertical" effect, in addition to its horizontal impact. Because legal means of tax avoidance are used mainly by wealthy families, they reduce actual income taxes paid by these families. Our actual rates on federal income taxes are progressive, as Table 20 · 2 shows, but the rates we pay are far below those that we would have to pay if loopholes and deductions were not available.

Loss of progressivity   Deductions greatly lessen the progressivity of taxes, as we can see by comparing the scheduled rates and the actual rates of taxation in different tax brackets. Deductions have this anti-progressive effect because a deduction is worth much more to a high-income family than to a low-income one. Example: charitable donations. A rich family, whose marginal tax bracket is 70 percent, gives away $100. As a result, its pretax income is reduced by $100, but its tax is reduced by

$70. The net cost of the $100 gift is therefore $30 in reduced after-tax spendable income. A poorer family, whose marginal tax bracket is 25 percent, also gives away $100. It thereby saves a tax of $25. Its spendable, after-tax income is reduced by $75. Not only is this loss of spendable income larger in *absolute* terms than for the richer family, but it is certainly larger as a percentage of its total income.

Is there a way around this inequity? One answer is to give tax credits instead of tax deductions. Take the case of mortgage interest. Because this interest is a deduction, the tax saving is proportionally much greater for a rich than for a poor family. But suppose that the government wanted to encourage home ownership (or charity donations) and gave a tax credit of $100 (or $1,000) for buying a home or for supporting a charity. Now all homeowners or philanthropists would find their tax bills reduced equally. Of course the difficulty is that some kinds of activities, such as buying homes, would probably not be much affected by this change, whereas other kinds, such as charitable donations, might be very seriously injured. Hence credits would have to be very selectively applied.

Corporate income taxes

Let us next take a look at the corporate income tax, the source of very substantial sums for federal government.

Who pays a corporation's income tax? Few questions are more uncertain. Some economists think the corporate income tax is essentially a sales tax, borne partly by consumers, partly by the business (in the form of reduced income), partly by the factors of production who suffer a loss in earnings. Others think it is a tax on capital, serving to reduce the flow of capital into the corporate sector. Still others believe that its impact cannot be clearly depicted because most corporate income taxes are paid by big oligopolistic companies, who may use tax increases as an excuse to raise prices in their industry, laying the blame for this on "the government." Some economists even go so far as to say that one of the virtues of the corporate tax is that no one can state with certainty who pays it; therefore, it serves as an excellent way for the government to raise money without clearly "imposing" a tax on anyone!

Tax integration?

The fact of the matter is that we do not know who ultimately bears the cost of the corporation income tax. This is merely another way of saying that we do not know how economic activity would change if the tax were eliminated.

As we have already learned, many economists have come to favor an integration of the tax system that would eliminate the income tax on corporations but would force individuals to include their share of corporate earnings in their own taxable incomes (see "Extra word" at the end of Chapter 17). Some critics assume that this would be a tax change in favor of the rich, lowering the overall progressivity of the tax structure. But this is not true. Because the bulk of corporate stock, as we have seen, is held by a very small number of wealthy households, the effective rate of taxation on upper income households would rise, not fall.

In all likelihood, however, if this change comes on the national agenda, the great debate will focus mainly on the effect of tax integration on the national savings rate. As our next "Extra word" notes, this is a matter about which we have little knowledge.

Social Security taxes

Social Security taxes pose another problem. There is no question who pays them. They reduce the income of the wage earner and the employer, who may or may not be able to pass forward his share of the tax. The more interesting question is whether this tax is regressive.

At first glance there is no doubt in the matter. Social Security taxes today take 11.7 percent of all wages, half paid by a reduction in the salary check, the other half by the employer. This percentage is the same on all taxed wages, so that the tax seems quite proportional. But there is no tax levied above an established level ($14,-300 in 1976), so that high wage earners pay smaller proportions of their earnings. In addition, although Social Security taxes are taken from even the lowest earned income, property income of any kind—interest, rent, dividends, or royalties—is exempt from Social Security. Thus, measured against total income, the Social Security levy is highly regressive.

Yet matters are not quite that simple. The "payout" formula for Social Security is set to give low-income earners more dollars of benefit, per dollar paid in, than high earners. If we offset the regressive tax with the progressive payment schedule, the net impact of Social Security becomes slightly progressive.

The difficulty is that Social Security taxes are paid at one stage in an individual's life cycle, and the benefits are received at another, later stage. It is not easy to compare costs and benefits when they are separated by long periods of time This problem is worsened because the ratio between the number of persons working (and paying tax) and those not working (and receiving benefits) is changing in favor of the retired population. An ever larger proportion of our population is living on Social Security, at much higher benefit levels than formerly; and these trends will certainly continue.

This means that it will soon become impossible to finance Social Security by the conventional Social Security taxes unless they are very greatly increased. Because workers are already grumbling at the "cut" that Social Security takes, it is likely that part of Social Security costs—perhaps the portion that finances Medicare—will be met from general tax revenues, and that Social Security taxes will be lifted much higher. All these changes would further improve the overall progressivity of the Social Security system.

Property taxes   Property taxes, like sales taxes, are certainly not paid just by the person who mails the check to the government. Property taxes are usually passed along at least to some degree in higher rents. They are regressive because rents bulk much larger in low-income than in high-income budgets, especially in slums. Rent payments are often outrageously high for slum dwellers, who cannot afford to move or are not accepted as tenants elsewhere.

But property taxes have two very im-portant aspects that are frequently over-looked. Some property taxes are assessed against land values; some against commercial property or rentable space. There is a big difference between the two. Land is essentially in inelastic, short-run supply. Thus its supply curve is vertical. A tax on land value must therefore fall on the owners of land because they cannot shift their supply curve to the left. A tax on land diminishes owners' economic rents but cannot be passed forward to consumers, as Fig. 20 • 5 shows:

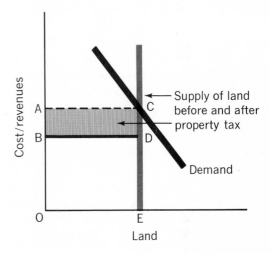

FIG. 20 • 5 Effect of property tax on supply of land.

Before the tax, landowners were offering quantity *OE* at rents *OA*. Their revenues were *OACE*. If a tax *AB* is levied on land, their incomes will simply be reduced by the amount *ABCD*. There is no way that rents can be increased above *OA*, so the landlord will bear all the tax.

Space vs. land   Compare the situation with a tax on space—a building property tax. Here the supply curve is very elastic. A tax on rentable space now raises the cost curve as

Fig. 20 • 6 shows. Thereafter the analysis is exactly as in the case of a sales tax. As we can see, the tax *AB* will be partly absorbed by landlords and partly passed along to users (consumers) of the space.

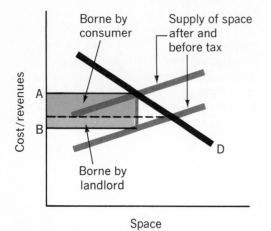

FIG. 20 • 6

Therefore a property tax on land may be progressive, hitting the landlord rather than the tenant, whereas a building property tax may be regressive, often hurting the tenant more than the landlord.

Property taxes and wealth

Second, property taxes have an impact on wealth as well as on income. Suppose that property taxes are $250,000 per year on a building whose rentals yield $1 million a year. Net earnings are therefore $750,000. As we know, the building is worth a capital sum that will yield $750,000 at the going rate of return for similar properties. At 10 percent, it will be worth $7,500,000.

Suppose that property taxes are now eliminated. Presumably this is a move toward a more progressive tax system. Is it? It will immediately raise the capitalized value of the building to $10,000,-000. The biggest gainer is the (presumably wealthy) owner of the building, not the tenants! The converse is also true. If we impose property taxes, the capitalized value of real estate will fall. Even though the taxes may be passed forward to renters, the heaviest cost will fall on the owner of the building whose capital has been diminished.

So it is not altogether clear that property taxes are as regressive as they are thought to be. They are regressive only if we estimate their incidence on incomes. If we include their impact of wealth, they can be a very progressive form of taxation!

Total incidence

Can we sum up the total incidence of the tax system? It must be clear that it is difficult to do so for two reasons. First, the horizontal variances are so great that "average" figures are often very little guide to reality. Second, incidence depends on elasticities of supply and demand that are often unknown to us.

In Table 20 • 3 we see the most recent and sophisticated effort to discover total tax incidence, carried out by Joseph Pechman and Benjamin Okner, both of the Brookings Institution.

Notice the tremendous difference between Variant 1 and Variant 2. In Variant 1, millionaires pay 49 percent of their incomes in taxes. In Variant 2, they pay less than 30 percent. In Variant 1, a very poor family pays less than 20 percent of its income in taxes. In Variant 2, it pays 28 percent.

The difference between the variants lies in the assumptions that are made about the elasticity of supply and demand curves. In Variant 1, where total taxation seems quite progressive, it is assumed that property taxes are borne mainly by landlords and that corporate income taxes ultimately descend on shareholders. In Variant 2, which is roughly proportional

Table 20·3   Effective rates of federal, state, and local taxes under two incidence assumptions, 1966

Adjusted family income ($000s)	VARIANT 1			VARIANT 2		
	Federal	State and local	Total	Federal	State and local	Total
$0–3	8.8%	9.8%	18.7%	14.1%	14.0%	28.1%
3–5	11.9	8.5	20.4	14.6	10.6	25.3
5–10	15.4	7.2	22.6	17.0	8.9	25.9
10–15	16.3	6.5	22.8	17.5	8.0	25.5
15–20	16.7	6.5	23.2	17.7	7.6	25.3
20–25	17.1	6.9	24.0	17.8	7.4	25.1
25–30	17.4	7.7	25.1	17.2	7.1	24.3
30–50	18.2	8.2	26.4	17.7	6.7	24.4
50–100	21.8	9.7	31.5	20.1	6.3	26.4
100–500	30.0	11.9	41.8	24.4	6.0	30.3
500–1,000	34.6	13.3	48.0	25.2	5.1	30.3
1,000 and over	35.5	13.8	49.3	24.8	4.2	29.0
Total	**17.6**	**7.6**	25.2	**17.9**	**8.0**	25.9

and regressive at the lowest and uppermost ends, it is assumed that property taxes are passed forward to the renter, and that corporate income taxes lower consumers' incomes through higher prices, not stockholders' incomes through lower dividends.

A proportional system

Which of these variants is more likely to be true? *We do not know.* The actual incidence of taxation remains a matter for conjecture. We should note, however, that the uncertainties relate to the very lowest and highest incomes. Under both sets of assumptions, the tax burden for the groups that we have called the Working Class, the Middle Class, and the Top 5 percent (although not the top 2 percent) are the same. Under both sets of assumptions, state and local taxes are regressive, and federal taxes are progressive—the two balancing each other out to produce an overall system that is roughly proportional.

Tax equity

Is this a fair tax system? Two issues are involved when we discuss this problem. The first is our preference for regressive, proportional, or progressive taxation. There is no economic law that makes one system better than another. Different systems have different economic, social and political effects. An economist or a social scientist may try to analyze the effects of each system on behavior, but in the end a preference for one system or another hinges on those value judgments that continue to dog our steps.

In the preceding "Extra word," we looked into the arguments for equality as a basic value premise, and it must be clear that our own preferences incline us in this direction. Therefore we favor a tax system that is progressive. We would like to lessen the regressivity of the Social Security tax, to minimize the use of sales taxes, and to increase the importance of the personal income tax, with a much reduced use of deductions.

But that is only a value preference. Senator Barry Goldwater, a distinguished conservative, prefers a proportional tax. He would therefore favor smaller adjustments in the Social Security levies and a less progressive schedule of rates for income taxes. Few (if any) spokesmen exist for regressive systems. If there are any, they must favor those taxes that lie most heavily on low incomes, and the lightening of the tax burden for the top 5 percent.

Horizontal equity again

The second issue requires us to return one last time to the problem of horizontal equity. Whatever the value preferences that may incline us toward progressive or proportional taxation, few people would go on record as favoring "preferential" taxation. Yet that is, in fact, the kind of tax system that we have.

Tax reform, in fact, is no longer basically focused on the question of progressivity or regressivity in general. There is a political consensus in favor of a mildly progressive system. The battle rages over the hundreds or thousands of loopholes that benefit small numbers of persons. Because the closing of any particular loophole would bring a tax saving of only a few dollars for most taxpayers, they cannot work up much enthusiasm in mounting an attack on any one provision.

The beneficiaries of that provision, on the other hand, stand to gain enormously by it, and they mount an all-out campaign in its favor. Thus lobbying for individual tax breaks is intense. Lobbying against any one loophole is weak.

Is tax reform possible?

There have been sporadic efforts to simplify and make more equitable the tax system of our 38,000 tax-levying governments. By and large they have been failures. Only wars, with their overriding imperatives, have proved capable of moving the vested interests and inertias that defend our complex system. Even advisers at the Internal Revenue services are often unable to specify which law applies to a taxpayer.

The pressures for tax reform, mainly by simplifying tax law and by removing loopholes and deductions, have been gathering for a long time. We may well see a major effort to overhaul the tax system during the next few years. Indeed, it has already begun, and Congress has recently passed a tax measure that contains some—although not nearly enough—improvements and only a few—although a few are too many—new loopholes and special provisions. We will have to wait to see what happens under the pressure of a slowly growing public impatience and indignation.

Focus Perhaps the most important lesson of this chapter is that the person or business writing a check to the government is not necessarily the ultimate taxpayer. Because of the shifts in prices and outputs that a tax often gives rise to, the "legal taxpayer" may not be at all the person on whom the burden of the tax falls. (The most vivid illustration is a business that sells a necessary good on which a sales or excise tax is imposed. Such a business raises its prices by the amount of the tax and becomes a tax collector for the government, taking the tax payments from its consumers and sending them to the city, state or federal taxing authority.)

How can we determine who is the true taxpayer? Often we cannot, because we lack enough information. But economic analysis tells us the kind of information that we need—above all, information about the elasticity of supply and demand curves.

The second main lesson of the chapter concerns the progressivity and regressivity of taxes. Our chapter contains many examples of taxes that seem to be progressive but are really regressive, or vice versa. The Social Security system (as contrasted with Social Security taxes) is one example of a concealed progressivity. Another is the effect of property taxes on land (not space) or on wealth (not income). These examples warn us that it is very difficult to come to simple conclusions as to the overall progressivity or regressivity of the composite tax structure of the United States, especially when we know nothing about who finally pays corporate income taxes.

Probably our national system is a mixture of a regressive state and local system plus a progressive federal system. It appears to be proportional for most income brackets. But much hinges on assumptions we make as to the incidence of taxes at the bottom and top, and our pronouncements about the "equity" of the system.

Third, we learn about horizontal inequities, one of the most important imperfections of the system. What are we to do about these? That is a matter for political action. But political action without some thoughtful economic analysis may not bring the results we want. Loopholes presumably exist to serve a purpose. The trick in reforming our tax system is to determine whether that purpose is worth the cost, or whether the activity that the loophole promotes or allows could not be better financed in some other way. That is a problem we will be pursuing in our next chapter.

Finally, values once more. Is the tax system just? Horizontal variations aside (or even including these), our conclusion is a matter of judgment, not of a calculus that transcends preferences. There is no one tax system that is better than another by any criterion other than our moral or political opinions. Even a system that is more "efficient" is not preferable in itself. Efficiency, like all other criteria for social performance, reflects our conception of what constitutes a better world.

WORDS AND CONCEPTS YOU SHOULD KNOW

Incidence of sales taxes, 291–93
Effects of elasticity, 291–92
Incidence of income taxes, 293–94
Deductions, 294
Tax expenditures, 294
Horizontal inequities, 294

Loopholes, 294
Vertical inequities, 295
Corporate income taxes, 296
Social Security taxes, 296–97
Incidence of property taxes, 297–98

QUESTIONS

1. Can you think of arguments that would incline you to favor a regressive tax system? How about encouraging the rate of saving? Or how about "Those who are richer deserve to be given preference because they have made a larger contribution to society"?

2. Assume that a payroll tax is imposed on all firms. Using supply and demand curves, show who might bear such a tax if the demand for factors were extremely inelastic. If it were not.

3. A building sells for $1 million and yields a rent of $100,000. A tax of $25,000 is placed on the value of the building. Assuming no other expenses, what is the new value of the building? (We assume that the rent yield before the tax reflected the market rate of return.) Can the owner recoup loss of wealth in any way, assuming that he or she was an income maximizer to begin with? Who then bears the new tax most painfully?

4. Suppose that Family A has $1 million in stocks and bonds and an income of $25,000. Family B has no property but an income of the same amount. How would you decide what tax system would yield horizontal equity with respect to such families? For example, would corporate income taxes affect each alike? Capital gains taxes? Straight income taxes? Sales taxes? Is total horizontal equity possible, when wealth differs, although income is alike?

5. How would you go about making a determination of whether a business's expenses were a "legitimate" deduction from its gross income? Assume that no entertainment expenses were allowed for any business. Would this result in horizontal inequities? Suppose that eliminating business entertainment *did* favor some businesses against others. Would this be a sufficient argument not to press for this tax change?

6. Do you think that the marginal utility of income decreases as our income increases? Is this a valid rationale in favor of progressive taxation? Why or why not?

Taxing wealth

Should wealth be taxed, the same as income? This has been a longstanding controversy in many countries. Taxes on wealth, if pressed vigorously, would certainly lessen the degree of wealth inequality that we find in all capitalist systems. We can also expect that they would meet with powerful opposition from owners of wealth, including owners of modest wealth who hope that someday they may be among the lucky ones.

Politics aside, what would be the effects of such a tax? We should begin by recognizing that a tax on wealth would only redistribute existing financial assets. It would not lessen the real wealth of the nation, which consists of its physical plant and equipment, its skills, its organizational morale.

There is, however, an important economic effect that a wealth tax would bring. It would almost certainly change the rate of saving—of additions to wealth. The question is: which way would it change it? Opponents of the tax declare that it would lower the savings rate, because savers would no longer be able to keep all the money that they had succeeded in accumulating. Proponents of the tax claim that a wealth tax would actually accelerate the rate of saving or improve the efficiency of its allocation, because owners of wealth would have to keep adding to their fortunes in order to maintain them after payment of the annual tax.

We do not know which of these two effects would be more important. Perhaps the answer depends on the rate of tax. A small wealth tax might well stimulate more saving or the more efficient use of savings. A severe wealth tax might discourage savers. Sweden already imposes a mild tax on wealth, and perhaps we will be able to verify this supposition by their experience.

Meanwhile, taxes on wealth already exist in our own country. One such tax is the levy that we impose on capital gains; that is, on gains from property. In the United States, taxes on gains from selling property held only a short period have usually been heavier than taxes on gains from selling property held for a "long-term" period, newly defined as more than a year.*

Some economists feel that this division between short- and long-term gains is artificial. However, proposals to remedy the present distinction go in opposite directions. One school feels that we should make a distinction between quick "killings," which are properly taxable as income, and long-term gains that should be protected as personal capital. It has been suggested that the rate on capital gains should be graduated over time, with rates going lower each year that the asset is held, down to some very low long-term rate.

---

*There is one important exception to this. If you sell a house on which you realize a capital gain, you need not pay any tax at all provided you buy another residence within a period of one year. This special provision was passed by Congress to eliminate difficulties caused by inflation. Often homeowners would sell a house for much more than it cost them, because they needed the full sales price to buy an equivalent home elsewhere. Obviously, if they had to pay a capital gains tax on their inflationary gains, they would not be able to maintain their previous standard of living.

In a contrary direction, other economists propose that we should tax capital gains more steeply, although perhaps not quite at the same rate as income. Their aim is to diminish the inequalities in wealth that result from capital gains. A higher capital gains tax is thus, in effect, a tax on wealth, although its aim is only to lessen the accumulation of new personal wealth, not to change the distribution of existing wealth.

Another kind of tax on wealth is the tax that we impose on estates. After all, a tax on wealth can be applied each year or each five years or once in a lifetime. Our estate tax system is, in fact, a once-in-a-lifetime wealth tax. As we have seen, it is a very ineffective form of taxation. There has been virtually no change in the pattern of wealth distribution despite many years of estate taxation. This static condition is due to numerous loopholes for transmission of wealth tax-free, such as trusts that allow wealth to go untaxed for two generations.

One suggested reform is the replacement of the present estate tax by an accessions tax. Instead of taxing the person who has accumulated wealth, an accessions tax would tax the person who inherits wealth. Each fresh inheritance or gift, whether from the same person or from different persons, would be subject to tax, presumably at rising rates. If a serious effort is to be made to lessen the extreme concentration of personal wealth, this is probably the most effective tax means that we could use.

Economics of public expenditure

Taxing is, of course, only half the government's fiscal activity. The other half is spending. Later, in our study of macroeconomics, we will devote a great deal of time to examining the flow of spending (and taxing) from a view that emphasizes the total volume of government activity. But before we conclude our present investigations, we want to look into the question of public spending from a microeconomic point of view.

Microeconomic approach

What is a "microeconomic" approach to government expenditure? It is one that studies how government allocates its expenditures among various competing ends, rather than one that stresses how much total spending government will carry out. What we are looking for, in other words, are counterparts in the public sphere for the guides to spending that we find in the private sphere. In private business, the imperatives of profit-seeking, and the principle of balancing marginal costs and marginal revenues give us a general theoretical understanding of how spending is divided among possible uses. Now we need to discover similar principles that will give us some guide to understanding the allocation of public spending.

21

305

Types and kinds of expenditure

In Chapter 2, we looked at the basic division of tasks among federal and state and local government. Nonetheless, it will help us to zero in on our analytic problem if we remind ourselves briefly of the tasks that government undertakes. In Table 21 • 1, we present a breakdown of government spending from a functional point of view.

Table 21 · 1   Government purchases, 1975

	Federal	State and local
	(Percent of budget)	
International affairs and defense, (incl. veterans)	34.0	—
Administration	11.0	13.0
Education	3.0	46.0
Health and welfare (incl. social sec. & grants)	34.0	18.0
Civilian safety (police, fire, etc.)	0.2	9.0
Labor	7.0	—
Regulation of business	0.1	0.9
Transportation and other commerce	4.3	9.0
Utilities and sanitation	1.0	4.0
Housing and community dev.	2.0	—
Postal service	1.0	—
Agriculture	1.0	—
National resources	1.0	—
Nuclear research	0.5	—

Figures have been rounded and do not add up to 100.

Where markets do and do not apply

It may help if we begin by asking a very simple question. How does the private sector allocate its resources among various uses? How do we explain, for example, that the private sector devotes 4.3 percent of its output to housing or 2.2 percent to automobiles?

The answer is very simple. The amount of resources devoted to a particular use depends on the market demand for that activity. Within that overall demand, each enterprise guides its production by the criterion of profitability. Another way of stating this is that each enterprise in the private sector must finance itself by selling its output.

The public sector is intrinsically different from the private sector. With minor exceptions, it does not sell its output. Therefore there is no indication from the marketplace as to how large the demand for each item of public output may be. Moreover, as we have seen, much of public output consists of "public goods," from whose use individuals cannot be excluded, even if they have not themselves helped pay for the good. For such goods there is no way, even in the imagination, to use the market to determine the "proper" distribution of expenditures among numerous ends.

Difficulties of local financing

Even if public expenditures cannot look to the market as a guide for a rational allocation of effort, is there not another aspect of the private sector that it could utilize? This is the self-financing properties of private enterprises. Could not government activity also be guided by the ability to finance—matching outgo to income and using the levels of revenue to determine what their expenditures should be?

Here the difficulty lies in another area; namely, the differing spending responsibilities and taxing capabilities of the federal and the state and local governments. Actually, the federal government *could* use its ability to raise taxes as a guide to its "proper" level of spending, because the federal tax power is very great.* It is great not just because the federal government *has* a relatively high income tax but because only the federal government *can* impose a stiff income tax. If any one state or city levied such a tax it could drive its residents to other states or cities.

A policy of guiding expenditure by the ability to tax would therefore allow the federal government to finance whatever expenditure it desired (within the limits of political acceptability), but would leave the states and localities the victims of a mutual competition that would inhibit any given state or locality from moving very far ahead of its neighbors.

under financial pressure. In the 1970s, under easier conditions, some state and local governments have fared much better and have even run an aggregate surplus of tax revenues over expenditures. But the geographic distribution of this surplus is very uneven. Houston, in the booming Southwest, has enjoyed a huge budget surplus. New York, in the stagnating East, has run a colossal deficit. Cities like New York or Newark or Detroit or St. Louis all need large expenditures to revitalize and renew their services and structures. But they cannot finance these expenditures from local taxes without driving out the very middle-class citizens and small businesses they desperately wish to keep.

Rising state and local responsibilities   This problem is intensified because we have traditionally looked to state and local spending for the provision of the "household" functions of government: schooling, taking care of the needy, safety, road building, local transportation facilities, and the like. With the growth of population and the increase in cost of services, state and local budgets for these purposes have soared. State and local expenditures are today 15 percent of GNP, double the proportion of the 1920s.

As we would expect, local financing capabilities have fallen behind local expenditure needs. During the 1960s, for example, when the baby boom created an immense surge in education expenditures, the state and local sector was continually

Grants-in-aid   Thus the capacity to "self-finance" cannot provide a useful guide for the allocation of public expenditures, especially at the state and local level. This dilemma has been overcome by the development of grants-in-aid: federal transfers of tax funds to the states (and for some purposes, directly to the cities) under various kinds of sharing-out formulae and with various kinds of restrictions.

In 1975, these grants-in-aid came to about $54 billions. This was about 15 percent of the federal budget, the third largest category of federal spending after defense and income support. From the recipients' point of view, grants-in-aid amounted to about one-fifth of all state and local receipts. Moreover, the principle of grants-in-aid is continued at the state level. The states are better tax raisers than the cities, for the same reason that the nation is a better tax raiser than the state. Thus the states have also used the grants system to help out cities that could not finance themselves by local taxation.

---

*Whether it *should* use its tax powers to establish limits on its spending is a question we will investigate in macroeconomics. Briefly, the answer is no. The federal government is a balance wheel for the economy. Sometimes the government should spend more than its tax receipts (borrowing the difference); sometimes less.

This dependence on grants-in-aid will continue in the future. The spectacle of mayors besieging state capitals and of governments badgering Washington is not, therefore, evidence of wastefulness or profligacy on the part of localities or states. **It is the consequence of a mismatch between taxing capacity and spending responsibility, a mismatch that forces nonfederal spending authorities to go outside for taxes to pay for activities that cannot be financed by their own tax revenues.**

Voting

We have seen that we cannot use the principle of market demand or of self-financing capability as a sensible guide to allocation of public resources. Then how are public moneys divided among various functions at federal or state and local levels?

The answer, as we all know, is through voting. Where there is no economic mechanism applicable, we turn to the political mechanism. We vote for or against the general economic programs of candidates or parties. Within Congress or the state legislatures, our representatives vote again. The voting process is the subject of intense efforts to influence its outcome: lobbying, pressure from constituents, log-rolling deals of many sorts. From this pulling and hauling emerges the national economic budget with its appropriations for different public purposes, a process duplicated again at state and local levels.

The budgetary process

Federal budgeting process itself is better covered in a text on the political process than in one on economics. However, we ought to have at least a general idea of the process of consultation, bargaining, and reconciliation, by which the budget is shaped. In Fig. 21 • 1 we see this process in outline, showing the new budgeting methods put into effect in Congress.

The aim of the new process is to coordinate revenue raising and budgetary appropriations, traditionally assigned to different committees in each House. It is designed to give Congress better control over a process that had gradually slipped into the hands of the executive branch. The system has been in operation too short a time to allow an appraisal of its merits, but economists agree that it is a long overdue improvement in rational budgeting procedures.

Establishing the level of expenditure

The process of voting leads to many difficulties in establishing an intelligent level of government spending. One of these difficulties is that, paradoxically, both increasing and reducing government expenditures are vote-getting, popular policies.

As income maximizers, most citizens will vote for government programs that increase *their* incomes. They will vote to lower those expenditures that increase the incomes of others. Thus if each of us were to scrutinize the government's budget we could easily find areas to cut. The problem is, of course, that another citizen may gain from the very activity that we would eliminate. The objective, then, is to find cuts in expenditures that will win voting majorities. As with tax reform, expenditure reform runs into difficulties because particular cuts in spending help most voters only marginally while hurting some voters severely. Thus the beneficiaries of some expenditures form intense lobbying or pressure groups just as tax beneficiaries do. (See the "Extra word" on arms spending at the end of this chapter.)

The asymmetry of spending and taxing

For this reason there is an interesting difference between appeals for increasing government expenditures and for decreasing them. Expenditure increases are always discussed in terms of the specific programs to be expanded. This rallies a group of intense supporters and arouses only mild opposition from those who are not among the favored, because taxes will be only slightly raised. Conversely, when expenditure reductions are discussed, the emphasis is always placed on the general relief to all taxpayers, and the particular hurt to a few previously favored beneficiaries is passed over in silence.

The presence of staunch supporters and the absence of strong objectors demanding *specific* reductions tips the scale in favor of raising, not lowering, total expenditure. The only true budget cutter is one who would be willing to reduce an expenditure from which he or she benefited, and such fiscal saints are few. On the other hand, the bias in favor of raising expenditures does not mean that the public sector is therefore too large relative to the private sector. Many other biases exist in the system to reduce the valuation that we place on public spending and to inflate the value that we ascribe to private spending. As we have seen, economic analysis can give us no ultimately correct division between public and private expenditure.

Rational Government Expenditure

If voting actually determines government expenditure, what microeconomic principles, if any, apply to public allocations? How would we, as economists, advise a group of legislators who were trying to improve the rationing system of the budgetary process?

Marginal utilities

We must know what we cannot do, as well as what we can, so let us quickly dispose of two ideas that are not very useful.

The first impracticable idea is to apply the principle of equimarginal benefits to public spending, the way we do to private spending. Ideally, the marginal utility of the last dollar spent in the public sector should be equal to that of the last dollar spent in the private sector. If the marginal utility of the public sector dollar is higher than that of the private sector, we ought to spend more public dollars. If it is lower, we ought to spend fewer. And the same principle applies, needless to say, in comparing the amounts we spend for one program versus another.

What is the trouble with this tried and true principle of microeconomics? It is that we have no way of measuring marginal utilities. Even in the private sector, we simply assume that individuals buy goods or services in proportion to the marginal utilities they yield. But the public sector, as we have so often stressed, does not offer its goods for sale. We have no way of judging or even guessing the marginal utilities of goods, public or private, when they have no prices attached. Even if we could establish some kind of usefulness index of public goods for different citizens, how could we add these indices together? How much weight could the index of one person have in relation to another?

Hence marginal utility cannot be used as a guide for public allocations. It tells us what we should be doing, but it leaves us in the dark as to how to go about doing it.

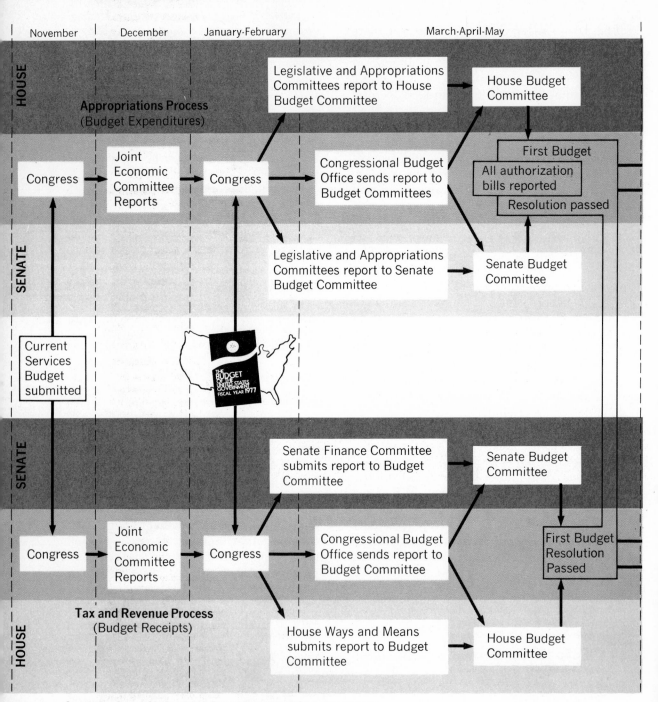

	November	December	January-February	March-April-May

HOUSE

Appropriations Process
(Budget Expenditures)

Legislative and Appropriations Committees report to House Budget Committee → House Budget Committee

Congress → Joint Economic Committee Reports → Congress → Congressional Budget Office sends report to Budget Committees

First Budget
All authorization bills reported
Resolution passed

SENATE

Legislative and Appropriations Committees report to Senate Budget Committee → Senate Budget Committee

Current Services Budget submitted

SENATE

Senate Finance Committee submits report to Budget Committee → Senate Budget Committee

Congress → Joint Economic Committee Reports → Congress → Congressional Budget Office sends report to Budget Committee

First Budget Resolution Passed

HOUSE

Tax and Revenue Process
(Budget Receipts)

House Ways and Means submits report to Budget Committee → House Budget Committee

Source: The Conference Board, *The Federal Budget: Its Impact on the Economy*

FIG. 21·1 Congressional budget timetable

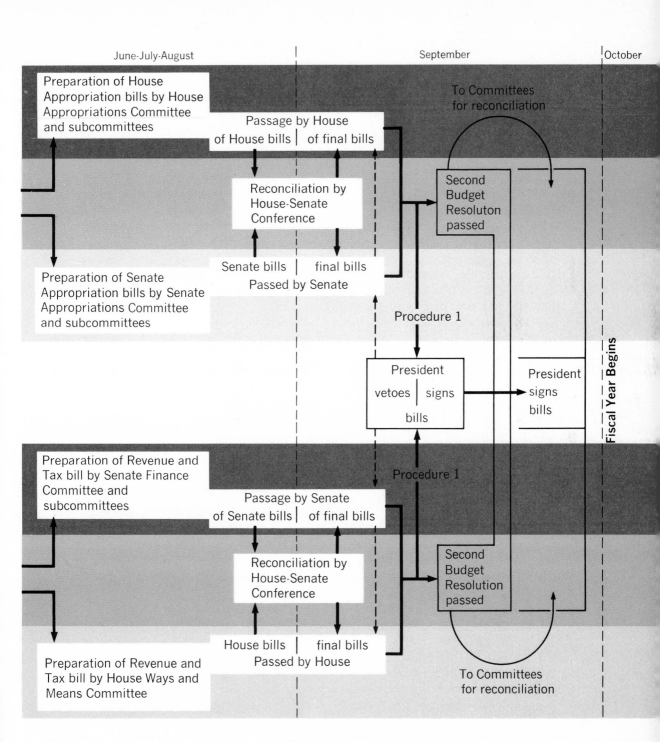

Cost-benefit analysis Somewhat related to marginal utility as a criterion for the allocation of public goods, is cost-benefit analysis. Here again the principles are simple, but the implementation is hard.

Cost-benefit analysis essentially tells us that any economic action will have costs and benefits. In private industry the benefits come in terms of dollar revenues. Private industry undertakes activities only if revenues exceed costs. Cost-benefit analysis tells us that we should apply the same principle to government. We should not undertake activities whose benefits are less than their costs.

Here we find two problems. One of them has to do with discounting the future. A dollar of revenues or benefits that will not accrue for 10 years is not worth $1 today, simply because we have to wait 10 years before we enjoy the benefit. Therefore we discount future income, reducing it by some percentage to measure the cost of waiting. One dollar, a year hence, discounted at 10 percent, is worth only 91¢ today. A dollar 2 years hence is worth only 83¢ because we discount each year in turn. Discounted at 5 percent, a dollar 2 years hence is worth 91¢.

Thus discount rates matter a lot. The Teton Dam that failed in 1976 was "justified" by using a discount rate of just over 3 percent. At a rate of 6 percent it would have been a clear loser.

But what discount rate should we use? Industry uses the going rate of interest, but government cannot use that rate because it helps *set* the rate of interest, as we shall learn in macroeconomics. There is no "right" discount rate to rely on.

An even greater handicap is the fact that we often cannot accurately evaluate the magnitude of public benefits. A private firm is interested only in the revenues that will accrue to it because it undertakes a certain activity. But the government cannot measure the benefits of a dam just by the additional tax revenues that it may generate. It must compute the increases in income and well-being of the nation—the increased volume of agricultural output, the lessening of flood damage, the cost of relocation, the enhancement of tourism, the loss of wilderness, the effect on ecology. These are much more elusive magnitudes to calculate than simple sales revenues.

Overall usefulness For these reasons and for others that we have not discussed, the application of cost-benefit analysis is disappointing in practice. In a rough and ready way it serves as a useful first approximation of winnowing out wasteful projects from useful ones, especially because it calls our attention to indirect, or external, benefits (or costs) that might otherwise escape our notice. When we try to calculate these external effects, it is often so difficult, so beclouded with uncertainty, that in practice, cost benefit—like equal marginal utilities—does little more than tantalize us with a method that defies practical application.

Microeconomic Methods

Let us now turn to a more positive view of how microeconomic methods can help a legislator vote intelligently for public expenditures.

Cost effectiveness The first method is simple and self-evident. Once a public project has been decided upon—a road, a school, a training program—considerations of "cost effectiveness" are exactly the same as they are in a factory, a private house, or any other private venture.

The principle is the use of the most economical combination of inputs to achieve a given output. In theory, as we know, this is achieved by adjusting the marginal productivities of factors so that the marginal revenue product of each grade of labor, or of labor and capital and land, are equal. The same guide obviously applies in public projects. "Wastefulness" has the same definition in public and private. It simply means that marginal productivity, insofar as it can be measured, has not been equalized for all factors.

It is true, of course, that marginal productivity is often difficult to measure. But it is no more difficult to measure in building a road than in building an airplane. It is certainly not easy to translate the principles of efficiency, as an economist describes them, into the complex specifications of a construction job. But the aim is in no way different between the public and private sectors.

Opportunity costs and budgeting

A second consideration that economists can offer to legislators is the concept of opportunity cost. The true "cost" of any public project (like that of any private one) is not the dollars it takes but the alternative projects that cannot be undertaken because resources are committed to the first.

Opportunity costs are difficult to apply to public projects because the "returns" from these projects, as we have emphasized, include so many nonmonetary gains. Hence in practice, most legislators consider each year's appropriations in terms of marginal increases or decreases to existing commitments. Suppose, for example, that you are considering the federal budgetary appropriation for housing and community development, a $7 billion commitment in 1975. In all likelihood, most of your discussion would be concentrated on whether the appropriation should be increased or diminished by, say, $0.5 billion. Your review of the opportunity costs of the project, or of its cost-benefit ratio, would focus on whether or not that $0.5 billion would be a useful addition to the program.

Zero-based budgeting

Yet the true opportunity cost of the program is not the $0.5 billion. It is the entire $7 billion annual commitment. Measuring opportunity costs requires that we do more than think about marginal budgeting. We must reflect on total, or "zero-based," budgeting. There is, in fact, only one reason why we do not perform zero-based budgeting on each and every item in all government budgets. The reason is simply that the accounting proceedures are too lengthy and costly. It is too arduous, each year, to justify a housing and community program again "from scratch" and to judge its merits against all other programs. Hence marginal budgeting is the path of least administrative resistance.

Yet on occasion we should certainly indulge in zero-based budgeting to grasp the full opportunity costs of what we are doing. One current suggestion is that all government programs should have "sunset" provisions, calling for the expiration of the total program after a given number of years. This would force us, every five years or so, to review the full opportunity costs of public expenditure, while using marginal budgeting in the years between.

The irrelevance of sunk costs   The concept of zero-based budgeting, in which we review the opportunity cost of an entire project, brings us to another guide to efficient budgeting. This is the idea of *sunk costs*, expenditures that have been made in the past and that can no longer be "undone."

Here, too, is a distinct similarity between private and public efficiencies. Suppose that you have a dam or a factory half built. A decision must be made whether to continue with the project or abandon it. At this point neither the public legislator nor the private entrepreneur should go back and review whether or not the project should have been started in the first place. The money that has been spent on it is irretrievably lost, both to the public and the private enterprise. The question that is relevant is whether the remaining costs will be justified by the benefits or revenues that are expected ultimately to accrue.

Although a private firm may regret having decided to start up a new branch, an intelligent decision on going through with the project will measure only the remaining costs against the expected revenues. A legislator may rue having voted for a public project, but he will intelligently vote to complete it if the remaining costs will be justified by the total ensuing benefits.

In other words, all sunk costs are irrelevant in making decisions about future actions. Rather, they should be irrelevant. In fact, it is very difficult for decision makers, private or public, to understand that costs incurred in the past are now beyond recall and can be recouped, in part if not in full, only by continuing with a project even though the total undertaking is now deemed to be a losing proposition. The impulse is to stop a project once it has been decided that the initial decision was in error. The common phrases are "not to throw good money after bad" or "to cut our losses."

Curiously, the same failure to evaluate the remaining costs against the total benefits of a project can also lead both entrepreneurs and legislators to complete projects that ought to be dropped. A half-built dam or a half-completed factory is testimony to a decision that was made. An honest computation of remaining costs measured against total benefits may show that the project should remain half complete. Since that would be an admission that the initial decision was in error, many projects are completed with hope that unexpected benefits will rescue the decision maker.

Expenditure incidence   In our previous chapter we looked at tax incidence, how the burden of taxation is distributed across different income classes. We can ask exactly the same questions with respect to expenditures. An expenditure, like a tax, affects different income strata in different ways. It may be progressive, proportional, or regressive in its impact, depending on whether its benefits raise the incomes of the rich more than, in equal proportions with, or less than incomes of the poor. The incidence of $1 million spent for university research will be a great deal more progressive than $1 million spent for unemployment relief. Recall that the incidence of social security expenditures was more regressive than the incidence of social security taxes, making the system as a whole slightly progressive in its impact. Note that the meaning of *progressive* and *regressive* are reversed, so that from an egalitarian point of view we would favor regressive expenditures for the same reasons that we favor progressive taxation.

Expenditure incidence can also study

both the direct and the indirect benefici-aries of government spending. Expendi-tures for school programs, for example, will directly benefit school children (and their parents) but will also indirectly benefit teachers by increasing the demand for teaching skills. Spending for unem-ployment relief will directly benefit the jobless, but will spread its indirect benefits to the whole range of businesses whose products the unemployed will be able to buy. Expenditures on flood control will directly benefit the residents of a region, but will indirectly benefit the construction companies and suppliers who specialize in this sort of work.

Like taxes, spending has direct or in-direct impacts that are not always easy to determine. This is particularly the case when we try to assess the benefits of spending for such purposes as defense or "law and order." The standard procedure is to assume that such expenditures are half used to defend lives, which spreads their benefits proportionally, and half to protect property, which gives them a progressive (anti-egalitarian) incidence.

Another problem in assessing the inci-dence of expenditures is that we do not know if the value to the recipient is equal to the per capita amount of the expendi-ture. This is difficult to determine because the recipient does not *buy* the benefits. An expenditure program may cost $1,000 for each tenant of a public housing project, but we do not really know if the benefit is worth that much to the tenant, because he or she has not actually put out the money for it.

The role of judgment

There are no satisfac-tory solutions to these kinds of problems, just as there are none to many of the earlier difficulties we examined. No doubt that is why the economics of government expen-diture (and especially of expenditure inci-dence) has been relatively neglected, com-pared with that of government revenue raising. The market has clear-cut price in-dicators. Public expenditure has none. Removed from the seeming exactitude and impersonal calculus of the market, public economic activities rely on naked human judgment.

The market in a final retrospect

This seems a good place to make a final assessment of alloca-tion of resources publicly through votes and through spend-ing. Many people look askance at how the public sector allocates its resources. No one needs to be reminded of innumerable scandals having to do with influence ped-dling or abuse of the public trust by members of federal or state legislatures.

What we should remember, however, is that the voting process is a substitute ra-tioning mechanism. One-person-one vote must replace the market mechanism's ra-tioning on the basis of one-dollar-one-vote.

The abuses of the voting mechanism may be many, and its problems are assuredly difficult (you might look again at the "Extra word" to Chapter 10). Nonethe-less, voting is the way a democracy rations its public output, just as spending is the way a market system rations its private output. Before we wax too indignant about the shortcomings of the voting process, pointing to the waste that accompanies government programs, etc., etc., we should remind ourselves of the inequities that ac-company private rationing decisions.

The market mechanism has enormous strengths, but it is certainly not perfect. In fact, we know that it must be imperfect. There are problems the market cannot cope with at all. Moreover, those it does handle reveal the pervasive bias of a vot-ing system in which individuals are measured by their incomes, not by any other gauge of their human value.

Thus all market systems must have public counterparts and complements. It is impossible to have an economic system in which government would play no role whatsoever. The exercise of the political will that is so much (and so properly) distrusted is also essential for social survival itself. In this struggle between the authority of politics and that of economics lies a central issue, not merely of microeconomics but of modern economic society.

FOCUS   Here is the last look at microeconomics. The lesson ends, appropriately, with a warning: the price system that microeconomics studies is a limited system, incapable of providing by itself for social survival. Government is inescapable, a fact of which we have to be reminded only because the market works so silently and smoothly that we sometimes ascribe all the faults of our economic system to the clumsiness or misuse of the public sector.

Thus, a survey of public expenditure is really an effort to see once again where the boundaries of the market system lie. Beyond these boundaries the public sector begins, and we seek to discover if we can use some of the principles of microeconomics within this sector.

The answer is mixed. There are concepts of microeconomics, such as marginal utility, that cannot be translated into the world of public goods because they are based on individual, not on collective enjoyments. There are general guides, such as cost benefit, that make the transition from the private to the public sector only with great difficulty because the purpose of the public sector is to maximize the nation's welfare, not the revenues of a single enterprise.

Of the various analytical points covered in the chapter, the most useful—and the most difficult to act on—is that of "sunk costs." Look at the questions in the section to follow. Test your understanding of this idea, as valid for private enterprise as for public.

WORDS AND CONCEPTS YOU SHOULD KNOW

Difficulties of local financing, 306–7
Grants-in-aid, 307
Asymmetry of spending and taxing, 309
Cost-benefit analysis, 312
Discounting the future, 312

Opportunity cost, 313
Zero based budgeting, 313
Sunk costs, 314
Expenditure incidence, 314–15

QUESTIONS

1. A congressional committee is considering the construction of a moving sidewalk to facilitate transportation for office workers in Washington, D.C. The costs will be $1 billion. How could the committee estimate the benefits? Should the cost be entirely financed by charging admission to the sidewalk, as to a subway? What benefits should be added to those of the proposed fare receipts? Reductions in traffic jams? Increased productivity in government work? Can you think of others?

2. Suppose that the project is undertaken. After a year $500 million has been expended, and Washington workers have said that they will not pay a toll to avoid walking. The sidewalk cannot count on any paid receipts. Its benefits will therefore consist entirely in the secondary savings of traffic, efficiency, and the like. It is estimated that these will amount to $75 million a year. Will the expected $75 million, stretched over 10 years, be enough to justify the remaining $500 million in costs? Does the answer depend on your discount rate?

3. Assume that the total benefits are *not* enough to cover the remaining costs. How would you explain a decision to halt all construction work? Assume, on the other side, that the total benefits, conservatively discounted, are worth $600 million ($400 million less than total costs, but $100 million more than remaining expenditures). Can you justify completing the project?

4. Is the process of voting for expenditure "democratic" just because each person (or each representative) has only one vote? If so, can we call the "voting" of the marketplace democratic? If we think that the marketplace allocates goods more efficiently than voting, why not use the market system in the voting booth, giving each citizen as many votes as he or she has dollars?

The military subsector

The problem of expenditure allocation really comes home to roost with the issue of defense. Here is a brief description of the actual size of the defense establishment, followed by some analysis of why it is difficult to escape from this expensive commitment.

THE DOD

The Department of Defense (DOD) is the largest planned economy outside the Soviet Union. Its property—plant and equipment, land, inventories of war and other commodities—amounts to over $240 billion, equal to about 7 percent of the assets of the entire American economy. It owns 39 million acres of land, roughly an area the size of Hawaii. It rules over a population of more than 3 million—direct employees or soldiers—and spends an "official" budget of roughly $93 billion, a budget 40% as large as the entire gross national product of Great Britain.

This makes the DOD richer than any small nation in the world and, of course, incomparably more powerful. That part of its assets represented by nuclear explosives alone gives it the equivalent of 6 tons of TNT for every living inhabitant of the globe, to which must be added the awesome military power of its "conventional" weapons. The conventional explosives dropped in Indochina *before* the extension of the war to Laos amounted to well over 3 million tons, or 50 percent *more* than the total bomb tonnage dropped on all nations in both European and Pacific theaters during World War II.

The DOD system embraces both people and industry. In the mid-1970s the people included, first, some 2.2 million soldiers deployed in more than 2,000 bases or locations abroad and at home, plus another 3 million civilians located within the United States and abroad. No less important are about one million civilian workers who are directly employed on war production, in addition to a much larger number employed in the secondary echelon of defense-related output. This does not include still further millions who owe their livelihood to the civilian services they render to the military.

THE WEB OF MILITARY SPENDING

The web of DOD expenditures extends to more areas of the economy than one might think. All in all, some twenty-odd thousand firms are prime contractors with the DOD, although the widespread practice of subcontracting means that a much larger number of enterprises—perhaps 100,000 in all—look to defense spending for a portion of their income. Within the main constituency, however, a very few firms are the bastion of the DOD economy. The hundred largest defense contractors supply about two-thirds of the $40-odd billion of manufactured deliveries; and within this group, an inner group of 10 firms by themselves accounted for 30 percent of the total.

The military establishment, as the largest single customer in the economy, not only supports a central core of industry but also penetrates that core with 2,072 retired military officers who were employed in 1969 by the 95 biggest contractors (the 10 largest firms averaging 106 officers each). Meanwhile, the establishment has a powerful political arm as well. In the early 1970s the DOD employed more than 300 lobbyists on Capital Hill and (a conservative estimate) some 2,700 public relations men in the U.S. and abroad. This close political relationship undoubtedly has some bearing on the Pentagon's requests for funds being given, until recently, only the most cursory congressional inspection, leading among other things to cost "over-runs" of $24 billion on 38 weapons systems.

This is not to say, of course, that the United States does not need a strong defense capability today. But there is no question that the Pentagon subeconomy has become a major element in, and a major problem for, American capitalism. Indeed, the questions it raises are central: how important is this subeconomy to our economic vitality? How difficult would it be to reduce? Can our economy get along without a military subsector?

MILITARY DEPENDENCY

Let us begin by reviewing a few important facts. At the height of the Vietnam War in 1968, more than 10 percent of our labor force was employed in defense-related work. As the Vietnam War gradually decelerated, this percentage fell to about 5.5 percent. Defense expenditures, however, rose to $93 billion in 1976 and are slated to rise slightly, the next few years.

These global figures do not, however, give a clear picture of the strategic position of defense spending within the economy. The problem is that war-related spending and employment are not distributed evenly across the system but are bunched in special areas and industries. In a survey made in 1967, the Defense Department found that 72 employment areas depended on war output for 12 percent or more of their employment and that four-fifths of these areas were communities with labor forces of less than 50,000. This concentration of defense activity is still a fact of economic life in the mid 1970s. The impact of a cutback on these middle-sized communities can be devastating.

In addition, defense-employment is concentrated among special skills as well as in a nucleus of defense-oriented companies. In the late 1960s, about one scientist or engineer out of every five in private industry was employed on a defense-related job. Thirty-eight percent of all physicists depended on war-work. Twenty-five percent of all sheet-metal workers, the same proportion of pattern-makers, and 54 percent of all airplane mechanics worked on defense projects. These proportions have declined, but "defense" is still a major employer of these skills. And as we have already remarked, there is a core of companies dependent on military spending for their very existence. These are not usually the largest companies in the economy (for whom, on the average, defense receipts amount to about 10 percent of total revenues) but the second echelon of corporations: of 30 companies with assets in the $250 million to $1 billion range, 6 depended on war spending for half their incomes, and 7 depended on it for a quarter of theirs.

Thus a cutback in defense spending is always felt very sharply in particular areas, where there may be no other jobs available, or among occupational groups who have no alternative employment at equivalent pay or in companies that are "captives" of the DOD. Such companies and areas naturally lobby hard for defense expenditure on which their livelihood depends. So do their representatives in Congress. It is this interweaving of economic and political interests that makes the problem of defense cutbacks so difficult.

CONVERSION POSSIBILITIES

Yet a cutback is not economically impossible. *What is crucial, economically, is that the decline in war-related spending be offset by increases in peace-related spending, to be sure that the overall level of demand would remain high enough to act as a magnet, attracting the displaced workers to other jobs.* Unless we were willing to undertake an ambitious program of public spending or tax cuts the conversion would certainly generate severe unemployment—and consequent political pressures to maintain military spending.

Meanwhile, it is clear that the armaments economy is not only costing us a vast sum of money, but is also weighing heavily on the Russians. The annual military expenditure of the U.S. and the U.S.S.R. together amounts to about two-thirds of the entire output of the billion people of Latin America, Southeast Asia, and the Near East. If we add in the arms expenditures of the rest of the world, we reach the total of more than $50 for every inhabitant of the globe. Not only is this an opportunity cost of tragically large dimensions, if we consider the uses to which those resources might otherwise be applied, but even in terms of a strictly military calculus, much of it is *total waste, since neither side has been able to gain a decisive advantage despite its enormous expenditures.*

PRISONERS' DILEMMA

How does such a senseless course commend itself to national governments? Needless to say, the answers lie deep in the web of political, economic, and social forces of our times. Analytical reasoning can nonetheless throw some light on the matter by unraveling a peculiar situation involving two prisoners, each of whom knows something about the other and who are being interrogated separately. If *both* prisoners remain silent, both will get very light terms, since the evidence against each is not conclusive. If one prisoner squeals on the other, he will get off scot-free as a reward for turning state's evidence, while the other prisoner gets a heavy term. If both prisoners squeal, both will get severe terms, convicted by each other's testimony.

Now, if the two prisoners could confer—and if they trusted each other absolutely—they would obviously agree that the strategy of shared silence was the best for each. But if the prisoners are separated or unsure of each other's trustworthiness, each will be powerfully tempted to rat on the other in order to reduce his own sentence. As a result, since the two are equally tempted, the outcome is likely to end in both sides ratting—and in *both* sides getting heavy punishment. Thus the pursuit of individual "self-interest" lures the two prisoners into a strategy that penalizes them both.

Something very like a Prisoners' Dilemma afflicts the nations of the world, especially the two superpowers, America and Russia. Although a policy of limited arms spending would clearly be to their mutual best advantage, their distrust of each other leads each to try to get ahead of the other. This state of mutual suspicion is then worsened when special interest groups in each nation deliberately play on the fears of the public. The end result is that both spend vast sums on armaments that yield them no advantage, while the world (including them) suffers an opportunity cost on an enormous scale. Only with a frank and candid exploration of shared gains and losses can both prisoners hope to get out of their dilemma. Prospects for a massive conversion of the U.S. arms economy may hinge on our understanding of this central military and political reality of our time.

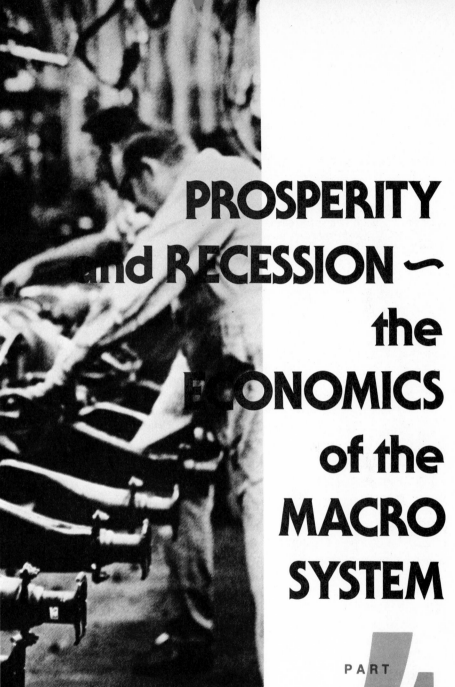

PROSPERITY and RECESSION — the ECONOMICS of the MACRO SYSTEM

PART

4

Wealth and output

What is "macroeconomics"? The word derives from the Greek *macro* meaning "big," and the implication is therefore that it is concerned with bigger problems than in microeconomics (*micro* = small). Yet microeconomics wrestles with problems that are quite as large as those of macroeconomics. The difference is really not one of scale. It is one of approach, of original angle of incidence. *Macroeconomics begins from a viewpoint that initially draws our attention to aggregate economic phenomena and processes,* such as the growth of total output. Microeconomics begins from a vantage point that first directs our analysis to the workings of the marketplace. Both views are needed to comprehend the economy as a whole, just as it takes two different lenses to make a stereophoto jump into the round. Since we can learn only one view at a time, we now turn to the spectacle of the entire national economy as it unfolds to the macroscopic gaze.

22

The macro perspective

What does the economy look like from this perspective? The view is not unlike that from a plane. What we see first is the fundamental tableau of nature—fields and forests, lakes and seas, with their inherent riches; then the diverse artifacts of man—cities and towns, road and rail networks, factories and machines, stocks of half-completed or unsold goods; finally the human actors themselves with all their skills and talents, their energies, their social organization.

Thus our perspective shows us a vast panorama from which we single out for special attention one process that we can see taking place in every corner of the economy. This process is the vast flux of economic activity. We saw it earlier as the circular chain of buying and selling that makes up the market system. This time, however, we begin by paying less attention to the circle of transactions and emphasize instead another aspect: *the vast river of output, the ceaseless flow of production that emerges from the nation's economic activity.*

Output

How does this flow of production arise? In microeconomics we investigate motives that lead factors of production to offer their services to business firms, and motives of entrepreneurs in hiring factors. A macro perspective studies the market process from a somewhat different standpoint, one that focuses on the stream of output as a whole, rather than tracing it back to its individual springs and rivulets.

Following the flow of output

It may help us picture the flow as a whole if we imagine that each and every good and service that is produced—each loaf of bread, each nut and bolt, each doctor's service, each theatrical performance, each car, ship, lathe, or bolt of cloth—can be identified in the way that a radioactive isotope allows us to follow the circulation of certain kinds of cells through the body. Then if we look down on the economic panorama, we can see the continuous combination of land, labor, and capital giving off a continuous flow of "lights" as goods and services emerge in their saleable form.

Intermediate goods

Where do these lights go? Many, as we can see, are soon extinguished. *The goods or services they represent are* intermediate goods *that have been incorporated into other products to form more fully finished items of output.* Thus from our aerial perspective we can follow a product such as cotton from the fields to the spinning mill, where its light is extinguished, for there the cotton disappears into a new product: yarn. In turn, the light of the yarn traces a path as it leaves the spinning mill by way of sale to the textile mill, there to be doused as the yarn disappears into a new good: cloth. Again, cloth leaving the textile mill lights a way to the factory where it will become part of an article of clothing.

Final goods: consumption

And what of the clothing? *Here at last we have what the economist calls a* final good. *Why "final"? Because once in the possession of its ultimate owner, the clothing passes out of the active economic flow.* As a good in the hands of a consumer, it is no longer an object on the marketplace. Its light is now extinguished permanently; or if we wish to complete our image, we can imagine it fading gradually as the clothing "disappears" into the utility of the consumer. In the case of consumer goods like food or of consumer services like recreation, the light goes out faster, for these items are "consumed" when they reach their final destination.*

We shall have a good deal to learn in later chapters about the macroeconomic behavior of consumers. What we should notice in this first view is the supreme importance of this flow of production into consumers' hands. By this vital process, the population replenishes or increases its energies and ministers to its wants and needs. If the process were halted very long, society would perish. That is why we speak of consumption as the ultimate end and aim of all economic activity.

A second final good: investment

Nevertheless, for all the importance of consumption, if we look down on the illuminated flow of output we see a surprising thing. Whereas the greater portion of the final goods and services of the economy is bought by the human agents of production for their consumption, we also find that a lesser but still considerable flow of final products is not. What happens to it?

If we follow an appropriate good, we may find out. Watch the destination of steel leaving a Pittsburgh mill. Some of it, like our cotton cloth, will become incorporated into consumers' goods, ending up as cans, automobiles, or household articles. Some will not find its way to a consumer at all. Instead, it will end up as part of a machine or an office building or a railroad track.

Now in a way, these goods are not "final," for they are used to produce still further goods or services. The machine produces output of some kind; the building produces office space, the rail track produces transportation. Yet there is a dif-

ference between such goods, used for production, and consumer goods, like clothing. The difference is that the machine, the office building, and the track are goods that are used by business enterprises as part of their permanent productive equipment. In terms of our image, these goods slowly lose their light-giving powers as their services pass into flows of production, but usually they are replaced with new goods before their light is totally extinguished.

That is why we call them *capital goods* or *investment goods*, distinguished from consumers' goods. *As part of our capital, they will be preserved, maintained, and renewed, perhaps indefinitely. Hence the stock of capital, like consumers, constitutes a final destination for output.*

Gross and net investment

We call the great stream of output that goes to capital gross investment. The very word *gross* suggests that it conceals a finer breakdown; and looking more closely, we can see that the flow of output going to capital does indeed serve two distinct purposes. Part of it is used to replace the capital—machines, buildings, track, or whatever—that has been used up in the process of production. Just as the human agents of production have to be replenished by a flow of consumption goods, so the material agents of production need to be maintained and renewed if their contribution to output is to remain undiminished. We call the part of gross investment, whose purpose is to keep society's stock of capital intact, replacement investment, or simply replacement.

Sometimes the total flow of output going to capital is not large enough to maintain the existing stock; for instance, if we allow inventories (a form of capital) to become depleted, or if we simply fail to re-

*In fact, of course, they are not *really* consumed but remain behind as garbage, junk, wastes, and so on. Economics used to ignore these residuals, but it does so no longer.

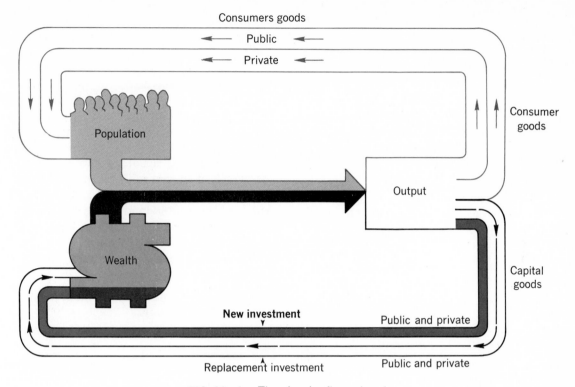

Consumers goods

Public

Private

Population

Consumer goods

Output

Wealth

Capital goods

New investment

Public and private

Replacement investment

Public and private

FIG. 22 · 1   The circular flow, view 1

place wornout equipment or plant. This running-down of capital, we call *disinvestment*, meaning the very opposite of investment. Instead of maintaining or building up capital, we are literally consuming it.

Not all gross investment is used for replacement purposes, however. Some of the flow may *increase* the stock of capital by adding buildings, machines, track, inventory, and so on.* If the total output consigned to capital is sufficiently great not only to make up for wear and tear but to increase the capital stock, we say there has been new or net investment, or net capital formation.

*Note carefully that increased inventory is a form of investment. Later this will receive special attention.

Consumption and investment

A simple diagram may help us picture the attributes of the flow of final output that we have been discussing. Figure 22 · 1 calls our attention to these paramount attributes of the output process:

1. The flow of output is circular, self-renewing, self-feeding. This circularity, which we have encountered before, is one of the dominant elements in the macroeconomic processes we will study.

2. Societies must make a choice between consumption and investment. At any given level of output, consumption and investment uses are rivals for the current output of society. Furthermore, we can see that so-

ciety can add to its capital only the output that it refrains from consuming. Even if it increases its output, it cannot invest the increase except by not consuming it.

3. Both consumption and investment flows are split between public and private use. Like consumption and investment, these are also rival uses for output. A society can devote whatever portion of output it pleases to public consumption or public investment, but only by refraining from using that portion for private consumption or investment.

4. Output is the nation's budget constraint. Our output is the total quantity of goods and services available for all public and private uses (unless we want to use up our past wealth). More goods and services may be desired, but if output is not large enough, they cannot be had.

Wealth

The flow of output interests us for many reasons. Perhaps we can already see that many macroproblems—the level of GNP, volume of employment, rate of growth—will depend directly on the size of the flow of total production. It must also be apparent that our standard of living as consumers will depend very largely on the size of that part of the total flow of output that goes into private or public consumption.

Not so obvious, perhaps, is the strategic role of another aspect of the overall flow: the portion of total output that goes into the creation of new capital goods. This investment flow is the main source of our stock of national wealth.

Kinds of wealth   What exactly is our wealth? In Table 22•1 we show the most recent inventory

of our national wealth. Note that it consists of the value of those physical objects we noticed in our aerial overview: land, buildings, equipment, and the like. Yet a closer examination reveals some odd things.

To begin with, our wealth does not include *all* our material goods. Immense economic treasures such as the contents of the Library of Congress or the Patent Office cannot be accurately valued. Nor can works of art, nor military equipment— not any of them included in the total. Much of our public land is valued at only nominal amounts. Hence at best this is the roughest of estimates of the economic endowment at our disposal.

Table 22•1   U.S. national physical wealth 1975 value

	Billions of dollars, rounded
Structures	
Residential	$ 953
Business	857
Government	745
Equipment	
Producers (machines, factories, etc.)	544
Consumers durables (autos, appliances)	497
Inventories, business	707
Monetary gold and foreign exchange	16
Land	
Farm	336
Residential & business	706
Public	243
Net foreign assets	78
Total	5,682

What is more important, the table omits the most important constituent of our wealth: the value of skills and knowledge in our population. If we estimate the value of those skills for 1976 they come to $8.9 trillion—more than the value

HUMAN WEALTH

Why do we not include the value of human skills in our inventory of wealth? The reason is that all our inventory consists of *property* that can be sold; that is, marketable goods. When our economy included slaves, they were part of our wealth; but in today's market system, people are not property. They can sell their labor but not themselves. See box, p. 11.

Ideally, our inventory of wealth should therefore include the "asset value" of that labor, or the human capital that gives rise to the various tasks, skilled and unskilled, that people perform. How could we estimate that value? The method is much the same as that used to estimate the value of a machine. If a lathe produces a flow of output worth, say, $1,000 a year, we can "capitalize" the value of that flow of output to arrive at the current value of the machine itself. On page 252 we have explained how this process of capitalization works.

In the same way we can capitalize the flow of output of humans. The value of human output is measured by the *incomes* that the factor of production labor earns. In 1976 that stream of income was worth $890 billion. If we capitalize it at 10 percent—a rough and ready figure that is comparable to the rate at which we might capitalize many assets—the value of our human capital was therefore $8.9 trillion.

of the material equipment with which they work! For reasons that we explain in the box, "Human Wealth," we do not usually include human wealth along with physical wealth, although we shall return again and again to this strategic element of our economic system. Here we shall familiarize ourselves with the material side of our national balance sheet, leaving the human side for later.

Capital

One portion of the endowment of a nation's physical wealth has a special significance. *This is its national* capital—*the portion of its productive wealth that is* man-made *and therefore* reproducible. In Table 22·1 we can see that our own national capital in 1975 consisted of the sum total of all our structures, producers' equipment and consumer durables, inventories, monetary gold and foreign assets—$4,397 billion in all.

We can think of this national capital as consisting of everything of use that has been preserved out of the sum total of everything that has ever been produced from the very beginning of the economic history of the United States up to a certain date—here December 31, 1975. Some of that capital—inventories for example—might be used up the very next day. On the other hand, inventories might also be increased. In fact, our national capital changes from date to date, as we do add to our inventories or to our stocks of equipment or structures, etc., or more rarely, as we consume them and do not replace them. At any date, our capital still represents *all the output that the nation has produced*—yesterday or a century ago—*and has not used up or destroyed.*

The reason that we identify our national capital within the larger frame of our wealth is that it is constantly changing and usually growing. Not that a nation's inheritance of natural resources is trivial. Indeed, the ability of a people to build capital depends to no small degree on the bounties or obstacles offered by its geography and geology. Think of the economic limitations imposed by desert and ice on the Bushman and the Eskimo. The point in singling out our capital is that it represents the portion of our total national endowment over which we have the most immediate control. As we shall later see, much of a nation's current economic fortune is intimately related to the rate at which it is adding to its capital wealth.

Wealth and claims

There remains to be noted one more thing before we leave the subject of wealth. *Our table of national wealth omits two items that would be the very first to be counted in an inventory of personal wealth: bank accounts and financial assets such as stocks or bonds or deeds or mortgages.* Why are these essentials of personal wealth excluded from our summary of national wealth?

The answer to this seeming paradox is that we have already counted the *things*—houses, factories, machines, etc.,—that constitute the real assets behind stocks, bonds, deeds, and the like. Indeed these certificates tell us only who *owns* the various items of our national capital. Stocks and bonds and mortgages and deeds are *claims* on assets, not those assets in themselves. The reality of General Motors is its physical plant and its going organization, not the shares of stock that organization has issued. If by some curious mischance all its shares disintegrated, General Motors would still be there. If the plants and the organization disintegrated instead, the shares would not magically constitute for us another enterprise.

So, too, with our bank accounts. The dollars we spend or hold in our accounts are part of our personal wealth only insofar as they command goods or services. The value of coin or currency as "objects" is much less than their official and legal value as money. But most of the goods over which our money exerts its claims (although not, it must be admitted, the services it also buys) are already on our balance sheet. **To count our money as part of national wealth would thus be to count a claim as it if were an asset, much as in the case of stocks and bonds.**

Why, then, do we have an item for monetary gold in our table of national wealth? The answer is that foreigners will accept gold in exchange for their own real assets (whereas they are not bound to accept our dollar bills). Therefore, monetary gold gives us a claim against *foreign* wealth* In much the same way, the item of *net foreign assets* represents the value of all real assets such as factories located abroad and owned by U.S. citizens, less the value of any real wealth located in the United States and owned by foreigners.

Real wealth vs. financial wealth

Thus *national wealth is not quite the same thing as the sum of personal wealth.* When we add up our individual wealth, we include first of all our holdings of money or stocks or bonds—all items that are excluded from our national register of wealth. The difference is that as individuals we properly consider our own wealth to be the *claims* we have against one another, whereas as a society we consider our wealth to be the stock of material *assets* we possess, and the only claims we consider are those that we may have against other societies.

National wealth is therefore a *real* phenomenon, the tangible consequence of past activity. Financial wealth, on the other hand—the form in which individuals hold their wealth—is only the way the claims of ownership are established vis-à-vis the underlying real assets of the community. The contrast between the underlying, slow-changing reality of national wealth and the overlying, sometimes fast-changing financial representation of that wealth is one of the differences between economic life viewed from the vantage

---

*Gold has, of course, a value in itself—we can use it for jewelry and dentistry. However, in the balance sheet of our national wealth, we value the gold at its formal international exchange price, rather than merely as a commodity.

point of the economist and that same life seen through the eyes of a participant in the process. We shall encounter many more such contrasts as our study proceeds.

Wealth and output

Why must we pay so much attention to national wealth? Exactly what is the connection between the wealth of nations and the well-being of their citizens?

The question is not an idle one, for the connection between wealth and well-being is not a matter of direct physical cause and effect. For example, India has the largest inventory of livestock in the world, but its contribution to Indian living standards is far less than that of our livestock wealth. Or again, our national stock of capital goods in 1933 was not significantly different from that in 1929, but one year was marked by widespread misery and the other by booming prosperity.

Clearly then, the existence of great physical wealth by itself does not guarantee—it only holds out the possibility of—a high standard of living. It is only insofar as physical wealth interacts with the working population that it exerts its enormous economic leverage, and this interaction is not a mechanical phenomenon that we can take for granted but a complex *social* process, whose motivations we must now start to explore.

FOCUS The essential point of this chapter is to bring a macroeconomic perspective into sharp focus. We do so by beginning to examine the flow of output, a subject that will occupy us for many more chapters, and by learning something about our treasury of national wealth.

Studying the flow of output introduces us to a number of concepts and vocabulary items that we will be using regularly from now on. This is the time to learn very carefully the difference between intermediate goods and final goods. Be sure you understand why we divide all final goods into two broad categories: consumption and capital. As part of that learning process, pay attention to the ideas of gross and net investment, which will also recur frequently in the chapters to come.

Finally, in learning about the output, pay close heed to Figure 22 · 1 on page 325 and the accompanying 4 attributes of the output process. You want to understand why output is self-renewing. Notice how it replenishes the factors of production and the worn-out wealth of the economy. Make sure you see how output divides twice: once between consumption and investment; the other between public and private.

A look at our national wealth is interesting in its own right, but it is especially useful because it enables us to see how the flow of output into investment becomes part of our stock of wealth. Because we tend to think of "wealth" as consisting of money or financial assets, we take a moment to separate "real" wealth from claims. That's an important idea to grasp. And now we are ready to move into a study of how output is generated.

WORDS AND CONCEPTS YOU SHOULD KNOW

Remember that each chapter of our text is followed by a "Focus"—not a full-scale review of the chapter, but a section that will help you center your attention on main issues and set for yourself central learning objectives. Beyond these issues remains the always necessary, always tricky business of learning the new vocabulary that you encounter in each chapter, a vocabulary that you must eventually master in order to "speak economics."

That is the purpose of these Words and Concepts sections. Sometimes they repeat terms or phrases that you will already have met in the "Focus," sometimes not. All these words and ideas are important for you to know. Thus you should pause for a moment to see if you can give a clear, short definition of each term. If in doubt, look back to the page or pages indicated. Make a note opposite the items about which your memory failed you. Then in a few days look over the section again and see if you have added these words and concepts to your working knowledge.

Macroeconomics, 322
Intermediate goods, 323
Final goods, 323–24
Consumption goods, 323–24
Investment goods, 324–25
Gross investment, 324–25

Replacement, 324
Disinvestment, 325
Capital, 327
Wealth vs. claims, 328
Financial vs. real wealth, 328–29

QUESTIONS

1. Why is capital so vital a part of national wealth? Why is money not considered capital? Why are stocks and bonds not part of national wealth?

2. Explain how the "circularity" of the economic process means that the outputs of the system are returned to it as fresh inputs.

3. What is meant by net investment? How is it different from gross investment? How is investment related to wealth?

4. Why is investment considered a final rather than an intermediate good?

5. What is the physical relation between the stock of wealth and the flow of output? Is it the same as the social relationship? Can a society be "rich" yet "broke"? How do you think that can happen? (This is one of the main subjects that we will be studying. You might think about it now, even if you're not sure of the answer.)

Public vs. private goods and services

What is the right division of the national output between public and private goods and services? This question has been debated since the first economists began to study society, but it has recently been the focus of even more than the normal amount of attention. Is government too big? Do we have too many public goods and services relative to private goods and services? Too little? Here are some facts.

In the post-World War II period there has certainly been an upward trend in the share of GNP going to government. Surprisingly, President by President, the largest increase in the share of the GNP going to government occurred in the Nixon-Ford administration.

Table 22 · 2   Share of GNP originating in federal government expenditures

	Percent
Truman, 1946–1952	17.0–20.5
Eisenhower, 1952–1960	20.5–18.4
Kennedy-Johnson, 1960–1968	18.4–20.8
Nixon-Ford, 1968–1976	20.8–23.0
Carter, 1976–	23.0–

In addition to buying goods and services, government also reallocates private goods and services by taxing some individuals and giving transfer payments, such as social security, to others. Transfer payments do not require public production of goods and services, but they do represent a government intervention in the economy. The biggest growth in government expenditures has not been in public production but in transfer payments. From 1948 to 1976 these have gone from 4.1 to 10.9 percent of the GNP. Many of those who object to the size of government are not really talking about the division between the public and private output of goods and services, but about the extent to which governments should reallocate incomes among individuals.

Big government is also usually taken to mean federal government. In fact, the federal government's purchases of goods and services have grown from 6.3 percent to 7.8 percent of the GNP from 1950 to 1976, but purchases of state and local governments have grown from 6.8 percent to 13.7 percent of the GNP. The governments that have grown have in fact been little governments, at least relative to the federal government. Thus the issue is not really big government, but government in general.

The issue arises because we have no concrete way of measuring gains or losses of social welfare. We often do not know whether public or private expenditures yield more benefits. Each of us may have an opinion, but we have not agreed upon a way of deciding which opinion is correct. Lacking a better means of deciding the question, we rely on the political process. Thus public expenditures grew because, as a society, we wanted them to grow.

What economics does tell us, however, is that the correct allocation of the national output cannot be made by debating what fraction of the GNP should go to "government." The question must be decided at a more disaggregated level. Do we have too much education or too little? Do we have too many roads or too few? Too many or too few sewage treatment plants, missiles, post offices, policemen? Advocates of budget cuts often find a general agreement to cut expenditures in the abstract, but no agreement on which individual expenditures should be cut. To be more truthful, each of us believes that those expenditures which benefit *others* should be cut, but not those which benefit us. The litmus test of a serious budget cutter is to be willing to cut expenditures that he enjoys.

It is also well to remember that in many cases, public and private purchases of goods and services are not substitutes for each other; they complement each other. Private cars need public roads; private boats need public lakes; private farms use public weather forecasters; national defense exists at least in part to defend private property.

Gross national product

We have had a first view of the overall flow of national output that will play so large a role in our macroeconomic studies. Now we want to look into the flow more closely. Here we can begin by using a term that is already familiar to us from Chapter 1. We **call the dollar value of the total annual output of final goods and services in the nation its gross national product.** The gross national product (or GNP as it is usually abbreviated) is thus nothing but the dollar value of the total output of all consumption goods and of all investment goods produced in a year. We are already familiar with this general meaning, but now we must define GNP a little more precisely.

Final goods   We are interested, through the concept of GNP, in measuring the value of the *ultimate* production of the economic system; that is, the total value of all goods and services *enjoyed by its consumers or accumulated as new or replacement capital.*

Hence we do not count the intermediate goods we have already noted in our economic panorama. We do not add up the value of the cotton *and* the yarn *and* the cloth *and* the final clothing when we

23

compute the value of GNP. That kind of multiple counting might be very useful if we wanted certain information about our total economic activity, but it would not tell us accurately about the final value of output. When we buy a shirt, the price we pay includes the cost of the cloth to the shirtmaker. In turn, the amount the shirtmaker paid for his cloth included the cost of the yarn. In turn, again, the seller of yarn included in his price the amount he paid for raw cotton. Embodied in the price of the shirt, therefore, is the value of all the intermediate products that went into it.

Thus in figuring the value for GNP, we add only the values of all final goods, both for consumption and for investment purposes. Note as well that GNP includes only a given year's production of goods and services. Therefore sales of used car dealers, antique dealers, etc., are not included, because the value of these goods was picked up in GNP the year they were produced.

Types of final goods

In our first view of macroeconomic activity we divided the flow of output into two great streams: consumption and gross investment. Now, for purposes of a closer analysis, we must impose a few refinements on this basic scheme.

First we must pay heed to a small flow of production that has previously escaped our notice. That is the net flow of goods or services that leaves this country; that is, the total flow going abroad minus the flow that enters. This international branch of our economy will play a relatively minor role in our analysis for quite a while. We will largely ignore it until Chapter 29, then again until Part 5. But we must give it its proper name: *net exports.* Because these net exports are a kind of investment (they are goods we produce but do not

consume), we must now rename the great bulk of investment that remains in this country. We will henceforth call it *gross private domestic investment.*

By convention, gross private domestic investment refers only to investments in physical assets such as factories, inventories, homes. Personal expenditures on acquiring human skills, as well as expenditures for regular use, are considered *personal consumption expenditures*—the technical accounting term for *consumption.* As these accounting terms indicate, *public* consumption and investment are included in neither personal consumption expenditures nor gross private domestic investment. Here is our last flow of final output: all public buying of final goods and services is kept in a separate category called *government purchases of goods and services.*

Four streams of final output

We now have four streams of "final" output, each going to a final purchaser of economic output. Therefore we can speak of gross national product as being the sum of personal consumption expenditure (C), gross private domestic investment (I), government purchases (G), and net exports (X), or (to abbreviate a long sentence) we can write that

$$GNP \equiv C + I + G + X$$

This is a descriptive identity that should be remembered.

It helps, at this juncture, to look at GNP over the past decades. In Fig. 23·1 we show the long irregular upward flow of GNP from 1929 to the present, with the four component streams of expenditures visible. Later we will be talking at length about the behavior of each stream, but first we need to be introduced to the overall flow itself.

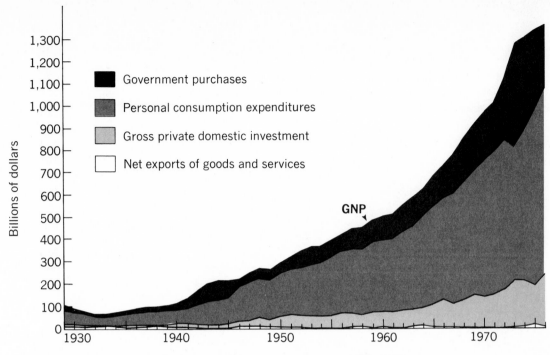

FIG. 23·1   GNP and components, 1929–1976

Stocks and flows   One final point should be made about our basic identity. All through our discussion of GNP we have talked about *flows* of output. We do so to distinguish GNP, a "flow concept," from wealth or capital (or any asset) that is a *stock,* or a sum of wealth that exists at any given time.

A moment's reflection may make the distinction clear. When we speak of a stock of business capital or of land or structures, we mean a sum of wealth that we could actually inspect on a given date. GNP, however, does not "exist" in quite the same way. If our gross national product for a year is, say $1.5 trillion, this does not mean that on any day of that year we could actually discover this much value of goods and services. Rather, GNP tells us the rate, for that year, at which production was carried out; so that if the year's flow of output had been collected in a huge reservoir without being consumed, at the end of the year the volume in the reservoir would

indeed have totaled $1.5 trillion. GNP is, however, constantly being consumed as well as produced. Hence the $1.5 trillion figure refers to the value of the *flow of production over the year* and should not be pictured as constituting a given sum of output existing at any moment in time.

GNP as a Measure

GNP is an indispensable concept in dealing with the performance of our economy, but it is well to understand the weaknesses as well as the strengths of this most important single economic indicator.

1. GNP deals in dollar values, not in physical units.

That is, it does not tell us how many goods and services were produced; only what their sales value was. As we know from Chapter 2, trouble then arises when we

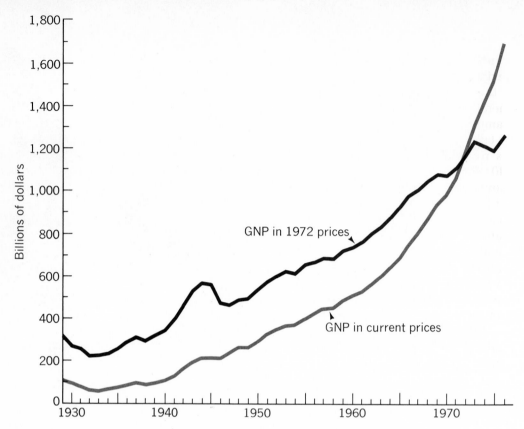

GNP in 1972 prices

GNP in current prices

FIG. 23·2   GNP in constant and current prices, 1929–1976

compare the GNP of one year with that of another, to determine whether or not the nation is better off. If prices in the second year are higher, GNP will appear higher, even though the actual volume of output is unchanged or even lower!

We could correct for this price change very easily if all prices moved in the same degree or proportion. Then it would be easy to speak of "real" GNP—that is, the current money value of GNP adjusted for price changes—as reflecting the actual rise or fall of output. The price problem becomes more difficult, however, when prices change in different degrees or even in different directions, as they often do. Then a comparison of "real" GNP from one year to the next, and especially over a long span of years, is unavoidably arbitrary to some extent.

Figure 23·2 shows us the previous

totals for GNP corrected as best we can for price changes. In this chart, 1972 is used as the "base," and the GNP's of other years use 1972 prices, so that the price changes are eliminated to the greatest possible extent. One can, of course, choose any year for a base. Choosing a different year would alter the basic dollar measuring rod, but it would not change the profile of "real" year-to-year changes. (See more on this problem, if you wish, in Chapter 44.)

2. **Changes in the quality of output may not be accurately reflected in GNP.**

The second weakness of GNP also involves its inaccuracy as an indicator of "real" trends over time. The difficulty revolves around changes in the utility of goods and services. In a technologically advancing society, goods are usually improved from one decade to the next, or even more rapidly, and new goods are constantly being introduced. In an urbanizing, increasingly high-density society, the utility of other goods may be lessened over time. An airplane trip today, for example, is certainly highly preferable to one taken 20 or 30 years ago; a subway ride is not. Television sets did not even exist 40 years ago.

Government statisticians attempt to correct for changes in the quality of goods and services. Committees composed of government statisticians and industry representatives meet to decide on the extent to which price increases represent quality improvements. It is very difficult to determine whether these committees over- or under-adjust for quality improvements. In the 1950s these committees counted the cost of putting "fins" on cars as a quality improvement rather than as a price increase. The fins did not affect the performance of the car, but they were thought to improve its beauty.

Completely new goods, such as the picture phones that have been demonstrated in some part of the country, present an even more difficult problem. Clearly, a picture phone is not an ordinary telephone. Yet, how much of a quality improvement is it? Since there is no satisfactory answer to this question, picture phones will be valued at their selling price in any given year. If picture phones fall in price as they are introduced into the mass market, an evaluation of GNP in 1980 prices will give a much higher "weight" to picture phones than an evaluation of GNP in 1990 prices. This is a prime reason why base years and deflating formulas are periodically reconsidered.

REAL AND CURRENT GNP

It's worth a moment to review the ideas on p. 336.

How do we arrive at a figure for "real" GNP? *The answer is that we "correct" the value of GNP (or any other magnitude measured in dollars) for the price changes that affect the value of our dollars but not the real quantities of goods and services our dollars buy.*

We make this correction by applying a *price index*. Such an index is a series of numbers showing the variation in prices, year to year, from a starting or *base year* for which the price level is set at 100. Thus if prices go up 5 percent a year, a price index starting in year one will read 105 for year two, 110.25+ for year three (105 × 1.05), 115.8 for year four, and so on.

In correcting GNP we use a very complex price index called a GNP *price deflator*. This index, constructed by the Department of Commerce, allows for the fact that different parts of GNP, such as consumers goods and investment goods may change in price at different rates. The present price deflator uses GNP price levels in 1972 as a "base." In 1975, the value of the deflator was 126.37. That is, the price index was up 26% from 1972.

Now let us work out an actual example. *To arrive at a corrected GNP, we divide the current GNP by the deflator and then multiply by 100.* For example, GNP in current figures was $1,171 billion for 1972; $1,306 billion for 1973; $1,413 billion for 1974; and $1,499 billion for 1975. The deflators for those years were 100, 106, 116, and 127. Here are the results:

$$\frac{\$1171}{100} = \$11.71 \times 100 = \$1{,}171 \text{ billion}$$

$$\frac{\$1306}{106} = \$12.32 \times 100 = \$1{,}232 \text{ billion}$$

$$\frac{\$1413}{116} = \$12.18 \times 100 = \$1{,}218 \text{ billion}$$

$$\frac{\$1499}{127} = \$1180 \times 100 = 1{,}180 \text{ billion}$$

Thus the "real value" of GNP in 1974 was $1218 billion, *in terms of 1972 prices*, rather than the $1413 billion of its current value. Two things should be noted in this process of correction. First, the "real value" of any series will differ, depending on the base year that is chosen. For instance, if we started a series in 1975, the "real value" of GNP for that year would be $1,413, the same as its money value.

Second, the process of constructing a GNP deflator is enormously difficult. In fact there is no single "accurate" way of constructing an index that will reflect all the variations of prices of the goods within GNP. To put it differently, we can construct different kinds of indexes, with different "weights" for different sectors, and these will give us differing results. The point then is to be cautious in using corrected figures. Be sure you know what the base year is. And remember that complex indexes, such as the GNP deflator, are only approximations of a change that defies wholly accurate measurement.*

*For a fuller discussion of price indexes and related problems, you might look into Part 6, pp. 694 ff.

3. **GNP does not reflect the purpose of production.**

A third difficulty with GNP lies in its blindness to the ultimate use of production. If in one year GNP rises by a billion dollars, owing to an increase in expenditure on education, and in another year it rises by the same amount because of a rise in cigarette production, the figures in each case show the same amount of "growth" of GNP. Even output that turns out to be wide of the mark or totally wasteful—such as the famous Edsel car that no one wanted or military weapons that are obsolete from the moment they appear—all are counted as part of GNP.

The problem of environmental deterioration adds another difficulty. Some types of GNP growth directly contribute to pollution—cars, paper or steel production, for example. Other types of GNP growth are necessary to stop pollution—sewage disposal plants or the production of a clean internal combustion engine. Still other types of GNP have little direct impact on the environment. Most personal services fall into this category.

As we know from Chapter 3, growth is not a process without its dangers, and nobody would count all kinds of output as being equally compatible with safe, long-term growth. But the sheer measure of GNP tells us nothing with respect to such a problem. For example, our conventional measure of GNP makes no allowances for the harmful goods and services that are often generated by production. Actually, all forms of pollution and congestion diminish individual pleasure or utility and should be *subtracted* from GNP. Yet under our accounting procedures, they are included in GNP! So too, we fail to factor out of GNP those expenditures taken to repair the damage caused by other elements in the total. For instance, the cleaning bills we pay to undo damage caused by smoke from the neighborhood factory become part of GNP, although cleaning our clothes does not increase our well-being. It only brings it back to what it was in the first place.

These costs of cleaning up the harmful effects of economic growth are just one of a large number of *defensive expenditures* in GNP. Defensive expenditures are designed to prevent bad things from happening or to offset the impacts of adverse circumstances, rather than to cause good things to happen. In addition to environmental expenditures, other major examples include military and police expenditures, flood control, repair bills, many medical outlays. These outlays are not desired in their own right; they are simply forced on us by man-made circumstances.

4. **GNP does not include most goods and services that are not for sale.**

Presumably GNP tells us how large our final output is. Yet it does not include one of the most useful kinds of work and chief sources of consumer pleasure—the labor of women in maintaining their households. Yet, curiously, if this labor were paid for—that is, if we engaged cooks and maids and babysitters instead of depending on wives for these services, GNP *would* include their services as final output, since they would be purchased on the market. The labor of wives being unpaid, it is excluded from GNP.

The difficulty here is that we are constantly moving toward purchasing "outside" services in place of home services. Laundries, bakeries, restaurants, etc., all perform work that used to be performed at home. Thus the process of *monetizing* activity gives an upward trend to GNP statistics that is not fully mirrored in actual output.

A related problem is that some parts of GNP are paid for by some members of the population and not by others. Rent, for example, measures the services of landlords for homeowners and is therefore included in GNP, but what of the homeowner who pays no rent? Similarly, what of the family that grows part of its food at home and therefore does not pay for it? In order to include such items of "free" consumption into GNP, the statisticians of the Commerce Department add an "imputed" value figure to include goods and services like these not tallied on a cash register.

5. GNP does not consider the value of leisure.

Leisure time, enjoyable in its own right, is also *necessary* in order to consume material goods and services. A boat without the time to use it is of little consumption value. Over the years, individual enjoyment and national well-being go up because each person has more leisure time, *but leisure time does not show up in GNP.*

Leisure time has not been integrated into measured GNP, since economists have not managed to find either a good technique for measuring its extent or for placing a value upon it. What should be subtracted from the 24-hour day to indicate hours of leisure?

If you were asked to divide your own day into the hours that give pleasure (utility) and the hours that give you pain (disutility), how would you divide your day? Most of us would find many ambiguous hours that we could not really categorize one way or another. If you cannot do it yourself, economists cannot do it for you.

Consequently, GNP suffers as a realistic measure of our changing true standard of living.

6. GNP does not indicate anything about the distribution of goods and services among the population.

Societies differ widely in how they allocate their production of purchasable goods and services among their populations. A pure egalitarian society might allocate everyone the same quantity of goods and services. Many societies establish minimum consumption standards for individuals and families. Few deliberately decide to let someone starve if they have the economic resources to prevent such a possibility. *Yet to know a nation's GNP, or even to know its average (per capita) GNP, is to know nothing about how broadly or how narrowly this output is shared. A wealthy country can be composed mainly of poor families. A poor country can have many wealthy families.**

---

*See the section on averages and bimodal distributions, Part 6, for more on this important statistical problem.

GNP and economic welfare

These problems lead economists to treat GNP in a skeptical and gingerly manner, particularly insofar as its "welfare" considerations are concerned. Kenneth Boulding has suggested that we relabel the monster *Gross National Cost* to disabuse ourselves once and for all of the notion that a bigger GNP is necessarily a better one. Paul Samuelson suggests a new measure—Net Economic Welfare, or NEW—to supplement GNP, the difference being mostly the maintenance or defensive or negative outputs we have mentioned. Economists Tobin and Nordhaus propose MEW—Measure of Economic Welfare—for much the same purposes, subtracting the outputs that contribute nothing to the sum of individuals' utilities and adding back other sums, mainly housewives' services, that are conventionally omitted. (We might note in passing that MEW, as calculated by Tobin and Nordhaus, grows much less rapidly per capita than does GNP. From 1929 to 1965, real per capita GNP mounted at 1.7 percent per year; MEW, at 1.1 percent.)

All these doubts and reservations should instill in us a permanent caution against using GNP as if it were a clear-cut measure of social contentment or happiness. Economist Edward Denison once remarked that perhaps nothing affects national economic welfare so much as the weather, which certainly does not get into the GNP accounts. Hence, because the U.S. may have a GNP per capita that is higher than that of say, Denmark, it does not mean that life is better here. It may be worse. In fact, by the indices of health care or quality of environment, it probably *is* worse.

Yet, with all its shortcomings, GNP is still the simplest way we possess of summarizing the overall level of market activity of the economy. If we want to summarize its welfare, we had better turn to specific social indicators of how long we live, how healthy we are, how cheaply we provide good medical care, how varied and abundant is our diet, etc.—none of which we can tell from GNP figures alone. But we are not always interested in welfare, partly because it is too complex to be summed up in a single measure. For better or worse, therefore, GNP has become the yardstick used by most nations in the world. Although other yardsticks are sure to become more important, GNP will be a central term in the economic lexicon for a long time to come.

FOCUS   Here is a chapter that is essentially definitional. Its purpose is to introduce you, at a technical level, to the nomenclature and basic conceptual problems of gross national product.

Accordingly, that is the thing to study. What you want to understand is:

1. Why GNP is a measure of final output (not final plus intermediate output).

2. The four kinds of final goods or services.

3. What we mean by GNP as a "flow" and by wealth as a "stock."

4. The main conceptual difficulties with GNP: the problem of prices, of qualities, of purpose, of nonmarketed output, of leisure, and distribution. Perhaps the best way to sum up this whole problem is to ask you to reflect carefully on why GNP may not accurately measure *welfare*.

WORDS AND CONCEPTS YOU SHOULD KNOW

Gross national product, defined, 333
Gross private domestic investment, 334
Government purchases, 334
Net exports, 334

Stocks vs. flows, 335
Real GNP, 336–37
Imputed incomes, 338–39

QUESTIONS

1. Write the basic identity for GNP and state *carefully* the exact names of each of the four constituents of GNP.

2. Suppose we had an island economy with an output of 100 tons of grain, each ton selling for $90. If grain is the only product sold, what is the value of GNP? Now suppose that production stays the same but that prices rise to $110. What is the value of GNP now? How could we "correct" for the price rise? If we didn't, would GNP be an accurate measure of output from one year to the next?

3. Now suppose that production rose to 110 tons but that prices fell to $81. The value of GNP, in terms of current prices, has fallen from $9,000 to $8,910. Yet, actual output, measured in tons of grain, has increased. Can you devise a price index that will show the change in real GNP?

4. Presumably, the quality of most products improves over time. If their price is unchanged, does that mean that GNP understates or overstates the real value of output?

5. When more and more consumers buy do-it-yourself kits, does the value of GNP (which includes the sale price of these kits) understate or overstate the true final output of the nation?

6. What is an intermediate good, and why are such goods not included in the value of GNP? Is coal sold to a utility company an intermediate good? Coal sold to a homeowner? Coal sold to the army? What determines whether a good will or will not be counted in the total of GNP?

7. A bachelor pays a cook $100 a week. Is this part of GNP? He then marries her and gives her an allowance of $100 a week. Allowances do not count in GNP. Hence the measure of GNP falls. Does welfare fall?

8. Do you think that we should develop measures other than GNP to indicate changes in our basic well-being? What sorts of measures? After thinking about this, see the "Extra word" at the end of this chapter.

Social indicators

Many people object to the gross national product on the grounds that it focuses our attention on too narrow a band of human activity. Many of the things that improve or degrade our society are left out. Worse still, because they are left out they are ignored. These are not the previously mentioned items, such as imputed income for housewives or negative economic outputs in the form of pollution, that might be added to the GNP to make it a more comprehensive measure of economic *output.* These omissions are measurements of life expectancy, morbidity, mental illness, crime, social unrest and other areas of human activity.

The Social Indicators "movement" is an effort to expand our system of social accounts to measure progress (or the lack of progress) in these other dimensions. The GNP would not be eliminated but would be just one of a number of measurements in an expanded set of social accounts, some of them listed in Table 23 • 1.

Table 23 • 1   Some social indicators

Life expectancy at birth	71.1 years (1971)
Days of disability	24 days per year per person (1969)
Violent crimes	397.7 per 100,000 (1972)
Property crimes	2,432 per 100,000 (1972)
High school graduate rate	76.2 percent (1972)
Job satisfaction	3.44 on scale of 1 to 4 (1973)
Substandard housing units	7.4 percent (1970)

Ideally, such a wide-ranging set of social accounts would give us a better indication of the trend of general welfare than that provided by simple GNP measurements. Yet, although the federal government now issues a social report every other year, the Social Indicators movement has never had the impact that was imagined when it started in the mid1960s. There are two fundamental reasons for its weakness.

First, there are many aspects of human existence that are important to welfare but *unmeasurable.* Consider friendship. Without doubt, social relationships influence our welfare; but could we measure whether the average American has more or fewer friends, better or less helpful friends? Clearly we cannot. Unfortunately, the Social Indicators movement has been so closely linked to the idea of measurement that such problems have led to less and less political interest in the idea.

Second, there is the aggregation problem. We have seen that dollar values are used as the common denominator to aggregate different economic goods and services. What is to be the common denominator used to aggregate life expectancy, crime, and mental illness? Nothing obvious suggests itself. Although there is nothing wrong in presenting three dozen different indices of social progress, one cannot easily say, if indicators point in different directions, whether society is improving.

Lacking an aggregate measure of general welfare, social indicators have had very little impact on public opinion. A declining GNP is front-page news. General welfare may also be declining, but no one social indicator is able to show us this. The net result is that the GNP, for all its shortcomings, is not about to be eclipsed by a more general indicator of social welfare in the near future.

Supply
of
output

Macroeconomics is essentially concerned with growth. At the center of its focus is the question: How does an economy expand its output of goods and services? Or if it fails to expand them, why does growth not take place? Chapter 3 opened a discussion of the long upward trend of U.S. output and the reasons for this trend. In Chapter 23, we began to analyze this process by familiarizing ourselves with the way our stock of wealth interacts with our labor force to yield a flow of output that we call gross national product.

Now we are going to push forward by learning much more about the underlying trends and causes of growth in the American economy. That will set the stage for the work that still lies ahead, when we will narrow our focus down to the present and inquire into the reasons for the problems of our macrosystem—unemployment and inflation, booms and busts.

Historical record   In Fig. 24•1 we see the American experience from the middle of the nineteenth century, in terms of real per capita GNP in 1929 prices. Viewed from the long perspective of history, our average rate of growth has been astonishingly consistent.

24

343

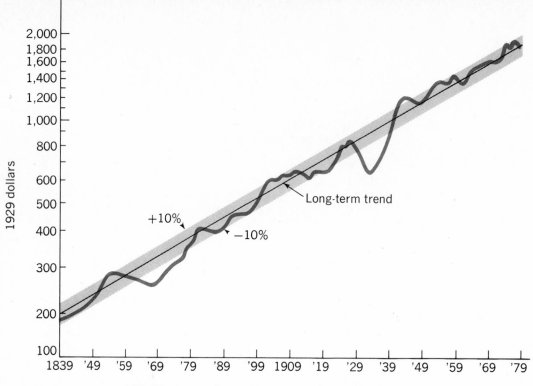

FIG. 24 · 1   Trend in real GNP per head, 1839–1977

This holds true for an average over the past thirty-odd years since the Great Depression or back to the 1870s (or even 1830s). As the chart shows, the swings are almost all contained within a range of 10 percent above or below the trend. The trend itself comes to about 3.5 percent a year in real terms, or a little over 1.5 percent a year per capita. Although 1.5 percent a year may not sound like much, remember that this figure allows us to double our real per capita living standards every 47 years. If we could raise the rate to 2.0 percent, real living standards could double every 35 years.

What determines our rate of growth? As with so many economic processes, we can think of growth as the outcome of a contest between two forces: an active driving force of demand and a constraining, limiting force of supply. We shall learn more about the driving force when we arrive at the study of business investment and government expansionary policy. Here, we focus on the question of supply, equally important in determining our final growth rate. That leads to a fundamental question from the supply side: How much can an economy produce?

Production-possibility curve   If the economy produced only a single good, like wheat, the answer would be simple. Maximum output would be some number of bushels that result from the use of every available acre, every tractor, every hour of work.

Obviously, economies produce many kinds of goods. Thus we cannot answer the question in terms of a single figure, but in terms of a range of possibilities, depending on which goods we produce. It would be difficult to represent this range of possibilities in a simple graph, so we abstract the range of possible outputs to two goods,

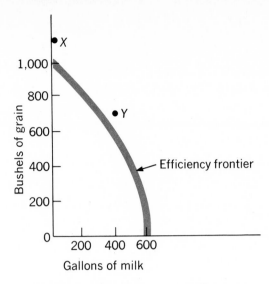

FIG. 24 · 2   Production-possibility curve

within the production possibilities of the economy. *What the curve shows us is that we cannot have both at the same time. If we want 700 bushels of grain, we must be content with less than 400 gallons of milk. If we want 400 gallons of milk, we will have to settle for about 600 bushels of grain.*

say grain and milk, and *we then show what combinations of outputs are possible, using all factors. We call such a schedule of alternative possibilities a production-possibility curve,* and we draw such a curve in Fig. 24 · 2.

Efficiency frontier   The production-possibility curve shows us a number of things. First it makes vivid the material meaning of the word *scarcity. Any point outside the frontier of the curve is unattainable for our community with its present resources.* If the economy uses all available inputs in the most efficient manner, it can produce 1,000 bushels of wheat or 600 gallons of milk. If it had more inputs or were more productive, it could produce more; but with its present supply of inputs and its present level of productivity, it cannot. That is why we call the boundary of the production-possibilities curve *the efficiency frontier.*

It is easy to see that point X is unattainable, but look at point Y. This is an output that represents roughly 700 bushels of grain and 400 gallons of milk. Either one of these goals, taken separately, lies well

Importance of the frontiers   Such a two-commodity diagram may seem unreal, but remember that "milk" and "grain" can stand for consumption and investment (or any other choices available to an economy). In fact, with a little imagination we can construct a three-dimensional production-possibility *surface* showing the limits imposed by scarcity on a society that divides its output among three uses such as consumption, investment, and government. Figure 24 · 3 shows what such a diagram looks like.

FIG. 24 · 3   A production-possibility surface

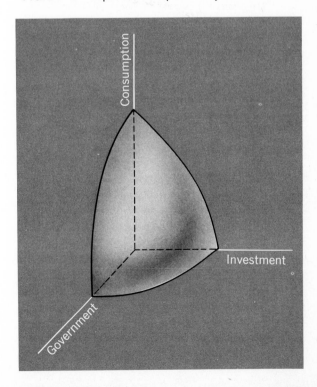

Note how the production-possibility surface swells out from the origin like a windfilled spinnaker sail. Any place on the sail represents some combination of consumption, investment, and government spending that is within the reach of the community. *Any place "behind" the efficiency frontier represents a failure of the economy to employ all its resources. It is a graphic depiction of unemployment of men or materials.*

Very few economies actually operate on their efficiency frontiers. Most economies have at least *some* unemployed inputs or are not using their inputs with all possible efficiency. Perhaps only in wartime do we reach the frontiers of our production-possibility map. Nonetheless, we can see that a major job of economic policy makers is to move the economy as close to its frontiers as possible, under normal conditions.

Law of increasing cost

One point deserves clarification before we move on. The alert student may have noticed that all the production-possibility curves have bowed shapes. The reason for this lies in the *changing efficiency* of our resources as we shift them from one use to another. This is a basic constraint we first met in Chapter 3. *We call this changing efficiency, represented by the bowed curve, the* law of increasing costs. *Note that it is a law imposed by nature, rather than behavior.*

What would it mean if the curve connecting the two points of all-out grain or milk production were a straight line as in Fig. 24·4 *It would mean that as we shifted resources from one use to the other, we would always get exactly the same results. The last man and the last acre put into milk would give us exactly as much milk, at the loss of exactly as much grain, as the first man and the first acre.*

Such a straight-line production-possibility curve is said to exhibit constant returns to specialization. Except perhaps in a very simple economy, where a population might choose between hunting or fishing, constant returns to specialization is an unrealistic assumption, for it implies that there is no difference from one man or acre to another, or that it made no difference as to the *proportions* in which factors, even if they were homogenous, were combined.

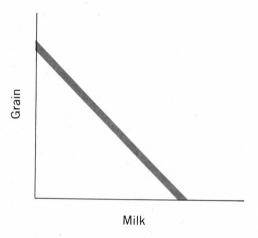

FIG. 24 · 4   Constant returns to specialization

That is a very unrealistic assumption. Men and land (and any other resource) *are* different. Different products *do* utilize them in different proportions. Hence, as we shift them from one use to another, assuming that we always choose the resources best suited for the job, society's efficiency changes. *At first we enjoy a very low opportunity cost in terms of what we must give up for what we get. Thereafter we pay an increasing opportunity cost.* (see box p. 347). Although the shapes of production-possibility curves may have considerably different contours, the unevenness of nature's gifts make most of them bowed, or concave from below.

The production-possibility curve gives a new meaning to *cost*. Suppose we were producing both grain and milk, as shown by the lines *OA* and *OA'*. If we move a given quantity of resources *AB* out of grain and into milk, grain production will fall by the length of the line *AB*. Milk production will rise by *A'B'*. Now imagine that we continue to concentrate on milk at the expense of grain, until we are producing only *OC* worth of grain and *OC'* worth of milk. Once again we move the *same amount* of resources from grain to milk (*CD* = *AB*). Look how much smaller is the gain in milk production: *C'D'* compared with *A'B'*.

Note that the cost of a given quantity of milk is the amount of grain we have to give up to get that milk. The cost of producing a quantity of grain is the amount of milk we would have to give up to get that much grain. **We must trade off gains in one commodity against losses in another.**

A VERY IMPORTANT LOOK AT OPPORTUNITY COST

Economists call this trade-off *opportunity* cost. The term drills home a fundamental truth: there is no economic activity that does not have a cost. That cost is the measure of other actions we might have taken but could not, because we were engaged in the course we chose. As the saying goes, economics teaches us that there is no such thing as a free lunch. Everything that utilizes labor or resources has a cost, whether a charge is levied or not.

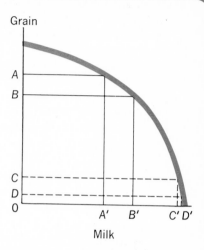

The cost is the alternative benefits that could have been enjoyed by using those resources for some other purpose. *Costs are foregone opportunities.*

Shifting frontiers outward

One last point about production - possibility curves will relate them more specifically to growth. P-p *curves are not static. Changes in factor supplies can move* *frontiers to the right.* If all factors grew at the same rate, the p-p frontier would shift evenly outward as in Fig. 24 • 5, panel I. If only the factors that specialized in milk production increased, it would shift as in panel II.

FIG. 24 • 5   Shifts in the production frontier

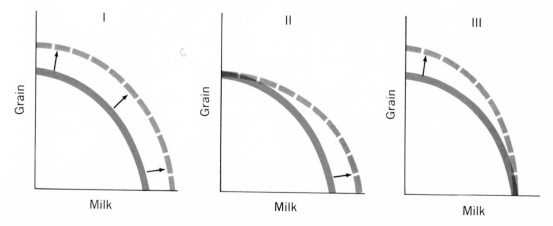

Exerting more influence, as we know, technical progress or changes in skill increase the amount of output we can derive from a given input. These changes also move the *p-p* frontier out. In panel I we enjoy a general increase in productivity that enables us to have both more grain and milk, whereas in panels II and III, productivity has increased only in one area of production, so that the maximum output available for the other good remains the same, regardless of increases in the output of the first.

Thus, changes in the quantity or quality—in sheer volume or productivity—of the factors of production is once again highlighted as the two sources of economic growth. We say "once again," for we first made the acquaintance of these two sources of growth in Chapter 3 (pp. 33–34). Now we must look into them further.

The Supply of Growth

Labor input and production   Output depends on work, and work depends on people working. Thus, the first source of growth that we study is the rise in the sheer numbers of people in the *labor force*. As we shall see, this is a more complicated matter than might at first appear.

Figure 24 • 6 gives us a picture of the population and the labor force over the past almost half-century. As we would expect, the size of the force has been rising because our population has been rising. One might expect that as our society grew richer and more affluent, fewer people would seek employment, but that is not

the case. Looking back to 1890 or 1900, we find that only 52 out of every 100 persons over 14 sought paid work. Today about 60 out of every 100 persons of working age seek employment. Looking forward is more uncertain; but if we can extrapolate (extend) the trend of the past several decades to the year 2000, we can expect perhaps as many as 65 persons out of 100 to be in the labor market by that date.

Participation in the labor force   How can we explain this upward drift of the labor force itself? The answer is to be found in the *different labor participation trends* of different ages and different sexes. We have already glanced into this on p. 18. Figure 24 • 7 shows the different participation rates more clearly.

Thus the overall trend toward a larger participation rate for the entire population masks a number of significant trends.

1. **Young males entering the labor force are older than were those who entered in the past.**
A larger number of young men remain in high school now or go on to college. Only a third of elementary school pupils now go on to college, but the ratio is steadily growing.
2. **Older males show a dramatic withdrawal from the labor force.**
Almost 7 out of 10 older males used to work. Now only 2 to 3 work. The reason is the advent of Social Security and private pension plans. It is probable that the proportion of older males in the labor force will continue to fall as the retirement age is slowly reduced.
3. **Counterbalancing this fall in male participation is a spectacular rise in total female participation. Indeed, the overall trend toward an increasing**

search for work within the population at large is entirely the result of the mass entrance of women into the labor force.

This surge of women into the labor market reflects several changing factors in the American scene (many of these changes can be found abroad, as well). One factor is the growth of nonmanual, as contrasted with manual, jobs. Another is the widening cultural approval of working women and working wives. The average American girl who marries today in her early twenties and goes on to raise a family will nevertheless spend 25 *years* of her life in paid employment after her children are grown. Yet another reason for the influx of women is that technology has released them from household work. Finally there is the pressure to raise living standards by having two incomes within the household.

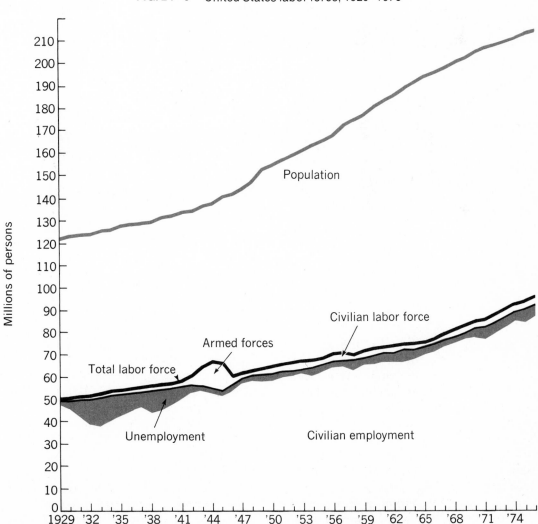

FIG. 24 · 6   United States labor force, 1929–1975

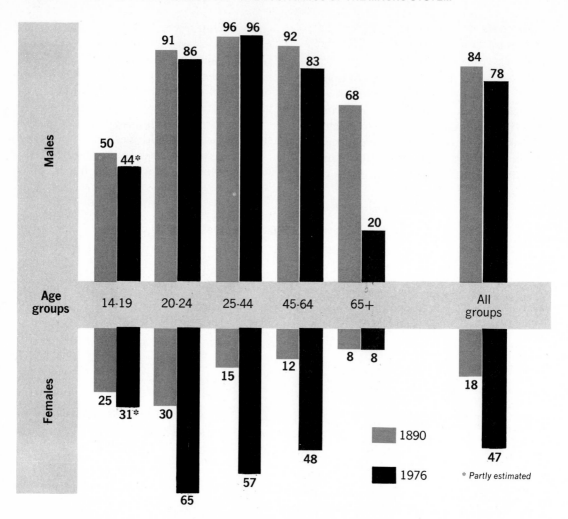

FIG. 24 · 7   Participation rates

Monetization of work

Actually, the upward trend of female participation does not imply an increasing amount of labor performed within society. Rather, it measures a larger amount of *paid* labor. In the 1890s, many persons worked long and hard hours on a family farm or in a family enterprise, and above all within a household, *without getting paid* and, therefore, were not counted as members of the "labor force." To a very considerable

extent, the rising numbers of female participants in the labor force mirror the transfer of these unpaid jobs onto the marketplace where the same labor is now performed in an economically visible way. There is every likelihood this process will continue.

These are not, of course, the only factors that bear on the fundamental question of how many persons will seek work out of a given population. The drift from country to city, the decline in the number of hours of labor per day expected of a jobholder, the general lengthening of life, the growth of general well-being—all these changes bear on the decision to work or not. *Overall, what the complex trends seem to show is that we are moving in the direction of a society where employment absorbs a larger fraction of the life (but not of the day) of an average woman, and a diminishing fraction of the life and of the day of an average man.*

Hours of work   In addition to deciding whether to participate in the labor force, individuals decide how much labor they wish to contribute as members of the labor force. That is, they must decide how many hours of work they wish to offer during a week or how many weeks they wish to work in a year.

Had we asked this question in the days of Adam Smith, it would have been relatively simple to answer. Wages were so close to subsistence that someone in the labor force was obliged to work extremely long hours to keep body and soul together. Paid vacations were unknown to the employees of the cotton mills. Unpaid vacations would have been tantamount to starvation.

MEASURING PRODUCTIVITY

As the accompanying table shows, the average increase in productivity of 3.5 percent masks wide swings from year to year. Compare 1950, when productivity per man grew at 9.2 percent, with 1956, when it actually declined by 0.1!

There is a caution here. These sharp ups and downs do not so much reflect real variations in output per man-hour as they reflect the way in which we measure productivity. *Productivity is measured by dividing total output by total man-hours.* When recessions occur and output falls, businesses reduce their labor forces as much as possible, but they find considerable numbers of overhead workers who cannot profitably be let go simply because output is down. If General Motors' production falls by 25 percent, it does not reduce the working time of its president by 25 percent.

Hence, in recession years, a smaller output is divided by a number of man-hours that has been "kept high." The underlying normal growth in productivity of the labor force may still be occurring, but it is masked by the overhead labor that is not reduced as much as output. In booming years, just the opposite occurs. Output increases faster than employment, since the company does not need to add overhead as rapidly as output. Result: *year-to-year productivity figures must be interpreted with great care.*

	Productivity index (GNP/ man-hour)	% change in productivity per man-hour in the private economy
1947	100	
1948	103.4	3.4%
1949	105.9	2.4
1950	115.7	9.2
1951	121.0	4.6
1952	124.5	2.9
1953	130.2	4.6
1954	133.7	2.7
1955	139.5	4.3
1956	139.5	−0.1
1957	143.3	2.7
1958	146.6	2.3
1959	152.5	4.0
1960	154.2	1.1
1961	158.4	2.7
1962	166.8	5.3
1963	172.3	3.3
1964	178.7	3.7
1965	184.6	3.3
1966	193.1	4.6
1967	197.0	2.0
1968	204.9	4.0
1969	207.1	1.1
1970	206.8	1.0
1971	214.6	4.1
1972	222.2	3.8
1973	227.9	2.9
1974	221.5	−3.4
1975	222.2	2.1
1976	231.6	5.8

With the slow rise in productivity, working men and women gradually found their income rising above "subsistence," and a new possibility came into being: the possibility of deliberately working less than their physical maximum, *using part of their increased productivity to buy leisure for themselves instead of wages.* * Thus, beginning in the early nineteenth century we find that labor organizations (still very small and weak) sought to shorten the workweek. In England, in 1847 a signal victory was won with the introduction of the Ten (!) Hour Day as the legal maximum for women and children. In America, in the prosperity of the 1920s, the 48-hour week finally became standard. More recently, the two-day weekend has become the general practice. Now we hear of the coming of the three-day weekend.

Thus the total supply of labor-time has not risen as fast as the labor force, because a decline in average hours has offset the rise in participation rates and population. On balance, the total supply of labor-hours has increased, but the supply of labor-hours *per employee*, male and female, has fallen.

Labor productivity
As we have seen, we can trace part of our long-term growth to increases in the total supply of man-hours of production. But this is by no means the main source of growth. Far outpacing the growth in the sheer volume of labor-time has been the increase in the amounts of goods and services that each hour of labor-time gives rise to.

Economists measure the productivity of the labor force by dividing the total output of goods by the total number of man-hours. *In Chapter 3, p. 34, we saw the wide margin by which changes in labor productivity outweigh changes in labor-time as a source of increased output.*

Over the post World War II period, the *average* increase in productivity per man-hour has been growing at about 3½ percent a year (see box). At that rate, productivity per man-hour doubles in just under 20 years. Of course, this increase varies from one sector to another. Over the last two decades it increased by 80 percent in manufacturing and *tripled* in agriculture.

Sources of Labor Productivity

What is the explanation for this tremendous and persistent increase in the ability of labor to turn out goods? Here are the most pertinent answers.

1. Growth of human capital

By human capital, as we know, we mean the skills and knowledge possessed by the labor force. Even though the measurement of "human capital" is fraught with difficulties, we cannot ignore this vital contributory element in labor productivity. Ferenc Jánossy, a Hungarian economist, has suggested a vivid imaginary experiment to highlight the importance of skills and knowledge.

Suppose, he says, that the populations of two nations of the same size could be swapped overnight. Fifty million Englishmen would awake to find themselves in, say, Nepal, and 50 million Nepalese would find themselves in England. The newly transferred Englishmen would have to contend with all the poverty and difficulties of the Nepalese economy. Newly transferred Nepalese would confront the riches of England. Yet the

*See "An extra word," p. 104, on using income to buy time.

Englishmen would bring with them an immense reservoir of literacy, skills, discipline, and training, whereas the Nepalese would bring with them the very low levels of "human capital" that are characteristic of underdeveloped countries. Is there any doubt, asks Jánossy, that growth rates in Nepal with its new skilled population would in all likelihood rise dramatically, and that those of England would probably fall catastrophically?

One way of indicating in very general terms the rising "amount" of human capital is to trace the additions to the stock of education that the population embodies. Table 24 · 1 shows the change in the total number of years of schooling of the U.S. population over the past three quarters of a century, as well as the rise in formal education per capita. While these measures of human capital are far from exact or all-inclusive, they give some dimensions to the importance of skills and knowledge in increasing productivity.

Table 24 · 1   Stock of education, U.S.

	1900	1976
Total man-years of schooling embodied in population (million)	228	2098
Percent of labor force with high-school education or more	6.4%	71%
Percent of high-school graduates entering college	17.0	45%

2. Shifts in the occupations of the labor force

A second source of added productivity results from shifts in employment from low productivity areas to high productivity areas. If workers move from occupations in which their productivity is low relative to other occupations in which output per man-hour is high, the production possibility curve of the economy will move out,

even if there are no increases in productivity *within* the different sectors.

A glance at Table 24 · 2 shows that very profound and pervasive shifts in the location of labor have taken place. What have been the effects of this shift on our long-term ability to produce goods?

Table 24 · 2   Percent distribution of all employed workers

	1900	1976
Agriculture, forests, and fisheries	38.1	3.8
Manufacturing, mining, transportation, construction, utilities	37.7	36.1
Trade government, finance, professional and personal services*	24.2	60.1

Source: Calculated from *Historical Statistics,* p. 74; also from *Statistical Abstract.*

*It is customary to include transportation and utilities among the third, or service, area of activities. In this analysis, however, we group them with goods-producing or goods-handling activities, to highlight the drift into "purely" service occupations. Since domestic servants, proprietors, and the self-employed are omitted (owing to inadequate statistics), the table under-represents the labor force in the service and trade sector.

The answer is complex. In the early years of the twentieth century, the shift of labor out of agriculture into manufacturing and services probably increased the overall productivity of the economy, since manufacturing was then the most technologically advanced sector. In more recent years, however, we would have to arrive at a different conclusion. Agriculture is now a highly productive though very small sector, in terms of employment. Moreover, the proportion of the labor force employed in manufacturing is roughly constant, up or down only a few percentage points year to year, from its long-term level of 35 to 40 percent of all workers.

Today, growth in employment takes place mainly in the congeries (collection) of occupations we call the service sector: government, retail and wholesale trade, professions such as lawyers, accountants, and the like. The growth of output per capita is less evident in these occupations.* Thus the drift of labor into the service sector means that average GNP per worker is growing more slowly today than if labor were moving into manufacturing or agriculture.

Why is this growth-lowering shift taking place? The reason has to do with the changing pattern of demand in an affluent society. There seems to be a natural sequence of wants as a society grows richer: first for food and basic clothing, then for the output of a wide range of industrial goods, then for recreation, professional advice, public administration, and enjoyments of other services.

3. Economies of large-scale production

A third source of increasing productivity is the magnifying effect of mass production on output. As we have seen, when the organization of production reaches a certain critical size, especially in manufacturing, economies of scale become possible. Many of these are based on the possibility of dividing complex operations into a series of simpler ones, each performed at high speed by a worker aided by specially designed equipment. It is difficult to esti-

*It is only proper to note that we cannot measure productivity of output in the service sector nearly so unambiguously as in the goods sector, and there is no doubt that the *quality* of many services has increased substantially. Compare, for example, the "productivity" of a surgeon operating for appendicitis in 1900, 1930, and 1960. On the other hand, insofar as we are interested in increases of measurable output per capita, there seems little doubt of the considerable superiority of the goods-producing branches of the economy.

mate the degree of growth attributable to these economies of size. Certainly during the era of railroad-building and of the introduction of mass production, they contributed heavily to growth rate. In a careful study of the contemporary sources of U.S. growth, Edward F. Denison estimates that economies of large-scale production today are responsible for about one-tenth of our annual rate of productivity increase.

4. Increases in the amount of capital

A fourth basic reason for the rising productivity of labor again harks back to Adam Smith's day. It is the fact that each additional member of the labor force has been equipped with at least as much capital as earlier members had; and that all members of the labor force have worked with a steadily more productive stock of capital.

We call the first kind of capital growth a *widening* of capital. It consists of matching additional workers with the same amounts and kinds of equipment that their predecessors had. The streams of additional part-time women workers coming into offices and stores, for example, would not be able to match the productivity of those who preceded them if they did not also get typewriters, cash registers, or similar equipment.

But we must also notice a *deepening* of capital as a source of increased labor productivity. This means that each worker receives *more* capital equipment over time. The ditch digger becomes the operator of a power shovel; the pencil-and-paper accountant uses a computer.

Over the long course of economic growth, increased productivity has required the slow accumulation of very large capital stocks per working individual. Thus investment that increases capital per worker is, and will probably continue to

MASS PRODUCTION IN ACTION

Allan Nevins has described what mass production techniques looked like in the early Ford assembly lines.

Just how were the main assembly lines and lines of component production and supply kept in harmony? For the chassis alone, from 1,000 to 4,000 pieces of each component had to be furnished each day at just the right point and right minute; a single failure, and the whole mechanism would come to a jarring standstill. . . . Superintendents had to know every hour just how many components were being produced and how many were in stock. Whenever danger of shortage appeared, the shortage chaser—a familiar figure in all automobile factories—flung himself into the breach.

Counters and checkers reported to him. Verifying in person any ominous news, he mobilized the foreman concerned to repair deficiencies. Three times a day he made typed reports in manifold to the factory clearing-house, at the same time chalking on blackboards in the clearing-house office a statement of results in each factory-production department and each assembling department.[1]

Such systematizing in itself resulted in astonishing increases in productivity. With each operation analyzed and subdivided into its simplest components, with a steady stream of work passing before stationary men, with a relentless nevertheless manageable pace of work, the total time required to assemble a car dropped astonishingly. Within a single year, the time required to assemble a motor fell from 600 minutes to 226 minutes; to build a chassis, from 12 hours and 28 minutes to 1 hour and 33 minutes. A stopwatch man was told to observe a 3-minute assembly in which men assembled rods and pistons, a simple operation. The job was divided into three jobs, and half the men turned out the same output as before.

[1]*Ford, the Times, the Man, the Company* (New York: Scribner's, 1954), 1, 507.

be, one of the most effective levers for steadily raising output per worker. Unlike the steady widening of capital, however, the deepening of capital is not a regular process. Between 1929 and 1947 there was no additional capital added per worker! This was, of course, a time of severe depression and thereafter of enforced wartime stringencies. Since 1947, the value of our stock of capital worker has been growing at about 2.7 percent a year. As we shall see immediately following, however, the *size* of this additional stock of capital is less crucial than the *productivity* of that capital—that is, its technological character.

5. Technology

We have already implied the fifth and last main source of increases in productivity: technology. Even during the 1929–1947 era, for instance, when capital stock per worker remained fixed, the output of GNP per worker grew by 1.5 percent per year!

Part of this growth can be attributed to some of the sources of growth that we have itemized above, such as improvements in the skills of the labor force. But contemporary economic investigation increasingly attributes the bulk of the bonus rate of growth to the impact of new technology. In the long run, our real standard of living depends upon advances in applied knowledge rather than simply on increases in the supply of capital with which each laborer works (see box).

What we do not know about long-run growth

Last, we must take cognizance of an important fact. We have learned a good deal about the sources of growth in the United States, but we have not really unlocked the secret of the historical trajectory of that growth. In fact, we can now see this trajectory was the result of crosscurrents of many kinds. A rising participation rate, which is a potential sti-

DIFFERENT KINDS OF KNOWLEDGE

In thinking about technology and growth, it helps to differentiate among scientific knowledge, engineering knowledge, and economic knowledge. The relationship can best be understood if we look at the accompanying figure. Here we assume that knowledge can be arranged along a continuum from the least productive technologies to the most productive. On the extreme left are those techniques we have discarded; for example, water mills or treadmills for the production of energy. Next we come to the range of techniques in use. Here is a "bell curve" of plants, beginning with those that are still in use but almost obsolete—say, old-fashioned utilities—to the newest plant and equipment, perhaps nuclear power plants. Here we reach the *economic frontier,* the limit of knowledge that can be profitably used.

Still further to the right is another frontier—the limit of *engineering knowledge.* For instance, breeder reactors, still in "pilot plant stage" might be located near this point. Then to the far right is the boundary of *scientific knowledge*—for instance, fusion power—where our theoretical knowledge has not yet passed into the stage of engineering feasibility.

From an economist's point of view, the level of productivity in an economy depends not only on the location of all these techniques and frontiers, but on the distribution of plants *within* the bell curve. A high-productivity economy will have its curve of plants to the right of a low-productivity economy. Moreover, within that curve, its working equipment will be "bunched" toward the right-hand edge of *best-practice* plants; a low-productivity economy will have the opposite distribution. Incidentally, this is one reason why productivity is very high in industrial nations that have been severely damaged by war but have rebuilt their capital stock. Their factories will tend to incorporate the very newest and best in techniques, whereas an economy that was spared the damages of war will retain in use many older plants that still manage to show a small profit. The rate of growth of productivity depends on how fast the distribution of plants in operation is moving to the right. This depends partly on R&D (research and development), partly on application. For example, someone might invent a train that goes 200 mph, but it could not be used because the roadbeds would not permit trains to go faster than 50 mph. Or social resistances may get in the way: opposition of unions, environmental groups, and others.

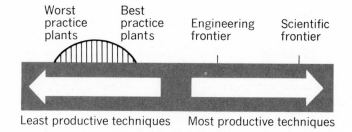

Least productive techniques   Most productive techniques

---

mulus to growth, was dampened by a decline in the numbers of hours worked per year. Increases in productivity of labor in manufacturing and agriculture were offset by a shift of labor into the "low productivity" service sector. Figure 24·8 shows the shifting importance of different sources of growth in different periods.

The overall effect of these complex trends is the "steady" rate of 3.5 percent growth evidenced in the United States for many years. We can now see that this steady rate was really the outcome of many contrary trends. Is there any underlying reason why the growth of GNP maintained such an even pace, or why that pace was 3.5 percent per year?

Not so far as we know. Other nations have different long-run growth rates. and those growth rates are not always as steady as those of the United States, by any means. Furthermore, within the United States, the steadiness of the average rate conceals a great deal of variation in short-run rates, as we have seen. The fact is, then, that we can describe but cannot really explain why our growth has followed the pattern shown in Fig. 24·8. This remains a profound problem for economists and economic historians.

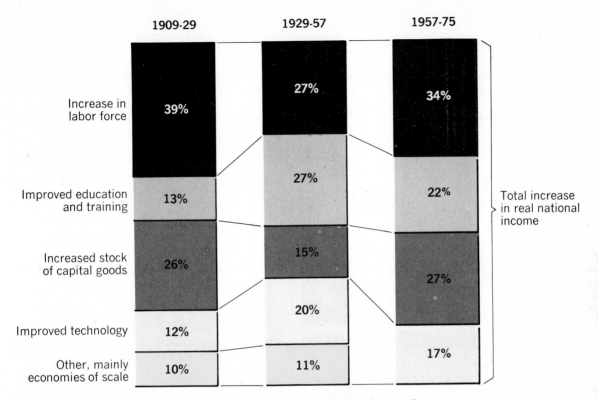

FIG. 24 · 8   Sources of U.S. economic growth

FOCUS   This is a chapter devoted to the subject of growth, a subject that we will be continually referring to in chapters to come. Therefore, you should use this review to fix a few basic ideas firmly in your mind.

At the top of the heap is the matter discussed at the end of our chapter: the "supply" of growth. You must certainly understand how growth can be achieved by increasing the quantity or by improving the quality of the services of the factors of production. You should be able to list the major causes for the increased quality (productivity) of labor and capital.

One way to conceptualize the idea of growth is to draw a production-possibility curve and to see how the efficiency frontier of such a curve moves out as quantities or qualities of inputs rise. At the same time, the *p-p* curve serves a very useful lesson in showing us that there are constraints on the production of combinations of goods that arise from the operation of the law of increasing cost. Because factors are not homogenous, we can produce more and more of one good only by giving up larger and larger quantities of another good. This idea of a "trade-off" gives us a basic insight into the nature of cost as foregone opportunities. Be sure you read the box on p. 347

WORDS AND CONCEPTS YOU SHOULD KNOW

Production possibility curve, 344–45
Efficiency frontiers, 345
Law of increasing cost, 346–47
Opportunity cost, 346–47 (box)

Participation rate, 348–50
Quantities vs. qualities of inputs, 352–53
Productivity and its sources, 352–55

QUESTIONS

1. Set up a production-possibility curve for an economy producing food and steel. Show how combination of goods cannot be produced, *although a quantity of either good alone is within reach of the economy.*

2. What kind of economy might display constant returns to specialization? Would a very simple, low-technology economy show such a straight-line efficiency frontier if it chose, for example, to hunt or fish? Would this depend on the abundance of game or fish?

3. Explain why an economy might not want to operate on its efficiency frontier.

4. How do you account for the fact there are more people per hundred who want to work today than there were 70 years ago, when the nation was so much poorer? How much does the monetization of labor have to do with this? How much is it a change in life-styles, especially for women? What do you expect for the very long run—say 100 years from now?

5. Why is productivity so essential in achieving growth? What are its main sources? What would you recommend as a long-term program to raise American productivity? Asian productivity?

U.S. standard of living

Americans have traditionally prided themselves on having the world's highest standard of living. But recently we have been passed by a number of oil-rich countries in the Middle East, and we either have been, or are about to be, passed by a number of countries in Europe. Here are the most recent figures:

	Per capita GNP 1975
U.S.A.	$ 7,099
Kuwait	11,094
Qatar	19,819
Switzerland	8,754
Sweden	8,450
Norway	6,944
West Germany	6,842

The oil-rich countries are often dismissed on the grounds that they simply "inherited" wealth, rather than having had to do anything to earn it.* Perhaps this is true, but critics must remember the extent to which U.S. wealth has also been built on inherited resources, including vast quantities of oil, coal, minerals, and the best agricultural land in the world.

Certainly the claim of inherited wealth cannot be applied to the newly-rich nations of Europe. What, then, is the reason for the declining relative position of the U.S. in the world?

If we examine the rates of growth of the U.S. and its new superiors, we discover that the turnabout has not occurred because the United States is doing worse than it used to. Output has been growing in the U.S. at about 3 percent a year (1.9 percent per capita) for over a century. Rather, what has changed dramatically is the performance of other countries. The oil-rich countries have suddenly leaped ahead, owing to the boost in the price of oil after the Arab-Israeli war. The new top GNP countries of Europe and Japan got there because their productivity has been growing twice, even three times as fast as ours for the last decade (see Fig. 24 • 9).

To what do they owe their performance? It used to be popular to explain their rapid growth in terms of "catching up." It was said that Europe and Japan speeded up their economic pace by importing U.S. techniques in place of their old-fashioned ways. If this explanation were true, the new winners would have stopped growing faster than the U.S., once they caught up with us. Instead, they have continued to forge ahead. Evidently it is now they, not we, who are pioneering in the techniques of economic efficiency.

*Their average GNP is so high, of course, because a small number of families have gigantic incomes. See Chapter 44, pp. 691–94, on "averages."

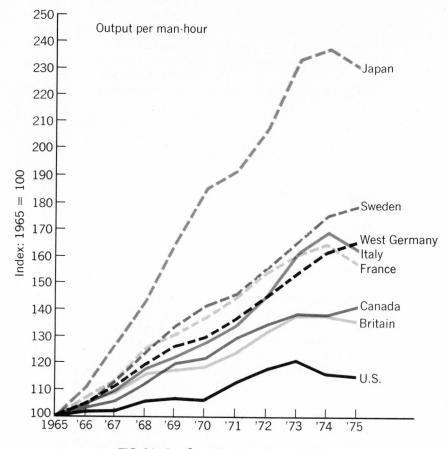

FIG. 24 · 9   Growth rates of productivity

In what ways are they pioneering? Industrial technology tends to spread around the world fairly rapidly, so that is not likely that Europe or Japan possesses industrial secrets unknown to us. They may, however, have some other secrets. Some of these may have to do with the way in which workers' morale is encouraged, especially in Japan and Sweden. In part, the "secret" may have to do with more effective national planning. In part, it may reflect the fact that Europe and Japan live under an American military umbrella and are not saddled with a cumbersome military sector.

These are only guesses. The fact is that nobody is certain why other nations have learned how to combine the factors of production more efficiently than we have, and no one knows exactly what sorts of changes would be needed in this country if we are to try once more to be Number One in per capita output. Very likely this will be a matter for national discussion over the coming years.

Demand
for
output

So far, we have talked about GNP from the supply point of view. First we familiarized ourselves with the actual process of production itself—the interaction of the factors of production and the accumulated wealth of the past as they cooperated to bring a flow of output into being. Next we examined the forces that swelled that volume of output over time, mainly the increase in skills and capital equipment and technology that are responsible for our long-term trend of growth.

Now we are going to turn to the other side of the picture, emphasizing the driving forces that generate GNP, rather than the constraining ones that hold it back. To put it differently, we are going to move from a perspective of supply to one of demand.

Before we can go very deeply into the question of demand, we need to understand something about the meaning of demand, as it affects our total output. Hence in this chapter we will not look into the question of growth. Instead, we shall look into the prior question of how the flow of purchasing power is generated in an economy, and how it can be constantly regenerated.

25

Output and Demand

Let us start with a basic question—at once very simple and surprisingly complex. *How do we know that there will be enough demand to buy the amount of output that the factors produce?* Once we understand that, we will be well on the way to unlocking the puzzle of macro-economies.

The question leads us to understand a fundamental linkage between demand and output, for how does output actually come into existence? Anyone in business will give you the answer. The crucial factor in running a business is *demand* or *purchasing power;* that is, the presence of buyers who are willing and able to buy some good or service at a price the seller is willing to accept.

But how does demand or purchasing power come into existence? Any buyer will tell us that dollars come in as part of *income* or cash receipts. But where, in

turn, do the dollar receipts or incomes of buyers come from? If we inquire again, most buyers will tell us that they have money in their pockets because in one fashion or another they have contributed to the process of production; that is, because they have helped to make the output that is now being sold.

Thus output is generated by demand—and demand is generated by output! Our quest for the motive force behind the flow of production therefore leads us in a great circle through the market system. Here is the circular flow we first met in Chapter 10, this time approached from a macro rather than micro perspective. We can see this in Fig. 25 • 1.

At the top of the circle we see payments flowing from households to firms or government units (cities, states, federal agencies, etc.), thereby creating the demand that brings forth production. At the bottom of the circle, we see more payments, this time flowing from firms or governments back to households, as busi-

FIG. 25 • 1   The circular flow, view II

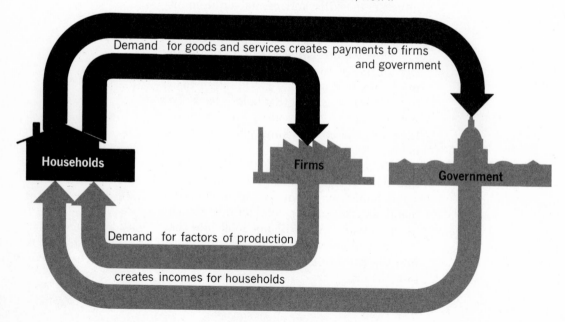

Demand for goods and services creates payments to firms and government

Households

Firms

Government

Demand for factors of production

creates incomes for households

nesses hire the services of the various factors in order to carry out production. *Thus we can see that there is a constant regeneration of demand as money is first spent by the public on the output of firms and governments, and then in turn spent by firms and governments for the services of the public.*

An economic model

Let us begin by examining this chain of payments and receipts as a model of the macro system.

Our model, to begin with, will be a very simple one. We must simplify it, at first, by ruling out some of the very events to which we will later turn as the climax of our study. For instance, we shall ignore changes in *people's tastes*, so that we can assume that everyone will regularly buy the same kinds of goods. We shall ignore differences in the *structure of firms* or *markets*, so that we can forget about differences in competitive pressures. We shall rule out *population growth* and, even more important, *inventive progress*, so that we can deal with a very stable imaginary world. For the time being, we will exclude even *saving* and *net investment* (although of course we must permit replacement investment), so that we can ignore growth. Later, of course, we are to be deeply concerned with just such problems of dynamic change. In order to come to grips with them, we must first understand an economic world as "pure" and changeless as possible.

Cost and output

The very abstract model we have created may seem too far removed from the real world to tell us much about its operation. But if we now go back to the circle of economic activity in which payments to firms, governments, and factors become their incomes, and in turn reappear on the marketplace as demand, our model will enable us to explain a very important problem. *It is how an economy that has produced a given GNP is able to buy it back.*

This is by no means a self-evident matter. Indeed, one of the most common misconceptions about the flow of economic activity is that there will not be enough purchasing power to buy everything we have produced—that somehow we are unable to buy enough to keep up with the output of our factories. So it is well to understand once and for all how an economy can sustain a given level of production through its purchases on the market.

We start, then, with an imaginary economy in full operation. We can, if we wish, imagine ourselves as having collected a year's output, which is now sitting on the economic front doorstep looking for a buyer. What we must now see is whether it will be possible to *sell* this gross national product to the people who have been engaged in producing it. We must ask whether enough income or receipts have been generated in the process of production to buy back all the products themselves.

Costs and Incomes

How does production create income? Businesspeople do not think about "incomes" when they assemble the factors of production to meet the demand for their product. They worry about *cost*. All the money they pay out during the production process is paid under the heading of *cost*, whether it be wage or salary cost, cost of materials, depreciation cost, tax cost, or whatever. Thus it seems that the concept of cost may offer us a useful point of entry into the economic chain. *If we can show how all costs become incomes,* we will have taken a major step toward understanding whether our gross national product can in fact be sold to those who produced it.

It may help us if we begin by looking at the kinds of costs incurred by business firms in real life. Since governments also produce goods and services, this hypothetical firm should be taken to represent government agencies as well as business firms. Both incur the same kinds of costs; only the labels differ.

Table 25 • 1, a hypothetical expense summary of General Output Company, will serve as an example typical of all business firms, large or small, and all government agencies. (If you examine the year-end statements of any business, you will find that costs all fall into one or more of the cost categories shown.)

Table 25 • 1   General Output Company cost summary

Wages, salaries, and employee benefits	$100,000,000
Rental, interest, and profits payments	5,000,000
Materials, supplies, etc.	60,000,000
Taxes other than income	25,000,000
Depreciation	20,000,000
Total	$210,000,000

Factor costs and national income   Some of these costs we recognize immediately as payments to factors of production. The item for "wages and salaries" is obviously a payment to the factor *labor.* The item "interest" (perhaps not so obviously) is a payment to the factor *capital;* that is, to those who have lent the

company money in order to help it carry on its productive operation. The item for rent is, of course, a payment for the rental of *land* or natural resources from their owners.

Note that we have included profits with rent and interest. In actual accounting practice, profits are not shown as an expense. For our purposes, however, it will be quite legitimate and very helpful to regard profits as a special kind of factor cost going to entrepreneurs for their risk-taking function. Later we shall go more thoroughly into the matter of profits.

Two things strike us about these factor costs. First, it is clear that they represent payments that have been made to secure production. In more technical language, they are payments for factor inputs that result in commodity outputs. All the production actually carried on within the company or government agency, all the value it has added to the economy has been compensated by the payments the company or the agency has made to land, labor, and capital. To be sure, there are other costs, for materials and taxes and depreciation, and we shall soon turn to these. But whatever production or assembly or distribution the company or agency has carried out during the course of the year has required the use of land, labor, or capital. Thus *the total of its factor costs represents the value of the total new output that General Output by itself has given to the economy.*

From here it is a simple step to add up *all* the factor costs paid out by *all* the companies and government agencies in the economy, in order to measure the total new *value added* by all productive efforts in the year. This measure is called *national income.* As we can see, it is less than gross national product, for it does not include other costs of output; namely, certain taxes and depreciation.

Factor costs and household incomes   A second fact that strikes us is that *all factor costs are income payments.* The wages, salaries, interest, rents, etc., that were costs to the company or agency were income to its recipients. So are any profits, which will accrue as income to the owners of the business.

Thus, just as it sounds, national income means the total amount of earnings of the factors of production within the nation. If we think of these factors as constituting the households of the economy, we can see that *factor costs result directly in incomes to the household sector.* Thus, if factor costs were the only costs involved in production, the problem of buying back the gross national product would be a very simple one. We should simply be paying out to households, as the cost of production, the very sum needed to buy GNP when we turned around to sell it. A glance at the General Output expense summary shows that this is not the case. There are other costs besides factor costs. How shall we deal with them?

Costs of materials   The next item of the expense summary is puzzling. Called payments for "materials, supplies, etc.," it represents all the money General Output has paid, not to its own factors, but to other companies for other products it has needed. We may even recognize these costs as payments for those *intermediate products* that lose their identity in a later stage of production. How do such payments become part of the income available to buy GNP on the marketplace?

Perhaps the answer is already intuitively clear. When General Output sends its checks to, let us say, U.S. Steel or General Electric or to a local supplier of stationery, each of these recipient firms now uses the proceeds of General Output's checks to pay its own costs. (Actually, of course, they have probably long since paid their own costs and now use General Output's payment only to reimburse themselves. But if we want to picture our model economy in the simplest way, we can imagine U.S. Steel and other firms sending their products to General Output and waiting until checks arrive to pay their own costs.)

And what are those costs? What must U.S. Steel or all the other suppliers now do with their checks? The answer is obvious. They must now reimburse their own factors and then pay any other costs that remain.

Figure 25 • 2 may make the matter plain. It shows us, looking back down the chain of intermediate payments, that what constitutes material costs to one firm is made up of factor and other costs to another. Indeed, as we unravel the chain from company to company, it is clear that all the contribution to new output must have come from the contribution of factors somewhere down the line, and that *all the costs of new output—all the value added—must ultimately be resolvable into payments to land, labor, and capital.*

Another way of picturing the same thing is to imagine that all firms or agencies in the country were bought up by a single gigantic corporation. The various production units of the new supercorporation would then ship components and semifinished items back and forth to one another, but there would not have to be any payment from one division to another. The only payments that would be necessary would be those required to buy the services of factors—that is, various kinds of labor or the use of property or capital—so that at the end of the year, the supercorporation would show on its expense summary only items for wages

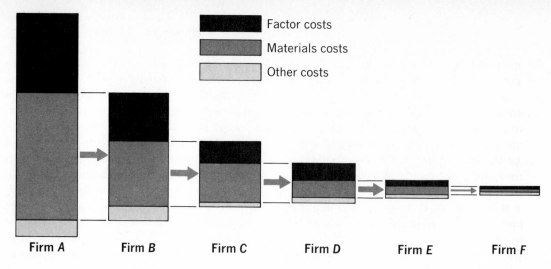

Firm *A*   Firm *B*   Firm *C*   Firm *D*   Firm *E*   Firm *F*

FIG. 25 · 2   How materials costs become other costs

and salaries, rent, and interest (and as we shall see, taxes and depreciation), but it would have no item for materials cost.

We have come a bit further toward seeing how our gross national product can be sold. **To the extent that GNP represents new output made during the course of the year, the income to buy back this output has already been handed out as factor costs, either paid at the last stage of production or "carried along" in the guise of materials costs.**

But a glance at the General Output expense summary shows that entrepreneurs incur two kinds of costs that we have still not taken into account: taxes and depreciation. Here are costs employers have incurred that have not been accounted for on the income side. What can we say about them?

Tax costs   Let us begin by tracing the taxes that General Output pays, just as we have traced its materials payments.* In the first instance, its taxes will go to government

units—federal, state, and local. But we need not stop there. Just as we saw that General Output's checks to supplier firms paid for the suppliers' factor costs and for still further interfirm transactions, so we can see that its checks to government agencies pay for goods and services that these agencies have produced—goods such as roads, buildings, or defense equipment; or services such as teaching, police protection, and the administration of justice. General Output's tax checks are thus used to help pay for factors of production—land, labor, and capital—that are used in the *public sector*.

In many ways, General Output's payments to government units resemble its payments to other firms for raw materials. Indeed, if the government *sold* its services to General Output, charging for the use of the roads, police services, or defense protection it affords the company, there would be *no* difference whatsoever. The reason we differentiate between a company's payment to the public sector and its payments for intermediate products is important, however, and worth looking into.

The first reason is clearly that with few exceptions, the government does *not* sell its output. This is partly because the community has decided that certain things the government produces (education, justice, or the use of public parks, for instance) should not be for sale but should be supplied to all citizens without direct charge. In part, it is also because some things the government produces, such as defense or law and order, cannot be equitably charged to individual buyers, since it is impossible to say to what degree anyone benefits from—or even uses—these communal facilities. Hence General Output, like every other producer, is billed, justly or otherwise, for a share of the cost of government.

There is also a second reason why we consider the cost of taxes as a new kind of cost, distinct from factor payments. It is that when business firms have finished paying the factors, they have not yet paid all the sums that employers must lay out. *Some taxes, in other words, are an addition to the cost of production.*

Indirect vs. direct taxes

These taxes—so-called *indirect taxes*—are levied on the productive enterprise itself or on its actual physical output. Taxes on real estate, for instance, or taxes that are levied on each unit of output (such as excise taxes on cigarettes) or taxes levied on goods sold at retail (sales taxes) are all payments that entrepreneurs must make as part of their costs of doing business.

Note that not all taxes collected by the government are costs of production. Many taxes will be paid, not by the entrepreneurs as an expense of doing business, but by the *factors* themselves. These so-called *direct* taxes (such as income taxes) are *not* part of the cost of production. When General Output adds up its total cost of production, it naturally includes the wages and salaries it has paid, but it does not include the taxes its workers or executives have paid out of their incomes. Such direct taxes transfer income from earners to government, but they are not a cost to the company itself.

In the same way, the income taxes on the profits of a company do *not* constitute a cost of production. General Output does not pay income taxes as a regular charge on its operations but waits until a year's production has taken place and then pays income taxes on the profits it makes *after* paying its costs. If it finds that it has lost money over the year, it will not pay any income taxes—although it will have paid other costs, including indirect taxes. *Thus direct taxes are not a cost that is paid out in the course of production and must be recouped, but a payment made by factors (including owners of the business) from the incomes they have earned through the process of production.*

Taxes as cost

Thus we can see two reasons why taxes are handled as a separate item in GNP and are not telescoped into factor costs, the way materials costs are. One reason is that taxes are a payment to a *sector different* from that of business and thus indicate a separate stream of economic activity. But the second reason, and the one that interests us more at this moment, is that *certain taxes*—indirect taxes—*are an entirely new kind of cost of production, not previously picked up.* As an expense paid out by entrepreneurs, over and above factor costs (or materials costs), these tax costs must be part of the total selling price of GNP.

Will there be enough incomes handed out in the process of production to cover this item of cost? We have seen that there will be. The indirect tax costs paid out by firms will be received by government agencies who will use these tax receipts to pay income to factors working for the government. Any direct taxes (income taxes) paid by General Output or by its factors will also wind up in the hands of a government. Thus all tax payments result in the transfer of purchasing power from the private to the public sector, and when spent by the public sector, they will again become demand on the marketplace.

Depreciation

But there is still one last item of cost. At the end of the year, when the company is totting up its expenses to see if it has made a profit for the period, its accountants do not stop with factor costs, material costs, and indirect taxes. If they did, the company would soon be in serious straits. In producing its goods, General Output has also used up a certain amount of its assets—its buildings and equipment—and a cost must now be charged for this wear and tear if the company is to be able to preserve the value of its physical plant intact. If it did not make this cost allowance, it would have failed to include all the resources that were used up in the process of production, and it would therefore be overstating its profits.

Yet, this cost has something about it clearly different from other costs that General Output has paid. Unlike factor costs or taxes or materials costs, depreciation is not paid for by check. When the company's accountants make an allowance for depreciation, all they do is make an entry on the company's book, stating that plant and equipment are now worth a certain amount less than in the beginning of the year.

At the same time, however, General Output *includes* the amount of depreciation in the price it intends to charge for its goods. As we have seen, part of the resources used up in production was its own capital equipment, and it is certainly

entitled to consider the depreciation as a cost. Yet, it has not paid anyone a sum of money equal to this cost! How, then, will there be enough income in the marketplace to buy back its product?

Replacement expenditure

The answer is that in essence it has paid depreciation charges to itself. Depreciation is thus part of its gross income. Together with after-tax profits, these depreciation charges are called a business's *cash flow*.

A business does not *have to* spend its depreciation accruals, but normally it will, *to maintain and replace its capital stock*. To be sure, an individual firm may not replace its worn-out capital exactly on schedule. But when we consider the economy as a whole, with its vast assemblage of firms, that problem tends to disappear. Suppose we have 1,000 firms, each with machines worth $1,000 and each depreciating its machines at $100 per year. Provided that all the machines were bought in different years, this means that in any given year, about 10 percent of the capital stock will wear out and have to be replaced. It's reasonable to assume that among them, the 1,000 firms will spend $100,000 to replace their old equipment over a ten-year span.*

This enables us to see that insofar as there is a steady stream of replacement expenditures going to firms that make capital goods, there will be payments just large enough to balance the addition to costs

---

*What if the machines *were* all bought in one year or over a small number of years? Then replacement expenditures will *not* be evenly distributed over time, and we may indeed have problems. This takes us into the dynamics of prosperity and recession, to which we will turn in due course. For the purpose of our explanatory model, we will stick with our (not too unrealistic) assumption that machines wear out on a steady schedule and that aggregate replacement expenditures therefore also display a steady, relatively unfluctuating pattern.

due to depreciation. As with all other payments to firms, these replacement expenditures will, of course, become incomes to factors, etc., and thus can reappear on the marketplace.

Another view of costs and incomes

Because it is very important to understand the relationship between the "selling price" of GNP and the amount of income available to buy it back, it may help to look at the matter from a different point of view.

This time let us approach it by seeing how the economy arranges things so that consumers and government and business, the three great sectors of final demand, are provided with enough purchasing power to claim the whole of GNP. Suppose, to begin with, that the economy paid out income only to its factors and priced its goods and services accordingly. In that case, consumers could purchase the entire value of the year's output, but business would be unable to purchase any portion of the output to replace its wornout equipment. (Also it raises the awkward question of how we would pay factors working for the government, since government agencies would have very little income.)

That would obviously lead to serious trouble. Hence we must arrange for business to have a claim on output and for government factors to be paid for their services. The latter is simple. By imposing direct (income) taxes on factors, we divert income from the private to the public sector. And by imposing indirect taxes on output, we price output above its factor cost, thus making it impossible for consumers to claim the entire output.

In exactly the same way, business also reserves a claim on output by pricing its products to include a charge for depreciation. By so doing, it again reduces the ability of consumers to buy back the entire output of the economy, while it gives business the purchasing power to claim the output it needs (just as taxes give purchasing power to government). Now, after paying direct and indirect taxes and depreciation, the consumer is finally free to spend all the remainder of his income without danger of encroaching on the output that must be reserved for public activity and for the replacement of capital.

In other words, we can look at taxes and depreciation not merely as "costs" that the consumer has to pay or as "incomes" that accrue to government and business, but also as the means by which the output of the economy is made available to two important claimants besides private households.

The three streams of expenditure

Our analysis is now essentially complete. Item by item, we have traced each element of cost into an income payment, so that we now know there is enough income paid out to buy back our GNP at a price that represents its full cost. Perhaps this was a conclusion we anticipated all along. After all, ours would be an impossibly difficult economy to manage if somewhere along the line purchasing power dropped out of existence, so that we were always faced with a shortage of income to buy back the product we made. But our analysis has also shown us something more unexpected. We are accustomed to thinking that all the purchasing power in the economy is received and spent through the hands of "people"—usually meaning households. Now we can see that this is not true. There is not only one, but there are *three* streams of incomes and costs, all quite distinct from one another (although linked by direct taxes).

1. Factor costs → Households → Consumers goods

    Direct Taxes

2. Indirect taxes → Government agencies → Government goods

    Direct Taxes

3. Depreciation → Business firms → Replacement investment

The one major crossover in the three streams is the direct taxes of households and business firms that go to governments. This flow permits governments to buy more goods and services than could be purchased with indirect taxes alone.

There is a simple way of explaining this seemingly complex triple flow. Each stream indicates the existence of a *final taker* of gross national product: consumers, government, and business itself.* Since output has final claimants other than consumers, we can obviously have a flow of purchasing power that does not enter consumers' or factors' hands.

*We continue to forget about net exports until Chapter 29. We can think of them perfectly satisfactorily as a component of gross private investment.

The Completed Circuit of Demand

The realization that factor owners do not get paid incomes equal to the total gross value of output brings us back to the central question of this chapter: can we be certain that we will be able to sell our GNP at its full cost? Has there surely been generated enough purchasing power to buy back our total output?

We have thus far carefully analyzed and answered half the question. We know that all costs will become incomes to factors or receipts of government agencies or of firms making replacement items. To sum up again, factor costs become the incomes of workers, managements, owners

---

THE THREE FLOWS

To help visualize these three flows, imagine for an instant that our money comes in colors (all of equal value): black, gray, and red. Now suppose that firms always pay their factors in red money, their taxes in gray money, and their replacement expenditures in black money. In point of fact, of course, the colors would soon be mixed. A factor that is paid in red bills will be paying some of his red income for taxes; or a government agency will be paying out gray money as factor incomes; or firms will be using black dollars to pay taxes or factors, and gray or red dollars to pay for replacement capital.

But at least in our mind we could picture the streams being kept separate. A gray tax dollar paid by General Output to the Internal Revenue Service for taxes could go from the government to another firm, let us say in payment for office supplies, and we can think of the office supply firm keeping these gray dollars apart from its other receipts, to pay its taxes with. Such a gray dollar could circulate indefinitely, from government agencies to firms and back again, helping to bring about production but never entering a consumer's pocket! In the same way, a black replacement expenditure dollar going from General Output to, let us say, U.S. Steel could be set aside by U.S. Steel to pay for *its* replacement needs; and the firm that received this black dollar might, in turn, set it aside for its own use as replacement expenditure. We could, that is, imagine a circuit of expenditures in which black dollars went from firm to firm, to pay for replacement investment, and never ended up in a pay envelope or as a tax payment.

of natural resources and of capital; and all these incomes together can be thought of as comprising the receipts of the household sector. Tax costs are paid to government agencies and become receipts of the government sector. Depreciation costs are initially accrued within business firms, and these accruals belong to the business sector. As long as worn-out capital is regularly replaced, these accruals will be matched by equivalent new receipts of firms that make capital goods.

Crucial role of expenditures

What we have not yet established, however, is that these sector receipts will become sector expenditures. That is, we have not demonstrated that all households will now *spend* all their incomes on goods and services, or that government units will necessarily *spend* all their tax receipts on public goods and services, or that all firms will assuredly *spend* their depreciation accruals for new replacement equipment.

What happens if some receipts are not spent? The answer is of key importance in understanding the operation of the economy. A failure of the sectors to spend as much money as they have received means that some of the costs that have been laid out will *not* come back to the original entrepreneurs. As a result, they will suffer losses. If, for instance, our gross national product costs $1 trillion to produce but the various sectors spend only $900 billion in all, then some entrepreneurs, will find themselves failing to sell all their output. Inventories of unsold goods will begin piling up, and businessmen will soon be worried about overproducing. The natural thing to do when you can't sell all your output is to stop making so much of it, so that businesses will begin cutting back on production. As they do so, they will also cut back on the number of

people they employ. As a result, business costs will go down; but so will factor incomes, for we have seen that costs and incomes are but opposite sides of one coin. As incomes fall, the expenditures of the sectors might very well fall further, bringing about another twist in the spiral of recession.

This is not yet the place to go into the mechanics of such a downward spiral of business. But the point is clear. A failure of the sectors to bring all their receipts back to the marketplace as demand can initiate profound economic problems. In the contrast between an unshakable equality of costs and incomes on the one hand and the uncertain connection between incomes and expenditures on the other, we have come to grips with one of the most important problems in macroeconomics.

The closed circuit

We shall have ample opportunity later to observe exactly what happens when incomes are not spent. Now let us be sure that we understand how the great circle of the economic flow is closed when the sectors *do* spend their receipts. Figure 25 · 3 shows how we can trace our three streams of dollars through the economy and how these flows suffice to buy back GNP for its total cost. For simplicity, we assume that there are no direct taxes.

We can trace the flow from left to right. We begin on the left with the bar representing the total cost of our freshly produced GNP. As we know, this cost consists of all the factor costs of all the firms and government units in the nation, all the indirect tax costs incurred during production, and all the depreciation charges made during production. The bar also shows us the amount of money demand our economy must generate in order to buy back its own output.

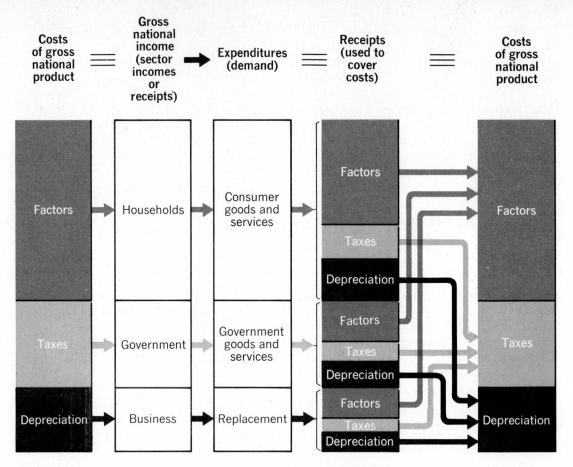

FIG. 25 · 3   The circular flow, view III

From GNP to GNI

The next bars show us the transmutation of costs into sector receipts for householders, government units, and business firms (who retain their own depreciation accruals). This relationship between costs and sector receipts is one of *identity*—all costs *must* be receipts. Hence we use the sign ≡ to indicate that this is a relation of identities—of definitional differences only. If we use GNI to stand for gross national income (the gross incomes of all the sectors), then:

$$\text{GNP} \equiv \text{GNI}$$

That is an identity to be remembered—and understood.

Incomes and expenditures

Thereafter we notice the crucial link. We assume that each sector dutifully spends all its receipts, as it is supposed to. Our household sector buys the kinds of goods and services householders do in fact buy—consumption goods and services. Our government sector buys government goods and services, and our business sector buys replacement investment. This time we use an arrow (→) because this is emphatically *not* a relationship of identity. Our sectors may not spend all their incomes. Later we will see what happens if they don't.

Now note the next bar. Here we see what happens to these expenditures when they are received by the firms that make consumer goods or by the firms or individuals who make goods and services bought by governments or by the manufacturers of capital equipment. Each of these recipients will use the money he has received to cover factor payments, taxes, and depreciation for his own business. (What we show in our diagram are not these costs for each and every firm but the aggregate costs for all firms selling to each sector.)*

We are almost done. It remains only to aggregate the sector costs; that is, to add up all the factor costs, all the taxes, and all the depreciation accruals of *all* firms and government agencies—to reproduce a bar just like the one we started with. A circle of production has been completed. Firms and government units have received back, on the marketplace, a sum just large enough to cover their initial costs, including their profits for risk. The stage is set for another round of production, similar to the last.

GNP as a Sum of Costs and a Sum of Expenditures

Our bar graph also enables us to examine again the concept of gross national product, for now we can see that GNP can be looked at in one of two ways. One way is to think of GNP as representing the total costs of a year's final output. As we know, these are factors costs, indirect tax costs, and depreciation costs. We also know that these costs are identical with the incomes or receipts of sectors. Therefore GNP measures total incomes as well as total costs.

*Recall that for ease of exposition we are treating government agencies like firms and therefore show them as taxpayers.

But we can also look at GNP as a sum of expenditures. For every item of output has been paid for by someone—a household, a government unit, or a business. Even items that have not been sold belong to (and have been paid for) by the business that produced them. Therefore we can look at GNP as the sum of all these expenditures on output—the sum of household or consumption expenditure, government expenditure, and business expenditure, plus a small amount bought by foreigners: net exports.

Two ways of measuring GNP

An illustration may make it easier to grasp this identity of the two ways of measuring GNP. Suppose once again that we picture the economy as a gigantic factory from which the flow of production emerges onto a shipping platform, each item tagged with its selling price. There the items are examined by two clerks. One of them notes down in his book the selling price of each item and then analyzes that price into its cost (as income) components; factor cost (including profit), indirect taxes, and depreciation. The second clerk keeps a similar book in which each item's selling price is also entered, but his job is to note which sector—consumer, government, business investment, or export—is its buyer. Clearly, at the end of the year, the two clerks must show the same value of total output. But whereas the books of the first will show that total value separated into various costs, the books of the second will show it analyzed by its "customers"; that is, by the expenditures of the various sectors.

But wait! Suppose that an item comes onto the shipping platform without an order waiting for it! Would that not make the sum of costs larger than the sum of expenditures?

The answer will give us our final insight into the necessary equality of the two measures of GNP. For what happens to an item that is not bought by one of the sectors? It will be sent by the shipping clerk into inventory *where it will count as part of the business investment of the economy!* Do not forget that increases in inventory are treated as investment because they are a part of output that has not been consumed. In this case it is a very unwelcome kind of investment; and if it continues, it will shortly lead to changes in the production of the firm. Such dynamic changes will soon lie at the very center of our attention. In the meantime, however, *the fact that unbought goods are counted as investment*—as if they were "bought" by the firm that produced but cannot sell them—establishes the absolute identity of GNP measured as a sum of costs or as a sum of expenditures.

GNP and GNI

To express the equality with the conciseness and clarity of mathematics, we can write, as we know:

$$GNP \equiv GNI$$

We already know that:

$$GNP \equiv C + I + G + X$$

and

$$GNI \equiv F + T + D$$

where C, I, G, and X are the familiar categories of expenditure, and F, T, and D stand for factor costs (income to land, capital, and labor), indirect taxes, and depreciation. Therefore, we know that:

$$C + I + G + X \equiv F + T + D$$

It is important to remember that these are all accounting identities, true by definition. The *National Income and Product Accounts*, the official government accounts for the economy, are kept in such a manner as to make them true.* As the name implies, these accounts are kept in two sets of "books," one on the products produced in the economy and one on the costs of production, which we know to be identical with the incomes generated in the economy. Since both sets of accounts are measuring the same output, the two totals must be equal.

NNP and national income

It is now easy to understand the meaning of two other measures of output. One of these is called *net national product* (NNP). As the name indicates, it is exactly equal to the gross national product minus depreciation. GNP is used much more than NNP, since the measures of depreciation are very unreliable. The other measure, national income, we have already met. It is *GNP minus both depreciation and indirect taxes*. This makes it equal to the sum of factor costs only. Figure 25 • 4 should make this relationship clear. The aim of this last measure is to identify the net income that actually reaches the hands of factors of production. Consequently, the measure is sometimes called the *national income at factor cost*. Its abbreviation is Y.

The circular flow

The "self-reproducing" model economy we have now sketched out is obviously still very far from reality. Nevertheless, the particular kind of unreality that we have deliberately constructed serves a highly useful purpose. An economy that regularly and dependably buys back everything it produces gives us a kind of bench mark from which to begin our subsequent inves-

*There is an "Extra word" on these accounts at the end of Chapter 32.

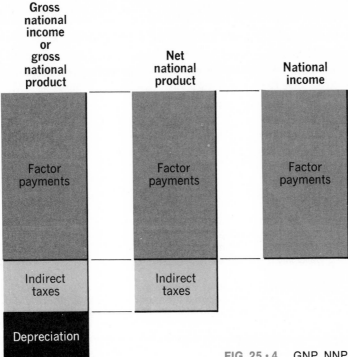

FIG. 25 · 4   GNP, NNP, and NY

tigations. We call such an economy, whose internal relationships we have outlined, an economy in *stationary equilibrium,* and we denote the changeless flow of costs into business receipts, and receipts back into costs, a *circular flow.*

We shall return many times to the model of a circular flow economy for insights into a more complex and dynamic system. Hence it is well that we summarize briefly two of the salient characteristics of such a system.

1. A circular flow economy will never experience a "recession."

Year in and year out, its total output will remain unchanged. Indeed, the very concept of a circular flow is useful in showing us that an economic system can maintain a given level of activity *indefinitely,* so long as all the sectors convert all their receipts into expenditures.

2. A circular flow economy also will never know a "boom."

That is, it will not grow, and its standard of living will remain unchanged. That standard of living may be high or low, for we could have a circular flow economy of poverty or of abundance. But in either state, changelessness will be its essence.

The great puzzle   What we have demonstrated in this chapter is an exceedingly important idea. There *can* always be enough purchasing power generated by the process of output to buy back that output.

Yet we all know, from our most casual acquaintance with economics, that in fact there is not always enough purchasing power around, or that on occasions there is too much purchasing power. With too little, we have slumps and recessions; with too much, booms and inflation.

Hence the circular flow sets the stage for the next step in our study of macroeconomics. If there *can be* the right amount of purchasing power generated, why isn't there? Or to put the question more perplexingly: if there *can be* enough purchasing power to buy *any* size output, small or large, what determines how large purchasing power will actually be, and therefore how large output will actually be?

These questions point the way for the next stage of our investigation. We must study the workings of demand much more realistically than heretofore, by removing some of the assumptions that were necessary to create a model of a circular flow system.

Focus

This chapter must be given careful study, for it holds the key to understanding how the flow of GNP is generated by demand. The purpose of the chapter is to show that it is possible for an economy to create sufficient demand (purchasing power) to buy all the output that it produces.

This purpose involves us in a step-by-step demonstration that all costs incurred in the process of output become incomes or receipts. First we analyze factor (and materials) costs, then the costs of indirect taxes, and finally those of depreciation. Through this analysis we see that all costs are in fact only one side of a transaction that always creates an equivalent receipt. It is impossible to incur a cost without giving rise to an equivalent income. Thus we trace the three categories of cost—F, T, and D—into the incomes of three sectors: the household sector, the government sector, and the business sector.

Crucial to the analysis is our understanding that this identity of costs and receipts is only half the circular flow. To create enough demand to buy output, all the sectors must spend their incomes. And expenditure is not the other side of the act of receiving an income. If incomes are not all spent by the three sectors, there will not be enough demand to complete the circuit, and GNP will fall. We will study this in greater detail in coming chapters. Now is the time to master the mechanics of a "successful" economy.

We suggest that you carefully answer the questions that follow. If you get them right, you will have no trouble with the essential idea of this chapter. If you cannot answer them correctly, go back through the chapter again and see where you have missed out.

WORDS AND CONCEPTS YOU SHOULD KNOW

Purchasing power, 362
Factor costs, 364–65
Materials costs, 365–66
Direct tax costs, 367–68
Indirect tax costs, 367
Depreciation costs, 368
Costs and incomes, 363–68, 369

Three streams of expenditure, 369–70, 371
GNP as costs and expenditure, 373–74
GNI ≡ GNP, 374
NNP, 374–75
Y, 374–75
A circular flow economy, 374–75

QUESTIONS

1. How can a model elucidate reality when it is deliberately stripped of the very things that make reality interesting?

2. Why do we need a model to show that an economy can buy back its own production?

3. What are factor costs? What kinds of factor costs are there? To what sector do factor costs go?

4. What are direct taxes? What are indirect taxes? Which are considered part of production costs? Why?

5. To whom are materials costs paid? Why are they not counted separately as part of the sum total of costs in GNP?

6. What is depreciation? Why is it a part of costs? Who receives the payments or accruals made for depreciation purposes?

7. Show in a carefully drawn diagram how costs become income or receipts of the different sectors.

8. Show in a second diagram how the incomes of the various sectors can become expenditures.

9. Why is the link between expenditure and receipt different from that between receipt and expenditure?

10. What is meant by a circular flow economy? Why does such an economy have neither growth nor fluctuation?

11. Explain the two different ways of looking at GNP and write the simple formula for each. Why is GNP the same thing as GNI?

12. Can we have demand without expenditure?

Input-output analysis

Input-output is another means of understanding the production process. It is an analytical procedure developed during the last two decades under the leadership of Wassily Leontieff of Harvard University, who won the Nobel prize for his efforts.

Input-output analysis is an effort to clarify the way the economy literally fits together in terms of the flows of goods from one producer to another or from the last producer to the final buyer. In our normal aggregative way of looking at GNP, we do not see the immensely complex interaction of production flows down the various "stages" of production. All these flows are ignored as we concentrate on *final* production. Input-output analysis concentrates on *all* production, final or intermediate. It thereby gives us a much more detailed understanding of the linkages of output than we can get from normal GNP analysis.

Input-output analysis begins by classifying production into basic inputs or industries. Today the Department of Commerce operates with an input-output table that lists 87 different industries, such as livestock and livestock products, ordnance and accessories, household appliances, amusements. These 87 industries are listed one below the other. Then the output of each industry is placed in a "cell" or "cells" corresponding to the industries to which it is sold. An actual input-output table or *matrix* is too large to be shown here. Instead, Table 25·2 gives us a look at a model of such a matrix for an extremely simple hypothetical economy.

Table 25·2

	Wheat	Machines	Automobiles	Labor	Total
Wheat (000 bushels)	100	0	0	500	600
Machines (units)	10	5	25	0	40
Automobiles (units)	5	10	3	50	68
Labor (000 man-years)	20	30	60	10	120

What is such a matrix good for? First, let us read across the rows of the table, to trace where output goes. For example, of the total wheat crop of 600 (thousand bushels), 100 are kept back to sow next year's crop, none go to the machine or auto industry, and 500 are used for food (and sold to labor). Machines have a different pattern. Forty machines are produced. Ten are used in harvesting wheat, 5 are used in making more machines (machine tools), 25 go to the auto industry, none are sold to labor. Automobiles are sold to wheat farms (trucks), used by the machinery and auto industry, as trucks or vehicles for salesmen, and sold in large numbers to consumers. Labor is used by all producers, including labor itself (barbers, lawyers, teachers).

This shows us the flow of production "horizontally" through the economy. But we can also use the table to trace its "vertical" distribution. That is, we can see that the production of 600 "units" of wheat (last figure in the top row) required *inputs* (the column under wheat) of 100 units of wheat, 10 machines, 5 automobiles (trucks), and 20 units of labor. To make 40 machines, it takes no wheat, 5 machines, 10 autos, and 30 units of labor. The production of 68 automobiles needs 25 machines, 3 cars, and 60 labor units. To "produce" 120 "units" of labor—to feed and sustain that much labor—takes 500 units of wheat, 50 cars, 10 units of personal services.

Thus our input-output analysis enables us to penetrate deeply into the interstices of the economy. But more than that, it *enables us to calculate production requirements* in a way that far exceeds in accuracy any previously known method. Suppose, for example, that the economy wanted to double its output of autos. Forget for a moment about economies of scale. To begin with, we can see that it will need 25 more machines, 3 additional autos, and 60 more units of labor.

But that is only a list of its *direct demands.* There is also a long series of *indirect demands.* For when the auto industry buys five additional machines, the machine industry will have to increase its output by one-eighth. This means it will need one-eighth more inputs of machines, autos, and labor. But in turn this sets up still further requirements. To "produce" more labor will require more outputs of wheat and cars. To produce more wheat will require still further output of machines and autos. Thus a whole series of secondary, indirect demands spread out through the economy, each generating still further demands.

Input-output analysis uses a technique known as *matrix algebra* to sum up the total effects of any original change. This is not a subject that we will explore here. It is enough to understand how the matrix enables us to calculate production requirements, very much in the manner of an aggregate production function, but in finer detail.

We should note one difficulty with input-output analysis. When we took our example of doubling auto output, we assumed that there would be no changes in the proportions of inputs required to double output and that the input "mixes" for the other industries would be unaffected by increases in their outputs. This assumption of *fixed production coefficients* is not in accord with reality. Increases in output, such as a doubling of auto output, not only usually lead to economies of scale, but may also result from wholly new techniques. Input-output analysis has no way of handling or predicting these kinds of changes. At best it gives us a picture of the production requirements of an economy under the assumption that production methods and products are fixed, although we know they are not.

Nonetheless, no more powerful tool has yet been developed to examine the interactions of the economic system. Input-output analysis is used more and more, not only by government planners or economists, but by large corporations that want to calculate how changes in various sectors of the economy affect demand for their products. Input-output tables enable them to do this because they show the indirect as well as direct demands that economic changes generate.

Saving
and
investment

Our model of a circular flow economy, continually buying back all the output it has produced, begins to explain the role of demand in determining our gross national product. Yet in one vital particular, our model lacks the illumination we seek. We are ultimately interested in understanding the phenomenon of growth, for we know that in an economy where population and productivity are rising, a failure to grow will result in serious economic difficulties. But our circular flow model, as we have just seen, portrays a stationary economy in which growth (or decline) are never present.

Therefore we must now take a long step toward reality by introducing into our system the key element of growth—the process of saving and investing that is the subject of our chapter.

The meaning of saving

We begin by making sure that we understand a key word in this dynamic analysis—*saving*. We have come across saving many times by now in this book, and so we should be ready for a final mastery of this centrally important economic term. In Chapter 22, "Wealth and Output," we spoke of saving in *real* terms as the act by which society relinquished resources that might have been

26

used for consumption, thereby making them available for the capital-building stream of output. Now we must translate that underlying real meaning of saving into terms corresponding with the buying and selling, paying and receiving discussed in the preceding chapter.

What is saving in these terms? It is very simply *not spending all or part of income for consumption goods or services.** It should be very clear then why saving is such a key term. In our discussion of the circular flow, it became apparent that expenditure was the critical link in the steady operation of the economy. If saving is not-spending, then it would seem that saving could be the cause of just that kind of downward spiral of which we caught a glimpse in our preceding chapter.

And yet this clearly is not the whole story. We also know that the act of investing—of spending money to direct factors into the production of capital goods—requires an act of saving; that is, of not using that same money to direct those factors instead into the production of consumers goods. Hence, saving is clearly necessary for the process of investment. Now, how can one and the same act be necessary for economic expansion and a threat to its stability? This is a problem that will occupy us during much of the coming chapters.

Gross vs. net saving

It will help us understand the problem if we again have recourse to the now familiar diagram of the

circular flow. But this time we must introduce into it the crucial new fact of net saving. Note *net* saving. Quite unnoticed, we have already encountered saving in our circular flow. In our model economy, when business made expenditures for the replacement of capital, it used money that *could* have been paid in dividends to stockholders or in additional compensation to employees. Before a replacement expenditure was made, someone had to decide not to allocate that money for dividends or bonuses. Thus, there is a flow of saving—that is, of nonconsumption—even in the circular flow.

But this saving is not *net* saving. Like the regular flow investment itself, the flow of saving that finances this replacement serves only to maintain the existing level of capital wealth, not to increase it. Hence, just as with investment, we reserve the term *net saving* for saving that makes possible a rise in the total of our capital assets.

Gross and net saving are thus easy to define. **By gross saving we mean all saving, both for replacement and for expansion of our capital assets, exactly like gross investment. By net saving, we mean any saving that makes possible an increase in the stock of capital, again exactly as in the definition of net investment.**

We have already seen that an economy can maintain a circular flow when it saves only as much as is needed to maintain its capital. But now suppose that it saves more than that, as is shown in Fig. 26·1. Here householders save a portion of their incomes, over and above the amount saved by business to insure the maintenance of its assets.*

---

*Note "for consumption goods or services." Purchasing stocks or bonds or life insurance is also an act of saving, even though you must spend money to acquire these items. What you acquire, however, are assets, not consumption goods and services. Some acts of spending are difficult to classify. Is a college education, for instance, a consumption good or an investment? As we know, it is probably better thought of as an investment, even though in the statistics of GNP it is treated as consumption.

*Figure 26·1 represents all net saving as occurring in households, but it should be emphasized that a large fraction of this household savings actually takes place in corporations. We discuss this in the "Extra word" at the end of this chapter.

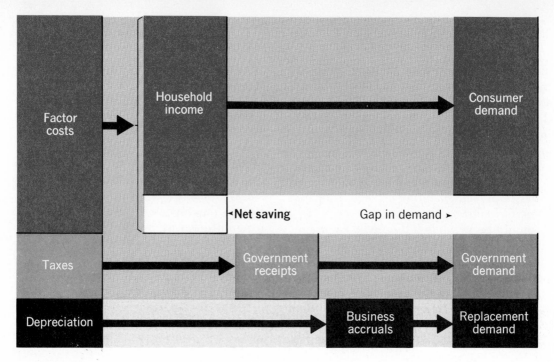

FIG. 26·1 The demand gap

The demand gap What we see is precisely what we would expect. *There is a gap in demand introduced by the deficiency of consumer spending.* This means that the total receipts of employers who make consumer goods will be less than the total amounts they laid out. It begins to look as if we were approaching the cause of economic recession and unemployment.

Yet, whereas we have introduced net saving, we have forgotten about its counterpart, net investment. Cannot the investment activity of a growing economy in some way close the demand gap?

The dilemma of saving This is indeed, as we shall soon see, the way out of the dilemma. But before we trace the way investment compensates for saving, let us draw some important conclusions from the analysis we have made up to this point.

1. Any act of saving, in and by itself, creates a gap in demand, a shortage of spending. Unless this gap is closed, there will be trouble in the economic system, for employers will not be getting back as receipts all the sums they laid out

2. If the gap is caused by saving that is implicit in depreciation, it can be closed by replacement expenditures. But if it is caused by net saving, over and above the flow needed to maintain the stock of capital, it will require net investment to be closed.

3. The presence of a demand gap forces us to make a choice. If we want a dynamic, investing economy, we will have to be prepared to cope with the problems that net saving raises. If we want to avoid these problems, we can close the gap by urging consumers or corporations not to save. Then we would have a dependable circular flow, but we would no longer enjoy economic growth.

382

The Offset to Savings

How, then, shall we manage to make our way out of the dilemma of saving? The previous diagram makes clear what must be done. If a gap in demand is due to the savings of households, then *that gap must be closed by the expanded spending of some other sector.* There are only two other such sectors: government or business. Thus in some fashion or other, the savings of one sector must be "offset" by the increased activity of another.

But how is this offset to take place? How are the resources that are relinquished by consumers to be made available to entrepreneurs in the business sector or to government officials? In a market economy there is only one way that resources or factors not being used in one place can be used in another. Someone must be willing and able to hire them.

Whether or not government and business *are* willing to employ the factors that are not needed in the consumer goods sector is a very critical matter, soon to command much of our attention. But suppose that they are willing. How will they be able to do so? How can they get the necessary funds to expand their activity?

Increasing expenditure   There are six principal methods of accomplishing this essential increase in expenditure.

1. The business sector can increase its expenditures by *borrowing* the savings of the public through the sale of new corporate bonds.
2. The government sector can increase its expenditures by *borrowing* savings from the other sectors through the sale of new government bonds.
3. Both business and government sectors can increase expenditures by *borrowing* additional funds from commercial banks.*
4. The business sector can increase its expenditures by attracting household savings into partnerships, new stock, or other *ownership (or equity).*
5. The government sector can increase its expenditures by *taxing* the other sectors.
6. Both business and government sectors can increase their expenditures by drawing on *accumulated past savings,* such as unexpended profits or tax receipts from previous years.

Claims   The first four methods above have one attribute that calls them especially to our attention. *They give rise to claims that reveal from whom the funds have been obtained and to whom they have been made available, as well as on what terms.* Bonds, corporate or government, show that savings have been borrowed from individuals or banks or firms by business and government units. Shares of stock reveal that savings have been obtained on an equity (ownership) basis, as do new partnership agreements. Borrowing from banks gives rise to loans that also represent the claims of one part of the community against another.

We can note a few additional points about claims, now that we see how many of them arise in the economy. First, many household savings are first put into banks and insurance companies—so-called financial intermediaries—so that the transfer of funds from households to business or government may go through several stages: e.g., from household to insurance company and then from insurance company to corporation.

Second, not *all* claims involve the offsetting of savings of one sector by expendi-

---

*Actually, they are borrowing from the public through the means of banks. We shall learn about this in Chapter 33.

tures of another. Many claims, once they have arisen, are traded back and forth and bought and sold, as is the case with most stocks and bonds. These purchases and sales involve the *transfer of existing claims*, not the creation of new claims.

Finally, not every claim necessarily involves the creation of an asset. If A borrows $5 from B, bets it on the races, and gives B his note, there has been an increase in claims, but no new asset has been brought into being to match it.

Public and private claims   Now let us look at Fig. 26·2. This time we show what happens when savings are made available to the business sector by direct borrowing from households. Note the claim (or equity) that arises.

If the government were doing the borrowing, rather than the business sector, the diagram would look like Fig. 26·3. Notice that the claim is now a government bond.

We have not looked at a diagram showing business or government borrowing its funds from the banking system. (This process will be better understood when we take up the problem of money and banking, in Chapter 33.) The basic concept, however, although more complex, is much the same as above.

Completed act of offsetting savings   There remains only a last step, which must now be fully anticipated. We have seen how it is possible to offset the savings in one sector, where they were going to cause an expenditure gap, by increasing the funds available to another sector. It remains only to *spend* those additional funds in the form of additional investment or, in the case of the government, for additional public goods and services. The two

completed expenditure circuits now appear in Fig. 26·4, p. 386.

While Fig. 26·4 is drawn so that the new investment demand or new government demand is exactly equal to net saving, it is important to understand that there is nothing in the economic system guaranteeing that these demands will exactly equal net saving. The desire for new investment or new government goods and services may be either higher or lower than new saving. The need to regulate these new demands so that they will equal net savings is an important objective of *fiscal and monetary policies*, a problem we will study later.

Intersectoral offsets   We shall not investigate further at this point the differences between increased public spending and increased business investment. What we must heed is the crucial point at issue: *if saving in any one sector is to be offset, some other sector (or sectors) must spend more than its income.* A gap in demand due to insufficient expenditure in one sector can be compensated only by an increase in demand—that is, in expenditure—of another.

Once this simple but fundamental point is clearly understood, much of the mystery of macroeconomics disappears, for we can then begin to see that an economy in movement, as contrasted with one in a stationary circular flow, is one in which sectors must *cooperate* to maintain the closed circuit of income and output. In a dynamic economy, we no longer enjoy the steady translation of incomes into expenditure which, as we have seen, is the key to an uninterrupted flow of output. Rather, we are faced with the presence of net saving and the possibility of a gap in final demand. Difficult though the ensuing problems are, let us not forget that net sav-

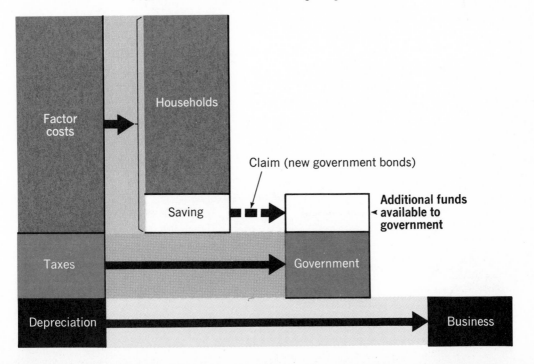

FIG. 26 · 2 ''Transfer'' of savings to business

FIG. 26 · 3 ''Transfer'' of savings to government

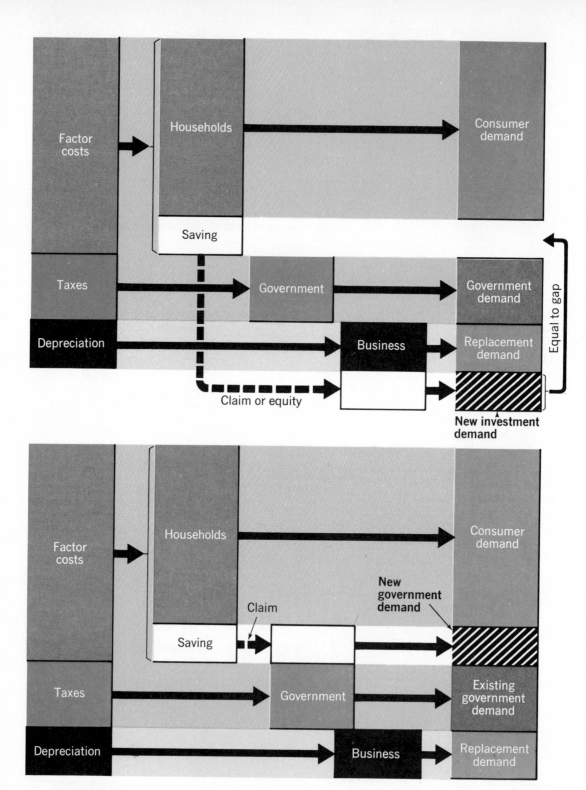

FIG. 26 · 4 Two ways of closing the demand gap

ing is the necessary condition for the accumulation of capital. *The price of economic growth, in other words, is the risk of economic decline.*

Real and money saving

This central importance of saving in a growing economy will become a familiar problem. At this juncture, where we have first encountered the difficulties it can pose, we must be certain that we understand two different aspects that saving assumes.

One aspect, noticed in our initial overview of the economy, is the decision to relinquish *resources* that can be redeployed into capital-building. This is the real significance of saving. But this "real" aspect of saving is not the way we encounter the act of saving in our ordinary lives. We think of saving as a *monetary* phenomenon, not a "real" one. When we save, we are conscious of not using all our incomes for consumption, but we scarcely, if ever, think of releasing resources for alternative employments.

There is a reason for this dichotomy of real and money saving. In our society, with its extraordinary degree of specialization, the individuals or institutions that do the actual saving are not always those that do the actual capital-building. In a simple society, this dichotomy between saving and investing need not, and usually does not, occur. A farmer who decides to build new capital—for example, to build a barn—is very much aware of giving up a consumption activity—the raising of food—in order to carry out his investment. So is an artisan who stops weaving clothing to repair the loom. Where the saver and the investor are one and the same person, there need be no "financial" saving, and the underlying real phenomenon of saving as the diversion of activity from consumption to investment is immediately apparent.

Savers and investors

In the modern world, savers and investors are often the same individual or group—as in the case of a business management that spends profits on new productive capacity rather than on higher executive salaries, or government leaders who use tax revenues to build roads or dams rather than to increase welfare payments.

Frequently, however, savers are not investors. Certainly householders do not personally decide and direct the process of capital formation in the nation. Furthermore, the workers and materials that households voluntarily relinquish by not using all their incomes to buy consumers goods have to be physically transferred to different industries, often to different occupations and locations, in order to carry out their investment tasks. This requires funds in the hands of the investors, so that they can tempt resources from one use to another.

Hence we need an elaborate system for directly or indirectly "transferring" money saving into the hands of those who will be in a position to employ factors for capital construction purposes. Nevertheless, underlying this complex mechanism for transferring purchasing power remains the same simple purpose that we initially witnessed. Resources that have been relinquished from the production of consumption goods or services are now employed in the production of capital goods. Thus, *saving and investing are essentially real phenomena*, even though it may take a great deal of financial manipulation to bring them about.

A final important point. The fact that the decisions to save and the decisions to invest are lodged in different individuals or groups alerts us to a basic reason why the savings-investment process may not always work smoothly. Savers may choose to consume less than their total incomes at times when investors have no interest in expanding their capital assets. Alternatively, business firms may wish to form new capital when savers are interested in spending money only on themselves. This separation of decision-making can give rise to situations in which savings are not offset by investment or in which investment plans race out ahead of savings capabilities. In our next chapters we will be investigating what happens in these cases.

Even in the case where savers and investors are the same people, problems arise. A business may wish to save *this* year and invest *next* year. Thus savings and investment decisions may not be coordinated in the shortrun. In our next chapters we will be investigating what happens in these cases.

Transfer Payments and Profits

We have talked about the transfer of purchasing power from savers to investors, but we have not yet mentioned another kind of transfer, also of great importance in the overall operation of the economy. This is the transfer of incomes from sector to sector (and sometimes within sectors).

Transfers As we already know, income transfers (called *transfer payments*) are a very useful and important means of reallocating purchasing power in society. Through transfer payments, members of the community who do not participate in production are given an opportunity to enjoy incomes that would otherwise not be available to them. Thus Social Security transfer payments make it possible for the old or

the handicapped to be given an "income" of their own (not, to be sure, a currently *earned* income), or unemployment benefits give purchasing power to those who cannot get it through employment.

Not all transfers are in the nature of welfare payments, however. The distribution of money *within* a household is a transfer payment. So is the payment of interest on the national debt.* So is the grant of a subsidy to a private enterprise, such as an airline, or of a scholarship to a college student. Any income payment that is not earned by selling one's productive services on the market falls in the transfer category.

It may help to understand this process if we visualize it in our flow diagram. Figure 26 • 5 shows two kinds of transfers. The upper one, from government to the household sector, shows a typical transfer of incomes, such as veterans' pensions or Social Security; the transfer below it reflects the flow of income that might be illustrated by a payment to agriculture for crop support. Transfers *within* sectors, such as household allowances, are not shown in the diagram.

One thing we may well note about transfers is that they can only rearrange *the incomes created in the production process; they cannot increase those incomes.* Income, as we learned in the last chapter, is inextricably tied to output—indeed, income is only the financial counterpart of output.

Tranfer payments, on the other hand, are a way of arranging individual claims to production in some fashion that strikes the community as fairer or more efficient or more decorous than the way the market

---

*As we know, the payment of interest on corporate debt is not considered a transfer payment, but a payment to a factor of production. Actually, much government interest should also be thought of as a factor payment (for the loan of capital for purposes of public output); but by convention, all government interest is classified as a transfer payment.

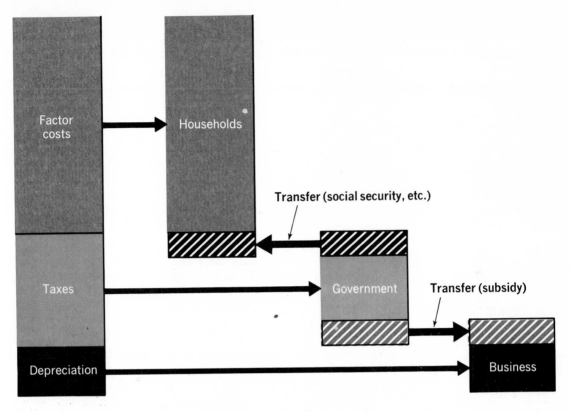

FIG. 26 · 5 Transfer payments

process allocates them through the production process. As such, transfer payments are an indispensable and often invaluable agency of social policy. But it is important to understand that no amount of transfers can, in themselves, increase the total that is to be shared. That can happen only by raising output itself.

Transfer payments and taxes We have mentioned, but only in passing, another means of transferring purchasing power from one sector to another: taxation. Heretofore, however, we have often spoken as though all government tax receipts were derived from indirect taxes that were added onto the cost of production.

In fact, this is not the only source of government revenue. Indirect taxes are an important part of state and local revenues, but they are only a minor part of federal tax receipts. Most federal taxes are levied on the incomes of the factors of production or on the profits of businesses after the other factors have been paid.

Once again it is worth remembering that the government taxes consumers (and businesses) because it is in the nature of much government output that it cannot be *sold*. Taxes are the way we are billed for our share—rightly or wrongly figured—of government production that has been collectively decided upon. As we can now see, taxes—both on business and on the household sector—also finance many transfer payments. That is, the government

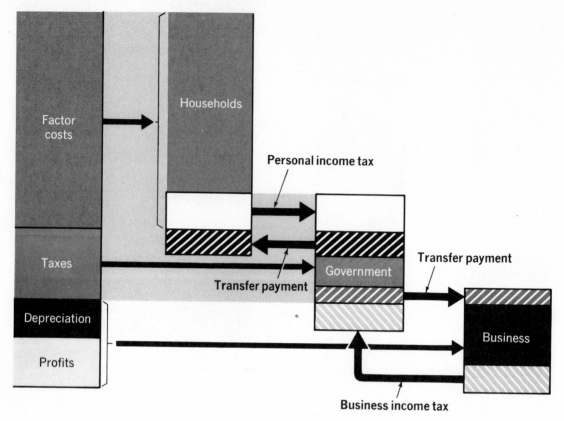

FIG. 26 · 6   Transfers and income taxes

intervenes in the distribution process to make it conform to our politically expressed social purposes, taking away some incomes from certain individuals and groups and providing incomes to others. Figure 26 · 6 shows what this looks like in the flow of GNP. (Note that the business sector is drawn with profits, as our next section will explain.)

As we can see, the exchanges of income between the household and the government sectors can be very complex. Income can flow from households to government units via taxation and return to the household sector via transfer payments; and the same two-way flows can take place between government and business.

Profits and demand

The last diagram has already introduced a new element of reality in our discussion. Taxes on business *income* presuppose that businesses make *profits*. Let us see how these profits fit into the savings-investment process.

During our discussion of the circular flow, we spoke of profits as a special kind of factor cost—a payment to the factor *capital*. Now we can think of profits not merely as a factor cost (although there is always a certain element of risk-remuneration in profits), but as a return to especially efficient or forward-thinking firms who have used the investment process to introduce new products or processes ahead of the run of their industries. We also know that profits accrue to powerful firms who exact a semimonopolistic return from their customers.

What matters in our analysis at this stage is not the precise explanation we give to the origin of profits, but a precise explanation of their role in maintaining a "closed-circuit" economy in which all costs are returned to the marketplace as demand. A commonly heard diagnosis for economic maladies is that profits are at the root of the matter, in that they cause a "withdrawal" of spending power or income from the community. If profits are "hoarded," or kept unspent, this can be true. In fact, however, profits are usually spent in three ways. They may be

1. **Distributed as income to the household sector in the form of dividends or profit shares, to become part of household spending**

2. **Spent by business firms for new plant and equipment**

3. **Taxed by the government and spent in the public sector**

All three methods of offsetting profits appear in Fig. 26 • 7.

Thus, we can see that profits need not constitute a withdrawal from the income stream. Indeed, unless profits are adequate, businesses will very likely not invest enough to offset the savings of the household sector. They may, in fact, even fail to make normal replacement expenditures, aggravating the demand gap still further in this way.

Thus the existence of profits, far from being deflationary—that is, far from causing a fall in income—is, in fact, essential for the maintenance of a given level of income or for an advance to a higher level. Nonetheless, there is a germ of truth in the

FIG. 26 • 7   Profits in the circular flow

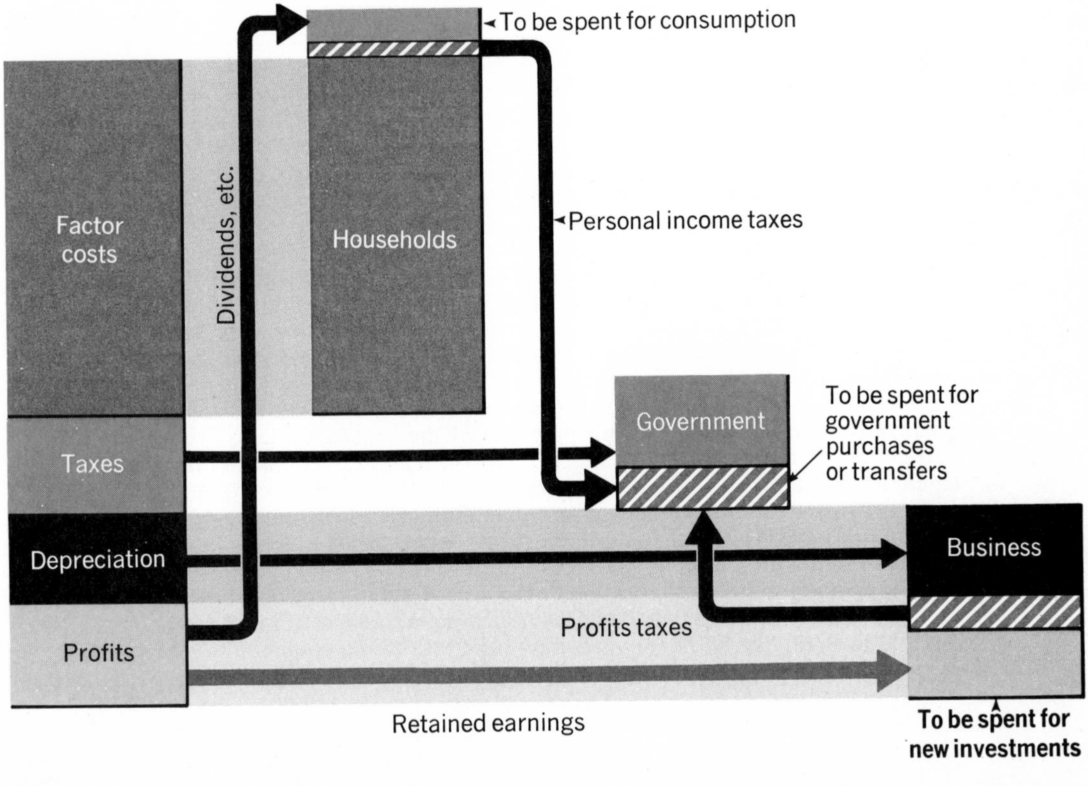

contentions of those who have maintained that profits can cause an insufficiency of purchasing power. For unless profits are returned to the flow of purchasing power as dividends that are spent by their recipients or as new capital expenditures made by business or as taxes that lead to additional public spending, there will be a gap in the community's demand. Thus we can think of profits just as we think of saving—an indispensable source of economic growth or a potential source of economic decline.

Saving, investment, and growth

We are almost ready to leave our analysis of the circle of production and income and to proceed to a much closer study of the individual dynamic elements that create and close demand gaps. Before we do, however, it is well that we take note of one last fact of the greatest importance. In offsetting the savings of any sector by investment, we have closed the production and income circuit, much as in the stationary circular flow, but there is one crucial difference from the circular flow. Now we have closed the flow by diverting savings into the creation of *additional* capital. Unlike the stationary circular flow where the handing around of incomes did no more than to maintain unchanged the original configuration of the system, in our new dynamic saving-and-investment model *each closing of the circuit results in a quantitative change—the addition of a new "layer" of capital.*

Hence, more and more physical wealth is being added to our system; and thinking back to our first impressions of the interaction of wealth and population, we would expect more and more productiveness from our human factors. With complications that we shall have to deal with in due course, *growth* has entered our economic model.

Focus

This lesson continues our exploration of how demand is generated. It takes up the vital question of how saving is accomodated by the system, and the crucial role of saving in making growth possible.

The central idea of the chapter is the interaction among sectors in offsetting demand gaps. Demand gaps arise when any sector fails to spend all its income, so that instead of a completed circular flow, we have a failure to turn all incomes into expenditure. When such a demand gap occurs, the financial savings of that sector must be made available to another sector for investment spending. The transfer of saving is made by borrowing or taxing or creating new equities. The sector that gains savings will often create a claim—a stock or a bond—that shows the transfer of savings to its account.

Once you see how the savings and investment process works, you are well along the way to understanding the operation of the macro system. Probably no single process is as central to the "secret" of growth and recession as the creation of new capital through the process of saving and investment. Be sure to draw all the diagrams in the questions that follow and check them with the originals.

A secondary but by no means unimportant lesson of the chapter is the role of transfer payments and profits in the circular flow. It is important to understand how transfers rearrange but do not create income, and the diagrams on pages 389 and 391 are a good way to grasp this. It is essential also to understand that profits must be returned to GNP, like all flows of income, and that if returned, do not become a "drag" on income, but rather a source of new growth.

WORDS AND CONCEPTS YOU SHOULD KNOW

Real vs. monetary saving, 380–81
Gross vs. net saving, 381
Demand gap, 382
Claims, 383–84

Intersectoral offsets to saving, 384–86
Transfers, 388
Profits in a circular flow, 390–92
Saving and growth, 392

QUESTIONS

1. What do we mean by a demand gap? Show diagrammatically.

2. How is a demand gap filled by business investment? Show diagrammatically.

3. Why is saving indispensable for growth?

4. Can we have planned business investment without saving? Saving without planned business investment?

5. Draw carefully a diagram that shows how savings can be offset by government spending.

6. How is it possible for a sector to spend more than its income? How does it get the additional money?

7. What is a transfer payment? Draw diagrams of transfers from government to consumers, from government to business. Is charity a transfer? Is a lottery?

8. Diagram the three ways in which profits can be returned to the expenditure flow. What happens if they are not?

9. Why is a problem presented by the fact that those who make the decision to invest may not be the same people who decide to save?

10. In what way is a stationary circular flow economy different from an economy that saves and invests?

Raising the savings rate

One of the sharpest arguments, these days, is whether or not there is a "capital shortage"—an insufficient amount of capital to give us the growth, the new energy, the pollution suppression, the capital-using services we require. In another "Extra word" (p. 428) we will look into some aspects of that problem. But if we assume for the moment that there *is* such a shortage, one important remedy would certainly be to raise the national savings rate. How could we do that?

Let us begin by inquiring into the sources of saving. In our chapter we concentrated almost wholly on the generation of savings in the household sector. But in fact households are by no means the main savers in the economy as we can see:

SOURCES OF SAVINGS, 1976

	$ Billion	%		$ Billion	%
Households	$ 78	34	State and local government	14	6
Businesses	199	86	Federal government	−58	−26

In this table, the household sector shows up as a substantial provider of funds. And so it is. But a very large fraction of those personal savings go into the purchase of homes. If we subtract this flow residential investment, we fine that individuals provide only 4 percent of the funds borrowed by business and government.

Business provides most of its savings through retained earnings—that fraction of its profits, usually about one-third, that is not paid out to shareholders or to government as taxes. And governments save when they use their incomes for capital-building rather than consumption purposes. We are not accustomed to dividing government spending into consumption and investment purposes, but when local, state, or federal governments build roads, schools, hospitals, housing projects, and the like, they are saving-and-investing just as certainly as when corporations use their retained earnings to build plant and equipment. The difference is that the government creates public investment, rather than private investment.

If we were to look for government savings that were available for the use of other sectors of the economy, we would find that state and local governments saved $14 billion over what they invested in 1976, while the federal government absorbed $58 billion in savings from other sectors of the economy. How could the savings rates of these three sectors be increased? Let us begin with the household sector. In Table 26 · 1 we see that high-income families do most of the sector's savings.

Table 26 · 1 Savings rates by income class ($000)

$0–3	$3–6	$6–10	$10–15	$15 +
−12%	2%	15%	18%	37%

NOTE: These savings rates are defined as the ratio of change in net assets to current income, rather than the more conventional savings out of current income.

Thus one way of raising household savings would be to reduce income tax rates for upper-income families, who would almost certainly save a large amount of their tax cuts. Opponents of such a proposal argue that a tax cut for the rich would have to be matched by tax increases for the middle and lower groups. They admit that savings might go up and that this would lead to investment and growth. But they object to the pattern of increased inequality that such a policy would bring.

Both the proponents and the opponents of tax cuts for the upper-income groups are right. Tax cuts would create more capital and thus more per capita income; and tax cuts would also increase inequality. The pertinent question is one of magnitudes. How much inequality are we willing to accept to gain additional savings or additional income?

What about raising corporate savings rates? They could be raised by reducing corporate income taxes—with exactly the same arguments pro and con, because corporate stock is largely owned by upper-income individuals, so that a corporate tax cut is equivalent to a personal tax cut for the rich.

Table 26 · 2   Ownership of stock by income class

Quintile	Lowest	Second	Third	Fourth	Highest
Percent	7%	5%	9%	9%	70%

Could governments increase their savings available for other sectors of the economy? One way would be for government to plan budgets that had surpluses—excesses of tax income over expenditures. It could do this by raising taxes or by cutting back on its consumption outlays. The problem here, it need hardly be said, is the political opposition that would be generated by tax increases or by reduced government outlays for consumption purposes, such as schooling, police, health care, recreation, sanitation, and the like.

There are still other ways of raising the savings rate—for example by reducing the ease with which households can get consumer or mortgage credit. If we had a very tough consumer credit policy, households would have to save up *before* they could buy a car or a house, and those savings could be used (via the banking system) to build new industrial capital. The trouble, of course, is that such a policy would deal a terrific blow, in the short run, to the housing or automobile or appliance industry.

Thus there exist many ways of raising the savings rate, but all of them carry social costs. In fact the key thing to note is that all these options require reductions in consumption for some groups. If saving is to go up, someone's consumption must go down. In the case of a tax break for the wealthy, the cut in consumption will be felt by the middle and lower classes whose taxes will rise. A cut in corporation income taxes may induce corporations to save and invest, but that must mean that they pay less taxes. Someone else will have to pay those taxes. And if governments save, as we have seen, this too means less public consumption or higher tax rates.

Thus, if we want to raise the savings rate, someone must pay the cost. Who should that be? This question plunges us into the debate between equity and efficiency that economist Arthur Okun has called "the big trade-off." There is no magic answer to this question. The big trade-off is a value-laden question that forces both proponents and opponents of higher savings rates to declare their preferences for one kind of society or another.

Consumption demand

With a basic understanding of the crucial role of expenditure and of the complex relationship of saving and investment behind us, we are in a position to look more deeply into the question of the determination of gross national product. For what we have discovered heretofore is only the *mechanism* by which a market economy can sustain or fail to sustain a given level of output through a circuit of expenditure and receipt. Now we must try to discover the *forces* that dynamize the system, creating or closing gaps between income and outgo. What causes a demand for the goods and services measured in the GNP? Let us begin to answer that question by examining the flow of demand most familiar to us—consumption.

The Household Sector

27

Largest and in many respects most important of all the sectors in the economy is that of the nation's households—that is, its families and single-dwelling individuals (the two categories together called consumer units) considered as receivers of

All figures in billions*

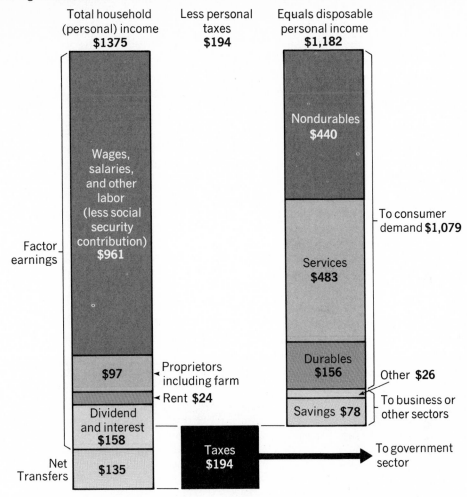

* Totals do not always add, owing to rounding

Consumption sector 1976

income and transfer payments or as savers and spenders of money for consumption.

How big is this sector? In 1976 it comprised some 57 million families and some 21 million independent individuals who collectively gathered in $1,375 billion in income and spent $1,104 billion.* As Fig.

27 · 1 shows, the great bulk of receipts was from factor earnings, and transfer payments played only a relatively small role. As we can also see, we must subtract per-

*The Department of Commerce has redefined some categories of the national income accounts, and the word *consumption* today applies, strictly speaking, only to personal expenditures for goods and services. Included in total consumer spending, however, are sizeable amounts for interest (mainly on installment loans) and for remittances abroad, neither of which sums are included in the amount for goods and services. The proper

nomenclature for the total of consumer spending (goods and services plus interest and remittances) is now *personal outlays*. We shall, however, continue to use the simpler term, *consumption,* although our figures will be those for personal outlays.

Note, also, that the compilation of these figures is a time-consuming process in which earlier estimates are frequently subject to revision. Hence, figures for the components of consumption or, for that matter, for almost all magnitudes in the economic process are apt to vary slightly in successive printed statistics until, eventually, the "final" figures are arrived at. Note our caution about preliminary data in the box "Cautions about Data," p. 117.

sonal tax payments from household income (or *personal income* as it is officially designated) before we get *disposable personal income*—income actually available for spending. It is from disposable personal income that the crucial choice is made to spend or save. Much of this chapter will focus on that choice.

Subcomponents of consumption

Finally we note that consumer spending itself divides into three main streams. The largest of these is for *nondurable* goods, such as food and clothing or other items whose economic life is (or is assumed to be) short. Second largest is an assortment of expenditures we call consumer *services,* comprising things such as rent, doctors' or lawyers' or barbers' ministrations, theater or movie admissions, bus or taxi or plane transportation, and other purchases that are not a physical good but work performed by someone or some equipment. Last is a substream of expenditure for consumer *durable* goods, which, as the name suggests, include items such as cars or household appliances whose economic life is considerably greater than that of most nondurables. We can think of these goods as comprising consumers' physical capital.

There are complicated patterns and interrelations among these three major streams of consumer spending. As we would expect, consumer spending for durables is extremely volatile. In bad times, such as 1933, it has sunk to less than 8 percent of all consumer outlays; in the peak of good times in the early 1970s, it came to nearly double that. Meanwhile, outlays for services have been a steadily swelling area for consumer spending in the postwar economy. As a consequence of the growth of consumer buying of durables

and of services, the relative share of the consumer dollar going to "soft goods" has been slowly declining.

Consumption and GNP

The internal dynamics of consumption are of great interest to someone who seeks to project consumer spending patterns into the future—perhaps as an aid to merchandising. But here we are interested in the larger phenomenon of the relationship of consumption as a whole to the flow of gross national product.

Figure 27·2 shows us this historic relationship since 1929. Certain things stand out.

1. Consumption spending is by far the largest category of spending in GNP.

Total consumer expenditures—for durable goods such as automobiles or washing machines, for nondurables like food or clothing, and for services such as recreation or medical care—account for approximately two-thirds of all the final buying in the economy.

2. Consumption is not only the biggest, but the most stable of all the streams of expenditure.

Consumption, as we have mentioned, is *the* essential economic activity. Even if there is a total breakdown in the social system, households will consume some bare minimum. Further, it is a fact of common experience that even in adverse circumstances, households seek to maintain their accustomed living standards. Thus consumption activities constitute a kind of floor for the level of overall economic activity. Investment and government spending, as we shall see, are capable of

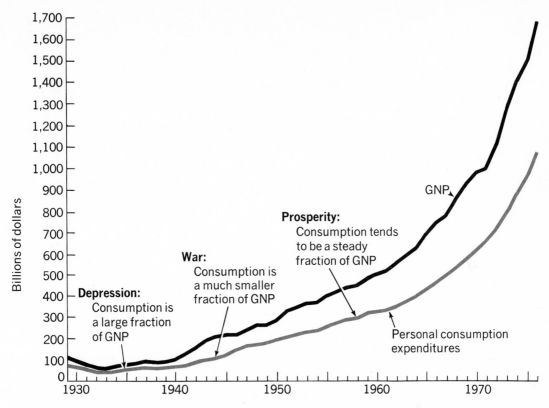

FIG. 27 · 2 Consumption and GNP, current prices

sudden reversals; but the streams of consumer spending tend to display a measure of stability over time.

3. **Consumption is nonetheless capable of considerable fluctuation as a proportion of GNP.**

Remembering our previous diagrams, we can see that this proportionate fluctuation must reflect changes in the relative importance of investment and government spending. And indeed this is the case. As investment spending declined in the Depression, consumption bulked relatively larger in GNP; as government spending increased during the war, consumption bulked relatively smaller.

The changing *relative* size of consumption, in other words, reflects broad changes in *other* sectors rather than sharp changes in consuming habits.

4. **Despite its importance, consumption alone will not "buy back" GNP.**

It is well to recall that consumption, although the largest component of GNP, is still *only* two-thirds of GNP. Government buying and business buying of investment goods are essential if the income-expenditure circuit is to be closed. During our subsequent analysis it will help to remember that consumption expenditure by itself does not provide the only impetus of demand.

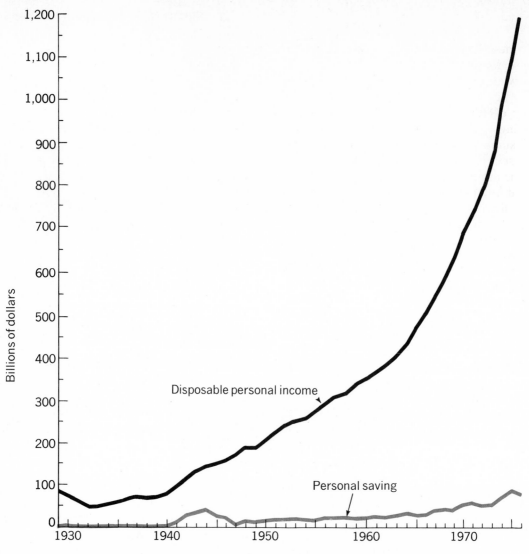

FIG. 27 · 3   Saving and disposable income

Saving in Historic Perspective

This first view of consumption activity sets the stage for our inquiry into the dynamic causes of fluctuations in GNP. We already know that the saving-investment relationship lies at the center of this problem and that much saving arises from the household sector. Hence, let us see what

we can learn about the saving process in historic perspective.

We begin with Fig. 27.3 showing the relationship of household saving to disposable income—that is, to household sector incomes after the payment of taxes.

What we see here are two interesting facts. First, during the bottom of the Great Depression there were *no* savings in the household sector. In fact, under the duress of unemployment, millions of households were forced to *dissave*—to borrow or to draw on their old savings (hence the negative figure for the sector as a whole). By way of contrast, we notice the immense savings of the peak war years when consumers' goods were rationed and households were urged to save. Clearly, then, the *amount* of saving is capable of great fluctuation, falling to zero or to negative figures in periods of great economic distress and rising to as much as a quarter of income during periods of goods shortages.

In Fig. 27·4, we are struck by another fact. However variable the amounts, the savings *ratio* shows a considerable stability in "normal" years. This steadiness is particularly noteworthy in the postwar period. From 1950 to the present, consumption has ranged between roughly 92 to 95 percent of disposable personal income—which is, of course, the same as saying that savings have ranged roughly between 8 percent and 5 percent. If we take the postwar period as a whole, *we can see that in an average year we have consumed a little more than 94 cents of each dollar of income and that this ratio has remained fairly constant even though our incomes have increased markedly.*

Long-run savings behavior

This stability of the long-run savings ratio is an interesting, important phenomenon and something of a puzzling one, for we might easily imagine that the savings ratio would rise over time. Statistical investigations of cross sections of the nation show that rich families tend to save not only larger amounts, but larger *percentages* of their income, than poor families do.* Thus as the entire nation has grown richer and as families have moved from lower income brackets to higher ones, it seems natural to suppose that they would also take on the higher savings characteristics that accompany upper incomes.

Were this so, the economy would face a very serious problem. In order to sustain its higher levels of aggregate income, it would have to invest an ever larger *proportion* of its income to offset its growing ratio of savings to income. As we shall see in our next chapter, investment is always a source of potential trouble because it is so much riskier than any other business function. If we had to keep on making proportionally larger investments each year to keep pace with our proportionally growing

*See Table 26·1 on p. 394.

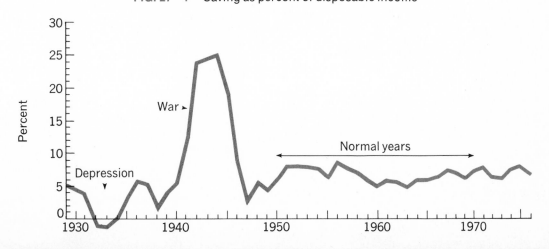

FIG. 27·4 Saving as percent of disposable income

How do we reconcile the stability of the long-run savings ratio with the fact that statistical studies always reveal that rich families save a larger percentage of their incomes than do poor families? As the nation has moved, en masse, into higher income brackets, why has it not also saved proportionately more of its income?

The explanation for the long-run stability of savings behavior revolves around the importance of *relative* incomes, or "keeping up with the Joneses," in consumption decisions. If a family earned $15,000 in 1940, it was a wealthy family with an income far above the average. It could save a large fraction of its income and still have more than other families in the community had to spend on consump-

tion. By 1975 the family with an $15,-000 annual income was simply an average family. To keep up with consumption standards of other families in the community, it needed to spend a large fraction of its income. As a result, the savings rates for families with $15,000 gradually fell over time as the families changed from wealthy to average.

The same relative income effect is seen in the savings rates of black families. For any given income level, the average black family saves more than the average white family. Since black family incomes are lower than white family incomes, any given in-

come has a higher relative position among blacks than it does among whites. To keep up with their peer group, whites must consequently spend more than blacks.

As a result of these and still other motivations, savings behavior in the long run differs considerably from that in the short run. Over the years, American households have shown a remarkable stability in their rate of overall savings. Its importance has already been mentioned. In a shorter period of time, however—over a few months or perhaps a year—households tend to save higher fractions of increases in their incomes than they do in the long run. The very great importance of this fact we shall subsequently note.

---

savings, we should live in an exceedingly vulnerable economic environment.

Fortunately, we are rescued from this dangerous situation, because our long-run savings ratio, as we have seen, displays a reassuring steadiness. In fact, there has been no significant upward trend in the savings ratio for the nation's households since the mid-1800s, and there may have been a slight downward trend.*

The Consumption-Income Relationship

What we have heretofore seen are some of the historical and empirical relationships of consumption and personal saving to income. We have taken the trouble to investigate these relationships in some detail, since they are among the most important causes of the gaps that have to be closed by investment. But the statistical facts in

themselves are only a halfway stage in our macroeconomic investigation. Now we want to go beyond the facts to a generalized understanding of the behavior that gives rise to them. Thus our next task is to extract from the facts certain behavioral *relationships* that are sufficiently regular and dependable for us to build into a new dynamic model of the economy.

If we think back over the data we have examined, one primary conclusion comes to mind. This is the indisputable fact that the *amount* of saving generated by the household sector depends in the first instance upon the income enjoyed by the household sector. Despite the stability of the savings ratio, we have seen that the dollar volume of saving in the economy is susceptible to great variation, from negative amounts in the Great Depression to very large amounts in boom times. Now we must see if we can find a systematic connection between the changing size of income and the changing size of saving.

Propensity to consume

There is indeed such a relationship, lying at the heart of macroeconomic analysis. We call it the

*Economists maintain a certain tentativeness in their assertions about long-run trends, since the statistical foundation on which they are based is inevitably subject to some error and uncertainty.

consumption function or, more formally, the *propensity to consume*, the name invented by John Maynard Keynes, the famous English economist who first formulated it in 1936.* What is this "propensity" to consume? It means that the relationship between consumption behavior and income is sufficiently dependable so that we can actually *predict* how much consumption (or how much saving) will be associated with a given level of income.

We base such predictions on a *schedule* that enables us to see the income-consumption relationship over a considerable range of variation. Table 27·1 is such a schedule, a purely hypothetical one, for us to examine.

Table 27·1 A propensity to consume schedule

BILLIONS OF DOLLARS

Income	Consumption	Savings
$100	$80	$20
110	87	23
120	92	28
130	95	35
140	97	43

One could imagine, of course, innumerable different consumption schedules; in one society a given income might be accompanied by a much higher propensity to consume (or propensity to save) than in another. But the basic hypothesis of Keynes—a hypothesis amply confirmed by research—was that the consumption schedule in all modern industrial societies had a particular basic configuration, despite these variations. The propensity to consume, said Keynes, reflected the fact that on the average, men tended to increase their consumption as

*More about Keynes in the box on p. 450. Note that his name is pronounced "Kanes," not "Keenes."

their incomes rose, but not by as much as their income increased. In other words, as the incomes of individuals rose, so did both their consumption *and their savings*.

Note that Keynes did not say that the proportion of saving rose. We have seen how involved is the dynamic determination of savings ratios. Keynes merely suggested that in the short run, the *amount* of saving would rise as income rose—or to put it conversely again, that families would not use *all* their increases in income for consumption purposes alone. It is well to remember that these conclusions hold in going down the schedule as well as up. Keynes' basic "law" implies that when there is a decrease in income, there will be some decrease in the *amount of saving*, or that a family will not absorb a fall in its income entirely by contracting its consumption.

What does the consumption schedule look like in the United States? We will come to that shortly. First, however, let us fill in our understanding of the terms we will need for our generalized study.

Average propensity to consume The consumption schedule gives us two ways of measuring the fundamental economic relationship of income and saving. One way is simply to take any given level

Table 27·2 Calculation of the average propensity to consume

BILLIONS OF DOLLARS		Consumption ÷ income (Avg. propensity to consume)
Income	Consumption	
$100	$80	.80
110	87	.79
120	92	.77
130	95	.73
140	97	.69

of income and to compute the percentage relation of consumption to that income. This gives us the *average propensity to consume*. In Table 27 • 2, using the same hypothetical schedule as before, we make this computation.

The average propensity to consume, in other words, tells us how a society at any given moment divides its total income between consumption and saving. It it thus a kind of measure of long-run savings behavior, for households divide their incomes between saving and consuming in ratios that reflect established habits and, as we have seen, do not ordinarily change rapidly.

Marginal propensity to consume

But we can also use our schedule to measure another very important aspect of saving behavior: the way households divide *increases* (or decreases) in income between consumption and saving. This *marginal propensity to consume* is quite different from the average propensity to consume, as the figures in Table 27 • 3 (still from our original hypothetical schedule) demonstrate.

Note carefully that the last column in Table 27 • 3 is designed to show us something quite different from the last column of the previous table. Take a given

income level—say $110 billion. In Table 27 • 2 the average propensity to consume for that income level is .79, meaning that we will actually spend on consumption 79 percent of our income of $110 billion. But the corresponding figure opposite $110 billion in the marginal propensity to consume table (27 • 3 is .70. This does *not* mean that out of our $110 billion income we somehow spend only 70 percent, instead of 79 percent, on consumption. It *does* mean that we spend on consumption only 70 percent *of the $10 billion increase* that lifted us from a previous income of $100 billion to the $110 billion level. The rest of that $10 billion increase we saved.

As we know, much of economics, in micro- as well as macroanalysis, is concerned with studying the effects of *changes* in economic life. It is precisely here that marginal concepts take on their importance. When we speak of the average propensity to consume, we relate all consumption and all income from the bottom up, so to speak, and thus we call attention to behavior covering a great variety of situations and conditions. But when we speak of the marginal propensity to consume, we are focusing only on our behavior toward *changes* in our incomes. Thus the marginal approach is invaluable, as we shall see, in dealing with the effects of shortrun fluctuations in GNP.

Table 27 • 3   Calculation of the marginal propensity to consume

	BILLIONS OF DOLLARS			Marginal propensity to consume = Change in consumption ÷ change in income
Income	Consumption	Change in income	Change in consumption	
$100	$80	—	—	—
110	87	$10	$7	.70
120	92	10	5	.50
130	95	10	3	.30
140	97	10	2	.20

A scatter diagram   The essentially simple idea of a systematic, behavioral relationship between income and consumption will play an extremely important part in the model of the economy we shall soon construct. But the relationships we have thus far defined are too vague to be of much use. We want to know if we can extract from the facts of experience not only a general dependence of consumption on income, but a *fairly precise method of determining exactly how much saving will be associated with a given amount of income.*

Here we reach a place where it will help us to use diagrams and simple equations rather than words alone. So let us begin by transferring our conception of a propensity to consume schedule to a new kind of diagram directly showing the interrelation of income and consumption.

The *scatter diagram* (Fig. 27•5) shows precisely that. Along the vertical axis on the left we have marked off intervals to measure total consumer expenditure in billions of dollars; along the horizontal axis on the bottom we measure disposable personal income, also in billions of dollars. The dots tell us, for the years enumerated, how large consumption and income were. For instance, if we take the dot for 1966 and look directly below it to the horizontal axis, we can see that disposable personal income for that year was roughly $510 billion. The same dot measured against the vertical axis tells us that consumption for 1966 was a little more than $475 billion. If we now divide the figure for consumption by that for income, we get a value of 93.1 percent for our propensity to consume. If we subtract that from 100, our propensity to save must have been 6.9 percent.*

*It is difficult to read figures accurately from a graph. The actual values are: disposable income, $512 billion; consumption, $479 billion; average propensity to consume, 93.4 percent. For more information on "fitting" a line to such a graph, see Chapter 44, Part 6, Section VI.

Returning to the diagram itself, we notice that the black line which "fits" the trend of the dots does not go evenly from corner to corner. If it did, it would mean that each amount of income was matched by an *equal* amount of consumption—in other words, that there was no saving. Instead, the line leans slightly downward, indicating that as income goes higher, consumption also increases, but not by quite as much.

Does the chart also show us marginal propensity to consume? Not really. As we know, our short-run savings propensities are higher than our long-run propensities. This chart shows our "settled" position, from year to year, after the long-run, upward drift of spending has washed out our marginal (short-run) savings behavior.

Nevertheless, if we look at the movement from one dot to the next, we get some notion of the short-run forces at work. During the war years, for instance, as the result of a shortage of many consumer goods and a general exhortation to save, the average propensity to consume was unusually low. That is why the dots during those years form a bulge below the trend line. After the war, we can also see that the marginal propensity to consume must have been very high. As a matter of fact, for a few years consumption actually rose faster than income, as people used their wartime savings to buy things that were unavailable during the war. Between 1946 and 1947, for example, disposable income rose by some $9.8 billion, but personal outlays rose by almost $18 billion! By 1950, however, the consumption-income relationship was back to virtually the same ratio as during the 1930s.

In simple mathematics   There is another way of reducing to shorthand clarity the propensity to consume. For obviously, what we are looking for is a functional rela-

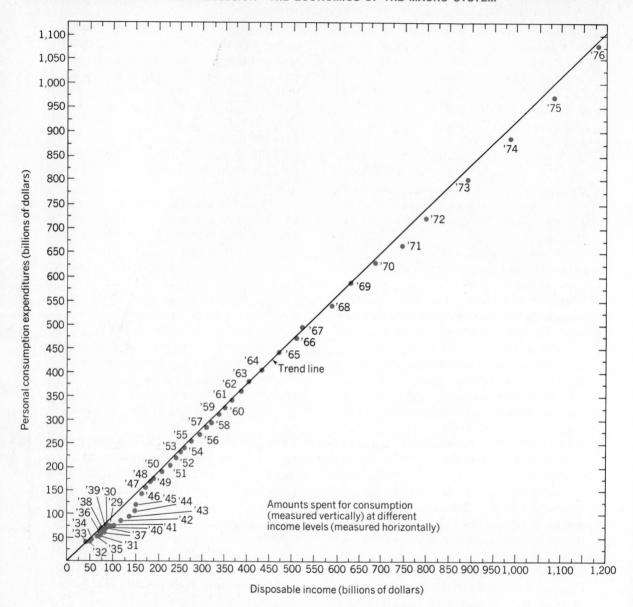

FIG. 27 · 5   United States' propensity to consume, 1929–1976

tionship between income (Y), the independent variable, and consumption (C), the dependent variable. In the mathematical language now familiar to us, we write

$$C = f(Y)$$

and we want to discover what f looks like.

Highly sophisticated and complex formulas have been tried to "fit" values of C and Y. Their economics and their mathematics both are beyond the scope of this book. But we can at least get a clearer idea of what it means to devise a *consumption function* by trying to make a very simple one ourselves. If we look at Fig. 27·5 we can see that during the Depression years, at very low levels of income, around $50 billion, consumption was just as large as income itself. (In some years it was actually bigger; as we have seen, there was net dissaving in 1933). Hence, we might hypothesize that a consumption function for the United States might have a fixed value representing this "bottom," plus some regular fraction designating the amount of income that would be saved for all income over that amount.

A generalized consumption function

This is a very important hypothesis. It enables us to describe the consumption function as an amount that represents rock-bottom consumption, to which we add additional consumption spending as income rises. If *a* is the "bottom," and subsequent spending out of additional income is $b(Y)$, where *b* represents this spending "propensity," we can now write the consumption function as a whole as:

$$C = a + b(Y)$$

We have seen that *a* is $50 billion, and we know that our actual spending propensity, *b*, is about 94 percent. Therefore, we can get a *very rough* approximation of consumption by taking $50 billion and adding to it 94 percent of our disposable income over $50 billion. In 1973 for example, disposable income was $883 billion. If we add $50 billion and .94 (883 − 50), we get $833. Actual consumption in 1973 was $828 billion.*

Let the reader be warned, however, that devising a reliable consumption func-

*Would you like to know a little more about the mathematics of the consumption function? Look at Chapter 44, Section V.

tion is much more difficult than this simple formula would indicate. The process of translating economics into *econometrics*— that is, of finding ways to represent abstract theoretical relationships in terms of specific empirical relations—is a very difficult one. Nonetheless, even our simple example gives one an idea of what the economist and the econometrician hope to find: a precise way of expressing functional interrelations (like those between consumption and income), so that the relations will be useful in making predictions.

Individual vs. aggregate consumption

Here an important warning is in order. The consumption function should not be taken as a representation of individual consumption patterns. Individual preferences vary enormously, and a wide variety of random factors causes individuals to purchase different commodities at different times. But the task of predicting the consumption expenditures of a large group of people is much easier than the task of predicting the consumption of any individual in the group. The random factors that make individual predictions difficult average out in a large group. Some individuals will spend more than we would predict on the basis of their income, but others will spend less.

Age

In addition to random disturbances, systematic factors other than incomes influence consumption. Age is a critical variable. When individuals marry and establish households of their own they are confronted with the need to acquire many consumer durables. As a result, young families are apt to have low or even negative savings rates—they consume more than they earn by using installment pay-

What about consumer credit, someone will ask. Aren't many families in debt up to their ears? Doesn't the ability to buy "on time" enable consumers as a group to spend more than their incomes?

Consumer credit indeed enables families to spend a larger amount than they earn as incomes or receive as transfers, for short periods of time. Nonetheless, consumers do not use credit to spend more than their total receipts: some consumers do, but consumers as a group do not. We know this is true because the value of all consumption spending includes purchases that are made on credit, such as cars or many other kinds of items bought on household loans or on installment. But this total spending is still less than the total receipts of the consumer sector. Thus there is net household saving, even though purchases are made on credit.

Would there be more saving if there were no credit? In that situation, many families would put income aside until they had accumulated enough to buy cars, refrigerators, houses, and other big items. During the period that they were saving up to buy these goods, their savings rates would certainly be higher than if they had consumer credit at their disposal. But after they had bought their "lumpy" goods, their savings rates would again fall, perhaps below the level of a consumer credit economy, which tempts us to buy lumpy items and to perform our saving through installment payments.

As a result, we would expect to find high savings rates in an economy where desires for lumpy items were increasing but where consumer credit was not available. Economists cite this as one explanation of the fact that Japanese families have savings rates that are more than three times as high as American families, even though Japanese incomes are lower. In Japan you cannot "buy now, pay later"; so you save now and buy later.

---

ments. When individuals reach middle age, they have already incurred those expenditures necessary to raise a family and are starting to think about retirement. Their consumption propensities fall, and their savings propensities rise.

If the age distribution of the population were changing rapidly the marginal propensity to consume would not be as stable and constant as it is. Age can be ignored only in the aggregate, since the age distribution of the population does not change rapidly.

Passivity of consumption   Throughout this chapter we have talked of the dynamics of consuming and saving. Now it is important that we recall the main conclusion of our analysis, *the essential passivity of consumption as an economic process.* Consumption spending, we will recall, is a function of income. This means it is a *dependent* variable in the economic process, a factor that is acted *on,* but that does not itself generate spontaneous action.

To be sure, it is well to qualify this assertion. We have earlier paid special attention to the long-term stability of the national savings ratio and pointed out that one cause of this stability was a general upward tendency of consumption, as families "learned" to spend their rising incomes. This dynamic, although slow-acting, behavioral trend has exerted a strong background force on the trend of the economy. Then, too, there have been occasions, the most famous being the years just following World War II, when consumption seemed to generate its own momentum and—as we have seen—raced out ahead of income. But this was a period when wants were intense, following wartime shortages, and when huge amounts of wartime savings were available to translate those wants into action. During the normal course of things, no matter how intense "wants" may be, consumers ordinarily lack the spendable cash to translate their desires into effective demand. Brief swings in consumption—for example for automobiles—may give rise to short-run fluctuations in saving, but these savings are short-lived and therefore cannot drive the economy upward or downward for any extended period of time.

This highlights an extremely important point. Wants and appetites *alone* do not drive the economy upward; if they did, we should experience a more impelling demand in depressions, when people are hungry, than in booms, when they are well off. Hence the futility of those who urge the cure of depressions by suggesting that consumers should buy more! There is nothing consumers would rather do than buy more, if only they could. Let us not forget, furthermore, that consumers are at all times being cajoled and exhorted to increase their expenditures by the multibillion dollar pressures exerted by the advertising industry.

The trouble is, however, that consumers cannot buy more unless they have more incomes to buy with.

of course, that for short periods they can borrow or they may temporarily sharply reduce their rate of savings; but each household's borrowing capacity or accumulated savings are limited, so that once these bursts are over, the steady habitual ways of saving and spending are apt to reassert themselves.

Thus it is clear that in considering the consumer sector we study a part of the economy that, however ultimately important, is not in itself the source of major changes in activity. Consumption mirrors and, as we shall see, can magnify disturbances elsewhere in the economy, but it does not initiate the greater part of our economic fortunes or misfortunes.

FOCUS

The most important thing to remember from this chapter is the very last point: consumption is a passive element in the flow of demand that generates GNP. If you understand the reason for this, all the rest of the chapter will fall in line.

Consumption is passive (not absolutely passive, since people do go on spending sprees) for two reasons:

1. We spend for consumption largely out of income; therefore, the amount of consuming we can do depends on how much income we have.

2. We are by habit regular savers. Thus as the national income goes up, national consumption goes up, and so does national saving. The percentages remain about the same, in the long run, but the amounts rise.

This average "propensity" to consume must be carefully distinguished from our *marginal* propensity to consume. The latter is a short-run phenomenon and describes the way we divide increases (or decreases) in income between spending and saving. What we do in the short run is not the same as what we do in the long run, and later we shall see that the marginal propensity to consume is an important behavioral characteristic accounting for fluctuations in GNP.

Be sure to learn the formula $C = a + b(Y)$. Think carefully about what a (the bottom) stands for, and about the meaning of b, the marginal propensity to consume. This is a simple formula that you should not forget. Don't forget, also, that this is not an identity, like $GNP \equiv C + I + G + X$. This new formula describes behavior. It can be tested—and frequently has been.

WORDS AND CONCEPTS YOU SHOULD KNOW

Household sector, 396–97
Disposable personal income, 397–98
Durable and nondurable goods, 398
Services, 398
Consumption-income relationship, 402–9
Average propensity to consume, 402–4

Marginal propensity to consume, 404
Scatter diagram, 405
$C = f(Y)$, 406
$C = a + b(Y)$, 407
Passivity of consumption, 408–9

QUESTIONS

1. What are the main components of consumption? Why are some of these components more dynamic than others?

2. "The reason we have depressions is that consumption isn't big enough to buy the output of all our factories." What is wrong with this statement?

3. What do you think accounts for the relative stability of the savings ratio over the long run? Would you expect the savings ratio in the short run to be relatively stable? Why or why not?

4. What is meant by the consumption function? Could we also speak of a savings function? What would be the relation between the two?

5. Suppose that a given family had an income of $8,000 and saved $400. What would be its average propensity to consume? Could you tell from this information what its marginal propensity to consume was?

6. Suppose the same family now increased its income to $9,000 and its saving to $500. What is its new average propensity to consume? Can you figure out the family's marginal propensity to consume?

7. Draw a scatter diagram to show the following:

Family income	Savings
$4,000	$ 0
5,000	50
6,000	150
7,000	300
8,000	500

From the figures above, calculate the average propensity to consume at each level of income. Can you calculate the marginal propensity to consume for each jump in income?

8. How do you read $S = f(Y)$? From what you know of the propensity to consume, how would you describe the relation of S to Y?

9. Why can't we cure depressions by urging people to go out and spend?

Aid in cash or kind

Over the past 15 years there has been a gradual expansion in the public provision of *private* consumption goods—not roads, but actual consumers' goods. For example, food stamps have risen from $.03 billion in 1965 to $5.6 billion in the 1978 budget. Government medical expenditures rose from $7 billion to $26 billion from 1965 to 1975. Why is the government getting increasingly involved in the distribution of private kinds of goods?

Food stamps and medical expenditures can both be viewed as income redistribution measures. Both raise the real incomes of recipients, who are mainly poor. But what arguments can be mustered in favor of giving the poor food or medical aid, rather than cash? Cash, such as welfare payments, could always be used to buy food or medical treatment; and it might yield a much higher real income to the recipient, if he or she did not happen to need food or medical assistance, but something else, such as better housing. Why force the poor to consume things that they may not rank at the top of their lists of needs?

There are two classic arguments in favor of aid-in-kind, rather than aid-in-cash. One is that the poor cannot be trusted to buy what is best for them. They may actually *need* food or medical care, it is said, but if given the money they will spend it on luxuries or liquor. Thus, by "tying" their aid, we are really doing them a favor.

Is this a valid argument? We need hardly point out that it involves value judgments. Indeed, the argument has a patronizing ring about it. To be sure, there probably are people on welfare who *would* spend a cash bonus for luxuries or liquor instead of food or medical help, but the poor are not alone in spending their incomes in ways that maximize short-run pleasures rather than long-run benefits.

The second argument for aid-in-kind is more sophisticated. It revolves around the distinction between luxuries and necessaries. As a society we have quite egalitarian beliefs about how necessaries should be distributed, but we have no such beliefs about luxuries. We look with favor on rationing of a very scarce "necessity," such as a new vaccine, but we easily tolerate a high degree of inequality in the distribution of new Cadillacs. This distinction puts us on the horns of a dilemma. If we distribute welfare through equal amounts of cash, we are helping to bring about a more egalitarian distribution of luxuries, since the poor are free to spend their money on luxuries if they wish. On the other hand, if we distribute cash welfare unequally, we are possibly contributing to the unequal distribution of necessities, where we would like the poor to get a "fair share."

Aid-in-kind is an effort to get around this dilemma. When we distribute medical care equally, we are lending support to the equal sharing of medical care, which we consider a necessity. When we distribute food stamps, we are actually printing a different kind of money, usable only for food, and distributing this money in special ways. Thus aid-in-kind ties egalitarianism to "necessaries."

Does this justify aid-in-kind? Most economists, including ourselves, would prefer to give aid in cash, allowing each recipient to do with it as he or she wished. But to the extent that the preferences of the public are to be taken into account—and the taxpaying public far outnumbers the recipients of aid—the distribution of aid-in-kind may commend itself simply because it seems to accord with the political and social wishes of the public, the supreme arbiter in these matters.

Investment demand

In studying the behavior of the consumption sector, we have begun to understand how the demand for GNP arises. Now we must turn to a second source of demand— investment demand. This requires a shift in our vantage point. As experienced consumers, we know about consumption, but the activity of investing is foreign to most of us. Worse, we are apt to begin by confusing the meaning of investment, as a source of demand for GNP, with "investing" in the sense familiar to most of us when we think about buying stocks or bonds.

Investment: real and financial We had best begin, then, by making certain that our vocabulary is correct. *Investing, or investment, as the economist uses the term in describing the demand for GNP, is an activity that uses the resources of the community to maintain or add to its stock of physical capital.*

Now this may or may not coincide with the purchase of a security. When we buy an ordinary stock or bond, we usually buy it from someone who has previously owned it, and therefore our personal act of "investment" becomes, in the economic view of things, merely a *transfer* of claims without any direct bearing on the creation of new wealth. A pays B cash and takes his

28

412

General Output stock; B takes A's cash and doubtless uses it to buy stock from C; but the transactions between A and B and C in no way alter the actual amount of real capital in the economy. Only when we buy *newly issued* shares or bonds, and then only when their proceeds are directly allocated to new equipment or plant, does our act of personal financial investment result in the addition of wealth to the community. In that case, A buys his stock directly (or through an investment banker) from General Output itself, and not from B. A's cash can now be spent by General Output for new capital goods, as presumably it will be.

Thus, much of investment, as economists see it, is a little-known form of activity for the majority of us. This is true not only because real investment is not the same as personal financial investment, but because the real investors of the nation usually act on behalf of an institution other than the familiar one of the household. The unit of behavior in the world of investment is typically the business firm, just as in the world of consumption it is the household. Boards of directors, chief executives, or small-business proprietors are the persons who decide whether or not to devote business cash to the construction of new facilities or to the addition of inventory; and this decision, as we shall see, is very different in character and motivation from the decisions familiar to us as members of the household sector.

with the sector as a whole, much as we did with the consumption sector.

Figure 28·1 gives a first general impression of the investment sector in a recent year. Note that the main source of gross private domestic investment expenditure is the retained earnings of business; that is, the expenditures come from depreciation accruals or from profits that have been kept in the business. However, as the next bar shows, gross investment *expenditures* are considerably larger than retained earnings. The difference represents funds that business obtains in several ways.

1. It may draw on cash (or securities) accumulated out of retained earnings or depreciation accruals of previous years.
2. It may obtain savings from the household sector by direct borrowing or by sale of new issues of shares of stock or indirectly via insurance companies or savings banks or pension funds, and so on.
3. It may borrow from commercial banks.
4. The difference also represents investment in housing, which is not typically financed by corporate earnings but by consumers, borrowing from banks.

The last two sources of funds we will not fully understand until we reach Chapter 33, when we study the money mechanism. But our chart enables us to see that most gross investment is financed by business itself from its *internal* sources—retained earnings plus depreciation accruals—and that external sources play only a secondary role. In particular, this is true of new stock issues, which, during most of the 1960s and early 1970s, raised only some 3 to 8 percent of the funds spent by the business sector for new plant and equipment.

The Investment Sector in Profile

Before we begin an investigation into the dynamics of investment decisions, however, let us gain a quick acquaintance

Categories of investment

From the total funds at its disposal, the business sector now renews its worn-out capital and adds new capital. Let us say a word concerning some of the main categories of investment expenditure.

1. Inventories

At the top of the expenditure bar in Fig. 28 • 1 we note an item of $14 billion for *additions to inventory*. Note that this figure does not represent total inventories, but only *changes* in inventories, upwards or downwards. If there had been no change in inventory over the year, the item would have been zero, even if existing inventories were huge. Why? Because those huge inventories would have been included in the investment expenditure flow of *previous* years when they were built up.

Additions to inventories are capital, but they need not be additions to capital

goods. Indeed, they are likely to include farm stocks, consumer goods, and other items of all kinds. Of course, these are goods held by business, and not by consumers. But that is the very point. We count inventory additions as net investment because they are output that has been produced but that has not been consumed. In another year, if these goods pass from the hands of business into consumers' hands, and inventories decline, we will have a negative figure for net inventory investment. This will mean, just as it appears, that we are consuming goods faster than we are producing them—that we are disinvesting.

Inventories are often visualized as completed TV sets sitting in some warehouse. While some inventories are completed goods sitting in storage, most

FIG. 28 • 1   Business sector 1976

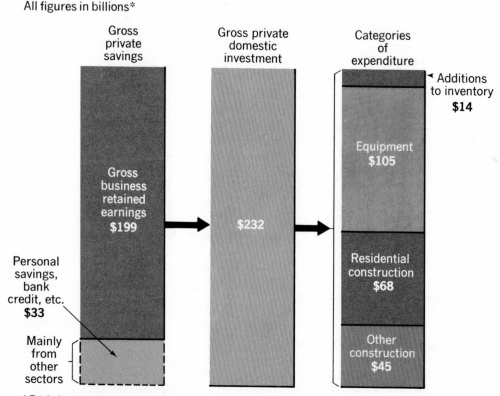

All figures in billions*

Gross private savings

Gross private domestic investment

Categories of expenditure

◄ Additions to inventory **$14**

Gross business retained earnings **$199**

$232

Equipment **$105**

Personal savings, bank credit, etc. **$33**

Residential construction **$68**

Mainly from other sectors

Other construction **$45**

* Totals do not always add, owing to rounding

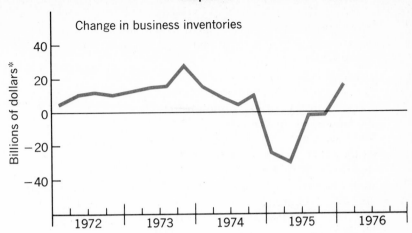

FIG. 28 · 2   Inventory swings

*Seasonally adjusted annual rates

are in the form of goods on display in stores, half-finished goods in the process of production, or raw materials to be used in production. When a steel company adds to its stock of iron ore, it is adding to its inventories.

Investments in inventory are particularly significant for one reason. Alone among the investment categories, inventories can be *rapidly* used up as well as increased. A positive figure for one year or even one calendar quarter can quickly turn into a negative figure the next. This means that expenditures for inventory are usually the most volatile element of any in gross national product. A glance at Fig. 28 · 2 shows a particularly dramatic instance of how rapidly inventory spending can change. In the fourth quarter of 1973, we were investing in inventories at an annual rate of over $20 billion. Five quarters later, we were working off inventories— *disinvesting* in inventories—by roughly the same amount. Thus, within a span of a year and a half, there was a swing of almost $50 billion in spending. Rapid inventory swings, although not quite of this magnitude, are by no means uncommon.

As we shall see more clearly later, this volatility of investment has much significance for business conditions. Note

that while inventories are being built up, they serve as an offset to saving—that is, some of the resources released from consumption are used by business firms to build up stocks of inventory capital. But when inventories are being "worked off," we are actually making the demand gap bigger. As we would expect, this can give rise to serious economic troubles.

2. Equipment

The next item in the expenditure bar (Fig. 28 · 1) is more familiar: $105 billion for *equipment*. Here we find expenditures for goods of a varied sort—lathes, trucks, generators, computers, office typewriters.* The total includes both *new equipment* and *replacement equipment*, and we need a word of caution here. Exactly what does it mean to "replace" a given item of equipment? Suppose we have a textile loom that cost $100,000 and that is now on its last legs. Is the loom "replaced" by spending another $100,000, regardless of what kind of machine the money will buy? What if loom prices have gone up and $100,000 no longer buys a loom of the same capacity?

*But *not* typewriters bought by consumers. Thus the same good can be classified as a consumption item or an investment item, depending on the use to which it is put.

Or suppose that prices have remained steady but that owing to technological advance, $100,000 now buys a loom of double the old capacity.

From an economic perspective, replacement is the dollar amount that would be necessary to buy the same productive capacity. But this is an amount that is seldom known with great accuracy. It may not be possible to buy new equipment with exactly the same productive capacity as old equipment. Often businesses replace whole factories rather than individual pieces of equipment. These new factories are likely to have very different configurations of equipment as well as different productive capacities. Such problems make the definition of "replacement" an accountant's headache and an economist's nightmare. At the moment there isn't even a generally accepted estimate of replacement investment. We need not involve ourselves deeper in the question, but we should note the complexities introduced into a seemingly simple matter once we leave the changeless world of stationary flow and enter the world of invention and innovation.

3. Constuction—residential

Our next section on the expenditure bar (Fig. 28 • 1) is total *residential construction*. Why do we include this $68 billion in the investment sector when most of it is represented by new houses that householders buy for their own use?

Part of the answer is that most houses are built by business firms, such as contractors and developers, who put up the houses *before* they are sold. Thus the original expenditures involved in building houses typically come from businesses, not from households. Later, when the householder buys a house, it is an existing asset, and his or her expenditure does not pump new incomes into the economy but only repays the contractor who *did* contribute new incomes.

Actually, this is a somewhat arbitrary definition, since, after all, business owns *all* output before consumers buy it. However, another reason for considering residential construction as investment is that, unlike most "consumer goods," houses are typically maintained as if they were capital goods. Thus their durability also enters into their classification as investment goods.

Finally, we class housing as investment because residential purchases "behave" very much like other items of construction. Therefore it simplifies our understanding of the forces at work in the economy if we classify residential construction as an investment expenditure rather than as a consumer expenditure.

4. Other construction—plant

Last on the bar, $45 billion of *other construction* is largely made up of the "plant" in "plant and equipment"—factories and stores and private office buildings and warehouses. (It does not, however, include public construction such as roads, dams, harbors, or public buildings, all of which are picked up under government purchases.) It is interesting to note that the building of structures, as represented by the total of residential construction plus other private construction, accounts for over half of all investment expenditure, and this total would be further swelled if public construction were included herein. This accords with the dominant role of structures in the panorama of national wealth we first encountered in Table 22 • 1 (p. 326). It tells us, too, that swings in construction expenditure can be a major lever for economic change.

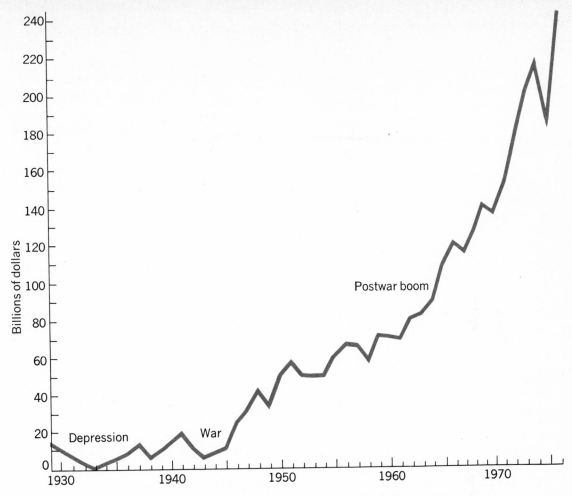

FIG. 28 · 3   Gross private domestic investment, 1929–1976

Investment in Historic Perspective

With this introduction behind us, let us take a look at the flow of investment, not over a single year, but over many years.

In Fig. 28 · 3 several things spring to our notice. Clearly, investment demand is not nearly so smooth and unperturbed a flow of spending as consumption. Note that gross investment in the depths of the Depression virtually disappeared—that we almost failed to *maintain,* much less add to, our stock of wealth. (Net invest-

ment was, in fact, a negative figure for several years.) Note also investment was reduced during the war years as private capital formation was deliberately limited through government allocations.

Three important conclusions emerge from this examination of investment spending:

First, as we have already seen, investment spending contains a component—net additions to inventory—that is capable of drastic, sudden shifts. This accounts for much of the wavelike movement of the total flow of investment expenditure.

Second, investment spending as a whole is capable of more or less total collapses, of a severity and degree that are never to be found in consumption.

Third, unlike household spending, investment can fluctuate independently of income. It may rise when GNP is low, perhaps to usher in a boom. It can fall when GNP is high, perhaps to trigger a recession. It is an independent variable in the determination of demand.

The prime example of such a collapse was, of course, the Great Depression. From 1929 to 1933, while consumption fell by 41 percent, investment fell by *91 percent,* as we can see in Fig. 28 • 3. Similarly, whereas consumption rose by a little more than half from 1933 to 1940, investment in the same period rose by *nine times.*

Importance of investment   This potential for collapse or spectacular boom always makes investment a source of special concern in the economic picture. But even the tendency toward inventory fluctuations, or toward milder declines in other capital expenditures, is sufficient to identify investment as a prime source of economic instability. As we have said before, there is often a tendency among noneconomists to equate all buying in the economy with consumer buying. Let us never lose sight of the fact that the maintenance of, and addition to, capital is also a part of GNP spending and that a considerable part of the labor force depends for its livelihood on the making of investment goods. At the bottom of the Great Depression in 1933, it was estimated that one-third of total unemployment was directly associated with the shrinkage in the capital goods industry.

The Multiplier

In our next chapter we shall look more closely into the reasons for the sensitivity of investment spending. But first a question must surely have occurred to the reader. For all its susceptibility to change, the investment sector is, after all, a fairly small sector. In 1976, total expenditures for gross private domestic investment came to only about one-seventh of GNP, and the normal year-to-year variation in investment spending in the 1960s and 1970s is only about 1 to 2 percent of GNP. To devote so much time to such small fluctuations seems a disproportionate emphasis. How could so small a tail as investment wag so large a dog as GNP?

Snowball effect   The answer lies in a relationship of economic activities known as the *multiplier.* The multiplier describes the fact that *additions to spending (or diminutions in spending) have an impact on income that is greater than the original increase or decrease in spending itself.* In other words, even small increments in spending can *multiply* their effects (whence the name).

It is not difficult to understand the general idea of the multiplier. Suppose that we have an island community whose economy is in a perfect circular flow, unchanging from year to year. Next, let us introduce the stimulus of a new investment expenditure in the form of a stranger who arrives from another island (with a supply of acceptable money) and who proceeds to build a house. This immediately increases the islanders' incomes. In our case, we will assume that the stranger spends $1,000 on wages for construction workers, and we will ignore all other expenditures he may make. (We also make the assumption that these workers were previously unemployed, so that the builder is not merely taking them from some other task.)

Now the construction workers, who have had their incomes increased by $1,000, are very unlikely to sit on this money. As we know from our study of the marginal propensity to consume, they are apt to save some of the increase (and they may have to pay some to the government as income taxes), but the rest they will spend on additional consumption goods. Let us suppose that they save 10 percent and pay taxes of 20 percent on the $1,000 they get. They will then have $700 left over to spend for additional consumer goods and services.

But this is not an end to it. The sellers of these goods and services will now have received $700 over and above their former incomes, and they, too, will be certain to spend a considerable amount of their new income. If we assume that their family spending patterns (and their tax brackets) are the same as the construction workers, they will also spend 70 percent of their new incomes, or $490. And now the wheel takes another turn, as still *another* group receives new income and spends a fraction of it—in turn.

Continuing impact of respending

If the newcomer then departed as mysteriously as he came, we would have to describe the economic impact of his investment as constituting a single "bulge" of income that gradually disappeared. The bulge would consist of the original $1,000, the secondary $700, the tertiary $490, and so on. If everyone continued to spend 70 percent of his new income, after ten rounds all that would remain by way of new spending traceable to the original $1,000 would be about $28. Soon, the impact of the new investment on incomes would have virtually disappeared.

But now let us suppose that after our visitor builds his house and leaves, another visitor arrives to build another house. This time, in other words, we assume that the level of investment spending *continues* at the higher level to which it was raised by the first expenditure for a new house. We can see that the second house will set into motion precisely the same repercussive effects as did the first, and that the new series of respendings will be added to the dwindling echoes of the original injection of incomes.

In Fig. 28 • 4, we can trace this effect. The succession of colored bars at the bot-

---

INTENDED AND UNINTENDED INVENTORY INVESTMENT

Changes in inventories reflect both the desires of firms and their planning errors. *Investment in inventories can therefore be intended or unintended.* If an automobile manufacturer expects to sell 1 million cars and is disappointed in this expectation, actual sales will lag behind expected sales. Since production was planned on the basis of expected sales, it will exceed actual sales until production can be readjusted to the new sales levels. Autos built but not sold will be added to inventories. In

this case, inventories go up not because the firm wanted more inventories, but because it made a mistake.

If actual sales exceed expected sales, the reverse will happen. Inventories fall. But again, the firm did not lower inventories because lower inventories were more profitable, but by

mistake. Low inventories can be extremely unprofitable. If certain models are not available or in limited supply, the auto maker will find that he is losing potential sales to a competitor that can give the consumer the kind of car he wants at the time he wants it.

These unintended changes in inventories enter into the statistics of GNP, just as do intended changes in inventories. But they obviously have very different significances regarding future economic behavior.

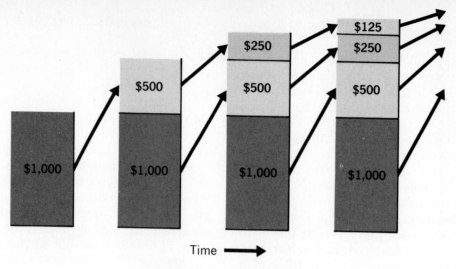

FIG. 28 · 4   The multiplier

tom of the graph stands for the continuing injections of $1,000 as new houses are steadily built. (Note that this means the level of new investment is only being maintained, not that it is rising.) Each of these colored bars now generates a series of secondary, tertiary, etc., bars that represent the respending of income after taxes and savings. In our example we have assumed that the respending fraction is 50 percent.

Let us now examine the effects of investment spending in a generalized fashion, without paying attention to specific dollar amounts. In Fig. 28 · 5, we see the effects of a single, *once-and-for-all* investment expenditure (the stranger who came and went), contrasted with the effects of a *continuing* stream of investment.

Our diagrams show us two important things:

1. A single burst of investment creates a bulge of incomes larger than the initial expenditure, but a bulge that disappears.

2. A continuing flow of investment creates a new steady level of income, higher than the investment expenditures themselves.

FIG. 28 · 5   Once-over and continuing effects of investment

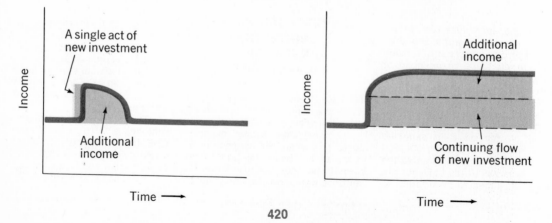

Marginal propensity to save

We can understand now that *the multiplier is the numerical relation between the initial new investment and the total increase in income.* If the initial investment is $1,000 and the total addition to income due to the respending of that $1,000 is $3,000, we have a multiplier of 3; if the total addition is $2,000, the multiplier is 2.

What determines how large the multiplier will be? The answer depends entirely on our marginal consumption (or, if you will, our marginal saving) habits—that is, on how much we consume (or save) out of each dollar of additional income that comes to us. Let us follow two cases below. In the first, we will assume that each recipient spends only one-half of any new income that comes to him, saving the rest. In the second case, he spends three-quarters of it and saves one-quarter.

It is very clear that the amount of income that will be passed along from one receiver to the next will be much larger where the marginal propensity to consume

is higher. In fact, we can see that the total amount of new incomes (total amount of boxes below) must be mathematically related to the proportion that is spent each time.

What is this relationship? The arithmetic is easier to figure if we use not the consumption fraction, but the *saving fraction* (the two are, of course, as intimately related as the first slice of cake and the remaining cake). If we use the saving fraction, the sum of new incomes is obtained by taking the reciprocal of (i.e., inverting, or turning upside down) the fraction we save. Thus, if we save ½ our income, the total amount of new incomes generated by respending will be ½ inverted, or 2 (twice the original increase in income). If we save ¼, it will be the reciprocal of ¼, or 4 times the original change.

Basic multiplier formula

We call the fraction of new income that is saved the *marginal propensity to save* (often abbreviated as mps). As we have just seen, this fraction is

FIG. 28 · 6   Comparison of two multipliers

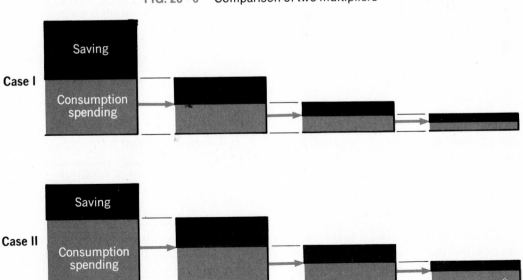

MATHEMATICS FOR THE CURIOUS

How do we know that the multiplier will be 4, if the marginal propensity to save is ¼? Most of us "intuitively" see that the sum of respending hinges on the savings fraction, and we take on faith the simple formula that tells us how to calculate that sum by taking the reciprocal of the mps and multiplying it by the change in spending.

But some students may want to go beyond faith, to understanding. Here is a simple mathematical demonstration that the multiplier formula is "really" true.

What we are trying to get at, with the multiplier formula, is the *sum of a series,* in which an initial term is multiplied again and again by some number that is less than 1 (and greater than 0). Suppose the initial term is $10 and the number-less-than-one is .8. Then we want to know the sum of the following problem:

$$10 + .8(10) + .8[.8(10)]\ldots$$

This is the same as if we wrote:

$$10 + .8(10) + .8^2(10) + .8^3(10)\ldots$$
$$+\ldots.8^n(10)$$

If we think of .8 as designating the marginal propensity to consume, we are looking for the sum of an initial new expenditure of $10, of which $8 will be spent in the first round (.8 × $10); $6.40 (.8² × $10) in the second round; $5.12 (.8³ × $10) in the third, and so on. From the textbook, we "know" that this sum is found by taking the mps, which is .2, or 1/5, and multiplying the original expenditure by its reciprocal. Thus, $10 × 5 = $50. Now let's prove it.

We can restate our multiplier series in simple algebra by calling the initial term a and the number-less-than-one (.8 above) b. Then the series looks like this:

$$a + b \cdot a + b^2 \cdot a\ldots + \ldots b^n \cdot a$$

where b^n stands for the fraction spent on the last (nth) round.

Suppose we call the sum of this series S. Now we are going to perform a truly magical (but perfectly legitimate) mathematical trick. We will first write the formula we have just described, and below it we will write the same formula, after we have multiplied both sides of the equation by b.

$$S = a + b \cdot a + b2 \cdot a\ldots + \ldots b^n a$$
$$b \cdot S = b \cdot a + b2 \cdot a\ldots + \ldots b^{n+1} \cdot a$$

We have strung out the second equation so that terms such as $b \cdot a$ lie underneath their counterparts in the first equation.

Now we subtract the second equation from the first. All the terms that are under one another just disappear. This leaves us:

$$S - b \cdot S = a - b^{n+1} \cdot a$$

Next we factor out S on the left side, giving us $S(1 - b)$, and divide both sides by $(1 - b)$. The result:

$$S = a - b^{n+1} \cdot a/(1 - b)$$

We are almost at the end. Now we examine what happens as the ex-

ponent n approaches infinity. Remember that by definition b is a number less than 1, so that with each successive increase in the exponent, b becomes *smaller.* Thus we can assume that the final term approaches zero, as its exponent approaches infinity. That is to say, it "vanishes." This is very convenient because it leaves us with the much simpler formula:

$$S = a/(1 - b)$$

Do you see the connection with the multiplier? The term b was the fraction (.8) by which we constantly multiplied the initial sum ($10). *Thus this fraction was exactly like the marginal propensity to consume!* Therefore, $1 - b$ must be the difference between 1 and the mpc (or .2).

We know this is the mps. Therefore we can write mps in place of $1 - b$; and while we are about it, we can write $10, or Δl, or any other number in place of a.

Hence our formula becomes translated into economic terms and looks like this:

$$S = \Delta l/mps$$

The term S stood for the sum of the series. An economist will call it ΔY since this is the sum of the additional incomes generated by each round of spending.

ΔY is therefore $10 ÷ .2 (or $50). And that is why the formula is true.

---

the complement of an already familiar one, the marginal propensity to consume. If our marginal propensity to consume is 80 percent, our marginal propensity to save must be 20 percent; if our mpc is three-quarters, our mps must be one-quarter. In brief, mps + mp ≡ 1.

Understanding the relationship between the marginal propensity to save and the size of the resulting respending

fractions allows us to state a very simple (but very important) formula for the multiplier:

change in income = multiplier ×
change in investment

Since we have just learned that the multiplier is determined by the reciprocal of the marginal propensity to save, we can write:

$$\text{multiplier} = \frac{1}{\text{mps}}$$

If we now use the symbols we are familiar with, plus a Greek letter Δ, delta, that means "change in," we can write the important economic relationship above as follows:

$$\Delta Y = \left(\frac{1}{\text{mps}}\right) \times \Delta I$$

Thus, if our mps is 1/4 (meaning, let us not forget, that we save a quarter of increases in income and spend the rest), then an increase in investment of $1 billion will lead to a total increase in incomes of $4 billion

$$(\$4 \text{ billion} = 1/(\tfrac{1}{4}) \times \$1 \text{ billion}$$

Note that the multiplier is a complex or *double* fraction:

it is 1/(1/4) and *not* 1/4.

If the mps is 1/10, $1 billion gives rise to incomes of $10 billion; if the mps is 50 percent, the billion will multiply to $2 billion. And if mps is 1? This means that the entire increase in income is unspent, that our island construction workers tuck away (or find taxed away) their entire newly earned pay. In that case, the multiplier will be 1 also, and the impact of the new investment on the island economy will be no more than the $1,000 earned by the construction workers in the first place.

Leakages

The importance of the size of the marginal savings ratio in determining the effect that additional investment will have on income is thus apparent. Now, however, we must pass from the simple example of our island economy to the more complex behavioral patterns and institutional arrangements of real life. The average propensity to save (the ratio of saving to disposable income) runs around 6 to 7 percent. In recent years, the *marginal* propensity to save (the ratio of additional saving to increases in income) figured over the period of a year has not departed very much from this figure. If this is the case, then, following our analysis, the multiplier would be very high. If mps were even as much as 10 percent of income, a change in investment of $1 billion would bring a $10 billion change in income. If mps were nearer 6 percent—the approximate level of the average propensity to save—a change of $1 billion would bring a swing of over $16 billion. Were this the case, the economy would be subject to the most violent disturbances whenever the level of spending shifted. For example, the $50 billion swing in inventory investment from late 1973 to early 1975 would have produced a sixteenfold fall in GNP—a fall of $800 billion!

In fact, however, the impact of the multiplier is greatly reduced because the successive rounds of spending are dampened by factors other than personal saving. One of them we have already introduced in our imaginary island economy. This is the tendency of *taxation* to "mop up" a fraction of income as it passes from hand to hand. This mopping-up effect of taxation is in actuality much larger than that of saving. For every dollar of change in income, federal taxes will take about 30 cents, and state and local taxes another 6 cents.

Another dampener is the tendency of respending to swell *business savings* as well as personal incomes. Of each dollar of new spending, perhaps 10 cents goes into business profits, and this sum is typically saved, at least for a time, rather than immediately respent.

Still another source of dampening is the tendency of consumers and businesses to increase purchases from abroad as their incomes rise. These rising *imports* divert 3 to 4 percent of new spending to foreign nations and accordingly reduce the successive impact of each round of expenditure.

All these withdrawals from the respending cycle are called *leakages*, and the total effect of all leakages together (personal savings, business savings, taxes, and imports) is to reduce the overall impact of the multiplier from an impossibly large figure to a very manageable one. In dealing with the multiplier equation ($\Delta Y = 1/\text{mps} \times \Delta I$), we usually interpret mps to mean the total withdrawal from spending due to all leakages. The combined effect of all leakages brings the actual multiplier in the United States in the 1970s to a little more than 2 over a period of 2 years.*

To be sure—and this is very important—all these leakages *can* return to the income stream. Household saving can be turned into capital formation; business profits can be invested; tax receipts can be disbursed in government spending programs; and purchases from foreign sellers can be returned as purchases *by* foreigners. What is at stake here is the regularity and reliability with which these circuits will be closed. In the case of ordinary income going to a household, we can count with considerable assurance on a "return expenditure" of consumption. In the case of the other recipients of funds, the assurance is much less; hence we count their receipts as money that has leaked out of the expenditure flow, for the time being.

*It is interesting to note that the leakages all tend to increase somewhat in boom times and to decline in recessions, which results in a multiplier slightly larger in bad times than in good.

The downward multiplier

The multiplier, with its important magnifying action, rests at the very center of our understanding of economic fluctuations. Not only does it explain how relatively small stimuli can exert considerable upward pushes, but it also makes much clearer than before how the failure to offset a small savings gap can snowball into a serious fall in income and employment.

For just as additional income is respent to create still further new income, a loss in income will not stop with the affected households. On the contrary, as families lose income, they cut down on their spending, although the behavior pattern of the propensity to consume schedule suggests that they will not cut their consumption by as much as their loss in income. Yet each reduction in consumption, large or small, lessens to that extent the income or receipts of some other household or firm.

We have already noted that personal savings alone do not determine the full impact of the multiplier. This is even more fortunate on the way down than on the way up. If the size of the multiplier were solely dependent on the marginal propensity to save, an original fall in spending would result in a catastrophic contraction of consumption through the economy. But the leakages that cushion the upward pressure of the multiplier also cushion its downward effect. As spending falls, business savings (profits) fall, tax receipts dwindle, and the flow of imports declines. We shall discuss this cushioning effect when we look into the government sector.

All of these leakages now work in the direction of mitigating the repercussions of the original fall in spending. The fall in business profits means that less will be saved by business and thus less withdrawn from respending; the decline in taxes means that more money will be left to consumers; and the drop in imports similarly releases additional spending power for the domestic market. Thus, just as the various leakages pulled money away from consumption on the way up, on the way down they lessen their siphoning effect and in this way restore purchasing power to consumers' hands. As a result, in the downward direction as in the upward, the actual impact of the multiplier is about 2, so that a fall in investment of, say, $5 billion will lower GNP by $10 billion.

Even with a reduced figure, we can now understand how a relatively small change in investment can magnify its impact on GNP. If the typical year-to-year change in investment is around $10 billion to $20 billion, a multiplier of 2 will produce a change in GNP of $20 billion to $40 billion, by no means a negligible figure. In addition, as we shall shortly see, the multiplier may set up repercussions that feed back onto investment. But more of that momentarily. First let us make three final points in regard to the multiplier.

1. Other multipliers

We have talked of the multiplier in connection with changes in investment spending. But we must also realize that any original change in any spending has a multiplier effect. We have used investment as the "trigger" for the multiplier because it is, in fact, a component of spending that is likely to evidence *large* and *sudden* changes. But an increase in foreigners' purchases of our exports has a multiplier effect, as does an increase in government spending or a decrease in taxes, or a spontaneous increase in consumption itself due to, say, a drop in the propensity to save.

Any stimulus to the economy is thus not confined to its original impact, but gives a series of successive pushes to the system until it has finally been absorbed in leakages. We shall come back to this important fact in our next chapter.

2. Idle resources

Finally, there is a very important proviso to recognize, although we will not study its full significance until Chapter 34. This is the important difference between an economy with idle resources—unemployed labor or unused machines or land—and one without them.

For it is only when we have idle resources that the respending impetus of the multiplier is useful. Then each round of new expenditure can bring idle resources into use, creating not only new money incomes but *new production and employment*. The situation is considerably different when there are no, or few, idle men or machines. Then the expenditure rounds of the multiplier bring higher money incomes, but these are not matched by increased real output.

In both cases, the multiplier exerts its leverage, bringing about an increase in total expenditure larger than the original injection of new spending. In the case without idle resources, however, the results are solely *inflationary*, as the increased spending results in higher incomes and higher prices, but not in higher output. In the case where idle resources exist, we can avoid this mere "money" multiplication and enjoy a rise in output as a result of our increased spending. Indeed, we can even speak of the *employment multiplier* in situations where there is considerable unemployment, meaning by this the total increase in employment brought about by a given increase in spending. We shall return in subsequent chapters to a fuller scrutiny of the difference between the case of idle and of fully employed resources, but we must bear the distinction in mind henceforth.

3. The importance of time lags

Last we must distinguish between the multiplier as a mathematical relationship and the multiplier in real life.

In equations, the multiplier is "instantaneous." If investment rises by $10 billions and the multiplier is 2, we "instantly" have a $20 billion rise in output. In actuality, the successive "rounds" of spending display very important time lags. Investment expenditures of $10 billion will first show up as increased sales of businesses. Businesses usually will draw down on inventories rather than immediately increasing production (and factor incomes), to hedge

against the possibility that the increase is only temporary. This leads to a smaller increase in incomes, other than profits, than might be expected. And for the same hedging reason, businesses are unlikely at first to use their additional profits to pay higher incomes or to finance new investment.

Moreover, incomes that do go to consumers are also not instantaneously spent. One recent study has shown that families spent only 66 cents out of each dollar of new income in the first three months during which they received that income. Only gradually did their spending propensities build up to "normal." And even when they *did* spend their additional incomes, the businesses that enjoyed larger sales were again likely to display the cautious hedging attitudes we have described. That is another reason why the multiplier, 2 years after an investment increase, is in fact only about 2.

FOCUS   There are two central ideas in this chapter, one of which is easy to learn; the other demands some time and thought. The easy but absolutely central idea is that investment is a flow of demand capable of deep, sudden shifts. Unlike changes in consumption, which reflect prior changes in income, investment can go "against" the trend of income, rising in bad times, perhaps to lead the way to recovery; falling in good times, perhaps to set off a recession. This idea is very important to grasp. It also calls attention to the role of inventory change, as the most volatile component of a volatile flow.

The second main idea is the multiplier. The multiplier is important because it explains why changes in spending—investment or government or export or whatever—can lift or lower the economy by more than the original change itself. This multiplying effect is the consequence of the marginal propensity to consume—the fact that we respend large fractions of increases on our income, thereby creating incomes for others. (Look at question 4.) The very high respending fraction of the marginal propensity to consume is greatly reduced by leakages into business profits, taxes and imports, reducing the effect of the multiplier to about 2, over 2 years.

It should be needless to say—but it is critical to see—the effect of the multiplier will be useful going "up" when we have unemployed resources, but not when we do not. We shall come back to that critical difference later on when we study inflation.

WORDS AND CONCEPTS YOU SHOULD KNOW

Real vs. financial investment, 412–13
Four types of investment, 414, 415, 416
The multiplier, 418–20
Marginal propensity to save, 421
$\Delta Y = 1/mps \times \Delta I$, 423

Four kinds of leakage, 423–24
The downward multiplier, 424
The multiplier and idle resources, 425–26
The multiplier and time, 424

QUESTIONS

1. If you buy a share of stock on the New York Stock Exchange, does that always create new capital? Why, or why not?

2. Why are additions to inventory so much more liable to rapid fluctuation than are other kinds of investment?

3. Why do we face the possibility of a total collapse of investment, but not of consumption?

4. Draw a diagram of boxes showing the multiplier effect of a $1,000 expenditure when the marginal propensity to save is one-tenth. Draw a second diagram, showing the effect when the marginal propensity to consume is nine-tenths?

5. Compare two multiplier diagrams: one where the marginal propensity to save is one-quarter; the other where it is one-third. The *larger* the saving ratio, the larger or smaller the multiplier?

6. Calculate the impact on income if investment rises by $10 billion and the multiplier is 2. If the multiplier is 3. If it is 1.

7. Income is $500 billion; investment is $50 billion. The multiplier is 2. If inventories decline by $10 billion, what happens to income?

8. Draw a diagram showing what happens to $1 billion of new investment given the following leakages: mps 10 percent; marginal taxation 20 percent; marginal propensity to import 5 percent; marginal addition to business saving 15 percent. What will be the size of the second round of spending? the third? the final total?

9. If the marginal propensity to consume is three-quarters, what is the size of the marginal propensity to save? If it is five-sixths? If it is 70 percent?

10. What is the formula for the multiplier?

A capital shortage

Many businessmen and some economists argue that there will be a "capital shortage" in the 1980s. They point to the rising needs for capital equipment for such new purposes as pollution control or energy, and they warn that the demand for capital will grow much faster than in the past. This will mean that capital will become scarce relative to other goods, and that its price—the rate of interest—will rise.

It is difficult to know, yet, exactly how large the demand for capital will be over the next decade. But we can at least clarify some issues in the capital shortage argument. The first is that it would be incorrect to calculate the degree of "shortage" simply by adding prospective expenditures on pollution or energy investment to the normal expectations of investment. To do so ignores the shifts in demands that will take place as a consequence of these very additional expenditures. Goods that are "pollution-intensive" or "energy-intensive" will cost more, relative to other goods. They will thereby probably absorb more of our spending. Thus, as the sales of other goods fall behind, less capital will be required to keep their production abreast of national demand.

In other words, the extra capital needed in some branches will be offset to some degree by less capital needed in others. Statisticians estimate the net effect on total capital may raise the demand for it by ½ to 1 percent of GNP at current interest rates. Is this a large number? In actual dollar amounts, it comes to something like $250 billion over the next decade. On the other hand, total GNP over the same period, assuming present rates of growth and inflation, comes to a staggering $31 trillion. Thus the additional capital sums, although large, are not likely to distort the traditional patterns of GNP significantly.

The second main issue is how to raise the added new capital. We have already looked into the problem of trying to raise saving rates, and we have seen that there is a real social cost in trying to do so. So suppose that we do nothing. Then the new capital demands will certainly raise interest rates. In turn this will exert an effect—and a very uneven effect—across the economy. As we shall see later on (see page 528), a credit squeeze most hurts small business, residential construction, and state and local government. It means more business failures for small enterprise, fewer homes, less urban services.

This puts a different light on the question of raising the savings rate. For the course of leaving things alone will also impose costs—perhaps more severe costs than in trying to raise the flow of savings. These costs will, however, be borne by different groups. Which policy is best? The policy that lessens the costs on those groups whose well-being you happen to prefer. It would be nice if there were a more "scientific" answer, but there is not.

Motivation of investment

The inherent instability of investment, and the multiplier repercussions that arise from changes in investment, begin to give us an understanding of the special importance of the business sector in determining the demand for GNP. In our next chapter we shall look into equally special characteristics of government demand before assembling the demand functions of all the sectors, to match them against the supply of GNP.

But before we proceed to that goal, we must learn something further about the nature of investment demand—in particular, about the motivations that give rise to it—for if we compare the underlying behavioral drives that impel consumption and investment, we can see a fundamental difference of the greatest significance.

Utility vs. profit   Consumption demand, we remember, is essentially directed at the satisfaction of the individual—at providing him with the "utilities" of the goods and services he buys. An increasingly affluent society may not be able to say that consumer expenditure is any longer solely geared to necessity, but at least it obeys the fairly constant promptings of the cultural and social environment, with the result that

29

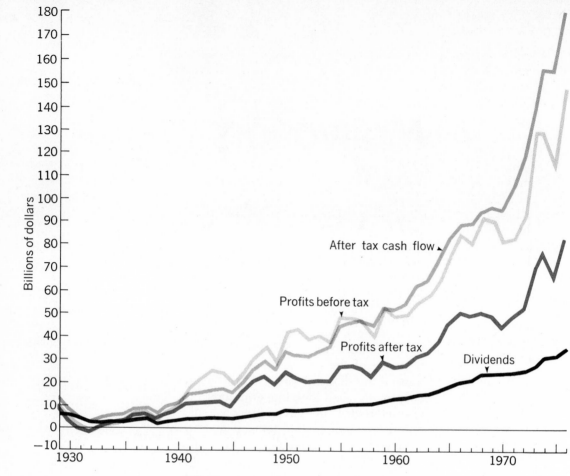

FIG. 29 · 1   Profits, taxes, and dividends

consumer spending, in the aggregate, fluctuates relatively little, except as income fluctuates.

A quite different set of motivations drives the investment impulse. Whether the investment is for replacement of old capital or for the installation of new capital, the ruling consideration is not apt to be the personal use or satisfaction that the investment yields to the owners of the firm. Instead, the touchstone of investment decisions is *profit*.

Figure 29·1 shows corporate profits since 1929 and their division into retained earnings, dividends, and taxes. What is strikingly apparent, of course, is the

extreme fluctuation of profits between prosperity and recession. Note that corporations as a whole lost money in the depths of the Depression years, but that even in the lush postwar period, the swings from year to year have been considerable (compare 1958 and 1959).

Expectations   The chart shows us how corporate profits looked to business when the books were tallied at the end of each year. But the results of last year's operation, although very important, is not the main thing that motivates business to invest. Primarily, it is interested in the profits expected from *next year's* operations. The view is never backward, but always forward.

Note the important stress on *expectations*. One firm may be enjoying large profits on its existing plant and equipment at the moment; but if it anticipates no profits from the sale of goods that an *additional* investment would make possible, the firm will make no additions to capital. Another firm may be suffering current losses; but if it anticipates a large profit from the production of a new good, it may launch a considerable capital expenditure.

There is a sound reason for this anticipatory quality of investment decisions. Typically, the capital goods bought by investment expenditures are expected to last for years and to pay for themselves only slowly. In addition, they are often highly specialized. If capital expenditures could be recouped in a few weeks or months, or even in a matter of a year or two, or if capital goods were easily transferred from one use to another, they would not be so risky and their dependence on expectations not so great. But it is characteristic of most capital goods that they *are* durable, with life expectancies of ten or more years, and that they tend to be limited in their alternative uses, or to have no alternative uses at all. You cannot spin cloth in a steel mill or make steel in a cotton mill.

The decision to invest is thus always forward-looking. Even when the stimulus to build is felt in the present, the calculations that determine whether or not an investment will be made necessarily concern the flow of income to the firm in the future. These expectations are inherently much more volatile than the current drives and desires that guide the consumer. Expectations, whether based on guesses or forecasts, are capable of sudden and sharp reversals of a sort rare in consumption spending. Thus in its orientation to the future we find a main cause for the volatility of investment expenditures.

Induced and Autonomous Investment

One kind of profit expectation, and the investment that stems from it, derives from *an observed rise in current consumption spending*, as a result of higher incomes.

Many business firms decide to invest because they must expand their capacity to maintain a given share of a growing market. Real estate developers who build to accommodate an already visible suburban exodus, or supermarkets that build to serve a booming metropolis, or gas stations that must be built to serve a new highway, or additions to manufacturing ca-

---

HAVE CORPORATE PROFITS CHANGED?

Have corporate profits changed as a percent of GNP? This question is not easy to answer for a number of reasons. Corporate profits are very sensitive to the business cycle (rising and falling much faster than output). Averages will be very misleading if they cover different phases of the business cycle. Depreciation charges must also be subtracted from gross corporate earnings before profits can be estimated. But no one knows exactly how fast equipment wears out or becomes technologically obsolete.

In addition, worn out equipment is almost never replaced by exactly the same equipment, because technical advances lead to new configurations. What new configuration is equivalent to what old configuration?

If we compare the periods from 1947 through 1953 and the period from 1965 through 1972, we have two periods with both a war and a mild recession. Corporate gross cash flow was 15.4 percent of the GNP in the first period and 14.2 percent of the GNP in the second. Thus there was a slight decline between the two periods; but in the recessionary period from 1973 through 1976, corporate gross cash flow was also 14.2 percent of the GNP. The fact that there was no decline in corporate profits (as a share of GNP) during a very severe recession indicates a shift toward corporate profits that may have eliminated, or more than eliminated, the previous decline.

pacity that must be made because existing facilities cannot keep up with demand—these are all examples of what we call *induced investment*.

The acceleration principle — When rising incomes and consumption lead to induced investment, the relationship is called the *acceleration principle* or the *accelerator*. The name springs from the fact that the amount of induced investment depends upon the rate of growth of the economy. An economy that is not growing has no induced investment. Also, an economy that has unutilized capacity will not have induced investment.

Table 29·1 is a model that explains this phenomenon. It shows us an industry whose sales rise for six years, then level off, and finally decline. We assume it has no unused equipment and that its equipment wears out every ten years. Also, we will make the assumption that it requires a capital investment of $2 to produce a flow of output of $1.

Now let us see the accelerator at work.

In our first view of the industry, we find it in equilibrium with sales of, let us say, 100 units, capital equipment valued at 200 units, and regular replacement demand of 20 units, or 10 percent of its stock of equipment. Now we assume that its sales rise to 120 units. To produce 120 units of goods, the firm will need (according to our assumptions) 240 units of capital. This is 40 units more than it has, so it must order them. Note that its demand for capital goods now shoots from 20 units to 60 units: 20 units for replacement as before, and 40 new ones. Thus investment expenditures *triple*, even though sales have risen but 20 percent!

Now assume that in the next year sales rise further, to 130 units. How large will our firm's investment demand be? Its replacement demand will not be larger, since its new capital will not wear out for ten years. And the amount of new capital needed to handle its new sales will be only 20 units, not 40 as before. Its total investment demand has *fallen* from 60 units to 40.

What is the surprising fact here? It is that *we can have an actual fall in induced investment, though sales are still rising!* In fact, as soon as the *rate of increase* of consumption begins to fall, *the absolute amount* of induced investment declines. Thus a slowdown in the rate of improve-

Table 29·1 A model of the accelerator

Year	Sales	Existing capital	Needed capital (2 × sales)	Replacement investment	Induced new investment (2 × addition to sales)	Total investment
1	$100	$200	$200	$20	—	$20
2	120	200	240	20	$40	60
3	130	240	260	20	20	40
4	135	260	270	20	10	30
5	138	270	276	20	6	26
6	140	276	280	20	4	24
7	140	280	280	20	—	20
8	130	280	260	—	—	0
9	130	260	260	20	—	20

ment in sales can cause an absolute decline in the orders sent to capital goods makers. This helps us to explain how weakness can appear in some branches of the economy while prosperity seems still to be reigning in the market at large. It will play a role when we come to explain the phenomenon of the business cycle.

Now look at what happens to our model in the eighth year, when we assume that sales slip back to 130. Our existing captal (280 units) will be greater by 20 units than our needed capital. That year the industry will have no new orders for capital goods and may not even make any replacements, because it can produce all it needs with its old machines. Its orders to capital goods makers will fall to zero, even though its level of sales is 30 percent higher than at the beginning. The next year, however, if sales remain steady, it will again have to replace one of its old machines. Its replacement demand again jumps to 20. No wonder capital goods industries traditionally experience feast or famine years!

There is, in addition, an extremely important point to bear in mind. **The accelerator's upward leverage usually takes effect only when an industry is operating at or near capacity.** When an industry is not near capacity, it is relatively simple for it to satisfy a larger demand for its goods by raising output on its underutilized equipment. Thus, unlike the multiplier, which yields its effects on output only when we have unemployed resources, the accelerator yields its effects only when we do *not* have unemployed capital.

Autonomous investment

Not all investment is induced by prior rises in consumption. A very important category of investment is that undertaken in the expectation of a profit to be derived from a *new* good or a *new* way of making a good. This type of investment is usually called *autonomous* investment.

In autonomous investment decisions, prior trends in consumption have little or nothing to do with the decision to invest. This is particularly the case when new technologies provide the stimulus for investment. Then the question in the minds of the managers of the firm is whether the new product will create *new* demand for itself.

433

Technological advance is not, however, the only cause for autonomous investment, and therefore we cannot statistically separate autonomous from induced investment. With some economic stimuli, such as the opening of a new territory or shifts in population or population growth, the motivations of both autonomous and induced investment are undoubtedly present. Yet there is a meaningful distinction between the two, insofar as induced investment is sensitive and responsive to sales, whereas autonomous investment is not. This means that induced investment, by its nature, is more foreseeable than autonomous investment.

At the same time, both spontaneous and induced investments are powerfully affected by the overall investment "climate"—not alone the economic climate of confidence, the level and direction of the stock market, etc., but the political scene, international developments, and so on. Hence it is not surprising that investment is often an unpredictable component of GNP, and thus a key "independent" variable in any model of GNP.

The Determinants of Investment

As we have seen, profit expectations that guide investment decisions are largely unpredictable. But there exists one influence on investment decisions that seems to offer a more determinable guide. This is the influence of the *rate of interest* on the investment decisions of business firms.

Interest costs   The rate of interest should offer two guides to the investing firm. If the business must borrow capital, a higher rate of interest makes it more expensive to undertake an investment. For huge firms that target a return of 15 to 20 percent on their investment projects, a change in the interest rate from 7 to 8 percent may be negligible. But for certain kinds of investment—notably utilities and home construction—interest rates constitute an important component of the cost of investment funds. To these firms, the lower the cost of borrowed capital, the more stimulus for investment. The difference in *interest costs* for $1 million borrowed for 20 years at 7 percent (instead of 8 percent) is $200,000, by no means a negligible sum. Since construction is the largest single component of investment, the interest rate therefore becomes an important influence on the value of total capital formation.

A second guide is offered to business not directly seeking to borrow money for investment but debating whether to invest the savings (retained earnings) of the firms. This problem of deciding on investments introduces us to an important idea: the discounting of future income.

Discounting the future   Suppose that someone gave you an ironclad promise to pay you $100 a year hence. Would you pay him $100 *now* to get back the same sum 365 days in the future? Certainly not, for in parting with the money you are suffering an *opportunity cost* or a cost that can be measured in terms of the opportunities that your action (to pay $100 now) has foreclosed for you. Had the going rate of interest been 5 percent, for example, you could have loaned your $100 at 5 percent and had $105 at the end of the year. Hence, friendship aside, you are unlikely to lend your money unless you are paid something to compensate you for the opportunities you must give up while you are waiting for your money to return. Another way of saying exactly the same thing is that we arrive at the *present value* of a specified sum in the future by discounting it by some percentage. If the discount rate is 5 percent, the present value of $100 one year in the future is $100 ÷ 1.05, or approximately $95.24.

This brings us back to the business that is considering whether or not to make an investment. Suppose it is considering investing $100,000 in a machine that is expected to earn $25,000 a year for 5 years, over and above all expenses, after which it will be worthless. Does this mean that the expected profit on the machine is therefore $25,000—the $125,000 of expected earnings less the $100,000 of original cost? No, it does not, for the expected earnings will have to be discounted by some appropriate percentage to find their present value. Thus the first $25,000 to be earned by the machine must be reduced by some discount rate; and the second $25,000 must be discounted *twice* (just as $100 to be repaid in *two* year's time will have to yield the equivalent of *two* years' worth of interest); the third $25,000, three times, etc.*

Clearly, this process of discounting will cause the present value of the expected future returns of the machine to be less than the sum of the undiscounted returns. If, for example, its returns are discounted at a rate of 10 percent, the business will find that the present value of a five-year flow of $25,000 per annum comes not to $125,000 but to only $94,700. This is *less* than the actual expenditure for the machine ($100,000). Hence, at a discount rate

---

*The formula for calculating the present value of a flow of future income that does not change from year to year is:

$$\text{Present value} = \frac{R}{(1+i)} + \frac{R}{(1+i)^2} + \dots + \frac{R}{(1+i)^n}$$

where R is the annual flow of income, i is the interest rate, and n is the number of years over which the flow will last.

of 10 percent, the business would not undertake the venture.

On the other hand, if it used a discount rate of 5 percent, the present value of the same future flow would be worth (in round numbers) $109,000. In that case, the machine *would* be a worthwhile investment.

Interest rates and investment

What rate should our business use to discount future earnings? Here is where the rate of interest enters the picture. Looking out at the economy, the business manager sees that there is a whole spectrum of interest rates, ranging from very low rates on bonds (usually government bonds) where the element of risk is very small, to high rates on securities of the same maturity (that is, coming due in the same number of years) where the risk is much greater, such as "low-grade" corporate bonds or mortgages. Among this spectrum of rates, there will be a rate at which he or she can borrow—high or low, depending on each one's credit worthiness in the eyes of the banking community. By applying that rate the manager can discover whether the estimated future earning from the venture, properly discounted, is actually profitable or not.

We can see the expected effect of interest rates on investment in Fig. 29 • 2. Suppose that a businessman has a choice among different investment projects from which he anticipates different returns. The technical name for these returns is the *marginal efficiency of investment.* Suppose he ranks those projects, as we have in Fig. 29 • 2, starting with the most profitable (*A*) and proceeding to the least profitable (*G*). How far down the list should he go? The rate of interest gives the answer. Let us say that the rate (for projects of comparable risk) is shown by *OX*. Then all his

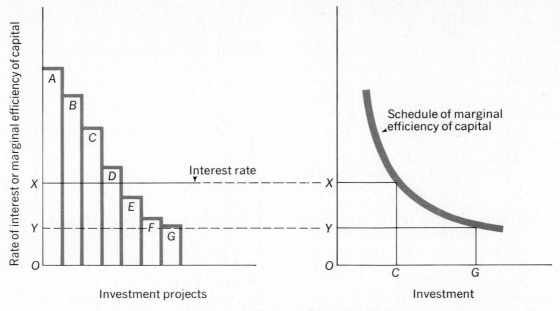

FIG. 29 · 2   Marginal efficiency of capital

investment projects whose marginal efficiency is higher than OX (investments A through D) will be profitable, and all those whose marginal efficiency falls below OX (E through G) will be discarded or at least postponed.

Note that if the interest rate falls, more investments will be worthwhile; and that if it rises, fewer will be. As the figure on the right shows in generalized form, a fall in the rate of interest (e.g., from OX to OY) induces a rise in the quantity of investment (from OC to OG).

Increases in autonomous investment or induced investment can be represented as the marginal efficiency of capital schedule shifting to the right. New opportunities, either arising from the development of new goods and services or because of increasing sales of old goods, mean that a given amount of capital can earn a higher rate of return or that more investment will occur at any given rate of interest. Draw in a new marginal efficiency curve in Fig. 29 · 2 and prove this to yourself.

Thus, whether we figure interest as a cost or as a guideline against which we measure the expected returns of a capital investment, we reach the important conclusion that *low interest rates should encourage investment spending*—or in more formal language, that *investment should be inversely related to the rate of interest.* To be sure, the fact that a given investment, such as project *B* above, has a marginal efficiency higher than the interest rate is no guarantee that a business actually will undertake it. Other considerations—perhaps political, perhaps psychological—may deter management, despite its encouraging calculations. But assuredly a business will not carry out a project that yields less than the interest rate, because it can make more profit by lending the money, at the same degree of risk, than by investing it.*

The Export Sector

Before we go on to the problem of public demand, we must mention, if only in passing, a sector we have so far largely overlooked. This is the foreign sector, or more properly the sector of net exports.

If we lived in Europe, South America, or Asia, we could not be so casual in our treatment of foreign trade, for this sector constitutes the very lifeline of many, perhaps even most, countries. Our own highly self-sustained economy in which foreign trade plays only a small quantitative (although a much more important qualitative) role in generating total output

is very much the exception rather than the rule.*

In part, it is the relatively marginal role played by foreign trade in the American economy that allows us to treat it so cavalierly. But there is also another problem. The forces that enter into the flows of international trade are much more complex than any we have heretofore discussed. Not alone the reactions of American consumers and firms, but those of foreign consumers and firms must be taken into account. Thus comparisons between international price levels, the availability of foreign or domestic goods, credit and monetary controls, exchange rates—a whole host of other such considerations—lie at the very heart of foreign trade. To begin to unravel these interrelationships, one must study international trade as a subject in itself, and that we will defer until Part Five. Nevertheless, we should try to understand the main impact of foreign trade on the demand for GNP, even if we cannot yet investigate the forces and institutions of foreign trade as thoroughly as we might like.

Impact of foreign trade We must begin by repeating that our initial overview of the economic system, with its twin streams of consumption and investment, was actually incomplete. It portrayed what we call a "closed" system, an economy with no flows of goods or services from within its borders to other nations or from other nations to itself.

Yet such flows must, of course, be taken into account in computing our national output. Let us therefore look at a chart that shows us the main streams of

---

*The relation between the interest rate and housing investment or investment in utilities is as we have described it. The matter is more complicated with regard to manufacturing investment. See "An extra word" at the end of this chapter for details.

*In Chapter 39 we shall see, however, that international currency problems can play a very important role in our economic affairs.

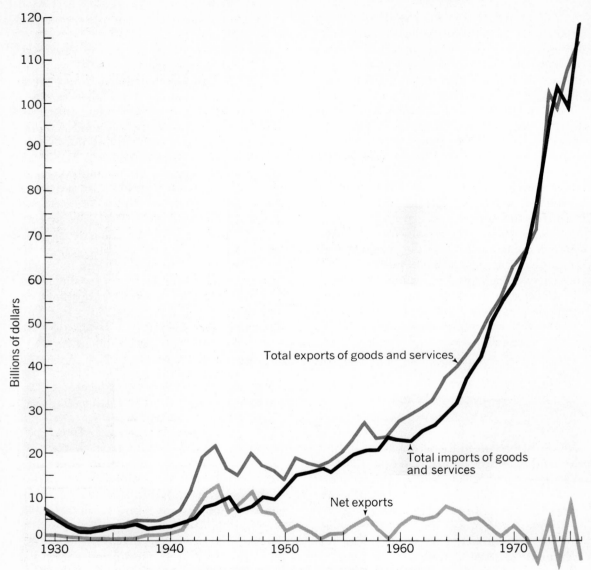

FIG. 29 · 3 Exports, imports, and net exports

goods and services that cross our borders, as well as a table of the magnitudes in our benchmark years (see Fig. 29 • 3).

First a word of explanation. Exports show the total value of all goods and services we sold to foreigners. Imports show the total value of all goods and services we bought from foreigners. Our bottom line shows the net difference between exports and imports, or the difference between the value of the goods we sold abroad and the value we bought from abroad. This difference is called *net exports,* and it constitutes the net contribution of foreign trade to the demand for GNP.

If we think of it in terms of expenditures, it is not difficult to see what the net contribution is. When exports are sold to foreigners, their expenditures add to American incomes. Imports, on the contrary, are expenditures that we make to other countries (and hence that we do not make at home). If we add the foreign expenditures made here and subtract the domestic expenditures made abroad, we will have left a net figure that will show the contribution (if any) made by foreigners to GNP.

The export multiplier

What is the impact of this net expenditure on GNP? It is much the same as net private domestic investment. If we have a rising net export balance, we will have a net increase in spending in the economy.

Conversely, if our net foreign trade balance falls, our demand for GNP will decline, exactly as if the demand for domestic investment fell. Thus, even though we must defer for a while a study of the actual forces at work in international trade, we can quickly include the effects of foreign trade on the level of GNP by considering the net trade balance as a part of our investment demand for output.

One point in particular should be noted. If there is a rise in the net demand generated by foreigners, this will have a *multiplier effect*, exactly as an increase in investment will have. Here is, in fact, the parable of an individual visiting an island (p. 418) come to life. Additional net foreign spending will generate new incomes which will generate new buying; and decreased net foreign spending will diminish incomes, with a similar train of secondary and tertiary effects. We will look into this problem again when we study the foreign trade difficulties of the United States in Chapter 40.

FOCUS This chapter continues the exploration and explanation of investment as a source of the demand for GNP. The reason that we take two chapters to do so is that investment opens the way to many other subjects, such as the multiplier analysis of our last chapter. Here we concentrate on a complementary aspect of the investment flow, the accelerator. Together with the multiplier, the accelerator helps us explain the phenomenon of economic instability. The multiplier tells us how relatively small changes in spending can give rise to larger changes in income. The acceleration principle tells us how relatively small changes in consumption spending can give rise to bigger changes in investment. That is a key thing to learn.

Investment, unlike consumption, looks to expected profit for its motivation. Whether investment is induced or autonomous, it is always hoped-for profit that lies behind the decision to invest. Thus investment is not simply a function of current GNP.

But the interest rate also plays a role in establishing the level of investment, especially in certain industries such as housing. Interest rates affect the actual cost of investment and also help to establish the profitability of investment. That's a second main idea of this chapter.

We conclude with a brief glance at the export sector, to which we will return when we study foreign trade in depth.

WORDS AND CONCEPTS YOU SHOULD KNOW

Utility vs. expected profit, 429–30
Induced investment, 431–33
Acceleration principle (accelerator), 432–33
Autonomous investment, 433–34
Interest costs, 434

Discounting the future, 434–35
Interest rates and investment, 435–37
Export sector, 437–39
Marginal efficiency of investment, 435–37
The export multiplier, 439

QUESTIONS

1. Discuss the difference in the motivation of a consumer buying a car for pleasure and the same person buying a car for business.

2. Which of the following are induced and which autonomous investment decisions: a developer builds homes in a growing community; a city enlarges its water supply after a period of water shortage; a firm builds a laboratory for basic research; an entrepreneur invests in a new gadget.

3. What is the basic idea of the acceleration principle? Describe carefully how the acceleration principle helps explain the instability of investment.

4. What is meant by "discounting" the value of an expected return? If the rate of interest were 10 percent, what would be the *present value* of $100 due a year hence? What would be its present value two years hence? (HINT: the first year's discounted value has to be discounted a *second time*.)

5. Assume that it costs 7 percent to borrow from a bank. What is the minimum profit that must be expected from an investment before it becomes worthwhile? Could we write that $I = f(r)$ where r stands for the rate of interest? What would be the relation between a change in r and I? Would $I = f(r)$ be a complete description of the motivation for investment? Why should future costs as well as profits be discounted?

6. Why doesn't the accelerator work when there is idle equipment? What significance does this have for the flow of investment as the economy moves from a position of underutilization to one of high utilization?

7. Explain how exports stimulate income. Does this mean that imports are bad? Are savings bad?

The elusive investment function

We are familiar with the consumption function that relates income to consumption. If our analysis in this chapter is valid, there should also be an *investment function* relating investment to the rate of interest. That is, we should be able to specify that for each percentage point fall in interest, investment rises by such-and-such a percent. We would expect the function to show a curve like the hypothetical one in Fig. 29 • 4.

In fact, when econometricians first began to inquire into the interest-investment relationship, they found exactly this kind of relation between interest rates and residential construction. As they expected, when it became cheaper to borrow or take out a mortgage, home-building increased. But to their consternation, when they investigated the relation between interest rates and plant and equipment investment, no such relationship appeared. Worse, the data seemed to show a "wrong" relationship: when interest rates went up, plant and equipment investment also went up! Figure 29 • 5 shows the kind of relation that research established between plant and equipment investment (shown as a proportion of GNP) and interest rates, *i*.

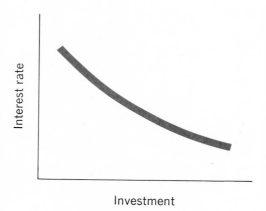

FIG. 29 • 4   The hypothetical interest-investment function

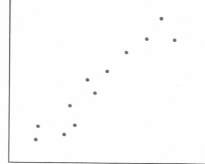

FIG. 29 • 5   The econometric interest-investment function

Plant and equipment (% of GNP)

Does this mean that our theory is wrong in some fundamental sense? Econometricians have tried a number of ways to make it come out right. One method was to correct the money rate of interest to the *real rate of interest*. The real rate of interest is the money rate reduced by the rate of inflation. If you get 5 percent on a savings bank deposit, but prices rise by 5 percent, your real interest return is zero. So, too, if businessmen could borrow at 8 percent, but prices rose by 5 percent, their real interest cost was only 3 percent. Unhappily, when money interest rates were corrected for inflation, the expected investment functions still did not appear.

Numerous other attempts have also been made to "specify" an investment function that would reconcile the observed phenomenon of investment perversely rising with interest rates. Econometricians have struggled to incorporate after-tax profit rates and many other possible influences into their investment function term, but all to no avail. No testable interest rate—manufacturing investment function has yet been devised!

Is there no way, then, of explaining a phenomenon that seems to fly in the face of common sense as well as theory? One plausible explanation has been advanced. Historically, interest rates rise during periods of rapid growth. This happens for two reasons. During these periods, the demand curve for *induced* investment shifts to the right. Therefore, even if higher interest rates tend to discourage autonomous investment, this effect may be overridden by the accelerator taking hold elsewhere.

Second, periods of rapid growth push economies toward full employment. Governments thereupon deliberately raise interest rates through the money mechanism to try to cool off the economy. In this complex of cross currents we can have the curious parallel of higher interest rates and higher investment in plant and equipment, but we can see that the influence of interest rates alone is difficult—even impossible—to isolate. Therefore we continue to assume that *if* we could isolate those effects, they would show the negatively sloped investment function we use in economic theory. We make this assumption because it is logical, and because we believe we can explain away the seeming disconfirmation of our theory in real life. Nevertheless, the interest rate—investment relationship remains something of a puzzle and a source of discomfiture to economists.

Government demand

We turn now to the last of the main sources of demand for GNP—the government. As before, we should begin by familiarizing ourselves with its long historical profile. Figure 30 • 1 at once shows the signal fact that will underlie the discussion in this chapter. It is that up to 1940 the government was almost insignificant as a source of economic demand. More important, the New Deal (1933–1940) and the postwar era marked a turning point in the *philosophy* of government, from a passive to an active force in macroeconomic affairs. In Europe, government has played a substantial economic role for a longer period; but in Europe as well as America, the deliberate *public management* of demand is a modern phenomenon on which this chapter will focus.

Government in the Expenditure Flow

Before we begin our analysis, let us take a closer look at a recent year, to help us fit the government sector into the flow of national expenditure. Figure 30 • 2 has the fa-

30

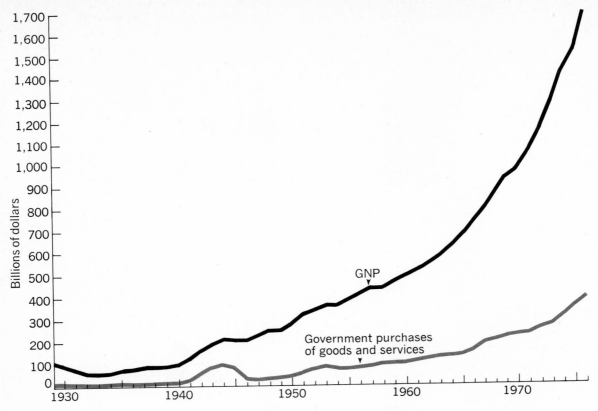

FIG. 30 · 1   GNP and the government sector

miliar bars of our flow diagram. Note that indirect taxes, totaling some $150 billion in 1976, amounted to almost 10 percent of the value of GNP. As can be seen, however, income taxes on households and businesses are much more important than indirect taxes in providing total government revenues. (What the diagram does not show is that about two-thirds of the indirect taxes are state and local in origin: property taxes, excise taxes, motor vehicle and gasoline taxes, and others. Income taxes and Social Security contributions constitute about nine-tenths of the income of the federal government.)

On the expenditure side, we see once again that state and local purchases of goods and services are more important than federal purchases in providing public demand; however, since two-thirds of all transfer payments are federal in origin, total federal *expenditures* (as contrasted with purchases of goods and services) run about one-fifth higher than all state and local expenditures.

Purchases vs. transfers   Finally, it is worth reminding ourselves of the different significance and impact of public purchases and transfers. *Public purchases of goods and services, whether they originate with local or federal government, require the use of land, labor and capital. They thus contribute to GNP. Transfer payments, on the other hand, do not increase output. They are simply a reallocation of income, from factors to various groups of the community in the business sector or the household sector.*

Transfers, therefore, do not require new production and therefore do not add to GNP.

Government sector in historical perspective

How large does the public sector bulk in the total flow of GNP? Let us again try to put a perspective into our answer by observing the trend of government purchases over the years.

We have already pointed out the striking change from prewar to postwar years. The government sector, taken as a whole, has changed from a very small sector to a very large one. In 1929, total government purchases of goods and services were only half of total private investment spending; in 1976 total government purchases were almost 50 percent *larger* than private investment. In terms of its contributions to

GNP, government is now second only to consumption.

Thus, the public sector, whose operation we will have to examine closely, has become a major factor in the economy as a whole. Let us begin by learning to distinguish carefully among various aspects of what we call "government spending." As we shall see, it is very easy to get confused between "expenditures" and "purchases of goods and services"; between federal spending and total government spending (which includes the states and localities); and between war and nonwar spending.

1. Government expenditures vs. purchases of goods and services

When we speak of government spending, we must take care to specify whether we mean total *expenditures of the govern-*

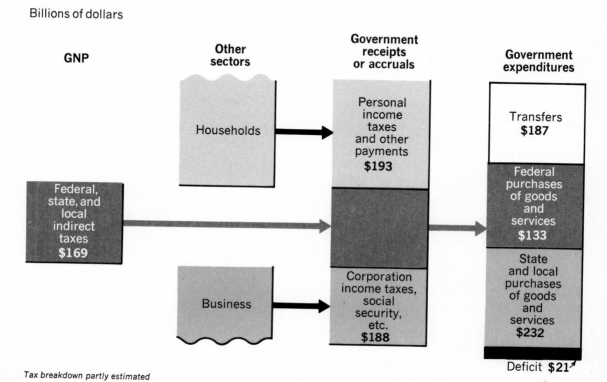

FIG. 30 · 2   Government sector, 1976

Billions of dollars

Tax breakdown partly estimated

ment, which include transfer payments, or *purchases of goods and services by the government,* which represent only actual economic activity performed for, and bought by, the government. In the latter category we include all "production" that owes its existence to public demand, whether from federal, state, or local agencies; in the former we include activities performed for the government *plus* transfer payments made by government, at all levels, as part of the redistribution of income. Thus, under "purchases" we include items such as arms and education and police and roads; under "expenditures" we count all these plus Social Security; interest on the debts of localities, states, and the federal government; welfare and other such transfers.

The distinction is important in terms of the relative bulk of what we call government spending. The purchases of goods and services by all government agencies amounted in 1976 to about $365 billion (of which, as Fig. 30·2 shows, the federal government accounted for $133 billion). *The term "G" in our GNP equation stands for these total purchases.* The larger "expenditure" category came to $531 billion. Thus government purchases were the direct cause of the production of about 22 percent of GNP itself, whereas government expenditures amounted in all to not quite one-third of GNP. Remember that a rise in transfers does not increase GNP, so that you must be careful not to use "expenditures" and "purchases" indiscriminately.

2. Federal vs. state and local spending

In dealing with the public sector we must also be careful to distinguish between expenditures or purchases that originate with the federal government and those that stem from state and local agencies. As we noted in Figure 30·2, state and local spending for goods and services is *larger* than federal purchasing. This is the consequence of the rise of an urbanized, motorized, education-minded society that has imposed vast new burdens on state and local authorities: the supervision of vehicular traffic alone requires the employment of roughly one out of every ten state and local employees, and the support of education now runs to $100 billion a year. These services have been increasing during the last decade, and now, annual state and local spending for such goods and services runs about 75 percent ahead of federal purchases.

On the other hand, federal expenditures, *including transfers,* make *total* federal spending larger than total state-and-local spending. In 1976, for example, federal expenditures, including transfers such as Social Security, interest on the debt, various subsidies, grants to the states, etc., brought total federal outlays of all kinds to more than double the amount it spent for goods and services alone.

3. Welfare vs. warfare

Most of the rise in federal purchases of goods and services is the result of our swollen armaments economy. Defense spending in 1976 amounted to almost 30 percent of our federal expenditures of all kinds including transfers, and to a much larger fraction—about two-thirds—of federal purchases of goods and services. In contrast, Table 30·1 shows that federal purchases of nonwar goods and services as a percent of GNP are actually smaller than in the prewar days and have shown only a slight rise during the last decade.

Meanwhile, social welfare expenditures of all kinds and of all government agencies (federal, state, and local), including such payments as Social Security,

Table 30 · 1   Federal nondefense purchases

Selected years	1929	1933	1940	1960–65	1966	1967	1968	1969	1970	1971	1972	1973	1974	1975	1976
Percent of GNP	1.0*	3.0*	4.0	2.1	2.2	2.3	2.5	2.5	2.4	2.5	2.6	2.6	2.4	2.6	2.7

*Estimated.

health and medical programs, public education, public housing, welfare assistance, etc., have risen from about 10 percent of GNP in the mid-1930s to about 19 percent today. This is not a large percentage by international standards. In recent years at least 4 other nations spent a higher proportion of their GNP on education than we did. Other social welfare spending (excluding education) amounted to about 13 percent of our GNP, compared with an average of more than 15 percent among the industrialized nations of Europe. It is noteworthy that in 1975 the average monthly Social Security check per married couple came to just over $340. In Scandinavian countries the payments, compared to average earnings, were roughly twice as generous as ours.

The Main Tasks of Government

The forms and functions of government spending are so complex that it may help us if we now step back and simplify the picture. Basically the federal government has three major economic functions. Measured in terms of expenditures, its largest responsibility lies in the conduct of *international affairs.* Here we find expenditures for defense, foreign aid, veterans' expenditures, military research including space exploration. In 1975 this was 33 percent of all federal spending.

Second, the federal government writes checks in the form of *transfer payments* and *interest payments* to individuals and businesses. Here are the farm

PUBLIC AND PRIVATE BUYING

It is important to realize that government buying can be divided into consumption and investment expenditures, just as private expenditures are. In 1975 for example, governments—federal, state, and local— spent $66 billion for structures and durable goods such as roads, schools, parks, sewage disposal plants and the like, as well as $97 billion on manpower training programs and education to upgrade human skills. These are all *public investment* programs.

Governments also spend large sums on *public consumption;* that is, on providing goods that are enjoyable or necessary for the public at large. Streets are swept, zoos operated, bombers flown, criminals caught.

Why do we separate government consumption and investment from private consumption and investment?

The immediate answer is that the money is spent by some government agency rather than by a household or a firm. But there is a deeper reason behind this. It is that a *political decision* has been made to put certain types of expenditures into the hands of the public authorities.

This decision varies from nation to nation. Some countries, like the U.S., have private airlines. Others, such as most of the nations of Europe, have public airlines. In the old days, roads were private; today roads are public, although occasionally one finds a privately owned road. (Note, by the way, that we could not utilize our private consumption of automobile travel unless we simultaneously "consumed" the public road on which we travel.) All nations provide public defense, justice, administration; most provide some public health; a few provide public entertainment. Ideology draws the line, not only between socialist and capitalist governments, but within socialist and capitalist governments: there is a large private agricultural sector in Yugoslavia, a very small one in Russia; many municipally owned power stations in Europe; far fewer here.

What is important to realize is that government expenditure is not a form of economic activity different from consumption or investment. It is the same kind of economic activity, undertaken collectively, through a public agency, rather than privately.

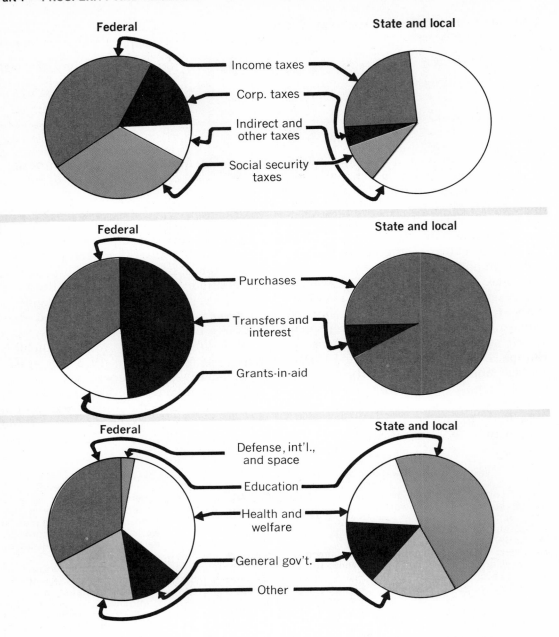

FIG. 30 · 3   Federal, state, and local finances

subsidies, subsidies for the merchant marine, and the very large outflow for Social Security and other welfare. In all, this adds up to another 41 percent of federal expenditure.

Third, the federal government writes checks, in the form of *grants-in-aid* to states and local governments. This accounts for 15 percent of federal outlays. The remainder of federal spending—11 percent—represents direct federal government operating costs and various miscellaneous functions.

It will help us review the main outlines of government spending if we look at Fig. 30·3. The first chart shows us the strikingly different *sources of funds* that flow to the federal and to state and local governments. Note the much heavier reliance of the federal government on income taxes, and the corresponding dependence of state and local governments on indirect taxes. The middle chart shows us the difference in the division of activity between federal and other governments by kinds of payments. But this table obscures a still more basic division, which we see in the third chart. Here we contrast the functions of federal and state and local governments. Now the importance of the three main functions of the federal government clearly emerges.

Economics of the Public Sector

So far we have been mainly concerned with problems of a definitional kind—in finding out what the government does. Now we want to examine the public sector from a different angle; namely, its unique *economic* character. And here the appropriate place to begin seems to be in the difference in *motivations* that guide public, as contrasted with private, spending.

We recall that the motivations for the household sector and the business sector are lodged in the free decisions of their respective units. Householders decide to spend or save their incomes as they wish, and we are able to construct a propensity to consume schedule only because there seem to be spending and saving patterns that emerge spontaneously from the householders themselves. Similarly, business firms exercise their own judgments on their capital expenditures, and as a result we have seen the inherent variability of investment decisions.

But when we turn to the expenditures of the public sector, we enter an entirely new area of motivation. It is no longer fixed habit or profit that determines the rate of spending, but *political decision*— that is, the collective will of the people as it is formulated and expressed through their local, state, and federal legislatures and executives.

As we shall soon see, this does not mean that government is therefore an entirely unpredictable economic force. There are regularities and patterns in the government's economic behavior, as there are in other sectors. Yet the presence of an explicit political will that can direct the income or outgo of the sector *as a whole* (especially its federal component) gives to the public sector a special significance. *This is the only sector whose expenditures and receipts are open to deliberate control.* We can exert (through public action) very important influences on the behavior of households and firms. But we cannot directly alter their economic activity in the manner that is open to us with the public sector.

JOHN MAYNARD KEYNES

Few economists have left so deep a mark on their own times as John Maynard Keynes, and few have roused such passions, pro and con. It is difficult now, when (as a famous conservative economist has said) "We are all Keynesians," to recall the impact of Keynes's seminal book, *The General Theory of Employment, Interest and Money,* when it appeared in 1936. Yet there were debates in the halls of academe in which voices shook and faces became empurpled over questions such as whether or not savings and investment were equal, as Keynes *defined* them to be! (We shall come to that question shortly.)

What made Keynes so controversial? Partly it was the economic philosophy that lay half explicit, half implicit in his great book—a philosophy of active government intervention. In a period when the reigning philosophy in many circles was still laissez faire, this was reason enough for Keynes's disturbing impact.

But perhaps another reason was Keynes's personality. Inordinately gifted, he was successful at a dozen things: a brilliant mathematician, a major diplomat, a great collector of modern French art, a dazzlingly skillful investor and speculator—here was one theoretical economist who *did* make a lot of money—a fascinating speaker, a consummate stylist. Keynes was not one to wear these talents modestly, and his wit was savage. Sir Harry Goshen, chairman of a Scottish bank, once deplored a Keynesian proposal and urged that things should be allowed to take "their natural course." "Is it more appropriate to smile or rage at these artless sentiments?" Keynes asked. "Best perhaps to let Sir Harry take *his* natural course."

Fiscal policy

The deliberate use of the government sector as an active economic force is a relatively new conception in economics. Much of the apparatus of macroeconomic analysis stems essentially from the work of John Maynard Keynes during the Great Depression. At that time his proposals were regarded as extremely daring, but they have become increasingly accepted by both major political parties. Although the bold use of the economic powers of the public sector is far from commanding unanimous assent in the United States today, there is a steadily growing consensus in the use of fiscal policy—that is, the deliberate utilization of the government's taxing and spending powers—to help insure the stability and growth of the national economy.

The basic idea behind modern fiscal policy is simple enough. We have seen that economic recessions have their roots in a failure of the business sector to offset the savings of the economy through sufficient investment. If savings or leakages are larger than intended investment, there will be a gap in the circuit of incomes and expenditures that can cumulate downward, at first by the effect of the multiplier, thereafter, and even more seriously, by further decreases in investment brought about by falling sales and gloomy expectations.

But if a falling GNP is caused by an inadequacy of expenditures in one sector, our analysis suggests an answer. Could not the insufficiency of spending in the business sector be offset by higher spending in another sector, the public sector? Could not the public sector serve as a supplementary avenue for the "transfer" of savings into expenditure?

As Fig. 30 · 4 shows, a demand gap can indeed be closed by "transferring" savings to the public sector and spending them. The diagram shows savings in the household sector partly offset by business investment and partly by government spending. It makes clear that at least so far as the mechanics of the economic flow are concerned, the public sector can serve to offset savings or other leakages equally as well as the private sector.

How is the "transfer" accomplished? It can be done much as business does it, by offering bonds that individuals or institutions may buy with their savings. Unlike business, the government cannot offer stock, for it is not run as a profit-making enterprise. However, government has a source of funds quite different from business; namely, *taxes. In effect, government can "commandeer" purchasing power in a way that business cannot.*

Taxes, expenditures, and GNP

We shall look more carefully into the question of how the government can serve as a kind of counterbalance for the private economy. But first we must discover something about the normal behavior of the public sector; for despite the importance of political decisions in determining the action of the public sector, and

despite the multiplicity of government units and activities, *we can nonetheless discern "propensities" in government spending and receiving*—propensities that play their compensating role in the economy quite independently of any direct political intervention.

The reason for these propensities is that both government income and government outgo are closely tied to private activity. Government receipts are derived in the main from taxes, and taxes—direct or indirect—tend to reflect the trend of business and personal income. In fact, we can generalize about tax payments in much the same fashion as we can about consumption, describing them as a predictable function of GNP. To be sure,

FIG. 30 · 4 Public expenditure and the demand gap

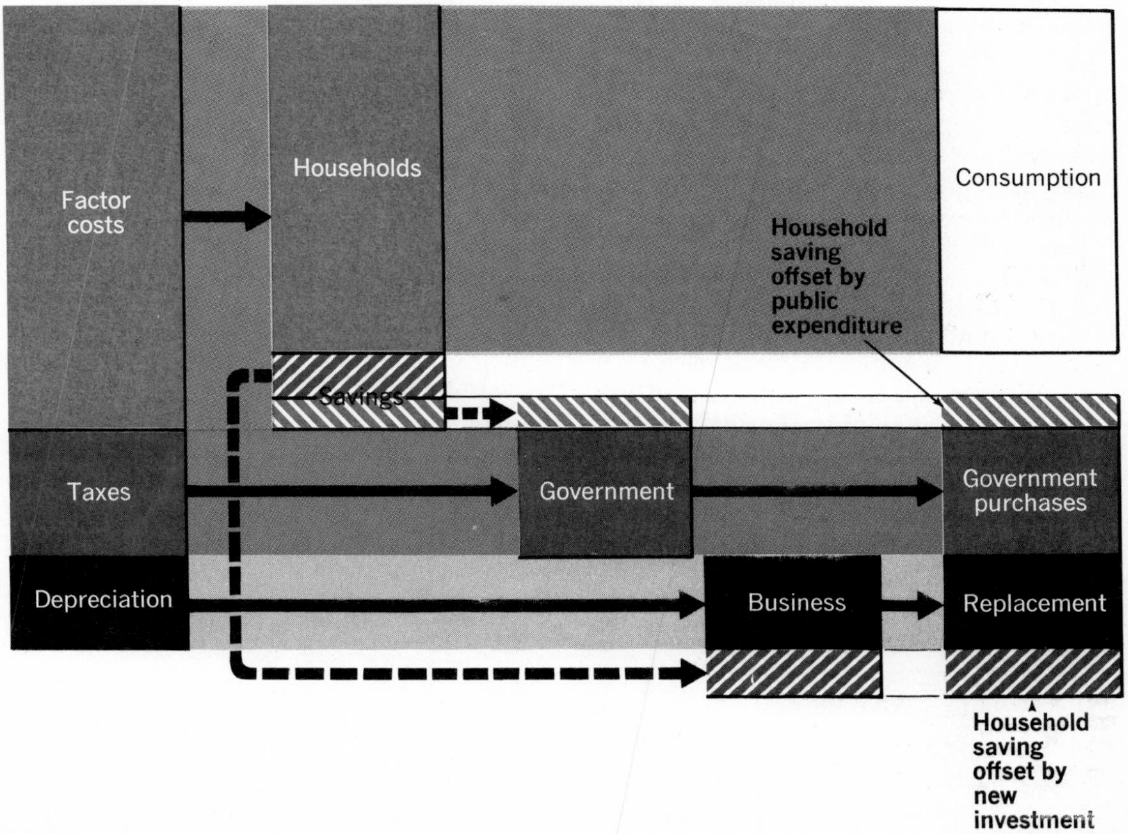

- Factor costs
- Households
- Consumption
- Savings
- Household saving offset by public expenditure
- Taxes
- Government
- Government purchases
- Depreciation
- Business
- Replacement
- Household saving offset by new investment

this assumes that tax *rates* do not change. But since rates change only infrequently, we can draw up a general schedule that relates tax receipts and the level of GNP. The schedule will show not only that taxes rise as GNP rises, but that they rise *faster than GNP*.

Why faster? Largely because of the progressive structure of the federal income tax. As household and business incomes rise to higher levels, the percentage "bite" of income taxes increases (see Table 20 · 2, p. 295). Thus as incomes rise, tax liabilities rise even more. Conversely, the tax bite works downward in the opposite way. As incomes fall, taxes fall even faster, since households or businesses with lowered incomes find themselves in less steep tax brackets.

Government expenditures also show certain "propensities," which is to say, *some government spending is also functionally related to the level of GNP.* A number of government programs are directly correlated to the level of economic activity in such a way that spending *decreases* as GNP *increases,* and vice versa. For instance, unemployment benefits are naturally higher when GNP is low or falling. Many payments such as food stamps, aid to dependent children, or various welfare programs are highly sensitive to unemployment: in 1976, for example, when unemployment neared 9 percent, such outlays were $20 billion higher than if unemployment had been 5 percent. So, too, disbursements to farmers under various agricultural programs also vary inversely with GNP.

Automatic stabilizers   All these automatic effects taken together are called the *automatic stabilizers* or the *built-in stabilizers* of the economy. What they add up to is an automatic government counterbalance to the private sector. As GNP falls because private spending is insufficient, taxes decline even faster and public expenditures grow, thereby automatically causing the government sector to offset the private sector to some extent. In similar fashion, as GNP rises, taxes tend to rise even faster and public expenditures decline, thereby causing the government sector to act as a brake.

The public sector therefore acts as an automatic compensator, even without direct action to alter tax or expenditure levels, pumping out more public demand when private demand is slowing, and curbing public demand when private demand is brisk.

How effective are the built-in stabilizers? It is estimated that the increase in transfer payments plus the reduction in taxes offset about 35¢ of each dollar of original decline in spending. Here is how this works. Suppose that private investment were to fall by $10 billion. If there were no stabilizers, household spending might fall by another $10 billion (the multiplier effect), causing a total decline of $20 billion in incomes.

The action of the stabilizers, however, will prevent the full force of this fall. First, the reduction in incomes of both households and firms will lower their tax liabilities. Since taxes take about 35¢ from each dollar, the initial drop of $10 billion in incomes will reduce tax liabilities by about $3.5 billion. Most of this—let us say $3 billion—is likely to be spent. Meanwhile some public expenditures for unemployment insurance and farm payments will rise, pumping out perhaps $1 billion into the consumption sector, all of which we assume to be spent by its recipients.

Thus, the incomes of firms and households, having originally fallen by

$10 billion, will be offset by roughly $4 billion—$1 billion in additional transfer incomes and $3 billion in income spent by households because their taxes are lower. As a result, the decline in expenditure will be reduced from $10 billion to about $6 billion (actually $6.5 billion, according to the calculations of the Council of Economic Advisers).

This is certainly an improvement over a situation with no stabilizers. Yet if the drop in investment is not to bring about some fall in GNP, it will have to be *fully* compensated by an equivalent increase in government spending or by a fall in taxes large enough to induce an equivalent amount of private spending. This will require public action more vigorous than that brought about automatically. Indeed, it requires that the government take on a task very different from any we have heretofore studied, the task of "demand management," or acting as the *deliberate* balancing mechanism of the economy.

Demand management

How does the government manage demand? It has three basic alternatives. It can

1. increase or decrease expenditures
2. raise or lower taxes
3. alter its monetary policy

We have already looked into the mechanics of the first option in Fig. 30 • 4, where we showed that government expenditure fills a demand gap exactly like private expenditure. It follows that a decrease in government spending will also create a decrease in final demand, just as a drop in the spending of any other sector.

Our diagram did not show the direct effect of tax changes, simply because it is difficult to draw such a diagram clearly.

But it is not difficult to understand the effect of a tax change. When the government lowers taxes it diminishes the transfer of income from households or firms into the public sector. Households and firms therefore have more income to spend. Contrariwise, in raising taxes, a government withdraws spending power from households and firms. As a result, we can expect that private spending will fall.

Full employment budgets

The direct effects of expenditures and taxes are thus easy to picture, and the rule for demand management should be simple: establish a government budget that will have an expansionary influence when GNP is too low and a restraining influence when it is too high; and balance the budget when GNP is at desired levels.

But this seemingly obvious guideline is not as simple as it looks. Suppose that we are suffering from mild unemployment and the President's advisers accordingly recommend a level of expenditure that, combined with existing tax rates, would produce a small deficit. Isn't this following the proper guide?

The answer is: not necessarily. For if we calculate the flow of tax receipts that the government would be receiving *if we were operating at full employment*, the planned level of expenditure may in fact be so small that it would not even produce a neutral budget, but a deflationary one at the *desired* level of GNP! A glance at Fig. 30 • 5 shows that this can indeed be the case. In 1974, for example, the actual budget was in substantial deficit, as the colored line shows. But if we calculate the budget *at full employment levels* of tax receipts, we find that our flow of expenditure was far too short of the levels needed

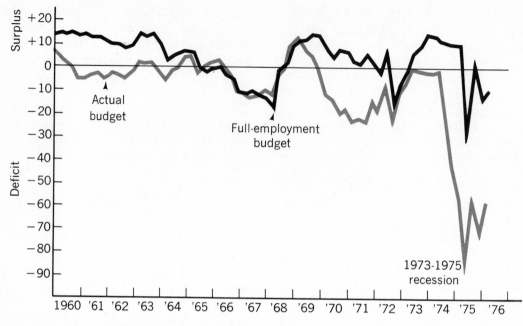

FIG. 30 · 5   Full-employment and actual budget deficits

to spend our receipts *at that level.* As the black line shows, our flows of taxes and expenditures would have given us a surplus at full employment! Therefore the $12 billion deficit was too little to give us the stimulus we needed to reach full employment. A true full-employment budget would have raised expenditures (or cut taxes) to bring the economy up to a high level of operation.

Paradoxically, although this would have required more expenditures or a lower tax rate, the effect at full employment might have been a government budget that was balanced, rather than one in deficit. That would have depended on how the other sectors behaved. If the flow of investment spending was strong, the net budget contribution of the government at full employment might well have been zero. If investment was weak, the government might—and should—plan to run a

deficit at full employment *to bring us there.*

Time lags   Second, there is a long delay between the adoption of a new tax or expenditure policy and the realization of its effects.[*] Increased expenditures or new tax proposals have to move through Congress, often a time-consuming process. In addition, if expenditures require capital construction, it may take months, even years, before spending really gets rolling. Thus by the time the new expenditures begin to give their boosting effect, the economic situation may have changed in a

[*]The other side of the same coin is the lag before a changed economic condition is *recognized*. How do we know when a recession begins? When unemployment goes up? By the time that statistics are in, it is already too late—the recession isn't beginning, it's begun. When the stock market dips? That may be a false alarm. The very great difficulties of knowing what is going on directly under our own noses is a major reason why demand management is inherently difficult.

way that makes those expenditures unwelcome. So, too, with expenditure cuts. It takes a long time to turn off most government programs. By the time the spending ceases, we may wish it were still with us!

Some economists have therefore suggested that we should have "stockpiles" of approved expenditure projects and "standby" authority to permit the President to raise or lower tax rates, within stated limits, in order to speed up the process of demand management. Other countries have successfully used such expenditure "stockpiles" as a means of accelerating the demand management process, and the last several U.S. administrations have sought—so far in vain—for executive power to adjust tax rates. Most economists would probably favor both proposals, but neither is yet an actuality. As a result, *very long time lags must be taken into account in the normal process of demand management.*

Tax cuts vs. expenditures

Which of these two methods of managing demand—taxes or spending—is preferable? The question basically asks us which we need more: public goods or private goods. But there are a number of technical economic criteria that we must also bear in mind.

First, tax cuts and expenditures tend to favor different groups. Tax cuts benefit those who pay taxes, and expenditures benefit those who receive them. This simple fact reveals a good deal about the political and economic pros and cons of each method. Tax cuts help well-to-do families and are of little direct benefit to poor families whose incomes are so low that they pay little or no income taxes. Expenditure programs *can* benefit these disadvantaged groups or areas—for example, by slum clearance in specific cities, training programs, or simply higher welfare payments. Expenditure programs can also help special groups, such as military or road contractors, or middle-income families who usually benefit from housing programs.

The difference, then, is that tax programs have a widespread impact, whereas expenditure programs tend to have a concentrated impact: *tax cuts or increases are diffused across the economy, exerting their influences on different income strata, whereas expenditure programs are often concentrated geographically or occupationally.* (Some expenditure programs, such as Social Security or medical aid, can have a broad "horizontal effect" as well.)

Second, expenditure programs tend to be more reliable as a means of increasing demand, whereas tax programs tend to be effective in decreasing demand. The reason is clear enough. If the government wishes to increase final demand and chooses to lower taxes, it makes possible a higher level of private spending, but there is no guarantee that firms or households will in fact spend all their tax savings. Indeed, the marginal propensity to consume leads us to be quite certain that firms and households will not spend all their tax reductions, at least for a time. Thus if the government wants to increase demand by say $7 billion, it may have to cut taxes by about $10 billion.

On the other hand, tax increases are a very reliable method of decreasing demand. Individuals or firms *can* "defy" tax increases and maintain their former level of spending by going out and borrowing money or by spending their savings, but it is unlikely they will do so. If the government tries to hold back total demand by cutting its own expenditure programs, however, there is the chance that firms and individuals will undo the government's effort to cut demand by borrowing and spending more themselves.

There is no magic formula that will enable us to declare once and for all what policy is best for demand management. It is often impossible to raise taxes for political reasons, in which case a decrease in expenditures is certainly the next best way to keep total demand from rising too fast. So too, it may be impossible to push through a program of public expenditure because public opinion or congressional tempers are opposed to spending. In that case, a tax cut is certainly the best available way to keep demand up if the nation is threatened with a recession.*

Fiscal drag

Thus the management of demand is fraught with difficulties. One of these is the problem known as *fiscal drag*, a problem that arises from the same mechanism that gives rise to the automatic stabilizers. We have seen that most taxes depend on the level of income and that the federal government tends to increase its tax collections faster than income grows. At present tax rates, federal revenues rise about 1.2 percent for every 1 percent of GNP growth, while federal outlays rise by only 0.8 percent. As a result, if the government maintains a more or less "do nothing" policy, there will be a tendency toward a chronic, rising surplus in the federal budget. In macroeconomic terms, this means the government is taking income away from the household and business sectors and failing to spend it. Such a surplus could seriously hold back the economy from attaining its maximum output. Thus the government would have to declare a "fiscal dividend" by cutting taxes or increasing expenditures, if it is to prevent a slowdown. It is the pressure of fiscal drag that lies behind the idea of a full-employment budget.

Grants-in-aid vs. revenue sharing

A different kind of demand management problem relates to the fiscal aid that the federal government gives to the states. As we have seen, this is a major function of our federal sector. Traditionally it has been accomplished through grants-in-aid—cash transfers, some of which are tied to specific purposes, others of which are available for whatever purposes the recipient states wish. These grants-in-aid have risen from $12.7 billion in 1966 to $60.2 in 1976.

During the Nixon administration, however, many of these grants were replaced by a system of *revenue sharing*, under which the states were automatically given a percentage of federal tax revenues. Proponents of this plan stress two advantages. One is that the federal government is a much more effective tax gatherer than the states or cities. By agreeing to share its revenues with states and localities it will give them spending abilities they could not otherwise enjoy. Second, the plan accords with the general philosophy of those who would like to see economic power deconcentrated and brought back toward local government.

Opponents of the plan fear that the more-or-less unrestricted granting of funds may lead to state and local tax cuts instead of to additional state and local spending. These cuts may occur because states tend

---

*We should also note that different kinds of private and public spending programs may have different multipliers if they go to different spending groups. A government public works program that uses unskilled labor is apt to have a larger initial repercussion on GNP than a private investment project in computers. Additional transfer expenditures may also have initial multiplier effects different from direct purchases of goods and services. And finally, different tax structures will cause changes in GNP to affect private spending differently.

to compete with one another for new industry, each state trying to keep its taxes lower than its neighbors. When all states do this, no one gains a competitive advantage, but the result is too little spending for domestic purposes. The danger is that the assurance of federal aid will take the pressure off states and localities, who will use their revenue shares to cut down on local taxation, thereby cutting down as well on local programs. Proponents of revenue sharing reply that the share of revenue going to each state can be determined by formulas that will reward states for making a strong local tax effort. Opponents then charge that this will benefit rich states that can afford higher taxes and penalize poor ones that cannot.

These complex considerations force us to confront the difficult question of what level of government should make various expenditure and tax decisions. There is disagreement over which functions are best "reserved" for the federal government (e.g., highways?); over how much intervention the federal government should have in economic activities traditionally reserved for the states (education?); and over what sorts of strictly local programs should be aided by categorical grants (such as local police forces). These are matters for political determination, but their effects on the level and distribution of public demand can be very considerable. We shall come back to these questions in Chapters 35 and 36.

Responsibility of public demand

All these considerations point out how difficult it is to conduct demand management as smoothly in practice as in textbooks. There was a time, not too long ago, when economists talked rather glibly of "fine-tuning" the economy. That was in the first flush of triumph of the *idea* of managed demand, before the hard realities of full-employment budgets and fiscal drag and other problems had been fully faced. Economists are a good deal more modest in their claims these days.

Nevertheless, the basic idea of using the government as a balancing mechanism for the economy remains valid, however difficult it may be to realize the perfect balance in fact. It is valid because the federal sector is the only sector whose operations we can collectively control. There is no way for business to determine how much it should spend as a sector, no way for consumers to concert their activity. More important, even if there were such a way, business and consumer actions might not accord with the needs of the macroeconomy. Only the public sector can act consciously on behalf of the public interest; only the public sector can attempt to reconcile the needs of all groups. However exasperating or inefficient or clumsy public demand management may be, it remains a major accomplishment, both in theory and fact, of twentieth-century economics.

FOCUS   The central idea of this chapter should by now be very easy to grasp: the government is an economic sector whose expenditures are subject to public (political) control. This places a special responsibility on government for the management of demand; that is, for the adoption of fiscal and monetary policies that will compensate for deficiencies or offset excesses in the expenditures of the private sectors. We have seen how this can be done by government taxing and borrowing (and in our next chapter we shall look into the associated problem of the federal budget).

The issue of demand management is simple to state but surrounded with thorny side issues. Some of these have to do with the operation of the automatic stabilizers—the propensity for taxes to rise, and for certain welfare expenditures to fall, when GNP rises, and vice versa. Other issues concern the choice of tax cuts or expenditures to boost or restrain the economy, the pressures of fiscal drag, the choice between helping states through grants-in-aid or general revenue sharing, and the very important need to plan the government contribution at full-employment rates of flow.

There are no "answers" to these issues. Your purpose in learning them is to acquaint you with the complexity of the real business of managing demand. You should bring away from this chapter a clear picture of the big role of government in the economy and a keen understanding of how hard it is to go from general purposes to specific policy decisions.

WORDS AND CONCEPTS YOU SHOULD KNOW

Government purchases vs. transfers, 444–45
Government purchases vs. expenditures, 445–46
Federal vs. state and local spending, 446
Tasks vs. revenues of federal and state & local government, 447–49
Fiscal policy, 450

Automatic stabilizers, 452–53
Demand management, 453
Full employment budgets, 453
Tax cuts vs. expenditures, 455–56
Fiscal drag, 456
Revenue sharing, 456–57
Grants-in-aid, 456–57

QUESTIONS

1. What are the main differences between the public and the private sectors? Are these differences economic or political?

2. Show in a diagram how increased government expenditure can offset a demand gap. Show also how decreased government taxation can do the same.

3. What is meant by the automatic stabilizers? Give an example of how they might work if we had an increase in investment of $20 billion and the multiplier were 2; and if the increase in taxes and the decrease in public expenditure associated with the boom in investment were $3 billion and $1 billion, respectively.

4. What do you consider a better way of combating a mild recession—tax cuts or higher expenditures? Why? Suppose we had a deep recession, then what would you do?

5. In what sorts of economic conditions should the government run a surplus? Explain the idea of a full-employment budget.

6. Suppose the government cuts taxes by $10 billion and also cuts its expenditures by the same amount. Will this stimulate the economy? Suppose it raises its expenditures and also raises taxes? Would this be a good antirecession policy?

State and local finances

State and local finances are very sensitive to the condition of the economy. When national output goes down, state and local revenues (in real terms) also decline. Occasionally a state goes up against the national trend, but usually a national slowdown pulls down all state and local revenues. As household incomes fall, state and local income taxes decline. As household spending weakens, sales tax receipts fall. As employment worsens, revenues from payroll taxes fall off. All this results in pressure to cut back state and local budgets. And this, in turn, adds its undertow to the national picture, giving the recession additional force.

One suggested remedy for this built-in weakness of state and local finance is *countercyclical revenue sharing.* This remedy would automatically authorize federal grants-in-aid to state and local governments, when times were bad. Such grants would be sufficiently large to maintain state and local spending at the levels they would have reached if the recession has not occurred. This would allow state and local governments to make long-range plans without having to worry about short-run fluctuations in their revenues, and it would also prevent these governments from inadvertently worsening a national recession by cutting back on their own expenditures.

A difficulty in countercyclical revenue sharing lies in different regional growth rates. Incomes and output have been growing faster in the West and South, for example, than in the Midwest or Northeast. This uneven pace has been going on for some years, but has recently been exaggerated by high energy prices. The slower-growing Northeast and Midwest have to use expensive oil, whereas the faster-growing South and West have available to them the relatively cheaper energy source of regulated natural gas.

As a result, the lucky states in high-growth regions may show budget surpluses when the unlucky states in slow-growth regions show deficits. Countercyclical revenue sharing would then have to make the difficult choice of whether or not to seek to equalize differences or to ignore them.

There is a natural tendency to say ''Ignore them,'' because such differences hardly seem a matter of federal concern. But a second look shows us that the matter is not as simple as this. For the federal government itself is a partial cause of some of these very differences! When we look at federal individual income taxes received and grants-in-aid paid out in different areas, it is clear that the federal government is taking net spending power out of the slow-growing Northeast and Midwest and injecting it in the fast-growing South and West.

**Table 30 · 2   Ratio of federal expenditures to
federal tax collections, 1975**

Northeast	.86
Midwest	.76
South	1.14
West	1.20

Source: *National Journal,* June 26, 1976, p. 881.

Thus the federal government is contributing to the differences in growth rates, although we should stress that this is only one cause of the differences, and certainly not the main one.

What should the federal government do? Beginning with Franklin Roosevelt, it has followed a deliberate policy of trying to equalize regional differentials. TVA is probably the most well-known effort to aid one particular region, but actually nearly all federal programs are structured to give more help to low-income states than to high-income ones. If the South, for example, has been, and still is, favored in federal policy it is because, despite its rapid growth, its average family income remains below that of the Northeast, $12,236 compared to $14,481 in 1975.

Most people favor this federal equalizing role. The question today is whether, and to what degree, the policy should now be extended within states to localities. New York City, for example, lies in the middle of one of the richest regions in the nation, but it is a pocket of serious poverty. (In our next "Extra word" we shall look into the financial plight of New York.) If the federal government decides that it wants to help low-income localities, as well as low-income states, how should this be done? By federalizing welfare? By relieving localities of hospital expenses through federal health insurance? By giving federal aid to primary education in low-income cities? These are some of the suggestions that have been put forth. None of them is without problems. But at issue is the basic question whether we want the federal government to play the same role with localities that it has long played with regions. Once that issue is clarified, the problems will begin to take care of themselves.

Deficit spending

Up to this moment, we have been analyzing the public sector in terms of its effect on the demand for GNP. Now we are going to take a brief but necessary respite from our systematic examination of the various sources of demand for output. The use of the public sector as a source of deliberate demand management poses a question that we must understand before we can comfortably resume our inquiry. This is the question of the government debt.

Any government that uses its budget as a stabilizing device must be prepared to spend more than it takes in in taxes. On occasion it must purposefully plan a budget in which outgo exceeds income, leaving a negative figure called a *deficit*.

That raises a problem that alarms and perplexes many people. Like a business or consumer, the government cannot spend money it does not have. Therefore it must *borrow* the needed funds from individuals, firms, or banks in order to cover its deficit. Deficit spending, in other words, means the spending of borrowed money, money derived from the sale of government bonds.

31

461

Deficits and losses

Can the government safely run up a deficit? Let us begin to unravel this important but perplexing question by asking another: can a private business afford to run up a deficit?

There is one kind of deficit that a private business *cannot* afford: a deficit that comes from spending more money on current production than it will realize from its sale. This kind of deficit is called a *business loss;* and if losses are severe enough, a business firm will be forced to discontinue its operations.

But there is another kind of deficit, although it is not called by that name, in the operations of a private firm. This is an excess of expenditures over receipts brought about by spending money on *capital assets.* When the American Telephone and Telegraph Company or the Exxon Corporation uses its own savings or those of the public to build a new plant and new equipment, it does not show a "loss" on its annual statement to stockholders, even though its total expenditures on current costs and on capital may have been greater than sales. Instead, expenditures are divided into two kinds, one relating current costs to current income, and the other relegating expenditures on capital goods to an entirely separate "capital account." Instead of calling the excess of expenditures a deficit, they call it investment.*

Debts and assets

Can A.T.&T. or Exxon afford to run deficits of the latter kind indefinitely? We can answer the question by imagining

*Investment does not *require* a "deficit," since it can be financed out of current profits. But many expanding companies do spend more money on current and capital account than they take in through sales, and thereby incur a "deficit" for at least a part of their investment.

ourselves in an economic landscape with no disturbing changes in technology or in consumers' tastes, so that entrepreneurs can plan ahead with great safety. Now let us assume that in this comfortable economy, Exxon decides to build a new refinery, perhaps to take care of the growing population. To finance the plant, it issues new bonds, so that its new asset is matched by a new debt.

Now what about this debt? How long can Exxon afford to have its bonds outstanding?

The answer is—forever!

Remember that we have assumed an economy remaining changeless in tastes and techniques, so that each year the new refinery can turn out a quota of output, perfectly confident that it will be sold; and each year it can set aside a reserve for wear and tear, perfectly confident that the refinery is being properly depreciated. As a result, each year the debt must be as good as the year before—no better and no worse. The bondholder is sure of getting his interest, steadily earned, and he knows that the underlying asset is being fully maintained.

Admittedly, after a certain number of years the new factory will be worn out. But if our imaginary economy remains unchanged and if depreciation accruals have been properly set aside, when the old plant gives out, an identical new one will be built from these depreciation reserves. Meanwhile, the old debt, like the old plant, will also come to an end, for debts usually run for a fixed term of years. The Exxon Corporation must now pay back its debtholders in full. But how? The firm has accumulated a reserve to buy a new plant, but it has not accumulated a second reserve to repay its bondholders.

Nevertheless, the answer is simple enough. When the bonds come due in our

Table 31 · 1   Corporate net long-term debt*

Year	1929	1933	1940	1950	1960	1970	1971	1972	1973	1974	1975	1976
Billions of dollars	47	48	44	60	231	360	402	447	484	524	574	616

*Maturity over one year.

imaginary situation, the Exxon Corporation issues *new* bonds equal in value to the old ones. It then sells the new bonds and uses the new money it raises to pay off the old bondholders. When the transaction is done, a whole cycle is complete: both a new refinery and a new issue of bonds exist in place of the old. Everything is exactly as it was in the first place. Furthermore, as long as this cycle can be repeated, such a debt could safely exist in perpetuity! And why not? Its underlying asset also exists, eternally renewed, in perpetuity.

Real corporate debts

To be sure, not many businesses are run this way, for the obvious reason that tastes and techniques in the real world are anything but changeless. Indeed, there is every reason to believe that when a factory wears out it will *not* be replaced by another costing exactly as much and producing just the same commodity. Yet, highly stable businesses such as the Exxon Corporation or A.T.&T. do, in fact, continuously "refund" their bond issues, paying off old bonds with new ones, and never "paying back" their indebtedness as a whole. A.T.&T., for instance, actually increased its total indebtedness from $1.1 billion in 1929 to $31.8 billion in 1975. Exxon ran up its debt from $170.1 million in 1929 to $3.5 billion in 1975. And the credit rating of both companies today is as good as, or better than, it was in 1929.

Thus some individual enterprises that face conditions of stability similar to our imaginary situations do actually issue bonds "in perpetuity," paying back each issue when it is due, only to replace it with another (and, as we have seen, *bigger*) issue.

Total business debts

Most strong individual businesses can carry their debts indefinitely, and the business sector *as a whole* can easily do so. For although individual businesses may seek to retire their debts, as we look over the whole economy we can see that as one business extinguishes its debt, another is borrowing an even larger sum. Why larger? Because the *assets* of the total business sector are also steadily rising.

Table 31 · 1 shows this trend in the growth of corporate debt.*

Note that from 1929 through 1940, corporate debt *declined.* The shrinkage coincided with the years of depression and slow recovery, when additions to capital plant were small. But beginning with the onset of the postwar period, we see a very rapid increase in business indebtedness, an increase that continues down to our present day.

*We do not show the parallel rise in new equities (shares of stock), since changes in stock market prices play so large a role here. We might, however, add a mental note to the effect that business issues new stock each year, as well as new bonds. During the 1960s and early 1970s, net new stock issues have ranged from about $2 to $9 billion per annum.

If we think of this creation of debt (and equity) as part of the savings-investment process, the relationship between debts and assets should be clear. Debts are claims, and we remember how claims can arise as the financial counterpart of the process of real capital formation. Thus, rising debts on capital account are a sign that assets are also increasing. It is important to emphasize the *capital account*. Debts incurred to buy capital assets are very different from those incurred to pay current expenses. The latter have very little close connection with rising wealth, whereas when we see that debts on corporate capital account are rising, we can take for granted that assets are probably rising as well. The same is true, incidentally, for the ever-rising total of consumer debts that mirror a corresponding increase in consumers' assets. As our stock of houses grows, so does our total mortgage debt; as our personal inventories of cars, washing machines, and other appliances grow, so does our outstanding consumer indebtedness.

Government deficits

Can government, like business, borrow "indefinitely"? The question is important enough to warrant a careful answer. Hence, let us begin by comparing government borrowing and business borrowing.

One difference that springs quickly to mind is that businesses borrow in order to acquire productive assets. That is, matching the new claims on the business sector is additional real wealth that will provide for larger output. From this additional wealth, business will also receive the income to pay interest on its debt or dividends on its stock. But what of the government? Where are its productive assets?

We have already noted that the government budget includes dams, roads,

housing projects, and many other items that might be classified as assets. During the 1960s, federal expenditures for such civil construction projects averaged about $5 billion a year. Thus the total addition to the gross public debt during the 1960s (it rose from roughly $239 billion in 1960 to $619 billion in 1976) could be construed as merely the financial counterpart of the creation of public assets.

Why is it not so considered? Mainly because, as we have seen, the peculiar character of public expenditures leads us to lump together all public spending, regardless of kind. In many European countries, however, public capital expenditures are sharply differentiated from public current expenditures. If we had such a system, the government's deficit on capital account could then be viewed as the public equivalent of business's deficit on capital account. Such a change might considerably improve the rationality of much discussion concerning the government's deficit.

Sales vs. taxes

But there is still a difference. Private capital enhances the earning capacity of a private business, whereas most public capital, save for such assets as toll roads, does not "make money" for the public sector. Does this constitute a meaningful distinction?

We can understand, of course, why an individual business insists that its investment must be profitable. The actual money that the business will pay out in the course of making an investment will almost surely not return to the business that spent it. A shirt manufacturer, for instance, who invests in a new factory cannot hope that the builders of that factory will spend all their wages on the firm's shirts. The manufacturer knows that the money spent through investment will soon be dissipated throughout the economy and that it can be recaptured only through strenuous selling efforts.

Not quite so with a national government, however. Its income does not come from sales but from taxes, and those taxes reflect the general level of income of the country. Thus any and all that government lays out, just because it enters the general stream of incomes, redounds to the taxing capacity or, we might say, the "earning capacity" of government.

How much will come back to the government in taxes? That depends on two main factors: the impact of government spending on income via the multipler, and the incidence and progressivity of the tax structure. Under today's normal conditions, the government will recover about half or a little more of its expenditure.* But in any event, note that the government does not "lose" its money in the way that a business does. Whatever goes into the income stream is always *available* to the government as a source of taxes; but whatever goes into the income stream is not necessarily available to any single business as a source of sales.

This reasoning helps us understand why federal finance is different from state and local government finance. An expenditure made by New York City or New York State is apt to be respent in many other areas of the country. Thus taxable incomes in New York will not, in all probability, rise to match local spending. As a result, *state and local governments must look on their finances much as an individual business does.* The power of full fiscal recapture belongs solely to the federal government.

*We can make a rough estimate of the multiplier effect of additional public expenditure as 2 and of the share of an additional dollar of GNP going to federal taxes as about ⅓ (see p. 423). Thus $1 of public spending will create $2 of GNP, of which 65¢ will go back to the federal government.

The National Debt

Internal and external debts
This difference between the limited powers of recoupment of a single firm and the relatively limitless powers of a national government lies at the heart of the basic difference between business and government deficit spending. It helps us understand why the government has a capacity for financial operation that is inherently of a far higher order of magnitude than that of business. We can sum up this fundamental difference in the contrast between the *externality of business debts* and the *internality of national government debts.*

What do we mean by the externality of business debts? We simply mean that business firms owe their debts to someone distinct from themselves—someone over whom they have no control—whether this be bondholders or the bank from which they borrowed. Thus, to service or to pay back its debts, business must transfer funds from its own possession into the possession of outsiders. If this transfer cannot be made, if a business does not have the funds to pay its bondholders or its bank, it will go bankrupt.

The government is in a radically different position. Its bondholders, banks, and other people or institutions to whom it owes its debts belong to the same community as that whence it extracts its receipts. In other words, the government does not have to transfer its funds to an "outside" group to pay its bonds. It transfers them, instead, from some members of the national community over which it has legal powers (taxpayers) to other members of the *same* community (bondholders). The contrast is much the same as that between a family that owes a debt to another family, and a family in which the husband has borrowed money from his wife; or again between a firm that owes money to another, and a firm in which one branch has borrowed money from another. **Internal debts do not drain the resources of one community into another, but merely redistribute the claims among members of the same community.**

To help bring home the point, imagine that you and your roommate exchange $1000 IOUs. Each of you now has a $1,000 asset (an IOU from the other person) but each of you also has a $1,000 liability (the IOU each owes the other). The total debt of the room is now $2,000. But is your room richer or poorer, or is any individual in the room richer or poorer? The answer is obviously no. No one is better or worse off than before. And what happens if you now each pay off your IOUs? Once again no one is richer or poorer than before. The same thing is true at the national level. The national debt makes us neither richer nor poorer, since we (as taxpayers) owe it to ourselves (as bondholders).

Problems of a national debt

A government cannot always borrow without trouble, however. Important and difficult problems of money management are inseparable from a large debt. More important, the people or institutions from whom taxes are collected are not always exactly the same people and institutions to whom interest is paid, so that servicing a government debt often poses problems of *redistribution of income*. For instance, if all government bonds were owned by rich people and if all government taxation were regressive (i.e., proportionately heavier on low incomes), then servicing a government debt would mean transferring income from the poor to the rich. Considerations of equity aside, this would also probably involve distributing income from spenders to savers and would thereby intensify the problem of closing the savings gap.

In addition, a debt that a government owes to foreign citizens is *not* an internal debt. It is exactly like a debt that a corporation owes to an "outside" public, and it can involve payments that can cripple a nation. Do not forget that the internality of debts applies only to *national* debts held as bonds by members of the same community of people whose incomes contribute to government revenues.

Perpetual public debts

Can a national government therefore have a perpetual debt? We have seen that it can. To be sure, the debt must be constantly refunded, much as business refunds its debts, with new issues of bonds replacing the old. But like the business sector, we can expect the government debt in this way to be maintained indefinitely.

Will our public debt grow forever? That depends largely on what happens to our business debts and equities. If business debts and equities grow fast enough—that is, if we are creating enough assets through investment—there is no reason why government debts should grow. Government deficits, after all, are designed as *supplements* to private deficits. The rationale behind public borrowing is that it will be used only when the private sector is not providing enough expenditure to give us a large enough GNP to provide reasonably full employment.

Nonetheless, the prospect of a rising national debt bothers many people. Some day, they say, it will have to be repaid. Is this true? It may aid us to think about the problem if we try to answer the following questions:

1. Can we afford to pay interest on a rising debt?

The capacity to expand debts, both public and private, depends largely on the willingness of people to lend money, and this willingness in turn reflects their confidence that they will be paid interest regularly and will have their principal returned to them when their bonds are due.

We have seen how refunding can take care of the repayment problem. But what about interest? With a private firm, this requires that interest costs be kept to a modest fraction of sales, so that they can easily be covered. With government, similar financial prudence requires that interest costs stay well within the taxable capacity of government. The figures in Table 31·2 give us some perspective on this problem today.

It can be seen that interest is a much higher percentage of federal revenues than of corporate revenues. But there is a reason for this. Corporations are supposed to maximize their revenues; the government is not supposed to maximize its tax income. Hence we must also judge the size of the federal interest cost in comparison with the size of GNP, the total tax base from which the government can draw. Finally, we should know that interest as a percentage of all federal receipts has remained very steady in recent years, and it is actually much lower than in the

1920s, when interest costs amounted to about 20 to 30 percent of the federal budget.

2. Can we afford the burden of a rising debt?

What is the "burden" of a debt? For a firm, the question is easy to answer. It is the *interest cost* that must be borne by those who owe the debt. Here, of course, we are back to the externality of debts. The burden of a debt is the obligation it imposes to pay funds from one firm or community to another.

But we have seen that there is no such cost for an internal debt, such as that of a nation. The *cost* of the debt—that is, the taxes that must be levied to pay interest—becomes *income* to the very same community, as checks sent to bondholders for their interest income. Every penny that the debt costs our economy in taxes returns to our economy as income.

The same is also true of the principal of the debt. The debts we owe inside the nation we also *own* inside the nation—just as the case of the IOUs, or, again, just as an amount borrowed by Branch A of a multibranch firm is owed to Branch B of the same firm.

There is a further point here. Internal debts are debts that are considered as financial *assets* within the "family." Nobody within A.T.&T. considers its debts to be part of the assets of the firm, but many

Table 31 · 2   Debt and interest costs

	Net interest ($ billions)	Interest as proportionate cost
Nonfinancial corporations (1976)	$36	3.7 percent of gross corporate revenues
Federal government (1976)	28	{8.4 percent of receipts {1.7 percent of GNP

thousands of people in the U.S. consider the country's debts to be their assets. Indeed, everyone who owns a government bond considers it an asset. Thus in contrast to external debts, paying back an internal debt does not "lift a burden" from a community, because no burden existed in the first place! When a corporation pays off a debt to a bank, it is rid of an obligation to an outside claimant on its property. But when a husband pays his wife, the *family* is no richer, any more than the *firm* is better off if one branch reimburses another. So, too, with a nation. If a national debt is repaid, the national economy is not rid of an obligation to an outside claimant. We would be rid only of obligations owed to one another.

Real burdens

This is not to say— and the point is important—that government spending is costless. Consider for a moment the main cause of government spending over the past fifty years: the prosecution of three wars. There was surely a terrific cost in lives, health, and (in economic terms) in the use of factors of production to produce guns instead of butter. But note also that all of this cost is irrevocably and unbudgeably situated in the past. The cost of all wars is borne during the years when the wars are fought and must be measured in the destruction that was then caused and the opportunities for creating real wealth that were then missed. The debt inherited from these wars is no longer a "cost." Today it is only an instrument for the transfer of incomes within the American community.

So, too, with debts incurred to fight unemployment. The cost of unemployment is also borne once and for all at the time it occurs, and the benefits of the government spending to combat unem-

ployment will be enjoyed (or if the spending is ill-advised, the wastes of spending will be suffered) when that spending takes place. Afterward, the debt persists as a continuing means of transferring incomes, but the debt no longer has any connection to the "cost" for which it was incurred.

Costs, in other words, are *missed opportunities*, potential well-being not achieved. Debts, on the other hand (when they are held within a country) only transfer purchasing power and do not involve the nation in giving up its output to anyone else.

Indirect effects

Does this mean that there are no disadvantages whatsoever in a large national debt?

We have talked of one possible disadvantage, that of transferring incomes from spenders to savers, or possibly of transferring purchasing power from productive groups to unproductive groups. But we must pay heed to one other problem. This is the problem a rising debt may cause indirectly, but nonetheless painfully, *if it discourages private investment.*

This could be a very serious, real cost of government debts, were such a reaction to be widespread and long-lasting. It may well be (we are not sure) that the long drawn-out and never entirely successful recovery from the Great Depression was caused, to a considerable extent, by the adverse psychological impact of government deficit spending on business investment intentions. Business did not understand deficit spending and interpreted it either as the entering wedge of socialism (instead of a crash program to save capitalism) or as a wastrel and a harebrained economic scheme. To make matters worse, the amount of the government deficit (at its peak $4 billion), while large enough to

PERSONAL DEBTS AND PUBLIC DEBTS

In view of the fact that our national debt today figures out to approximately $2,880 for every man, woman, and child, it is not surprising that we frequently hear appeals to "common sense," telling us how much better we would be without this debt, and how our grandchildren will groan under its weight.

Is this true? We have already discussed the fact that internal debts are different from external debts, but let us press the point home from a different vantage point. Suppose we decided that we would "pay off" the debt. This would mean that our government bonds would be redeemed for cash. To get the cash, we would have to tax ourselves (unless we wanted to roll the printing presses), so that what we would really be doing would be transferring money from taxpayers to bondholders.

Would that be a net gain for the nation? Consider the typical holder of a government bond—a family, a bank, or a corporation. It now holds the world's safest and most readily-sold paper asset from which a regular income is obtained. After our debt is redeemed, our families, banks, and corporations will have two choices: (1) they can hold cash and get *no* income, or (2) they can invest in other securities that are slightly *less* safe. Are these investors better off? As for our grandchildren, it is true that if we pay off the debt they will not have to "carry" its weight. But to offset that, neither will they be carried by the comfortable government bonds they would otherwise have inherited. They will also be relieved from paying taxes to meet the interest on the debt. Alas, they will be relieved as well of the pleasure of depositing the green Treasury checks for interest payments that used to arrive twice a year.

---

frighten the business community, was not big enough to begin to exert an effective leverage on total demand, particularly under conditions of widespread unemployment and financial catastrophe.

Today, however, it is much less likely that deficit spending would be attended by a drop in private spending. A great deal that was new and frightening in thought and practice in the 1930s is today well-understood and tested. World War II was, after all, an immense laboratory demonstration of what public spending could do for GNP. The experience of recent years gives good reason to believe that deficit spending in the future will not cause a significant slowdown in private investment expenditure.

A modern version of this old fear is that the large demands for funds needed to finance and refinance the federal budget will "crowd out" private borrowers or force up interest rates to levels that will interfere with private expansion. The pros and cons of this argument need not delay us here. So far, there has been no demonstrated crowding-out of private borrowing.

The public sector again in perspective

We have spent enough time on the question of the debt. Now we must ask what is it that close examination of the problems of government finance reveals, making them look so different from what we expect. The answer is largely that we think of the government as if it were a firm or a household, when it is actually something else. *The government is a sector;* and if we want to think clearly about it, we must compare it, not to the maxims and activities of a household or a firm, but to those of the entire consumer sector or the entire business sector.

Then we can see that the government sector plays a role not too dissimilar from that of the business sector. We have seen how businesses, through their individual decisions to add to plant and equipment, act in concert to offset the savings of consumers. The government, we now see, acts in precisely the same way, except that its decisions, rather than reflecting the behavior of innumerable entrepreneurs in a search for profit, reflect the deliberate political will of the community itself.

Persons who do not understand the intersectoral relationships of the economy like to say that business must "live within its income" and that government acts irresponsibly in failing to do so. These critics fail to see that business does *not* live within its income, but borrows the savings of other sectors and thus typically and normally spends more than it takes in from its sales alone. By doing so, of course, it serves the invaluable function of providing an offset for saving that would otherwise create a demand gap and thereby precipitate a downward movement in economic activity.

Once this offsetting function is understood, it is not difficult to see that government, as well as business, can serve as a "spender" to offset savings, and that in the course of doing so, both government and business typically create new assets for the community.

Public and
private assets

Finally, we have seen something else that gives us a last insight into government spending. We have seen that the creation of earning assets is indispensable for business, because each asset constitutes the means by which an individual business seeks to recoup its own investment spending. But with the government, the definition of an "earning asset" can properly be much larger than with a business firm. The government does not need its assets to make money for itself directly, for the government's economic capability arises from its capacity to tax *all* incomes. So far as government is concerned, then, all that matters is that savings be turned into expenditures, and thereby into taxable incomes.

As a result, government can and should be motivated—even in a self-interested way—by a much wider view of the economic process than would be possible or proper for a single firm. Whereas a firm's assets are largely its capital goods, the assets of a nation are not only capital wealth but the whole productive capacity of its people. Thus government expenditures that redound to the health or well-being or education of its citizens are just as properly considered asset-building expenditures as are its expenditures on dams and roads.

FOCUS   The object of this lesson must be very plain. It is to reveal that most of the fears with regard to government "deficits" and "unbalanced budgets" are unfounded. People do not understand how government can safely go into debt, although households often cannot. The answer, of course, lies in the fact that the government is a sector and a household is not. The government can command revenues through taxation; no household can demand that society pay it an income. Moreover, a government debt is owed by some members of the national community to others; a household debt is owed to individuals or institutions who are outside the household. Of course these same arguments apply to the difference between national government and business debts or between federal and state debts.

This is not to say that national debts, even when internally held, are costless. They involve flows of income from taxpayers to interest receivers. The taxpayers may be households of modest means; the bondholders may be wealthy individuals or banks. Thus financing the debt may worsen income distribution or cause political friction. Moreover, even though government debts do not pose a burden on the nation as a whole, government spending is certainly not costless or burdenless.

These central ideas should be carefully mastered, for they recur constantly in the press or in political discussion. The best way to master the argument is to explain to yourself exactly how government debts resemble and differ from business debts. The questions will help you do this.

WORDS AND CONCEPTS YOU SHOULD KNOW

Deficits vs. losses, 462
Debts and assets, 462
Refunding a debt, 462–63
Business debts, 463–64

Government deficits, 464–65
Internal vs. external debts, 465–66
Perpetual public debts, 466–68
Problems of a national debt, 466–69

QUESTIONS

1. In what ways is a government deficit comparable to business spending for investment purposes? In what ways is it not?

2. If the government is going to go into debt, does it matter if it spends money for roads or for relief? For education or for weapons? Is there any connection between the use to which government spending is put and *the economic analysis of deficit spending?* Think hard about this; suppose you could show that some spending increased the productivity of the country and that other spending didn't. Would that influence your answer?

3. What is meant by the internality of debts? Is the debt of New York State internal? The debt of a country like Israel?

4. What relation do debts generally have to assets? Can business debts increase indefinitely? Can a family's? Can the debt of all consumers?

5. What are the real burdens of a national debt?

6. Trace out carefully all the consequences of paying back the national debt.

7. How would you explain to someone who is adamantly opposed to socialism that government deficit spending was (a) safe and (b) not necessarily "socialistic"? Or do you think it is not safe and that it is socialistic?

The New York City debt crisis

New York City's 1976 debt crisis was a vivid illustration of how even very large and seemingly rich government institutions *that are not national in scope* have limits to the amount of deficit finance they can safely undertake. Because any resident can leave New York, all the city's debt is potentially "external" to it.

As Table 31 • 3 shows, New York City's debt has been building up for a long period. But over most of these years its bonds were rated very highly by various companies, such as Standard and Poor's, that give ratings (risk designations) to private and public bonds. We can also see that the debt build-up accelerated after 1970, partly the consequence of financially imprudent actions on the part of New York City officials, partly the result of the 1974–1975 recession that hit many northeastern cities hard.

Table 31 • 3   New York City's debt ($ billions)

1950	$ 3
1960	6
1970	8
1974	14

To pay its bills, the city had to borrow larger and larger sums at the very time that the federal government had created a very tight situation in the money markets—a "credit crunch"—as part of its efforts to curb inflation. In a tight-money period, everyone has trouble borrowing, and banks and other lenders reexamine their credit applicants to determine who should be first in line and who should be last.

In this reexamination, New York City fared very badly. Its bond ratings suddenly fell. Overnight it became apparent to everyone that its debt and deficit had reached levels that could not be sustained in the long run. As a result, New York suddenly found itself unable to borrow. Not only was no one willing to lend funds to cover its current deficit, which had reached a staggering $700 million for the year 1974, but banks or other lenders would not even lend the city money to finance its outstanding debt. That is, the normal process of "rolling over" the debt, by replacing bonds that had become due with new bonds, was impossible.

What were the city's options at this point? All were unpleasant. One was to slash expenditures to the point at which the deficit would be eliminated, and revenues would cover debt repayments. This would have required so drastic a cut in expenditures (something on the order of 25 percent) that city officials feared the city could not be safely operated—too few police, firemen, sanitation workers, teachers.

Another option was to raise taxes by the amount needed to cover debt repayment. There were two problems here. First, the course would have required additional taxing powers for the city, which the state legislature was loathe to hand over. Second, city taxes, already among the highest in the nation, would have soared to such astronomical levels that many taxpayers would have voted with their feet, by moving out of the city to the suburbs or to neighboring states.

A third option was to default on debt repayments—simply not to honor the old bonds that came due. Here the difficulties were obvious. A default would still have left the city short of funds to cover its current deficit. And, of course, a default would have terribly damaged its prospects for selling bonds in the future. Once burned, twice shy in the bond market. Then, too, many worried lest a default in New York's bonds might not set off a series of defaults in other municipal bonds, giving rise to a serious panic in the capital markets.

Last was the hope that the federal government would save the situation, and city officials pled with the Ford administration to add a federal guarantee to city bonds, thereby assuring their salability, or for outright federal loans or grants to cover the deficit. But the Ford administration was not eager to rescue the city on easy terms. It felt that the city was itself responsible for much of its financial plight and that a rescue operation for New York could lead to requests from many other hard-pressed cities.

What happened in the end? All options were used to some extent. The city did cut its services. City taxes were raised. Default was technically avoided, but holders of city bonds were forced to exchange their securities for long-term bonds that carried lower interest rates. And the federal government made some necessary loans.

As part of the rescue operation, city finances were placed under the scrutiny of a committee of state, federal, and private representatives, who will monitor its union contracts and other expenditures, its taxes, and its budgets. If all goes well, the city should be back in the black by 1980. In all likelihood, however, by then the burden of local finance for other cities as well as New York will have been lightened through some kind of federalization of welfare payments, some kind of health insurance, and perhaps by still other revenue-sharing procedures. Short of such basic remedies, it is unlikely that New York or any other major municipality can enjoy fiscal health in the decades ahead.

The determination of GNP

We have reached the destination toward which we have been traveling for many chapters. We are finally in a position to understand how the forces of supply and demand determine the actual level of GNP that confronts us in daily life—"the state of the economy" that affects our employment prospects, our immediate well-being, our satisfaction or dissatisfaction with the way things are going.

Supply and Demand in Macro

As we have begun to see, the short-run, level of GNP is determined by the outcome of two opposing tendencies of supply and demand, just as the level of prices and quantities in a marketplace is "set" by the counterplay of these forces. In fact, the opposition of supply and demand play just as central a role in macroeconomics as in microeconomics. The crucial difference is that in macroeconomics we talk of supply and demand in relation to GNP, whereas in microeconomics we speak of them mainly in relation to price.

Short-run fixed supply

Here we come to an interesting analog with microeconomics. Perhaps we remember (and those who have not had microeconomics will easily understand) that in the short run we often take the supply curve in a given market as fixed. It may, for example, represent the catch of fish that a fishing fleet has brought back. The crucial thing is that this short-run supply of goods is unalterable, so that the only "active" force in determining price is the position and movement of the demand curve. Of course this does not mean that the supply curve plays no role in the price-determining process, for without supply there would be no market in the first place. But demand is where the action lies.

Exactly the same situation confronts us in considering the short-run determination of GNP. In the long run, of course, the supply of GNP expands as our production possibilities curve moves outward, as we saw in Chapter 24, "Supply of Output." But in the short run we take the p-p curve as given, and we are interested only in determining how much of our potential GNP will in fact be produced. Just to create a sharp image in your mind, you might think of the supply of GNP in the short run as the range of possibilities before an economy suffering a total general strike that brought its production down to zero, and that same economy using every resource at its command to bring production up to its limits.

Demand curve for GNP

What do the demand and supply curves for GNP look like? We will begin with the demand curve, for we are already very familiar with the forces that give rise to it. The demand curve will show us the amount of spending (demand for output) that will be generated by the community, as output rises from zero (the general strike) to the full utilization of existing resources.

Of course such a curve will slope upward. In Fig. 32 · 1 we see why this is so. The total spending on output, as we know, will consist of the sum of the spending for consumer goods, investment goods (we'll lump exports in here for convenience sake), and government goods. Panel I shows the spending for consumer goods (on the vertical axis). Even if output is zero, consumers will still spend money out of past savings to buy necessaries; and as production grows, pumping incomes into households, consumer spending will rise. Consumer demand is therefore a graphic representation of our familiar consumption function, $a + b(Y)$.

It is not so simple to draw an accurate investment or government demand function. Once again we assume that in the event of zero production (our general strike), both business and government would wish to make certain expenditures. As output rises, their expenditures would also increase because their incomes will rise, although we know that the relation between investment and government outlays and incomes is by no means so passive as is the case with household. Therefore we have drawn their respective demand functions with only a small upward slope, to emphasize the independent nature of these components of demand.

Panel IV shows that total demand is obtained by summing the demand of consumption, investment, and government. *It shows that total spending will rise as output rises: here is our upward sloping demand curve.*

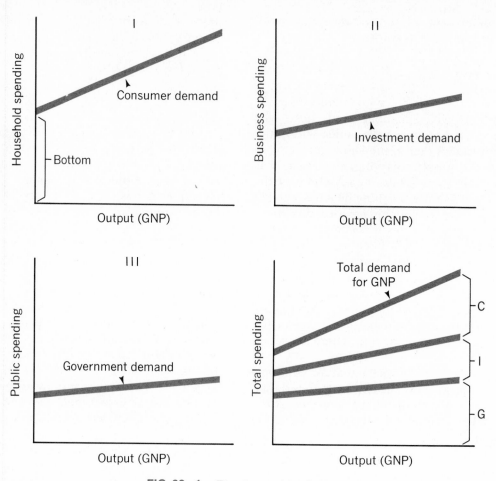

FIG. 32 · 1   The demand for GNP

***Short-run supply
curve***   Now what about the
short-run supply
curve? *It will show us
how much income—not spending—will
rise as we "relax" the general strike and
allow production to expand. Here we
make use of an identity that we learned in
Chapter 25. Incomes and output are always the same. The amount of income
made available to the community must
rise, dollar for dollar, with the amount of
production, because every dollar going*

*into production must become income to
some individual or institution.*

Our supply curve must show this
identity, and Fig. 32 · 2 makes clear that
the resulting curve will be a 45° line.
Notice that $OX = OY$, $OX' = OY'$, and so
on. Notice also that this supply curve is
fixed, in that the relation between incomes
(GNI) and output (GNP) is always the
same—identical. In our demand curve, the
relation between demand (or spending)
and output was not identical.

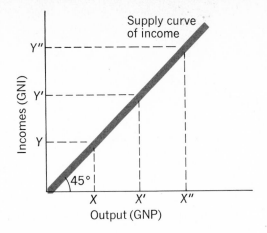

FIG. 32 · 2   Supply curve of income

This equilibrium shows us the money value of GNP brought about by the flow of demand against supply. It might, for example, indicate that this equilibrium value of GNP was $1.5 trillion. It does *not* tell us whether $1.5 trillion is a *good* size for GNP, any more than an equilibrium price of $20 for a commodity tells us whether that is a good or bad price from the viewpoint of buyers, producers, or the economy at large. We shall return to this critical point at the end of our chapter.

Equilibrium

It now remains only to put the demand and supply curves together, as in Fig. 32 · 3

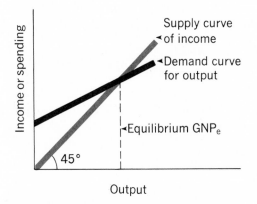

FIG. 32 · 3   Supply and demand for GNP

The circular flow

First, however, we must be sure we understand the nature of the GNP-establishing process, just as we must understand how a market works before we can get into issues of social policy connected with a market. Let us therefore take another step and connect our supply-demand equilibrium for GNP with our previous discussion of the circular flow. In Fig. 32 · 4 let us take out a thin slice of output at equilibrium and examine it under a magnifying glass.

As always, GNP can be analyzed into its component factor, indirect tax, and depreciation costs $(F + T + D)$ and into its

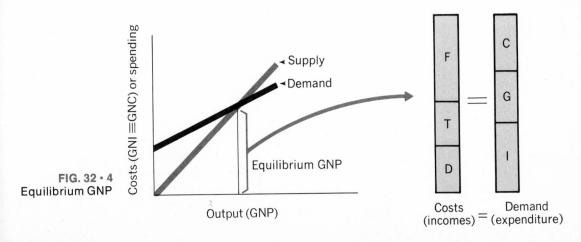

FIG. 32 · 4
Equilibrium GNP

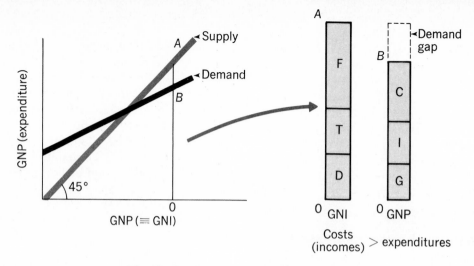

Fig. 32 · 5   Analysis of equilibrium GNP

component expenditures or demands (C + G + I). From our earlier discussion we recall that *all costs become incomes.* Therefore we could relabel the GNI axis Gross National Cost. What we see in our diagram is that at equilibrium, total demand for GNP equals total cost for GNP, much like our circular flow (p. 372).*

The demand gap   Now let us examine another slice of GNP that is above equilibrium, as in Fig. 32 · 5.

Here the cost of GNP is represented by *OA*, composed of *F + T + D*. But now the demand for GNP, *OB*, is less than *OA*. The difference consists of the demand gap, with which we are familiar.

If we had taken a slice below equilibrium, what would have been the situation? Now the demand curve lies above the supply curve. That is, total expenditures would have been larger than total costs. We would have had a demand surplus, rather than a demand gap. You might try

*But not *exactly* like our circular flow. We are now dealing with an economy that has saving and investing, profits and losses. Therefore we must think of the cost category "depreciation" (*D*) as including profits, and the expenditure category "investment" (*I*) as including net investment as well as replacement. We also continue to forget about exports, for simplicity.

drawing such a slice and seeing what the relation of *F + T + D* would be to *C + G + I*.

Movement to equilibrium   Now let us trace the forces that would push GNP toward the position of equilibrium. At the level of GNP that lies above equilibrium, entrepreneurs and public agencies would have paid out larger sums as costs (≡ incomes) than they would receive back as sales (≡ demand). Sales would be below the level of expectations that led to the employment of the factors in the first place. The first result would be a piling up of unsold inventories. Quickly, however, production plans would be revised downward. Fewer factors would be employed. With the fall in employment, incomes would fall; and as incomes fell, so would demand.

The analysis is exactly reversed if GNP is below equilibrium. Now demand (C + G + I) is greater than costs or incomes (F + T + D). Entrepreneurs will meet this extra demand out of inventories, and they will begin to plan for higher output, hiring more factors, and embarking on investment programs, thereby raising costs and incomes.

Note that in both cases, demand does not change as rapidly as income. In the first case it does not fall as fast as income; in the second it rises more slowly than income. This is mainly the result of the marginal propensity to consume, which, as we have seen, reflects the unwillingness of households to raise or lower their consumption spending as much as any change in their incomes.

Assuming for the moment that G and I remain unchanged, we can see that as the employment of factors increases because we have a demand surplus, or decreases because we have a gap, total demand must come closer to total costs or incomes. If there is a demand gap, employment will be reduced, but income will fall more rapidly than spending, and the gap will close. If there is a demand surplus, employment will rise, but income will rise faster than spending and the surplus will gradually disappear. In both cases, the economy will move toward equilibrium.

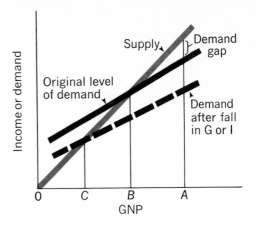

FIG. 32 · 6   A change in equilibrium GNP

Movement of equilibrium   If we now introduce changes in G and I, we can see that *the equilibrium point itself may move.* As the economy enters a downward spiral, investment spending may fall, outbalancing the supportive action of the automatic stabilizers. If this is the case, then the equilibrium level of GNP will move leftward, and the recession may not halt until we reach a very low level of GNP. This is, in fact, exactly what happens when a severe recession causes investment to fall, and the economy does not "bottom out" until GNP has fallen substantially, bringing with it considerable unemployment. Figure 32 · 6 shows us this process schematically.

Let us begin at a level of GNP indicated by output OA. A demand gap exists, and the level of output begins to fall toward OB, which is an equilibrium level at the *original level of demand.* But now the fall in GNP adversely affects I as well as C, so that the demand schedule for output shifts downward to the dotted line. Hence the economy will not settle at output OB but will continue downward until OC, where once again the demand for output equals the supply of output.

The expansion process   Just the opposite course of events helps us explain an upward movement. Suppose our economy "began" in equilibrium at output OC, following a severe recession. Now let us suppose that a rise in demand takes place. This could be the consequence of a burst of autonomous investment or simply the result of brighter expectations or the consequence of more government spending or any combination. If you will extend the line at OC up to the new demand curve (the upper line, this time), you can see that demand for output $(C + I + G)$ is now larger than the costs of output $(F + T + D)$.

As a result, entrepreneurs will find
their receipts rising. They will add factors,
rehiring labor that has been let go during
the recession and adding to their stock of
inventories or equipment. The economy
will begin to move toward the equilibrium
depicted by output OB.

Once again, however, we must be
careful not to imagine that the equilibrium
point is fixed. As the economy moves, so
will autonomous investment and government spending and taxing. Hence the final
equilibrium level may be less than, equal
to, or greater than OC, depending on
further shifts in the demand curve. But the
process by which an equilibrium level of
GNP is reached is always indicated by the
relationship between the supply curve of
GNI and the demand curve for GNP.

Another View of Equilibrium

*Saving and
investment*

Equilibrium is always
a complicated subject
to master, so let us fix
the matter in our minds by going over the
problem once more. Suppose that, by
means of a questionnaire, we are going to
predict the level of GNP for an island community. To simplify our task, we will ignore government and exports, so that we

can concentrate solely on consumption,
saving, and investment.

We begin by interrogating the island's
business community about their intentions
for next year's investment. Now we know
that some investment will be induced and
that, therefore, investment will partly be a
result of the island's level of income; but
again for simplification, we assume that
businesses have laid their plans for next
year. They tell us they intend to spend $30
million for new housing, plant, equipment, and other capital goods.

Next, our team of pollsters approaches
a carefully selected sample of the island's
householders and asks them what their
consumption and savings plans are for the
coming year. Here the answer will be a bit
disconcerting. Reflecting on their past
experience, our householders will reply:
"We can't say for sure. We'd *like* to spend
such-and-such an amount and save the
rest, but really it depends on what our incomes will be." Our poll, in other words,
will have to make inquiries about different
possibilities that reflect the island's
propensity to consume.

Now we tabulate our results, and find
that we have the schedule in Table 32 • 1

Table 32 • 1

Income	Consumption	Saving	Investment
		(In millions)	
$100	$75	$25	$30
110	80	30	30
120	85	35	30

Interplay of saving and investment

If we look at the last two columns, those for saving and investment, we can see a powerful cross play that will characterize our model economy at different levels of income, for the forces of investment and saving will not be in balance at all levels. At some levels, the propensity to save will outrun the act of purposeful investment; at others, the motivations to save will be less than the investment expenditures made by business firms. In fact, our island model shows that at only one level of income— $110 million—will the saving and investment schedules coincide.

What does it mean when intended savings are greater than the flow of intended investment? It means that people are *trying* to save out of their given incomes a larger amount than businesses are willing to invest. Now if we think back to the exposition of the economy in equilibrium, it will be clear what the result must be. The economy cannot maintain a closed circuit of income and expenditure if savings are larger than investment. This will simply give rise to a demand gap, the repercussions of which we have already explored.

But a similar lack of equilibrium results if intended savings are less than intended investment expenditure (or if in-vestment spending is greater than the propensity to save). Now business will be pumping out more than enough to offset the savings gap. The additional expenditures, over and above those that compensate for saving, will flow into the economy to create new incomes—and out of those new incomes, new savings.

Income and output will be stable, in other words, only when the flow of intended investment just compensates for the flow of intended saving. Investment and saving thus conduct a tug of war around this pivot point, driving the economy upward when intended investment exceeds the flow of intended saving; downward when it fails to offset saving. In Fig. 32•7 we show this crosscurrent in schematic form. Note that as incomes fall very low, householders will *dissave*.

Injections vs. leakages

We can easily make our graph more realistic by adding taxes (*T*) and imports (*M*) to savings, and exports (*X*) and government spending to investment. The vertical axis in Fig. 32•8 now shows all *leakages and injections*.

We recall that leakages are any acts, such as savings, increased taxes, profits or imports, that reduce spending. Similarly, injections are any acts, such as investment

FIG. 32•7   Saving and investment

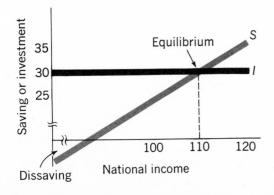

FIG. 32•8   Leakages and injections

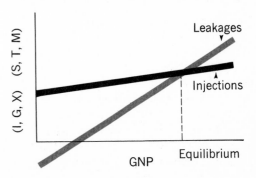

or higher government spending or rising exports or even a spontaneous jump in consumption, that lead to higher spending. And just to introduce another feature of the real world, we will tilt the injection line upward, on the assumption that induced investment will be an important constituent of total investment. The leakages curve will not be exactly the same shape as the savings curve, but it will reflect the general tendency of savings and imports and taxes to rise with income.

Intended and unintended S and I

The careful reader may have noted that we speak of *intended* savings and *intended* investment as the critical forces in establishing equilibrium. This is because there is a formal balance between *all* saving and investment (or all leakages and all injections) at every moment in the economy.

This sounds very strange. Are there not demand gaps, when saving is not offset by investment? Have we not just shown a schedule in which S was not equal to I at every level of income? How then can saving and investment be identities?

The answer is unexpectedly simple. Both saving and investment are made up of *intended* and *unintended* flows. I may intend to save a great deal, but if my income falls, my actual savings may be very small. As an entrepreneur, I may intend to invest nothing this year; but if sales are poor, I may end up with an unintended investment in unsold inventories. Thus, through fluctuations in incomes, profits, and inventories, people are constantly saving and investing more or less than they intended. These unintended changes make *total* savings equal to (identical with) *total* investment, whereas obviously the intended portions of saving or investment may be unequal.

Ex post and ex ante

Economists speak of the difference between intended and unintended activities as *ex ante* and *ex post. Ex ante* means "looking forward;" *ex post* means "looking backward." Ex ante savings and investment (or leakages and injections) are usually not equal. But at each and every moment, ex post savings and investment *will* be equal because someone will have been stuck with higher or lower inventories or greater or lesser saving than he intended ex ante.*

The strict balance between the formal accounting meanings of saving and investment and the tug-of-war between the active forces of *intended* saving and investment are sources of much confusion to students who ask why the terms are defined in this difficult way. In part we owe the answer to Keynes, who first defined S and I as identities. Since then the usage has become solidified because it is useful for purposes of national accounting.

For our purposes, we must learn to distinguish between the formal, ex post identity between total saving and investment (or between all leakages and all injections) and the active, ex ante difference between *intended* savings and investment (or *intended* saving, *intended* imports, *intended* business saving, etc., and *intended* additional expenditures of all kinds).

What matters in the determination of GNP are the *actions* people are taking—actions that lead them to try to save or to invest or that make them struggle to get rid of unintended inventories or to build up desired inventories. These are the kinds of activities that will be moving the economy up and down in the never-ending "quest"

*In the same way, purchases in any market must exactly equal sales at each and every moment, but that does not mean the market is in equilibrium at all times.

for its equilibrium point. The fact that at each moment ex post savings and investment are identical from the viewpoint of the economy's balance sheet is important only insofar as we are economic accountants. As analysts of the course of future GNP, we concentrate on the inequality of ex ante, intended actions.

The paradox of thrift

The fact that income must always move toward the level where the flows of intended saving and investment are equal leads to one of the most startling—and important—paradoxes of economics. This is the so-called paradox of thrift, a paradox that tells us that the *attempt to increase intended saving* may, under certain circumstances, lead to a *fall in actual saving.*

The paradox is not difficult for us to understand at this stage. An attempt to save, *when it is not matched with an equal willingness to invest or to increase government expenditure*, will cause a gap in demand. This means that business will not be getting back enough money to cover costs. Hence, production will be curtailed or costs will be slashed, with the result that incomes will fall. As incomes fall, savings will also fall, because the ability to save will be reduced. Thus, by a chain of activities working their influence on income and output, the effort to *increase* savings may end up with an actual *reduction* of savings.

This frustration of individual desires is perhaps the most striking instance of a common situation in economic life, the incompatibility between some kinds of individual behavior and some collective results. An individual farmer, for instance, may produce a larger crop in order to enjoy a bigger income; but if all farmers produce bigger crops, farm prices are apt to fall so heavily that farmers end up with less income. So too, a single family may wish to save a very large fraction of its income for reasons of financial prudence; but if all families seek to save a great deal of their incomes, the result—unless investment also rises—will be a fall in expenditure and a common failure to realize savings objectives. The paradox of thrift, in other words, teaches us that the freedom of behavior available to a few individuals cannot always be generalized to all individuals.*

The Multiplier

There remains only one part of the jigsaw puzzle to put into place. This is the integration of the *multiplier* into our analysis of the determination of GNP.

We remember that the essential point about the multiplier was that changes in investment, government spending, or exports resulted in larger changes in GNP because the additions to income were respent, creating still more new incomes. Further, we remember that the size of the multiplier effect depended on the marginal propensity to consume, the marginal propensity to tax, and the marginal propensity to buy imports as GNP rises. Now it remains only to show how this basic analytic concept enters into the determination of equilibrium GNP.

*The paradox of thrift is actually only a subtle instance of that type of faulty reasoning called the fallacy of composition. The fallacy consists of assuming that what is true of the individual case must also be true of all cases combined. The flaw in reasoning lies in our tendency to overlook "side effects" of individual actions (such as the decrease in spending associated with an individual's attempt to save more, or the increase in supply when a farmer markets his larger crop) which may be negligible in isolation but which are very important in the aggregate. See p. 111.

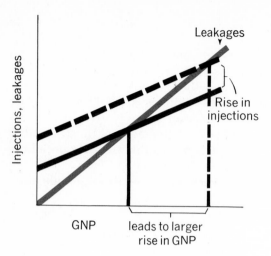

FIG. 32 • 9   Multiplier in graphic form

Let us begin with the diagram that shows injections and leakages, and let us now draw a new line showing an increase in injections (Fig. 32 • 9). Notice that the increase in GNP is larger than the increase in injections. *This is the multiplier itself in graphic form.*

We can see exactly the same result in our diagram of the supply and demand for GNP. Notice how a rise in the demand for GNP (a rise in injections) leads to a larger rise in the output of GNP (see Fig. 32 • 10).

FIG. 32 • 10   Multiplier and GNP

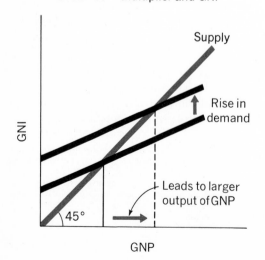

Slope of the leakage curve

Both diagrams also show that the relation between the original increase in injections and the resulting increase in GNP depends on the *slope* of the leakage line. Figure 32 • 11 shows us two different injection-GNP relationships that arise from differing slopes.

Notice how the *same* increase in spending (from *OA* to *OB* on the injections axis) leads to a much smaller increase in panel I GNP (from *OX* to *OY*), where the leakage slope is high, than in panel II (from *OX'* to *OY'*), where the slope is more gradual.

Why is the increase greater when the slope is more gradual? The answer should be obvious. The slope represents the marginal propensity to save, to tax, to import—in short, all the marginal propensities that give rise to leakages. If these propensities are high—if there are high leakages—then the slope of the leakage curve will be high. If it is low, the leakage curve will be flat.

A last look at equilibrium

Thus we finally understand how GNP reaches an equilibrium position after a change in demand. Here it is well to reiterate, however, that the word "equilibrium" does not imply a static, motionless state. Nor does it mean a desired state. We use the word only to denote the fact that *given* certain behavior patterns, there will be a determinate point to which their interaction will push the level of income; and *so long as the underlying patterns of injections and leakages remain unchanged, the forces they exert will keep income at this level.*

In fact, of course, the flows of spending and saving are continually changing, so that the equilibrium level of the economy is constantly shifting, like a Ping-Pong ball suspended in a rising jet of water. Equilibrium

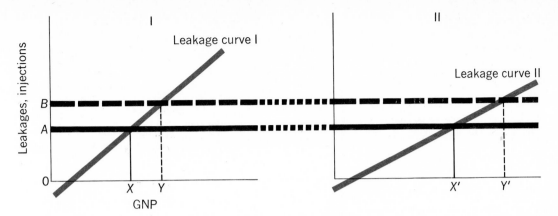

Leakage curve I

B

A

0

X   Y

GNP

II

Leakage curve II

X'   Y'

FIG. 32·11   Two multipliers

can thus be regarded as a target toward which the economy is constantly propelled by the push-pull between leakages and injections. The target may be attained but momentarily before the economy is again impelled to seek a new point of rest. What our diagrams and the underlying analysis explain for us, then, is not a single determinate point at which our economy will in fact settle down, but the *direction* it will go in quest of a resting place, as the dynamic forces of the system exert their pressures.

Equilibrium and full employment

Like the market for any single good or service, the market for all goods and services will find its equilibrium where the total quantity of goods demanded equals that supplied. But now we must note something of paramount importance. While the economy will automatically move to this equilibrium point, the point need not bring about the full employment of the factors of production, particularly labor. In Fig. 32 · 12, the economy at equilibrium produces a GNP indicated by GNP_e, but as our diagram indicates this may be well short of the volume of production needed to bring about full employment (GNP_f). Equilibrium can thus occur at any level of capacity utilization. All we can say about it—exactly as in the market

for goods and services—is that it is the level toward which the system will move, and from which it will not budge unless the demand curve shifts. It is certainly not necessarily the "right" level in any sense, and it may indeed be a very poor or unsatisfactory level, as during the Great Depression.

The aim of macroeconomic policy making is therefore to raise or lower the demand curve for GNP so that it crosses the supply curve at, or near, full employment or some other desired level of output. As we have already seen, this is an objective that is exceedingly difficult to accomplish; but at least we possess, in the body of macroeconomics itself, the basic intellectual tools needed to understand the nature of the task.

FIG. 32·12   Supply and demand for GNP

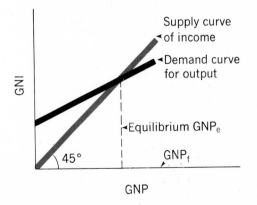

Supply curve of income

Demand curve for output

GNI

Equilibrium GNP_e

GNP_f

45°

GNP

You can see the relation between our multiplier analysis and our graphical analysis by thinking about the following two examples.

1. Suppose that the leakage fraction is 1; in other words, that we absorb *all* increases in income in additional savings, taxes, imports. What will the multiplier be? We know that the multiplier is 1/*mps*. If *mps* = 1,

THE MULTIPLIER ONCE AGAIN

then the multiplier fraction will be 1, and the increase in income will be 1 times the injection. In graphical terms, this looks like the figure on the left, below.

The leakage curve shows that each dollar of additional GNP leads to

another dollar of leakage. Hence the increase in GNP arising from an increase in injections is exactly equal to the original increase in injections. The multiplier is unity.

2. Now suppose that the leakage fraction is .5. The multiplier, once again, is 1/.5 or 2. In the figure on the right, we show the same relationship in graphical terms.

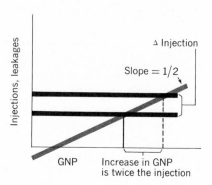

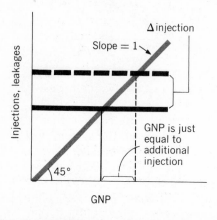

FOCUS There is one big idea to master in this lesson—how the level of GNP is determined by the outcome of two forces, supply and demand. We have now spent a number of chapters on the components of demand, so that it should not be difficult to grasp the idea of the demand curve. We see that it slopes upward because we are relating the volume of spending with the short-run level of "utilization" of output.

The supply curve is less self-evident. It is not a curve showing the growth of GNP over time, such as we might draw from a study of history. The supply curve shows us the amount of income that will be made available to households, firms, and government agencies at various levels of utilization of the economy. Keep in mind the parable of a functioning economy shut down by a general strike and then going back into full blast production. As we go from zero to full production, income payments will rise exactly as rapidly as the value of production. This is because, as we know, incomes are an identity with costs. Demand (spending) will rise more slowly than production, because demand will not fall to zero, even if production comes to a full stop.

Thus the supply curve becomes a fixed 45° slope, showing the income-cost identity; and against it we match the force of demand, represented by our upward sloping demand curve.

After this basic and essential idea, you must master the idea of a shift in demand. This will happen every time the flow of spending of any sector—usually business or government—suddenly changes.* With the shift in demand will come a new equilibrium, which will be determined by the amount of the shift in demand times the multiplier. You should be able to show that diagrammatically.

Finally, keep in mind that equilibrium is only a technical term. At equilibrium, savings and investment are equal. Costs and expenditures are also equal: $F + T + D = C + G + I$. There is no meaning to equilibrium other than that it is a stable level of GNP. That level may, however, be far below the point of full employment or optimum social benefit. The task of fiscal and monetary policy will then be to change the demand curve so that a socially satisfactory equilibrium is reached.

*As in microeconomics, a change in demand means a shift in the position of the demand curve, not a movement along it.

WORDS AND CONCEPTS YOU SHOULD KNOW

Demand for GNP, 475–76
Supply curve of GNP ≡ GNI, 475, 477
Equilibrium of GNP, 477–78
Changing equilibrium, 479
Saving and investment and GNP
   equilibrium, 480–81
Leakages and injections, 481–82

Intended and unintended S and I, 482
Ex post vs. ex ante, 482–83
Paradox of thrift, 483
Multiplier and slope of leadage curve, 483–
  84
Equilibrium and full employment, 485–86

QUESTIONS

1. Explain equilibrium in terms of the demand and supply for output. Why does the supply curve begin at the origin? Why doesn't the demand curve?

2. Draw an equilibrium diagram and indicate the volume of GNP it implies. Can you tell from the diagram if this is a full-employment GNP? What information would you need to draw in the various ranges of employment on the GNP axis?

3. Why is GNP an identity with GNI? Why does the "curve" of an identity always have a 45° slope? Demonstrate this by plotting a curve that relates the number of bachelors (horizontal axis) with the number of unmarried men (vertical axis).

4. Describe the "scenario" by which GNP is "pushed" from a point above equilibrium back to equilibrium. Do the same for a GNP below equilibrium.

5. Can you show why there is no demand gap at equilibrium?

6. Now show how a shift in the demand curve will bring about a new equilibrium point. What is the difference between this and the scenario in Question 4?

7. Show the interplay in the simplest form between savings and investment. Enlarge the saving/investment diagram to a leakage/injection diagram.

8. Show how the multiplier affects the size of changes in GNP, according to the slope of the leakage curve. What does this slope represent? Relate the slope to the *mps.*

9. What is the paradox of thrift? Can you turn it upside down? Suppose no one wanted to save, and everyone tried to spend all his income. What would happen to total income? What would probably happen to saving?

10. Suppose that an economy turns out to have the following consumption and saving schedule (in billions):

Income	Saving	Consumption
$400	$50	$350
450	55	395
500	60	440
550	70	480
600	85	515

Now suppose that firms intend to make investments of $60 billion during the year. What will be the level of income for the economy? If investment rises to $85 billion, then what will be its income? What would be the multiplier in this case?

National income and product accounts

The computation of GNP—requires a vast array of statistics. But behind the numbers lie very important concepts about what the statistics are supposed to represent. Every July issue of the *Survey of Current Business* (a publication of the U.S. Department of Commerce) contains a detailed set of National Accounts for the previous year. Here are a few of the basic tables, indispensable for anyone who wants to become a practicing economist in business or government.

As we now know, there are two ways of viewing the economy's output. One can add up all the costs of the outputs that the economy produces, or one can add up the expenditures of the groups in society who buy this output. Because every item of output is bought by someone, the sum of all costs must be identical with the sum of all expenditures.

Table 32·2 presents the official breakdown of these two ways of viewing total output. To avoid the confusion of calling the same total by two different names—GNP and GNI—the official National Income and Product Accounts refer to the sum of both columns as gross national product.

Table 32·2   National income and product accounts: 1976

Expenditures on output		Income (costs)	
Personal consumption expenditures	1078	1. Compensation of employees	1028
Durable goods	156	2. Proprietors income	97
Nondurable goods	440	3. Rental income	24
Services	482	4. Corporate profits and	
Gross private domestic investment	241	inventory valuation	
Nonresidential structures and		adjustment	119
equipment	160	5. Net interest	82
Residential structures	68	6. National income	1349
Change in inventories	13	7. Indirect business taxes	
Net exports of goods and services	7	and nontax liability	150
Exports	162	8. Business transfer payments	7
Imports	155	9. Statistical discrepancy	8
Government purchases	366	10. Minus: subsidies less current	
Federal	133	surplus of government	
defense	88	enterprises	1
nondefense	45	11. Net national product	1512
State and local	232	12. Capital consumption allowances	180
Gross national product	1692	13. Gross national (income) product	1692

A BREAKDOWN OF THE ACCOUNTS

Many of the terms in the table are now familiar to us. But let us examine a few that need special attention.

First, note (on the output side) that *change in inventories,* not inventories, enters the GNP. Since GNP measures goods and services produced during a given year, it takes into account goods that have been made and put into inventory only during that year. Goods held over in inventory from last year do not count.

What happens, then, if we sell goods out of last year's inventory and do not replace them? From the point of view of overall output, this is exactly the same as if a business firm did not replace its worn-out capital. By convention, we count this diminution in the level of our capital stock as a fall in the total value of output. Hence, the item "change in inventories" is the only item on the product side of GNP that can have a negative value. We cannot produce less than zero consumers goods or government output, but we can produce less goods for inventories than we need to maintain their levels.

The first strange term on the income side is the *inventory valuation adjustment* (no. 4 on the list). Remember than the GNP accounts attempt to measure incomes that are produced this year. If a corporation made a good last year but did not sell it, it will add that good to its inventories. If the good is actually sold this year when prices and costs have risen, measured corporate profits will be higher than they would have been if the good had been produced in the year in which it was sold. The good is sold for this year's higher prices, but the cost of making it is last year's lower cost. As a result, measured profits are higher because of production undertaken in the past. If we are trying to measure the profits that are produced this year, we must subtract these extra profits; and that is what the "valuation adjustment" attempts to do. (If prices and costs were falling, we would make a similar adjustment to increase this year's true profits.)

Indirect business taxes (no. 7) are already known to us. They are the sales and excise taxes (gas taxes, liquor taxes, etc.) that are assessed on the value of some products. Nontax *liabilities* (no. 7) refer to the public fees (licenses, etc.) that are collected from businesses. *Business transfer payments* (no. 8) are corporate gifts to nonprofit institutions, consumer bad debts, and a few other minor payments.

DISCREPANCIES AND SUBSIDIES

Now for the *statistical discrepancy* (no. 9). As we have seen, theoretically the gross national product must equal the gross national income. In practice, however, if you gave one group of statisticians the task of estimating the gross national product and another the task of estimating the gross national income, they would not come up with identical numbers. Why? Each side of the accounts is subject to measurement errors, and there is no reason why the errors should be identical. The statistical discrepancy is an estimate of these errors. Since the GNP and the GNI must be equal, we add a term (positive or negative) to the income side of the accounts to make them equal. The statistical discrepancy is simply the number that will make the final sum of both sides of the accounts the same.

Let's move on to *subsidies less current surplus of government enterprises* (no. 10). This entry refers to the profits and losses of TVA, state liquor stores, and other such government businesses. When the government loses money on one of its enterprises, these losses must be subtracted from the other income flows, because a loss means that incomes have been paid out, but no corresponding product has been produced.* If the losses were not subtracted, the gross national product would not equal the gross national income.

This loss is an example of a true but misleading number. The loss occurs because some activities that the ordinary individual would not consider a business are counted as a business. The agriculture support programs of the federal government are such a "business." When the government pays the farmer $2.00 for a bushel of corn and then sells it for $1.50, it incurs a loss. The purpose is to raise farm incomes through subsidies, but this shows up in the GNP accounts as though it were an accidental loss. Most government businesses that are designed to make money do in fact make money.

Subtracting subsidies less surpluses is just a convention. One could just as easily add surpluses less subsidies. In the former case you are subtracting a positive number; in the latter case you are adding a negative number.

NET VS. GROSS NATIONAL PRODUCT

In theory, the net national product (no. 11) is a more useful number than the gross national product. NNP measures the output of the economy that can be used for consumption or net investment after capital consumption allowances (no. 12)—funds that have been set aside to replace the capital equipment that has worn out in the process of production.

In fact, however, most analysts use the gross national product, GNP. There are three major reasons for this. First, it is very difficult to estimate how much capital equipment has in fact worn out during the year. As a result, the gross national product is a more accurate figure than the net national product. Second, the gross national product shows the value of all goods and services that are actually available for different uses. If we wished to use it all for consumption, we could. Third, old capital equipment is almost never replaced with identical equipment. We replace it instead

---

*If a private business loses money, this shows up in negative corporate profits or proprietor's income. Thus, this is really a government counterpart to these private income categories.

with the latest available equipment. Thus "replacement" investment actually becomes a source of economic growth. As a result, the net national product is much less useful than might be supposed from simply looking at definitions. Recent revisions of GNP accounts have attempted to make the figures for NNP more accurate by adjusting depreciation to reflect replacement prices. We will have to wait and see if this leads to a greater use of NNP as a measure of output.

PRODUCTION OF GNP

We have examined only the most basic table of GNP; and as we have said, there are dozens more. One of them is worth looking at. It shows who *produces* GNP, rather than who buys it or who earns it.

Table 32 · 3   Production of GNP, 1976

Private gross national product	1692.4
Business	1428.4
Farm	50.8
Nonfarm	1377.6
Households and institutions	55.9
Rest of the world	13.3
Gross government product	194.8

NOTE: Institutions are nonprofit private institutions such as universities and hospitals. They are added together with households, since neither attempts to earn profits. The *household* production of GNP includes the paid services of domestic servants and others.

Notice also that in this table, consumption and investment disappear, since all sectors—farms, households, governments, etc.—both consume and invest.

Many other tables are to be found in the Department of Commerce publications, including tables that show in much finer detail the large figures that appear on these tables. For anyone doing research on the activity of the economy, the annual July issue of the *Survey of Current Business* is indispensable. But before using these tables, one must understand the problems and pitfalls we have discussed in this introduction to the U.S. Income and Product Accounts.

Money

We have almost completed our analysis of the major elements of macroeconomics, and soon we can bring our analysis to bear on some major problems of the economy. But first there is a matter that we must integrate into our discussion. This is the role that money plays in fixing or changing the level of GNP, along with the other forces that we have come to know.

Actually, we have been talking about money throughout our exposition. After all, one cannot discuss expenditure without assuming the existence of money. But now we must look behind this unexamined assumption and find out exactly what we mean when we speak of money. This will entail two tasks. In this chapter we shall investigate the question of what money *is*—for, as we said in our Introduction, money is surely one of the most perplexing inventions of human society. Then in our next chapter, once we have come to understand what currency and gold and bank deposits are and how they come into being, we will look into the effect that money has on our economic operations.

33

The Supply of Money

Let us begin by asking "What is money?" Coin and currency are certainly money. But are checks money? Are the deposits from which we draw checks money? Are savings accounts money? Government bonds?

The answer is somewhat arbitrary. Basically, money is anything we can use to make purchases with. But there exists a spectrum of financial instruments that serve this purpose—a continuum that varies in liquidity, or the ease with which it can be used for purchasing. By law, coin and currency are money because they are defined by law as "legal tender": a seller *must* accept them as payment. Checks do not have to be accepted (we have all seen signs in restaurants saying, "WE DO NOT ACCEPT CHECKS"), although in fact checks are overwhelmingly the most prevalent means of payment. In some states checks can be written on savings accounts as well as on checking accounts. On occasion, government bonds are accepted as a means of payment.

Thus, a variety of things can be counted as money. Most economists, however, agree that what we mean by "money" is cash in the hands of the public plus checking accounts, and they call this sum M_1. Some economists prefer to include savings accounts, along with cash and checking accounts, and call this M_2. And some definitions of money go as high as M_8. (If savings banks expand their new accounts on which checks can be drawn, there will no longer be any difference between M_1 and M_2.)

Currency

Money, then, is mainly currency and checking accounts. In 1976 for example, our total money supply was $312 billion, of which $81 billion was currency in the hands of the public, and $231 billion was the total of checking accounts (or demand deposits, as they are also called).

Of the two kinds of "money," currency is the form most familiar to us. Yet there is a considerable mystery even about currency. Who determines how much currency there is? How is the supply of coins or bills regulated?

We often assume that the supply of currency is "set" by the government that "issues" it. Yet when we think about it, we realize that the government does not just

---

CREDIT CARDS

Money serves as a mechanism for storing potential purchasing power and for actually purchasing goods and services. Since cash and personal checks are the principal means for making these purchases, money has come to be defined as cash outside banks plus checking accounts. But what about credit cards. Shouldn't they be considered money?

Credit cards clearly can be used to make purchases, so that they appear on the surface to have a vital attribute of money. But a moment's reflection shows that in fact they *substitute* for cash or checks in which payment is finally made. The moment you pay your credit card bill, or the moment the credit card company pays the local merchant, the credit card is replaced by standard money. *Thus credit cards play the role of money only to the extent that credit bills are unpaid!*

In this role credit cards are not unique. Any unpaid bill or charge account is like money, in that you are able to purchase goods and services in exchange for your personal IOU. In a sense, each person is able to "print" money to the extent that he can persuade people to accept his IOUs.

For most of us, that extent is very limited.

From an economist's point of view, the value of all outstanding trade credit (unpaid bills, unpaid charge accounts, or credit cards) *should* be considered money. It is not included in the official statistics for two reasons. First, it is difficult or impossible to figure how much trade credit is outstanding at any moment. Second, fluctuations in trade credit do not have a big impact on the economy. Ordinarily, the value of trade credit does not vary much, and therefore trade credit does not give rise to substantial changes in the effective money supply.

hand out money, and certainly not coins or bills. When the government pays people, it is nearly always by check.

Then who does fix the amount of currency in circulation? You can answer the question by asking how you yourself determine how much currency you will carry. If you think about it, the answer is that you "cash" a check when you need more currency than you have, and you put the currency back into your checking account when you have more than you need.

What you do, everyone does. The amount of cash that the public holds at any time is no more and no less than the amount that it *wants* to hold. When it needs more—at Christmas, for instance—the public draws currency by cashing checks on its own checking accounts; and when Christmas is past, shopkeepers (who have received the public's currency) return it to their checking accounts.

Thus the amount of currency we have bears an obvious, important relation to the size of our bank accounts, for we can't write checks for cash if our accounts will not cover them.

Does this mean, then, that the banks have as much currency in their vaults as the total of our checking accounts? No, it does not. But to understand that, let us follow the course of some currency that we deposit in our banks for credit to our accounts.

Bookkeeping money

When you put money into a commercial bank,* the bank does not hold that money for you as a pile of specially earmarked bills or as a bundle of checks made out to you from some payer. The bank takes notice of your deposit simply by crediting your "account," a bookkeeping page recording your present "balance." After the amount of the currency or check has been credited to you, the currency is put away with the bank's general store of vault cash and the checks are sent to the banks from which they came, where they will be charged against the accounts of the people who wrote them.

There is probably no misconception in economics harder to dispel than the idea that banks are warehouses stuffed with money. In point of fact, however, you might search as hard as you pleased in your bank, but you would find no money that was yours other than a bookkeeping account in your name. This seems like a very unreal form of money; and yet, the fact that you can present a check at the teller's window and convert your bookkeeping account into cash proves that your account must nonetheless be "real."

But suppose that you and all the other depositors tried to convert your accounts into cash on the same day. You would then find something shocking. There would not be nearly enough cash in the bank's till to cover the total withdrawals. In 1976 for instance, total demand deposits in the United States amounted to about $231 billion. But the total amount of coin currency held by the banks was only $9 billion!

At first blush, this seems like a highly dangerous state of affairs. But second thoughts are more reassuring. After all, most of us put money into a bank because we do *not* need it immediately, or because making payments in cash is a nuisance compared with making them by check. Yet, there is always the chance—more than that, the certainty—that some depositors *will* want their money in currency. How much currency will the banks need then? What will be a proper reserve for them to hold?

---

*A commercial bank is a bank that is empowered by law to offer checking services. It may also have savings accounts.

Federal reserve system

For many years, the banks themselves decided what reserve ratio constituted a safe proportion of currency to hold against their demand deposits (the technical name for checking accounts). Today, however, most large banks are members of the Federal Reserve, a central banking system established in 1913 to strengthen the banking activities of the nation. Under the Federal Reserve System, the nation is divided into twelve districts, each with a Federal Reserve Bank owned (but not really controlled) by the member banks of its district. In turn, the twelve Reserve Banks are themselves coordinated by a seven-member Federal Reserve Board in Washington. Since the President, with the advice and consent of the Senate, appoints members of the board for fourteen-year terms, they constitute a body that has been purposely established as an independent nonpolitical monetary authority.*

One of the most important functions of the Federal Reserve Board is to establish reserve ratios for different categories of banks, within limits set by Congress. Historically these reserve ratios have ranged between 13 and 26 percent of demand deposits for city banks, with a somewhat smaller reserve ratio for country banks. Today, reserve ratios are determined by size, and they vary between 16 percent for the largest banks and 7 percent for the smallest. The Federal Reserve Board also sets reserve requirements for "time" deposits (the technical term for savings deposits). These range from 1 to 6 percent, depending on the ease of withdrawal.

The banks' bank

Yet here is something odd! We noticed that in 1976 the total amount of deposits was $231 billion and that banks' holdings of coin and currency were only $9 billion. This is much less than the 18 percent—or even 8 percent—reserve against deposits established by the Federal Reserve Board. How can this be?

The answer is that cash is not the only reserve a bank holds against deposits. Claims on other banks are also held as its reserve.

What are these claims? Suppose, in your account in Bank A, you deposit a check from someone who has an account in Bank B. Bank A credits your account and then presents the check to Bank B for "payment." By "payment" Bank A does not mean coin and currency, however. Instead, Bank A and Bank B settle their transaction at still *another* bank where both Bank A and Bank B have their own accounts. These accounts are with the twelve Federal Reserve Banks of the country, where all banks who are members of the Federal Reserve System (and this accounts for banks holding most of the deposits in our banking system) *must* open accounts. Thus at the Federal Reserve Bank, Bank A's account will be credited, and Bank B's account will be debited, in this way moving reserves from one bank to the other.†

The Federal Reserve Banks serve their member banks in exactly the same way as the member banks serve the public. Member banks automatically deposit in their Federal Reserve accounts all checks they get from other banks. As a result, banks are constantly "clearing" their checks with one another through the Federal Reserve System, because their depositors are constantly writing checks on their own banks payable to someone who

---

*The independence of the Federal Reserve is a perennially controversial issue. See "An extra word" at the end of this chapter.

†When money is put into a bank account, the account is credited; when money is taken out, the account is debited.

banks elsewhere. Meanwhile, the balance that each bank maintains at the Federal Reserve—that is, the claim it has on other banks—counts, as much as any currency, as part of its reserve against deposits.

In 1976, therefore, when demand deposits were $231 billion and cash in the banks only $9 billion, we would expect the member banks to have had heavy accounts with the Federal Reserve banks. And so they did—$26 billion in all. Thus, total reserves of the banks were $35 billion ($9 billion in cash plus $26 billion in Federal Reserve accounts), enough to satisfy the legal requirements of the Fed.

Fractional reserves

Thus we see that our banks operate on what is called a *fractional reserve system*. That is, a certain specified fraction of all demand deposits must be kept "on hand" at all times in cash or at the Fed. The size of the minimum fraction is determined by the Federal Reserve, for reasons of control that we shall shortly learn about. It is *not* determined, as we might be tempted to think, to provide a "safe" backing for our bank deposits. For under *any* fractional system, if *all* depositors decided to draw out their accounts in currency and coin from all banks at the same time, the banks would be unable to meet the demand for cash and would have to close. We call this a "run" on the banking system. Needless to say, runs can be terrifying and destructive economic phenomena.*

Why, then, do we court the risk of runs, however small this risk may be? What is the benefit of a fractional banking system? To answer that, let us look into our bank again.

---

*A "run" on the banking system is no longer so much of a threat as in the past, because the Federal Reserve could supply its members with vast amounts of cash. We shall learn how, later in this chapter.

Loans and investments

Suppose its customers have given our bank $1 million in deposits and that the Federal Reserve Board requirements are 20 percent, a simpler figure to work with than the actual one. Then we know that our bank must at all times keep $200,000, either in currency in its own till or in its demand deposit at the Federal Reserve Bank.

But having taken care of that requirement, what does the bank do with the remaining deposits? If it simply lets them sit, either as vault cash or as a deposit at the Federal Reserve, our bank will be very "liquid," but it will have no way of making an income. Unless it charges a very high fee for its checking services, it will have to go out of business.

And yet there is an obvious way for the bank to make an income, while performing a valuable service. The bank can use all the cash and check claims it does not need for its reserve to make *loans* to businesses or families or to make financial *investments* in corporate or government bonds. It will thereby not only earn an income, but it will assist the process of business investment and government borrowing. Thus the mechanics of the banking system lead us back to the concerns at the very center of our previous analysis.

Inside the Banking System

Fractional reserves allow banks to lend, or to invest in securities, part of the funds that have been deposited with them. But that is not the only usefulness of the fractional reserve system. It works as well to help enlarge or diminish the supply of

ORIGINAL BANK

Assets	Liabilities
$1,000,000 (cash and checks)	$1,000,000 (money owed to depositors)
Total $1,000,000	**Total $1,000,000**

investible or loanable funds, as the occasion demands. Let us follow how this process works. To make the mechanics of banking clear, we are going to look at the actual books of the bank—in simplified form, of course—so that we can see how the process of lending and investing appears to the banker himself.

Assets and liabilities

We begin by introducing two basic elements of business accounting: *assets* and *liabilities*. Every student at some time or another has seen the balance sheet of a firm, and many have wondered how total assets always equal total liabilities. The reason is very simple. Assets are all the things or claims a business owns. Liabilities are claims against those assets—some of them the claims of creditors, some the claims of owners (called the Net Worth of the business). Since assets show everything that a business owns, and since liabilities show how claims against these self-same things are divided between creditors and owners, it is obvious that the two sides of the balance sheet must always come to exactly the same total. The total of assets and the total of liabilities are an identity.

T accounts

Businesses show their financial condition on a *balance sheet* on which all items on the left side represent assets and all those on the right side represent liabilities. By using a simple two-column balance sheet (called a "T account" because it looks like a T), we can follow very clearly what happens to our bank as we deposit money in it or as it makes loans or investments. (See T account above.)

We start off with the example we have just used, in which we open a brand new bank with $1 million in cash and checks on other banks. Accordingly, our first entry in the T account shows the two sides of this transaction. Notice that our bank has gained an asset of $1 million, the cash and checks it now owns, and that it has simultaneously gained $1 million in liabilities, the deposits it *owes* to its depositors (who can withdraw their money).

As we know, however, our bank will not keep all its newly-gained cash and checks in the till. It may hang on to some of the cash, but it will send all the checks it has received, plus any currency that it feels it does not need, to the Fed for deposit in its account there. As a result, its T account will now look like this:

ORIGINAL BANK

Assets		Liabilities	
Vault Cash	$100,000	Deposits	$1,000,000
Deposit at Fed	900,000		
Total	**$1,000,000***	**Total**	**$1,000,000**

*If you will examine some bank balance sheets, you will see these items listed as "Cash and due from banks." This means, of course, cash in their own vaults plus their balance at the Fed.

Excess reserves   Now we recall from our previous discussion that our bank does not want to remain in this very liquid, but very unprofitable, position. According to the law, it must retain only a certain percentage of its deposits in cash or at the Federal Reserve—20 percent in our hypothetical example. All the rest it is free to lend or invest. As things now stand, however, it has $1 million in reserves—$800,000 more than it needs. Hence, let us suppose that it decides to put these *excess reserves* to work by lending that amount to a sound business risk. (Note that banks do not lend the excess reserves themselves. These reserves, cash and deposits at the Fed, remain right where they are. Their function is to tell the banks how much they may loan or invest.)

Making a loan   Assume now that the Smith Corporation, a well-known firm, comes in for a loan of $800,000. Our bank is happy to lend them that amount. But "making a loan" does not mean that the bank now pays the company in cash out of its vaults. Rather, *it makes a loan by opening a new checking account for the firm* and by crediting that account with $800,000. (Of if, as is likely, the Smith firm already has an account with the bank, it will simply credit the proceeds of the loan to that account.)

Now our T account shows some interesting changes.

There are several things to note about this transaction. First, our bank's reserves (its cash and deposit at the Fed) have not yet changed. The $1 million in reserves are still there.

Second, notice that the Smith Corporation loan counts as a new asset for the bank because the bank now has a legal claim against the company for that amount. (The interest on the loan is not shown in the balance sheet; but when it is paid, it will show up as an addition to the bank's cash.)

Third, deposits have increased by $800,000. Note, however, that this $800,000 was not paid to the Smith firm out of anyone else's account in the bank. It is a new checking account, one that did not exist before. As a result, the supply of money is also up! More about this shortly.

The loan is spent   Was it safe to open this new account for the company? Well, we might see whether our reserves are now sufficient to cover the Smith Corporation's account as well as the original deposit accounts. A glance reveals that all is well. We still have $1 million in reserves against $1.8 million in deposits. Our reserve ratio is much higher than the 20 percent required by law.

It is so much higher, in fact, that we might be tempted to make another loan to the next customer who requests one, and in that way further increase our earning capacity. But an experienced banker shakes

ORIGINAL BANK

Assets		Liabilities	
Cash and at Fed	$1,000,000	Original deposits	$1,000,000
Loan (Smith Corp.)	800,000	New deposit (Smith Corp.)	800,000
Total	**$1,800,000**	**Total**	**$1,800,000**

his head. "The Smith Corporation did not take out a loan and agree to pay interest on it just for the pleasure of letting that money sit with you," he explains. "Very shortly, the company will be writing checks on its balance to pay for goods or services; and when it does, you will need every penny of the reserve you now have."

That, indeed, is the case. Within a few days we find that our bank's account at the Federal Reserve Bank has been charged with a check for $800,000 written by the Smith Corporation in favor of the Jones Corporation, which carries its account at another bank. Now we find that our T account has changed dramatically to look like this:

Now if we refigure our reserves we find that they are just right. We are required to have $200,000 in vault cash or in our Federal Reserve account against our $1 million in deposits. That is exactly the amount we have left. Our bank is now fully "loaned up."

Expanding the money supply

But the banking system is not yet fully loaned up. So far, we have traced what happened to only our bank when the Smith Corporation spent the money in its deposit account. Now we must trace the effect of this action on the deposits and reserves of other banks.

We begin with the bank in which the

ORIGINAL BANK

Assets		Liabilities	
Cash and at Fed	$ 200,000	Original deposits	$1,000,000
Loan (Smith Corp.)	800,000	Smith Corp. deposits	0
Total	**$1,000,000**	**Total**	**$1,000,000**

SECOND BANK

Assets		Liabilities	
Cash and at Fed	$800,000	Deposit (Jones Corp.)	$800,000
Total	**$800,000**	**Total**	**$800,000**

Let us see exactly what has happened. First, the Smith Corporation's check has been charged against our account at the Fed and has reduced it from $900,000 to $100,000. Together with the $100,000 cash in our vault, this gives us $200,000 in reserves.

Second, the Smith Corporation's deposit is entirely gone, although its loan agreement remains with us as an asset.

Jones Corporation deposits the check it has just received from the Smith Corporation. As the above T account shows, the Jones Corporation's bank now finds itself in exactly the same position as our bank was when we opened it with $1 million in new deposits, except that the addition to this "second generation" bank is smaller than the addition to the "first generation" bank.

SECOND BANK
(after Brown Co. spends the proceeds of its loan)

Assets		Liabilities	
Cash and at Fed	$160,000	Deposits (Jones Corp.)	$800,000
Loan (to Brown Co.)	640,000	Deposits (Brown Co.)	0
Total	**$800,000**	**Total**	**$800,000**

THIRD BANK
(after Black Co. gets the check of Brown Co.)

Assets		Liabilities	
Cash and at Fed	$640,000	Deposit (Black Co.)	$640,000
Total	**$640,000**	**Total**	**$640,000**

As we can see, our second generation bank has gained $800,000 in cash and in deposits. Since it needs only 20 percent of this for required reserves, it finds itself with $640,000 excess reserves, which it is now free to use to make loans as investments. Suppose that it extends a loan to the Brown Company and that the Brown Company shortly thereafter spends the proceeds of that loan at the Black Company, which banks at yet a third bank. The two T accounts above show how the total deposits will now be affected.

As Fig. 33 • 1 makes clear, the process will not stop here but can continue from one bank to the next as long as any lending power remains. Notice, however, that this lending power gets smaller and smaller and will eventually reach zero.

Expansion of the Money Supply

If we now look at the bottom of Fig. 33 • 1 we will see something very important.

Every time any bank in this chain of transactions has opened an account for a new borrower, *the supply of money has increased*. Remember that the supply of money is the sum of currency outside the banking system (i.e., in our own pockets) plus the total of demand deposits. As our chain of banks kept opening new accounts, it was simultaneously expanding the total check-writing capacity of the economy. Thus, money has materialized, seemingly out of thin air.

Now how can this be? If we tell any banker in the chain that he has "created" money, he will protest vehemently. The loans he made, he will insist, were backed at the time he made them by excess reserves as large as the loan itself. Just as we had $800,000 in excess reserves when we made our initial loan to the Smith Corporation, so every subsequent loan was always backed 100 percent by unused reserves when it was made.

Our bankers are perfectly correct when they tell us that they never, never lend a penny more than they have. Money is not created in the lending process be-

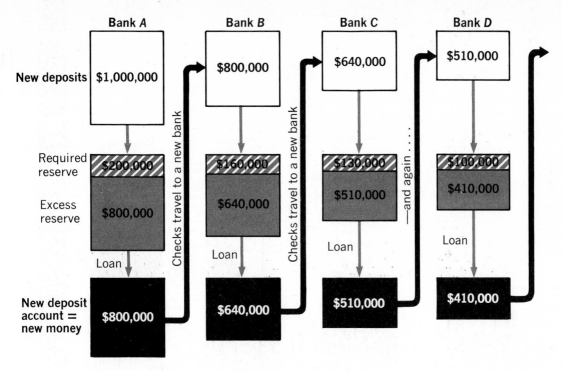

Bank A   **Bank B**   **Bank C**   **Bank D**

New deposits: $1,000,000 / $800,000 / $640,000 / $510,000

Required reserve: $200,000 / $160,000 / $130,000 / $100,000

Excess reserve: $800,000 / $640,000 / $510,000 / $410,000

Loan

New deposit account = new money: $800,000 / $640,000 / $510,000 / $410,000

Checks travel to a new bank — and again . . . . .

FIG. 33 · 1   Expansion of the money supply

cause a banker lends money he doesn't have. **Money is created because you and I generally pay each other by checks that give us claims against each other's bank.** If we constantly cashed the checks we exchanged, no new money would be created. But we do not. We deposit each other's checks in our own bank accounts; and in doing so, we give our banks more reserves than they need against the deposits we have just made. These new excess reserves make it possible for our banks to lend or invest, and thereby to open still more deposit accounts, which in turn lead to new reserves.

Limits on the expansion

This all sounds a little frightening. Does it mean that the money supply can go on expanding indefinitely from a single new deposit? Wouldn't that be extremely dangerous?

It would of course be very dangerous, but there is no possibility that it can happen. For having understood how the supply of money can expand from an original increase in deposits, we may now understand equally well what keeps an expansion within bounds.

1. **Not every loan generates an increase in bank deposits.**

If our bank had opened a loan account for the Smith Corporation at the same time that another firm had paid off a similar loan, there would have been no original expansion in bank deposits. In that case, the addition of $800,000 to the Smith account would have been exactly balanced by a decline of $800,000 in someone else's account. Even if that decline would have taken place in a different bank, it would still mean that the nation's total of bank deposits would not have risen, and therefore no new money would have been created. Thus, only net additions to loans have an expansionary effect. We will shortly see how such net additions arise in the first place.

2. **There is a limit to the rise in money supply from a single increase in deposits.**

As Fig. 33 • 1 shows, in the chain of deposit expansion each successive bank has a smaller increase in deposits, because each bank has to keep some of its newly gained cash or checks as reserve. Hence the amount of *excess* reserves, against which loans can be made, steadily falls.

Further, we can see that the amount of the total monetary expansion from an original net increase in deposits is governed by the size of the fraction that has to be kept aside each time as reserve. In fact, we can see that just as with the multiplier, the cumulative effect of an increase in deposits will be determined by the reciprocal of the reserve fraction. If each bank must keep one-fifth of its increased deposits as reserves, then the

cumulative effect of an original increase in deposits, when it has expanded through the system, is five times the original increase. If reserves are one-fourth, the expansion is limited to four times the original increase, and so on.

If M is the money supply, D is net new deposits, and r is the reserve ratio, it follows that:

$$\Delta M = 1/r \times \Delta D$$

Notice that this formula is exactly the same as that for the multiplier.*

3. **The monetary expansion process can work in reverse.**

Suppose that the banking system as a whole suffers a net loss of deposits. Instead of putting $1 million into a bank, the public takes it out in cash. The bank will now have too few reserves, and it will have to cut down its loans or sell its investments to gain the reserves it needs. In turn, as borrowers pay off their loans, or as bond buyers pay for their securities, cash will drain from other banks who will now find *their* reserves too small in relation to their deposits. In turn, they will therefore have to sell more investments or curtail still other loans, and this again will squeeze still other banks and reduce their reserves, with the same consequences.

Thus, just as an original expansion in deposits can lead to a multiple expansion, so an original contraction in deposits can lead to a multiple contraction. The size of this contraction is also limited by the reciprocal of the reserve fraction. If banks have to hold a 25 percent reserve, then an original fall of $100,000 in deposits will lead to a total fall of $400,000, assuming

---

*Why is ΔM determined by multiplying ΔD by $1/r$? Same reason as the multiplier. See box on p. 422.

that the system was fully "loaned up" to begin with. If they had to hold a 20 percent reserve, a fall of $100,000 could pyramid to $500,000.

4. The expansion process may not be fully carried through.

We have assumed that each bank in the chain always lends out an amount equal to its excess reserve, but this may not be the case. The third or fifth bank along the way may have trouble finding a credit-worthy customer and may decide—for the moment, anyway—to sit on its excess reserves. Or borrowers along the chain may take out cash from some of their new deposits and thereby reduce the banks' reserves and their lending powers. Thus the potential expansion may be only partially realized.

5. The expansion process takes time.

Like the multiplier process, the expansion of the money supply encounters many "frictions" in real life. Banks do not instantly expand loans when their reserves rise; bank customers do not instantly spend the proceeds of bank loans. The time lags in banking are too variable to enable us to make an estimate of how long it takes for an initial increase in new deposits to work its way through the system, but the time period is surely a matter of months for two or three "rounds."

Why banks must work together

There is an interesting problem concealed behind this crisscrossing of deposits that leads to a slowly rising level of the money supply. Suppose that an imaginary island economy was served by a single bank (and let us forget about all complications of international trade, etc.), and this bank, which

worked on a 20 percent reserve ratio, was suddenly presented with an extra one million dollars worth of reserves—let us say newly mined pure gold. Our bank could, of course, increase its loans to customers. By how much? *By five million dollars!*

In other words, our island bank, all by itself, could use an increase in its reserves to create a much larger increase in the money supply. It is not difficult to understand why. Any borrower of the new five million, no matter where he spent his money on the island, would only be giving his checks to someone who also banked at the single, solitary bank. The whole five million, in other words, would stay *within* the bank as its deposits, although the identity of those depositors would, of course, shift. Indeed, there is no reason why such a bank should limit its expansion of the money supply to five million. As long as the "soundness" of the currency was unquestioned, such a bank could create as much money as it wanted through new deposits, since all of those deposits would remain in its own keeping.

The imaginary bank makes it plain why ordinary commercial banks *cannot* expand deposits beyond their excess reserves. Unlike the monopoly bank, they must expect to *lose* their deposits to other banks when their borrowers write checks on their new accounts. As a result they will also lose their reserves, and this can lead to trouble.

Overlending

This situation is important enough to warrant taking a moment to examine. Suppose that in our previous example we had decided to lend the Smith Corporation not $800,000 but $900,000, and suppose as before that the Smith Corporation used the proceeds of that loan to pay the Jones Cor-

Original Bank

Assets		Liabilities	
Cash and at Fed	$ 100,000	Original deposits	$1,000,000
Loan (Smith Corp.)	900,000	Smith Corp. deposit	0
Total	**$1,000,000**	**Total**	**$1,000,000**

poration. Now look at the condition of our bank after the Smith payment has cleared.

Our reserves would now have dropped to 10 percent! Indeed, if we had loaned the company $1,000,000 we would be in danger of insolvency.

Banks are, in fact, very careful not to overlend. If they find that they have inadvertently exceeded their legal reserve requirements, they quickly take remedial action. One way that a bank may repair the situation is by borrowing reserves for a short period (paying interest on them, of course) from another bank that may have a temporary surplus at the Fed; this is called borrowing *federal funds.* Or a bank may quickly sell some of its government bonds and add the proceeds to its reserve account at the Fed. Or again, it may add to its reserves the proceeds of any loans that have come due and deliberately fail to replace these expired loans with new loans. Finally, a bank may borrow reserves directly from its Federal Reserve Bank and pay interest for the loan. We shall shortly look into this method when we talk about the role of the Federal Reserve in regulating the quantity of money.

The main point is clear. A bank is safe in lending only an amount that it can afford to lose to another bank. But of course one bank's loss is another's gain. That is why, by the exchange of checks, the banking system can accomplish the same result as the island monopoly bank, whereas no individual bank can hope to do so.

Investments and interest

If a bank uses its excess reserves to buy securities, does that lead to the same multiplication effect as a bank loan?

It can. When a bank buys government securities, it usually does so from a securities dealer, a professional trader in bonds.* Its check (for $800,000 in our example) drawn on its account at the Federal Reserve will be made out to a dealer, who will deposit it in his bank. As a result, the dealer's bank suddenly finds itself with an $800,000 new deposit. It must keep 20 percent of this as required reserve, but the remainder is excess reserve against which it can make loans or investments as it wishes.

Is there a new deposit, corresponding to that of the borrower? There is: the new deposit of the securities dealer. Note that in his case, as in the case of the borrower, the new deposit on the books of the bank has not been put there by the transfer of money from some other commercial bank. The $800,000 deposit has come into being through the deposit of a check of the Federal Reserve Bank, which is not a commercial bank. Thus it represents a new addition to the deposits of the private banking system.

Let us see this in the T accounts. After our first bank has bought its $800,000 in

---

*The dealer may be only a middleman, who will in turn buy from, or sell to, corporations or individuals. This doesn't change our analysis, however.

bonds (paying for them with its Federal Reserve checking account) its T account looks like this.

than a 4 percent return ($40 is only 3.6 percent of $1,100). If the price should fall to $900, the $40 return will be more than 4

Original Bank

Assets		Liabilities	
Cash at Fed	$ 200,000	Deposits	$1,000,000
Government bonds	800,000		
Total	**$1,000,000**	**Total**	**$1,000,000**

As we can see, there are no excess reserves here. But look at the bank in which the seller of the government bond has deposited the check he has just received from our bank. Here there are excess reserves of $640,000 with which additional investments can be made. It is possible for such new deposits, albeit diminishing each time, to remain in the financial circuit for some time, moving from bank to bank as an active business is done in buying government bonds.

percent ($40 is 4.4 percent of $900). Thus the *yield* of a bond varies inversely—in the other direction—from its market price.

When the price of government bonds changes, all bond prices tend to change in the same direction. This is because all bonds are competing for investors' funds. If the yield on "governments" falls, investors will switch from governments to other, higher yielding bonds. But as they bid for these other bonds, the prices of these bonds will rise—and their yields will fall,

Second Bank

Assets		Liabilities	
Cash	$800,000	New deposit of bond seller	$800,000
Total	**$800,000**	**Total**	**$800,000**

Yields

Meanwhile, however, the very activity in bidding for government bonds is likely to raise their price and thereby lower their rate of interest.

This is a situation that you will probably be faced with in your personal life, so you should understand it. A bond has a *fixed* rate of return and a stated face value. If it is a 4 percent, $1,000 bond, this means it will pay $40 interest yearly. If the bond now sells on the marketplace for $1,100, the $40 yearly interest will be less

too!

In this way, a change in yields spreads from one group of bonds to another. A lower rate of interest or a lower yield on government securities is quickly reflected in lower rates or yields for other kinds of bonds. In turn, a lower rate of interest on bonds makes loans to business look more attractive. Thus, sooner or later, excess reserves are apt to be channeled to new loans as well as new investments. Thereafter the deposit-building process follows its familiar course.

Controlling the Money Supply

We have now seen how a banking system can create money through the successive creation of excess reserves. But the key to the process is the creation of the *original* excess reserves, for without them the cumulative process will not be set in motion. We remember, for example, that a loan will not result in an increase in the money supply if it is offset by a decline in lending somewhere else in the banking system; neither will the purchase of a bond by one commercial bank if it is only buying a security sold by another. **To get a net addition to loans or investments, however, a banking system—assuming that it is fully loaned up—needs an increase in its reserves.** Where do these extra reserves come from? That is the question we must turn to next.

Role of the Federal Reserve

In our example we have already met one source of changes in reserves. When the public needs less currency, and it deposits its extra holdings in the banks, reserves rise, as we have seen. Contrariwise, when the public wants more currency, it depletes the banks' holdings of currency and thereby lowers their reserves. In the latter case, the banks may find that they have insufficient reserves behind their deposits. To get more currency or claims on other banks, they will have to sell securities or reduce their loans. This might put a very severe crimp in the economy. Hence, to allow bank reserves to be regulated by the public's fluctuating demand for cash would seem to be an impossible way to run our monetary system.

But we remember that bank reserves are not mainly currency; in fact, currency is a relatively minor item. Most reserves are the accounts that member banks hold at the Federal Reserve. Hence, if these accounts could somehow be increased or decreased, we could regulate the amount of reserves—and thus the permissible total of deposits—without regard to the public's changing need for cash.

This is precisely what the Federal Reserve System is designed to do. Essentially, the system is set up to regulate the supply of money by raising or lowering the reserves of its member banks. When these reserves are raised, member banks find themselves with excess reserves and are thus in a position to make loans and investments by which the supply of money will increase further. Conversely, when the Federal Reserve lowers the reserves of its member banks, they will no longer be able to make loans and investments, or they may even have to reduce loans or get rid of investments, thereby extinguishing deposit accounts and contracting the supply of money.

Monetary control mechanisms

How does the Federal Reserve operate? There are three ways.

1. Changing reserve requirements

It was the Federal Reserve itself, we will remember, that originally determined how much in reserves its member banks should hold against their deposits. Hence by changing that reserve requirement for a given level of deposits, it can give its member banks excess reserves or can create a shortage of reserves.

In our imaginary bank we have assumed that reserves were set at 20 percent of deposits. Suppose now that the Federal Reserve determined to lower reserve requirements to 15 percent. It would thereby automatically create extra lending or investing power for our *existing* reserves. Our bank with $1 million in deposits and $200,000 in reserves could now lend or invest an additional $50,000 without any new funds coming in from depositors. On the other hand, if requirements were raised to, say, 30 percent, we would find that our original $200,000 reserve was $100,000 short of requirements, and we would have to curtail lending or investing until we were again in line with requirements.

Do not forget that these new reserve requirements affect *all* banks. Therefore, changing reserve ratios is a very effective way of freeing or contracting bank credit on a large scale. But it is an instrument that sweeps across the entire banking system in an undiscriminating fashion. It is therefore used only rarely, when the Federal Reserve Board feels that the supply of money is seriously short or dangerously excessive and needs remedy on a countrywide basis. For instance, in early 1973, the board raised reserve requirements one-half percent for all banks, partly to mop up excess reserves and partly to sound a general warning against what it considered to be a potentially dangerous inflationary state of affairs.

2. Changing discount rates

A second means of control uses interest rates as the money-controlling device. Recall that member banks that are short on reserves have a special privilege, if they wish to exercise it. They can *borrow* reserve balances from the Federal Reserve Bank itself and add them to their regular reserve account at the bank.

The Federal Reserve Bank, of course, charges interest for lending reserves, and this interest is called the *discount rate*. By raising or lowering this rate, the Federal Reserve can make it attractive or unattractive for member banks to borrow to augment reserves. Thus in contrast with changing the reserve ratio itself, changing the discount rate is a mild device that allows each bank to decide for itself whether it wishes to increase its reserves. In addition, changes in the discount rate tend to influence the whole structure of interest rates, either tightening or loosening money.*

Although changes in the discount rate can be used as a major means of controlling the money supply and are used to control it in some countries, they are not used for this purpose in the U. S. The Federal Reserve Board does not allow banks to borrow whatever they would like at the current discount rate. The discount "window" is a place where a bank can borrow small amounts of money to cover a small deficiency in its reserves, but it is not a place where banks can borrow major amounts of money to expand their lending portfolios. As a result, the discount rate serves more as a signal of what the Federal Reserve would like to see happen than as an active force in determining the total borrowings of banks.

3. Open-market operations

Most frequently used, however, is a third technique called open-market operations. This technique permits the Federal Reserve Banks to change the supply of reserves by buying or selling U.S. government bonds on the open market.

How does this work? Let us suppose that the Federal Reserve authorities wish to increase the reserves of member banks. They will begin to buy government securities from dealers in the bond market, and

---

*When interest rates are high, money is called tight. This means not only that borrowers have to pay higher rates, but that banks are stricter and more selective in judging the credit worthiness of business applications for loans. Conversely, when interest rates decline, money is called easy, meaning that it is not only cheaper but literally easier to borrow.

they will pay these dealers with Federal Reserve checks.

Notice something about these checks: *they are not drawn on any commercial bank!* They are drawn on the Federal Reserve Bank itself. The security dealer who sells the bond will, of course, deposit the Fed's check, as if it were any other check, in his own commercial bank; and his bank will send the Fed's check through for credit to its own account, as if it were any other check. *As a result, the dealer's bank will have gained reserves, although*

no other commercial bank has lost reserves. On balance, then, the system has more lending and investing capacity than it had before. In fact, it now has *excess* reserves, and these, as we have seen, will spread out through the system. **Thus by buying bonds, the Federal Reserve has, in fact, deposited money in the accounts of its members, thereby giving them the extra reserves that it set out to create** (see box).

Conversely, if the authorities decide that member banks' reserves are too large, they will sell securities. Now the process

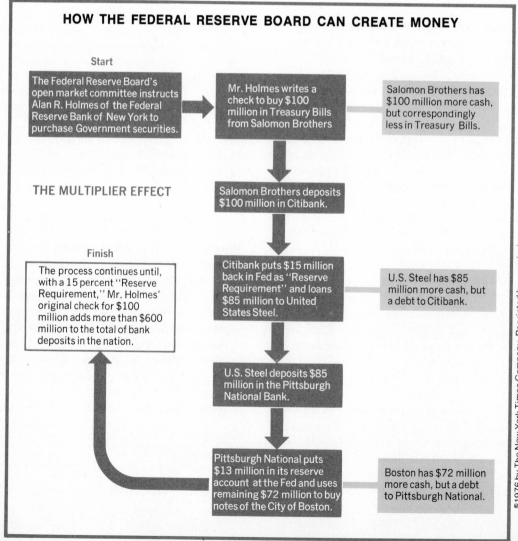

HOW THE FEDERAL RESERVE BOARD CAN CREATE MONEY

Start

The Federal Reserve Board's open market committee instructs Alan R. Holmes of the Federal Reserve Bank of New York to purchase Government securities.

Mr. Holmes writes a check to buy $100 million in Treasury Bills from Salomon Brothers

Salomon Brothers has $100 million more cash, but correspondingly less in Treasury Bills.

THE MULTIPLIER EFFECT

Salomon Brothers deposits $100 million in Citibank.

Finish

The process continues until, with a 15 percent "Reserve Requirement," Mr. Holmes' original check for $100 million adds more than $600 million to the total of bank deposits in the nation.

Citibank puts $15 million back in Fed as "Reserve Requirement" and loans $85 million to United States Steel.

U.S. Steel has $85 million more cash, but a debt to Citibank.

U.S. Steel deposits $85 million in the Pittsburgh National Bank.

Pittsburgh National puts $13 million in its reserve account at the Fed and uses remaining $72 million to buy notes of the City of Boston.

Boston has $72 million more cash, but a debt to Pittsburgh National.

works in reverse. Security dealers or other buyers of bonds will send their own checks on their own regular commercial banks to the Federal Reserve in payment for these bonds. This time the Fed will take the checks of its member banks and charge their accounts, thereby reducing their reserves. Since these checks will not find their way to another commercial bank, the system as a whole will have suffered a diminution of its reserves. By selling securities, in other words, the Federal Reserve authorities lower the Federal Reserve accounts of member banks, thereby diminishing their reserves.*

Asymmetric control

How effective are all these powers over the money supply? The Federal Reserve Board's capacity to control money is often compared to our ability to manipulate a string. If the Federal Reserve Board wishes to *reduce* the money supply, it can increase the discount rate or sell bonds. Sooner or later, this tends to be effective. If banks have free or excess reserves, they will not immediately have to reduce their lending portfolios; but eventually, by pulling on the string hard enough, the Fed can force a reduction in bank loans and the money supply.

*Isn't this, you might ask, really the same thing as raising or lowering the reserve ratio? If the Fed is really just putting money into member bank accounts when it buys bonds and taking money out when it sells them, why does it bother to go through the open market? Why not just tell the member banks that their reserves are larger or smaller?

Analytically, you are entirely right. There are however cogent reasons for working through the bond market. The open-market technique allows banks to *compete* for their share of the excess reserves that are being made available or taken away. Banks that are good at attracting depositors will thereby get extra benefit from an increase in the money supply. Thus, rather than assigning excess reserves by executive fiat, the Fed uses the open market as an allocation device.

In addition, open-market operations allow the Fed to make very small changes in the money supply, whereas changes in reserve requirements would be difficult to adjust in very fine amounts.

The Federal Reserve Board's capacity to increase the money supply is not equally great. It can reduce reserve rates and buy bonds, but it cannot *force* banks to make loans if they do not wish to do so. Banks can, if they wish, simply increase their excess reserves. Normally, banks wish to make loans and earn profits; but if risks are high, they may not wish to do so. Such a situation occurred in the Great Depression. Banks piled up vast reserves rather than make loans, since the risks of defaults were too high to make most loans an attractive economic gamble. In terms of our analogy, the Federal Reserve Board can pull, but it cannot push on its string of controls.

Sticky prices

We are almost ready to look into the dynamics of money, in our next chapter, but we must examine a question that we have heretofore passed over in silence. We have taken for granted that we need a larger supply of money in order to expand output. But why should we? Why could we not grow just as well if the supply of money were fixed?

Theoretically we could. If we cut prices as we increased output, a given amount of money (or a given amount of expenditure) could cover an indefinitely large real output. Furthermore, as prices fell, workers would be content not to ask for higher wages (or would even accept lower wages), since in real terms they would be just as well or better off.

It is not difficult to spot the flaw in this argument. In the real world, prices of many goods cannot be cut easily. If the price of steel rose and fell as quickly and easily as prices on the stock exchange or if wages went down without a murmur of resistance or if rents and other contractual items could be quickly adjusted, then prices would be flexible and we would not require any enlargement of our money supply to cover a growing real output.

In fact, as we know, prices are extremely "sticky" in the downward direction. Union leaders do not look with approval on wage cuts, even when living costs fall. Contractual prices cannot be quickly adjusted. Many big firms administer their prices and carefully avoid price competition: note, for example, that the prices of many customer items are printed on the package months before the item will be sold.

Thus we can see that a fixed supply of money would put the economy into something of a straitjacket. As output tended to increase, business would need more money to finance production, and consumers would need more money to make their larger expenditures. If business could get more money from the banks, all would be well. But suppose it could not. Then the only way it could get a larger supply of cash would be to persuade someone to lend the money, and persuasion would be in the form of a higher rate of interest. But this rising interest rate would discourage other businesses from going ahead with their plans. Hence the would-be-boom would be stopped dead in its tracks by a sheer shortage of spending power.

A flexible money supply obviates this economic suffocation. The fact that banks can create money (provided that they have excess reserves) enables them to take care of businesses that wish to make additional expenditures. The expenditures themselves put additional money into the hands of consumers. And the spending of consumers in turn sends the enlarged volume of purchasing power back to business firms to complete the great flow of expenditures and receipt.

Paper Money and Gold

Finally, let us clear up one last mystery of the monetary system—the mystery of where currency (coin and bills) actually comes from and where it goes. If we examine most of our paper currency, we will find that it has "Federal Reserve Note" on it: that is, it is paper money issued by the Federal Reserve System. We understand, by now, how the public gets these notes: it simply draws them from its checking accounts. When it does so, the commercial banks, finding their supplies of vault cash low, ask their Federal Reserve district banks to ship them as much new cash as they need.

And what does the Federal Reserve Bank do? It takes packets of bills ($1 and $5 and $10) out of its vaults, *where these stacks of printed paper have no monetary significance at all,* charges the requisite amount against its member banks' balances, and ships the cash out by armored truck. So long as these new stacks of bills remain in the member banks' possession, they are still not money! But soon they will pass out to the public, where they will be money. Do not forget, of course, that as a result, the public will have that much *less* money left in its checking accounts.

Could this currency-issuing process go on forever? Could the Federal Reserve ship out as much money as it wanted to? Suppose that the authorities at the Fed decided to order a trillion dollars worth of bills from the Treasury mints. What would happen when those bills arrived at the Federal Reserve Banks? The answer is that they would simply gather dust in their vaults. There would be no way for the Fed to "issue" its money unless the public wanted cash. And the amount of cash the

GOLDFINGER AT WORK

Some years ago a patriotic women's organization, alarmed lest the Communists had tunneled under the Atlantic, forced an inspection of the gold stock buried at Fort Knox. It proved to be all there. An interesting question arises as to the repercussions, had they found the great vault to be bare. Perhaps we might have followed the famous anthropo-

logical example of the island of Yap in the South Seas, where heavy stone cartwheels are the symbol of wealth for the leading families. One such family was particularly remarkable insofar as its cartwheel lay at the bottom

of a lagoon, where it had fallen from a canoe. Although it was absolutely irretrievable and even invisible, the family's wealth was considered unimpaired, since everyone knew the stone was there. If the Kentucky depository had been empty, a patriotic declaration by the ladies that the gold really was in Fort Knox might have saved the day for the United States.

public could want is always limited by the amount of money it has in its checking accounts.

The gold cover Are there no limitations on this note-issuing or reserve-creating process? Until 1967 there *were* limitations imposed by Congress, requiring the Federal Reserve to hold gold certificates equal in value to at least 25 percent of all outstanding notes. (Gold certificates are a special kind of paper money issued by the U.S. Treasury and backed 100 percent by gold bullion in Fort Knox.) Prior to 1964 there was a further requirement that the amount of gold certificates also be sufficient to give a 25 percent backing as well to the total amount of member bank deposits held by the Fed. Thus the legal obligation not to go beyond this 25 percent gold cover provided a strict ceiling on the amount of member bank reserves the Federal Reserve system could create or on the amount of notes it could ship at the request of its member banks.

All this presented no problem in, say, 1940, when the total of member bank reserves plus Federal Reserve notes came to only $20 billion, against which we held gold certificates worth almost $22 billion. Trouble began to develop, however, in the

1960s when a soaring GNP was accompanied by a steadily rising volume of both member bank reserves and Federal Reserve notes. By 1964, for example, member bank reserves had grown to $22 billion, and outstanding Reserve notes to nearly $35 billion. At the same time, for reasons that we shall learn more about in Part Five, our gold stock had declined to just over $15 billion. With $57 billion in liabilities ($22 billion in member bank reserves plus $35 billion in notes) and only $15 billion in gold certificates, the 25 percent cover requirement was clearly imperiled.

Congress thereupon removed the cover requirement from member bank reserves, leaving all our gold certificates available as "backing" for our Federal Reserve notes. But even that did not solve the problem. Currency in circulation continued to rise with a record GNP until it exceeded $40 billion in 1967. Our gold stock meanwhile continued to decline to $12 billion in that year and threatened to fall further. The handwriting on the wall indicated that the 25 percent cover could not long be maintained.

There were basically two ways out. One would have been to change the gold cover requirements from 25 percent to, say, 10 percent. That would have made our gold stock more than adequate to "back" our paper money (and our member bank deposits, too).*

The second way was much simpler: *eliminate the gold cover entirely.* With very little fuss, this is what Congress did in 1967.

Gold and money   Does the presence or absence of a gold cover make any difference? From the economist's point of view it does not. Gold is a metal with a long and rich history of hypnotic influence, so there is undeniably a psychological usefulness in having gold "behind" a currency. But unless that currency is 100 percent convertible into gold, *any* money demands an act of faith on the part of its users. If that faith is destroyed, the money becomes valueless; so long as it is unquestioned, the money is "as good as gold."

Thus the presence or absence of a gold backing for currency is purely a psychological problem, so far as the value of a domestic currency is concerned. In Chapter 40 we will look into its international significance. But the point is worth pursuing a little further. Suppose our currency *were* 100 percent convertible into gold—suppose, in fact, that we used only gold coins as currency. Would that improve the operation of our economy?

A moment's reflection should reveal that it would not. We would still have to cope with a very difficult problem that our bank deposit money handles rather easily. This is the problem of how we could increase the supply of money or diminish it, as the needs of the economy changed. With gold coins as money, we would either have a frozen stock of money (with

consequences that we shall trace in the next chapter), or our supply of money would be at the mercy of our luck in gold-mining or the currents of international trade that funneled gold into our hands or took it away. And incidentally, a gold currency would not obviate inflation, as many countries have discovered when the vagaries of international trade or a fortuitous discovery of gold mines increased their holdings of gold faster than their actual output.

Money and belief   As we cautioned at the outset, money is a highly sophisticated and curious invention. At one time or another nearly everything imaginable has served as the magic symbol of money: whales' teeth, shells, feathers, bark, furs, blankets, butter, tobacco, leather, copper, silver, gold, and (in the most advanced nations) pieces of paper with pictures on them or simply numbers on a computer printout. In fact, anything is usable as money, provided that there is a natural or enforceable scarcity of it, so that men can usually come into its possession only through carefully designated ways. Behind all the symbols, however, rests the central requirement of faith. Money serves its indispensable purposes as long as we believe in it. It ceases to function the moment we do not. Money has well been called "the promises men live by."

But the creation of money and the control over its supply is still only half the question. We have yet to trace how our money supply influences the flow of output itself—or to put it differently, how the elaborate institutions through which men promise to honor one another's work and property affect the amount of work they do and the amount of new wealth they accumulate. This is the subject to which our next chapter will be devoted.

---

*Actually as we shall see in the box on the gold standard on p. 614—the gold never really backed our currency, since no American was legally permitted to buy gold bullion.

FOCUS This is the first time we have had a chance to investigate the "mystery" of money. Your central purpose should be to dispel whatever shrouds of mystery still cling to the idea of money.

Money is mysterious because it is not simply gold coins; it is a *symbol* of wealth. For that matter, gold coins are also symbols of wealth which, in the last analysis, is production. Therefore, we have to understand how the symbolic pieces of paper we use, both currency and checks, come into being. We should also see that "money" can be defined to include other symbols of wealth, such as savings accounts or even government bonds.

Most money consists of checking accounts owned by individuals or firms or government agencies at banks. Money "circulates" when owners of deposits draw checks on these accounts. Money can also take the form of currency whenever the public exchanges its deposits for coins or bills. But most money is "in" the bank, where it is nothing more than a bookkeeping entry showing the size of your account.

Each commercial bank must keep a certain fraction of its demand deposits in cash or as a deposit at its Federal Reserve Bank. This fraction is set by the Fed. The remaining "excess reserves" indicate the amount that a bank can lend or invest, in order to make money. When a loan or investment is made, a bank opens a new account in the name of the borrower or bond seller. When these new accounts are subsequently used, they become new deposits for other banks, and in this way the money supply can be expanded (or contracted if the first bank curtails a loan or sells a bond). You should study the diagram on p. 501 and the series of T accounts, to be sure you understand this process. Better yet, using T accounts, work your way through questions 4 to 8.

The second main point to learn is how the Federal Reserve System controls the money supply. We have seen that the reserve ratio is established by the Fed. This is not to "safeguard" deposits. In the case of a real panic only 100 percent reserves would be a safeguard (and the Fed could easily print up and ship out trillions of dollars of Federal Reserve Notes if the public had a mass, panicky urge to get into cash.) The Fed sets reserve ratios as one of its ways of controlling the supply of money. The other ways are to change the discount rate and to buy or sell U.S. government bonds—"open market" operations. Be sure that you understand these three methods: they are crucial to understanding how our money mechanism works. Questions 11, 12, and 13 should help you here.

Any mysteries left?

WORDS AND CONCEPTS YOU SHOULD KNOW

Currency, 493–94
Money, 493–94
Bank deposits, 494
Federal Reserve System, 495
Reserve ratio, 495, 506
Bank reserves, 496
Fractional reserves, 496
T accounts, 497
Excess reserves, 498
Bank lending, 498–500

Five limits on expansion of money supply, 501–3
Overlending, 503–4
Yields, 505
Reserve requirements, 506–7
Discount rates, 507
Open-market operations, 507–9
Asymmetric control, 509
Sticky prices, 509
Gold "cover," 511

QUESTIONS

1. Why do we not count cash in the tills of commercial banks in the money supply? When you deposit currency in a commercial bank, what happens to it? Can you ask for your particular bills again? If you demanded to see "your" account, what would it be?

2. What determines how much vault cash a bank must hold against its deposits? Would you expect this proportion to change in some seasons, such as Christmas? Do you think it would be the same in worried times as in placid times? In new countries as in old ones?

3. Is currency the main reserve of a bank? Do reserves ensure the safety of a currency? What function do they have?

4. What are excess reserves? Suppose a bank has $500,000 in deposits and that there is a reserve ratio of 30 percent imposed by law. What is its required reserve? Suppose it happens to hold $200,000 in vault cash or at its account at the Fed. What, if any, is its excess reserve?

5. If the bank above wanted to make loans or investments, how much would it be entitled to lend or invest?

6. Suppose its deposits increased by another $50,000. Could it lend or invest this entire amount? Any of it? How much?

7. If a bank lends money, it opens an account in the name of the borrower. Now suppose the borrower draws down his new account. What happens to the reserves of the lending bank? Show this in a T account.

8. Suppose the borrower sends his check for $1,000 to someone who banks at another bank. Describe what happens to the deposits of the second bank. If the reserve ratio is 20 percent, how much new lending or investing can it do?

9. If the reserve ratio is 20 percent, and the original addition to reserves is $1,000, what will be the total potential amount of new money that can be created by the banking system? If the ratio is 25 percent?

10. What is the difference between a banking system and a single competitive bank? Can a single bank create new money? Can it create more new money than an amount equal to its excess reserves? Can a banking system create more money than its excess reserves?

11. Suppose that a bank has $1 million in deposits, $100,000 in reserves, and is fully loaned up. Now suppose the Federal Reserve System lowers reserve requirements from 10 percent to 8 percent. What happens to the lending capacity of the bank?

12. The Federal Reserve Banks buy $100 million in U.S. Treasury notes. How do they pay for these notes? What happens to the checks? Do they affect the reserves of member banks? Will buying bonds increase or decrease the money supply?

13. Now explain what happens when the Fed sells Treasury notes. Who buys them? How do they pay for them? Where do the checks go? How does payment affect the accounts of the member banks at the Federal Reserve Banks?

14. Why do you think gold has held such a place of prestige in the minds of men?

Independence of the Fed

The Federal Reserve Board is run by 7 governors, each appointed to a 14-year term by the President with the approval of Congress. The governors of the Federal Reserve System cannot be removed during their terms of office except for wrongdoing. Thus, although fiscal policy is located in the executive and legislative branches of the government, monetary policy is vested in an independent board.

There were two initial justifications for this institutional arrangement. The first was that monetary policies were necessarily subject to quick changes. Second, it was felt that monetary policies ought to be insulated from the political process.

Are these reasons still valid? Some economists think so; others, including ourselves, think not. To take the first argument, it is true that Congress cannot be expected to operate an efficient open-market system on a daily basis. But this is not an argument for divorcing the responsibility for such operations from the *executive* branch. In most of the world's governments, Central Banks (the equivalent of the Fed) are located within the executive establishment, usually as a part of the Treasury or Finance ministries or departments. These banks have no trouble making quick decisions. Moreover, even if Congress could not be expected to approve of every jiggle in monetary measures, there is no reason why it could not endorse or direct the major thrust of monetary strategy toward an expansionary or a contractive general objective.

The argument about "insulation" depends on one's view of democracy, where values once again reign supreme. There is a curious inconsistency, however, in trying to insulate only monetary policies, not fiscal policies. Why should we trust the democratic mechanism to establish expenditures and taxes, but not the supply of money?

As in most institutional debates, dramatic changes are unlikely to happen, although we seem to be moving in a more "democratic" direction in our monetary management. Congress now expects to be briefed every quarter on the Fed's monetary targets for the following year. There are also bills pending in Congress to integrate the Fed more fully by altering the tenure of the Chairman to be concomitant with that of the President; or to require the Fed to issue an economic report directly after the President's Economic Report, stating what differences, if any, lie between them, and justifying the Fed's course of action if it differs from that of the Administration.

Meanwhile, a high degree of integration exists in fact, although not in law. More and more, the Fed bows to public pressure or to pressure from the Administration. This is hardly surprising. As we shall see in our next chapter, we live at a time when the importance of money in the economy is more highly regarded than it used to be. The idea of an "independent" Fed does not sit so well in an era when we think of the Fed as bearing a prime responsibility for our economic well-being. Having created the Federal Reserve Board in the first place, Congress can alter it, as it wishes; and it undoubtedly would alter it, were the Fed to risk a direct confrontation with congressional or presidential economic objectives. The more important money management becomes, the more powerful are the pressures to place it within, not outside of, the main political mechanisms of the nation.

Money
and the
macro system

In our preceding chapter, we found out something about what money is and how it comes into being. Now we must turn to the much more complicated question of how money works—the level of output. What happens when the banks create or destroy deposits? Can we directly raise or lower incomes by altering the quantity of money? Can we control inflation or recession by using the monetary management powers of the Federal Reserve System? These extremely important questions will be the focus of discussion in this chapter.

The Quantity Theory of Money

Quantity equation

One relation between money and economic activity must have occurred to us. It is that the quantity of money must have something to do with *prices*. Does it not stand to reason that if we increase the supply of money, prices will go up, and that if we decrease the amount of money, prices will fall?

Something very much like this belief lies behind one of the most famous equations (really identities) in economics. The equation looks like this:

$$MV \equiv PT$$

where

M = *quantity of money* (currency outside banks plus demand deposits)
V = *velocity of circulation,* or the number of times per period or per year that an average dollar changes hands
P = *the general level of prices,* or a price index
T = *the number of transactions made in the economy* in a year, or a measure of *physical output*

If we think about this equation, its meaning is not hard to grasp. What the quantity equation says is that the amount of *expenditure* (M times V, or the quantity of money times the frequency of its use) equals the amount of *receipts* (P times T, or the price of an average sale times the number of sales). Naturally, this is an identity. In fact, it is our old familiar circular flow. What all factors of production receive (PT) must equal what all factors of production spend (MV).

Just as our GNP identities are true at every moment, so are the quantity theory of money identities true at every instant. They merely look at the circular flow from a different vantage point. And just as our GNP identities yielded useful economic insights when we began to inquire into the functional relationships within those identities, so the quantity theory can also shed light on economic activity if we can find functional relationships concealed within its self-evident "truth."

Assumptions of the quantity theory

To move from tautologies to operationally useful relationships, we need to make assumptions that lend themselves to investigation and evidence. In the case of the GNP $\equiv C + G + I + X$ identity, for instance, we made a critical assumption about the propensity to consume, which led to the multiplier and to predictive statements about the influence of injections on GNP. In the case of $MV \equiv PT$, we need another assumption. What will it be?

The crucial assumptions made by the economists who first formulated the quantity theory were two: (1) the velocity of money—the number of times an average dollar was used per year—*was constant*; and (2) transactions (sales) *were always at a full-employment level*. If these assumptions were true, it followed that the price level was a simple function of the supply of money:

$$P = \frac{V}{T} \cdot M$$
$$P = kM$$

where k was a constant defined by V/T.

If the money supply went up, prices went up; if the quantity of money went down, prices went down. Since the government controlled the money supply, it could easily regulate the price level.

Testing the quantity theory

Is this causal relation true? Can we directly manipulate the price level by changing the size of our stock of money?

The original inventors of the quantity equation, over half a century ago, thought this was indeed the case. And of course it *would* be the case if everything else in the equation held steady while we moved the quantity of money up or down. In other words, if the velocity of circulation, V, and the number of transactions, T, were fixed, changes in M would have to operate directly on P.

Can we test the validity of this assumption? There is an easy way to do so. Figure 34•1 shows us changes in the supply of money compared with changes in the level of prices.

A glance at Fig. 34•1 answers our question. Between 1929 and 1973, the supply of money in the United States increased over eightfold, while prices rose only a little more than twofold. Clearly, something *must* have happened to V or to T to prevent the eightfold increase in M from bringing about a similar increase in P. Let us see what those changes were.

Changes in V

Figure 34•2 gives us a first clue as to what is wrong with a purely mechanical interpretation of the quantity theory. In it we show how many times an average dollar was used to help pay for each year's output.* We derive this number by dividing the total expenditure for each year's output (which is, of course, the familiar figure for GNP) by the actual supply of money—currency plus checking accounts—for each year. As the chart shows, the velocity of money fell by 50 percent between 1929 and 1946, only to rise again to the 1929 level over the postwar years.

We shall return later to an inquiry into why people spend money less or more quickly, but it is clear beyond question that they do. This has two important implications for our study of money. First, it gives a very cogent reason why we cannot apply the quantity theory in a mechanical way, asserting that an increase in the supply of money will *always* raise prices. For if people choose to spend the increased quantity of money more slowly, its impact on the quantity of goods may not change at all: whereas if they spend the same

quantity of money more rapidly, prices can rise without any change in M.

Second and more clearly than we have seen, the variability of V reveals that money itself can be a destabilizing force—destabilizing because it enables us to do two things that would be impossible in a pure barter economy. We can:

1. delay between receiving and expending our rewards for economic effort

2. spend more or less than our receipts by drawing on, or adding to, our cash balances

Classical economists used to speak of money as a "veil," implying that it did not itself play an active role in influencing the behavior of the economic players. But we can see that the ability of those players to vary the rate of their expenditure—to hang onto their money longer or to get rid of it more rapidly than usual—makes money much more than a veil. Money (or rather, people's wish to hold or to spend money) becomes an independent source of change in a complex economic society. To put it differently, the use of money introduces an independent element of uncertainty into the circular flow.*

Changes in T

Now we must turn to a last and perhaps most important reason why we cannot relate the supply of money to the price level in a mechanical fashion. This reason lies in the role played by T; that is, by the volume of output.

Just as the early quantity theorists thought of V as essentially unvarying, so they thought of T as a relatively fixed term in the quantity equation. In the minds of nearly all economic theorists before the Depression, output was always assumed to

---

*Note that final output is not quite the same as T, which embraces *all* transactions, including those for intermediate goods. But if we define T so that it includes only *transactions that enter into final output*, PT becomes a measure of gross national product. In the same way, we can count only those expenditures that enter into GNP when we calculate MV. It does no violence to the idea of the quantity theory to apply it only to final output, and it makes statistical computation far simpler.

*Technically, the standard economic definition of money is that it is both a means of exchange and a store of value. It is the latter characteristic that makes money a potentially disturbing influence.

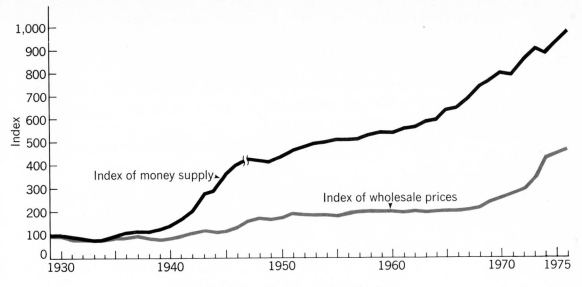

FIG. 34 · 1   Money supply and prices

be as large as the available resources and the willingness of the factors of production would permit. While everyone was aware that there might be minor variations from this state of full output, virtually no one thought they would be of sufficient importance to matter. **Hence the quantity theory implicitly assumed full employment or full output as the normal condition of the economy.** With such an assumption, it was easy to picture T as an unimportant term in the equation and to focus the full effect of changes in money on P.

The trauma of the Great Depression effectively removed the comfortable assumption that the economy "naturally" tended to full employment and output. At the bottom of the Depression, real output had fallen by 25 percent. Aside from what the Depression taught us in other ways, it made unmistakably clear that changes in the volume of output (and employment) were of crucial importance in the overall economic picture, and that the economy does not "naturally" graduate to full employment levels.

FIG. 34 · 2   Velocity of money

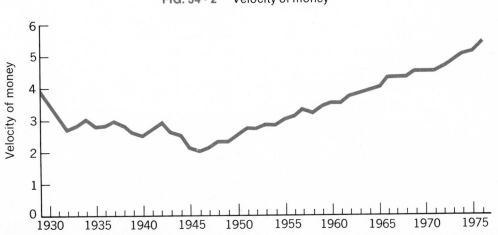

Output and prices

How does our modern emphasis on the variability of output and employment fit into the overall question of money and prices? The answer is very simple, but very important. We have come to see that the effect of more money on prices cannot be determined unless we also take into account the effect of spending on the volume of transactions or output.

It is not difficult to grasp the point. Let us picture an increase in spending, perhaps initiated by a business launching a new investment program or by the government inaugurating a new public works project. These new expenditures will be received by many other entrepreneurs, as the multiplier mechansim spreads the new spending through the economy. But now we come to the key question. What will entrepreneurs do as their receipts increase?

It is at this point that the question of output enters. For if factories or stores are operating *at less than full capacity*, and if there is an *employable supply of labor available*, the result of their new receipts is almost certain to be an increase in output. That is, employers will take advantage of the rise in demand, to produce and sell more goods and services. They may also try to raise prices and increase their profits further; but *if their industries*

are reasonably competitive, it is doubtful that prices can be raised very much. Other firms with idle plants will simply undercut them and take their business away. An example is provided by the period 1934 through 1940, when output increased by 50 percent while prices rose by less than 5 percent. The reason, of course, lay in the great amount of unemployed resources, making it easy to expand output without price increases.

Prices and employment

Thus we reach a general conclusion of the greatest importance. *An increase in spending of any kind tends to result in more output and employment, with or without price increases, whenever there are considerable amounts of unemployed resources.* But this is no longer true when we reach a level of high employment or very full plant utilization. Now an increase in spending *cannot* quickly lead to an increase in output, simply because the resources for more production are lacking. The result, instead, can only be a rise in prices, for no firm can lose business to competitors when competitors are unable to fill additional orders. Thus the corollary of our general conclusion is that *additional spending from any source is inflationary when it is difficult to raise output.*

Full employment vs. under-employment

It is impossible to overstress the importance of this finding for macroeconomic policy. Policies that make sense when we are fully employed may make no sense when we are badly underemployed, and vice versa.

To spend more in the public or in the private sector is clearly good for an economy that is suffering from underutilized resources, but equally clearly inflationary and bad for an economy that is bumping up against the ceiling of output. Similarly, to balance budgets or run budget surpluses makes little sense when people are looking for work and business is looking for orders, but it is the course of wisdom when there are no idle resources to absorb the additional expenditure.

One of the main differences between contemporary economic thought and that of the past is precisely this sharp division between policies that make sense in full employment and those that make sense in conditions of underemployment. It was not that the economists of the past did not recognize the tragedy of unemployment or did not wish to remedy it. It was rather that they did not see how an economy could be in *equilibrium* even though there was heavy unemployment.

The dragging years of the Great Depression taught us not only that output could fall far below the levels of full utilization, but—perhaps this was its most intellectually unsettling feature—that an economy could be plagued with unemployed men and machines for almost a decade and yet not spontaneously generate the momentum to reabsorb them. Today we understand this condition of unemployment equilibrium, and we have devised various remedial measures to raise the equilibrium point to a satisfactory level, including, not least, additional public expenditure. But this new understanding must be balanced with a keen appreciation of its relevance to the underlying situation of employment. Remedies for an underemployed economy can be ills for a fully employed one.

Inflation and public finance

We can see that the conclusion we have reached puts a capstone on our previous analysis of deficit spending. It is now possible to add a major criterion to the question of whether or not to use the public sector as a supplement to the private sector. That criterion is whether or not substantially "full" employment has been reached.

If the economy is operating at or near the point of full employment, additional net public spending will only add more MV to a situation in which T is already at capacity and where, therefore, P will rise.

MAXIMUM VS. FULL EMPLOYMENT

What is "full" employment? Presumably government spending is guided by the objectives of the Employment Act of 1946, which declares the attainment of "maximum employment" to be a central economic objective of the government.

But what is "maximum" employment? Does it mean zero unemployment? This would mean that no one could quit his job even to look for a better one. Or consider the problem of inflation. Zero unemployment would probably mean extremely high rates of inflation, for reasons we will look into more carefully later. Hence no one claims that "full" employment is maximum employment in the sense of an absence of *any* unemployment whatsoever.

But this opens the question of how much *unemployment* is accepted as consistent with "maximum" employment. Under Presidents Kennedy and Johnson, the permissible unemployment rate was 4 percent. Under Presidents Nixon and Ford the permissible unemployment rate rose to a range of 4.5 to 5 or even 6 percent, largely because inflation had worsened. Hence the meaning of "full employment" is open to the discretion of the economic authorities, and their policies may vary from one period to another.

But note that this conclusion attaches to more than additional *public* spending. When full employment is reached, additional spending of any kind—public or private, consumption or investment—will increase MV and, given the ceiling on T, affect P.

A different conclusion is reached when there is large-scale unemployment. Now additional public (or private) spending will result not in higher prices, but in larger output and higher employment. Thus we cannot say that public spending in itself is "inflationary." Rather, we must see that *any kind of additional spending can be inflationary in a fully employed economy.*

Money and Expenditure

We have almost lost sight of our subject, which is not really inflation (we will come back to that in Chapter 35), but how money affects GNP. And here there is an important point. How does an increased supply of money get "into" GNP? People who have not studied economics often discuss changes in the money supply as if the government "put" money into circulation, mailing out dollar bills to taxpayers. The actual connection between an increase in M and an increase in MV is much more complex. Let us look into it.

Interest rates and the transactions demand for money   From our previous chapter, we know the immediate results of an increased supply of money, whether brought about by open-market operations or a change in reserve ratios. *The effect in both cases is a rise in the lendable or investible reserves of banks.* Ceteris paribus, this will lead to a fall in interest rates as banks compete with one another in lending their additional unused reserves to firms or individuals.

As interest rates decline, some firms and individuals will be tempted to increase their borrowings. It becomes cheaper to take out a mortgage, to buy a car on an installment loan, to finance inventories. Thus, as we would expect, the demand curve for "spending money," like that for most commodities, slopes downward. As money gets cheaper, people want to "buy" (borrow) more of it. To put it differently, the lower the price of money, the larger the quantity demanded. We speak of this demand curve for money to be used for expenditure as the *transactions demand for money.*

Financial demand   But there is also another, quite separate source of the demand for money. This is the demand for money for *financial purposes*, to be held by individuals or corporations as part of their assets.

What happens to the demand for money for financial purposes as its price goes down? Financial demand also increases, although for different reasons. When interest rates are high, individuals and firms tend to keep their wealth as fully invested as possible, in order to earn the high return that is available. But when interest rates fall, the opportunity cost of keeping money idle is much less. If you are an investor with a portfolio of $10,000, and the rate of interest is 7 percent, you give up $700 a year if you are very "liquid" (i.e., all in cash); whereas if the interest rate is only 3 percent, your opportunity cost for liquidity falls to $300.

Liquidity preference

Economists call this increased willingness to be in cash as interest rates fall *liquidity preference*. The motives behind liquidity preferences are complex—partly speculative, partly precautionary. With low opportunity costs for holding money, we can afford to hold cash for any good investment or consumption opportunity that happens to come along. Similarly, it is cheaper to hold more money to protect ourselves against any unexpected emergencies.

In this way, both the speculative and precautionary motives make us more and more willing or eager to be in cash when interest rates are low, and less and less willing when rates are higher. Thus the financial demand for cash, like the transactions demand, is a downward sloping demand curve.

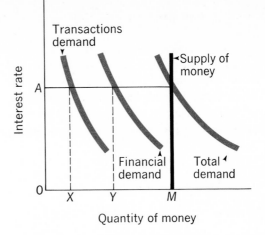

FIG. 34·3 Transactions and financial demands for money

Demand curve for money

We can now put together the two demand curves for money and add the supply curve of money—the actual stock of money available. The result looks like Fig. 34·3.

PRECAUTIONARY AND SPECULATIVE DEMAND

Both the precautionary and the speculative demand for money can be illustrated in the problem of buying or selling bonds. Most bonds are a promise to pay a certain stated amount of interest and to repay the principal at some fixed date. To simplify things, forget the repayment for a moment and focus on the interest. Suppose that you paid $1,000 for a perpetual bond that had a "coupon"— an interest return—of $100 per year with no date of repayment. And suppose that you wanted to sell that bond. What would it be worth?

The answer depends wholly on the current market rate of interest for bonds of equal risk. Suppose that this rate of interest was 10 percent. Your bond would then still be worth $1,000, because the coupon would yield the buyer of the bond 10 percent on his money. But suppose that interest rates had risen to 20 percent. You would now find that your bond was only worth $500. A buyer can go into the market and purchase other bonds that will give him a 20 percent yield on his money. Therefore he will pay you only $500 for your bond, because your $100

coupon is 20 percent of $500. If you want to sell your bond, that is the price you will have to accept.

On the other hand, if interest rates have fallen to 5 percent, you can get $2,000 for your bond, for you can show the buyer that your $100 coupon will give him the going market return of 5 percent at a price of $2,000. (If you were to buy a *new* $1,000 bond at the going 5 percent interest rates, it would carry a coupon of only $50.)

As these numbers indicate, enormous capital gains or losses can be made as market rates of interest change. Your $1,000 bond can fluctuate from $500 to $2,000 if interest rates rise to 20 percent and then drop to 5 percent.

These calculations also show that it can be very profitable at times to hold money. When interest rates are rising, bond prices are falling. Therefore, the longer you wait before

you buy, the bigger will be your chances for a capital gain if interest rates turn around and go the other way. This means that we tend to get "liquid" whenever we think that interest rates are below "normal" levels and bonds are too high; and that we tend to get out of money and into bonds whenever we think that interest rates are above normal levels, and therefore bonds are cheap. The trick, of course, is being right about the course of interest rates before everyone else.

Actual operations in the bond market are complicated, because we must take into account not only interest rates but the time left until a bond becomes "mature" (i.e., is repaid). The closer it is to maturity, the less its price will depart from its face value or principal. Nonetheless, very great gains and losses can be made in bonds that have some years to go before maturity. Even the most "conservative" bonds, such as government bonds, will swing in price as our speculative and precautionary impulses incline us now toward liquidity, now towards a fully-invested position.

Our diagram shows us that at interest rate *OA*, there will be *OX* amount of money demanded for transactions purposes and *OY* amount demanded for liquidity purposes. The total demand for money will be *OM* (= *OX* + *OY*), which is just equal to the total supply.

Changing the supply of money

Now let us suppose that the monetary authorities reduce the supply of money. We show this in Fig. 34 • 4. Now we have a curious situation. The supply of money has declined from *OM* to *OM'*. But notice that the demand curve for money shows that firms and individuals want to hold *OM*, at the given rate of interest *OA*. *Yet they cannot hold amount* OM, *because the monetary authorities have cut the supply to* OM'. What will happen?

The answer is very neat. As bank reserves fall, banks will "tighten" money—raise lending rates and screen loan applications more carefully. Therefore individuals and firms will be competing for a reduced supply of loans and will bid more for them. At the same

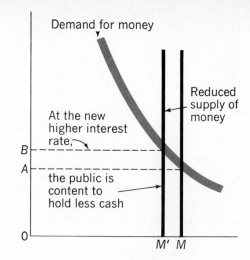

FIG. 34 • 5   Determination of new equilibrium

time, individuals and firms will feel the pinch of reduced supplies of cash and will try to get more money to fulfill their liquidity desires. The easiest way to get more money is to sell securities, to get out of bonds and into cash. Note, however, that selling securities does not create a single additional dollar of money. It simply transfers money from one holder to another. But it does change the rate of interest. As bonds are sold, their price falls; and as the price of bonds falls, the interest yield on bonds rises (see p. 505).

Our next diagram (Fig. 34 • 5) shows what happens. As interest rates rise, the public is content to hold a smaller quantity of money. Hence a new interest rate, *OB*, will emerge, at which the public is *willing* to hold the money that there *is to hold*. The attempt to become more liquid ceases, and a new equilibrium interest rate prevails.

Suppose the authorities had increased the supply of money. In that case, individuals and firms would be holding more money than they wanted at the going rate of interest. They would try to get out of money, into bonds, sending bond prices up and yields down. Simultaneously, banks would find themselves with extra

FIG. 34 • 4   Reducing the supply of money

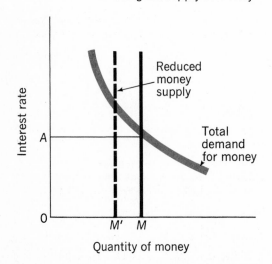

Quantity of money

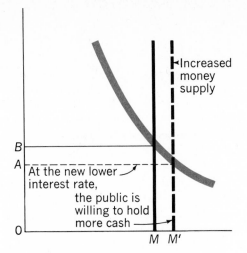

Increased money supply

B

A

At the new lower interest rate, the public is willing to hold more cash

O

M M'

FIG. 34·6   Increasing the supply of money

reserves and would compete with one another for loans, also driving interest rates down. As interest rates fell, firms and individuals would be content to hold more money either for transactions or liquidity purposes, until a new equilibrium was again established. Fig. 34·6 shows the process at work.

Determination of interest rates

This gives us the final link in our argument. We have seen that interest rates determine whether we wish to hold larger or smaller balances, either for transactions or financial (liquidity) purposes. But what determines the interest rate itself? We can now see that the *answer is the interplay of our demand for money and the supply of money.*

Our demand for money is made up of our transactions demand curve and our financial (liquidity) demand curve. The supply of money is given to us by the monetary authorities. The price of money—interest—is therefore determined by the demand for, and supply of, money, exactly as the price of any commodity is determined by the demand and supply for it.

Money and expenditure

What our analysis enables us to see, however, is that once the interest rate is determined, it will affect the use to which we put a given supply of money. Now we begin to understand the full answer to the question of how changes in the supply of money affect GNP (and prices). Let us review the argument one last time.

1. Suppose that the monetary authorities want to increase the supply of money. They will lower reserve ratios or buy government bonds on the open market.

2. Banks will find that they have larger reserves. They will compete with one another and lower lending rates.

3. Individuals and firms will also find that they have larger cash balances than they want at the going rate of interest. They will try to get rid of their extra cash by buying bonds, thereby sending bond yields down.

4. As interest rates fall, both as a result of bank competition and rising bond prices, the new, larger supply of money will find its way into use. *Part of it will be used for additional transactions purposes, as individuals and firms take advantage of cheaper money and increase their borrowings. Part of it will be used for larger financial balances, as the public's desire for liquidity grows with falling interest rates.*

The process in diagram

We can see the process very clearly in Fig. 34·7. We begin with *OM* money supply and a rate of interest *OA.* As we can see, *OL* amount of money is held for liquidity purposes, and *OY* for transactions purposes. Now the stock of money is increased to *OM'.* The interest rate falls, for the reasons we now understand, until it reaches *OB.* At the

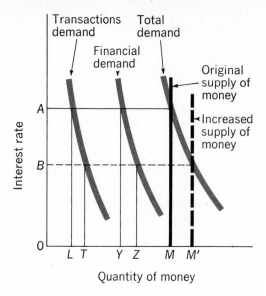

FIG. 34 · 7   Using money for two purposes

new interest rate, liquidity balances have increased to OT, and transactions balances to OZ.

Exactly the same process would take place in reverse if the stock of money were decreased from OM' to OM. Can you see that the decreased supply of money will result partly in smaller transactions balances and partly in smaller liquidity balances? Do you understand that it is the higher rate of interest that causes the public to hold these smaller balances?

Monetarism

We have traced the circuitous manner in which a change in M "gets into" GNP. But there is yet another route that bypasses the rate of interest entirely. The "monetarist" school suggests that increases in M directly affect our spending habits, *even though interest rates remain unchanged.*

The monetarists suggest that changes in the supply of money directly affect our spending propensities because changes in the money supply alter our portfolios. A portfolio describes the way in which we hold our assets—in cash, savings accounts, checking accounts, various kinds of bonds, stocks, real estate, etc. When the money supply is altered, for example through open-market operations, the government is tempting the public to shift its portfolios into cash. But there is no reason to believe that the public wants this much cash. If it *had* wanted it, it would not have held the bonds (at their going rate of interest) in the first place. Therefore the public will seek to reduce its undesired cash holdings by buying real assets—cars, homes, inventories, and other things.

Most economists are willing to add this *liquidity effect* to the *interest rate effect,* so that monetary policy is believed to affect the economy both through its impact on the price of money and also directly through its impact on our portfolio preferences. What remains in doubt is the degree of influence that should be attributed to interest or to liquidity.

Modern quantity theory

We are now in a position to reformulate the quantity theory. Modern proponents of the theory recognize that economies do not always operate at full employment and that the velocity of money changes (we can see that liquidity preferences must be closely related to velocity). Hence they do not argue that an increase in the quantity of money is mechanically reflected in a proportionate rise in prices.

Instead, they contend that the demands for money for transaction purposes and liquidity purposes are *calculable functions,* just as consumption is a calculable function of income. The variables on which the demand for money depend are very complex—too complex to warrant explanation here. What is important is the idea that the relation between an increase in money supply and in transactions and financial demand can be estimated, much as the propensity to consume is estimated.

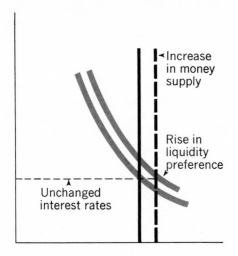

Increase
in money
supply

Rise in
liquidity
preference

Unchanged
interest rates

FIG. 34 · 8   A shift in liquidity preference

The Art of Money Management

We finally have all the pieces of the puzzle. We understand the curiously complex way in which changes in the supply of money affect changes in the expenditures of the public. It remains only to consider one aspect of the problem: the art of managing the supply of money so that the *right* increases in the supply of money will be forthcoming at the right time.

Why "art"? Is not the task of the monetary authority very clear? By increasing the supply of money, it pushes down interest rates and encourages expenditure. Hence all it has to do is to regulate the quantity of money to maintain a level of spending that will keep us at a high, but not too high, level of employment.

We have already seen some of the reasons why things are not that simple. The effect of interest rates on investment expenditure, as we previously learned, is obscure. So is the effect of liquidity on expenditure. We know that unwanted liquidity will encourage spending, but

there is a time lag involved, and this lag may vary considerably at different phases of the business cycle. To add to the problem, the Federal Reserve Board can control the money supply with an eye on interest rates, or it can control it with an eye on liquidity effects, but it cannot do both at the same time. As a result, sometimes the board seems to focus entirely on the "price effect" of interest rates, and at other times on the liquidity effect of money supply. When two policies clash and there is no scientific means of judging between them, we trust to good sense or to a "feel" of the economy. Hence the need for an "art" of money management.

Shifting liquidity preferences Still another difficulty enforces the need for artful control. Suppose, for example, that the Federal Reserve creates excess reserves, in the expectation that interest rates will go down and that new loans will be pumped into investment. But suppose that at the same time, the public's "liquidity preferences" are rising because investors feel nervous and want to be more liquid. Then the shift in the quantity of money, as shown in Fig. 34 · 8, will be offset by a shift in liquidity preferences, and the rate of interest will not change at all! The new money will simply wind up in larger financial cash holdings, and none will be available for more transactions.

In other words, an attempt by the monetary authorities to drive down the rate of interest in order to encourage expenditure may be frustrated if the public uses all the additional funds for liquidity. At the bottom of the Great Depression, for example, banks had huge excess reserves because business would not risk expenditure for new capital projects. People had an insatiable desire for liquidity, and no attempted reductions of the rate of interest could persuade them to spend the money they held for security.

In the same way, an attempt to raise interest rates and to halt price inflation by making credit tight may come to naught if the public reacts to higher interest rates by giving up its liquidity, thereby making funds available to others to finance increased transactions expenditure. Or take another instance: if the Fed tries to lower interest rates by increasing M, the effort may result in a general expectation of inflation and a movement out of bonds into stocks. In that case, interest rates, instead of falling, will go up! This actually happened in 1968.

Credit crunches   Still another difficulty of monetary management lies in *credit crunches*. These occur whenever the monetary authorities attempt to brake the economy quickly, as they did in 1974. Such braking periods are called crunches, since curtailments in the growth of the money supply do not evenly affect all sectors of the economy. Interest rates go up rapidly, but lending institutions also "ration" credit. Mortgage loans, for example, were almost unattainable at any rate of interest during the late fall of 1974. Banks also had to reduce their lending, and they directed their available funds toward large regular customers rather than small or less regular customers.

The uneven reduction in lending was very marked in the crunch of 1974. While residential and state and municipal lending declined by 24 percent, corporate lending rose by 114 percent. Even these figures understate the differences among sectors of the economy. Large corporations were not only able to gain more domestic loans than small business or local governments, but they also had access to international money markets. Thus to some extent they were exempt from the control of

domestic monetary authorities. Many large firms, for instance, borrowed in West Germany to make investments in the United States.

But even large corporations can run into trouble during credit crunches. In the 1968 crunch the Chrysler Corporation, one of the largest industrial enterprises in the nation, almost collapsed. And the Penn Central did collapse. Such disasters, together with the uneven effects of a crunch, place a limit on monetary policies. Very stringent restraints seem both institutionally and politically impossible. After the 1969–1970 credit crunch, efforts were made to develop financial intermediaries that would lend to the sectors most severely hurt and thus spread the effects of monetary policies more evenly across the economy. During the 1974 recession, however, these intermediaries proved to be ineffective. A painful credit crunch occurred despite these new institutions, and it will likely reoccur whenever monetary policies shift sharply toward restriction

Monetary and   All these problems of
fiscal policy   monetary management help us understand why economists are generally reluctant to entrust the overall regulation of the economy to monetary policy alone. There is too much slippage between changes in the money supply and changes in expenditure; too little reliability as to the effects of changes in M on desired changes in MV.

Thus we look for our overall controls to both monetary policies and fiscal policies. Few economists today would rely solely on the money mechanism to move the general economy. Instead, they seek a combination of monetary and fiscal policies—easy money and more government spending (or tax cuts), or tight money and a public budgetary surplus.

Focus The purpose of this lesson is to learn how monetary policy works—that is, how changes in the supply of money affect the economy. Therefore, we begin with a consideration of the quantity theory, one of the first attempts to explain the effects of a change in M.

The quantity theory erred because it believed that *V* and *T* were constants. We know now that they are not, especially *T* (the level of output). Hence, we must look for a better explanation of how changes in M will affect P or PT, the value of output (GNP). The critical link is through the rate of interest.

The monetary authorities cannot themselves decree that all interest rates must change. They can only alter the stock of money. But they know that changes in money must affect bank reserves. In turn, changes in bank reserves will usually lead banks to increase or decrease loans and investments. As a result, the public will be more or less liquid than before the change. If it is more liquid, it will try to get rid of its unwanted cash by buying bonds. This will send bond prices up and bond yields (interest rates) down. At lower interest rates, the public will hold its new larger cash balances. And at lower interest rates it will also be tempted to spend more.

This sequence of events or its reverse is not easy to understand immediately. The best way to master it is to trace very carefully, step by step, the effects of both an increase in money stock and a decrease. In imagination you can put yourself in the position of an entrepreneur and picture the effect of changing interest rates on your propensity to spend. You can also try to imagine how an investor would rearrange his or her holdings between a checking account and a portfolio of stocks and bonds if interest rates changed from 5 percent to 12 percent. Working through question 6 will help you here.

The purpose of learning this intricate web of connections must always be kept uppermost in your mind. We want to discover how the central bank can affect the level of GNP. This forces us to trace the elaborate chain of cause and effect from changes in bank reserves to the ultimate changes in spending.

Finally, as with fiscal policy, it is plain that monetary management is an art, not a mechanical procedure. Nonetheless, it is an art based on a scientific theory of behavior. It is this theory that you want to master in this chapter.

WORDS AND CONCEPTS YOU SHOULD KNOW

Quantity equation, 516–17
Quantity theory, 517, 526
Velocity of circulation, 518
Full employment and prices, 518–21
Transactions demand for money, 522
Financial demand for money, 522
Liquidity preference, 523

Supply and demand for money, 523–25
Bond prices and yields, 524
Money and expenditure, 525–26
Monetarism, 526, 531–32
Money management, 527–28
Credit crunches, 528

QUESTIONS

1. Why is the quantity equation a truism? Why is the interpretation of the quantity equation that M affects P not a truism?

2. The basic reason why the original quantity theorists thought that M affected P was their belief that V and T were fixed. Discuss the validity of these beliefs.

3. Why is the level of employment a critical determinant of fiscal policy?

4. If employment is "full," what will be the effects of an increase in private investment on prices and output, supposing that everything else stays the same?

5. In what way can an increase in excess reserves affect V or T? Is there any certainty that an increase in reserves will lead to an increase in V or T?

6. Suppose that you had $1,000 in the bank. Would you be more willing to invest it if you could earn 2 percent or 5 percent? What factors could make you change your mind about investing all or any part at, say, 5 percent? Could you imagine conditions that would make you unwilling to invest even at 10 percent? Other conditions that would lead you to invest your whole cash balance at, say, 3 percent?

7. Suppose that the going rate of interest is 7 percent and that the monetary authorities want to curb expenditures and act to lower the quantity of money. What will the effect be in terms of the public's feeling of liquidity? What will the public do if it feels short of cash? Will it buy or sell securities? What would this do to their price? What would thereupon happen to the rate of interest? To investment expenditures?

8. Suppose that the monetary and fiscal authorities want to encourage economic expansion. What are the general measures that each should take? What problems might changing liquidity preference interpose?

9. Do you unconsciously keep a "liquidity balance" among your assets? Suppose that your cash balance rose. Would you be tempted to spend more?

10. Show in a diagram how a decrease in the supply of money will be reflected in lower transactions balances and in lower financial balances. What is the mechanism that changes these balances?

11. Do you understand (a) how the rate of interest is determined; (b) how it affects our willingness to hold cash? Is this in any way different from the mechanism by which the price of shoes is determined or the way in which the price of shoes affects our willingness to buy them?

Monetarism

Monetarism is a theory that has had a great vogue during the past few years. In its purest form it is associated with the name of Milton Friedman, an eminent economist and staunch philosophic conservative (pp. 55, 550). Monetarism has two basic tenets. First, it claims that *only* monetary policies affect the long-run level of economic activity. In the slogan of the day, only money "matters"; fiscal policies don't count. Second, within the area of monetary policy proper, monetarists hold that central banks should concern themselves only with the supply of money (which should grow at a steady rate), and not with the level of interest rates. In other words, only the quantity of money counts, not its price!

Why do the monetarists take these seemingly extreme positions? Basically their argument rests on the assumption that any increase in government expenditures will lead to an equal and offsetting decrease in private expenditures (investment or consumption), unless the money supply rises to accommodate the larger public spending. The reasoning is that the government will have to gather the funds for additional spending either by taxing, which will dry up private spending, or by borrowing, which will cause interest rates to rise. Higher interest costs and less credit availability for the public sector will lead to a fall in investment or consumption spending. Thus what the government gains, the private sector loses.

Is this argument valid? Some economists believe that increased public expenditures do crowd out private expenditures. Others think that the "crowding out" is only a partial, not an entire, phenomenon. Still others stress that the "crowding out" is a long-run process and that the government can still effectively use short-run, antibusiness cycle spending, even if the long-run effect of higher spending is nil.

It will take more empirical investigation before we know how valid the first monetarist contention is. Meanwhile, there is an interesting implication in the monetarist position, quite in opposition to the conservative, generally antigovernment spending position of Professor Friedman and his followers. For if only money matters, it follows that inflations are wholly and solely monetary problems. That is, they must be caused by the monetary authorities, not by government fiscal policies. It follows, then, that the government can run a very large deficit with impunity, because its policies will exert no lasting effect on the economy! Curiously, what starts out as a conservative argument against the usefulness of government spending ends up as an argument that can justify rapidly rising government spending, because no monetarist can argue that it is inflationary unless financed by expanding the money supply!

Now what about central bank policy? Here the monetarist position also hinges on an empirical question: namely, is spending affected, in the long term, by the price of money or by its sheer availability, regardless of price? Once again, we do not have enough facts to give us an answer. Therefore, the Fed carries on its day-by-day activities with one eye on interest rates and one on the money supply. In times of accelerating inflation, it tends to lay more emphasis on credit availability; and by braking the expansion of credit, it brings about those crunches we have talked about. In periods of low inflation, the Fed pays more heed to interest rates. This mixed policy implies that credit availability is a more powerful deterrent to spending than are high interest rates, but that low interest rates are a more powerful stimulus for spending than easy money is, by itself.

Because business conditions can change rapidly, and because the monetary authorities necessarily rely on facts that are already "old" to determine policy for the future, monetary policies tend to move rapidly from expansionary to contractionary operations—the Fed buying bonds in the open market one week and selling them the next. The monetarists believe that these attempts to use money as a "fine tuning" device are bound to fail. They would like to hitch the growth in the supply of money to long-term steady factors, such as the growth in productivity. By expanding the money supply by a fixed amount—say, 0.3 percent—each month, the monetarists believe they would be introducing a powerful force for stability into the economy. Whether they are right depends on whether only the supply of money "matters." And that, as we have seen, we just don't know.

For all the uncertainty that surrounds its more extreme beliefs, monetarism has had a strong influence on modern economic thought. This is because many economists during the 1950s and 1960s tended to overlook the importance of money. Just as generals are said always to be prepared to fight the last war, so economists are ready to solve yesterday's problems. Brought up in the traumatic memory of the Great Depression, economists were inclined to place heavy emphasis on the power of spending to prevent this kind of collapse from recurring. But their emphasis on the power of spending and their disregard of the power of money were less relevant for an age dominated by inflation. It is almost certainly not true that *only* money matters. But there is no question that money does matter, and economists are grateful to Milton Friedman for calling to their attention this forgotten truth.

The problem
of
inflation

In Chapter 4 we looked at inflation, the problem Americans worry about most. Now we are finally in a position to examine that problem more thoroughly. This does not mean we will discover answers to questions we earlier described as ill-understood. Inflation remains something of an economic puzzle. But now we can do what was impossible before we had mastered a good deal of economics. We can divide inflation into its ABC, which we *do* understand, and its XYZ, which we don't.

The ABC of the Inflationary Process

What do we know about inflation? A good way to start is by refreshing our memories of how an individual price rises. As we have seen, prices go up when demand curves shift to the right or when supply curves shift to the left. This happens all the time in innumerable markets. Are these price rises "inflationary"?

35

Supply and demand once again

The question begins to sharpen our understanding of what we mean by inflation. In the first place, *inflation means that individual prices must be going up in all or nearly all markets at the same time.* Price rises in some markets, offset by price declines in others, are not an inflationary situation.

Second, *inflation means that the shift of supply and demand curves does not result in a new stable equilibrium.* In an inflationary economy there is no stable price level. Prices rise—and then rise higher. Inflation is a process, not a once-for-all shift.

Supply and demand curves

Our supply and demand apparatus can help us go deeper into the question, for we can see that an inflationary process must be characterized by two elements in the supply/demand picture. First, demand curves must be moving outwards, to the right. Second, supply curves must be upward sloping. That describes rather than explains things, but it also tells us where to look for explanations.

Changes in total demand

Part of the explanation we already understand. The continuing rightward shift in demand curves is the result of *a continuous rise in the volume of expenditure.* More and more dollars are earned and spent. This in turn means that the supply of money must be increasing, or that the velocity of circulation must be constantly increasing, or both. *MV* must be rising if the national price level is rising. You cannot have inflation unless demand curves in most markets are shifting to the right, and this in

turn cannot occur unless money incomes and expenditures are rising in the economy.

The supply constraint: bottlenecks

But this is only half the picture. There is also the question of supply. A rightward shift of a demand curve will not cause prices to rise in a market if the supply curve shifts outward to meet it or if the industry is producing under conditions of constant or decreasing cost. Thus, corresponding to the rightward shift in total demand must come an upward tilt in supply curves, as Fig. 35 • 1 shows.

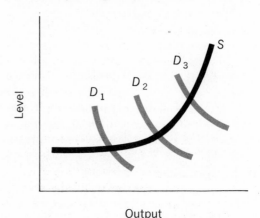

FIG. 35 • 1   The bottleneck supply curve

As demand moves from D_1 to D_2, prices hardly rise at all. But the shift from D_2 to D_3 brings a sharp increase because we run into *bottlenecks* where output cannot be further increased except at much higher cost. These bottlenecks, moreover, may begin to exert their constricting influence before the economy as a whole can be considered in a condition of overall full employment. Thus as demand curves for various goods and services move outward, we will experience price rises in some industries, even though there is unused capacity in others or even though considerable unemployment exists. If these industries bulk large in the pattern of production or in consumer budgets—for example, if we hit bottlenecks in steel or food output—the general price level will begin to rise.

Demand pull vs. cost push

Economists sometimes talk about the two processes that enter into inflation as *demand pull* or *cost push*. Demand pull focuses attention on forces that are causing thousands of demand curves to move to the right—for example, policies of easy money or expansionary fiscal policy. Cost push emphasizes the supply side, with cost curves moving to the left or becoming more vertical.

Cost-push analyses often concentrate on the wage level as a prime causative agency for inflation. Of course, rising wages can be a source of higher costs. But it is important to distinguish between increases in *wage costs per hour* and increases in *wage costs per unit*. Wages may rise; but if *labor productivity keeps pace, cost per unit will not rise* (see box on p. 50).

Corresponding to cost push from rising wage costs per unit, there is cost push from higher profits, an argument frequently put forward by labor. Again we must distinguish between higher profits for the company and higher profits per unit. The latter may occur if the increase in demand outruns the increase in productive capacity, strengthening the market power of large companies.

No doubt there are periods in which the immediate inflationary pressure seems to come from more spending or when it comes from a jump in costs, but it is wrong to separate the two entirely. *More spend-*

ing without higher unit costs will give us more output at the same price, and this is certainly not inflationary. Higher unit costs will lead to inflation only if they occur across the economy. Otherwise, higher unit costs in one area will simply cause people to rearrange their expenditure patterns, moderating the overall inflationary effect.

The Phillips curve

To determine the inflationary pressure in thousands of markets, each with a different configuration of supply and demand curves, would be an impossible task. Hence, the English economist A. W. Phillips has suggested that we show the general relationship between higher wages and/or profits per unit and the degree of capacity utilization. As industries move toward higher rates of utilization, their costs per unit begin to mount more steeply. This is because they are operating in ever tighter markets, especially for labor. Hence Phillips has drawn a curve showing the overall relationship between unemployment, a good indicator

FIG. 35 · 2   The Phillips curve

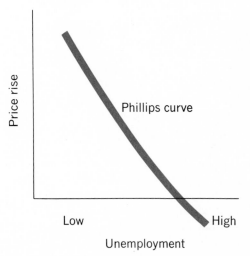

of capacity utilization, and the rise in prices. As Fig 35•2 shows, the lower unemployment falls, the higher is the tendency toward inflation.

Phillips curves are often interpreted as if they implied a causal relationship between employment and inflation, but that is not what the curves actually show. All that we can deduce from the Phillips curve is that there seems to be a statistical relation between high employment rates and high inflation rates. *That is not the same thing as saying that high employment is the cause of high inflation.* It may well be that both high employment and rapid inflation are the consequences of another element not shown on the chart; for example, rising aggregate demand or aggressive monetary expansion.

The trade-off dilemma   The Phillips curve does more than point out a general empirical relationship between employment and price rises. To the extent that the Phillips curve represents reality (a subject that we shall investigate later in this chapter), it also points up a fundamental dilemma. The dilemma is that we cannot choose one target for unemployment and another target for the price level, *independent of each other*. We cannot, for example, "decide" to have 2 percent inflation and 2 percent unemployment, because we do not know how to reconcile low unemployment and low inflation rates. *We have to trade off unemployment against price stability*. The dilemma thus imposes a cruel choice. Governments must choose between alternatives, *both* of which are painful and costly. Before we investigate the means by which they seek to bring about whatever choice they finally make, let us inquire into the costs of these alternatives.

Economic Costs of Unemployment

Suppose the government decides to lessen inflation by increasing the rate of unemployment. What does this cost?

The unemployment option   We can begin with a fairly straightforward estimate of the losses that result from unemployment. For each percentage point of increase in the official unemployment figures, United States' gross national product falls by about 3 percent, or roughly $51 billion. The percentage reduction in GNP is much larger than the percentage increase in officially measured unemployment because (as we shall see, page 552), the labor force and the hours worked per week both shrink as employment opportunities shrink.

Is this, then, the cost of choosing the unemployment "option"? Not quite. For the losses of output and income are by no means equally distributed. If increasing the unemployment rate from 4.5 to 5.5 percent meant that each person found himself unemployed for 14 instead of only 11 out of 250 working days, the income losses would be evenly shared among the labor force. On the other hand, if the additional one percent of unemployment meant that one percent of the working force was permanently unemployed all year, then the costs of unemployment would be entirely concentrated on this group.

If most people were asked which of the two ways of bearing the costs of unemployment were more equitable, they would probably choose the first. But in fact, the way unemployment is actually shared is closer to the second. Joblessness tends to concentrate in certain groups, especially in cyclical downswings. For instance, when the white unemployment rate rises by 1 percentage point, black unemployment rises by 2 percentage points. So, too, in 1976 when the average rate of unemployment among married men was only 4.2 percent, among young workers (16 to 19 years old) it was more than 19 percent. For white workers as a whole it was 7.0 percent; for black workers, 13.1 percent; among black teenagers it was 39 percent. To repeat a fact from Chapter 4: in 1975, 15 percent of the unemployed—over 1.3 million people—had been without work for over half a year.

To be sure, these costs are partly—but only partly—offset by unemployment insurance, as we shall see in our next chapter. But there is no doubt that the costs, psychic as well as economic, are very heavy. And they are not confined solely to workers without jobs. Capitalists also bear some of the loss of unemployment. When aggregate demand falls, output declines. As a result, profits fall; and because management is reluctant to fire overhead office staff, profits often fall more rapidly than output. As in the case of the labor force, the losses borne by firms are not evenly shared. Some industries, such as durable goods, tend to bear more than their share. Others, such as household staples, are relatively depression-proof.

Economic Costs of Inflation

As we have seen, the costs of unemployment tend to be concentrated among certain groups or industries, rather than diffusely shared by all. Now, what of the costs of inflation? Are they also concentrated? Do they resemble the costs of unemployment?

Inflation and income

Let us begin to answer this very important question by reviewing an important, familiar fact. It is our old identity between gross national product and gross national income. We recall that all costs of GNP must become the incomes of the factors of production. This gives us the knowledge that whenever the monetary value of GNP goes up, so must the monetary value of gross national income. This is true whether the increase in GNP results from increased output or higher prices, for in either case the factors of production must receive the monetary value of the output they have produced.

This provides a very important point of departure in comparing unemployment and inflation. For the nation as a whole, inflation cannot decrease the total of incomes. Here it differs sharply from unemployment. Whenever unemployment increases, there is a loss in potential GNP. But whatever the price at which GNP is sold, the real output of the nation remains the same—at least up to the point at which hyperinflation threatens to destroy the system itself.

A zero sum game

Discussions of inflation tend to overlook this fact. They often speak of the losses that inflation brings to this or that group. Of course inflation *can* lower an individual's standard of living by raising the prices he or she must pay. But since the total GNI is equal to GNP, one person's loss must be transferred as a gain to another. This in no way lessens the importance or even the dangers of inflations. But it makes clear that unlike unemployment, in which there are losers but no gainers, in inflation every loss is offset by an equal gain. We call this a *zero sum game*. What is important, then, is to try to weigh the benefits that inflation gives to some, against the losses it inflicts on others.

Who gains by inflation? Who loses?

Winners and losers

Speculators are one group of winners. During an inflation everything does not rise by the same amount or at the same rate. Some items will shoot up, others lag behind, just as in a booming stock market not all stocks share alike in the rise. Speculators are those lucky or skillful individuals who have bought goods that enjoy the sharpest rises. This may be land, gold, or (in hyperinflations) food. Indeed, one of the reasons that hyperinflations result in a collapse of GNP is that more and more persons are *forced* to become speculators, seeking to sell or trade possessions for basic necessities. As individuals spend more and more time trading or scrounging, they begin to spend less and less time at their regular jobs. Thus output begins to fall, and we have the strange coexistence of an economic collapse and soaring prices.

Fixed-income receivers

By definition, anyone who lives on a fixed income, such as an annuity, must be a loser in inflation. Therefore retirees, as a group, seem certain to be badly penalized when prices continually rise. Curiously, they are not. Undoubtedly, there exist the much advertised widows and orphans living off small pensions, but they are probably a very small group. Most retirees live on (or depend largely on) Social Security, and this is quite another story. Social Security benefits have been periodically hiked up by Congress, so that a typical recipient in 1973 was well ahead of the game in terms of the purchasing power of benefits he received. Moreover, in 1973, Congress added to Social Security a cost-of-living escalator clause that automatically adjusted Social Security payments to compensate for cost-of-living increases. Welfare recipients have also had their benefits periodically increased, and they too, have not come out behind in the race since 1950.

Labor and capital

What about labor and capital? Table 35·1 gives us a breakdown of the income shares of strategic groups as a percentage of GNP for the last 25 years.

Table 35 · 1   Pretax income shares as percentage of GNP*

Year	Capital income Cash flow (corp. profits + depreciation) and interest income	Labor income (wages and other income)	Proprietors' income	Rental income	Income redistribution Transfer income
1950	29.0%	54.1%	13.4%	3.5%	**5.3%**
1960	28.9	58.3	9.3	3.5	**5.7**
1970	28.8	62.0	6.6	2.6	**8.1**
1976	30.8	60.8	6.0	2.4	**11.3**

*Totals add to more than 100 percent because of transfers.

We must be cautious in reading this table, as we shall see, but it shows some important results. First, let us compare 1950 and 1975. Capital income as a percentage of GNP has barely changed during the last twenty-plus years. Many factors besides inflation influence corporate profits, but it is clear that inflation by itself has not been enough to increase profits.

Second, over the 25-year period, labor income has increased as a share of GNP. Here again a caution is needed: note the decline in proprietors' income in the third column. Much of that decline is the result of proprietors' giving up independent establishments to work for large enterprises. Their proprietors' income has become "wages." But if we add labor income and proprietors' income, we find that their combined share was just under 67.5 percent in 1950 and 66.8 percent in 1976 a trifling change. Landlords' income (rental income) has evidently fallen considerably as a share of GNP, as we would expect, since rents always lag behind rising prices. And transferees, as we have already seen, were strong gainers.

Changes in recent years

These are long-term trends. But what about the period from 1970 to 1975, when we had a combination of rapid inflation and high unemployment? As the table also shows, the shares of various sectors of the economy did not show any dramatic change.

Of course, just as in the case of unemployment, the impact of inflation is not evenly spread across all groups. Some unions made better settlements than others; some landlords may have made profits while others had losses. But this jockeying for position is a normal state of affairs, and there is no evidence to show that inflation has systematically biased the outcome of the race for real income in comparison with noninflationary times.

We buttress this conclusion if we examine the statistics for the distribution of income among families during the years of high inflation and mounting unemployment. Table 35 • 2 shows the shares of income going to various income groups in the nation in 1970 and 1975. Again, we see little or no evidence that inflation has brought about any substantial change.

Table 35 • 2   Shares of income by family, 1970 and 1975

	1970	1975
The poor (bottom 20 percent)	5.4	5.4
Working class (next 40 percent)	29.8	29.4
Middle class (next 35 percent)	49.2	49.7
Upper class (top 5 percent)	15.6	15.5

Why is inflation such a problem?

The figures raise an important question. Over the long run, there has been very little change in relative shares as a result of inflation. Moreover, even with inflation, real incomes are way up (see p. 35). *Why, then, the fuss about inflation?* Why is it not a popular economic process?

There are several plausible reasons. One is that *the losing groups, such as small proprietors and landlords, are politically influential and articulate and complain about their losses more loudly than the winners (labor or transferees) announce their gains.*

A second reason is that inflation is worrisome just because it affects everyone to some degree. Unlike the concentrated loss of unemployment, the diffuse gains-and-losses of inflation touch us all. *They give rise to the fear that the economy is*

HYPERINFLATIONS

Hyperinflations are among the most destructive economic experiences that a modern economic society can undergo. In the German hyperinflation of the 1920s, for example, prices rose so rapidly that hotels and restaurants with foreign guests would not reveal the price of a meal until the diner had finished; then they would determine the "going" value of marks at that moment. Inflation mounted until a common postage stamp cost 9 billion marks, and a worker's weekly wage came to 120 trillion marks. Newspapers and magazines of the period showed people bringing home their weekly pay in wheelbarrows—billions and billions of marks literally worth less than the paper they were printed on.

Hyperinflations have also occurred in Hungary in 1923 and in China after World War II. They are in large part psychological—even pathological—phenomena, rather than strictly economic ones. That is, they signal a collapse of faith in the vitality and viability of the economy. Farmers typically hoard foodstuffs, rather than accept payment in currencies that they fear will be only so much wallpaper in a matters of weeks.

Merchants and manufacturers are unable to make contracts, since suppliers ask for enormous prices in anticipation of price rises to follow. Shopkeepers are reluctant to sell to customers because this means giving up the true wealth of goods for the spurious wealth of paper money that no one trusts. Thus there is flight from all paper currency and a scramble to get into goods or into commodities such as gold, in which people retain faith. Meanwhile, governments find their expenses skyrocketing and are forced to turn to the printing presses as the only way to collect the revenues they require. Finally, people find that they must *barter* goods, as in primitive economic societies.

The only cure for a hyperinflation is the abandonment of the currency in which everyone has lost faith, and the institution of a new currency that people can be once again induced to believe will serve as a reasonably stable "store of value." For example, in 1958 General de Gaulle stopped an incipient runaway French inflation when he simply announced that there would be a new franc worth one hundred of the old, deteriorating francs. Because of de Gaulle's extraordinary prestige, Frenchmen willingly changed their old 100-franc notes for new one-franc coins and then stopped trying to get "out" of money and into goods. The same magic feat was performed in the 1920s in Germany when the government announced that there would be a new mark "backed" by land. People believed that, and hyperinflation stopped.

There is a curious aspect of hyperinflation that we might stop to notice. Why do workers trundle their wages home in wheelbarrows? Why doesn't the government simply print trillion-mark notes, so that a man's wage would fit into his pocketbook? The answer is purely bureaucratic. The printing presses are busy turning out notes in denominations that would have been suitable for the price level of, say, six months earlier. No one dares give orders for denominations that might meet needs when the notes will actually be issued. Why? Because an order to print, say, trillion-mark notes instead of billion-mark notes would be construed as *inflationary!*

"out of control"—which indeed, to a certain extent, it is.

Third *is the lurking fear that moderate inflation may give way to a galloping inflation.* The vision of a hyperinflation is a specter that chills everyone, and not one to be lightly dismissed. There is always the chance, albeit a small one, that a panic wave may seize the country and that prices may skyrocket while the production of goods declines. Fortunately, hyperinflations are rare. Nations have inflated as much as 200 or 300 percent per year without experiencing the breakdown and disorganization of a real runaway inflation.

Fourth, *the effect of inflation on incomes is not always mirrored in its effects on assets.* Some assets, such as land, typically rise markedly during inflation because they are fixed in supply and because people, forgetting about the land booms and crashes of the past, want to get into something that has "solid value." But many middle-class families have their assets in savings banks or in government bonds, and they watch with dismay as the value of their savings declines. For as interest rates rise, bond prices fall, and stock prices do not typically stay abreast of the price level, although most people think they do. For instance, in late 1968 there was a stock market fall that brought stocks below their levels of 1966–67; and again in early 1973, stock prices fell by a fifth, while consumer prices rose at record rates. Between 1968 and 1976, the cost of living rose by more than 60 percent, but the average of stock prices was basically unchanged.

Inflation vs. unemployment again

Can we now compare the costs of unemployment and inflation? Two points stand out from our analysis.

1. From the point of view of the economy as a whole, unemployment is more costly than moderate inflation. That is because unemployment results in less production, whereas inflation does not. From the point of view of winners and losers, unemployment is also more costly than inflation; for unlike inflation, unemployment is not a zero sum game. The losers in unemployment—the direct unemployed and the hidden unemployed—are not matched by winners who benefit from unemployment.

2. The psychological impact of moderate inflation is probably much greater than that of moderate unemployment. This is because we all feel affected by the inflationary process, whereas few of us worry too much about the unemployed—unless they happen to be ourselves.

Thus, there is a kind of myopia that inflation produces. We blame inflation for reducing our real incomes by raising prices, but we do not give it credit for raising our incomes to pay those higher prices. That is, for 364 days in the year we are painfully aware of price rises as part of the inflationary process, but we do not connect the income increase we receive on the 365th day (if we get a yearly hike in pay) as being part of that selfsame process. Or to put the last point differently: on the one day of the year that we get a raise and feel ahead of the game, our gain in pleasure is less than our 364 days of displeasure in which that gain is eroded by rising prices. In the end, we may still be ahead of the game, but it no longer *feels* that way.

Can we conclude from this that a nation should prefer inflation to unemployment—that a wise and humane policy would deliberately trade off a quite high degree of inflation in exchange for a low rate of unemployment? Some economists might recommend such a course, but it is doubtful that the nation as a whole would vote for it. Rightly or wrongly, most citizens feel that inflation is at least as great a danger as moderate unemployment, and they are not likely to support policies that reduce the joblessness of others in exchange for higher prices (or even higher prices and higher incomes!) for themselves.

The XYZ of Inflation

Until this point we have largely been concerned with conveying knowledge—what we know about inflation. Now we must change our track. The rest of this chapter is mainly concerned with conveying ignorance. There is a great deal that we do not know about inflation, and a student should be as aware of our ignorance as of our knowledge.

The elusive Phillips curve

Let us begin with the Phillips curve. Consider Fig. 35·3. The colored line shows that there is perhaps a *general* tendency of inflation to be inversely correlated with unemployment. When unemployment is *very* high, inflation is low, and vice versa, although there are exceptions: look at 1975! But now examine the scatter of dots within the tinted band representing the range from 3.5 to 6 percent unemployment. Compare 1964 and 1974, for instance. In 1964 an

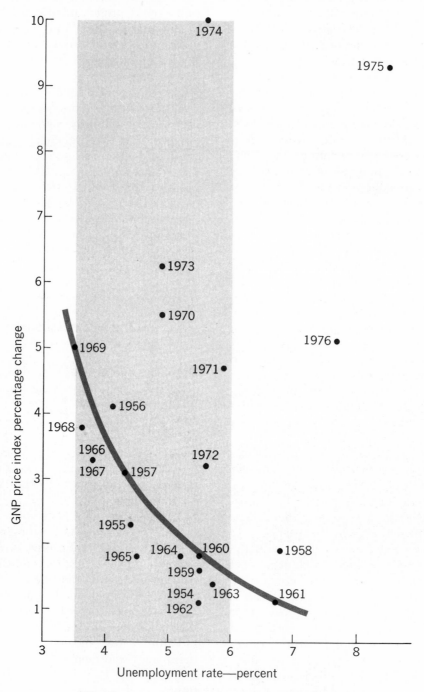

FIG. 35 · 3   The unemployment-inflation relation

unemployment rate of just over 5 percent was associated with a rate of inflation of less than 2 percent. In 1974 an unemployment rate of 5.6 percent was associated with an inflation of almost 10 percent.

What we have, in other words, is a relationship that is subject to such wide variations that economists have not been able to establish a function that enables them to *predict* what rate of unemployment will actually accompany a given inflation rate. This means that we cannot "target" a mix of inflation and unemployment, as our schematic diagram on p. 535 suggested, *because we do not know where the Phillips curve will be located.*

Indeed, given the lack of empirical evidence, we can even ask why the idea of a Phillips "curve" survives. The answer is that we continue to believe in the existence of an inflation-unemployment trade-off at extreme ranges. If we were willing to run the economy at Depression rates of 25 percent unemployment, few doubt that inflation would halt or even go into reverse. Conversely, if we were to strive for World War II rates of unemployment, when only 1 percent or 2 percent of the labor force was idle, there is little doubt that we would have to expect rampant inflation. The problem lies in the middle range—say between an unemployment rate of 3 percent and 7 percent. Here our knowledge is inadequate. We simply do not know what rate of inflation to associate with any given level of unemployment in this range.

The quantity theory

What about money? Is there not a clear theory of inflation in the quantity theory of money, especially in its new-fangled guise that we studied in our preceding chapter?

As with the relation between unemployment and inflation, no one denies the inflationary impact of increases in the supply of money, or the anti-inflationary effects of reductions in the supply of money, *at the extremes.* If the Fed were to go on an open-market buying spree, there isn't any question that spending would rise with inflationary consequences; or if the Fed were to put on the brakes hard, it would certainly bring about a credit crunch that would stop the economy (and the inflation) dead in its tracks.

The trouble once again lies in the middle range. And here the problem with the quantity theory is that it also has no predictive value. In our preceding chapter we saw how difficult it was for the Fed to know in advance whether an increase in money would lead to more transactions or simply to more liquidity. Add to that the fact that even "monetarists" admit that there is a lag of up to 9 months between the injection of new money by the Fed and a rise in prices, and we can see that for all practical purposes, the quantity theory, like the Phillips curve, fades away as a guide to policy. Just as we do not know what level of inflation will be associated with a given level of unemployment, so we do not know what effect a given change in the money supply will have on prices.

The problem of expectations

At the root of our problem is the question of expectations. As economist James Tobin has written:

To predict the rate of inflation next quarter or year, the most valuable single piece of information is the rate of inflation in the period immediately preceding. . . .The trend of prices is solidly built into the economy, with a powerful and persistent momentum.

Inflations thus perpetuate themselves, in part, because they breed expectations that lead to inflation-producing actions. Labor union leaders expect prices to rise, and they take that into account in setting wage goals. Business does likewise.

Not only do expectations help perpetuate inflation, but they also play hob with theory, for it is very difficult to predict the effects of pronouncements or news on expectations themselves. Will an announcement that the cost-of-living index is up over last month send people on a buying spree, in anticipation of next month's expected increase? Or will it result in a tightening of budgets for the very same reason?

Thus, our inability to predict the course of inflation stems in large part from those very uncertainties about expectations we discussed in Chapter 9. Until we learn to anticipate expectations or to influence expectations, the movements of the marketplace—and of that gigantic marketplace called the economy—are likely to take us by surprise.

Controlling Inflation

Can we stop inflation? Of course—at a price. For example, wage and price controls with terrific penalties for noncompliance would surely dampen inflation. So would a decision not to increase the money supply at all. The trouble is that no one is willing to pay so great a price—the price of a police state in the first case, or of massive unemployment in the second. Therefore, we seek to control inflation with *politically acceptable* measures, and these have not been too successful.

Since World War II every major government has tried to keep the lid on inflation, but with scant results. In the United States, the Kennedy administration inaugurated the idea of "wage-price guidelines" that were intended to serve as an official index of productivity, to which it was hoped labor leaders would conform their demands. But the wage-price guidelines allowed for increases of only about 3.4 percent per year and were not very effective. Some unions whose productivity had gone up more rapidly than 3.4 percent claimed that they had the *right* to higher wages; other unions simply ignored the guidelines; and most companies tried only halfheartedly to stick by them in wage bargaining sessions, because they counted on inflation itself to help them pass along any cost increases in higher prices.

Another tactic used by subsequent administrations was called "jawboning." This was simply the use of public pressure, usually through presidential statements, to get companies (or less frequently unions) to scale down price increases. For instance in 1971 Bethlehem Steel suddenly announced that it was about to raise steel prices by 12 percent. Angry comments from the White House, coupled with stories carefully leaked to the newspapers about the possibility of relaxing steel import quotas, brought the welcome response of a much smaller (6 percent) increase from Bethlehem's main competitors. In the end, Bethlehem had to back down to the 6 percent mark.

Wage and price controls   Still, 6 percent is a stiff price increase. Hence more and more pressure built up for the imposition of direct controls over wages and prices, which were finally instituted by the Nixon administration in 1971.

The problem with controls is that they are administratively clumsy, hard to enforce, and almost invariably evaded in one way or another. A wage and price freeze always catches someone at a disadvantage: a union that was just about to sign an advantageous but perhaps deserved contract, a store whose prices were at "sale" levels on the day that the freeze is announced, a business whose costs increase as a result of a rise in the prices of imported goods. Thus price controls lead to endless adjustment and adjudication. Moreover, unless there is a general sentiment of patriotic "pulling together" (as during World War II or the Korean war, when controls were fairly successful in repressing inflation), controls tend to lead to black or gray markets or to downgrading the quality of the "same" goods that are sold at fixed prices.

Not surprisingly, efforts to control wages tend to be more successful than efforts to control prices. This is because the government has an ally to help it enforce its wage regulations; namely, employers. Employers know what their employees make and have an interest in keeping wages within the legal limits. Consumers, on the other hand, usually do not know what products cost and cannot demand that stores refrain from marking up items. Renters are perhaps in the best position as consumers to enforce price controls on rents, but even they are in a weak position when they look for vacant apartments.

As a result, when controls are imposed, they tend to work fairly well for a short period of time on the wage side, while prices continue to creep upward. After a certain point, consumer resentment explodes in the form of demands from workers that their wage restraints be loosened. In nation after nation, this process has been repeated.

The Recession Approach

The Ford administration abandoned efforts to impose controls and substituted a policy of severe economic restraint. The administration, determined to hold federal spending as low as possible, encouraged the Fed to rein in the growth of the money supply. This does not mean that government spending or the money supply fell. It meant, rather, that the federal budget did not expand as rapidly as it would have under a different-minded administration and that the increase in the money supply was much slower than under past administrations.

The upshot of the new policies was a considerable rise in unemployment—indeed, a recession of severe magnitude. Grimly the administration clung to its policies of restriction while unemployment mounted at one point to almost 10 percent of the labor force. Meanwhile, each month the movement of prices was anxiously scanned. Was the restraining policy finally "paying off"? At the end of 1974 inflation had reached an annual rate of 13 percent. By early 1976 it had been brought down to 3.9 percent, although it again moved back to 5 and 6 percent.

Did the policy "work"? The answer is yes and no. Inflation certainly fell from its frightening levels of late 1974, probably (although not certainly) because of this deflationary policy. But a terrible price was exacted in joblessness and in public programs that were postponed or shelved. Whether the overall policy should be deemed a success therefore depends very much on the weight we place on unemployment as a social cost. There is no scientific way of declaring whether this cost is "justified." Our judgments, as we have so often said, reflect our values.

Stop-go   As a result of these partly economic, partly political difficulties, anti-inflationary policies here and abroad take on an aspect of "stop-go." When prices begin to rise too fast, remedial measures are put into effect. The money supply is tightened to curb spending. Governments trim their budgets. Taxes may be increased somewhat. Wage and price controls are put into effect.

For a time, these "stop" measures succeed. But then pressures mount in the opposite direction. High interest rates cut into home building. A slowdown in investment causes unemployment to rise. Tight government budgets mean that programs with important constituencies have to be cut back; Army bases are closed; social assistance programs abandoned. Business chafes under controls. Hence pressures mount for a relaxation. The red light changes to green. The money supply goes up again; investment is encouraged; public spending resumes its former upward trend; controls are taken off. Before long the expected happens: prices begin to move ahead too rapidly once more, and the pendulum starts its swing in the opposite direction.

Inflation as a way of life   Does this mean that inflation has become a chronic fact of life, uncurable except at levels of unemployment that would be socially disastrous or by the imposition of severe and unpopular wage, price, and income controls?

Probably. One fact of great significance is that inflation has been a worldwide experience. It has ravaged underdeveloped countries, where prices have often risen by 20 to 50 percent per year. Inflation has appeared in every industrialized nation, even though those nations did not participate in the Korean or Indochinese wars. As Table 35·3 shows, the United States' inflationary problem has generally been much *less* severe than the European or Japanese experience. In other words, contemporary inflation seems to be a new kind of economic problem that has appeared—and resisted attempts to remedy—in all industrialized nations.

Table 35 · 3   Worldwide inflation

PRICE RISES IN INDUSTRIALIZED COUNTRIES

Average annual percentage

	1959—69	1969—72	1973—75
U.S.	2.2	4.5	11
Australia	2.4	5.3	16
Canada	2.4	3.7	12
France	3.7	5.8	13
Italy	3.6	5.1	19
Japan	5.0	6.1	19
Sweden	3.7	6.9	11
Switzerland	3.0	5.6	9
U.K.	3.4	7.6	22
W. Germany	2.4	4.9	7

Global inflation   To what can we ultimately trace this global phenomenon? Here our knowledge becomes even less certain, and we are forced to resort to more or less plausible hypotheses that refer to social and political as much as economic causes.

In Chapter 4 (pp. 50–52) we mentioned some likely reasons for this endemic condition. One of them, we will recall, is a shift from high-productivity goods output to lower-productivity services output, a trend visible in all nations. Another is the worldwide growth of market power, in the hands of giant corporations, powerful labor unions, and government marketing agencies. A third is the rise of expansionist government policies in almost all nations. A fourth is the advent of new attitudes of high aspiration, coupled with greater "staying power," evinced by citizens of the more developed countries.

For these reasons it seems that we will have to live with inflation for a very long period.

What economists hope for is that a middle ground can be reached where the frictions generated by inflation and the real damage done by unemployment can be reduced to reasonable proportions. A price rise of 1 or 2 percent a year, for example, can be fairly easily tolerated, since a year-to-year increase in the quality of goods can be said to justify such an increase. Similarly, 3 or 4 percent unemployment (which includes voluntary unemployment and a hard core of "unemployables") is also socially acceptable, especially since both kinds of unemployment can be remedied by generous policies of unemployment compensation or by programs for retraining labor.

But it is one thing to announce such a goal and another to attain it. The simple fact remains that in no industrialized nation has anything like such an acceptable balance been achieved. In most nations, the claims of high employment quite properly take priority over those of inflation, and the rate of annual price increase has accordingly ranged from roughly 4 to 10 percent a year. As we have seen, in this chronicle of inflationary failure, the record of the United States is by no means the worst. Unhappily, its record in combating unemployment, as we shall see in our next chapter, is by no means the best.

Focus   There is a basic problem to be thought about in this chapter: the choice between the costs of unemployment and the frictions of inflation. This central dilemma affects all market economies. We can do no more than suggest that you read over the pages devoted to the subject (536–41) and review the main elements we stress.

Second, we hope you will bring from this chapter an understanding of both what we do and what we don't understand about inflation. You should clearly see why inflation must have some demand pull; that is, why it must have rightward moving demand curves in most markets. You should also see why it must have cost-push elements—bottlenecks or upward sloping demand curves. Do you understand why we could not have an inflation unless both conditions were present, regardless of which was the more "active" at the moment?

It is a little disconcerting to study a subject to find out what we don't know. Nonetheless, a knowledge of ignorance is a necessary part of wisdom. The elusive Phillips curve is a case in point. So is the unreliable guide of monetary policy, the happenstance of accidents, and the curious role of expectations. Can you see that we do not have a theory of inflation that compares in simplicity and explanatory power to the theory of underemployment equilibrium?

This brings us to the question of policy. When theory is weak, policy is apt to be catch-as-catch can. That is exactly what we find. You should try to understand the failures or partial successes of policy in terms of our inadequate theory. And you might look into the "Extra word" for two daring attempts to formulate much more effective policies than any that we discuss.

WORDS AND CONCEPTS YOU SHOULD KNOW

Bottlenecks, 534
Demand pull, 535
Cost push, 535
Phillips curve, 535–36
Trade-off dilemma, 536
Costs of unemployment, 541–43
Zero sum game, 537–38
Redistributive effects of inflation, 538–39

Four reasons why inflation is feared, 539–40
Hyperinflation, 540 (box)
Expectations, 543–44
Controls, 544–45
"Stop-go," 546
Incomes policies, 549
Indexing, 550

QUESTIONS

1. Distinguish between a change in prices in an individual market and an inflationary change. What is meant by calling inflation a "process"?

2. What is meant by "demand pull"? By "cost push"? What explanations can we give for the increase in demand? For the rise in costs? Can you have an inflationary *process* if both costs and demand are not rising?

3. What kind of event might give rise to a hyperinflation in the United States? Might a defeat in war trigger such an event? A victory? If we were to experience a runaway inflation, what measures would you counsel?

4. What is the importance of productivity in determining whether wage increases add to cost? Suppose that wages go up by 5 percent and that productivity goes up by 4 percent. Will there be an increase in costs per unit? Might this increase be absorbed by a fall in profits? Under what conditions is it likely to be passed on to consumers?

5. Is a war always inflationary? Does it depend on how it is financed? How should it be financed to minimize inflation? Does the same reasoning apply to an investment boom? (HINT: since corporations cannot tax, they must depend on savings for their expenditures.)

6. What is meant by the Phillips curve? Is it a concept that is useful for a general understanding of the inflationary process? Why is it of little use for prediction?

7. Suppose that you could add up the costs of unemployment in terms of income lost. Suppose that you could add up the losses incurred just by those groups who are left behind in inflation (forget about the "winners"). Suppose further, that the losses imposed by inflation were greater than those imposed by unemployment. Does this mean that inflation is necessarily a worse economic disaster than unemployment? Must personal values enter into such a calculation? (If you simply compare amounts, is this also a value judgment?)

8. Why have measures to control inflation been so unsatisfactory? Why are price controls more difficult to monitor than wage controls?

9. Suppose that unemployment and inflation rise again to about 10 percent a year. What measures would you propose?

Incomes policy and indexing

One of the most ambitious efforts to bring inflation under control is incomes policy, an effort to form a "social contract" that will establish the shares of national income going to each major power group. England, Sweden, and a few other European countries have been trying to bring labor and capital and other major interests (such as farmers and civil service employees) into an agreement about how much each will receive from the national income.

Incomes policies are not only efforts to deal with inflation but are, in fact, implicit theories of inflation. They assume that inflation is the result of power groups striving to outdo one another when the expansion of demand cannot be matched by a comparable increase in supply. The hope is that by bringing the free-for-all to a halt, all groups will gain secure shares of the national income, without the inflation-breeding struggle of the past.

Incomes policies have not yet been attended with great success. In part, the reason is that inflation is not always caused by domestic jockeying for place, but sometimes by outside factors, such as the "oil shock" that dealt European economies a fierce inflationary blow. Second, the idea of a social contract assumes that all groups can agree on "fair shares," and this is often difficult to do. Third, it also assumes that all members of society will be represented in a social contract. Otherwise the weak will simply be trampled on by the well-organized. And not least, the theory takes for granted that a bargain, once reached, will be respected by all.

Thus an effective incomes policy based on a "social contract" has very great problems. It is possible that some European nations where there already exists a high degree of social organization (such as Sweden) may succeed in forging such a new approach to inflation control over the coming years. In the United States, where most of the big economic interest groups are relatively unorganized, a social contract seems very unlikely, at least for the immediate future.

INDEXING

An entirely different approach to inflation has been suggested by Milton Friedman, whom we have already encountered as the leading protagonist of monetarism and as a staunch defender of a laissez-faire approach to economics (see Chap. 4, p. 55). As we know, Friedman believes that inflation is wholly caused by excess money supply. He proposes, however, that if we cannot bring our money supply under strict control for political reasons, we can at least learn to live much less painfully with inflation by "indexing."

Indexing means that as many contracts or institutional arrangements as possible, such as wages and interest and rent and bond values and welfare payments, should have "escalator" provisions that would regularly adjust their nominal money price in terms of some index of prices. Suppose you were hired at $200 a week and had a $2,000 savings account in Year 1. If prices doubled in Year 2, your pay would automatically jump to $400 a week, and your savings account would be revalued at $4,000. If all prices were indexed in this fashion, it would make very little difference if inflation were fast or slow. Your relative position in society, your relative wealth and income would be unaffected, although of course you could try to get ahead faster than your neighbor, as so many now do.

Indexing has two major problems. First, it presents an array of difficult questions about how to index certain kinds of wealth or income. How do you index a lawyer's income? An artist's fees? The wages of the nonunionized? The price of foreign raw materials? The value of stocks, land, houses?

More troubling is that indexing would remove any reason whatever to oppose inflation. The inertia that is built into our system because some contracts are not indexed would disappear. As long as everyone is protected, what difference how high the prices go? With this philosophy might come the beginning of a self-fulfilling prophecy in which expectations of an ever faster rising rate of inflation in fact brought into being just such a state of affairs. From there to hyperinflation is too close for comfort. And though hyperinflation in a perfectly indexed world theoretically would not make any difference, no one is very eager to put the theory of indexing to such a test.

Unlike the social contract, however, indexing will certainly be used to some extent in the United States. Already much of the American economy is indexed. Social Security payments, many union pay arrangements, most long-run business supply contracts have built-in cost-of-living adjustments or some other form of indexing. These arrangements are likely to be extended to more groups in society. One idea that has long been urged is the indexing of government bonds for small savers, so that when the bond comes due, an investor in U.S. Savings Bonds will get back the full real purchasing power invested. Such a step would be a useful means of lessening the erosion of wealth (especially of small wealthholders) that *is* one of the real costs of inflation.

The problem of unemployment

We have already looked briefly into the problem of unemployment in Chapter 4 (on pp. 52–55), and the reader might do well to begin by looking back over those pages. Now, however, we are ready to examine the question in a much more searching and detailed manner than before. And we begin by acquainting ourselves with the meaning of the word "unemployment" itself.

The meaning of unemployment

The measure of unemployment is determined by a household-to-household survey conducted each month by the Bureau of the Census among a carefully selected sample.* An "unemployed" person is thereupon defined not merely as a person without a job—for perhaps such a person does not *want* a job—but as someone who is "actively" seeking work but is unable to find it. Since, however, the number of people who will be seeking work will rise in good times and fall in bad times, figures for any given period must be viewed with caution.

*Sampling is an important statistical tool. If you would like to learn more about it, consult Section IV, Part 6.

36

As employment opportunities drop, unemployment will not rise by an equivalent amount. Some of those looking for work when job opportunities are plentiful will withdraw from the labor force and become part of *hidden unemployment*. When job opportunities expand, these "hidden unemployed" will reenter the labor force, so that unemployment will not fall as fast as employment rises. Thus the ups and downs in the measured unemployment rate reflect the state of the economy, but the swings are not as large as they would be if the term "unemployment" measured the hidden unemployed.

The elastic labor force

This gives rise to a curious and important result. Measured unemployment is not simply the difference between the number of people working and a fixed labor force. It is the difference between the number working and an elastic, changeable labor force.

The result of measuring unemployment is seemingly paradoxical. It is that employment and unemployment can both rise and fall at the same time, as workers (mainly youths and women) enter the labor market in good times, or as they withdraw in discouragement in bad times. Table 36 • 1 shows us this parallel rise in both the number working and the number without work. Look at the change from 1970 and 1971 or again between 1973 and 1974.

Participation rates

We call this elasticity of the labor force its *short-run participation rate*. In Chapter 2 (on p. 18) we learned something about long-run participation rates, marked by historical changes in the ratios of men and women in the labor force, or in the proportions of the young and the old at work. Now we see that short-run changes play a significant role in determining the meaning of the phenomenon we call unemployment. The average number of hours worked per week also varies with good and bad times because employees can or cannot get overtime work or can or cannot "moonlight" (take on a second job).

These considerations mean that economists do not judge the severity of a given unemployment rate just by the percentage of the jobless. They also look to participation rates and hours of work. Relatively low participation rates and a fall in average hours worked per week indicate that the impact of a given unemployment rate is more serious than it appears to be.

Severity of unemployment

How serious is unemployment as a national economic problem? Table 36 • 2 shows us the record of the past few years and gives us the data for earlier, benchmark years to serve as a point of comparison. (In this discussion we ignore participation rates, to concentrate on more deep-lying problems.)

Table 36 • 1   Short-run changes in the labor force (millions)

	1970	1971	1972	1973	1974	1975	1976
Number in civilian labor force	82.7	84.1	86.5	88.7	91.0	92.6	94.8
Civilian employment	78.6	79.1	81.7	84.4	85.9	84.8	87.5
Unemployment	4.1	5.0	4.8	4.3	5.1	7.8	7.3

Table 36 · 2   Unemployment in the U.S.

Year	Unemployed (thousands)	Percent of civilian labor force
1929	1,550	3.2
1933	12,830	24.9
1940	8,120	14.6
1944	670	1.2
1960–65 av.	4,100	5.5
1966	2,875	3.8
1967	2,975	3.8
1968	2,817	3.6
1969	2,832	3.5
1970	4,085	4.9
1971	4,993	5.9
1972	4,840	5.6
1973	4,304	4.9
1974	5,076	5.6
1975	7,530	8.5
1976	7,288	7.7

The terrible percentages of the Depression years speak for themselves. At the very depth of the Depression, a quarter of the work force was jobless, at a time when unemployment insurance and welfare was largely nonexistent. Note, too, that massive unemployment persisted until 1940. Only the advent of World War II finally brought unemployment below 1929 levels.

The record of the 1960s and 1970s is mixed. During the early 1960s, unemployment was at a level considered to be uncomfortably high—roughly between 5 and 6 percent of the labor force. This percentage dropped in the second half of the decade, partly as a consequence of higher spending on armaments. At the end of this chapter we will ask whether arms spending is necessary to absorb unemployment in capitalism.

It is the record of the 1970s that is disturbing. First, we watched the number of unemployed soar to a peak of over 8 million in May 1975. Second, we saw unemployment rates approach 9 percent of

the labor force, a rate more serious than any recession (barring only the 1933–1940 collapse) in this century.

Impact of unemployment

Moreover, as we recall from Chapter 4, the impact of an unemployment rate of, say, 7 percent does not mean that everyone who works will be laid off for 7 percent of the year, or about two weeks. Rather, the effect of unemployment hits very hard at particular groups, as Table 36 · 3 allows us to see in considerable detail.

Table 36 · 3   Composition of the unemployed

	1969	1975
Total	3.5	8.5
Male	2.8	7.9
16–19	11.4	20.4
20–24	5.1	14.3
25–64	1.7	5.2
65 up	2.2	5.4
Female	4.7	9.3
16–19	13.3	19.7
20–24	6.3	12.7
25–64	3.2	7.1
65 up	2.3	5.1
Black, total	6.4	13.9
16–19	23.9	37.4
White, total	3.1	7.8
16–19	10.7	18.1
White collar	2.1	4.7
Blue collar	3.9	11.7
Service	4.2	8.6
Farm	1.9	3.5

Duration (weeks)	Percent of unemployed	
0–5	57.5	37.0
6–10	22.2	22.2
11–14	7.1	9.1
15–26	8.5	16.5
27 and over	4.7	15.2

An analysis of unemployment

The table is long and complicated, but it repays some careful study. Let us begin by comparing total unemployment in 1969 and 1975. The year 1969 was the last year of a long period of real growth in GNP; 1975 was the bottom of the sharpest decline since the Great Depression. The effect on unemployment was to raise the national rate by more than 100 percent.

First look at the data for 1969. Notice that the seemingly low rate of 3.5 percent unemployment for the nation as a whole was a weighted average of very low rates (1.7 percent) for male workers between the ages of 25 and 64 and horrendous rates (23.9 percent) for black teenagers. Notice something else. At every age level, female unemployment rates exceeded male rates by substantial margins; and approximately twice as many blacks were jobless as whites. We can also see that unemployment hits different occupations differently. Service and blue-collar workers were twice as likely to be unemployed as white-collar or farm workers.

Now switch to 1975. With the rise in the national rate to 8.5 percent, unemployment rates for blacks and women have skyrocketed. Blue-collar rates are also relatively worse, compared with white-collar rates. And perhaps the most dramatic change has been in the duration of unemployment. In 1969 only 4.7 percent of the population had been without work for more than half a year. In 1975, as we noted in Chapter 4, this proportion had risen to 15.2 percent.

Easing the cost of unemployment

To some extent, this concentrated cost of unemployment is offset by transfer payments made to some of the unemployed. Because these payments come from taxes that are mainly paid by employed persons, transfers help to some small degree to spread the burden.

Unemployment compensation in the United States differs widely among the states. In general, it provides for payment of one-half of an unemployed person's income, up to some maximum weekly benefit. Actual weekly benefits range from $99 in Washington, D.C. to $48 in Mississippi. There is also a limit on how many weeks' unemployment compensation can be claimed. Usually 20 weeks can be collected, although that was temporarily upped to 65 weeks by federal legislation during the 1975–1976 recession.

However, many individuals, such as new entrants into the labor force or employees of government and nonprofit institutions are not eligible for any benefits at all. If a person is not eligible or has exhausted his or her benefits, there is welfare, which also varies from state to state in terms of benefits and eligibility.

Causes and Cures

What causes unemployment, and what will cure it? We have already more than once studied the principal reason for joblessness—a lack of sufficient aggregate demand. For reasons that we understand very well, when total spending declines, employers let workers go. **Thus the first cause of unemployment lies in too little demand, and the first cure lies in restoring demand to a "full employment level."**

Level of demand   This is only the first step in our analysis, however, for we must recognize that a

A special kind of unemployment arises because the age composition of the labor force changes, sometimes flooding the market with young untrained workers, sometimes with older workers. Take the group aged 14 to 24. This includes those who are finishing their educations, as well as those who have finished and are entering the work force. The "cohort" as a whole increased in numbers by roughly 8 to 10 percent from decade to decade in the period 1890 to 1960.

Then in the 1960s an explosion occurred. The so-called baby boom in the years immediately following World War II began to enter these age ranks. In the decade of the 1960s, the 14-to-24-year-old group increased by 52 percent. In the 1970s it will increase by a "normal" 11 percent; in the 1980s it will *decline* by 8 percent. We can confidently predict these changes, because the members of this age group are already born.

Beginning in mid 1980s, however, the rate of growth of the labor force will be very slow, except for women. Job prospects should then be very bright.

level of demand adequate to produce "full" or high employment in one year will not be adequate the next. First, there is a normal growth of the labor force as a consequence of population growth. This growth may accelerate if an unusually large number of young people, products of an earlier "baby boom," are leaving school. In the 1960s there was a flood of such young entrants; now, fortunately, the flood has ebbed (see box).

Second, even if there were no increase in the labor force, we experience a normal growth in productivity as the consequence of adding capital equipment, of improving our techniques of production, and of increasing our stock of skill and knowledge. This year-to-year increase in per capita productivity is about 3 percent. Therefore, unless GNP grows by at least that amount, there will not be enough demand to absorb the output of the given labor force.

Full employment growth

Thus we need a growth of GNP equal to the increase in the labor force, plus the increase in productivity, to insure a constant rate of employment. In ordinary times, this means that GNP, in real terms, must grow at about 4 to 4½ percent per year to give us steady high employment.

But suppose that we have too much unemployment and want to grow fast enough to absorb it? Now comes an important twist that results from the elasticity of the labor force. As employment grows, more people enter the labor force, and hours lengthen. This means that we have to increase the level of GNP enough to absorb the "original" unemployed, plus the addition to the labor force that results from higher participation rates and more hours worked. Arthur Okun, former Chairman of the Council of Economic Advisors, has estimated that it takes a 2½ percent increase in GNP just to hold the unemployment rate constant, and a 3½ percent increase in GNP to bring about a 1 percentage point fall in unemployment.

The difficulty with revving up GNP to eliminate unemployment is that we rapidly run into inflationary bottlenecks, once unemployment reaches the 5 to 6 percent level. This brings us to familiar terrain, where we must fight out the battle between unemployment and inflation. **We know how to reduce unemployment by raising aggregate demand, but we do not know how to do so without creating unacceptable levels of inflation.**

Technological unemployment

Aggregate demand—or rather, the lack of it—is the prime cause of unemployment, but it is not the only cause. Let us now begin to take up a series of subsidiary reasons for the existence of unemployment—conditions that may create unemployment or make difficult its cure, even if the level of national spending is high.

The first candidate on our list is technological unemployment, the joblessness caused by the introduction of machines. This is a problem that vexes and worries us, partly because it is real, partly because we do not understand it very well. For example, we constantly hear references to "automation" as a great unemployment-creating force, although in the very next breath we speak of the need for "growth industries" (like automation!) to *create* employment. In this next section, therefore, we shall try to sort out the different effects that technology can have on employment. And the reader will note a box just after the questions at the end of the chapter, in which we look into automation from a different, historical angle.

Technology and the demand for labor

We should begin by realizing that not all technology economizes on labor. Fertilizer, for example, saves land; miniaturization saves capital; new technologies may save labor *and* capital to make the "same" product (e.g., a mass-produced Volkswagen and a hand-tooled Rolls-Royce are both cars). But the inventions that interest us here are *labor-saving* inventions or innovations, changes in technique or technology that enable an entrepreneur to turn out the same output as before, with less labor, or a larger output than before, with the same amount of labor.

Do such inventions "permanently" displace labor? Let us trace an imaginary instance and find out.

We shall assume that an inventor has perfected a technique that makes it possible for a local shoe factory to reduce its production force from 10 men to 8 workers, while still turning out the same number of shoes. Forgetting for the moment about the possible stimulatory effects of buying a new labor-saving machine,* let us see what happens to purchasing power and employment if the shoe manufacturer simply goes on selling the same number of shoes at the same prices as before, utilizing the new lower-cost process to increase profits.

Suppose our manufacturer now spends the increased profits in increased consumption. Will that bring an equivalent increase in the total spending of the community? If we think twice we can see why not, for the increased spending of the manufacturer will be offset to a large extent by the decreased spending of the two displaced workers.

Exactly the same conclusion follows if the entrepreneur used the cost-cutting invention to lower the price of shoes, in the hope of snaring a larger market. Now it is *consumers* who are given an increase in purchasing power equivalent to the cut in prices. But again, their gain is exactly balanced by the lost purchasing power of the displaced workers.

Incomes vs. employment

Thus we can see that the introduction of labor-saving machinery does not necessarily imperil *incomes;* it merely shifts purchasing power from previously employed workers into the hands of consumers or into profits. But note also that *the unchanged volume of incomes is now associated with a smaller volume of employment.* **The fact that there**

---

*This is not an unfair assumption. The labor-saving technology might be no more than a more effective arrangement of labor within the existing plant, and thus require no new equipment; or the new equipment might be bought with regular capital replacement funds.

is no purchasing power "lost" when a labor-saving machine is introduced does not mean that there is no employment lost.

Is this the end to our analysis of labor-displacing technology? It can be. It is possible that the introduction of labor-saving machinery will have no effect other than that of the example above: transferring consumer spending from previously employed labor to consumers or to entrepreneurs.

But it is also possible that an employment-generating secondary effect may result. The entrepreneur may be so encouraged by higher profits from the new process that he uses them to invest in additional plant and equipment and thereby sets in motion, via the multiplier, a rise in total expenditure sufficient to reemploy the displaced workers. Or in our second instance, consumers may evidence such a brisk demand for shoes at lower prices that, once again, our employer is encouraged to invest in additional plant and equipment, with the same salutary results as above.

Do not fall into the trap of thinking that the new higher demand for shoes, will, *by itself*, suffice to eradicate unemployment. To be sure, shoe purchases may now increase to previous levels or even higher. But unless their incomes rise, consumer spending on other items will suffer to the exact degree that spending on shoes gains.

The moral is clear. *Labor-saving technology can offset the unemployment created by its immediate introduction only if it induces sufficient investment to absorb the unemployed.*

New demands Now let us take a second case of technology. Suppose that an inventor patents a new product—a stove that auto-matically cooks things to perfection. Will such an invention create employment?

We will suppose that our inventor personally assembles and sells original models in local stores, and we will ignore the small increase in spending (and perhaps in employment) due to the inventor's orders for raw materials. Instead, let us fasten our attention on the consumer who first decides to buy the new product in a store, because it has stimulated her demand.

Will the consumer's purchase result in a *net* increase in consumer spending in the economy? If this is so—and if the new product is generally liked—it is easy to see how the new product could result in sizeable additional employment.

But will it be true? Our consumer has, to be sure, bought a new item. *But unless her income has increased, there is no reason to believe that this is a net addition to her consumption expenditures.* The chances are, rather, that this unforeseen expenditure will be balanced by lessened spending for some other item. Almost surely she will not buy a regular stove. (When consumers first began buying television sets, they stopped buying as many radios and going to the movies as often.) But even where there is no direct competition, where the product is quite "new," everything that we know about the stability of the propensity to consume schedule leads us to believe that *total* consumer spending will not rise.

Thus we reach the important conclusion that new products do not automatically create *additional* spending, even though they may mobilize consumer demand for themselves. Indeed, many new products emerge onto the market every year and merely shoulder old products off. Must we then conclude that demand-creating inventions do not affect employment?

Employment and investment

We are by no means ready to jump to that conclusion. Rather, what we have seen enables us to understand that if a new product is to create employment, it must give rise to new *investment* (and to the consumption it induces in turn). If the automatic stove is successful, it may induce the inventor to borrow money from a bank and to build a plant to mass-produce the item. If consumer demand for it continues to rise, a very large factory may have to be built to accommodate demand. As a result of the investment expenditures on the new plant, GNP rises, consumers' incomes rise, and more employment will be created as they spend their incomes on various consumer items.

To be sure, investment will decline in those areas that are now selling less to consumers. At most, however, this decline can affect only their replacement expenditures, which probably averaged 5 to 10 percent of the value of their capital equipment. Meanwhile, in the new industry, an entire capital structure must be built from scratch. We can expect the total amount of investment spending to increase substantially, with its usual repercussive effects.

When we think of a new product not in terms of a household gadget but in terms of the automobile, airplane, or perhaps the transistor, we can understand how large the employment-creating potential of certain kinds of inventions can be. Originally the automobile merely resulted in consumer spending being diverted from buggies; the airplane merely cut into railroad income; the transistor, into vacuum tubes. But each of these inventions became in time the source of enormous investment expenditures. The automobile not only gave us the huge auto plants in Detroit, but indirectly brought into being multibillion-dollar in-

vestment in highways, gasoline refineries, service stations, tourism—all industries whose impact on employment has been gigantic. On a smaller, but still very large scale, the airplane gave rise not alone to huge aircraft building plants, but to airfields, radio and beacon equipment industries, international tourism, etc., whose employment totals are substantial. In turn, the transistor offered entirely new design possibilities for miniaturization and thus gave many businesses an impetus for expansion.

Industry-building inventions

What sorts of inventions have this industry-building capacity? We can perhaps generalize by describing them as inventions that are of sufficient importance to become "indispensable" to the consumer or the manufacturer, and of sufficient mechanical or physical variance from the existing technical environment to necessitate the creation of a large amount of supporting capital equipment to integrate them into economic life.

Demand-creating inventions, then, can indeed create employment. They do so indirectly, however—not by inducing new consumer spending, but by generating new investment spending.*

Unfortunately, there is no guarantee that these highly employment-generative inventions will come along precisely when they are needed. There have been long periods when the economy has not been adequately stimulated by this type of invention and when employment has lagged as a result.

---

*We should stress another effect of demand-creating inventions on consumption. It is probable that without the steady emergence of new products, the long-run propensity to consume would decline instead of remaining constant, as we have seen in Chapter 27. In this way, demand-creating technology is directly responsible for the creation of employment, by helping to keep consumer spending higher than it would be without a flow of new products.

Automation and employment   This discussion brings us to that cluster of new, versatile inventions we call automation. We have discussed the squeeze that these inventions might exert on employment in our long box at the end of the chapter. But we can see that a crucial aspect of the question is whether the technology of automation will be industry-building or labor-saving. We do not yet know. It is possible that the computer, the transistor, the myriad new possibilities in feed-back engineering will play the same role as the automobile and the railroad, not only giving rise to an enormous flow of investment, but opening new fields of endeavor for other new industries that will also expand. If this is the case, the demand for labor will grow fast enough to match the increase in the productivity of labor, and there will be nothing unusual to worry about.

But it is also possible that the impact of automation will make itself felt like our labor-saving shoe invention, cutting costs where it is used, but not giving an immediate expansionary push to investment. In that case, the new equipment would be likely to create unemployment in those industries in which it was used, and we would be in the anxious position of seeing unemployment mount without a strong new expanding industry to offer new jobs.

Other Causes of Unemployment

If automation does bring about unemployment, could we not take care of it through demand management? The question opens up new aspects of the unemployment problem that we have not yet studied. Unemployment is not solely a matter of people losing jobs, but of people not being able to find new jobs. As we saw in our first glimpse of the problem (pp. 54–55 and accompanying box), we can have unemployment that results from a lack of skills or from a mismatch between existing skills and required skills or because workers looking for jobs do not have the characteristics (such as literacy, or ethnic backgrounds, or education) that employers want.

Structural unemployment   This kind of unemployment is called *structural unemployment*. Because it is lodged so strongly in specific attributes of the individual, it resists the "easy" cure of higher aggregate demand. Business may be better for an employer, but he may prefer to pay his existing work force overtime, rather than to take on a new labor force that does not meet his specifications.

The remedy for structural unemployment is more difficult than for general lack-of-demand unemployment. New skills or new attributes (such as punctuality) are needed by the "structurally" unemployed, and these are expensive to impart. The Job Corps program of the 1960s, for example, found that it cost about $10,000 to $12,000 to make an unemployed person—often a member of a ghetto group—acceptable to employers. Society was not willing to pay so large a fee, and employers also resisted (or asked large subsidies for) programs to hire and train "unemployables."

The high cost of retraining or of imparting desired work characteristics is one reason why structural unemployment is a difficult problem. Perhaps even more difficult is the question: for what jobs shall the unemployed be trained? Unless we very clearly know the shape of future demand, the risk is that a retraining program will prepare workers for jobs that may no longer exist when the workers are ready for them. And unless the *level* of future demand is high, even a foresighted program will not effectively solve the unemployment problem.

Employer of last resort

One solution to this problem would be to create a program aimed at creating permanent jobs in specific areas of the public sector, such as the repair, maintenance, and beautification of our inner cities, or the care of the aged. Once again, however, we encounter public resistance. The use of the government as the "employer of last resort" is a potentially powerful weapon for the alleviation of unemployment, but it is a departure that does not yet have the wholehearted endorsement of the public. Because this is likely to become a lively political issue in the future, we discuss it in "An extra word" at the end of this chapter.

Frictional unemployment

We should not leave this discussion of the causes of unemployment without mentioning the "normal" unemployment that occurs when workers voluntarily leave one job in search of a better one. This kind of unemployment is actually a source of benefit for the economy, because it is one of the ways in which productivity is enhanced, as workers move from declining industries to growing ones.

Nonetheless, we can increase the efficiency of this productivity-promoting flow of labor by reducing the period of "frictional" unemployment as much as possible. The most frequently suggested means of doing so is to provide a nation-wide employment service that would make job information available to job searchers, so that a carpenter, wishing to leave an area where work was slow, would know what areas were booming; or a secretary who felt there was no room for promotion in a sluggish business would have available a roster of many other possibilities.

Want ads are a partial, but incomplete kind of employment service. A full-scale national information service would provide much more complete information; and a full national commitment to minimizing frictional unemployment would even help defray the costs of relocating. Sweden and some other European countries run such labor exchanges, but we have yet to establish one in the United States.

Capitalism and Unemployment

This is by no means a full discussion of all the causes of, or cures for, unemployment. We have, for example, ignored the problem of wage policy, although it must be obvious that unemployment can be generated if unions succeed in pushing up wage rates for certain jobs above the jobs' marginal productivity. And we have paid no heed to the long-run remedy for unemployment played by lengthening the years of schooling, lowering the age of retirement, liberalizing vacation policies, and other changes in social institutions.

But we have covered enough to enable us to draw up a preliminary report on the performance of the economy as a generator of employment. As we saw, when we first examined the data for the 1960s and 1970s, that report is not good.

Unemployment has ranged from 3.5 percent in the war-boom years to nearly 9 percent in the 1975 recession. Some of this was frictional unemployment—perhaps 2 to 3 percent of the labor force. All the rest was structural unemployment or the unemployment that resulted from inadequate levels of aggregate demand.

"Reserve Army of the Unemployed"

Is this a consequence of the inherent sluggishness of a capitalist system incapable of attaining high levels of employment except under armaments spending?

Marxists have argued that this is the case and have pointed to the very large workless bottom layer of the American economy. First there are the officially acknowledged unemployed—7.8 million in 1975. Then there are the underemployed, those who want full-time work but can get only part-time. These are another 3.7 million. Then there are 1 million who are not looking for work because they think they cannot find it. This gives us a very large "reserve army of the unemployed," to use Karl Marx's term for the jobless whose presence, he argued, served to keep down the wages of those who were employed. Really full employment, a Marxist would claim, would raise wages so high that profits—and capitalism—would disappear.

This is not an analysis to be lightly brushed aside. In Europe, for example, a similar "reserve army" has been created by importing cheap labor from Greece, Spain, Yugoslavia, and Turkey to man the great factories of the Continent. When times are bad, many of these "guest workers" are encouraged to return to their countries of origin; so that the European nations, in fact, export some of their unemployed.

U.S. vs. European performance

It may well be, in other words, that some unemployment above the frictional level is needed to prevent wages from squeezing out profits or sending prices skyhigh. Leaders in many countries speak candidly of the need to keep labor "in line," and unemployment is openly acknowledged to be a disciplinary force toward that end. Some degree of unemployment may indeed be inseparable from the operation of a capitalist system.

But what degree? It is also clear that the levels of unemployment that have been generated and tolerated in the United States are not necessary. In Western Europe the levels of unemployment have been far below that of the United States, as Table 36 • 4 shows—a record of years in which European nations were not "exporting" unemployment but were enjoying a strong boom.

Table 36 • 4 Unemployment rates 1960–1974

Country	Highest	Lowest	Average
United States	6.7%	3.5%	4.9%
Canada	7.1	3.9	5.4
Japan	1.7	1.1	1.3
France	3.0	1.6	2.3
West Germany	2.1	0.3	0.8
Italy	4.3	2.7	3.6
United Kingdom	5.3	1.2	3.2
Sweden	2.7	1.2	1.9

Source: Eva Christina Horowitz, "Unemployment Rates—An International Comparison," *The Nordic Economic Outlook*, mimeographed series B12 of the Federation of Swedish Industries, June 1975.

European nations have generally gone much further than we have in providing labor exchanges or in seeking to remedy structural unemployment, and they have been willing to accept a higher level of inflation as a lesser evil than a high level of unemployment.

What is lacking in our nation, to date, is a willingness to place employment at the very head of all the benefits that we expect from an economy, a willingness to bend every effort to achieve the right to work for all. We may still not wholly eliminate structural or aggregate demand employment, but at least we could not then be faulted for having failed to try to do so.

Focus The most thought-provoking question of this chapter is the one that we raise at the very end. Is unemployment necessary for capitalism to function? Would really full employment bring such inflation or such a squeeze on profits that the system could no longer operate, at least not on the basis of free markets? This opens a question of much greater depth than we can explore in this text. But our quick look suggests that whereas, indeed, some unemployment may be necessary to maintain a working capitalist system, it is far less than the rates that we have permitted in the United States.

That leads us to a consideration of the causes of unemployment. Here we cover some ground that is familiar, some that is new. We learn about necessary, frictional unemployment. We look into structural unemployment. And we study, above all, the need for GNP to grow, merely to maintain a given rate of unemployment, because the labor force swells and productivity rises. In turn, this ties in with what we have learned about the elasticity of the labor force, resulting from variable short-run participation rates. To reduce a given level of unemployment, we must raise aggregate demand by an amount large enough both to create the new jobs we want and to create jobs for those who enter the labor force because jobs are more plentiful.

A side theme that runs through this chapter is the problem of technological unemployment or, rather, the impact of machines on work. Here the crucial thing to understand is that a new process or a new product does not directly create new employment. Its first effect is to change the flow of incomes or expenditures, not to augment them. Only if the technology creates a wave of investment will it bring strong employment effects in tow.

This is useful to keep in mind when thinking about the problem of automation, a recurrent worry of our times. It will help you also to think about the interplay between the entrance of technology (of any kind, automation or not) in different sectors and the elasticity of demand for the outputs of different sectors. (This is covered in the long box that follows.) This problem will have an important bearing on the severity of U.S. unemployment in the years ahead.

WORDS AND CONCEPTS YOU SHOULD KNOW

Participation rates, 552
Impact of unemployment, 553–54
Full-employment growth, 554–55
Technological unemployment, 555–56
Employment and investment, 557–59
Structural unemployment, 559–60

Frictional unemployment, 560
"Reserve army" of unemployed, 560–61
Government as "employer of last resort" (see "An extra word" at the end of this chapter), 566–67
Automation, 559, 564–65

QUESTIONS

1. Suppose that an inventor puts a wrist radio-telephone on the market. What would be the effects on consumer spending? What would ultimately determine whether the new invention was labor-attracting or labor-saving?

2. Suppose that another new invention halved the cost of making cars. Would this create new purchasing power? What losses in income would have to be balanced against what gains in incomes? What would be the most likely way that such an invention could increase employment? Would employment increase if the demand for cars were inelastic, like the demand for farm products—that is, if people bought very few more cars despite the fall in prices?

3. Unemployment among the black population in many cities in the late 1960s was worse than it was during the Great Depression. What steps would you propose to remedy this situation?

4. Do you believe that there exists general support for large public employment-generating programs? Why or why not? What sorts of programs would you propose?

5. Do you think that the computer, on net balance, has created unemployment? How would you go about trying to ascertain whether your hunch was accurate? Would you have to take into account the indirect effects of computers on investment?

6. How much inflation would you willingly accept, to lower unemployment to, say, 3 percent?

7. Why is frictional unemployment useful, and structural unemployment not? If frictional unemployment is useful, why try to reduce it?

8. Explain why we need a rising GNP to maintain a constant level of employment. Would this be true if we had zero population growth, but rising productivity? Zero productivity growth but rising population? If we have both, will the target be constant employment? Constant unemployment? Constant unemployment rates?

THE PROBLEM OF AUTOMATION

For years, men have feared the effect of machinery on the demand for labor. The first-century Roman emperor Vespasian turned down a road-building machine, saying "I must have work for my poor." Shortly after Adam Smith's time, revolts of workers led by a mythical General Ludd smashed the hated and feared machines of the new textile manufacturers, which they believed to be stealing the very bread from their mouths.

In our own day, this lurking fear of machinery has focused on that extraordinary technology that "reads" and "hears" and "thinks" and puts human dexterity to shame. We call it automation. One of its characteristics is a feedback loop, by which the machine corrects itself, rather like a thermostat maintains a constant temperature. When such machines can make an engine block for a car almost without human supervision, it is understandable that thoughtful men should worry. There is a well-known story of Henry Ford II showing his newly automated engine plant to the late Walter Reuther, the famed head of the United Auto Workers, and asking, "Well, Walter, how will you organize these machines?" Reuther replied, "How will you sell them cars?"

Does automation impose a wholly new and dangerous threat to employment? Let us begin to answer the question by using the tried and true method of supply and demand.

MACHINES AND SUPPLY

What has the introduction of machinery done to the supply of labor? We know that its main effect has been vastly to increase the *productivity* of labor: a man with a tractor is incomparably more productive than a man with a shovel, not to speak of one with his bare hands.

But the effect of capital on productivity has not been evenly distributed among all parts of the labor force. On the contrary, one of the most striking characteristics of technology has been its *uneven entry* into production. In some sectors, such as agriculture, the effects of technology on output have been startling. Between

1880 and today, for instance, the time required to harvest an acre of wheat on the Great Plains has fallen from 20 hours to 3. Between the late 1930s and the mid-1960s, the manhours needed to obtain a hundredweight of milk were slashed from 3.4 to 0.9; a hundredweight of chickens from 8.5 to 0.6.

Not quite so dramatic but also far-reaching in their effect have been technological impacts in other areas. Output per worker has roughly doubled or tripled in most manufacturing industries over the last 20 years.

By way of contrast to the very great advances of productivity in the agricultural and manufacturing sectors, we must note the laggard advance in productivity in the tertiary sector of activity. Output per manhour in trade, for instance, or in education or in the service professions such as law or medicine or, again, in domestic or personal services such as barbering or repair work or in government has not increased nearly so much as in the primary and secondary sectors.

INFLUENCE OF DEMAND

These strikingly different rates of increase in productivity begin to suggest a way of analyzing the effects of automation, or for that matter, any kind of labor-saving machinery. Clearly, capital equipment increases the *potential output* of a given number of workers. But will increased output be absorbed through expanded demand, allowing the workers to keep their jobs? Let us look at the question first in its broadest scope. We have seen that productivity has increased fastest in agriculture, next in manufacturing, least in services. What has happened to demand for the output of these sectors? The table shows us the answers.

DOMESTIC DEMAND FOR OUTPUT

	Distribution of demand (%)	
	1899–1908	1976
Primary sector (agriculture)	16.7	3.2
Secondary sector (mining, construction, mfg.)	26.0	32.3
Tertiary sector transportation, communication, govt., other services)	57.2	64.5

What we see here is a shift working in a direction different from that of supply. As the productivity and potential output of the agricultural sector has risen, the demand for agricultural products has not followed suit but has lagged far behind. Demand has risen markedly for output coming from the secondary sector, but has remained roughly unchanged, in percentage terms, for the output of the tertiary service sector.

SQUEEZE ON EMPLOYMENT

If we now put together the forces of supply and demand, it is easy to understand what has happened to employment. The tremendous increase in productivity on the farm, faced with a shrinking proportionate demand for food, created a vast army of redundant labor in agriculture. Where did the labor go? It followed the route indicated by the growth of demand, migrating from the countryside into factory towns and cities where it found employment in manufacturing and service occupations. As the next table shows, the distribution of employment has steadily moved out of the primary and secondary, into the tertiary sector.

What we see here is the crucial role of technology in distributing employment among its various uses. As income rose, purchasing power no longer used for food was diverted to manufactured goods and homes. We would therefore expect that the proportion of the labor force employed in these pursuits would have risen rapidly. Instead, as we can see, it has fallen slightly. This is because technological improvements entered the secondary sector along with manpower, greatly increasing the productivity of workers in this area. Therefore a smaller portion of the national labor force could satisfy the larger proportional demands of the public for output from this sector.

DISTRIBUTION OF EMPLOYMENT

	Distribution of all employed workers (%)	
	1900	1976
Primary sector	38.1	3.8
Secondary sector	37.7	29.7
Tertiary sector	24.2	66.5

Most important of all is the service sector. As the first table shows us, the public has not much changed the share of income that it spends for the various outputs we call services. But technological advances have not exerted their leverage as dramatically here as elsewhere, so that it takes a much larger fraction of the work force to produce the services we demand.

IMPORTANCE OF THE TERTIARY SECTOR

The conclusion, then, is that the demand for labor reflects the interplay of technology (which exerts differing leverages on different industries and occupations at different times) and of changing demand for goods and services. Typically, the entrance of technology into industry has a twofold effect. The first is to raise the *potential* output of the industry, with its present labor force. The second is to enable the costs of the industry to decline, or its quality to improve, so that actual demand for the product will increase. But normally, the rise in demand is not great enough to enable the existing labor force to be retained along with the new techniques. Instead, some labor must now find its employment elsewhere.

There are exceptions, of course. But taking all industries and all technological changes together, the net result is unambiguous. **As our next table reveals, technology has**

THE PROBLEM OF AUTOMATION
(cont.)

steadily increased our ability to create goods, both on the farm and on the factory floor, more rapidly than we have wished to consume them, with the result that employment in these areas has lagged behind output.

OUTPUT AND EMPLOYMENT INDICES

	1950	1975
Agricultural output	100	130
Agricultural employment	100	47
Manufacturing output	100	206
Manufacturing employment	100	120
1950 = 100		

Note how agricultural output has increased rapidly in this period, while agricultural employment has shrunk by over 50 percent; and notice that whereas manufacturing output has more than doubled, employment in manufacturing is up by only 20 percent.

During this same period, however, our total civilian labor force increased by over 20 million. Where did these millions find employment? As we would expect, largely in the service sector. Figures for employment in various parts of the service sector appear in the fourth table. We might note that comparable shifts from agriculture "through" manufacturing into services are visible in all industrial nations.

SERVICE EMPLOYMENTS

	1950	1976	Increase
	(in millions)		1950–1976
Trade	9.4	17.5	86%
Services	5.4	14.6	170
Government	6.0	15.1	152
Finance and other	1.9	4.3	126
Total tertiary sector	22.7	51.5	127

IMPACT OF AUTOMATION

How does automation enter this picture? Our analysis reveals the threat that this new complicated technology may hold. It is that the whole complex of paper-handling, decision-making, service-generating devices we lump under the name of automation may represent the belated entry of technology into areas of economic activity that until now have been largely spared the impact of technical change. These are the areas of service and administrative tasks that we have previously marked as an important source of growing employment. *Thus the danger inherent in the new sensory, almost humanoid equipment is that it may put an end to the traditional employment-absorptive effects of the tertiary service and administrative sector.*

The implications of such a development would be very great. It would mean the end of the "safety valve" function provided by traditional service employments, and a corresponding need to find new ways to absorb labor that was rendered jobless in agriculture or manufacturing. What these methods might be we shall discuss further in the text.

But our analysis of the squeeze that machines have put on employment in some sectors and the absorption of employment in other sectors allows us to put the problem of automation in a historic perspective. We must wait to see if automation does indeed mean the full-scale invasion of the store and the office by machinery. If so, we shall have to find new ways of coping with a problem that an "old-fashioned" service sector has previously solved for us.

Government as employer of last resort

At the end of our chapter we broach a question of very great importance: can capitalism function with very low rates of unemployment? The danger, as we have mentioned, is that low unemployment would remove the "reserve army of the unemployed" and would create an upward pressure on wages. Prices would skyrocket; profits plummet.

There is a strong possibility that we will face a decisive test of that question in the reasonably near future. For on the agenda of possible legislation, there is the Humphrey-Hawkins bill, named after its principal cosponsors, Sen. Hubert H. Humphrey (D., Minn.) and Rep. Augustus F. Hawkins (D., Calif.), whose purpose is to assure that we make really full employment an official objective of U.S. economic policy.

We do not have such a policy today. The Employment Act of 1946, much heralded at its time of passage, commits the United States to the attainment of only "maximum feasible" employment. It makes no effort to define what this level might be or to designate the means of achieving it. The Humphrey-Hawkins bill, as it now stands, goes far beyond this. First, it defines "full employment" as 3 percent unemployment—barely above the frictional level. Second, it directs the government to attain this level by a number of fiscal and monetary means, but above all by the creation of permanent, desirable jobs open to all who want to work but cannot find acceptable work in the private sector. That is what is meant by making the government the employer of last resort. In effect, it makes the government a guarantor of full employment.

What sorts of problems will the Humphrey-Hawkins bill present if it is enacted into legislation? Here are some of them:

1. Will a guaranteed job program be limited to periods of recession or maintained during good times as well? The aim of the sponsors is certainly to maintain the program in operation year in, year out. But this means that during good times, the public and private sectors will compete for workers. As conditions improve, business will have to bid workers away from jobs, not from unemployment. This will raise the costs of creating new private employment—and may dampen the possibility for sustaining booms.

2. A related question has to do with the sorts of jobs that the public sector will offer. Will they be unskilled jobs, such as sweeping the streets or relaying the nation's roadbeds? This will hardly make them attractive to the skilled unemployed. Or will the jobs be creative, career-oriented work, such as redesigning the inner city, rehabilitating the handicapped, tending the young and the old? In that case, public jobs may be more attractive than private ones.

3. What will be the pay relation between similar jobs—say, a crane operator, a key punch operator, an office manager—in the public sector and the private sector? If we make the two sectors equal, will not the public sector, with its tradition of civil service, "outpull" the private? If we make public sector jobs pay less, are we really creating public employment or merely a fancy kind of public dole?

4. How will we determine what public jobs are worth creating? (This takes us into the question of national planning, a problem we examine in our next "Extra word.")

5. The biggest question of all: can we run an effective full-employment program without pushing wage rates up, accelerating inflation, and pushing down profits? This last crucial question ties back into some of the previous ones. If we keep the public service jobs at pay levels moderately below the private level—say 10 percent—then we could use public employment as a means of finding useful work for the "reserve army of the unemployed," adding to our output of needed goods and services with a minimal effect on the general level of wages.

But we can also see that this use of the public sector openly relegates public sector jobs beneath private sector jobs. It implies that we will use the public sector as a means of providing something better than unemployment insurance or welfare, but not that we are prepared to embark on imaginative, creative projects for which we would require first-rate talents who would not accept second-rate pay. In turn, this use of the public sector opens the dreary prospect of a public work force without morale or incentive.

We do not know, at this writing, whether the Humphrey-Hawkins bill or some similar bill will be passed. Our own inclinations strongly favor such a bill. The right to work strikes us as a fundamental element of a good society. But as this "Extra word" should make clear, we are far from blind to the range and difficulty of the problems that this new policy would create.

Problems of economic growth

Almost from the first pages of this book, and certainly from the first pages of the section on macroeconomics, growth has been at the center of our focus. Now, in this final chapter on that subject, we must return explicitly to the problem, adding to our previous knowledge and reflecting on issues that we have not yet had an opportunity to explore in depth.

The Business Cycle

Let us begin by investigating an aspect of growth that we have heretofore ignored. It is the uneven pace at which the historic trajectory of growth proceeds. If you will take a moment to look back at the chart of national growth on p. 30, you will notice its long, almost uninterrupted upward slope; or again, a glance at p. 32 will show the same thing.

Short vs. long run

But these long-run charts, on which only very large movements are visible, conceal from our view another aspect of the growth process that is of very great importance. In any short-run period,

568

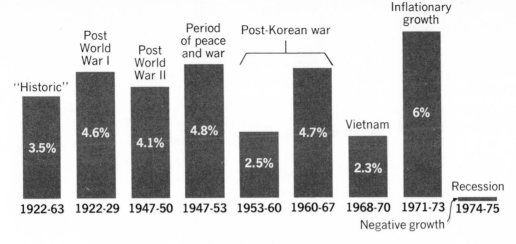

FIG. 37·1   Short-term variations in the rate of growth

the long-run consistency fades from view and the economy is marked by sharp ups and downs in the growth in output.

Take the years 1895 to 1905, very smooth-looking on the chart on p. 344. As Table 37·1 reveals, those years were, in fact, anything but steady.

Table 37·1   U.S. rates of growth 1895–1905

1895–1896	−2.5%	1900–1901	+11.5%
1896–1897	+9.4	1901–1902	+ 1.0
1897–1898	+2.3	1902–1903	+ 4.9
1898–1899	+9.1	1903–1904	− 1.2
1899–1900	+2.7	1904–1905	+ 7.4

Source: *Long Term Economic Growth* (U.S. Dept. of Commerce, 1966), p. 107.

Or examine a more recent period, not year by year, but in groups of years. As we can see in Fig. 37 • 1 the rate of growth has varied greatly over the last fifty years. At times, such as the 1974–1975 recession, the economy has even shown negative rates of growth. These episodes may show up only as small dips in the graph of our long-term advance, but they have meant suffering and deprivation for millions of persons who were robbed of work or income as a consequence of these dips.

Cycles

This sequence of ups and downs, riches of growth followed by doldrums, introduces us to the question of business cycles. For if we inspect the profile of the long ascent carefully, we can see that its entire length is marked with irregular tremors or peaks and valleys. Indeed, the more closely we examine year-to-year figures, the more of these tremors and deviations we discover, until the problem becomes one of selection: which vibrations to consider significant and which to discard as uninteresting.

The problem of sorting out the important fluctuations in output (or in statistics of prices or employment) is a difficult one. Economists have actually detected dozens of cycles of different lengths and amplitudes, from very short rhythms of expansion and contraction that can be found, for example, in patterns of inventory accumulation and decumulation, to large background pulsations of 17 or 18 years in the housing industry, and possibly (the evidence is unclear) swings of 40 to 50 years in the path of capitalist development as a whole.

Generally, however, when we speak of "the" business cycle we refer to a wavelike movement that lasts, on the average,

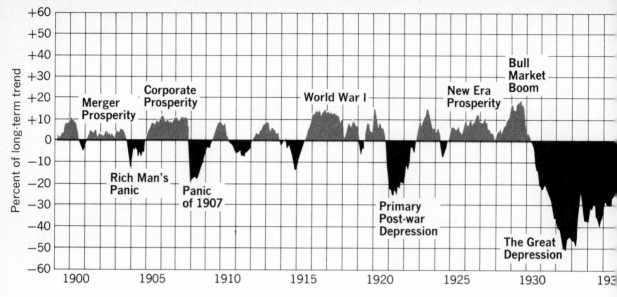

FIG. 37 · 2   The business cycle

about 8 to 10 years. In Fig. 37 • 2 this major oscillation of the American economy stands forth very clearly, for the chartist has eliminated the underlying tilt of growth, so that the profile of economic performance looks like a cross section at sea level rather than a cut through a long incline.

Reference cycles   In a general way we are all familiar with the meaning of business cycles, for the alternation of "boom and bust" or prosperity and recession (a polite name for a mild depression) is part of everyday parlance. It

will help us study cycles, however, if we learn to speak of them with a standard terminology. We can do this by taking the cycles from actual history, "superimposing" them, and drawing the general profile of the so-called *reference* cycle that emerges. It looks like Fig. 37 • 3. This model of a typical cycle enables us to speak of the "length" of a business cycle as the period from one peak to the next or from trough to trough. If we fail to measure from *similar* points on two or more cycles, we can easily get a distorted picture of short-term growth—for instance, one that begins at the upper turning point of one cycle and measures to the trough of the

FIG. 37 · 3   The reference cycle

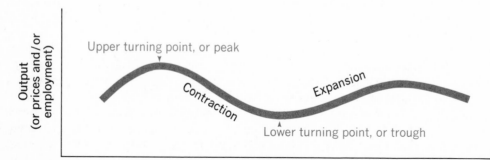

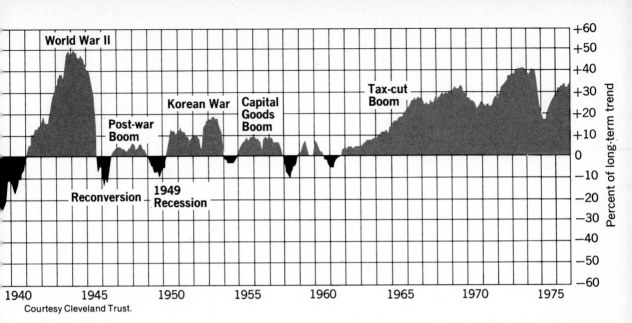

World War II

Korean War

Capital Goods Boom

Tax-cut Boom

Post-war Boom

Reconversion

1949 Recession

+60
+50
+40
+30
+20
+10
0
−10
−20
−30
−40
−50
−60

Percent of long-term trend

1940   1945   1950   1955   1960   1965   1970   1975

Courtesy Cleveland Trust.

next. Much of the political charge and coun(cid)tercharge about growth rates can be clarified if we examine the starting and terminating dates used by each side.

Causes of cycles   What lies behind this more or less regular alternation of good and bad times?

Innumerable theories, none of them entirely satisfactory, have been advanced to explain the business cycle. A common business explanation is that waves of op(cid)timism in the world of affairs alternate with waves of pessimism—a statement that may be true enough, but that seems to describe the sequence of events rather than to explain it. Hence economists have tried to find the underlying cyclical mechanism in firmer stuff than an alterna(cid)tion of moods. One famous late-nineteenth-century economist, W. S. Je(cid)vons, for example, explained business cy(cid)cles as the consequence of sunspots— perhaps not as occult a theory as it might seem, since Jevons believed that the sunspots caused weather cycles that caused crop cycles that caused business

cycles. The trouble was that subsequent investigation shows that the periodicity of sunspots was sufficiently different from that of rainfall cycles to make the connec(cid)tion impossible.

Other economists have turned to causes closer to home: to variations in the rate of gold mining (with its effects on the money supply); to fluctuations in the rate of invention; to the regular recurrence of war; and to yet many other factors. There is no doubt that many of these events can induce a business expansion or contrac(cid)tion. The persistent problem, however, is that none of the so-called underlying causes itself displays an inherent cycli(cid)cality—much less one with a periodicity of 8 to 10 years.

The multiplier accelerator cycle   Then how do we explain cycles? Economists no longer seek a single explana(cid)tion of the phenomenon in an exogenous (that is, external) cyclical force. Rather, they tend to see cycles as our own eye first

571

saw them on the growth curve—*as variations in the rate of growth that tend to be induced by the dynamics of growth itself.*

We can gain considerable insight into this uneven pace of growth if we combine our knowledge of the multiplier and the accelerator—the latter, we recall, showing us the investment induced by the growth of output.

Boom and bust

Let us, then, assume that some stimulus such as an important industry-building invention, has begun to increase investment expenditures. We can easily see how such an initial impetus can generate a cumulative and self-feeding boom. As the multiplier and accelerator interact, the first burst of investment stimulates additional consumption, the additional consumption induces more investment, and this in turn reinvigorates consumption. Meanwhile, this process of mutual stimulation serves to lift business expectations and to encourage still further expansionary spending. Inventories are built up in anticipation of larger sales. Prices "firm up," and the stock market rises. Optimism reigns. A boom is on.

What happens to end such a boom? There are many possible reasons why it may peter out or come to an abrupt halt. It may simply be that the new industry will get built, and thereafter an important stimulus to investment will be lacking. Or even before it is completed, wages and prices may have begun to rise as full employment is neared, and the climate of expectations may become wary. ("What goes up must come down," is an old adage in business, too.) Meanwhile, perhaps tight money will choke off spending plans or make new projects appear unprofitable.

Or investment may begin to decline because consumption, although still rising, is no longer rising at the earlier *rate* (the acceleration principle in action). We

have already noticed that the action of the accelerator, all by itself, could give rise to wavelike movements in total expenditure (see p. 432). The accelerator, of course, never works all by itself, but it can exert its upward and downward pressures within the flux of economic forces and in this way give rise to an underlying cyclical impetus.

Contraction and recovery

It is impossible to know in advance what particular cause will retard spending—a credit shortage, a very tight labor market, a saturation of demand for a key industry's products (such as automobiles). But it is all too easy to see how a hesitation in spending can turn into a general contraction. Perhaps warned by a falling stock market, perhaps by a slowdown in sales or an end to rising profits, business begins to cut back. Whatever the initial motivation, what follows thereafter is much like the preceding expansion, only in reverse. The multiplier mechanism now breeds smaller rather than larger incomes. Downward revisions of expectations reduce rather than enhance the attractiveness of investment projects. As consumption decreases, unemployment begins to rise. Inventories are worked off. Bankruptcies become more common. We experience all the economic and social problems of a recession.

But just as there is a "natural" ceiling to a boom, so there is a more or less "natural" floor to recessions. The fall in inventories, for example, will eventually come to an end: for even in the severest recessions, merchants and manufacturers must have *some* goods on their shelves and so must eventually begin stocking up. The decline in expenditures will lead to easy money, and the slack in output will tend to a lower level of costs: and both of these factors will encourage new investment projects. Meanwhile, the countercyclical effects of government fiscal policy will slowly make their effects known. Sooner or later, in other words, expenditures will cease falling, and the economy will tend to "bottom out."

Government-caused cycles

We have spoken about business cycles as if they were initially triggered by a spontaneous rise in investment or by natural cessation of investment. But our acquaintance with the relative sizes of the components of GNP should make us wary of placing the blame for recessions solely on industry. More and more, as government has become a major source of spending, cycles have resulted from variations in the rate of government spending, not business spending. Cycles these days, more often than not, are made in Washington.

Take the six recessions (periods of decline in real GNP lasting at least six months) since World War II. Every one of them can be traced to changes in government budgetary policies. The first four recessions—in 1949, 1954, 1957–1958 and 1960–1961—resulted from changes in the military budget. In each case, the federal government curtailed its rate of military expenditure without taking compensatory action by increasing expenditure elsewhere or by cutting taxes. The result in each instance was a slackening in the rate of growth.

The 1969–1970 and the 1974–1975 recessions are even more interesting. They represent the first cases in which the federal government deliberately created a recession, through fiscal and monetary policies aimed at slowing down the economy. The purpose, as we know, was to dampen inflation. The result was to reverse the trend of growth. Thus, it is no longer possible, as it once was, to discuss business cycles as if they were purely the outcome of the market process. *There is no doubt that the market mechanism has produced cycles in the past, and would continue to produce them if the government were miraculously removed from the economy. But given the size of the public sector these days, we need to look first to changes in government spending as the initiating source of a cycle.*

Curbing the business cycle

Can we do something about the cycle? Of course. All of our previous discussion of fiscal and monetary policy can be readily viewed in the context of trying to eliminate the fluctuations around a steady growth path.

Unhappily, the same problems that we have discussed at length in demand management and monetary policy also apply in the area of lessening the severity of the business cycle. The lags in time before we recognize a given situation, the delay before a remedy takes hold, the difficulty of measuring the appropriate dosage of our economic medicines, the continuous shifts in the spontaneous forces of investment spending or in government budgeting—all these enormously complicate the task of anti-business-cycle policy.

Nonetheless, difficult as it is to mitigate cycles, at least we have a clear picture of what we are doing. We know the basic causes, but our problems are in the difficulties of applying theory in the turmoil of real world events.

Long-Run Stable Growth

However difficult in practice, the aim of a fluctuation-free path of growth directs our attention once again to our long historic trajectory. Anti-business-cycle policy merely tries to iron out the wrinkles in our path of growth. But what about the path itself? What determines how rapid our historic advance should be?

Potential vs. actual growth

This brings us again to a consideration in our previous chapter—the need for GNP to grow in order to accommodate a growing labor force and a rising level of productivity. If we multiply the rise in our year-to-year hours of labor input by an index of the rising productivity of that labor, we can easily derive a curve showing our *potential output over time*. The question is therefore how much of that potential output we do in fact produce.

As Fig. 37 • 4 shows, all through much of the 1950s, 1960s, and the mid-1970s, potential output ran well ahead of the output we actually achieved. Indeed, between 1958 and 1962 the amount of lost output represented by this gap came to the staggering sum of $170 billion. Even in 1972, a prosperous prerecession year, we could have added another $55 billion to GNP—$1,000 per family—if we had brought unemployment down from the actual level of 5.6 percent to 4 percent. In 1975, the total of lost output was immense—$136 billion in 1958 dollars.

Demand vs. capacity

The idea of a potential growth rate opens an aspect of the investment process that we have not yet considered. Heretofore, we have always thought of investment primarily as an income-generating force, working through the multiplier to increase the level of ex-

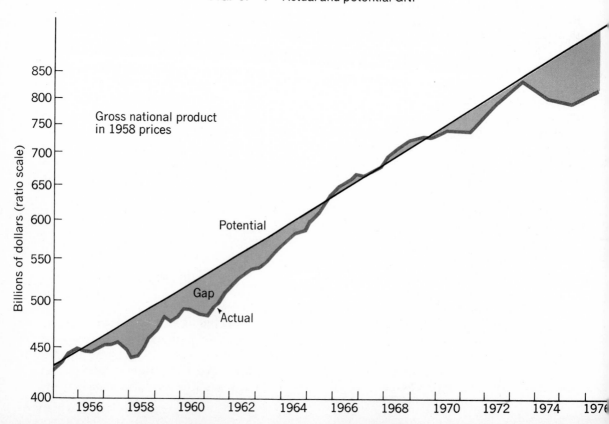

FIG. 37 • 4   Actual and potential GNP

penditure. Now we begin to consider investment also as a *capacity-generating* force, working through the actual addition to our plant and equipment to increase the productive potential of the system.

No sooner do we introduce the idea of capacity, however, than a new problem arises for our consideration. *If investment increases potential output as well as income, the obvious question is: will income rise fast enough to buy all this potential output? Thus at the end of our analysis of macroeconomics we revert to the question we posed at the beginning, but in a more dynamic context. At first, we asked whether an economy that saved could buy back its own output. Now we must ask whether an economy that grows can do the same.*

Marginal capital-output ratio

The question brings us to a new concept. The *marginal capital-output ratio*, as the formidable name suggests, is not a relationship that describes behavior, as the multiplier does. It describes a strictly technical or engineering or organizational relationship between an *increase in the stock of capital and the increase in output that this new capital will yield.*

Note that we are not interested in the ratio between our entire existing stock of capital (most of which is old) and the flow of total output, but only in the ratio between the *new* capital added during the period and the *new* output associated with that new capital. Thus the marginal capital-output ratio directs our attention to the *net investment* of the period and to the *change in output* of the period. If net investment was $60 billion and the change in output yielded by that investment was $20 billion, then the marginal capital-output ratio was 3.

Income vs. output

The marginal capital-output ratio gives us a powerful new concept to bring to bear on the problem of attaining and maintaining a high, steady rate of growth, for we can now see that the problem of steady growth requires the balancing out of two different economic processes. Investment raises productive capacity. *Increases* in investment raise income and demand. What we must now do is investigate the relationship between these two different, albeit related, economic variables.

Let us begin with a familiar formula that shows how a change in investment affects a change in income. This is

$$\Delta Y = \left(\frac{1}{\text{mps}}\right) \times \Delta I$$

which is nothing but the multiplier. For brevity, we will write it

$$\Delta Y = \left(\frac{1}{s}\right)\Delta I$$

where s stands for all leakages.

Now we need a new formula to relate I, the rate of new investment (not ΔI, the *change* in new investment), and ΔO, the change in dollar output. This will require a symbol for the marginal capital-output ratio, a symbol that expresses how many dollars' worth of output comes from a dollar's worth of investment. If we use the symbol σ (sigma), we can write this relationship as follows:

$$\Delta O = \left(\frac{I}{\sigma}\right)$$

showing that increased output (ΔO) is determined by investment (I) divided by the marginal capital/output ratio, σ.

For example, if we have $10 of new investment, and σ is 2, output will rise by $5.00. If σ is 3, output will rise by $3.33.

(Note that the smaller σ is, the larger is the addition to output of a given investment.)

Balanced growth in theory

We now have two formulas. The first tells us by how much *income* will rise as investment grows. The second tells us by how much *output* will rise from a given rate of investment. Thus we are ready to take the last and most important step. We can discover *by how much investment must rise each year, to give us the additional income we will need to buy the addition to output that has been created by this selfsame investment.*

Our formulas enable us to answer that question very clearly. Increased income is ΔY. Increased output is ΔO. Since $\Delta Y = \left(\dfrac{1}{s}\right) \Delta I$, and $\Delta O = \dfrac{I}{\sigma}$ then ΔY will equal ΔO if $\left(\dfrac{1}{s}\right) \Delta I = \dfrac{I}{\sigma}$. This is the formula for balanced growth.

If we now multiply both sides of the equation by s, and then divide both sides by I, we get

$$\frac{\Delta I}{I} = \frac{s}{\sigma}$$

Balanced growth in fact

What does this equation mean? It tells us what *rate of growth of investment* ($\Delta I/I$) is needed to make $\Delta Y = \Delta O$. In words, it tells us by what percentage investment spending must rise to make income payments keep pace with dollar output. That rate of growth is equal to the marginal savings (or leakage) ratio divided by the marginal capital-output ratio. Suppose, for instance, that the marginal leakage ratio is ⅓ and that the marginal capital-output ratio (σ) is 3. Then s/σ is ⅓ ÷ 3 (or ⅑), which means that investment would have to grow by ⅑ each year to create just enough income to match the growing flow of output. If the rate of investment grew faster than that, income and

demand would tend to grow ahead of output and we would be pushing beyond the path of balanced growth into inflation. If the rate of growth of investment were smaller than that, we would be experiencing chronic overproduction with falling prices and sagging employment.

What is the rate at which investment should rise for balanced growth in the United States? To determine that, we would have to deal with tricky statistical problems of marginal capital-output ratios; we would have to calculate *net* investment—not easy to do; and marginal leakages would have to behave as tamely as they do in textbooks—not always the case. Moreover, to include public as well as private capital formation in the terms "investment" and "marginal capital output ratio" would also greatly complicate our computations.

Therefore we shall sidestep here the difficult empirical problems posed by the requirements for balanced growth and concentrate on the general issue that the formulation opens up. For the purpose of our discussion is to explain that there is a complex relationship between the growth in income and the growth in output. Our analysis shows that we can have a *growth gap* if our leakages are too high, so that increases in injections do not generate enough new purchasing power, or if our marginal capital-output ratio is too low, so that a given amount of investment increases our potential output (our capacity) too fast.*

---

*One question may have occurred to the reader. Aren't incomes and outputs *identities*? Isn't it true that GNI ≡ GNP? Then how can a growth "gap" occur? The answer lies in our familiar ex ante and ex post perspectives (see page 482). Ex post, incomes are always the same as outputs. Ex ante they are not. The question, then, is not whether or not GNI will be equal to GNP, but *whether their identical values will be equal to potential output.* Our formula for balanced growth tells us which critical variables must be taken into account when we ask whether ex ante spending plans will bring us to a level of income and output that corresponds with *potential production.*

Policy for balanced growth

Suppose that we are not generating income fast enough to absorb our potential output. Suppose, to go back to Fig. 37·4, that we have a persistent growth gap similar to that of the late 1950s or middle 1970s. How can we bring the economy up to its potential?

Our formula for balanced growth gives us the answer. The relationship between the growth of incomes and the growth of output depends above all on the rate at which investment *increases*. Thus, if expenditures fall short of the amount needed to absorb potential output, the answer is to raise the rate of investment or, perhaps more realistically, to raise the rate of growth of all expenditures, public and private. Conversely, of course, if we find ourselves pushing over the trend line of potential growth into inflation, as in the late 1960s, the indicated policy is to lower the rate of growth of investment (or of investment and government and consumption) to bring the flow of rising incomes back into balance with the rise of output.

Thus the critical element in balancing a growing economy is not the *amount* of investment needed to fill a given demand gap, but the *increase* in investment (or other injection-expenditure) needed to match a growing output capacity with a large enough demand.

Here, one final time, we encounter the techniques and the problems familiar to us from our glance at anti-business-cycle policy and, before that, from our analysis of the means to combat unemployment and inflation. Demand management, through fiscal or monetary measures, remains the principal weapon at our disposal, supplemented in the future, perhaps, by measures for economic goal-setting (planning) that we will shortly discuss. And all the difficulties that we have considered heretofore remain to plague us in the pursuit of a policy of minimizing the growth gap.

Necessity for adequate growth

Nevertheless, the concept of a growth gap or a growth surplus enables us finally to put anti-business-cycle policy into a dynamic perspective. For we can now see that the objective of national economic policy is not merely to even out the ups and downs of a cycle but to assure a rate of expansion as close as possible to the line of our potential growth.

Here, of course, we come once again to the seemingly inescapable problem of choosing between inflation and unemployment. The line of potential growth gives us our target if we want to put full employment at the head of our list of priorities. But we know that the public does not want to do so. It prefers unemployment to inflation, hoping that the one will cure the other. *Nevertheless, the line of a rising potential GNP makes it clear that unless we grow at a sufficiently rapid rate, our unemployment will worsen. Even if we do not fully match income and potential output, income must grow to keep our condition of economic well-being unchanged. Growth is a prime essential for the healthy functioning of a capitalist system.*

The dangers of growth

But what about the dangers of growth that we discussed at the beginning of our studies (pp. 61f.)? Is there not a fundamental dilemma posed by the need to assure steady, high-level economic growth, on the one hand, and the dangers of resource stringency and pollution damage on the other?

There is indeed such a dilemma, and in the long run—over the next two or three

Growth means more income, and more income means more happiness. Or at least so we all believe. "For most Americans," writes economist Richard Easterlin, "the pursuit of happiness and the pursuit of money come to the same thing. More money means more goods (inflation aside), and this means more of the material benefits of life." But, Easterlin asks, "What is the evidence on the relation between money and happiness? Are the wealthier members of society usually happier than the poorer? Does raising the incomes of all increase the happiness of all?"

Easterlin has assembled data on the relation between wealth and happiness from some 30 surveys conducted in 19 developed and underdeveloped countries. The results are interesting—and paradoxical. In all societies, more money for the individual *is* reflected in a greater degree of happiness reported by the individual. However—and here is the paradox—raising the incomes of all does not increase the happiness of the entire society!

GROWTH AND HAPPINESS

How can we explain this paradoxical outcome? The answer seems to lie in the way people estimate their degree of material well-being. They do not measure their income or possessions starting from zero. Instead, people evaluate their places on the scale of wealth by *comparing themselves with others.* Thus it is not our "absolute" level of material well-being but our relative level that determines whether or not we feel "rich" or "poor." That relative level of well-being, in turn, depends on the distribution of income; and income distribution, as we know, is slow to evidence major shifts.

This situation has two major consequences for our own society. One is that poverty, with its associated unhappiness, cannot be eradicated by simply raising the incomes of the bottom portion of the population along with those of everyone else. The families that make up the bottom groups will continue to feel "poor" and therefore unhappier than the well-

to-do. Only a change in the pattern of income distribution could be expected to eliminate the feeling of poverty and its associated unhappiness. By the same consequence, however, a more equal distribution of income would reduce the feeling of being "rich" and its associated happiness! Whether a nation with a more equal distribution of income would be "happier" en masse therefore depends on our value judgments—specifically on the relative importance we would assign to an increase in the happiness of the bottom groups and a decrease in the happiness of top groups.

Second, Easterlin's findings suggest that we are all locked in a "hedonic treadmill." We are all engaged in an effort to acquire wealth, in the expectation that it will bring happiness; but unlike the race in *Alice in Wonderland,* the race for wealth has all winners but no prizes. Does this have something to do with the chronic feeling of dissatisfactions and the complaints about the "rat race" that are so much a part of our culture?

---

generations—it may well be that we shall have to take drastic steps to curtail or monitor growth, unless we achieve dramatic technological breakthroughs. Even in the middle run—say during the next generation—there are likely to be conflicts between the need for growth and the dangers of growth. There is likely to be a scramble for certain kinds of resources, especially as the underdeveloped nations exert their claims for goods and tighten their hold on minerals. There is certain to be a series of assaults on the environment—chemical wastes poisoning fish, fertilizers endangering water supplies, smogs affecting health.

We hope that we can use this middle period to lessen these risks, learn how to recycle materials, utilize less toxic processes, harness the forces of the sun and the tides, bring population growth to zero. If we could achieve these ends, we may learn how to maintain a high level of employment and a better distribution of output with a slower rate of growth, or without any reliance on dangerous growth. Further into the distance lies the possibility of approaching a stationary state, although that is a problematic question (see box, above).

All this will take time, however. *For another decade or two we shall need growth to assure a high level of employment, and we shall also have to cope with the particular dangers that growth may bring, in squeezes on certain resources or the disturbance of the environment.*

Growth and national planning

These two requirements strongly suggest that we will be moving in a direction of more national economic planning.

Planning is a word that disturbs many

people. This is not the place to discuss all its pros and cons or to spell out the ways in which planning might be carried out within a capitalist system. We shall look into some of these matters in the "Extra word" to this chapter and again in Chapter 43. Here we want to take up only two aspects of this very large and important question.

Plan or market? The first has to do with the need for planning. Can we not assure ourselves of safe and satisfactory growth without planning? Cannot the market mechanism, by itself, accomplish these objectives without more intrusive government activity?

Of course, in such matters, one can never be sure. But neither our historical record nor our analytical understanding gives us much reason to believe that an unsupervised and undirected market system would bring about growth that was either steady or adequate. The instability of the investment process (and of the government budget, as it is now used), the cumulative tendencies of the business cycle, the unpredictable effects of technology—now creating labor displacement, now building new industries—these and many other familiar problems make the present system a poor guarantor of steady economic growth. And we have seen that the market system is no guarantor at all of full employment growth.

The same doubts apply to the market's capacity to provide safe growth. To some extent, as we know, the market acts as a safety mechanism, using the signal of high prices to discourage the use of scarce resources. But as we saw in Chapter 12, the market has no way at all of signaling the presence of many dangerous processes. Nor can the market serve to set into motion research and development activities that may be needed today to

forestall a resource squeeze 25 years off—the very situation we face in our energy crisis.

Therefore, it seems probable that we shall extend our efforts to assure the pace and monitoring of growth. This will likely take the form of widening and strengthening our existing measures for demand management, and integrating these with democratically-chosen general macro and micro targets for the economy as a whole. National economic planning will not be so much a radical departure from present ways as it will be a coordination of existing institutions for the attainment of clearly articulated goals.

Planning and freedom A second issue is whether planning, even for such benign purposes as the promotion and protection of growth, is compatible with economic and political freedom.

This is not a question to which quick answers ought to be given, positive or negative. There are assuredly risks in planning, no matter how mild the institutions of planning may be. There are always dangers inherent in the expansion of government authority, no matter for what good end. It would be wrong to deny that planning might lead toward a more statist regime.

But it would be foolish to assert that planning *must* bring such unwanted changes. We have a long history of government authority within the economy, from the days of Theodore Roosevelt, through Franklin Roosevelt, down to present times; but it would be hard to claim that this expansion of government has come at the expense of capitalism or freedom. Rather, one can make a good case that the continued functioning of liberal capitalism has required government to extend its authority into new economic fields to forestall or remedy economic or social problems. Planning for safe, stable growth could well be another instance of that same process.

Then, too, for every risk associated with planning one must weigh the risk of not planning. Suppose that we consistently fail to reach high employment, through a lack of planning. What consequences, economic or political, might that bring? Suppose that we encounter resource or pollution crises because we have not taken the measures to avert them. What results could that bring?

A last word   There is no final judgment to be rendered in these matters. Some economists will remain opposed to planning because they believe that the economic system, more or less as it is presently constituted, will give us good enough growth and fewer risks of bureaucracy or oppression. Others, including the authors of this book, expect and welcome the development of planning to sustain and safeguard growth. In "An extra word" we shall discuss what such a plan might look like in operation.

What is important in these matters is not to overstate the case, either for or against one's judgment. In our view, planning will be an important step in making capitalism capable of better meeting the challenges of our time, but we want to emphasize that planning is certain to bring as many new problems as solutions to old ones. In economics, as in daily life, there are no lasting solutions. There is only the never-ending effort to cope with a changing reality as best we can.

FOCUS   This chapter takes us from business cycles through balanced growth into full-potential expansion and economic planning. Of all the topics, probably the last is the most important, although it is the least "technical." We suggest that you read "An extra word" to follow and that you try to think hard about the side opposite from that which you tend to favor. There are certainly cogent arguments to be raised against economic planning, and good or better arguments (we think) in its favor. You should know both.

The main technical points of the chapter are two. The first has to do with the idea of "balanced" growth—growth that balances the generation of additional income with that of additional output. The formulas that state this balance are very difficult to translate into actual statistical measurements, so that balanced growth is an idea rather than a working tool. But it is an idea that we need if we are to understand why a growing economy will not run out of purchasing power, provided its growth of investment is high enough. This is a concept as useful as that of closing a static demand gap.

Balanced growth also helps us grasp the idea of a growth gap—the loss we suffer from failing to grow up to our productive capacity—and of the measures needed to remedy it. Unlike balanced growth, the line of "potential output" is easily fleshed out with statistics, so that we can measure the loss in man-years of production from a failure to grow at an adequate rate.

Finally, business cycles. We do not have time or space fully to discuss the fascinating question of the periodicity of cycles—why they have lasted about eight to ten years—or of the many cyclical rhythms that can be discovered in the economy.

That is better reserved for an advanced course on business cycles. But you ought to understand how the multiplier-accelerator interaction acts to swell the recovery phase and to add momentum to a contraction. These are processes that lie behind the newspaper descriptions of "booms" and "recessions," and you should be sure that you can describe them clearly.

WORDS AND CONCEPTS YOU SHOULD KNOW

Business cycle, 569–73
Reference cycle, 570–71
Multiplier-accelerator interaction, 571–72
Potential growth, 574
Marginal capital output ratio, 575

Balanced growth, 575–76
Growth and full employment, 577
"Limits" to growth, 577–78
Growth and planning (see also "An extra word" at the end of this chapter), 578–80

QUESTIONS

1. Explain how the interaction of the accelerator and the multiplier can give rise to booms and busts. Why does a multiplier-accelerator model not tell us anything about the periodicity of cycles? Have you any ideas why the average cycle has been 8 to 10 years long? Suppose that capital goods tend to wear out and need to be replaced in about a decade. Would this by itself give rise to a cycle if the replacement (or original investment) were not bunched in time? Would it, if that were the case?

2. Try to get hold of a time series, such as a chart of stock market prices or GNP over a long time—say 10 years. Can you spot a cycle in the data? More than one?

3. What are the sources of growth for potential GNP? Explain why potential GNP is a kind of production possibility curve through time.

4. Investment adds both to capacity and the income. How does it add to capacity? Is this a behavioral function? What about the addition to income? Write the formula for balanced growth, carefully explaining to yourself the difference between the marginal capital-output ratio and the multiplier.

5. List the major policy problems in achieving balanced growth. Are they the same as those in minimizing business cycles?

6. How do you feel about the idea of national economic planning? Do you think it will infringe on economic liberty substantially? In what areas? What measures, if any, would you suggest instead?

National economic planning

For the reasons that we have seen, national economic planning is likely to become a reality—and is certain to be a topic of discussion—within the near future. What would such planning actually be like?

It is a great deal easier to say what American planning would *not* mean than to describe what it will be like. The first necessity is to disabuse ourselves of the idea that planning would mean the establishment of a giant apparatus resembling the cumbersome central planning system of the Soviet Union. In Chapter 43 we discuss some of the shortcomings of Soviet planning, which attempts to substitute computerized calculation and ministerial direction for the mechanism of the market. As we shall see, such a system can launch a stagnant society on a course of economic growth, but it is ill-adapted to the needs—not to speak of the traditions and values—of societies such as those of Europe or the United States.

Instead of central planning, we can expect that national economic planning in America will follow the course that is already emerging in Europe and Japan. This is an effort to use the market as a planning instrument and to confine the operation of planning to the establishment of long-term objectives, such as the national rate of growth or the level of unemployment or the rate of inflation or big micro objectives such as transportation, energy, or urban rehabilitation.

HOW PLANNING WORKS

How could this be done? As the planning process is currently envisaged by most economists, the first step is the formulation of a number of alternative micro and macro targets by a small group of economists and statisticians within the Executive branch. The initial task of planning is thus to work out a series of different "menus" of economic possibilities extending forward 3 to 5 years. Of course these menus will be political. They will present the preferences of the planners, or more realistically, of the Administration for whom the planners work.

But the menus are not just expressions of political preference. They are also efforts to discover what possibilities lie within the economy's grasp, given its labor force, its capital resources, its known technology, and so forth. In a sense, this first exercise is a translation of the idea of a production possibilities curve into reality.

How is such a set of menus drawn up? The first requirement is an extensive and reliable flow of economic statistics. Large as our present base of knowledge is, it is not large enough to allow us to make many economic calculations with much accuracy. (Just as an example: until the Arab oil crisis, there was no official statistical information regarding the size of total gasoline stocks in the country!)

These statistics would then be coordinated within an input-output matrix (see "An extra word" at the end of Chapter 25). This would give us the first general test of the feasibility of menus that might seem attractive. It could well turn out, for instance, that we could not undertake two major building programs simultaneously, although either one by itself would be feasible, just as in the case of the production possibility curve on p. 347 where we could not attain a desired output of both milk and wheat.

In making up our menus of choices, the big problem, however, is not so much apt to be the reconciliation of overambitious micro targets, but the reconciliation of macro targets; above all, targets for employment levels and rates of inflation. For the rate of growth will hinge, in the first instance, on the level of employment that we target; and that level, we know from experience, may not be easily matched with a desired rate of inflation, at least not without economic controls of various sorts.

Thus the planning economists are apt to offer us a range of two or three alternatives that might, for instance, include an option for 6 percent growth, 3 percent unemployment, and 5 percent inflation; or for 4 percent growth, 5 percent unemployment, and 4 percent inflation. In all likelihood the alternatives will not be so ambitious that we could realize them only by near-wartime measures (e.g., 10 percent growth and 1 percent unemployment with 2 percent inflation); or so unambitious that planning would be pointless—minus 2 percent growth, 9 percent inflation, and 8 percent unemployment, the combination we actually had in 1975.

FURTHER REVIEWS

In currently envisaged legislation, these alternative plans would then be reviewed by a standing committee, also within the Executive office. There the heads of the main departments and agencies, together with representatives from industry, labor, and the public, would voice their approval or disapproval of the various alternatives or perhaps ask the economists to devise still another feasible set of targets.

Thereafter, the plans, now perhaps reduced to one or two favored alternatives, would be presented to Congress, to be reexamined by the Joint Economic Committee of the House and Senate. Congress would then select a preferred plan or might even write a new one, heeding the advice of its own experts and the testimony it would gather from governors or other persons it might wish to consult.

The final plan would then be passed by both Houses and sent to the President for his signature. It would encompass both a set of targets and a set of means for achieving these targets—let us say 5 percent growth, 3 percent unemployment, 4 percent inflation, to be attained by new tax provisions, a major budget authorization for urban renewal, a general directive to the Fed, and so on. The plan might also include a number of environmental directives, accelerating research or investment in certain processes, discouraging it in others.

To a large extent, as we can see, this kind of planning resembles the process of law-making, with all its compromises, reconciliations, and efforts to achieve a workable consensus. The skepticism or faith that one holds out for planning is therefore closely related to that which one has for our capacity to produce just and workable laws. For those who hold democratic representative government in low esteem, there is no reason to assume that economic planning will rise above the level of a bureaucratic tangle or a sub rosa "takeover" by powerful groups.

But for those who hold a more sanguine view of the self-governing capabilities of a capitalist democracy, there is no reason to believe that a national planning effort could not achieve as acceptable a level of economic performance as our general legislation achieves for our political and social performance. The main purpose of economic planning, as we have seen, is to diminish the gap between potential output and actual output, and to achieve growth in ways that will not endanger the future.

The REST of the WORLD

PART **5**

Gains from trade

Americans have had the fortune to be extraordinarily sheltered from the currents of international economics that wash against other shores. British students are brought up knowing about exports and imports, because a quarter of their national income derives from foreign trade. A Canadian knows about international economics, because one Canadian dollar in five is earned or spent beyond Canadian borders. Any educated person in the underdeveloped world will tell you that the future of his country is critically affected by the exports it sells to the developed world and the capital it brings in from that world. Only the United States, among the nations of the West, is generally unconcerned and uneducated about foreign trade, for the general opinion is that we are relatively self-sufficient and could, if we had to, let the rest of the world go hang.

Could we? It is true that less than 10 percent of our gross national product is bought or sold overseas. Yet it is worth considering what would happen to our own economy if some mischance severed our ties with the rest of the world.

The first impact would be the loss of certain critical products needed for industrial production. In the earlier years of the country, we were inclined to treat our

38

natural resources as inexhaustible, but the astounding rate of our consumption of industrial raw materials has disabused us of that notion. Today the major fractions of our iron ore, our copper, and our wood pulp come to us from abroad. Ninety percent of the bauxite from which we make aluminum is imported. Ninety-four percent of the manganese needed for high-tempered steels, all our chrome, virtually all our cobalt, the great bulk of our nickel, tin, platinum, asbestos, a rising fraction of our petroleum is foreign-bought. Many of these materials are so strategic that we stockpile them against temporary disruption, but in a few years the stockpiles would be used up and we should be forced to make radical changes in some of our technology.

Then there would be other losses, less statistically impressive but no less irksome to consumer and industry: the loss of Japanese cameras, of British tweeds, of French perfume, of Italian movies, of Rolls Royce engines, Volkswagen cars, Danish silver, Indian jute and madras. Coffee and tea, the very mainstays of civilized existence, would no longer be available. Chocolate, the favorite flavor of a hundred million Americans, would be unobtainable. There would be no bananas in the morning, no pepper at supper, no Scotch whiskey at night. Clearly, shutting down the flow of the imports into America, however relatively self-sufficient we may be, would deal us a considerable blow. One can imagine what it would mean in the case of, say, Holland, where foreign products account for as much as 45 percent of all goods sold in that country.

But we have still not fully investigated the effects of international trade on the United States, for we have failed to consider the impact of a collapse of our exports. The farm country would feel such a collapse immediately of course, for a fifth of our cotton, almost a quarter of our grains, and more than a quarter of our tobacco go overseas. Mining country would feel it because a fifth of our coal and a third of our sulphur are sold abroad. Manufacturing enterprises in cities scattered all over the nation would feel the blow, as a quarter of our metalworking machinery and of our textile machinery, a third of our construction and mining machinery could no longer be sold overseas—not to speak of another thirty to forty industries in which at least a fifth of output is regularly sold to foreign buyers. In all, some three million to four million jobs, three-quarters of them in manufacturing or commerce, would cease to exist if our foreign markets should suddenly disappear.

Many of those jobs would be replaced by new industries that would be encouraged if our overseas markets and sources of supply vanished. If we could not buy watches or watch parts in Switzerland, we would make more of them here. If we could not sell machine tools to the world, we would no doubt try to use our unemployed skills to make some product or service that could be marketed at home—perhaps one of the items we no longer imported. With considerable effort (especially in the case of strategic materials) we *could* readjust. Hence the question: Why don't we? What is the purpose of international trade? Why do we not seek to improve our relative self-sufficiency by making it complete?

The bias of nationalism   No sooner do we ask the question of the aims of international trade than we encounter an obstacle that will present the single greatest difficulty in learning about international economies. This is the bias of nationalism—the curious fact that relationships and propositions that are perfectly self-evident in the context of "ordinary" economics suddenly appear suspect, not to say downright wrong, in the context of international economics.

For example, suppose that the governor of an eastern state—let us say New Jersey—wanted to raise the incomes of his constituents and decided that the best way to do so was to encourage some new industry to move there. Suppose furthermore that his son was very fond of grapefruit and suggested to him one morning that grapefruit growing would be an excellent addition to New Jersey's products.

The governor might object that grapefruit needed a milder climate than New Jersey had to offer. "That's no problem," his son might answer. "We could protect our grapefruit by growing them in hothouses. That way, in addition to the income from the crop, we would benefit the state from the incomes earned by the glaziers and electricians who would be needed."

The governor might murmur something about hothouse grapefruit costing more than ordinary grapefruit, so that New Jersey could not sell its crop on the competitive market. "Nonsense," his son would reply. "We can subsidize the grapefruit growers out of the proceeds of a general sales tax. Or we could pass a law requiring restaurants in this state to serve state grapefruit only. Or you could bar out-of-state grapefruit from New Jersey entirely."

"Now, my boy," the governor would return, "in the first place, that's unconstitutional. Second, even if it weren't, we would be making people in this state give up part of their incomes through the sales tax to benefit farmers, and that would

never be politically acceptable. And third, the whole scheme is so inefficient it's just downright ridiculous."

But if we now shift our attention to a similar scene played between the prime minister of Nova Jersia and his son, we find some interesting differences. Like his counterpart in New Jersey, the son of the prime minister recommends the growing of hothouse grapefruit in Nova Jersia's chilly climate. Admittedly, that would make the crop considerably dearer than that for sale on the international markets. "But that's all right," he tells his father. "We can put a tariff on foreign grapefruit, so none of the cheap fruit from abroad will undersell ours."

"My boy," says the prime minister after carefully considering the matter, "I think you are right. It is true that grapefruit in Nova Jersia will be more expensive as a result of the tariff, but there is no doubt that a tariff looks like a tax on them and not on us, and therefore no one will object to it. It is also true that our hothouse grapefruit may not taste as good as theirs, but we will have the immense satisfaction of eating our *own* grapefruit, which will make it taste better. Finally, there may be a few economists who will tell us that this is not the most efficient use of our resources, but I can tell them that the money we pay for hothouse grapefruit—even if it is a little more than it would be otherwise—stays in our own pockets and doesn't go to enrich foreigners. In addition to which, I would point out in my television appearances that the reason foreign grapefruit are so cheap is that foreign labor is so badly paid. We certainly don't want to drag down the price of our labor by making it compete with the cheap labor of other nations. All in all, hothouse grapefruit seems to me an eminently sensible proposal, and one that is certain to be politically popular."

Source of the difficulty

Is it a sensible proposal? Of course not, although it will take some careful thinking to expose all of its fallacies. Will it be politically popular? It may very well be, for economic policies that would be laughed out of court at home get a serious hearing when they crop up in the international arena. Here are some of the things that most of us tend to believe.

Trade between two nations usually harms one side or the other.

Rich countries can't compete with poor countries.

There is always the danger that a country may sell but refuse to buy.

Are these fears true? One way of testing their validity is to see how they ring in our ears when we rid them of our unconscious national bias by recasting them as propositions in ordinary economics.

Is it true that trade between businesses or persons usually harms one side or the other?

Is it true that rich companies can't compete with poor ones?

Is it true that one company might only sell but never buy—not even materials or the services of factors of production?

What is the source of this curious prejudice against international trade? It is not, as we might think, an excess of patriotism that leads us to recommend courses of action that will help our own country, regardless of the effect on others. For, curiously, the policies of the economic superpatriot, if put into practice, would demonstrably injure the economic interests of his own land. The trouble, then, springs from a root deeper than mere national interest. It lies in the peculiarly deceptive problems posed by international trade. What is deceptive about them,

however, is not that they involve principles that apply only to relations between nations. All the economic arguments that elucidate international trade apply equally well to domestic trade. The deception arises, rather, for two reasons:

1. International trade requires an understanding of how two countries, each dealing in its own currency, manage to buy and sell from each other in a world where there is no such thing as international money.
2. International trade requires a very thorough understanding of the advantages of and arguments for, trade itself.

Gains from trade

In a general way, of course, we are all aware of the importance of trade, although we have hardly mentioned it since the opening pages of our book. *It is trade that makes possible the division and specialization of labor on which our productivity is so largely based.* If we could not exchange the products of our specialized labor, each of us would have to be wholly self-supporting, and our standard of living would thereupon fall to that of subsistence farmers. Thus trade (international or domestic) is actually a means of *increasing productivity*, quite as much as investment or technological progress.

Gains from specialization

The importance of trade in making possible specialization is so great that we should take a moment to make it crystal clear. Let us consider two towns. Each produces two goods: wool and cotton; but Wooltown has good grazing lands and poor growing lands, while Cottontown's grazing is poor, but growing is good. Suppose, moreover, that the two towns had equal populations and that each town employed half its people in cotton and half in wool. The results might look like Table 38 • 1.

Table 38·1   Unspecialized production: Case 1

Production	Wooltown	Cottontown
Wool (lbs)	5,000	2,000
Cotton (lbs)	10,000	20,000

As we can see, the same number of grazers in Wooltown turn out two-and-one-half times as much wool as they do in Cottontown, whereas the same number of cotton farmers in Cottontown produce double the amount of cotton that they do in Wooltown. One does not have to be an economist to see that both towns are losing by this arrangement. If Cottontown would shift its woolworkers into cotton, and Wooltown would shift its cotton farmers into wool, the output of the two towns would look like Table 38·2 (assuming constant returns to scale).

Table 38·2   Specialized production

Output	Wooltown	Cottontown
Wool	10,000	0
Cotton	0	40,000

Now, if we compare total production of the two towns (see Table 38·3), we can see the gains from specialization.

Table 38·3   The gain from specialization

Output	Mixed	Specialized	Gain from specialization
Wool	7,000	10,000	3,000
Cotton	30,000	40,000	10,000

In other words, specialization followed by trade makes it possible for both towns to have more of both commodities than they had before. No matter how the gains from trade are distributed— and this will depend on many factors, such as the relative elasticities of demand for the two products—both towns can gain, even if one gains more than the other.

Unequal advantages

If all the world were divided into nations, like Wooltown and Cottontown, each producing for trade only a single item in which it has a clear advantage over all others, international trade would be a simple matter to understand. It would still present problems of international payment, and it might still inspire its prime ministers of Nova Jersias to forego the gains from trade for political reasons that we will examine at the end of this chapter. But the essential rationale of trade would be simple to understand.

It is unfortunate for the economics student as well as for the world that this is not the way international resources are distributed. Instead of giving each nation at least one commodity in which it has a clear advantage, many nations do not have such an advantage in a single product. How can trade possibly take place under such inauspicious circumstances?

To unravel the mystery, let us turn again to Cottontown and Wooltown, but this time call them Supraville and Infraville, to designate an important change in their respective abilities. Although both towns still enjoy equal populations, which are again divided equally between cotton and wool production, in this example Supraville is a more efficient producer than Infraville in *both* cotton and wool, as Table 38·4 shows.

Table 38·4   Unspecialized production: Case II

	Supraville	Infraville
Wool output	5,000	3,000
Cotton production	20,000	10,000

Is it possible for trade to benefit these two towns when one of them is so manifestly superior to the other in every product? It seems out of the question. But let us nonetheless test the case by supposing that each town began to specialize.

Trade-off relationships

But how to decide which trade each town should follow? A look at Fig. 38·1 may give us a clue. The production-possibility diagrams are familiar to us from Chapter 24, where we used them to clarify the nature of scarcity and economic choice. Here we put them to use to let us see the results of trade.

What do the diagrams show? First, they establish maximums that each town could produce if it devoted all its efforts to one product. Since we have assumed that the labor force is divided, this means that each town could double the amount of cotton or wool it enjoys when it divides its workers fifty-fifty. Next, a line between these points shows the production frontier that both towns face.* We see that Supraville is located at point *A* where it has 5,000 lbs of wool and 20,000 lbs of cotton, and that Infraville is at *B*, where it has 3,000 lbs of wool and 10,000 lbs of cotton.

But the diagrams (and the figures in the preceding table, on which they are based) also show us something else. It is that each town has a different "trade off" relationship between its two branches of production. When either town specializes in one branch, it must, of course, give up the output of the other. *But each town swaps one kind of output for the other in different proportions*, as the differing slopes of the two *p-p* curves show. Supraville, for example, can make only an extra pound of wool by giving up 4 pounds of cotton. That is, it gets its maximum potential output of 10,000 lbs of wool only by surrendering 40,000 lbs of cotton. Infraville can reach its production maximum of 6,000 lbs of wool at a loss of only 20,000 lbs of cotton. *Rather than having to give up 4 lbs of cotton to get one of wool, it gives up only 3.3 lbs.* Thus, in terms of how much cotton it must surrender, wool actually costs less in Infraville than in Supraville!

Not so the other way round, of course. As we would expect, cotton costs Supraville less in terms of wool than it costs Infraville. In Supraville, we get 40,000 lbs of cotton by relinquishing only 10,000 lbs of wool—a loss of a quarter of a pound of wool for a pound of the other. In Infraville, we can get the maximum output of 20,000 lbs of cotton only by a surrender of 6,000 lbs of wool—a loss of $\frac{1}{3}$ lb of wool rather than $\frac{1}{4}$ lb of wool for each unit of cotton.*

Comparative advantage

Perhaps the light is beginning to dawn. Despite the fact that Supraville is more productive than Infraville in terms of output per man in both cotton and wool, it is *relatively* more productive in cotton than in wool. And despite the fact that Infraville is absolutely less productive than Supraville, man for man, in both cotton and wool, it is *relatively* more productive in wool. To repeat, it requires a smaller sacrifice of wool to get another pound of cotton in Infraville than in Supraville.

---

*Why are these lines drawn straight, not bowed as in Chapter 24? As we know, the bowing reflects the law of increasing cost, which makes the gains from a shift in resource allocation less and less favorable as we move from one extreme of allocation to another. Here we ignore this complication for simplicity of exposition. We have also ignored the problem of variable returns when we assumed that each town could double its output of cotton or wool by doubling its labor force.

*It takes long practice to master the arithmetic of gains from trade. Practice on questions 2 through 5 will help. It is more important, at this point, to "get the idea" than to master the calculations.

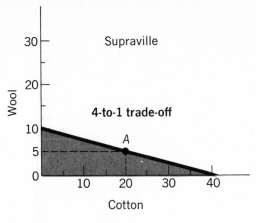
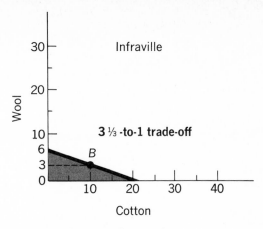

FIG. 38 · 1   Production possibilities in the two towns before trade

We call this kind of relative superiority *comparative advantage*. It is a concept that is often difficult to grasp at first but that is central to the reason for trade itself. When we speak of *comparative* advantage, we mean, as in the case of Supraville, that among *various* advantages of one producer or locale over another, there is one that is better than any other. *Comparatively* speaking, this is where its optimal returns lie. But just because it must abandon some lesser opportunity, its trading partner can now advantageously devote itself in the direction where *it* has a comparative advantage.

This is a relationship of logic, not economics. Take the example of the banker who is also the best carpenter in town. Will it pay him to build his own house? Clearly it will not, for he will make more money by devoting all his hours to banking, even though he then has to employ and pay for a carpenter less skillful than himself. True, he could save that expense by building his own house. But he would then have to give up the much more lucrative hours he could be spending at the bank!

Now let us return to the matter of trade. We have seen that wool is *relatively* cheaper in Infraville, where each additional pound cost only 3.3 lbs of cotton, rather than 4 lbs as in Supraville; and that

cotton is *relatively* cheaper in Supraville, where an additional pound costs but ¼ lb of wool, instead of ⅓ lb across the way in Infraville. Now let us suppose that each side begins to specialize in the trade in which it has the comparative advantage. Suppose that Supraville took half its labor force now in wool and put it into cotton. Its output would change as in Table 38 · 5.

Table 38 · 5   Supraville

	Before the shift	After the shift
Wool production	5,000	2,500
Cotton production	20,000	30,000

Supraville has lost 2,500 lbs of wool but gained 10,000 lbs of cotton. Now let us see if it can trade its cotton for Infraville's wool. In Infraville, where productivity is so much less, the entire labor force has shifted to wool output, where its greatly inferior productivity can be put to best use. Hence its production pattern now looks like Table 38 · 6.

Table 38 · 6   Infraville

	Before the shift	After the shift
Wool	3,000	6,000
Cotton	10,000	—

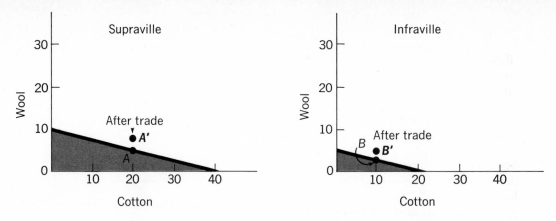

FIG. 38·2   Production possibilities in the two towns after trade

Infraville finds itself lacking 10,000 lbs of cotton, but it has 3,000 *additional* lbs of wool. Clearly, it can acquire the 10,000 lbs of cotton it needs from Supraville by giving Supraville *more* than the 2,500 lbs of wool it seeks. As a result, both Infraville and Supraville will have the same cotton consumption as before, but there will be a surplus of 500 lbs of wool to be shared between them. As Fig. 38·2 shows, *both towns will have gained by the exchange, for both will have moved beyond their former production frontiers* (from A to A' and from B to B').

This last point is the crucial one. If we remember the nature of production-possibility curves from our discussion of them in Chapter 24, any point lying outside the production frontier is simply unattainable by that society. In Fig. 38·2, points A' and B' do lie beyond the pre-trade p-p curves of the two towns, and yet trade has made it possible for both communities to enjoy what was formerly impossible.

Opportunity cost   Comparative advantage gives us an important insight into all exchange relationships, for it reveals again a fundamental economic truth that we have mentioned more than once before. It is that *cost, in economics, means opportunities that must be foregone.* The real cost of

wool in Supraville is the cotton that cannot be grown, because workers are engaged in wool production, just as the real cost of cotton is the wool that must be gone without. In fact, we can see that the basic reason for comparative advantage lies in the fact that opportunity costs vary, so that it "pays" (it costs less) for different parties to engage in different activities.

If opportunity costs for two producers are the same, then it follows that there cannot be any comparative advantage for either; and if there is no comparative advantage, there is nothing to be gained by specializing or trading. Suppose Supraville has a two-to-one edge over Infraville in *both* cotton and wool. Then, if either town specializes, neither will gain. Supraville may still gain 10,000 lbs of cotton for 2,500 lbs of wool, as before, but Infraville will gain only 2,500 lbs of wool (not 3,000) from its shift away from cotton. Thus, the key to trade lies in the existence of *different* opportunity costs.

Are opportunity costs usually different from country to country or from region to region? For most commodities they are. As we move from one part of the world to another—sometimes even short distances—climate, resources, skills, transportation costs, capital scarcity, or abundance all change; and as they change, so do opportunity costs. There is every possibility for rich countries to trade with poor ones, precisely because their opportunity costs are certain to differ.

Exchange ratios But we have not yet fully understood one last important aspect of trade—the *prices* at which goods will exchange. Suppose that Supraville and Infraville do specialize, each in the product in which it enjoys a comparative advantage. Does that mean they can swap their goods at any prices?

A quick series of calculations reveals otherwise. We remember that Supraville needed at least 2,500 lbs of wool for which it was going to offer some of its extra production of cotton in exchange. But how much? What price should it offer for its needed wool, in terms of cotton?

Suppose it offered 7,500 lbs of cotton. Would Infraville sell the wool? No, it would not. At home it can grow its own 7,500 lbs of cotton at a "cost" of only 2,273 lbs of wool, for we recall that Infraville traded off one pound of wool for 3.3 lbs of cotton (7,500 ÷ 3.3 = 2,273).

Suppose, then, that Infraville counteroffered to sell Supraville 2,500 lbs of wool for a price of 12,000 lbs of cotton. Would Supraville accept? Of course not. This would mean the equivalent of 4.8 lbs of cotton for a pound of wool. Supraville can do better than that by growing her own wool at her own trade-off ratio of only 4 lbs to one.

We begin to see, in other words, that the price of wool must lie between the trade-off ratios of Infraville and Supraville. Infraville wants to import cotton. If it did not trade with Supraville, it could grow its own cotton at the cost of one pound of wool for every 3.3 lbs of cotton. Hence, for trade to be advantageous, Infraville seeks to get *more* cotton than that, per pound of wool.

Supraville is in the opposite situation. It seeks to export cotton and to import wool. It could make its own wool at the sacrifice of 4 lbs of cotton per pound of wool. Thus it seeks to gain wool for a *lower* price than that, in terms of cotton. Clearly, any ratio between 3.3 and 4.0 lbs of cotton per pound of wool will profit both sides.

The role of prices Let us put this into ordinary price terms. Suppose that cotton sells for 30¢ per pound. Then wool would have to sell between 99¢ and $1.20 (30¢ × 3.3 and × 4) to make trade worthwhile.* Let us say that supply and demand established a price of $1.10 for wool. Supraville can then sell its 10,000 lbs of extra cotton production at 30¢, which will net it $3,000. How much wool can it buy for this sum? At the going price of $1.10 per lb, 2,727 lbs. Therefore Supraville will end up with the same amount of cotton (20,000 lbs) as it had before specialization and trade, and with 227 *more* lbs of wool than before (2,500 lbs produced at home plus 2,727 lbs imported from Infraville—a total of 5,227 lbs). It has gained by trade an amount equal to the price of this extra wool, or $249.70.

How has Infraville fared? It has 3,273 lbs of wool left after exporting 2,727 lbs to Supraville from its production of 6,000 lbs, and it also has 10,000 lbs of cotton imported from Supraville in exchange for its wool exports. Thus it, too, has a gain from trade—the 273 lbs of wool (worth $300.30) over the amount of 3,000 lbs that it would have produced without specialization and trade. In brief, *both* sides have profited from the exchange. To be sure, gains need not be distributed so evenly between the trading partners. If the price of wool had

---

*Obviously, these prices are used for illustrative purposes only. And once again, let us reassure you: these calculations are easy to follow but not easy to do by yourself. Familiarity will come only with practice.

been $1.00, trade still would have been worthwhile, but Supraville would have gained almost all of it. Had the price of wool been $1.19, both sides again would have come out ahead, but now Infraville would have been the larger beneficiary by far. The actual price at which wool would sell would be determined by the supply and demand schedules for it in both communities.

The Case for Free Trade

Would the prime minister of Nova Jersia be convinced by these arguments? Would his son? They might be weakened in their support for hothouse grapefruit, but some arguments would still linger in their minds. Let us consider them.

1. "Our workers cannot compete with low-wage workers overseas."

This is an argument one hears not only in Nova Jersia, but in every nation in the world, save only those with the very lowest wage rates. Swedish workers complain about "cheap" American labor; American workers complain about sweatshop labor in Hong Kong. And indeed it is true that American labor is paid less than Swedish and that Hong Kong labor is paid a great deal less than American. Does that not mean that American labor will be seriously injured if

we import goods made under "sweatshop" conditions, or that Swedish labor is right in complaining that its standard of living is undermined by importing goods from "exploited" American workers?

Like the answers to so many questions in economics, this one is not a simple yes or no. The American textile worker who loses his job because of low-priced textile imports *is* hurt; and so is the Swedish worker in an electronics company who loses his job because of American competition. We will come back to their legitimate grievances later. But we must note that both workers would also be injured if they lost their jobs as a result of domestic competition. Why do we feel so threatened when the competition comes from abroad?

Because, the answer goes, foreign competition isn't based on American efficiency. It is based on exploited labor. Hence it pulls down the standards of American labor to its own low level.

There is an easy reply to this argument. The reason Hong Kong textile labor is paid so much less than American textile labor is that *average* productivity in Hong Kong is so much lower than *average* productivity in America. To put it differently, the reason that American wages are high is that we use our workers in industries where their productivity is very high. If Hong Kong, with its very low productivity, can undersell us in textiles, then this is a clear signal that we must move our factors of production out of textiles into other areas where their contribution will be greater; for example,

594

in the production of machinery. It is no coincidence that machinery—one of the highest wage industries in America—is one of our leading exports, or that more than 75 percent of our manufactured exports are produced by industries paying hourly wage rates above the national average for all manufacturing industries. In fact, all nations tend to export the goods that are produced at the highest, not lowest, local wages! Why? Because those industries employ their labor most effectively.

This fact opens our eyes to another. Why is it that the American garment industry is worried about competition from Hong Kong, but not the American auto industry or the electrical machinery industry or the farm equipment industry? After all, the manufacturers of those products could also avail themselves of low wages in Hong Kong.

The answer is that American manufacturers can make these products at much lower cost in America. Why? Because the technical skills necessary to produce them are available in the U.S., not in Hong Kong. Thus, if Hong Kong has a comparative advantage over us in the garment trade, we have a comparative advantage over her in many other areas.

But suppose Hong Kong accumulated large amounts of capital and became a center for the manufacture of heavy equipment, so that it sold *both* garments and electrical generators more cheaply than we sold them. We are back to Supraville and Infraville. There would still be a *comparative* advantage in one or more of these products in which we would be wise to specialize, afterward trading with Hong Kong for our supplies of the other good.*

---

*Newspapers in Southeast Asia carry editorials seeking protection from American imports because, they say, we do not use labor in our production, and it is unfair to ask its citizens to compete with our machines that do not have to be paid wages.

2. "Tariffs are painless taxes because they are borne by foreigners."

This is a convincing-sounding argument advanced by the prime minister of Nova Jersia (and by some other prime ministers in their time). But is it true? Let us take the case of hothouse grapefruit, which can be produced in Nova Jersia only at a cost of 50 cents each, whereas foreign grapefruit (no doubt produced by sweated labor) can be unloaded at its ports at 25 cents. To prevent his home industry from being destroyed, the prime minister imposes a tariff of 25 cents on foreign grapefruit—which, he tells the newspapers, will be entirely paid by foreigners.

This is not, however, the way his political opponent (who has had a course in economics) sees it. "Without the tariff," she tells her constituency, "you could buy grapefruit for 25 cents. Now you have to pay 50 cents for it. Who is paying the extra 25 cents—the foreign grower or you? Even if not a single grapefuit entered the country, you would still be paying 25 cents more than you have to. In fact, *you are being asked to subsidize an inefficient domestic industry.* Not only that, but the tariff wall means they won't ever become efficient because there is no pressure of competition on them."

Whether or not our economic candidate will win the electoral battle, she surely has the better of the argument. Or does she? For the prime minister, stung by these unkind remarks, replies:

3. "But at least the tariff keeps spending power at home. Our own grapefruit growers, not foreigners, have our money."

There are two answers to this argument. First, the purchasing power acquired by foreigners can be used to buy goods from efficient Nova Jersia producers

If every industry must have a comparative advantage in one country or another, how can there be steel industries (or any other) in more than one country? The answer, quite aside from considerations of nationalism, lies in *transportation costs*, which compensate for lower production costs in many products and thereby allow a relatively inefficient industry to supply a home market.

Transportation costs also explain why some industries, such as brick-making, are spread out in many localities, whereas others, such as diamond cutting, are concentrated in one place. If diamonds were very bulky or bricks very light, the first industry would become more dispersed, and the second less so.

and will thus return to Nova Jersia's economy. Second, if productive resources are used in inefficient, low-productivity industries, then the resources available for use in efficient, high-productivity industries are less than they otherwise would be, and the total output of the country falls. To keep out foreign grapefruit is to lower the country's real standard of living. The people of Nova Jersia waste time and resources doing something they do not do very well.

4. "But tariffs are necessary to keep the work force of Nova Jersia employed."

This is the time to remember our investigation of macroeconomic policies. As we learned in macroeconomics, the governments of Nova Jersia and every other country can use fiscal and monetary policies to keep their resources fully employed. If textile workers become unemployed, governments can expand aggregate demand and generate domestic job opportunities in other areas.

Classical argument for free trade   Are there no arguments at all for tariffs? As we shall see, there are some rational arguments for restricting free trade. *But all of these arguments accept the fact that restrictions depress world incomes below what they would be otherwise. If world production is to be maximized, free trade is an essential ingredient.* Free trade must therefore be considered a means of increasing GNP, a means not essentially

different from technological improvement in its effect on output and growth. We may not want to maximize GNP, but we need to understand that to advocate restrictions on trade is to advocate lower real incomes. These arguments apply cogently to developed countries. They are less persuasive when applied to underdeveloped countries, as we shall see when we discuss imperialism in Chapter 42.

The Case for Tariffs

Are *all* arguments against tariffs? Not quite. But it is essential to recognize that these arguments take full cognizance of the inescapable costs of restricting trade. They do not contest the validity of the theory of free trade, but the difficulties of its application. Let us familiarize ourselves with them.

Mobility   *The first difficulty concerns the problem of mobility.* Explicit in Bastiat's case (see box) is the ease with which Crusoe and Friday move back and forth between hunting and gardening. Implicit in the case of Supraville and Infraville is the possibility of shifting workers and resources from cotton to wool production. But in fact is is sometimes exceedingly difficult to move resources from one industry to another.

Thus when Hong Kong textiles press hard against the garment worker in New

York, higher wages in the auto plants in Detroit are scant comfort. She has a lifetime of skills and a home in New York, and she does not want to move to another city where she will be a stranger and to a new trade in which she would be only an unskilled beginner. She certainly does not want to move to Hong Kong! Hence, the impact of foreign trade often brings serious dislocations that result in persistent local unemployment, rather than in a flow of resources from a relatively disadvantaged to a relatively advantaged one. If Crusoe had suggested that it was very difficult (perhaps because of the noonday sun) to work in the gardens in the morning when they usually went hunting, Friday would have been harder put for a reply.

The beclouding effect of national bias on our thinking was never more charmingly or effectively presented than in this argument by Frédéric Bastiat, a delightful exponent of mid-nineteenth-century classical economic ideals, in a little book entitled *Social Fallacies*.[1]

In Bastiat's book, Robinson Crusoe inhabits an island with Friday. In the morning, Crusoe and Friday hunt for six hours and bring home four baskets of game. In the evening, they garden for six hours and get four baskets of vegetables. But now let Bastiat take over:

One day a canoe touched at the island. A goodlooking foreigner landed and was admitted to the table of our two recluses. He tasted and commended very much the produce of the garden, and before taking leave of his entertainers, spoke as follows: "Generous islanders, I inhabit a country where game is much more plentiful than here, but where horticulture is quite unknown. It would be an easy matter to bring you every evening four baskets of game, if you will give me in exchange two baskets of vegetables."

At these words, Robinson and Friday retired to consult, and the debate that took place is too interesting not to be reported in extenso.

FRIDAY: What do you think of it?
ROBINSON: If we close with the proposal, we are ruined.
FRIDAY: Are you sure of that? Let us consider.
ROBINSON: The case is clear. Crushed by competition, our hunting as a branch of industry is annihilated.

ROBINSON CRUSOE

FRIDAY: What matters it, if we have the game?
ROBINSON: Theory! It will no longer be the product of our labour.
FRIDAY: I beg your pardon sir; for in order to have game we must part with vegetables.
ROBINSON: Then, what shall we gain?
FRIDAY: The four baskets of game cost us six hours' work. The foreigner gives us them in exchange for two baskets of vegetables, which cost us only three hours' work. This places three hours at our disposal. . . .
ROBINSON: You lose yourself in generalities! What should we make of these three hours?
FRIDAY: We would do something else.
ROBINSON: Ah! I understand you. You cannot come to particulars. Something else, something else—that is easily said.
FRIDAY: We can fish, we can ornament our cottage, we can read the Bible.
ROBINSON: Utopia! Is there any certainty we should do either the one or the other? . . . Moreover there are political reasons for rejecting the interested offers of the perfidious foreigner.

FRIDAY: Political reasons!
ROBINSON: Yes, he only makes us these offers because they are advantageous to him.
FRIDAY: So much the better, since they are for our advantage likewise. . . .
ROBINSON: Suppose the foreigner learns to cultivate a garden and that his island should prove more fertile than ours. Do you see the consequences?
FRIDAY: Yes; our relations with the foreigner would cease. He would take from us no more vegetables, since he could have them at home with less labour. He would bring us no more game, since we should have nothing to give him in exchange, and we should then be in precisely the situation that you wish us in now. . . .
The debate was prolonged, and, as often happens, each remained wedded to his own opinion. But Robinson possessing a great influence over Friday, his opinion prevailed, and when the foreigner arrived to demand a reply, Robinson said to him: "Stranger, in order to induce us to accept your proposal, we must be assured of two things: the first is, that your island is no better stocked with game than ours, for we want to fight only with equal weapons. The second is, that you will lose by the bargain. For, as in every exchange there is necessarily a gaining and a losing party, we should be dupes, if you were not the loser. What have you got to say?"
"Nothing," replied the foreigner; and, bursting out laughing, he regained his canoe.

[1]Translated by Frederick James Sterling (Santa Ana, Calif.: Register Publishing, 1944), pp. 203f.

Transition costs Second, we have seen that free trade is necessary to maximize world incomes and that it increases the incomes and real living standards of each country participating in trade. *But this does not mean that it increases the income and real living standards of each individual in each country.* Our New York textile worker may find herself with a substantial reduction in income for the rest of her life. She is being economically rational when she resists "cheap" foreign imports and attempts to get her congressman to impose tariffs or quotas.

There is, it should be noted, an answer to this argument—an answer, at any rate, that applies to industrial nations. Since the gains from trade are generally spread across the nation, the real transition costs of moving from one industry, skill, or region to another should also be generally spread across the nation. This means that government (the taxpayers), rather than the worker or businessman, should bear the costs of relocation and retraining. In this way we spread the costs in such a manner that a few need not suffer disproportionately to win the benefits of international trade that are shared by many.

We should also be aware of the possibility that transition costs may actually exceed the short-term benefits to be derived from international trade. Transition costs thus place a new element in the system, since the standard analysis of competitive systems—national or international—ignores them. A country may be wise to limit its international trade, if it calculates that the cost of reallocating its own factors is greater than the gains to be had in higher real income. Remember, however, that transition costs tend to be short-lived and that the gains from trade tend to last. Thus it is easy to exaggerate the costs of transition and to balk at making

changes that would ultimately improve conditions.

Full employment Third, *the argument for free trade rests on the very important assumption that there will be substantially full employment.*

In the days of the mid-nineteenth century when the free trade argument was first fully formulated, the idea of an underemployment equilibrium would have been considered absurd. When Crusoe asks what use they should make of their free time, Friday has no trouble replying that they should work or enjoy their leisure. But in a highly interdependent society, work may not be available, and leisure may be only a pseudonym for an inability to find work. In an economy of large enterprises and "sticky" wages and prices, we know that unemployment is a real and continuous object of concern for national policy.

Thus, it makes little sense to advocate policies to expand production via trade unless we are certain that the level of aggregate demand will be large enough to absorb that production. **Full employment policy therefore becomes an indispensable arm of trade policy.** Trade gives us the potential for maximizing production, but there is no point in laying the groundwork for the highest possible output, unless fiscal and monetary policy are also geared to bringing about a level of aggregate demand large enough to support that output.

National self-sufficiency Fourth, *there is the argument of nationalism pure and simple.* This argument does not impute spurious economic gains to tariffs. Rather, it says that free trade undoubtedly encourages production, but it does so at a certain cost. This is the cost of the vulnerability that comes from extensive and extreme specialization. This vulnerability is all very well within a nation where we assume that law and order will prevail, but it cannot be so easily justified among nations where the realistic assumption is just the other way. Tariffs, in other words, are defensible because they enable nations to attain a certain *self-sufficiency*—admittedly at some economic cost. Project Independence, the United States' effort to gain self-sufficiency in energy, is exactly such an undertaking.

When Crusoe argued that trade might cease, Friday properly scoffed. But the argument is much more valid for an economy of complex industrial processes and specialized know-how that cannot be quickly duplicated if trade is disrupted. In a world always threatened by war, self-sufficiency has a value that may properly override considerations of ideal economic efficiency. The problem is to hold the arguments for "national defense" down to proper proportions. When tariffs are periodically adjusted in international conferences, an astonishing variety of industries (in all countries) find it possible to claim protection from foreign competition in the name of national "indispensability."

Infant industries   Equally interesting is the nationalist argument for tariffs advanced by so-called infant industries, particularly in developing nations. These newly-formed or prospective enterprises claim that they cannot possibly compete with the giants in developed countries while they are small; but that if they are protected by a tariff, they will in time become large and efficient enough no longer to need a tariff. In addition, they claim, they will provide a more diversified spectrum of employments for their own people, as well as aiding in the national transition toward a more modern economy.

The argument is a valid one if it is applied to industries that have a fair chance of achieving a comparative advantage once grown up (otherwise one will be supporting them in infancy, maturity, and senility). Certainly it is an argument that was propounded by the youthful industries of the United States in the early nineteenth century and was sufficiently persuasive to bring them a moderate degree of protection (although it is inconclusive as to how much their growth was ultimately dependent on tariff help). And it is being listened to today by the underdeveloped nations who feel that their only chance of escaping from poverty is to develop a nucleus of industrial employment at almost any cost in the short run.

Producers'   Finally there is an
welfare   argument that comes
        down to desired life styles and the quality of life. Economists tend to think entirely of consumers' welfare and to ignore producers' welfare. They define work as a "disutility" that must create pain. But in fact, the quality of an individual's productive life may be as important to him as, or more important than, the quality of his consumptive life. Individuals can and do choose to have lower standards of consumption in exchange for a job that they enjoy. Whole countries may make the same choice.

Assume for the moment that the U.S. has a comparative advantage in agricultural production vis-à-vis France, but Frenchmen enjoy being farmers. In a world of free trade, Frenchmen would be driven out of farming. They would work in the cities and have more goods and services than they would have on their farms. But they would no longer be able to enjoy their farms. Is it irrational for France to place high tariffs and quotas on

American agricultural exports in this case? Clearly not. The only irrationality occurs when countries pretend that such actions do not impose costs and when they do not tell their populations that the whole country (farmers and nonfarmers) must reduce its material standard of living so that some can enjoy their work.

The problem of producers' welfare—the quality of work rather than consumption—is one with which neither economists nor society has adequately come to grips. It may become a key area in raising real standards of living.

The basic argument

Thus there are arguments for tariffs, or at least rational counterarguments against an extreme free trade position. Workers *are* hurt by international competition; and in the default of proper domestic plans for cushioning these blows, modest tariffs can buffer the pains of redeployment. Free trade *does* require a level of high employment; and when unemployment is already a national problem, tariffs may protect additional workers from losing their jobs. Strategic industries and development-stimulating industries *are* sometimes essential and may require protection from world competition. People may enjoy their jobs even though they work with less efficiency than they would in other jobs. All these arguments are but qualifications to the basic proposition on which the economist rests

his case for the freest *possible* trade, but they help to define "possible" in a realistic way.

Nonetheless it may help if we sum up the classical argument, for there is always a danger that the qualifications will take precedence over the main argument.

Free trade brings about the most efficient possible use of resources, and any interference with free trade lessens that efficiency.

Note that international trade is in no way different from interregional domestic trade in this regard. We recognize that we would suffer a loss in higher costs or smaller output by imposing restrictions on the exchange of goods between New York and Chicago. We suffer the same loss when we interfere with the exchange between New York and Hong Kong, whether by tariffs, quotas, or other means.

Frictional problems

International trade may indeed bring frictional problems, such as unemployment in an industry that cannot meet foreign competition. But the answer is not to block the imports but to cure the unemployment by finding better uses for our inefficiently used resources.

Once again, international trade is no different in this regard from domestic trade. When low-price textiles from the South cause unemployment in New En-

600

gland, we do not prevent the sale of southern goods. We try to find new jobs for New Englanders, in occupations in which they have a comparative advantage over the South.

Trade and welfare

Finally we must remember that the purpose of all trade is to improve the well-being of the consumer by giving him the best and cheapest goods and services possible. Thus imports, not exports, represent the gains from trade.

The whole point of trade is to exchange things that we make efficiently for other things in which our efficiency is less. Anything that diminishes imports will reduce our standard of living, just as anything that blocks a return flow of goods from Chicago to New York will obviously reduce the benefit to New Yorkers of trade with Chicago.

Actually, free trade works to improve total (national) income and may not serve the interests of every person in a nation. Under certain conditions, free trade can raise national income by favoring capital over labor or by raising the incomes of some groups at the expense of others. Thus this "welfare" argument must be taken with a certain caution, and in our last sec-

tion, when we turn to the troubles of the underdeveloped world, we will see some of these problems illustrated not in textbook example, but in reality.

However, it is encouraging that since 1948 the total value of world exports has risen from $54 billion to over $250 billion, and that the volume of world trade has been increasing at the rate of 6 percent a year since the 1960s.* For all its difficulties, trade is still "indirect production"; and in a world that needs production, trade is still very welcome.

---

*A considerable part of the impetus to the growth of world trade must be credited to the spread of more rational—i.e., lower and fewer—tariff barriers. The General Agreement on Tariffs and Trade (GATT), an international body formed in 1947 to work for wider world trade, has succeeded in steadily reducing tariff levels and in dismantling import quotas. It is pleasant to record that the United States initially played a major role in this movement. During the 1930s we had the unenviable reputation of being one of the most restrictive trading nations in the world, but our tariff wall has been far reduced since those irresponsible days. Today our average level of duties on dutiable imports is roughly 10 percent, compared with 53 percent in 1930; and in addition, a third of all our imports are admitted duty-free. On the negative side, however, it must be noted that we continue to discriminate against imports that affect our manufacturing interests. For example, coffee comes in free, but not instant coffee, so that the underdeveloped nations who would like to process coffee within their own economies are gravely disadvantaged. Moreover, in recent years there has been a revival of U.S. protectionism, resulting in "voluntary" agreements on the part of foreign producers to restrict certain kinds of exports, such as TV sets, to us, and (until very recently) in quotas on oil imports. The lessons of free trade continue to persuade economists more than business people.

FOCUS

Here is one of the central ideas of economics—the idea of the gains from trade. You will not really understand this idea until you have mastered the concept of comparative advantage. That is always a tricky and confusing idea because it forces us to think in terms of "tradeoffs" as costs (opportunity costs), rather than in our accustomed dollars-and-cents terms. There is no short cut to mastering this idea. We suggest you work through questions 2 to 5 carefully.

The arguments for and against free trade or tariffs hinge on a prior understanding of the gains from trade. These gains are entirely gains of efficiency—gains represented by a movement outward of production possibility frontiers. The arguments against free trade mainly have to do with the irrelevance of production (e.g., the very real importance of producers' welfare rather than consumers') or with the frictions that a movement of the p-p frontier generates or with other criteria such as the need to promote full employment or to protect national independence. The arguments for free trade—above all the arguments that counter the threats of "cheap foreign labor"—rest their case on the greater welfare of consumers, after the necessary production adjustments have been made.

You should approach this argument to understand both sides, because neither free trade nor protectionism rules the roost today. It must be clear there is something to be said for both sides. Your job is to know what that "something" is, so that you could intelligently take either side in a debate. Where your own preferences fall is, once again, a matter that will be determined by your values—which groups in society do you favor?—and not by an appeal to economic "science."

WORDS AND CONCEPTS YOU SHOULD KNOW

Specialization of labor, 588–89
Trade-off relationships, 590
Comparative advantage, 590–92
Opportunity cost, 592
Exchange rates, 593
Classical argument for free trade, 594–96

Mobility, 596–97
Transition costs, 598
Self-sufficiency, 598–99
Infant industries, 599
Producers' welfare, 599–600

QUESTIONS

1. What do we mean when we say that trade is "indirect production"?

2. Suppose that two towns, Coaltown and Irontown, have equal populations but differing resources. If Coaltown applies its whole population to coal production, it will produce 10,000 tons of coal; if it applies them to iron production, it will produce 5,000 tons of iron. If Irontown concentrates on iron, it will turn out 18,000 tons of iron; if it shifts to coal, it will produce 12,000 tons of coal. Is trade possible between these towns? Would it be possible if Irontown could produce 24,000 tons of iron? Why is there a comparative advantage in one case and not in the other?

3. In which product does Coaltown have a comparative advantage? How many tons of iron does a ton of coal cost her? How many does it cost Irontown? What is the cost of iron in Coaltown and Irontown? Draw a production-possibility diagram for each town. Show where the frontier lies before and after trade.

4. If iron sells for $10 a ton, what must be the price range of coal? Show that trade cannot be profitable if coal sells on either side of this range. What is the opportunity cost of coal to Irontown? Of iron to Irontown?

5. Is it possible that American watchmakers face unfair competition from Swiss watchmakers because wages are lower in Switzerland? If American watch workers are rendered unemployed by the lowpaid Swiss, what might be done to help them—impose a tariff?

6. Is it possible that mass-produced, low-cost American watches are a source of unfair competition for Switzerland? If Swiss watchmakers are unemployed as a result, what could be done to help them—impose a tariff? Is it possible that a mutually profitable trade in watches might take place between the two countries? What kinds of watches would each probably produce?

7. Are the duties on French wines borne by foreigners or by domestic consumers? Both? What, if any, is the rationale for these duties? How would you go about estimating the transition costs if we were to abolish the tariff on all wines and spirits? Who would be affected? What alternative employment would you suggest for the displaced labor? The displaced land?

Trade adjustment assistance

We have seen that free trade can increase the average real standard of living in a nation but that it may not increase the real living standard of every person. In fact, it usually will not do so. The losses are real, sharp, and concentrated. A textile mill goes out of business because it cannot meet foreign competition. Perhaps from the overall point of view, the gains outweigh the losses—the rise in purchasing power of the nation is greater than the loss in income to the workers and owners of the mill. But the workers and owners are outraged, and the consumers are largely unorganized or uninformed. Hence it is far from unusual that the minority interest prevails over the majority interest. Intensity overwhelms numbers, as in the case of tax reform. Thus we get special tariff preferences or protections—informally negotiated quotas on the amounts of textiles that low-cost countries will send us, limitations on imports of cheap steel, tariffs on French wine, and so on.

Can we find a way out? Economic theory suggests one. Because economic gains exceed economic losses, it should be possible for the winners to compensate the losers and still come out ahead. Here is an application of the Pareto Optimality principle that we learned about on page 281. Our Trade Adjustment Act, modified in 1974, is exactly such an effort. Under the Trade Adjustment Act, producers who can demonstrate injury from foreign competition are entitled to special compensation from the "winners"; that is, from the United States Treasury. Workers are provided with retraining allowances, moving allowances, and extra unemployment benefits. Companies are helped financially and technically to move into new kinds of enterprise. The assistance is not enough to remove all the losses from those who have been hurt, but it mitigates the injury.

The problem is that it is often difficult to determine whether an industry has been damaged by international competition or by other factors. Shoes are a good example. In the past decade American shoe manufacturers have seen imports take an ever larger share of the American shoe business. But was this because of low-wage foreign competition? The shoe companies say so. But some students of the industry argue that the American manufacturers lost their markets because they were slow to recognize that men had become style conscious, and because American companies were poorly managed. These are difficult questions to resolve. In the past, the Trade Adjustment Act has been narrowly interpreted, and few workers or companies have benefited. Recently, the interpretations have been more generous.

Yet, this raises a question. If winners can compensate losers from international trade, why should not the same principle apply to domestic trade? Why should not the winners from environmental clean-up programs compensate the companies and workers who have been economically hurt because of stricter pollution standards? The difficulty is that we cannot apply the principle of compensation to *every* economic change. Perhaps you can see the complexities to which this would lead, if we extended it far enough.

But in the field of international trade, there seems no reason why the Pareto Optimality idea cannot help us adjust to the pressures of liberalized trade. Do you think the winemakers of California will agree?

Mechanism of international transactions

We have learned something about one of the sources of confusion that surrounds international trade—the curiously concealed gains from trade itself. Yet our examples of trade have thus far not touched on another source of confusion—the fact that international trade is conducted in two (or sometimes more) currencies. After all, remember that Infraville and Supraville both trade in dollars. But suppose Infraville were Japan and Supraville America. Then how would things work out?

Foreign Money

The best way to find out would be to price the various items in Japan and America (assuming that Japan produces both wool and cotton, which she does not). Suppose the result looked like Table 39·1.

Table 39·1

	United States	*Japan*
Price of wool (lb)	$1.10	¥300
Price of cotton (lb)	.30	¥100

What would this tell us about the cheapness or dearness of Japanese products compared with those of the U.S.? Nothing, unless we knew one further fact: *the rate at which we could exchange dollars and yen.*

Suppose you could buy 400 yen for a dollar. Then a pound of Japanese wool imported into America (forgetting about shipping costs) would cost 75¢ (¥300 ÷ 400), and a pound of Japanese cotton in America would cost $0.25 (¥100 ÷ 400). Assuming that these are the only products that either country makes for export, here we have a case in which Japan can seemingly undersell America in everything.

But now suppose the rate of exchange were not 400 to one but 250 to one. In that event a pound of Japanese wool landed in America would cost $1.20 (¥300 ÷ 250); and a pound of cotton, $0.40. At this rate of exchange everything in Japan is more expensive than the same products produced in the United States.

The point is clear. *We cannot decide whether foreign products are cheaper or dearer than our own until we know the rate of exchange,* the number of units of their currency we get for ours.

Mechanism of exchange: imports

How does international exchange work? The simplest way to understand it is to follow through a single act of international exchange from start to finish. Suppose, for example, that we decide to buy a Japanese camera directly from a Tokyo manufacturer. The price of the camera as advertised in the catalog is ¥20,000, and to buy the camera we must therefore arrange for the Japanese manufacturer to get that many *yen.* Obviously we can't write him a check in that currency, since our own money is in dollars; and equally obviously

we can't send him a check for dollars, since he can't use dollars in Tokyo any more than we can use a check from him in yen.

Therefore, we go to our bank and ask if it can arrange to sell us yen to be delivered to the Tokyo manufacturer. Yes, our bank would be delighted to oblige. How can it do so? The answer is that our bank (or if not ours, another bank with whom it does business) keeps a regular checking account in its own name in a so-called correspondent bank in Tokyo. As we might expect, the bank in Tokyo also keeps a checking account in dollars in *its* own name at our bank. If our banker has enough yen in his Tokyo account, he can sell them to us himself. If not, he can buy yen (which he will then have available in Japan) from his correspondent bank in exchange for dollars which he will put into their account here.

Notice that two currencies change hands—not just one. Notice also that our American banker will not be able to buy yen unless the Japanese banker is willing to acquire dollars. And above all, note that banks are the intermediaries of the foreign exchange mechanism because they hold deposits in foreign banks.

When we go to our bank to buy ¥20,-000 the bank officer looks up the current exchange rate on yen. Suppose it is 385. He then tells us that it will cost us $51.95 (20,000 ÷ 385) to purchase the yen, plus a bank commission for his services. We write the check, which is deducted from our bank balance and added to the balance of the Tokyo bank's account in this country. Meanwhile, the manufacturer has been notified that if he goes to the Tokyo bank in which our bank keeps its deposits of yen, he will receive a check for ¥20,000. In other words, the Tokyo bank, having received dollars in the United States, will now pay out yen in Japan.

Exports   Exactly the opposite is true in the case of exports. Suppose that we were manufacturers of chemicals and that we sold a $1,000 order to Tokyo. In Japan, the importer of chemicals would go to his bank to find out how many yen that would cost. If the rate were 385, it would cost him ¥385,000 which he would then pay to the Japanese bank. The bank would charge his account and credit the yen to the Tokyo account of an American bank with which it did business, mean-time advising the bank here that the transaction had taken place. When the appropriate notice arrived from Japan, our U.S. bank would then take note of its increased holdings of yen and pay the equivalent amount in dollars into our account.

Foreign exchange   Thus the mechanism of foreign exchange involves the more or less simultaneous (or anyway, closely linked) operations of two banks in different countries. One bank accepts money in one national denomination, the other pays out money in another denomination. Both are able to do so because each need the other's currency, and each maintains accounts in the other country. Note that when payments are made in international trade, money does not physically leave the country. It travels back or forth between American-owned and foreign-owned bank accounts *in America*. The same is true in foreign nations, where their money will travel between an American-owned account there and the account of one of their nationals. *Taken collectively, these foreign-owned accounts (including our own overseas) are called "foreign exchange." They constitute the main pool of moneys available to finance foreign trade.*

Exchange Rates

Thus the mechanism of foreign exchange works through the cooperation of banks. But we must go beyond an understanding of the mechanism to see the actual forces of supply and demand at work. And this is confusing because we have to think in two money units at the same time.

Buying and selling money   We are used to thinking of the price of shoes in terms of dollars. We don't turn around and ask what is the price of dollars in terms of shoes, because consumers don't use shoes to buy dollars.

When we buy pounds or francs or yen, however, we are buying a commodity that is indeed usable to buy the very money we are using. Dollars buy francs and marks and yen; and marks, francs and yen buy dollars. We will have to bear this in mind when we seek to understand the supply and demand curves for international exchange.

Now let us consider an exchange market, say the market for yen (Fig. 39 · 1). The demand curve for yen is easy to understand. It shows us that we will want to acquire larger amounts of yen as they get cheaper. Why? Because cheap yen means relatively cheaper Japanese goods and services. Really our demand curve for foreign exchange is a picture of our changing demand for foreign goods and services as these goods get cheaper or dearer because the money we use to buy them gets cheaper or dearer.

Now the supply curve. We can most easily picture it as the changing willingness and ability of Japanese banks to offer yen as we pay high or low prices for yen. (There is a better way of explaining the

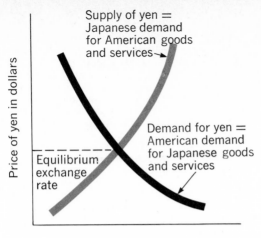

Supply of yen =
Japanese demand
for American goods
and services

Demand for yen =
American demand
for Japanese goods
and services

Equilibrium
exchange
rate

Price of yen in dollars

Quantity of yen

FIG. 39·1   The market for exchange

supply curve, but it takes some hard thought. Those who want to penetrate the mysteries of foreign exchange should look at the box, p. 608.)

Equilibrium prices

What is important is that our diagram shows that there is an equilibrium price for yen that just clears the market. At that price, the amounts of yen that Americans want are exactly equal to the amounts of yen that Japanese want to supply. If we look through the "veil of money," we can see that at this price the value of all Japanese goods and services that we will buy must also be equal to the value of all American goods and services that they will buy!

Appreciation and depreciation of exchange rates

From this, a very important result follows. Suppose that you are a U.S. importer who is eager to buy Japanese automobiles priced at ¥1 million per car. You go to the bank to finance the deal. Here you have an unpleasant surprise. Your banker tells you that exchange is very "tight" at the moment, meaning that the banker's own yen

balances in Japan are very small. As a result, the American banker can no longer offer yen at the old price of, say, 350 to the dollar. The Japanese banks with whom he does business are insisting on a higher price for yen—offering only 325 or perhaps even 300 yen for a dollar. Because of supply and demand, the yen has risen in price, or *appreciated;* and the dollar has fallen in price, or *depreciated.*

You now make a quick calculation. At 350 yen to the dollar, a Japanese car that costs ¥1 million will cost $2,857 (¥1,000,000 ÷ 350). At an exchange rate of 300, it would now cost $3,333 (¥1,000,000 ÷ 300). The new higher price is too steep for the American market. You decide not to place the order. Exactly the opposite situation faces the Japanese importer. Suppose he wants to buy a $50,000 IBM computer. How much will it cost *in yen* if he has to pay 350 yen for a dollar? 300 yen?

The principle is very clear. **Movements in exchange rates change relative prices among countries.** At different relative prices, imports will rise or fall, as will exports. If the price of the dollar falls, American exports will be increased and its imports diminished. If the price of the yen rises, Japanese exports will fall and its imports will rise.

Thus a moving exchange rate will automatically bring about an equilibrium between the demand for, and the supply of, foreign exchange, exactly as a moving price for shoes will bring about an equality between the value of the dollars offered for shoes and the value of the shoes offered for dollars! In one case as in the other, there may be time lags. **But the effect of a moving price in both cases is to eliminate "shortages" and "surpluses"; that is, to bring about a price at which quantity demanded (of a particular currency or any other commodity) equals quantity supplied.**

Let us trace the exchange process once more, very carefully. The chart of the New York market shows the demand for English pounds in dollars. When it costs $3 to buy £1, our demand is for one million pounds (we can think of them as commodities, like one million shoes). This is point A. When the price falls to $2 for £1, our demand rises to 2 million pounds, point B. The broken line AB is our demand curve for pounds.

Now we move to the London market on the right. We are going to show that the New York demand curve AB becomes a London supply curve A'B'. To do so, remember that when it costs $3 to buy £1, from the London point of view the price of $1 is 33 pence (one-third of a pound). What is the supply of dollars at this price? It is equal to the number of dollars spent for pounds in New York. At the $3 price, we bought one million pounds. Our supply of dollars is therefore $3 million. This gives us point A' in the London market.

It is now simple to get point B'. When £1 falls to $2 in New York, $1 rises to 50 pence (one-half pound) in London. How many dollars are supplied at this price? We can see in the New York diagram that we bought £2 million at $2 each, spending $4 million. Hence in the London market, we locate point B' at a price of 50 pence and a quantity of dollars equal to 4 million.

Now we have a demand curve in New York and a supply curve in London. We need a supply curve in New York and a demand curve in London. We'll start in London, with a high price for dollars. Point C shows us that when it costs £1 to buy $1, the

ANOTHER LOOK AT THE EXCHANGE PROBLEM

demand for dollars is small—only $.5 million are demanded. But this point on the demand curve also gives us a supply of pounds: .5 million "units" of dollars at £1 each, or a total of £.5 million. Back in New York this shows up as point C'. (Remember: $1 = £1.)

Now back to London. The price of dollars falls to 33 pence or ⅓ of a pound. At that price, suppose Britishers demand $4 million, point D. To buy $4 million at 33 pence each, Britishers will have to spend 132 million pence, or £1.32 million. This gives us the supply of pounds in the New York market at the price that corresponds to $1 = 33 pence. This price is $3 = 100 pence (one pound). Point D' locates the supply curve at that price. We suggest you draw the two new curves: CD, the demand for

dollars, and C'D', the supply of dollars.

Each panel now has an equilibrium price. In London it is a little over 33 pence, say 37 pence. *But the New York price must be the very same price, expressed in dollars instead of pounds.* If 37 pence = $1 in London, then in New York £1 must equal $2.70 ($1.00 ÷ .37). And if we look at the equilibrium price in New York, so it does.

This is not really surprising. The price of pounds in dollars is the same thing as the price of dollars in pounds "upside down." It is as if pounds were shoes and we were saying that a pair of shoes that cost $10 is the same thing as 10 dollars costing 1 pair of shoes. But it takes a while to get used to the idea of two markets in which supply and demand are linked, as in the case of international exchange. With a little practice, the mystery begins to evaporate.

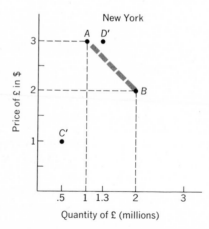

New York

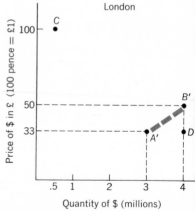

London

Balance of Payments

What does all this have to do with the U.S. balance of payments? To understand the answer, we first have to understand what we mean by the "balance" of payments. We don't speak of a "balance" of payments in, say, a market for shoes. Why, then, is

there one in the market of foreign exchange?

Disaggregating the balance of payments

The first part of the answer lies in an important attribute of this market. In a shoe market, all buyers want shoes, presumably to wear. In an exchange market, there are many kinds of buyers (or sellers) who want to buy or sell exchange for different purposes. That is, the so-called balance of payments represents supplies and demand for foreign exchange by *different groups* in each economy. When all supplies and all demands are added together, the two totals must balance because we then have an identity: Purchases ≡ Sales (i.e., the purchases of any currency, such as dollars, must equal the sales of that currency). But they need not balance for any particular group in the economy. As a result, deficits and surpluses refer to groups that are demanding more foreign exchange than they supply, or supplying more than they demand.

Items in the U.S. balance of payments

Let us learn more about these groups by examining the actual balance of payments for the United States for 1975 (Table 39·2). We begin with some obvious and self-explanatory figures—the exports and imports of *merchandise*. As we can see, in 1975 exporters sold 107.3 billion, earning that many dollars (foreign buyers had to supply us with dollars to that amount). U.S. importers bought $98.3 billion worth of foreign goods, supplying that many dollars to the foreign exchange market. On net balance, the merchandise trade showed a balance of $9.0 billion—a surplus arising from an excess of exports over

Table 39·2   The United States balance of payments, 1975 (billions of dollars)*

1. *Merchandise*		
Exports	+107.3	
Imports	−98.3	
Balance on merchandise	+9.0	
2. *Services*		
Military transactions	−0.9	
Travel & transportation	−2.5	
Investment income	+6.0	
Other	+4.7	
Balance on services	+7.3	
Balance on goods and services		+16.3
3. *Unilateral transfers*		
Remittances	−1.7	
Government transfers	−2.9	
Balance on transfers	−4.6	
Balance on current account		+11.7
4. *Capital outflow*		
Private	−27.1	
Government	−4.0	
Balance on long-term capital	−31.1	
5. *Capital inflow*	−0.5	
Private	+8.5	+28.0
Government	+6.4	
	+14.9	
6. *Statistical discrepancy*	+4.6	

*Based on first 3 quarters.

imports. This creates a net demand for dollars on the foreign exchange market.

The second group of items consists of supplies and demands for exchange to pay for *services* rather than goods. In our table we note a few of these major transactions. Note that *military transactions* gave rise to a small demand for foreign exchange to pay for expenses at U.S. bases abroad, a wind-up of the Indochina war, and the like. *Travel and transportation* mainly shows us that American tourists were demanding more foreign currencies to voyage abroad than foreigners were demanding dollars to travel here. It also shows the net balance between U.S. payments for foreign carriers (for example, a flight on Lufthansa or the charter of a Greek freighter) and foreign payments for U.S. transportation (flights on PanAm or cargo on a U.S. owned ship).

More interesting is the item for *investment income*. This reflects the flow of profits from U.S. companies in foreign nations to their home offices in the United States, minus the flow from foreign companies in the United States to their home offices abroad. When IBM in Italy sends profits back to its U.S. headquarters, it buys dollars with its local bank balances of lire, creating a demand for dollars. When Nestlé sends profits back to *its* headquarters country, it uses its dollar balances to buy Swiss francs. From this large inflow of earnings we must subtract a small outflow of government interest payments going abroad. When we net out these flows, we can see that investment income was a strong source of dollars for the United States in 1975, amounting to $6.0 billion.

Two partial balances

If we now sum up all items on the merchandise account and all items on service account we get the so-called *balance of goods and services*. In 1975 this showed a surplus of $16.3 billion.

Next we move to two further items, under the category of *unilateral transfers*. Here we find remittances, or the sums that persons residing in America send to private individuals abroad, less any sums coming the other way from Americans residing abroad and sending their pay home. The pay that an American working abroad might send home would be a remittance that would earn us dollars; the sums sent home by a Britisher working in the United States would require the purchase of pounds. As we can see, remittances cause a further deficit in our accounts.

This is augmented by *government unilateral transfers*—sums "sent abroad" by the government for foreign aid, emergency relief, and so on. Of course, these sums are not actually sent abroad; rather, the U.S. government opens a dollar account for the recipient nation, which then uses these dollars. But in using them, the recipient country again sells dollars for other currencies.

Summing up again, we now reach a new partial balance—*the balance on current account*, which showed a surplus of $11.7 billion in 1975.

Items on capital account

The next items reflect supplies and demands for foreign exchange associated with capital investments (not *income* from these investments, which we have already counted). This may include investment by U.S. companies in plant and equipment abroad, less investment by foreign companies in plant and equipment here; or purchases of foreign long-term securities by Americans less American stocks or bonds bought by foreigners. These *private capital* flows cost us a net $18.6 billion in 1975 (an outflow of $27.1 billion less an inflow of $8.5 billion). That outflow was slightly offset, however, by *government capital transactions*—the purchases of foreign government securities by the U.S. government, less any purchases of U.S. bonds by foreign governments. The net balance on *both* private and public capital account gave rise to a deficit or net supply of $16.2 billion ($31.1 billion of public and private outflow less $14.9 billion of inflow).

Capital inflows and outflows can also be divided into short-term and long-term capital inflows and outflows. (Not shown in Table 39 · 2.) In 1975 there was a short-term capital outflow of $11 billion. The most important of these consists of the transfer from one country to another of private balances, belonging to individuals or companies, that are moved about in response to interest rates or for speculative reasons. The treasurer of a multinational company may "park" his extra cash in Sweden one year and in the United States the next, depending on where he can earn more interest in short-term securities or special bank accounts. Some individuals and even some small governments move their bank balances from country to country in search of the best return or in anticipation of a move in exchange rates that will benefit them. This movement of short-term capital tends to be volatile and can on occasion give rise to speculative "flights" from one nation to another. In 1971, for example, when there was a general distrust of the American dollar, well over $7 billion was withdrawn from American accounts and "sent abroad," creating a deficit of that amount on short-term capital account.

Summing up the accounts

As we have seen, very different motivations apply to these different actors on the foreign exchange markets. Exports and imports reflect the relative price levels and growth of output of trading countries. Tourism is also affected by prices abroad, as well as by the relative affluence of different countries. Flows of corporate earnings arise from investments made in the past. Long-term private capital items reflect estimates of the *future* earning power of investments home or abroad. Short-term capital is guided by interest rates and speculative moods. Government flows hinge largely on foreign policy decisions.

Whatever the different motives affecting these flows, each gives rise to supplies of, or demands for, dollars. Thus we can sum up the net outcome of all these varied groups to discover the overall demand and supply for dollars. As must always be the case, they are in balance. The balance on current account plus the positive statistical discrepancy are exactly equal to the deficit on the capital account.

The "Balance"

What we have traced thus far are the various groups whose economic (or political) interests caused them to supply dollars to or demand dollars on the exchange market. But we have arrived at a curious stopping point.

Our description has shown that it is entirely possible that the quantity of foreign exchange demanded by one country will be larger (or smaller) than the quantity of foreign exchange supplied to it. In fact, only by chance would the total requirements of foreign exchange of importers and exporters of goods and services and capital balance out. But the existence of a difference between the total quantities supplied and demanded should present no problem. Just as in a market for shoes, the price of foreign exchange should change, exactly as we describe it on pp. 606 ff., altering the quantities that different groups would want to buy or sell. An equilibrium price for foreign exchange should clear the exchange market just as an equilibrium price for shoes clears the shoe market. No "balance" of exchange would remain, any more than there is a "balance" of shoes.

That will happen, however, only if the exchange market is as free as the shoe market. In fact, it is not quite so free, so that "balances" do remain, as we will see in our next chapter. In order to understand how these balances remain, we will have to take a moment to learn what happens in a foreign exchange market in which exchange rates are not free to move but are "fixed" in price by international agreements.

Fixed exchange rates

Suppose, for example, that the British pound is "pegged" at a price of $2.00 (we will soon learn how this is accomplished). This means that all transactions—all purchases or sales of pounds and dollars—will take place at that price, plus or minus a small fee for transaction costs. We can easily see that the quantity of pounds demanded at $2.00 may be greater than the quantity supplied at that price, or vice versa. In that case, some agency must provide the "missing" pounds to settle up any shortage that arises from market transactions, or it must provide some other currency to make up for the deficiency of some other currency, if more dollars (for example) are offered for pounds than are made available by the sale of pounds.

We call this a *fixed exchange rate system.* It is the system under which all international exchanges took place until quite recently. In our next chapter we shall review the dramatic events that led to its abandonment. But it is clear that under fixed rates our accounts do not necessarily "balance." How are accounts "settled" in such a case?

Central banks

The question leads us to a critically important group of institutions in international exchange called central banks. Central banks are the national banks we find in all countries. One of their functions, as we know, is to play a role in the determination of the appropriate quantity of money for domestic purposes. But a second role is equally important. Central banks are agencies of their governments, who buy or sell foreign exchange, making their own currencies available to foreigners when they buy foreign exchange and absorbing their own currency from foreigners when they sell foreign exchange. By buying at a price established by agreement, they "peg" the exchange of their currencies.

How do central banks acquire the capacity for these transactions in foreign exchange? The answer is that private banks in all countries have the option of transferring their own supplies of foreign exchange to their central bank, receiving payment in their own currency. For example, let us suppose that the Chase Manhattan Bank finds itself with large and unwanted supplies of francs. It can exchange these francs for dollars with the Federal Reserve. The Chase Manhattan Bank will then get a dollar credit at the Federal Reserve, and the Federal Reserve will be the owner of the francs formerly belonging to Chase. In the same way in their home countries, the Bank of Yokohama or Barclay's Bank or the Swiss Bank can exchange their holdings of dollars for yen or pounds or Swiss francs, in each case receiving a credit at their central bank in their own currencies and transferring their holdings of foreign currencies to their government bank.

How central banks work

Thus central banks are the holders of large amounts of foreign exchange, which they acquire indirectly from the activities of various groups in their own nations. The central banks are therefore the last "group" whose own actions must balance out the unbalanced flows that arise under "fixed" rates. There are two ways in which this can be done.

1. Gold flows

For many years, any balances "left over" were settled by the shipment of gold from one central bank to another. For example, all through the early 1960s, the United States balanced its accounts partly by selling gold to cover any deficit in its Official Reserve Transactions Balance. The sale of gold was exactly like an export. Foreign central banks paid us in dollars from their holdings of dollar exchange, and this dollar inflow offset any deficit of dollars arising from other transactions. (Recently, a new kind of "paper gold" called Special Drawing Rights has also served as another *reserve asset* available to balance accounts. We will learn more about SDRs in our next chapter.) For reasons that we will also investigate there, gold shipments have been discontinued since the international monetary crisis of 1971.

2. Holding reserve currencies

The second means by which the central banks balanced out the difference between demand and supply was to hold a foreign currency *as if it were a reserve asset*. This is exactly what the central banks of the world (reluctantly) agreed to do all through the 1960s and early 1970s in the case of the United States. The central banks of France, Germany, Japan and other nations allowed their dollar holdings to mount as a "reserve currency" without converting those holdings into gold.

Thus the major balancing item in the past consisted of increases in holdings of dollars owned by foreign governments. How did this increase in dollar holdings formally balance out the accounts? *The answer is that increased dollar holdings were counted in the overall balance of payments as a short-term credit for the United States.* They were, after all, foreign claims on U.S. wealth that have been "loaned" to us. In the official books they counted as a "plus" item that offsets the "minus" items.

Importance of liquidity

Our analysis has shown us a very important fact. Under fixed rates of exchange, we can run an unbalanced foreign exchange account only if we can "finance" it by one or the other of the two means described above. Suppose, for example, that we had no gold and that foreign central banks refused to hold any more dollars. Then an American importer or tourist who went to buy francs or marks would soon discover that there weren't any, because no bank would accept any more dollars. Since there weren't any, he or she could not finance imports or a trip abroad.

The balance of payments would then be brought into balance at the cost of a lower level of international transactions. Americans would have to do with fewer Toyotas. Fewer Americans could visit

THE GOLD STANDARD

Until the Great Depression, the international monetary system was run on a gold standard, under which any citizen at any time could demand gold for paper money. This led to two problems. One was the risk of a "run" on gold in times of panic. It was this that provided the rationale for the gold "backing" of currency in the original Federal Reserve System.

The second problem was that anyone at any time could convert his money into gold and then ship the gold abroad to buy francs or marks or any other currency, if that was profitable. This international ebb and flow of gold kept all currencies tightly tied together. The difficulty was that the gold link among currencies made it impossible for any nation to launch an expansionary program *if the rest of the world was experiencing a recession.* As a result of its expansion program, its prices would rise. As prices rose, its citizens found it profitable to turn their money into gold, to send the gold abroad and to buy cheaper foreign goods or assets. This drained gold from the expanding economy, caused credit to contract, and promptly brought the boom to a halt.

After World War II, nations used a gold-exchange standard. Under this standard, gold was reserved for foreign exchange use. The U.S. Treasury sold gold only to foreign official holders of dollars, such as central banks. No gold was sold to foreign private citizens or to domestic U.S. citizens. As we shall see, even this attempt to safeguard the system did not work.

Paris. No doubt more Fords would be sold instead, and Yellowstone Park would be more crowded. But the level of consumer well-being would be lower than if trade could have occurred; and the total of world production, as we saw in our preceding chapter, would suffer because countries could not take full use of their comparative advantages.

Thus the willingness of central banks to hold one another's currencies and the quantity of reserve assets that they can use to "settle up" was of the greatest importance in determining the level of world trade. That is the meaning of the phrase that was often heard as to the importance of having enough "liquidity" in the world. Not having enough liquidity means that the ability to finance imports is crippled because a country has no gold or SDRs or because no central bank is willing to accept its currency in the way that dollars have been accepted. This absence of liquidity is particularly difficult for poor nations that desperately need imports and cannot pay for them.

Why fixed rates? Why were exchange rates fixed? We shall look into some of the practical advantages of a fixed rate in our next chapter. But the basic cause must be sought in history and psychology. For centuries, the only commodities that have universally commanded the magic of belief have been gold and silver. No nation in the past would accept the curious pieces of paper that another nation called money. This led nations to "declare" the value of their paper monies in terms of their gold "content" and to agree that any foreign holder of its paper money (or of a checking account) could "redeem" that money in gold. In the United States, the value of a dollar from 1933 until very recent years was 1/35th of an ounce of gold.*

Numerous suggestions were put forward by economists for other international standards of value, and many economists urged that exchange rates should be cut loose entirely from any "fixed" value—that they should fluctuate like any other price. Until recent years, however, these proposals have been stubbornly resisted by most governments. But that leads us into the problems discussed in our next chapter.

---

*Nations that owned very little gold declared the value of their currencies in terms of a major "reserve currency" such as dollars or pounds.

Focus   This is certainly a difficult chapter, mainly because it deals with things that are unfamiliar to most of us. Therefore it may help to keep in mind two main objectives:

1. You must learn how imports and exports (or other transactions) give rise to demands for, and supplies of, foreign exchange. This is best done by tracing through the series of transactions that accompany a given import and the corresponding export from abroad; or reversing the coin and watching the chain of transactions that finances a given export (and the corresponding import abroad). This will show you how money in each country leaves domestic accounts to enter foreign owned accounts in that country, or vice versa. It will also show you the role of the banks in making possible the coordinated activities taking place simultaneously in two countries.

2. Once the mechanism of foreign exchange is understood, you must learn about the balance of payments. That is not so hard, once you see that "the" balance of payments is nothing but a collection of quite different demands for and supplies of foreign exchange—some for trade, some for tourism, some for military purposes, some for long-term capital investment, some for short-term capital investment. The "total" balance of payments always balances, just as a balance sheet always balances. Indeed, a balance of payments is a balance sheet of a kind, showing who has gained and who has lost claims on foreign exchange.

What complicates matters is *how* it balances. If exchange rates are free to move, the balance is achieved exactly the way it is in a market for shoes. Prices (foreign exchange in this case) rise or fall until quantities demanded and supplied are equal. There is no "surplus" or "shortage." Nothing has to be added to, or absorbed by, any institution. The marketers themselves pick up the tab.

This is not the case when rates are fixed. We then have a situation that is exactly analogous to shortages or surpluses in commodity markets. Just as the government has to buy the "surplus" of wheat offered in a price-supported market, so the government (through its central bank) has to buy the surplus of foreign exchange that arises when foreign exchange is officially priced too dearly vis-à-vis the dollar. In our next chapter we shall go into the history of the dissolution of this method of providing international liquidity.

WORDS AND CONCEPTS YOU SHOULD KNOW

Foreign exchange, 606
Appreciation of exchange, 607
Depreciation of exchange, 607
Balances in the balance of payments, 608–12

Current account, 610
Capital account, 610–11
Fixed exchange rate system, 612
Role of central banks, 612–13
Liquidity, 613–14

QUESTIONS

1. If you wanted to buy a Swiss watch and discovered that it cost 200 francs, what would you need to know to discover if it were cheaper or more expensive than a comparable American watch? Suppose that the price of francs was 20¢ and the American watch cost $50? What if the price of francs rose to 30¢?

2. If you now bought the watch, to be sent to you, how would you pay for it? What would happen to your bank check? How would the Swiss watchmaker be paid?

3. Suppose that the Swiss, in turn, now decided to buy an American radio that cost $40. He finds the rate of exchange is 5 Swiss francs to the dollar. Explain how he makes payment.

4. Now suppose that the rate of exchange rises for the Swiss, so that he has to pay 6 francs for a dollar. What happens to the price of the radio in Swiss terms? Suppose the rate cheapens, so that he pays only 4 francs? Now what is the price of the radio to him?

5. How is an exchange rate determined in a free market? Can you explain why the demand for a foreign currency increases as its price decreases? Why the supply increases?

6. Is the appreciation of the mark versus the franc the same thing as the depreciation of the franc versus the mark?

7. Show the relation between a "deficit" in the balance of payments and a surplus in a commodity market.

8. Suppose there were no central banks. Could a fixed exchange system work? A flexible exchange system?

The international monetary problem

In our preceding chapter we learned something about how the international monetary system works. Now we are going to use that knowledge in tracing the ups and downs of monetary affairs over the last several years. We shall divide our analysis into two parts. First we will watch the deterioration of the U.S. international trade position up to the middle of 1972. Then we will see the outcome of that great monetary crisis in the last few years.

The Pre-1972 Crisis

Bearing in mind that we are dealing only with the first act of the drama, let us watch what was going on in the international economic arena from 1967 to 1972.

Deterioration of trade

Figure 40 • 1 gives us a first clue to the problem. It shows the irregular but eventually precipitous fall in our earnings on current account. At the beginning of the period we were earning almost $1.5 billion in exchange. By the middle of 1972 we were running a deficit at almost the same rate. What was the cause of this fall?

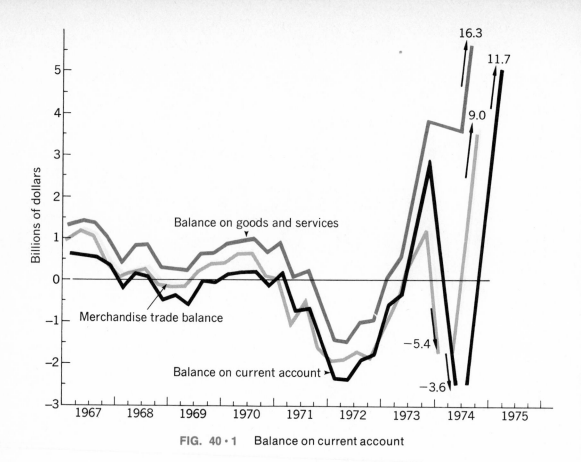

Balance on goods and services

Merchandise trade balance

Balance on current account ▸

16.3

11.7

9.0

−5.4

−3.6

FIG. 40 · 1 Balance on current account

We can find the answer by examining the main components of our balance on current account. The largest of these are our transactions on merchandise account. Here we find an immediate reason for the deterioration of the balance on current account.

Table 40 · 1 Balance on current account

	Exports	Imports (billions)	Net balance*
1967	$30.7	$26.9	$+3.8
1968	33.6	33.0	+0.6
1969	36.4	35.8	+0.6
1970	42.0	40.0	+2.1
1971	42.8	45.4	−2.7
1972	48.8	55.7	−6.8

*Figures are rounded.

The fall on current account

What was the cause of this tremendous decline in merchandise earnings? Many people tend to ascribe it to the inflation that was then rampant in the United States. Inflation in one country can indeed be a cause of balance of payment problems. But during the 1960s, inflation was even more pronounced in the lands of our major customers than at home. American export prices were actually cheapened on the international markets by the forces of inflation!

The real cause of the long-term decline was a much more rapid growth of productivity in Europe and Japan than in the United States (see "An Extra Word" to Chapter 24). Productivity grew approximately twice as fast in Europe and three times as fast in Japan as in the United States. As a result, during the late 1960s we became importers of commodities such as steel and autos, although we had traditionally been the major suppliers for many nations in the world.

Travel and transportation
This was not, however the only cause for the fall on current account. Travel and transportation added their drains to those of imports. At the beginning of the period, Americans were spending, net, $1.7 billion abroad for travel and transportation. By the end of the period, this figure had risen to $2.8 billion. Here, an enormous increase in tourism played a central role. A million and a half Americans traveled abroad in 1960 (creating a demand for foreign exchange). By 1971, this number had risen to 5.7 million, and the rise was not counterbalanced by an equivalent rise in foreign tourism in the U.S.

Military expenditures
These two large drains on American exchange were augmented by a third, this time originating from government rather than private persons. Every year, during the six-year period we are examining, the government ran up a large deficit for military purposes. In 1965 we were spending $3.0 billion in net foreign exchange to support U.S. military activities abroad. By 1972 this had risen to $4.7 billion, largely because of the Vietnam War. Notice that this is not the full cost of our military activities. Much of the war and nonwar military expenditure, such as the maintenance of U.S. troops in foreign bases, is paid in dollars and creates no demand for foreign exchange. The bombers we build or fly and the pay for soldiers (in U.S. dollars) create no exchange problems. But inextricably connected with foreign military activity is a need to make large expenditures in other currencies. Non-U.S. personnel must be paid in their currencies, not in ours. Supplies such as food or local supplies must also be paid for in foreign currencies.

Investment income
If we add up the deficits for 1972 (the worst year) on merchandise account, travel and transportation, and military, we get a total of $13 billion—far larger than the actual deficit of some $8 billion on current account for that year. What accounted for the difference?

Part of the difference is to be found in the other items we learned about in our last chapter, some of which helped and

EURODOLLARS

A student in international economics sooner or later hears about a mysterious currency called Eurodollars. Eurodollars are simply European bank accounts denominated in dollars rather than in the currency of the country. They represent a pool of funds that can be borrowed—*a pool of funds that are essentially unregulated by any government.* Since they are not held in the U.S., they are outside of the jurisdiction of the U.S. government. Since they are held in dollars and not in local currency, they are outside the jurisdiction of the local government.

Their main impact is to make it much more difficult for any country to control its own monetary policies. Suppose a firm wants to invest during a period when its own government is restricting the money supply and making it difficult to obtain loans. Unable to borrow in local currency, the firm borrows Eurodollars and exchanges these borrowed dollars for local currency. It now has the funds that it wished to have for investment purposes, and its government has been frustrated in its efforts to retard lending. In the United States credit crunch of 1969–1970, large U.S. firms were substantial borrowers of Eurodollars, to circumvent the Federal Reserve Board's policy of making it harder and harder to obtain local loans. Eurodollars are therefore one of the reasons for the uneven impact of monetary policies that we noted earlier.

Finally, Eurodollar accounts serve as a ready source of funds for speculating on international exchange rates. They are highly mobile and acceptable everywhere.

Table 40 · 2   Net private investment income (billions)

1967	1968	1969	1970	1971	1972	1973	1974	1975
$+5.8	$6.2	$5.8	$6.4	$9.0	$9.8	5.2	10.2	6.0

some of which hurt our balance on current account. During the 6-year period, for example, our remittances abroad increased, worsening our balance, whereas our sales of other services (such as insurance on cargoes), improved, helping the situation. But the main source of dollars to offset the huge total of our merchandise, travel, and military expenditures was a large and growing income from United States private investments abroad, mainly the flow of profits of U.S. corporations. Table 40 · 2 shows the substantial rise in these sources of foreign exchange for the United States (remember that every time a foreign branch of a U.S. company sends profit home, it must buy dollars).

Trends on capital account   We have still to look into the activities on capital account which, as we know, also enter into our official reserve transactions balance—the "balance" being achieved by sales of gold or other reserve assets or by holdings of currency by foreign central banks.

Table 40 · 3 shows the trends in both long-term and short-term capital.

What do these figures show? We see, first, that there has been a steady drain on the balance of payments from long-term government transactions. These largely reflect foreign aid loans, which are counted as claims against the U.S., although they are mainly spent *in* the U.S., creating additional exports.

More important, we see in the next column an irregular deficit earned on long-term private account. This is partially the result of companies purchasing foreign exchange to build plants and equipment abroad—a flow that ran between $1 billion and $2 billion all during the early 1960s. It is also partly the result of companies and individuals investing in long-term foreign securities in the early 1970s. They invested because they thought growth prospects were good for these companies, or because they wanted to protect themselves against a change in the value of the dollar, or were speculating that such a change would take place.

For example, a person who bought a World Bank Bond in Swiss francs in 1970 would have paid the fixed rate of exchange, then about 25¢ per franc. If the dollar then fell in price, so that each franc now cost 35¢ instead of 25¢, an owner of a

Table 40 · 3   Long- and short-term capital flows (billions)

	1967	1968	1969	1970	1971	1972
Long term						
Gov't.	$−2.4	$−2.2	$−1.9	$−2.0	$−2.4	$−1.3
Private	−2.9	+1.2	−0.1	−1.4	−4.1	−0.1
Short term	+1.2	+3.5	+8.8	−6.0	−7.8	−0.5

10,000 franc bond that cost $2,500 would be able to sell the bond for $3,500. (After the very large outflow of private capital in 1971, the United States placed a tax of 18 percent on purchases of most foreign securities, to deter just such speculative transactions. This tax has since been removed.)

Short-term trends

Finally, we come to the column of short-term capital flows. As we know, these are sums that travel from nation to nation in search of profitable short-term investment. They are partly guided by interest rates, partly by speculative considerations of the kind we have just considered. Note how volatile this item is. Between 1969 and 1970, there was a difference of $14 billion—$8 billion entering this country in the first year, $6 billion leaving it the next. Here was another serious cause for the crisis that finally erupted in 1971.

Now let us sum up our partial balances, to look at the trend in the official reserve transactions balance. As we can see in Table 40 • 4, this balance worsened seriously in 1970, "collapsed" in 1971, and remained badly in deficit in 1972.

The gold drain

How did the United States meet its worsening foreign exchange situation? As we have seen, there are only two ways to finance a deficit: by selling gold (or other reserve assets) or by persuading foreign central banks to hold the currency of the deficitary nation, in this case dollars.

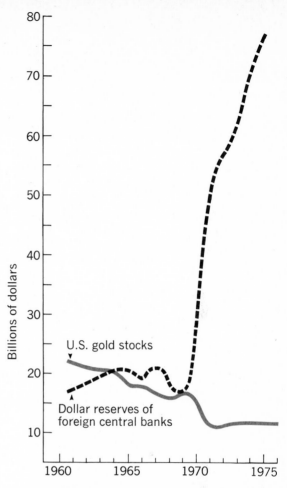

FIG. 40 • 2   Changes in U.S. gold stocks

Figure 40 • 2 shows that this is exactly what happened in the case of the United States. Beginning in the 1960s, our gold stock steadily declined, and the dollar reserves of foreign central banks rose. As we can see, as early as 1964 the holdings of dollars were so large that if foreign central banks had exercised their legal claims to gold, the entire gold stock of the nation would have been wiped out!

Table 40 • 4   Official reserve transactions balance (billions)

1967	1968	1969	1970	1971	1972
$−3.4	$+1.6	$+2.7	$−9.8	$−29.8	$−10.3

This would have been a major economic catastrophe—not because we would have no gold "behind" our currency, but because we would have cheated foreign nations out of hundreds of millions or billions worth of purchasing power. For if the gold supply ran out, foreigners could no longer repatriate their dollar holdings at a known exchange rate. Instead, their dollar holdings would now have to find their own price vis-à-vis their own currencies; and since dollars are held in very large quantities, this price might be very low.

Take, for example, a Netherlands bank that had allowed $1 million to remain in America, because it was confident that it could always get 28,571 ounces of gold for it (at $35 per ounce) *with which it could then purchase other currencies whose value in gold was also firmly fixed.* Suddenly it would find that its million-dollar deposit would be worth only as many ounces of gold as the market decreed—very possibly much less than the quantity it thought it owned. In turn, the amounts of other currencies available to the Netherlands bank would also fall, since it would have less gold to buy them with. *Thus, countries that had cooperated with us by allowing their dollars to remain here would be penalized.* They would never again allow dollars to pile up in U.S. banks.

Not less important in staying the hand of the central banks who might have claimed our gold was the fear of a terrible slump in trade that could have followed. Since World War II, the dollar had been *the* unit for settling balances among nations. If the dollar were no longer—at least in theory—convertible into gold, a main instrument for international "liquidity" would be wiped out. Unless another means of settling balances was put in its place, a straitjacket of gold could be placed on the volume of international trade, with an almost certain consequence of a drastic fall in the volume of trade.

The gold rush of 1967–68   Just because the consequences of a "run" on gold would be so disastrous, the central banks of foreign nations agreed not to demand their dollar balances in gold. This did not, however, prevent *private* speculators abroad from taking their holdings of dollars and converting them into gold. For many years there has been a perfectly legal market in gold in London and elsewhere, where private individuals could exchange their holdings of dollars or other currencies for gold bullion. The gold they bought was sold to them at the fixed price of $35 an ounce by an international gold pool comprised of the main goldholding nations. In the pool, the United States, as the largest

---

GOLD "FLOWS"

When the United States "loses" gold, the metal is not usually shipped abroad, as one might think. Instead, it is trucked to a vault many feet below the street surface in the Federal Reserve Bank of New York, where it is stacked in dull yellow bricks about the shape (but half the thickness) of a building brick. It is possible to visit this vault, which now holds some $13 billion of foreign gold, neatly separated into bins assigned to different countries. To see this modern equivalent of Montezuma's treasure is an astonishing sight. Gold may well be, as many have said, a kind of international psychosis, but its power over the imagination, no doubt the result of its traditional association with riches, is still remarkable. It is amusing to note that the Federal Reserve Bank, as custodian of this foreign gold, once suggested to its binholders that they might save a considerable sum if, instead of actually weighing the bricks and moving them from bin to bin whenever gold was bought and sold, both parties agreed to move the gold just on the books, the way bank balances are moved about. All governments demurred. They wanted the actual gold bricks in their bins. Hence, when gold moves from nation to nation to help settle up accounts, it is still actually pushed across the floor of the Fed's vault and carefully piled in the proper bin.

holder of gold in the world, was committed to providing 59 percent of all bullion supplied to the market.

In March, 1968, the gold pool suddenly faced a crisis. Alarmed at the shrinkage of U.S. gold reserves, private speculators converged on the London market to convert their dollars into bullion. On the first day of that month, the pool, which had normally sold 3 to 4 tons of gold per day, suddenly found itself obliged to sell 40 tons. A week later the demand had risen to 75 tons. On March 13, it was 100 tons; the next day, 200 tons.

At this rate of drainage, the United States Treasury was being forced to put $1 million of gold into the pool every two to three minutes. Officials in Washington nervously figured that if the gold hemorrhage were not checked, the nation's entire gold reserves would be used up in a few weeks. To prevent such a crisis, the world's central bankers hurriedly convened in Washington and after a weekend of continuous conferences, announced that the gold pool was to be discontinued and that a new "two-price" system would immediately begin. All *official* holders of dollars (i.e., governments and central banks) would still be able to buy gold at $35 an ounce from the Treasury. But there would no longer be any effort to maintain the price of gold at an "official" level in the private market by supplying whatever gold was needed there at that price. Instead, there would be no sales from any national reserve of gold into the private market, and "private" gold would be allowed to find its own price.*

*By late 1974, the price of gold on these private markets reached the astronomical price of $198 per ounce. This was far beyond any reasonable calculation of the equilibrium price of the dollar. It was simply an index of the capacity of that extraordinary metal to command belief in itself and, of course, evidence of the international private speculators' continuing feelings that the existing exchange rate structure was still untrustworthy. By 1976, the price was back to around $110.

The system worked fairly well for a while. But the continuing imbalance of American accounts made it clear that such a means of avoiding an international currency crisis was at best a stopgap.

Curing the Balance of Payments Deficit

Before we look into the next episode of the international monetary crisis of the early 1970s, let us take a moment to reflect on the problem. As we have seen, the United States had run a persisting deficit on its official reserve transactions balance—a deficit that had caused a drastic fall in its holdings of gold and an even more marked increase in the holdings of dollars by foreign central banks. American officials and businesspeople—especially bankers—were increasingly convinced that something should be done. What were the possibilities?

1. The classical medicine

One much-discussed option was to apply a stiff dose of what was called "the classical medicine." This consisted of higher interest rates and restrictive fiscal policies whose purpose was *to deflate the economy—forcing down our price level to make our exports more attractive, and lowering incomes to reduce imports.*

The problem with the classical medicine was twofold. In the first place, no one was sure that prices would fall, even if GNP did drop. The second was that few wanted to impose so drastic a remedy on the economy. Unemployment seemed too high a price to pay for a mistaken international exchange rate.

2. Restraints on capital flows

A second remedy was to discourage American spending abroad on capital account. Indeed, domestic short-term interest rates were raised to attract foreign short-term capital, and a tax was imposed on the American purchase of foreign securities.

This was a less deflationary solution to the balance of payments problem. But the difficulty with the solution was that capital exports, in the long run, earned us money on current account. Hence, discouraging the export of American capital (other than speculative capital) was killing the goose that laid the golden eggs of dividends and interest.

3. Cutting the government international deficit

A third possibility was to pare down the heavy government deficit on international account. Here there were two candidates for cutting. One was the flow of American foreign aid to the underdeveloped world. But as many economists pointed out, over 90 percent of this aid was directly "tied" to the purchase of American goods by its recipients and therefore cost us nothing in terms of a dollar drain. In addition, the spectacle of the richest nation on earth extricating itself from its international problems at the expense of the poorest nations on earth was not an attractive one.

The second candidate was the large American deficit on military account. In the eyes of many observers this was the real villain in the piece—the ultimate cause of our international economic (and political) problems. But the remedy of the military drain necessitated a change in our Vietnam and European military postures, and this was a course beyond the competence of economists to recommend or effect.

4. Devaluation

Another course of action, much talked about, was devaluation, a declaration that the gold content of the dollar had been reduced. Rather than an ounce of gold being worth $35, the President would state that henceforth it would be worth $45 or $75 or any other price that seemed likely to establish a balance in the supply and demand for American currency.

Devaluation had staunch advocates—and equally strong opponents. The advocates pointed out that it was an instant and painless cure. By devaluating the dollar sufficiently, the gold in America's possession could immediately be worth enough to cover all America's obligations to other central banks. A shipment of only a small quantity of our gold would then wipe out all of America's international obligations.

The opponents pointed to the obvious difficulties in this "solution." America would get rid of its problem by handing it to its creditors. Countries that had helped the United States by not demanding gold during the exchange crisis would now be penalized for their cooperation by receiving a much smaller amount of international purchasing power than they had expected and were originally entitled to.

Moreover, devaluation was a two-edged sword. If the United States devalued, so could its trading partners. If France, Germany, Japan, and other major nations also lowered the gold content of their currencies, there would be no gain to anyone, but a considerable friction and animosity shared by all. Finally, opponents pointed out that even if the United States' devaluation was tolerated, the cost of devaluation was a rise in the price of imports to the devaluing country. Imports were a strategic element in many aspects of America's economy. To devalue meant to raise their prices, and to give another boost to American inflation.

5. Creating new reserve assets: SDRs

A fifth method was more imaginative. It consisted of finding a reserve asset other than gold to enable central banks to "cover" any deficits. As we have seen, for many years the dollar itself was such an asset. Many foreign nations, especially in the less affluent nations, counted their holdings of dollars as if they were "as good as gold." But with the loss of faith in the ability of the United States to maintain the fixed exchange value of dollars, dollars ceased to become an acceptable reserve currency. Hence the effort was made to create a new reserve currency.

This effort was mounted by the International Monetary Fund (IMF), an institution which serves as a kind of central bank for many nations. Into the IMF, subscriber nations deposit both both gold and their own currencies. From the bank, they can borrow gold or other currencies to meet temporary shortages of reserve assets. In turn, the fund serves as a kind of monitor of exchange adjustments, because it will not lend reserves unless it approves of the borrower's exchange rates and overall economic policies.

To meet the growing crisis of liquidity, the IMF in 1970 took the very important step of creating a new reserve asset called Special Drawing Rights or SDRs. These new assets were, in fact, created out of thin air (as all money ultimately is); but because SDRs had the backing of the fund, they were just as "good" as gold in settling international accounts.

SDRs were a creative and important step in breaking the gold psychosis. The problem was the extreme difficulty in persuading the richer nations to accept this new form of international liquidity, and numerous technical difficulties in finding an acceptable formula for creating and distributing SDRs. The new step was promising, but very limited in its impact.

6. Flexible exchange rates

The sixth method was the simplest of all. It was simply to abandon the mechanism of fixed rates and to allow the price of exchange to fluctuate like any other price. As we have seen, under a "floating" exchange rate, a shortage or surplus of exchange could not develop, any more than under a free market price for shoes we find either shortages or surpluses of shoes.

Why was not this method tried at once? Partly the reasons have to do with the nationalistic feelings that obscure common sense in so many areas of international trade. Money is the very symbol of national sovereignty. To relinquish command over the international price of our money seemed tantamount to relinquishing a certain portion of sovereignty itself. And of course this was true. What was not considered was that sovereignty was also diminished by allowing the development of a balance of payments problem that, in the end, forced us to take actions against our best interests—a clear loss of sovereign powers.

There were also more thoughtful reasons for a general unwillingness to let rates "float." Most international transactions are not concluded immediately across a counter but extend over weeks or even months between the time that a sale is agreed upon and the time when the goods arrive and payment is due. If exchange rates changed during this period, either the importer or the exporter could be severely penalized. Although it is possible to insure oneself to some extent against exchange variations by buying "forward exchange," most traders would rather not deal in exchange rates that are likely to alter over the course of a transaction. More important, international investors who put money overseas for long periods have no way of protecting themselves against changes in rates, and they were even more concerned about the risks of flexible exchange.

In addition, many monetary experts feared that fluctuating rates would lead to speculative purchases and sales of foreign currencies just for the purpose of making a profit on swings in their price—and that these speculative "raids" would have the effect of self-fulfilling prophecies in still further aggravating those swings.

The Great Monetary Muddle

Now let us return to the situation of worsening tensions that we have traced up to 1971. *Between 1968 and August 1971, none of the six measures above was effectively applied.* The United States was unwilling to swallow the classical medicine. It tried to restrain capital outflows but with scant success. It did not cut down overseas government spending—in fact, it stepped up its military expenditures. It steadfastly opposed raising the number of dollars that an ounce of gold would buy (devaluation). It was unable to create a major addition to reserve assets, which in any case would not have solved the problem of persistent deficits. It did not allow the fixed exchange system to lapse and a new flexible exchange system to take over.

The Crisis of August 1971

Inevitably, therefore, the U.S. balance of payments deficit worsened, and foreign holdings of dollars grew. As they grew, so did fears that the U.S. would eventually be *forced* to devalue as the only way out of its dilemma. This brought worries that foreign governments who held dollars would suffer large losses.

To forestall this possibility, in August 1971 the British government apparently asked for a guarantee that our government would compensate the British Treasury for any losses on its dollar reserves in case we devalued. This placed the American government in a quandary. If it granted the English request, it would be forced to make similar concessions to other governments. This would have transferred the losses from devaluation from foreign governments to ourselves, since we would have had to give foreign central banks additional dollars to compensate for the fall in purchasing power of their "old" dollars.

Faced with this cost, and with the rapidly worsening climate of confidence, the United States government chose a drastic step. *It announced that it would no longer sell any gold to foreign central banks at any price.* In effect, it severed the tie of dollars to gold. Since dollars could no longer be "valued" in gold, in effect the United States allowed dollars to find their own market price. The dollar was "floated." To show that the United States meant business in correcting its balance of payments deficits, it imposed a temporary 10 percent tax on all imports.

Painful options   This immediately led to acrimonious debates as to what should be done next. The trouble was that all possibilities were painful. If nothing were done, foreign countries would be "stuck" with unwanted dollar holdings. If the dollar were formally devalued, then foreign currencies would appreciate. In that case, American goods would become cheaper, and foreign goods more expensive for Americans. Foreign producers who competed with American exporters, (such as French farmers) feared they would be flooded with cheap American goods; and foreign exporters, such as automobile makers, feared they might be priced out of America's enormous market.

Moreover, if the dollar were devalued in terms of gold, by raising the number of dollars that an ounce of gold was worth, this action would reward all the less cooperative countries in the world who had refused to allow their reserves to be

held in American dollars, while penalizing the very countries that had worked with us by agreeing not to exercise their option to exchange dollars for gold.

The fight to hold   Out of such conflicts
fixed rates   of interest no happy
   solution could ever
emerge, and none did. After long negotiations, European countries and Japan agreed to revalue (appreciate) their currencies vis-à-vis the dollar; the United States agreed to devalue its dollar in terms of gold, changing the price from $35 per ounce to $42, *and the nations of the world attempted to return to a new system of fixed exchange rates,* albeit rates that were different from those of the immediate past.

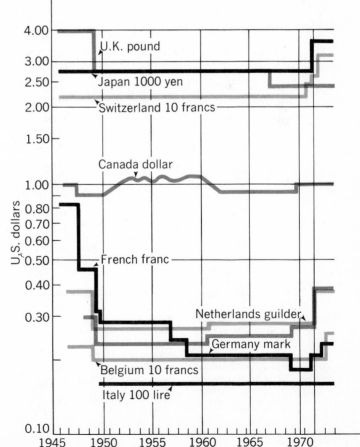

FIG. 40 · 3

How parities have changed

This patchwork lasted only a short time. Many individuals and corporations doubted that the exchange adjustments were large enough to correct the persisting deficit in America's balance of payments. Accordingly, they sought to buy currencies that were most likely to rise in value in the expected next round of devaluation. Once again a self-fulfilling prophecy fulfilled itself. During January and February of 1973, German reserves rose by $8 billion, or almost 50 percent, as speculators sought to buy German marks, the most obviously undervalued international currency (the Germans had been running persistent balance of payments *surpluses*). The German government then decided that it did not want its already huge dollar balances to rise further and announced that the mark would be allowed to "float." Once again the world was forced off a fixed exchange rate system and onto a floating one.

And once again the world tried to find a system of fixed rates that would hold up. The dollar was devalued again; calm was restored for a few weeks; but the rush into marks resumed, and the governments of

the world were again forced to abandon their fixed rates and to allow their currencies to float.

Figure 40 • 3 shows the gyrations of currencies during the turbulent years from 1946 to 1972. Note the dramatic fall in most currencies vis-á-vis the dollar just after the war, and the swing upward during the 1970 crisis years.

Recent Events

Dirty floating   The outcome of the long period of trial and error was thus a movement from fixed to floating rates. But as we have seen, the movement was resisted at each step along the way. Partly for reasons of international "prestige," partly because international bankers feared the possibility of diminishing trade, or of speculative raids, the world tried again and again—albeit unsuccessfully—to find a system of fixed rates that would withstand the pulls and tugs of

---

REJUVENATED SDRs

A heartening note. The need for liquidity—reserves of currency (or gold) that will be accepted by other nations as payment for their goods—remains a matter of anxious concern for the world, especially for the poorer nations whose currencies are not acceptable as international currencies. Hence the importance of raising the international supply of liquidity, and of distributing it among the needier nations, remains as great as ever, despite the advent of a more workable system of determining international currency prices.

Here we have seen a new development of promise. We have already traced the origin of Special Drawing

Rights (SDRs) as man-made equivalents of gold, to augment international buying power. The original SDRs were "backed" by gold and by "hard" currencies whose prices were established in terms of gold.

After the general abandonment of gold, the SDR had to be reconstituted. The new SDR consists of a "basket" of the currencies of the 16 IMF nations that accounted for at least 1 percent of world trade in 1968–1972. The value of an SDR on any day is found by valuing the basket on that day's exchange rates. Thus one SDR can rise or fall in

terms of the value of any given currency, although it tends to remain very stable in terms of an average of the world's major currencies.

Little by little the SDR is becoming a genuine international currency, rivaling gold in acceptability. OPEC has discussed stating the price of oil in SDRs; Suez Canal tolls have been set in SDRs, and similar action is being contemplated for international air transport rates. The day may come when tourists going abroad will buy SDR traveler's checks; and the day has arrived when corporations in international trade are beginning to write contracts in SDR-denominated amounts.

changes in international economic strength.

Today we have a system that is nominally free, but not entirely free—a system called "dirty floating." The major central banks have agreed not to intervene in the exchange market, except to stabilize it against speculative raids. They are supposed to offset short-run fluctuations that would make business difficult, but not to alter long-run trends.

Intervention of central banks   In fact, however, some central banks have intervened considerably beyond this point. The Japanese have frequently been accused of buying foreign currencies, thereby keeping down the price of the yen to encourage Japanese exports. Other countries have also intervened at crucial moments. The result is that exchange rates float, but they do not float all the way to the equilibrium price that a wholly free market would yield.

As a result, shortages and surpluses still appear in international accounts, evidenced by changes in the amounts of liquid liabilities (foreign-held bank accounts) held by most governments. We can see these in the case of the United States in 1975, when foreign liquid balances rose by $6.3 billion. If the liquid liabilities of any government are persistently large and positive, we can be sure that its central bank is intervening to buy foreign exchange in order to hold the price of its own currency down. If the balances are large and negative, we can be certain the bank is selling foreign exchange, in order to hold the value of its currency above the price that the free market would enforce.

The OPEC crisis   Will the new system work? There seems reason to be modestly hopeful. The near disastrous imbalance of the fixed-exchange crisis cannot recur under a regime of floating rates, even if the float is not quite "pure." And the new system has managed to weather some very serious blows.

The most serious was the OPEC oil crisis following the Arab-Israeli war of September 1973. Acting as a cartel, the Organization of Petroleum Exporting Countries (OPEC), largely concentrated in the oil-rich Middle East, dramatically raised the taxes imposed by its members on oil produced within their countries. In September 1973 every barrel of oil exported from an OPEC nation brought in $1.77 to the exporter. Within a year this had increased to $9.75. With transportation and other costs added, plus oil company profits, this increased the cost of oil to most Western nations to over $12—a four- to fivefold increase in a single year.

The OPEC price squeeze meant an enormous change in the world's balance of payments. The industrialized nations were forced to pay over $100 billions *a year* to the OPEC producers. Of this sum the OPEC nations utilized about half, mainly to pay for additional imports from the industrial nations and to provide some assistance to the underdeveloped world. But the remaining half—roughly $50 billion a year—simply piled up as "petrodollar" balances, largely deposited in German and American banks.

Considerable concern was raised by these balances, for had the OPEC countries shifted them about carelessly or tried to convert them all into the currencies of one or two preferred nations, this huge sum could have worked international financial havoc. In fact, the OPEC nations have sought to reinvest most of their petrodollar balances in the oil-buying industrial world, thereby "recycling" the money spent for oil and preventing a major financial crisis.

A workable system? Meanwhile the American position has recovered considerably. Shortly after the *de facto* abandonment of fixed rates, the dollar fell by an average of about 21 percent relative to the value of the currencies of its major trading partners. It then regained strength during the oil crisis. Because the United States is still a very large producer of oil within its own borders, the OPEC squeeze was a much smaller drain on our foreign exchange reserves than on those of our major Western allies. The dollar recovered about half of its relative fall after the "oil shock" began. In the last year or two, the dollar has essentially held its own, neither rising nor falling with respect to the average value of its trading partners' currencies, although some currencies, such as the pound, have fallen vis-à-vis the dollar. Others, such as the mark, have risen.

Even with the intervention of central banks, the system of floating rates should allow currencies to reflect the two basic forces that we have already identified as crucial in determining the international economic position of governments. One of these is the *relative rate of inflation* of different nations; the other is *the relative gain in productivity* among them. Other factors, such as threats of war, fears about certain governments, and similar political events, may cause a national currency to fall or rise temporarily, but the long-run trend should be governed by these underlying factors.

Thus a persistent "excess" rate of inflation, coupled with a persistent lag in productivity, will create serious problems for any nation. *But these problems will exist under any system of international payments.* To the extent that such a nation must sell abroad or provide inputs from abroad, its standard of living must fall, and no monetary arrangement in the world can prevent that.

But a system of floating rates can mitigate the damage by "signaling" its advent, as the price of the beleagured country's currency slowly falls, and a drastic and politically unmanageable sudden "crisis" can thereby be avoided. Thus there seems a fair change that the new system will work better than the old. In the imperfect world of international economic arrangements, that is perhaps as much as we can ask.

FOCUS   We do not ask you to learn a complicated story of monetary history, whose twists and turns read at times like a suspense novel. Rather, we suggest that you study the chapter as a "case history" of the difficulties that can develop when exchange rates are fixed at levels markedly divergent from those the free market would impose.

Today we live under a regime of "dirty" floating exchanges that, in all likelihood, will persist for a long time. The difficulties of going back to fixed exchange rates (and of determining those rates) now seem greater than the difficulties of living with free exchange rates, partially disturbed by the interventions of governments. Because the float seems here to stay, much of this chapter—such as the discussion of devaluation, the "classical medicine," and other cures for the pre-1971 chronic crisis—seems academic. It is a discussion of economic problems that were pressing at one time, but that are not likely to recur unless we go back to the system that got us into such trouble. Perhaps we should study them to understand why we should not try to resurrect the past.

No chapter on international monetary problems can ever come to a satisfactory end, because international monetary flows can change rapidly. The thing to understand is the mechanism by which these flows are generated and the way in which the supply and demand for foreign exchange establishes a price that clears the market for exchange. It will repay the time if you review the material of the previous chapter in the light of the more dynamic analysis of this one.

WORDS AND CONCEPTS YOU SHOULD KNOW

Flights of short-term capital, 621
The "classical medicine," 623–24
Devaluation, 624

SDRs, 625
Flexible exchange rates, 625–26
Dirty floating, 628–29

QUESTIONS

1. In the tables below we show the price of British pounds from 1971 to 1975. We also show the cost of living index in the two countries. Can you deduce what probably happened in the relationship of productivity between the U.S. and the U.K.? Are there other factors that could account for the slippage of the British pound?

	U.S. price of £	Rise in cost of living	
		U.S.	U.K.
1971	$2.44	4.3%	9.4%
1972	2.30	3.3	7.1
1973	2.45	6.2	9.2
1974	2.34	11.0	16.0
1975	2.22	9.1	24.2

2. Does gold or do SDRs serve a purpose under a system of free exchange rates if there is no intervention on the part of banks? If gold and SDRs were eliminated, what would provide "liquidity"?

3. Assuming that there was a general demand to return to fixed rates, what would you recommend as the proper basis for establishing the relation of various currencies to one another?

4. Can dirty floating persist in one direction only unless there is agreement to use some currency (or some asset) as a reserve currency?

The multinational corporation

Everything we have heretofore learned has had to do with the international *exchange* of goods and services. What we must now consider is a revolutionary development in international economics, based not on exchange, but on the *international production* of goods and services. To understand what this means we must learn about a new institution that has sprung up as the most important agency for international production: the multinational corporation.

What is a multinational corporation? Essentially, we mean a corporation that has producing branches or subsidiaries located in more than one nation. Take PepsiCo, for example. PepsiCo does not ship its famous product around the world from bottling plants in the United States. It *produces* Pepsi Cola in more than 500 plants in over 100 countries. When you buy a Pepsi in Mexico or the Philippines or Israel or Denmark, you are buying an American product that was manufactured in that country.

PepsiCo is a far-flung, but not a particularly large multinational corporation: in 1976 it was only the 77th largest company. More impressive by far is the Ford Motor Company, a multinational that consists of a network of 60 subsidiary corporations, 40 of them foreign-based. Of the corporation's total assets of $16 billion, over one-third is invested in 27 foreign nations; and of its 464,000 employees (as of 1974) more than 175,000 were employed outside the U.S. And if we studied the corporate structures of GM or IBM or the great oil companies, we would find that they, too, are multinational companies with substantial portions of their total wealth invested in productive facilities outside the United States.

Multinational corporations differ from international corporations in that they produce goods and services in more than one country, while international corporations produce most of their goods and services in one country, even though they sell them in many. Volkswagen is a large international corporation, since it sells Volkswagens all over the world; but it is not much of a multinational corporation, since most of its actual production is concentrated in Germany.

If we broaden our view to include the top 100 American firms, we find that two-thirds have such production facilities in at least 6 nations. Moreover, the value of output that is produced overseas by the largest corporations by far exceeds the value of the goods they still export from the United States. In 1974, sales of foreign affiliates of U.S. multinational firms (which means their wholly or partially owned overseas branches) came to over $115 billion. In the same year, our total exports of manufactures amounted to $47 billion, only 41 percent as much as American firms produced abroad.

International direct investment

Another way of establishing the spectacular rise of international production is to trace the increase in the value of U.S. foreign direct investment; that is, the value of foreign-located, U.S.-owned plant and equipment (*not* U.S.-owned foreign bonds and stocks). In 1950 the value of U.S. foreign direct investment was $11 billion. In 1976 it was over $133 billion. Moreover, this figure, too, needs an upward adjustment, because it includes only the value of American dollars invested abroad and not the additional value of foreign capital that may be controlled by those dollars. For example, if a U.S. company has invested $10 million in a foreign enterprise whose total net worth is $20 million, the U.S. official figures for our foreign investment take note only of the $10 million of American equity (ownership) and not of the $20 million wealth that our equity actually controls. If we include the capital controlled by our foreign direct investment as a whole, the value of American overseas productive assets may be as large as $300 billion. In general, something between a quarter and a half of the real assets of our biggest corporations are located abroad.

"The American Challenge"

The stunning expansion of American corporate production overseas, especially in Europe, has given rise to what has been called *The American Challenge*. In a book with that title, written in 1967, Jean-Jacques Servan-Schreiber described the "take over" of French markets by dynamic American firms that had seized 50 percent of Europe's semiconductor market, 80 percent of its computer market, and 95 percent of its integrated circuit production. Servan-Schreiber feared that the American Challenge portended the Americanization of Europe's fastest growing industries. "Fifteen years from now," he wrote, "it is quite possible that the world's third greatest industrial power, just after the United States and Russia, will not be

Europe, but American industry in Europe."

Servan-Schreiber argued that Europe must fend off this American threat by the formation of equally efficient, large pan-European corporations. But he failed to see that the movement toward the internationalization of production was not a strictly American but a truly multinational phenomenon. If the American multinationals are today the most imposing (of the world's biggest 500 corporations, over 300 are American), they are closely challenged by non-American multinationals. Philips Lamp Works, for example, is a huge Dutch multinational company with operations in 68 countries. Of its 225,000 employees, 167,000 work in nations other than the Netherlands "home" nation. Royal Dutch/Shell is another vast multinational, whose "home" is somewhere between the Netherlands and the United Kingdom (it is jointly owned by nationals of both countries): Shell *in the United States* ranks among "our" top 20 biggest companies. Another is Nestlé Chocolate, a Swiss firm, 97 percent of whose $2 billion revenues originate outside Switzerland.

The international challenge
Indeed, if we take the 10 leading capital-exporting nations together (including the United States), we find that in 1967 their combined exports came to over $130 billion, but their combined overseas production amounted to well over $240 billion. For 1970, an economist for the International Chamber of Commerce, estimated that total international production—U.S. production abroad, foreign production here, and foreign production in other foreign countries—accounted for as much as *one-sixth* of the total value of all world output, and a much higher fraction of the world output of industrial commodities.

Because we do not have complete statistics on many aspects of international production, the full extent of this new form of economic relationship is still uncertain. But a number of economists have made projections based on the continuance of the rapid growth of international production. Professor Harold Perlmutter, for example, predicts that by 1988 most non-communist trade will be dominated by 300 large corporations, of which 200 will be American, and that these corporations will account for roughly half of total world industrial output. Perhaps the reader will recall the comment in Chapter 4 that some corporations "can be thought of only in somewhat the way we have heretofore thought of nations." A glance at Table 41•1, comparing the GNPs of various countries with the sales of selected multinational corporations, shows that statement was not just rhetoric.

Table 41 • 1   GNP of various countries compared with sales of selected multinational corporations (billions of current dollars, 1975)

Netherlands	$64.9
Belgium	63.4
Switzerland	56.0
Exxon	44.9
Austria	38.0
Denmark	36.1
General Motors	35.7
Royal Dutch Shell	32.1
Norway	27.8
Texaco	24.5
Ford	24.0
Greece	22.8
Mobil	20.6
Portugal	14.8
Unilever	15.0
IBM	14.4
General Electric	13.4
Chrysler	11.7

THE TOP 15 MULTINATIONALS, 1971 (latest available data)

Company	Total sales (billions of dollars)	Foreign sales as percentage of total	Number of countries in which subsidiaries are located
General Motors	$28.3	19%	21
Exxon	18.7	50	25
Ford	16.4	26	30
Royal Dutch/Shell*	12.7	79	43
General Electric	9.4	16	32
IBM	8.3	39	80
Mobil Oil	8.2	45	62
Chrysler	8.0	24	26
Texaco	7.5	40	30
Unilever*	7.5	80	31
ITT	7.3	42	40
Gulf Oil	5.9	45	61
British Petroleum*	5.2	88	52
Philips Gloeilampenfabrieken*	5.2	NA	29
Standard Oil of California	5.1	45	26

*Not a U.S. firm.

Cautionary note: Corporate sales are not the equivalent of GNPs. The table vastly overstates the relative importance of corporations with respect to manpower: Portugal, for instance, has a population of over 9 million, whereas GM employs far less than 1 million. On the other hand, the table understates the economic strength of corporations: GM can borrow a great deal more easily than Portugal; and it controls *all* of its receipts, whereas Portugal gets only the taxes from its GNP. Nonetheless, the table makes it clear that Berle's comparison was not a wholly fanciful one.

Emergence of multinational production

Why has the multinational phenomenon arisen? After all, it is cheaper to export goods or to license production abroad than to establish a branch in a faraway nation and encounter troubles and risks, which we will look into. Why, then, has production itself leaped overseas?

The initial reason arises from a charac-teristic of the firm, to which we have here-tofore paid only passing attention. This is the drive for expansion that we find in nearly all capitalist enterprises.* This "logic" of expansion has driven firms, from early times, to expand their market overseas. Samuel Colt, the inventor of the first "assembly line" revolver, opened a foreign branch in London in the mid-1850s (and promptly failed). But in those same years, American entrepreneurs were already successfully pushing a railway line to completion across the Panama isthmus, and by the 1870s the Singer Sewing Machine was gaining half its revenues from overseas production and exports.

*Alfred Chandler has shown in a brilliant book, *Strategy and Structure* (Cambridge, Mass.: M.I.T. Press, 1962), that the typical domestic firm went through a series of "logical" changes in organization, growing from the single-product, single-plant firm (in which every operation was supervised personally by the founder-owner) to the multidivisional, multiproduct enterprise in which a tiered organizational structure became necessary to superintend the strategic requirements of national geographic scope and increasing technical complexity.

Motives for overseas production

But what drives a firm to *produce* overseas rather than just sell overseas? One possible answer is straightforward. A firm is successful at home. Its technology and organizational skills give it an edge on foreign competition. It begins to export its product. The foreign market grows. At some point, the firm begins to calculate whether it would be more profitable to organize an overseas production operation. By doing so, it would save transportation costs. It may be able to evade a tariff by producing goods "behind" a tariff wall. It may be able to take advantage of lower wage rates. Finally, it ceases shipping goods abroad and instead exports capital, technology, and management—and becomes a multinational.

Or calculations may be more complex. By degrees, a successful company may change its point of view. First it thinks of itself as a domestic company, perhaps with a small export market. Then it builds up its exports and thinks of itself as an international company with a substantial interest in exports. Finally its perspective changes to that of a multinational, considering the world (or substantial portions of it) to be its market. In that case, it may locate plants abroad *before* the market is fully developed, in order to be firmly established abroad ahead of its competition.*

In the multinational boom of the 1950s and 1960s, still other considerations may have played a role. For American corporations, one factor was probably our over-valued dollar, which made it possible to buy or build foreign plant and equipment cheaply. In fact, many experts

believe that the dollar devaluation of the early 1970s will slow down the multinational thrust of American companies, although by the same reasoning it would stimulate the thrust of foreign companies, now able to buy American dollars more cheaply. The added element of risk that results from floating exchange rates, however, may deter both American and foreign firms from investing large sums abroad, since domestic value may fall if the exchange rate fluctuates against them.

Economics of multinational production

Whether or not the multinational boom continues at its past rate, the startling rise of multinationals has already changed the face of international economic relationships. One major effect has been a dramatic shift in the *geographic location* and the *technological character* of international economic activity.

The shift away from exports to international production has introduced two changes into the international economic scene. One change is a movement of foreign investment away from its original concentration in the underdeveloped areas of the world toward the richer markets of the developed areas. Fifty years ago, in the era of high imperialism, most of the capital leaving one country for another flowed from rich to poor lands. Thus foreign investment in the late nineteenth and early twentieth centuries was largely associated with the creation of vast plantations, the building of railways through jungles, and the development of mineral resources.

But the growth of the multinational enterprise has coincided with a decisive shift away from investment in the underdeveloped world to investment in the industrial world. In 1897, 59 percent of American foreign direct investment was in

*The internal dynamics that send some firms overseas, but not others, are by no means wholly understood. The internationalization of production is much more widely spread in some industries, such as glass, than in others, such as steel. Drugs are widely produced on an international basis; machine tools are not.

agriculture, mining, or railways, mainly in the underdeveloped world. By the end of the 1960s, our investment in agriculture, mining, and railways, as a proportion of our total overseas assets, had fallen to about 20 percent; and its geographical location in the backward world came to only 36 percent of all our overseas direct investments. More striking, almost three-associated with large, unskilled labor forces, as in the building of railways or plantations—toward industries in which capital is perhaps less strategic than research and development, skilled technical manpower, and sophisticated management techniques typical of computer, petrochemical, and other new industries. Table 41 • 2 sums up the overall shift.

Table 41 · 2   Size and distribution of U.S. foreign direct investment

	1929	1950	1975
Total (millions)	$7,528	$11,788	$133,168
		Distribution by market (%)	
Canada	27	30	23
Europe	18	14	37
Latin America	47	41	12
Asia, Africa, other	8	15	28
		Distribution by industrial sector (%)	
Manufacturing	24	31	42
Petroleum	15	29	26
Transport and utilities	21	12	n.a.
Mining	15	9	8
Trade	5	7	n.a.
Agriculture	12	5	n.a.
Other	8	6	n.a.

quarters of our huge rise in direct investment during the decade of the 1960s had been in the developed world; and the vast bulk of it has been in manufacturing (and oil) rather than in plantations, railroads, or ores. Thus the multinational companies are investing in each others' territories rather than invading the territories of the underdeveloped world. This is not to say that they do not wield great power in the background regions, as we shall see, but their thrust of expansion has been in other industrial lands, not in the unindustrialized ones.

The second economic change is really implicit in the first. It is a shift away from "heavy technology" to "high technology" industries—away from enterprises in which often vast sums of capital were

Note the dramatic shift away from Latin America and away from transport, mining, and agriculture into Europe and manufacturing, a shift that would be even more accentuated if we were not still dependent on oil as a major source of the world's energy. If nuclear power or the fuel cell displace oil within the next two decades, we can expect a still more rapid decline in investment in the backward areas (especially in the Near East), and a proportionately still larger concentration of foreign direct investment in manufacturing.

Problems for policy makers

Multinationals have not only changed the face of international economic activity, but also have added considerably to the problem of controlling domestic economies. Assume that a country wants to slow down its economy through monetary policies designed to reduce plant and equipment spending. A restrictive monetary policy at home may be vitiated by the ability of a multinational to borrow *abroad* in order to finance investment at home. Conversely, a monetary policy designed to stimulate the home economy may end up in loans that increase production in someone else's economy. *Thus the effectiveness of national economic policy making is weakened.* Moreover, it is not easy to suggest that monetary policies should be coordinated among countries, since the economic needs of different countries may not be the same: what is right for one country at a given time may be wrong for another.

A second problem has already come to our attention when we considered the international movement of short-term capital. Multinationals are almost inevitably thrust into the role of international currency speculators. They can quickly move billions of dollars from one country to another—and as profit maximizers, they are motivated to carry out such movements. A multinational that allowed its balances to remain in a currency that seemed overpriced would be deliberately courting a loss. Thus the multinationals aggravate short-term capital flows, sometimes forcing the hand of governments. As we have seen, this contributed to the currency problems of the early 1970s.

Tax problems   Difficult problems also emerge in the area of taxation. Multinationals often produce components in one country and finished goods in another. When they ship components across national boundaries, they are in a position to charge high or low prices for these components. If they charge high prices, they will create profits for the component manufacturing country; if they charge low prices, profits will be higher in the component receiving country.

Since there are different tax laws in different countries, these pricing policies will be largely influenced by taxes rather than by other criteria. As a result, countries may not receive their fair share of total corporation tax payments. Indeed, countries may be forced to compete with one another in their tax rates, much as the various states in the United States who seek to attract industry by special tax arrangements. In one case as in the other, this is a zero-sum game, where the winner is the corporation who ends up paying less taxes than it should, and where the loser is the individual taxpayer who must pick up the burden.

Complications in the balance of payments   Last, there is the exceedingly difficult problem of determining whether a multinational helps or hurts its own country's balance of payments. Consider what happens when a corporation begins to produce abroad. To begin with, it will hurt the balance of payments by buying foreign exchange in order to build or buy foreign plant and equipment. Then it will further increase the balance of payments deficit by ceasing to export its goods, as production starts up abroad. To add insult to injury, it may begin to export goods *from* its new foreign facility back into the United States, increasing our imports. Doubtless it will increase the deficit on travel as its executives travel around the world.

But that is only half the picture. The

plants abroad will often require special machinery or parts or services from home, resulting in the export of goods or services that would not otherwise have been exported. Most important of all, the multinational will be sending home a steady and probably rising total of dividends. As we have seen, this homeward flow of profits is a major "plus" item in the balance on current account.

Can we then add up all the minuses and all the pluses and calculate whether a multinational is a net help or hindrance? It seems impossible to do so. The fact of overseas production changes the problem so markedly that we can no longer compare the situation under multinationals with that which preceded it. Foreign production is likely to be much larger than exports would have been. Therefore foreign-earned profits of the corporation may also be larger. It is really impossible to say whether, for example, GM earns more foreign exchange as a multinational than it would as a large exporter.

What does seem probable is that *domestic* employment will be less when a company goes multinational. GM will no longer employ American workers to make cars for export; instead, it employs workers in Germany. On the other hand, many American workers may work for a foreign company—Lever Brothers or BP Petroleum or Olivetti. If these companies were not also multinationals, they would be employing labor in their home countries rather than here.

Political economics of multinational enterprise

All these considerations make it difficult or impossible to draw up a balance sheet of the pluses and minuses of multinationals strictly in economic terms. Indeed, the problems posed by the multinationals make it necessary to view international production from a perspective that is different from the one we take toward international trade.

As we have seen, the "classical" conception of international trade was based on the familiar model of a competitive world in which factors of production were free to move about to find their points of highest return *within* their own national territories. The result, as our discussion of Infraville and Supraville revealed, was a final equilibrium in which each nation discovered the best allocation of resources both with regard to its own resources and to the advantageous exchanges it could make with other nations. In this final equilibrium, political considerations might enter in the form of tariffs or other trade barriers, but these were always considered by economists as the product of national nearsightedness, so that in theory—and to some extent in practice—it was possible to use the notion of *an equilibrium determined entirely by economic considerations.*

Not so, under the peculiar conditions of international production. For now the unit of economic activity is no longer the tiny "factor of production" subject to market forces, but a giant corporation capable of the maneuvers, tactics, and strategies characteristic of oligopolistic, rather than competitive economic units. *Within* a given country, as we have seen, oligopolies tend to "settle down" to a more or less steady division-of-the-market, usually by tacit agreement not to engage in price warfare. But this division-of-the-market becomes rudely disturbed when a newcomer from the "outside" establishes his production unit within the home market of another nation. Moreover, the new division-of-the-market between the invader and the established giants will not be determined solely by the economic growth potentials of the various contestants. *There is an inescapable political element that will also play an important, perhaps determinative, role.*

Creating pan-national enterprises

This political element has two aspects. On the one hand, it depends on the ability of smaller nations, such as those we find in Europe, to relinquish their feelings of national pride sufficiently to allow the creation of big enough pan-European enterprises to challenge the (American) invader successfully. (Here is Servan-Schreiber's problem in a nutshell.) The cost of IBM's research and development, for example, is more than the entire sales of its largest British competitor. To stand up against IBM, therefore, it may be necessary for British companies to merge with French or German ones, to form a competitor with the economies of scale, the ability to generate finance, the command over technical talent that will put it in a league with IBM. But that will require a *political* decision on the part of England or France or Germany to give up exclusive national control over "their" biggest computer companies.

A few such genuinely international companies have come into existence. Royal Dutch/Shell and Unilever are truly binational enterprises run by boards of directors that represent both Dutch and English directors, and an effort is being made to create more such genuinely "European" enterprises. Whether or not this effort will be successful, it is too early to tell. But surely the critical element in the final division of the market among the multinationals will depend fully as much on the politics of international merger as on the economics of market tactics.

National prerogatives

There is, moreover, a second political element that enters into the new multinational thrust. This is the question of the extent to which foreign governments will *permit* "foreign" corporations to operate within their borders.

This problem has its counterpart in the political decision on how much to tax (by tariffs) the goods that foreign companies sell to a given nation. But the problem of permitting the entry of a foreign-owned production unit is much more important—and much more difficult to resolve—because this may be the only way that a nation can "import" the *technology* and the *productivity* that the multinational invader will bring with it.

The French government, for example, has been extremely uneasy over the virtual preemption of its high technology computer industries by American firms. Thus when General Electric sought to buy a 20 percent interest in Machines Bull, a leading French manufacturer of computer and desk machinery, the French government balked at the "Americanization" of the firm and forbade the transaction. That was in 1962. Within a very few years it became apparent that without an infusion of American technology, Machines Bull could not stand up to the competition of IBM, and the French government unhappily acquiesced in the American "takeover." But then it *was* a takeover, for G.E. demanded (and got) 50 percent control of Machines Bull.*

Thus, the pan-national thrust of economic activity unavoidably hinges on political decisions concerning the national independence of the economies into which the multinationals seek to move.

---

*An investment that did not work out very successfully, by the way, for G.E.

Canadians, for example, have recently awakened to the fact that they own only *15* percent of their "own" industry. All the rest is foreign owned. Americans alone control 46 percent of Canadian manufacturing, 58 percent of its oil and gas, and almost 100 percent of its auto industry. The next biggest slice is owned by various European, mainly British, interests. Canada is thus a minority stockholder in its own economy, a situation that has led to strong sentiments to block further foreign ownership. But there would, of course, be a real economic price—a diminished rate of growth—for such a blockage.

Host and hostage This conflict between the jealous claims of nation-states who seek to retain national control over productive activity within their own borders and the powerful thrust of pan-national corporations for new markets in foreign territories introduces profound tensions into the political economics of multinational production. On the one hand, the multinational is in a position to win hard bargains from the "host" country into which it seeks to enter (as in the case of France and G.E.), because the corporation *is* the main bearer of new technologies and management techniques that every nation seeks. Therefore, if one country—say France— refuses to give a would-be entrant the right to come in (and possibly to cause financial losses to its established firms), the multinational may well place its plants, with their precious economic cargo of productivity, in another country, leaving the recalcitrant nation the loser in the race for international growth.

On the other hand, the power is by no means entirely one-sided; for once a multinational *has* entered a foreign nation, it becomes a *hostage* of the host country. It is now bound by the laws of that country and may find itself forced to undertake activities that are "foreign." In Japan, for example, it is an unwritten law that workers engaged by giant corporations are *never* fired, but become permanent employees. Japan has been extremely reluctant to allow foreign capital to establish manufacturing operations on Japanese soil, to the great annoyance of foreign companies. But if, as now seems likely, Japan is opened to American and European capital, we can be sure that American or European corporations will be expected to behave in the Japanese way with their employees. This will not be an easy course to follow, since these corporations are not likely to receive the special support that the Japanese government gives to its own big firms.

Or take the problem of a multinational that is forced by a fall in demand to cut back the volume of its output. A decision made along strictly economic lines would lead it to close its least profitable plant. But this may bring very serious economic repercussions in the particular nation in which that plant is located—so serious that the government will threaten to take "action" if the plant is closed. What dictates shall the multinational then follow: those of standard business accounting or those of political accounting?

Or consider the multinational seeking to expand or to alter its operations in an underdeveloped country. This, too, may lead to friction, for as former Under Secretary of State George Ball has candidly asked: "How can a national government make an economic plan with any confidence if a board of directors meeting 5,000 miles away can, by altering its pattern of purchasing and production, affect in a major way the country's economic life?"

As we have seen in Peru, Bolivia, and Libya, this incompatibility of aims may become so great that the underdeveloped country eventually seizes and nationalizes the local assets of the multinational.

Multinationals and world order

Is there a resolution to this conflict between the business rationality of the multinational corporation and the political priorities of the nation-state? At this stage in the development of both institutions, none is in sight. The very idea of pan-national production is itself so new that we lack even a conceptual model of how to deal with its problems, much less a set of practical rules and regulations to follow. Take something so simple—but so important—as the location of the "head office" of the corporation to which a nation would make representations if the action of an international corporation were contrary to national interest. From one nation to another, the legal definition of the head office differs: in the U.S. and the U.K., it is the place where the company is formally incorporated; in Morocco it is the location of the "registered" home office; in France, Germany, and Belgium, it is the main center of management; in Italy and Egypt, it is the place of principal business activity. Which of these will respond when a country in search of legal redress calls out: "Will the real head office please stand up?"

Or take the question of the patriotic accountability of the multinational enterprise. Suppose a company wishes to move its profits from country A to country B, but that country A has balance-of-payments difficulties. Is the company bound to obey the wishes of A? Suppose the government in B also has balance-of-payments difficulties and desires the company to import

capital? What should the corporation do? In 1966, for example, the United States government asked corporations not to export capital, lest our precarious balance of payments be worsened. But the Ford Motor Company decided that its long-term interests required the purchase of British Ford; so despite objections of the U.S. government, Ford exported $600 million of capital to make the purchase. Was Ford "unpatriotic," if its actions were in the long-term interests of the company? Was it similarly "unpatriotic" (from a British point of view) for a group of English investors to export British capital to finance the building of the PanAm skyscraper in New York?

Or suppose a multinational company, in one of its foreign plants, undertakes work that is integral to the defense of that nation and that the foreign policy of the nation in question brings its military strength to bear against another country where the multinational is also located? Is the company supposed to "take sides"?

Unresolved questions

There are no answers to such questions, only speculations. Here are some of them.

Speculation 1. Will the conglomerate serve as a means of mediation between the demands of business production efficiency and political "national" control? For example, why didn't Ford build the PanAm building, and why didn't the British investors put their pounds into autos? Both sides would have told you (in 1966) that they weren't "in the business" of real estate or cars, as the case may be. But the rise of the conglomerates opens new possibilities in this direction. If, in the future, the controlling center of Ford becomes (as ITT has already become) a capital-allocation office rather than the headquarters of an auto firm, it is possible that Ford *will* build buildings and that British realtors *will* make automobiles. In that case, the big corporation may surrender some of its multinationality in exchange for multi-industrial coverage.

Speculation 2. Will the multinationals, if they continue their growth, constitute the skeleton of a new form of world order? Some economists and businessmen see the rise of a pan-national system of oligopolies controlled by boards of directors that represent many nations (rather than mainly one, as is now the case), whose operations will pave the way for a much more pragmatic, down-to-earth, effective system of world production and distribution than the present competition of hostile, suspicious, and dangerous nation-states. Such an international rationalization of production, they believe, could bring a "businessman's peace," in which the big companies serve to accelerate world growth, to introduce efficiency into the backward areas, and to assert the logic of economic performance over the outmoded rivalries of jealous nation-states.

Speculation 3. Will the multinationals, on the contrary, serve to heighten the tension of a world which, for better or worse, must continue to use the powerful appeal of nationhood? How can giant corporations, necessarily dedicated to profit making, adjust their operations to the often unprofitable needs of national development? How can corporations, jockeying for market position, provide the basis for a stable world economic system? The opponents of the multinationals see in them not a force for progress but only a means of imposing a calculus of profits on a world whose needs at the moment often demand an entirely different set of fundamental values.

An unwritten ending

It is much too early to determine which of these arguments will eventually be proven correct. Perhaps the safest guess is that all will be, at least in our lifetimes. The big corporations are likely to continue to go in both multinational and conglomerate directions. To some extent they will be the international carriers of efficiency and development, especially in the high technology areas for which they seem to be the most effective form of organization. But if the power of the nation-state will be challenged by these international production units, it is not likely to be humbled by them. There are many things a nation can do that a corporation cannot, including, above all, the creation of the spirit of sacrifice necessary both for good purposes such as development and for evil ones such as war.

Perhaps all we can say at this stage of human development is that both nation-states and huge corporations are necessary, in that they seem to be the only ways in which we can organize mankind to perform the arduous and sustained labor without which humanity itself would rapidly perish. Perhaps after the long age of capital accumulation has finally come to an end and sufficient capital is available to all peoples, we may be able to think seriously about dismantling the giant enterprise and the nation-state, both of which overpower the individual with their massive organized strength. However desirable that ultimate goal may be, in our time both state and corporation promise to be with us, and the tension between them will be part of the evolutionary drama of our period of history.

FOCUS   There is no single lesson to be learned from this exploration of the multinational phenomenon. The problem itself is still too new, and too little understood, to enable us to wrap it up in a few salient "points."

Perhaps the central question that emerges is the tension that characterizes relations between huge corporations, organized along profit-maximizing lines, and nation-states, organized to achieve political objectives. This tension affects the "home" nations of big multinationals as well as the "host" nations. In the home nations, the multinational can often be quite independent of domestic policy (for example, it may borrow abroad, despite a credit squeeze at home) and thereby weaken the effective power of domestic policy makers. In host countries, the MNC finds itself both the possessor of vast power through its wealth and know-how, and the target of much hostile sentiment directed against the foreign control of the corporation's policy.

There is no resolution of these tensions yet in sight. The issues in this chapter will be with us for many years.

WORDS AND CONCEPTS YOU SHOULD KNOW

Multinational corporations, 632–33
Foreign direct investment, 637
Host and hostage, 641

Conflicts of the MNC, 642–43
Pan-national enterprises, 642

QUESTIONS

1. How many products *produced* in America can you identify as "foreign"? (You might start with the detergents and soaps produced by Lever Brothers, the office machinery produced by Olivetti-Underwood, the gas and oil refined by Shell.)

2. Can you suggest a hypothesis that might be testable as to why certain industries seem to go overseas more rapidly than others? Why autos and tractors but not washing machines? Why plate glass but not sheet steel? (Little is known about this, so you might become famous if you come up with an idea that tests out.)

3. Do you think a nation is right to exclude a foreign company from producing certain products? If you could get high-speed computers only by allowing a Japanese company to produce them in the U.S., would you still keep out the Japanese company?

4. What do you think is the duty of a company that is active in nations A, B, and C, when all have balance-of-payments problems and request domestic corporations not to make unnecessary international payments? Suppose the headquarters of the company is in A and the stockholders want the profits from B and C repatriated?

5. Can you draw up a plan for a company that would be privately owned and managed but not officially "headquartered" in any one nation? From whom would it receive its charter? Under what laws will it operate so far as the top management is concerned?

6. Do you think that the rise of multinational production opens the way for a more rational world or a more divided one?

Controlling the multinationals

During the 1960s, when the dollar was overvalued and foreign currencies cheap, the American multinational thrust was highly visible. One of the worries to which it gave rise was that American companies, by investing abroad, were creating foreign employment at the expense of domestic employment—that jobs were being "exported." A bill, the Burke-Hartley Act, was introduced into Congress to prevent this phenomenon through the imposition of taxes on foreign investment and by more direct measures.

Today the situation has changed. Currencies float and the American dollar is no longer overpriced. As a result, relative wage rates have changed: American labor is now cheap compared with some European labor. Therefore the flow of European capital *into* the United States is now accelerating. German workers in Volkswagen are complaining that their company is exporting jobs into the United States.

With this new development, political pressures have also changed. Newspapers report on foreign purchases of American firms as if these were threats to the economy. The specter of an Arab "takeover" of American companies has been frightening enough to be discussed in Congress as well as in *Time* magazine. We are now reacting to foreign investment just as others formerly reacted to our investment abroad. And we are beginning to see that foreign investment may improve productivity, but that it may not improve everyone's income. Arab investment in the U.S. will add to American output, just as American investment adds to Arab output. But American capitalists will feel the pressure of additional competition, whereas American workers will experience the pleasure of additional employers.

Interestingly, the most effective control on foreign investment in the United States are the antitrust laws. These laws were not originally designed to have any effect on multinational corporations. But in fact they have exerted their effect against the MNCs. Most multinationals expand into a foreign market by buying up a small or medium-sized producer and then strengthening it with capital and know-how. It is cheaper and quicker to "take over" and expand than to build from scratch.

But takeovers followed by expansion can bring foreign companies rapidly into conflict with American antitrust provisions. Under U.S. law, the Justice Department can prevent a foreign takeover on the grounds of the threat it would pose to "potential" competition. The rationale is that the foreigner could have started from scratch and that allowing him to buy an existing firm is therefore to lessen the potential competitiveness of the industry. Foreign investors complain that this is unfair treatment, *even though the same reasoning would be applied by the Justice Department against a takeover by an American firm.* The unfairness, claim the foreign MNCs, is that no such provisions exist in Europe and that they are therefore being prevented from pursuing the very policies that led to the success of the American MNC foreign thrust.

All this is a perfect example of the conflict that can exist between the rationale of economic growth and that of political self-governance. In fact, the Justice Department has generally permitted foreign companies to buy out American firms. This means that a double standard of conduct is being applied. If the doctrine of potential competition is valid, it should apply to all. If the Europeans feel unfairly treated, they can adopt similar antitrust legislation at home and apply it against American companies.

The underdeveloped world

Our account of the long sweep of Western economic advance has ignored the economic existence of almost four out of five human beings. Mere parochialism was not, however, the reason for this concentration on Western progress. Rather, it was the shocking fact that, taken in the large, *there was no economic progress in the rest of the world.*

This sobering realization does not mean that tides of fortune and misfortune did not mark these areas, that great cultural heights were not achieved, and that the political or social histories of these regions do not warrant interest and study. Yet the fact remains that the mounting tide of *economic* advance that has engaged our attention was a phenomenon limited to the West. It is no doubt something of an oversimplification, but it is basically true to claim that in Asia, Africa, South America, or the Near East, economic existence was not materially improved for the average inhabitant from the twelfth—and, in some cases, the second—to the beginning of the twentieth century. Indeed, for many of them it was worsened. A long graph of non-Western material well-being would depict irregular rises and falls but an almost total absence of cumulative betterment.

42

The near end of such a graph would show the standard of living of three-quarters of the human race who inhabit the so-called underdeveloped areas today. Most of this mass of humanity exists in conditions of poverty that are difficult for a Westerner to comprehend. When we sum up the plight of the underdeveloped nations by saying that a billion human beings have a standard of living of "less than $100 a year," and that another, more fortunate, billion people enjoy in a year one-quarter to one-half the income a typical American family spends in a single *month*, we give only a pale statistical meaning to a reality that we can scarcely grasp.

Background to underdevelopment

Why are the underdeveloped nations so pitiably poor? Only a half-century ago it was common to attribute their backwardness to geographic or climatic causes. The underdeveloped nations were poor, it was thought, either because the climate was too debilitating or because natural resources were lacking. Sometimes it was just said that the natives were too childlike or racially too inferior to improve their lot.

Bad climates may have had adverse effects. Yet, many hot areas have shown a capacity for sustained economic growth (for example, the Queensland areas of Australia), and we have come to recognize that a number of underdeveloped areas, such as Argentina and Korea, have completely temperate climates. So, too, we now regard the lack of resources in many areas more as a *symptom* of underdevelopment than a cause—which is to say that in many underdeveloped areas, resources have not yet been *looked for*. Libya, for instance, which used to be written off as a totally barren nation, has been discovered to be a huge reservoir of oil. Finally, little is heard today about native childishness or inherent inferiority. (Perhaps we remember how the wealthy classes in Europe similarly characterized the poor not too many centuries ago.) Climate and geography and cultural unpreparedness unquestionably constitute obstacles to rapid economic growth—and in some areas of the globe, very serious obstacles—but there are few economists who would look to these disadvantages as the main causes of economic backwardness.

Why then are these societies so poor?

The answer is that these are poor societies because they are *traditional* societies—that is, societies which have developed neither the mechanisms of ef-

---

DAMASCUS: In famine years the children of the poor examine the droppings of horses to extract morsels of undigested oats.

CALCUTTA: 250,000 people have no home whatsoever; they live, eat, defecate, mate, and die in the streets.

HONG KONG: Large numbers of families live in floating villages that tourists like to photograph. A family of six, eight, or ten occupies a home approximately the size of a rowboat.

CALI, COLOMBIA: When the rains come, the river rises and the sewers run through the homes of the poor.

SNAPSHOTS OF UNDERDEVELOPMENT

HYDERABAD: Child labor employed in sealing the ends of cheap bracelets is paid eight cents per *gross* of bracelets.

KATMANDU, Nepal: Life expectancy is between 35 and 40 years. Tu-

berculosis is chronic. One hears people coughing themselves to death at night.

NEW DELHI: "Oh, sir! Someone has dropped ice cream on your shoes! I will clean them." The tourist finds himself propped against a building, with two boys each shining one shoe. "Oh, sir! Your laces are frayed. See, they break! I will sell you a new pair." The tourist buys the new pair. As he leaves, an Old India Hand says to him: "Have to watch those little beggars. Fling mud on your shoes." These are the tactics which poverty generates.

fective command nor of the market by which they might launch into a sustained process of economic growth. Indeed, as we examine them further we shall have the feeling that we are encountering in the present the anachronistic counterparts of the static societies of antiquity.

Why did they remain traditional societies? Why, for instance, did Byzantium, which was economically so advanced in contrast with the Crusaders' Europe, fall into decline? Why did China, with so many natural advantages, not develop into a dynamic economic society? There are no simple or even fully satisfactory answers. Perhaps the absence of economic progress elsewhere on the globe forces us to look upon our Western experience not as the paradigm and standard for historic development, but as a very special case in which various activating factors met in an environment peculiarly favorable for the emergence of a new economic style in history. The problem is one into which we cannot go more deeply in this book. At any rate, it is today an academic question. The dominant reality of our times is that the backward areas are now striving desperately to enter the mainstream of economic progress of the West. Let us examine further their chances for doing so.

Conditions of backwardness

Every people, to exist, must first feed itself; there is a rough sequence to the order of demands in human society. But to go beyond existence, it must achieve a certain level of efficiency in agriculture, so that its efforts can be turned in other directions. What is tragically characteristic of the underdeveloped areas is that this first corner of economic progress has not yet been turned.

Consider the situation in that all-important crop of the East, rice. Table 42•1 shows the difference between the productivity of rice fields in the main Asiatic countries and those of the United States and Australia and Japan.

What is true of rice can be duplicated in most other crops.* It is a disconcerting fact that the backward peasant nations that depend desperately on their capacity to grow food cannot even compete in these main products with the advanced countries: Louisiana rice undersells Philippine rice, California oranges are not only better but cheaper than Indonesian oranges.

Table 42•1   Rice production

(100 kilograms per hectare)	1975
U.S.	51.0
Australia	51.2
Japan	61.9
India	18.3
Indonesia	26.9
Thailand	17.1
Philippines	17.6
China	32.4

Why is agriculture so unproductive? One apparent reason is that the typical unit of agricultural production in the underdeveloped lands is far too small to permit efficient farming. "Postage stamp cultivation" marks the pattern of farming throughout most of Asia and a good deal of Africa and South America. John Gunther, reporting the situation in India over a

*Table 42•1 shows only the productive differentials of equal areas of land. When we consider that a single American farmer tends up to a hundred times as large an acreage as a peasant in an underdeveloped area, the difference of output per man would be much more striking. The "Green Revolution" (discussed near the end of the chapter) has improved the situation, but we do not yet have the data we need to determine outputs for the new rice strains. Despite the improvement, a vast gulf still separates U.S. agricultural productivity from that of the underdeveloped nations.

generation ago, described it vividly. It has not changed materially since that time.

There is no primogeniture in India as a rule, and when the peasant dies his land is subdivided among all his sons with the result that most holdings are infinitesimally small. In one district in the Punjab, following fragmentation through generations, 584 owners cultivate no less than 16,000 fields; in another, 12,800 acres are split into actually 63,000 holdings. Three-quarters of the holdings in India as a whole are under ten acres. In many parts of India the average holding is less than an acre.[1]

In part, this terrible situation is the result of divisive inheritance practices which Gunther mentions. In part, it is due to landlord systems in which peasants cannot legally own or accumulate their own land; in part, to the pressure of too many people on too little soil. There are many causes, with one result: agriculture suffers from a devastatingly low productivity brought about by grotesque man/land ratios.

These are, however, only the first links in a chain of causes for low agricultural productivity. Another consequence of these tiny plots is an inability to apply sufficient capital to the land. Mechanical binders and reapers, tractors and trucks are not only impossible to use efficiently in such tiny spaces, but they are costly beyond the reach of the subsistence farmer. Even fertilizer is too expensive: in much of Asia, animal dung is used to provide free fuel rather than returned to the soil to enrich it.

This paralyzing lack of capital is by no means confined to agriculture. It pervades the entire range of an underdeveloped economy. The whole industrial landscape of a Western economy is missing: no factories, no power lines, no machines, no

[1]*Inside Asia* (New York: Harper, 1939), p. 385.

paved roads meet the eye for mile upon mile as one travels through an underdeveloped continent. Indeed, to a pitiable extent, an underdeveloped land is one in which human and animal muscle power provide the energy with which production is carried on. In India in 1953, for instance, 65 percent of the total amount of productive energy in the nation was the product of straining man and beast. The amount of usable electrical power generated in *all of India* would not have sufficed to light up New York City. Of course, progress has been made since. But in 1973, energy consumption in India averaged 188 kg per capita (coal equivalent). By way of contrast, in Ireland it averaged 3,461 kg; in Canada, 11,237.

Social inertia

A lack of agricultural and industrial capital is not the only reason for low productivity. As we would expect in traditional societies, an endemic cause of low per capita output lies in prevailing social attitudes. Typically, the people of an underdeveloped economy have not *learned* the "economic" attitudes that foster rapid industrialization. Instead of technology-conscious farmers, they are tradition-bound peasants. Instead of disciplined workers, they are reluctant and untrained laborers. Instead of production-minded business people, they are trading-oriented merchants.

For example, in the 1960s Alvin Hansen reported from his observations in India:

Agricultural practices are controlled by custom and tradition. A villager is fearful of science. For many villagers, insecticide is taboo because all life is sacred. A new and improved seed is suspect. To try it is a gamble. Fertilizers, for example, are indeed a risk. . . . To adopt these untried methods might be to risk failure. And failure could mean starvation.

In similar vein, a UNESCO report told us:

In the least developed areas, the worker's attitude toward labour may entirely lack time perspective, let alone the concept of productive investment. For example, the day labourer in a rural area on his way to work, who finds a fish in the net he placed in the river the night before, is observed to return home, his needs being met. . . .

An equally crippling attitude is evinced by the upper classes, who look with scorn or disdain upon business or production-oriented careers, or who see in economic change a threat to their station in society. More than a decade ago, UNESCO reported that of the many students from the underdeveloped lands studying in the United States—the majority of whom come from the more privileged classes—only 4 percent were studying a problem fundamental to all their nations: agriculture. This has not changed over time.

All these attitudes give rise to a *social inertia* that poses a tremendous hurdle to economic development. A suspicious peasantry, fearful of change that might jeopardize the slim margin yielding them life, a work force unused to the rhythms of industrial production, a privileged class not interested in social change, all these are part of the obdurate handicaps to be overcome by an underdeveloped nation.

Further problems: population growth

Many of these problems resemble the premarket economies of antiquity. But in addition to this, the underdeveloped lands face an obstacle with which the economies of antiquity did *not* have to cope; a crushing rate of population increase that threatens to nullify their efforts to emerge from backward conditions.

Only a few figures are needed to make the point. Let us begin with our southern neighbor, Mexico. Today, Mexico has a population equal to that of New York State, Pennsylvania, New Jersey, and Connecticut. Thirty years from now, if Mexico's present rate of population increase continues, it will have as many people as the present population of these four states *plus* the rest of New England, *plus* the entire South Atlantic seaboard, *plus* the entire West Coast, *plus* Ohio, Indiana, Illinois, Michigan, and Wisconsin. Or take the Caribbean and Central American area. In some thirty years, at present growth rates, that small part of the globe will outnumber the entire population of the United States. South America, now 5 percent less populous than we, will be 200 percent larger than our present population. India could then number a billion souls.

We have already seen one result of the relentless proliferation of people in the fragmentation of landholdings. But the problem goes beyond mere fragmentation. Eugene Black, formerly president of the International Bank for Reconstruction and Development (the World Bank) has written that in India a population equivalent to that of all Great Britain has been squeezed out of any landholding whatsoever—even though it still dwells in rural areas. Consequently, population pressure generates massive and widespread rural poverty, pushing inhabitants from the countryside into the already overcrowded cities. Five hundred families a day move into Jakarta from the surrounding Javanese countryside, where population has reached the fantastic figure of 1,100 per square mile.

Even these tragic repercussions of population growth are but side effects. The main problem is that population

Anyone interested in development soon comes up against the formidable problems of population growth, and this quickly leads to the field of demography, the study of the behavior of populations. Demography is a fascinating and immensely important subject, which we cannot go into in this book, but we must take a moment to introduce the student to some of its elements.

Let us begin by looking at two imaginary countries, both having zero population growth. We will call them Westernland and Easternland because the facts they represent, although somewhat exaggerated, are approximated by conditions in the developed Western and the underdeveloped Eastern (and Southern) nations.

First consider Westernland. The demographic facts are simple. Of 2,000 population (50 percent women), all marry. Each couple has two children, 1 girl, 1 boy. None die. At age 26 the original population has reproduced itself, and a new cycle can begin with no increase in numbers.

Now Easternland. The original population is again 2,000. But only 900 marriages take place, owing to various restrictions of caste, taboos, illnesses, and so forth. This 900 marriages now produce 4.2 children each. This is lower than the number they would produce if some of the husbands and wives did not die before the years of child-bearing were finished. It is roughly the family size we find in many underdeveloped areas. However, of the 3,780 births, 880 die during the first year and 900 in the next 25 years—again, "age-specific" mortality rates closely corresponding with the facts of the poorer regions. Hence we

A PRIMER ON DEMOGRAPHY

reach a new generation, at age 26, that is only 2,000 strong, just as in the case of Westernland. *There is no population growth.*

	Western-land	Eastern-land
Population, age 26	2,000	2,000
Number of marriages	1,000	900
Total births	2,000	3,780
Infant deaths	0	880
Number surviving to age 1	2,000	2,900
Child and young adult deaths	0	900
Population, age 26	**2,000**	**2,000**

There is, however, an enormous potential for population growth in the frustrated fertility of Easternland. One hundred additional marriages could take place. The total number of children born to the 2,000 potential marriages would be 5,250 if neither adult died and if prevailing family size were achieved by all. If all infant, childhood, and young adult deaths were prevented, 1,780 additional marriages could result. In that case, the population at the end of 26 years would not be 2,000 but 5,250—a rate of increase reminding us of Central America.

Now two important demographic terms. *The net reproduction rate* tells us the number of daughters who will be born to 1,000 girl babies by the end of their child-bearing years, *assuming that existing fertility and mortality rates prevail*. In both Westernland and Easternland this is 1,000, or a net re-

production rate of 1.00. Each girl baby in each land will eventually be succeeded by one potential mother at age 26. *Gross reproduction rates* tell us the number of female offspring, *ignoring mortality and other wastage, such as failure to marry*. In Westernland it is also 1.00. In Easternland it is 2,625 (half of 5,250), or a rate of 2.625. *The difference between the two rates is therefore the measure of frustrated fertility in a population.*

The table shows us that a population in equilibrium, with zero population growth, can be big with potential increase. It also reveals the surprising number of factors that enter into population growth rates. Age at marriage is one: if that age were 20 instead of 26, the average family in Easternland would have over 6 people. It calls attention to celibacy as an element in the population equation, a factor of some importance in certain areas. It points out the role of premature death, both in limiting the size of families that will be achieved, and in winnowing out the number of survivors who will eventually become parents. And of course it highlights the all-important factor of desired or traditional family size in determining how large the rate of population growth will be. Clearly, the limitation of population growth is a good deal more complicated than just birth control, important as the latter is.

Anyone wishing to learn more about this crucially important subject might look into E. A. Wrigley, *Population and History* (New York: McGraw-Hill, 1969) from which this example has been taken. This is an engrossing and easily accessible book on a subject every economist should know something about.

growth adds more mouths almost as fast as the underdeveloped nations manage to add more food. They cancel out much economic progress by literally eating up the small surpluses that might serve as a springboard for faster future growth.

Ironically, this population "explosion" in the underdeveloped countries is a fairly recent phenomenon, attributable largely to the incursion of Western medicine and public health into the low income areas. Prior to World War II, the poorer countries held their population growth in check because death rates were nearly as high as birth rates. With insecticides and antibiotics, death rates have plunged dramatically. In Ceylon, for example, death rates dropped 40 percent in one year following the adoption of malaria control and other health measures. As death rates dropped in the underdeveloped areas, birth rates, for many reasons, continued high, despite efforts to introduce birth control. In the backward lands, children are not only a source of prestige and of household labor for the peasant family, but also the only possible source of "social security" for old age. The childless older couple could very well starve. As parents or grandparents, they are at least assured of a roof over their heads.

The population outlook

Is there a solution to this problem? The mood of demographers has swung between despair and cautious hope over the past decades. New birth control methods have, from time to time, offered the chance for dramatic breakthroughs. Poor birth control programs have repeatedly dashed these hopes.

Today most demographers expect the population explosion to continue for at least another generation. Part of the problem lies in the disproportionately large numbers of the population under age 15 in the poorer regions—young people who are themselves the result of the population flood. Even if each young woman who comes of child-bearing age were to adopt birth control, the ever larger number of such child-bearers will result in rapid population growth for another generation, despite a declining birth rate. And in all probability, the newly wed women of the next generation in most parts of the world will *not* practice birth control.

Thus the population "explosion" continues, even though the rate of increase is gradually tapering off. According to United Nations estimates, the world passed the 4 billion population mark in 1975, and population is growing at a rate that doubles roughly every 35 years. However, this global growth rate is a weighted average of much slower rates in Western countries (where zero population growth exists or is within easy reach) and still rapid rates in the underdeveloped areas.

The upshot of these considerations can be presented in one depressing statistic. Today the population of the backward areas constitutes about 70 percent of the world's total. In 25 years it will constitute 80 percent.

Nineteenth-century imperialism

This gives us a brief introduction to underdevelopment as it exists today. Before we turn to the problem of how this condition can be remedied, we must inquire into one more question. Why did not the market society, with all its economic dynamism, spread into the backward areas?

The answer is that the active economies of the European and American worlds *did* make contact with the underdeveloped regions, beginning with the great exploratory and commercial voyages of the fifteenth and sixteenth centuries. Until the nineteenth century, unfortunately, that contact was little more than mere adventure and plunder. And then, starting in the first half of that century and gaining momentum until World War I, came that scramble for territory we call the Age of Imperialism.

What was this imperialism? It was, in retrospect, a compound of many things: militarism, jingoism, a search for markets and for sources of cheap raw materials to feed growing industrial enterprises. Insofar as the colonial areas were concerned, however, the first impact of imperialism was not solely that of exploitation. On the contrary, the incursion of Western empires into the backward areas brought some advantages. It injected the heavy doses of industrial capital: rail lines, mines, plantation equipment. It brought law and order, often into areas in which the most despotic personal rule had previously been the order of the day. It introduced the ideas of the West, including, most importantly, the idea of freedom, which was eventually to rouse the backward nations against the invading West itself.

Yet if imperialism brought these positive and stimulating influences, it also exerted a peculiarly deforming impulse to the underdeveloped—indeed, then, totally underdeveloped—economies of the East and South. In the eyes of the imperialist nations, the colonies were viewed not as areas to be brought along in balanced development, but essentially as immense supply dumps to be attached to the mother countries' industrial economies. Malaya became a vast tin mine; Indonesia, a huge tea and rubber plantation; Arabia, an oil field. In other words, the direction of economic development was steadily pushed in the direction that most benefited the imperial owner, not the colonial peoples themselves.

The result today is that the typical underdeveloped nation has a badly lopsided economy, unable to supply itself with a wide variety of goods. It is thereby thrust into the international market with its one basic commodity. For instance, in South America we find that Venezuela is dependent on oil for some 90 percent of its exports; Colombia, on coffee for three-quarters of its exports; Chile, on copper for two-thirds of its foreign earnings; Honduras, on bananas for half of its foreign earnings. On the surface, this looks like a healthy specialization of trade. We shall shortly see why it may not be.

Economic lopsidedness was one unhappy consequence of imperialism. No less important for the future course of development in the colonial areas was a second decisive influence of the West: its failure to achieve political and psychological relationships of mutual respect with its colonial peoples. In part, this was no doubt traceable to an often frankly exploitative economic attitude, in which the colonials were relegated to second-class jobs with third-class pay, while a handful of Western whites formed an insulated and highly paid managerial clique. But it ran deeper than that. A terrible color line, a callous indifference to colonial aspirations, a patronizing and sometimes contemptuous view of "the natives" runs all through the history of imperialism. It has left as a bitter heritage not only an identification of capitalism with its worst practices, but a political and social wariness toward the West, a wariness that deeply affects the general orientation of the developing areas.

Imperialism today   What about imperialism today? Certainly it has changed. The naked power grabs are in the past, when imperialism often meant only the acquisition of territory that would look good on a map. In the past, also, are the seizures of raw materials on the unfair terms characteristic of mineral empires built in the late nineteenth century. Less prominent, as well, are attitudes of racial "superiority," so infuriating to peoples whose culture was often of far greater delicacy and discrimination than that of the West.

Thus, the nature of this imperialism is now changing, partly under the pressures exerted by a restive Third World, partly as a result of developments within the advanced nations themselves. The rise of the multinational corporation, for example, puts the problem of the economic relationship of advanced and backward countries in a new light. The backward nations are extremely wary of the power inherent in a giant U.S. or European corporation. Yet they also want some of the things the multinationals offer. Big multinationals pay higher wages, keep more honest books, provide better working conditions and fancier career opportunities, and bring in more technological expertise than do the domestic enterprises of the "host" nation.

The result is that the problem of imperialism in our day, at least so far as the United States is concerned, has taken an unexpected turn. On the economic side of the question, the danger now is as much that the big companies will bypass the backward nations as that they will dominate them.

Meanwhile, the political element of imperialism seems to be diminishing. The erstwhile capitalist empires of Germany, Belgium, Netherlands, England, Portugal have disappeared. What is left is a strong effort on the part of the United States to preserve its ideological and political influence, particularly in Latin America and Southeast Asia, but the debacle of the American Vietnam policy indicates that the prospects for a "successful" imperialism of this kind are limited, at best.

The Engineering of Development

Up to this point we have concentrated our attention mainly on the background of underdevelopment. Now we must ask a more forward-looking, more technically "economic" question: How can an underdeveloped nation emerge from its poverty?

From what we have learned, we know the basic answer to this question. To grow, an underdeveloped economy must build capital.

But how is a starving country able to build capital? When 80 percent of a country is scrabbling on the land for a bare subsistence, how can it divert its energies to building dams and roads, ditches and houses, railroad embankments and factories that, however indispensable for progress tomorrow, cannot be eaten today? If our postage-stamp farmers were to halt work on their tiny unproductive plots and go to work on a great project like, say, the Aswan Dam, who would feed them? Whence would come the necessary food to sustain these capital workers?

Building capital from saved labor   At first glance the situation seems hopeless. Still, when we look again at the underdeveloped lands, the prospect is not entirely bleak. In the first place, these economies have unemployed factors. In the second place, we find that a large number of the peasants who till the fields are not feeding themselves. They are, also, in a sense, taking food from one another's mouths.

As we have seen, the crowding of peasants on the land in these areas has resulted in a diminution of agricultural productivity far below that of the advanced countries. Hence the abundance of peasants working in the fields obscures the fact that *a smaller number of peasants, with little more equipment—perhaps even with no more equipment—could raise a total output just as large.* One observer wrote twenty years ago: "An experiment carried out near Cairo by the American College seems to suggest that the present output, or something closely approaching it, could be produced by about half the present rural population of Egypt." Here is an extreme case, but it still applies, to some degree, to nearly every underdeveloped land.

Now we begin to see an answer to the predicament of the underdeveloped societies. In nearly all of these societies, there exists a disguised and hidden surplus of labor which, if it were taken off the land, could be used to build capital. Most emphatically, this does not mean that the rural population should be literally moved, en masse, to the cities where there is already a hideous lump of indigestible unemployment. It means, rather, that the inefficient scale of agriculture conceals a reservoir of both labor and the food to feed that labor if it were elsewhere employed. By raising the productivity of the tillers of the soil, a work force can be made available for the building of roads and dams, while this "transfer" to capital building need not result in a diminution of agricultural output.

Saving output   This rationalization of agriculture is not the only requirement for growth. When agricultural productivity is enhanced by the creation of larger farms (or by improved techniques on existing farms), *part of the ensuing larger output per person must be saved*. In other words, peasants who remain on the soil cannot enjoy their enhanced productivity by raising their standard of living and eating up all their larger crops. Instead, the gain in output per cultivator must be siphoned off the farm. It must be "saved" by the peasant cultivators and shared with their formerly unproductive cousins, nephews, sons, and daughters who are now at work on capital-building projects. We do not expect hungry peasants to do this voluntarily. Rather, by taxation or exaction, the government of an underdeveloped land must arrange for this indispensable transfer. Thus in the early stages of a *successful* development program there is apt to be no visible rise in the individual peasants' food *consumption*, although there must be a rise in their food *production*. What is apt to be visible is a more or less efficient—and sometimes harsh—mechanism for assuring that some portion of this newly added productivity is not consumed on the farm but is made available to support the capital-building worker. This is a problem that caused the Russian planners such trouble in the early days of Soviet industrialization.

What we have just outlined is not, let us repeat, a formula for immediate action. In many underdeveloped lands, as we

---

ZERO MARGINAL PRODUCTIVITY?

The suggestion that output could be increased if there were fewer people working on the land implies that the "last" people working must have *negative* marginal productivities—that they must, in fact, duplicate the seemingly far-fetched example on p. 172, where the addition of still more workers actually causes output to drop.

Do they really have negative marginal productivities? There has been considerable discussion about this in the professional literature and quite extensive investigations in the field. When we look at a peasant family at work, it seems impossible to find a case where an extra pair of hands does not produce some increment to the crop. The difficulty arises from the fact that average productivities are so low—in part a *consequence* of low productivity.

To unscramble that sentence, as a result of the low average productivity of peasant workers, diets are meager, and men and women cannot work nearly as successfully as if they were well-fed. Thus, taking men off the farm may permit the remaining members of the household to eat a little more (they cannot eat a lot more, or they would eat up all their productivity gains), and the result of eating more may, in turn, enhance their productive ability. Food thus becomes a capital good. Eating is investment, in conditions of extreme poverty.

have seen, the countryside already crawls with unemployment, and to create, overnight, a large and efficient farming operation would create an intolerable social situation. We should think of the process we have just outlined as a long-term blueprint which covers the course of development over many years. It shows us that the process of development takes the form of a huge internal migration from agricultural pursuits, where labor is wasted, to industrial and other pursuits, where it can yield a net contribution to the nation's progress.

Problem of equipment

Capital-building is not just a matter of freeing hands and providing them with food. Peasant labor may construct roads, but it cannot, with its bare hands, build the trucks to run over the roads. It may throw up dams, but it cannot fashion the generators and power lines through which a dam can produce energy. In other words, what is needed to engineer the great ascent is not just a pool of labor. It is also a vast array of industrial equipment.

How is this equipment obtained? In an industrialized economy, by expanding the machine-tool—that is, the capital-equipment-building—subsector. But an underdeveloped economy does not have a capital-equipment-building sector and cannot take the time to create one. Consequently, *in the first stages of industrialization, before the nucleus of a self-contained industrial sector has been laid down, a backward nation must obtain its equipment from abroad.*

This it can do in one of three ways. (1) It can buy the equipment from an industrialized nation by the normal process of *foreign trade*. Libya, for example, can sell its oil and use the foreign currency it receives to purchase abroad the tractors, lathes, and industrial equipment it needs. (2) It can receive the equipment by *foreign investment* when a corporation in an advanced nation chooses to build in a backward area. This is the route by which the United States got much of its capital from Britain during the nineteenth century, and it is the means by which the underdeveloped nations themselves received capital during their colonial days. (3) It may receive the foreign exchange needed to buy industrial equipment as a result of a grant or a loan from another nation or from a United Nations agency such as the World Bank. That is, it can buy industrial equipment with *foreign aid*.

Foreign trade

Of these three avenues of industrialization, the most important is foreign trade. In 1974 the underdeveloped nations earned just over $100 billion from exports. By no means all of this was available for new capital goods, however. About $60 billion was needed for food and vital raw materials. Some $10 billion was needed to

656

pay interest on foreign debts. This left $30 billion for *all* manufactures, from pharmaceuticals and Mercedes Benzes to lathes, tractors, and jet aircraft.

A problem that has plagued the underdeveloped world in seeking to increase its trade earnings is that their lopsided economies have typically made them sellers of raw materials on the world market.

As sellers of raw commodities—usually only one raw commodity—they face a highly inelastic demand for their goods. Like the American farmer, when they produce a bumper crop, prices tend to fall precipitously, and demand does not rise proportionately. At the same time, the industrial materials they buy in exchange tend to be firm or to rise in price over the years.

Terms of trade

Thus the "terms of trade"—the actual *quid pro quo* of goods received against goods offered—have usually moved against the poorer nations, who have given more and more coffee for the same amount of machinery. In 1957 and 1958, when commodity prices took a particularly bad tumble, the poor nations actually lost more in purchasing power than the total amount of all foreign aid they received. In effect, they subsidized the advanced nations! As another example, it has been estimated that falling prices cost the African nations more, in the first two decades since World War II, than all foreign funds given, loaned, or invested there.

It is possible–we do not yet know– that tightening markets in resources may now reverse this trend. The last few years have seen enormous sums flowing into the coffers of mid-Eastern governments, many of whom may become lenders, not borrowers, on the international capital markets. If the world resource picture worsens, along the lines we sketched out in Chapter 4, the underdeveloped countries may find themselves the beneficiaries of inelastic demand curves, and the developed nations may be the ones complaining about the terms of world trade.

Third and fourth worlds

In fact, the example of OPEC (the Organization of Petroleum Exporting Countries) has raised the possibility that the underdeveloped "world" must now be considered as consisting of at least two subworlds. One consists of those nations with low per capita GNPs that possess the raw material resources, or in some cases the organizational skills, to give promise of a potential fairly rapid rise in per capita incomes. Iran, with its huge oil and copper deposits is such a country; Brazil, another; Mexico, perhaps a third.

Contrasting with this Third World is a Fourth, made up of those nations that seem at present to offer little or no hope for rapid growth. Bangladesh, Burma, Egypt, Ethiopia, India, and Pakistan are among these least hopeful nations whose aggregate population is well over one billion.

Even among many Third World nations (except for the oil producers), foreign exchange reserves are still very scarce, and the effort to increase them by exports is intense. One way that has commanded more and more attention is through the development of *commodity stabilization agreements*, not dissimilar to the programs that have long supported American farm prices. Recently, the Western nations have recognized the need for some such device if the underdeveloped countries are to be able to plan ahead with any assurance of stability.

Another possibility lies in the prospect of encouraging diversified exports from the underdeveloped nations—handicrafts, light manufactures, and others. The difficulty here is that these exports may compete with the domestic industry of the advanced nations: witness the problems of the American textile industry in the face of textile shipments from Hong Kong. No doubt a large source of potential earnings lies along this path, and it is likely to rise as the advanced nations gradually allow the backward countries more equal access to their own markets.

Private foreign investment   A second main avenue of capital accumulation for the backward nations is foreign investment. Indeed, before World War II, this was *the* source of their industrial wealth. Today, however, it is a much diminished avenue of assistance, for reasons we have learned in our exploration of the multinational corporation. The former capital-exporting nations are no longer eager to invest private funds in areas over which they have lost control and in which they fear to lose any new investments they might make. For reasons that we have discussed, many of the poorer nations view Western capitalism with ambivalence. They need capital, technology, and expertise; but the arrival of a branch of a powerful corporation run by faraway "headquarters" looks to them like another form of the domination they have just escaped. As a result, foreign investment is often hampered by restrictive legislation in the underdeveloped nations, even though it is badly needed.

In 1975, $21 billion of private capital was invested in the developing countries, but nearly all of it went to the higher income nations. Probably not much more than $3 billion went overseas as foreign investment into the poorest Fourth World nations.

Another difficulty is that Western corporations partially offset the growth-producing effects of their investments by draining profits out of the country. In the period 1950–1965, for example, the flow of income remitted from Latin America to the United States was $11.3 billion, three times larger than the flow of new capital into Latin America. In 1975, income of $4.1 billion was transmitted to the United States, and only $1.9 billion was sent back to Latin America. This pattern of economic flows should not be misinterpreted as implying that foreign investment is a "negative" influence: the plant and equipment that the West has sent abroad remains in the underdeveloped world, where it continues to enhance the productivity of labor, or perhaps to generate ex-

THE GREEN REVOLUTION

In the critical life-and-death race between mushrooming populations and recalcitrant nature, hopes have been buoyed by the Green Revolution, the name given to efforts to discover high-yielding strains of rice and wheat. Working in field laboratories in Mexico and elsewhere, scientists of the Rockefeller Institute have developed a number of promising new varieties, including the famous IR-8 rice. Some of these new varieties allow two and even three crops to be grown where formerly only one was harvested.

The Green Revolution has been a considerable scientific triumph, but its impact on development has been less spectacular. For one thing, the new strains require vast amounts of fertilizer and water, both in short supply in those areas of the world where present yields are lowest. Second, because the seeds require complementary inputs of fertilizers or tubewell irrigation ditches, the new grains are mainly introduced by the richer peasants. In lands where transportation facilities are lacking, their bumper crops may not find a ready market, and local prices may fall, to the despair of the poor peasant whose output has not risen. Thus the Green Revolution may actually contribute to the poverty of the lowest classes.

These social repercussions, coupled with the vast costs needed to introduce the new seeds on a wide basis, have tempered the first rosy expectations of the food scientists. Nonetheless, the Green Revolution is vital in enabling the world to buy a little precious time while birth control efforts and new production and distribution techniques are worked out.

ports. But the *earnings* on this capital are not typically plowed back into still more capital goods, so that their potential growth-producing effect is far from realized.

The crucial avenue of aid

These considerations enable us to understand the special importance that attaches to the third channel of capital accumulation: foreign aid. Surprisingly, perhaps, in the light of the attention it attracts, foreign aid is not a very large figure. International assistance, from *all* individual nations and from the UN and its agencies, ran at a rate of about $6 billion per year throughout the 1960s and rose to $14 billion only after the OPEC nations devoted considerable sums from their oil earnings for development purposes.

Even $14 billion is an insignificant figure compared with the total GNP of the underdeveloped world. But it is a sizeable fraction—perhaps as much as 15 percent—of the gross investment of South Asia, and more than that in poorest Africa.

In addition, foreign aid plays a number of subsidiary roles not performed by private investment. It is the source of much technical assistance, which allows the underdeveloped countries to overcome handicaps imposed by their lack of skilled personnel. Aid also provides food, often desperately needed in times of crop failure—the United States food program has been a major source of famine relief to Asia and Africa. In addition, foreign aid is sometimes given in "soft" loans repayable in the currency of the developing nation rather than in scarce hard currencies. Such loans are unobtainable from private lenders.

All these forms of international assistance make possible the accumulation of industrial capital much faster than could

be accomplished solely as a result of the backward lands' export efforts or their ability to attract foreign private capital.* To be sure, an increase in foreign earnings or in private capital imports would have equally powerful effects on growth. But we have seen the difficulties in the way of rapidly increasing the receipts from these sources. For the near future, foreign aid represents the most effective channel for *quickly* raising the amount of industrial capital which the underdeveloped nations must obtain.

Economic possibilities for growth

Against these handicaps, can the underdeveloped nations grow? Can the terrible conditions of poverty be relegated to the past? Economic analysis allows us to ask these questions systematically, for growth depends on the interplay of three variables.

1. **The rate of investment that an underdeveloped nation can generate**

As we know, this depends on the proportion of current effort that it can devote to capital-creating activity. In turn, the rate of saving, the success in attracting foreign capital, the volume of foreign aid—all add to this critical fraction of effort on which growth hinges.

2. **Productivity of the new capital**

The saving that goes into new capital eventually results in higher output. But not all capital boosts output by an equal amount. A million-dollar steel mill, for

*Note "make possible." There is some disturbing evidence that foreign aid may displace domestic saving, so that an underdeveloped country receiving aid may relax its own efforts to generate capital. Much depends on the political will of the recipient country.

example, will have an impact on GNP very different from that of a million-dollar investment in schools. In the short run, the mill may yield a higher return of output per unit of capital investment; in the long run, the school may have the edge. But in any event, the effect on output will depend not merely on the amount of investment, but on the marginal capital-output ratio of the particular form of investment chosen.

3.   Population growth

Here, as we know, is the negative factor. If growth is to be achieved, output must rise faster than population. Otherwise, per capita output will be falling or static, despite seemingly large rates of overall growth.

The critical balance   With these basic variables, is growth a possibility for the backward lands? We can see that if investment were 10 percent of GNP and if each dollar of new investment gave rise to a third of a dollar of additional output,* a 10 percent rate of capital formation would yield a 3.3 percent rate of growth of output (10 percent × one-third). This is about equal to population growth rates in the nations with the higest rates of population income.

The trouble is that most of the backward nations, especially in the Fourth World, have investment rates that are closer to 5 than to 10 percent of GNP. In that case, even with a marginal capital-output ratio of one-half, growth rates would not be enough to begin a sustained climb against a population growth of 2.5 percent (5 percent × ½ = 2.5 percent). And this gloomy calculation is made

gloomier still when we confront the fact that the labor force is rising faster than the population as a whole, as vast numbers of children become vast numbers of workers. In the 1960s in Latin America it was estimated that at least 25 *percent* of the working-age population was unemployed. In the decade since then, unemployment as a percent of the labor force seems to have increased in virtually every underdeveloped country.

The economic outlook   No one can confront these economic realities and make optimistic forecasts for the developing countries. A few of these nations may fare well, even better than expected a few years ago. The oil-rich Arab states, perhaps the mineral producers, may grow at rapid rates.

Not so the remaining vast majority. As Nathan Keyfitz, a noted demographer, has written: "Currently 15 million people join the middle class [in all nations of the world] each year and 60 million join the poor. Even if the middle class increment could rise to 20 million per year, the poor would be increasing by 80 million per year at the end of the century. Therein lies the harm of rapid population growth."*

Social and political problems   But this is not the end of our analysis, for it is impossible to think of development only in terms of economics. As in the case of Western growth, *economic development is nothing less than the modernization of an entire society.* When we talk of building capital or redirecting agriculture, we must not imagine that this entails only the addition of machines and farm equipment

---

*This seems to be *roughly* what the marginal capital-output ratio of new investment in the underdeveloped areas may be.

*"World Resources and the World Middle Class," *Scientific American* (July 1976), pp. 33–34.

to a peasant society. It requires the conversion of a peasant society into another kind of society. It means a change in the whole tenor of life, in the expectations and motivations, the environment of daily existence itself.

We can easily anticipate the changes that economic development imposes on a society. Illiterate peasants must be made into literate farmers. Dispirited urban slum-dwellers must be made into disciplined factory workers. Old and powerful social classes, which have for generations, derived their wealth from feudal land tenure, must be deprived of their vested rights. New managerial attitudes must be implanted in new elites. Above all, the profligate generation of life, conceived in dark huts as the only solace available to a crushed humanity, must give way to a responsible and deliberate creation of children as the chosen heirs to a better future.

These changes will *in time* be facilitated by the realization of development itself. A growing industrial environment breeds industrial ways. The gradual realization of economic improvement brings about attitudes that will themselves accelerate economic growth. A slowly rising standard of living is likely to quicken the spread of birth control, as it did in the West.

All these changes, as we have said, may take place in time. But it is time itself that is so critically lacking. The changes must begin to take place now—today—so that the process of development can gain an initial momentum. Given the momentum of population growth, the transition from a backward, tradition-bound way of life to a modern and dynamic one cannot be allowed to mature at its own slow pace. Only an enormous effort can inaugurate, much less shorten, the transition from the past into the future.

Collectivism and underdevelopment

These sobering considerations converge in one main direction. They alert us to the fact that *in the great transformation of the underdeveloped areas, the market mechanism is apt to play a much smaller role than in the comparable transformation of the West during the industrial revolution.*

When the industrial revolution came into being in the West, it exploded within a historic situation in which market institutions, actions, customs had already become the dominant form of economic organization. None of this true in the underdeveloped nations today. Rather than having their transition to a market society behind them, many of those nations must leap overnight from essentially tradition-bound and archaic relationships to commercialized and industrialized ones. Many of them are not even fully monetized economies. None of them have the network of institutions—and behind that, the network of "economic" motivations—on which a market society is built.

Hence it is not difficult to foresee that the guiding force of development is apt to be tilted in the direction of planning. Regardless of the importance of private enterprise in carrying out the individual projects of development, the driving and organizing force of economic growth will have to be principally lodged with the government.

Political implications

But the outlook indicates more than a growth of economic command. Implicit also in the harsh demands of industrialization is the need for strong political leadership, not only to initiate and guide the course of development, but to *make it stick*. For it is not only wrong, but dangerously wrong, to picture

CHINESE ECONOMICS

Until very recently, information about the Chinese economy percolated into the United States only through roundabout sources, and our knowledge of how the Chinese economy operated was scanty indeed.* In the past few years, however, a number of American economists have been invited to visit China. One of them, David Gordon, has written this brief report of his impressions.

The Chinese have begun the long road toward industrialization. As many have reported in the American press during the recent burst of interest about China, the economy has made amazing progress in raising the basic standard of living of the entire population. Chinese planners now feel that agricultural production has grown rapidly enough to permit the diversion of substantial resources into industrial development. They are increasing the levels of investment in heavy industry, and they are also stepping up production in their key light industries. (Many Chinese are now able to buy the three most desired consumer durables: bicycles, sewing machines, and transistor radios.)

Although many other underdeveloped economies have begun to industrialize at analogous points in their economic histories, the Chinese industrial development strategy has some unique and unprecedented features. The Cultural Revolution (1966–1968) had a profound effect on that

strategy. It involved some fundamental struggles over power and ideology, eventually resolved through the consolidation of Chairman Mao Tse-tung's power and the clarification of the country's ideological direction. The forces which triumphed during the Cultural Revolution were waging ideological battle against Liu Shao-chi, Mao's former heir apparent and leading party official. They accused Liu Shao-chi of "revisionism" and of being a "capitalist-roader." In particular, they argued that Liu Shao-chi's economic development policies would lead China down the same economic paths already traveled by both the Western capitalist countries and the developed socialist nations like Russia. (The Chinese accuse the Russians of having abandoned socialism; they say the Soviet Union is the leading model of "state capitalism," or "bureaucratic capitalism.")

The problem with both these versions of economic development, according to the anti-Liu faction, is that the economy develops unevenly. The most advanced sectors become more advanced. Those workers with the greatest skills become even more skilled. Organizations become ever

more hierarchical and bureaucratic. In the pursuit of more and more economic growth, justified by arguments of efficiency, private capitalism and "state capitalism" both reinforce inequalities in the already uneven patterns of development.

Particularly since the rout of the Liu forces during the Cultural Revolution, the Chinese have been intensifying their efforts to promote a path of industrial development aimed at overcoming the inequalities inherited from history. They are trying to ensure that all regions and all people share both in the process and the fruits of increasing industrialization. For example, some regions in the country inherited a considerable industrial capacity (they had automobile and tractor factories in Shanghai). By conventional Western economic criteria, it would probably be more efficient to build on that existing capacity. Instead, the Chinese are encouraging the dispersion of industrial investment throughout the country. Four-fifths of the people live in the country; therefore, much of the new industrial building is occurring in rural areas where the bulk of the people live. Since many of these people have neither industrial skills nor large stocks of capital for investment, the scale of industry will initially be quite small and the technology quite primitive.

We saw a living, breathing, fuming

*One of the best sources of information is still a book by Barry Richman, a Canadian economist, Industrial Society in China (New York: Random House, 1969).

economic development as a long, invigorating climb from achievement to achievement. On the contrary, it is better imagined as a gigantic social and political earthquake. Eugene Black, ex-president of the World Bank, soberly pointed out that we delude ourselves with buoyant phrases such as "the revolution of rising expectations" when we describe the process—rather than the prospect—of development. To many of the people involved in the bewildering transformations of development,

the revolution is apt to be marked by a loss of traditional expectations, by a new awareness of deprivation, a new experience of frustration. For decades, perhaps generations, a developing nation must plow back its surplus into the ugly and unenjoyable shapes of lathes and drills, conveyor belts and factory smokestacks. Some change toward betterment is not ruled out, particularly in health, basic diet, and education; but beyond this first great step, material improvement in every-

illustration of these economic policies in rural Tsunhua County in the province of T'ang-shan (to the east of Peking). Following the new economic guidelines, the county government had begun to develop its own, admittedly crude, heavy industries. In 1970 the county began to build an iron and steel factory. Relying on what everyone in China calls "indigenous methods," the inexperienced local workers designed and built the iron and steel plant themselves. The plant was financed from the county's own "accumulation fund," earned from profits in other county-sponsored production. Almost 400 workers are now employed in the factory.

The plant looked primitive indeed. It comprised a series of open-air sheds, all small. The furnaces were tiny. The ores were conveyed almost entirely by horse-drawn carts. Molten steel was drawn and processed through simple machines that looked like clothes wringers; the long red-hot metal bars were pulled through with simple iron tongs. As the bars grew longer and longer, they would whip and lash as they came through the machine. The workers, wearing only rubber gloves for protection, would dodge the glowing metal like smaller Muhammad Alis, dancing nimbly like butterflies to escape its sting.

One of the members of our group was an industrial economist, schooled in American corporate technological perspectives. After we finished touring the plant, he whispered that he thought the plant was a joke. "What a

waste of money," he said, "to build such a primitive plant when you have better technologies available."

Many of us thought otherwise. There are many reasons why that little iron and steel plant made a great deal of sense. Building local industry on a small scale means that many peasants who would otherwise never leave their rural pursuits will participate in the process of industrialization. The fact that local people designed and built the plant gives them pride in its products and provides a strong incentive for them to work as hard as they can in production. Having involved themselves this far, they have started expanding their economic horizons. In order to be completely self-reliant in iron and steel production, for instance, they have begun exploring for iron ore in the local hills, hoping to find additional deposits that they could mine themselves. They have found 23 different ores, including iron, which they are now extracting. Building on a small scale has also taken advantage of crude scrap materials that could be incorporated into indigenous plant designs but could not possibly be built into more technologically advanced factory structures. And the local base of production has guaranteed, to a certain extent, that the products of their heavy industry are oriented to their own needs.

Gordon's comments point up the important difference between the criteria of "Western" economics and those of the Chinese. The Chinese have established as basic goals the

development of self-reliant communities, with as diverse a range of occupations as possible, rather than industrial complexes that achieve high standards of economic efficiency at the cost of the human problems associated with extreme regional and occupational specialization. In our terms, they are deliberately trading off a certain amount of efficiency for the attainment of social goals.

It should be added, of course, that this emphasis on rural diversification also adds an element of safety against military attack and may have an even more down-to-earth justification in saving the transportation costs that would be involved in moving men and materials to massive industrial centers. Nonetheless, with all these considerations, there is no doubt that the Chinese are attempting to modernize in a new way—a way that seeks to avoid the bureaucratic characteristics of big business and oversized ministries.

What remains to be seen is whether small-scale rural-based industry can achieve *enough* efficiency to allow China to develop rapidly enough to satisfy its leaders and its people. We will have to wait several years to find that out. If the Chinese succeed, they may be a pattern of development for much of the remainder of the underdeveloped world, now in a schizophrenic state of mind—eager to begin the "Western" industrialization process and yet fearful of the social costs that progress has imposed on the West.

day living will not—cannot—materialize quickly.

As a consequence, many of the policies and programs required for development, rather than being eagerly accepted by all levels of society, are apt to be resisted. Tax reform, land reform, the curtailment of luxury consumption are virtually certain to be opposed by the old order. In addition, as the long march begins, latent resentments of the poorer classes are likely to become mobilized; the

underdog wakens to his lowly position. Even if his lot improves, he may well feel a new fury if his *relative* well-being is impaired.

Social stresses   These considerations enable us to understand how social tensions and economic standards can rise at the same time. And this prospect, in turn, enables us to appreciate the fearful demands on political leadership, which must provide impetus, inspiration, and, if necessary, discipline to keep the great ascent in motion. The strains of the early industrial revolution in England, with its widening chasm between the proletariat and capitalist, are not to be forgotten when we project the likely course of affairs in the developing nations.

In the politically immature and labile areas of the underdeveloped world, this exercise of leadership typically assumes the form of "strong-man" government. In large part, this is only the perpetuation of age-old tendencies in these areas; but in the special environment of development, a new source of encouragement for dictatorial government arises from the exigencies of the economic process itself. Powerful, even ruthless government may be needed, not only to begin the development process, but to cope with the strains of a *successful* development program.

It is not surprising, then, that the political map reveals the presence of authoritarian governments in many developing nations today. The communist areas aside, we find more or less authoritarian rule in Egypt, Pakistan, Burma, South Korea, Indonesia, India, and a succession of South American junta governments. From country to country, the severity and ideological coloring of these governments varies. Yet in all of them we find that the problems of economic development provide a large rationale for the tightening of political control. At least in the arduous early stages of growth, some form of political command seems as integral to economic development as the accumulation of capital itself.

The ecological problem

To this endless list of problems one last one must now be added. As we have seen in Chapter 4, there may

well be limits to the amount of industrialization the planet can sustain. These limits are likely to impose a ceiling on material output in the underdeveloped areas that would leave them far below Western standards.

This problem reinforces the political argument above. For it is clear that the free play of market forces, *insofar as these are permitted to develop along the lines of traditional capitalism*, would lead rapidly to an ecological impasse. Instead, the development of the backward nations, once an initial momentum has been attained, will have to be planned to economize on materials and production to a degree unknown in the West. The absurd waste of resources involved in providing transportation through the proliferation of private automobiles instead of public conveyances; the encouragement of individual ownership of washing machines and television sets and domestic conveniences—the very center of the Western ideal of a "high standard of living"—will probably be impossible to duplicate on a global scale.

What will be required in their place is a new pattern of *public consumption,* perhaps even a wholly new conception of what is meant by an advanced society. All this will be required not as a matter of ideological preference, but as one of long-run necessity. The ecological barriers of resource availability and the absorption capacity of the earth pose truly staggering problems for the underdeveloped nations, once they manage to escape from the stagnation that still characterizes most of them. No one knows how these constraints of nature will be translated into the realities of social life, but it is doubtful that the relatively laissez-faire attitudes of Western capitalism will not be adequate to the task.

FOCUS

This chapter has one obvious purpose: to make you thoughtful about the problems facing the underdeveloped world. That requires two learning efforts. First, you must begin to appreciate the empirical realities of underdevelopment. This means a comprehension of the population problem, the extent and effects of poverty, the sheer statistical magnitudes of the Third and Fourth Worlds. An essential first step toward becoming knowledgeable about the development problem is an awareness of the size of this problem. Our coming "An extra word" may help here.

Second, you should begin to understand the basic elements in the process of development. This means understanding the interplay of the three main variables we discuss on pages 659–60. It means, as well, understanding the relative importance of, and the problems associated with, exports, foreign investment, and foreign aid—the main avenues for the accumulation of capital from abroad. And not least, it means becoming aware of the inextricable manner in which the process that we call economic development is also a process of social change and political will.

WORDS AND CONCEPTS YOU SHOULD KNOW

Population "explosion," 650–52
Demography, 651
Imperialism, 652–54
Building capital, 654–56
Foreign trade, 656–57
Terms of trade, 657

Third and Fourth Worlds, 657
Private foreign investment, 658
Green revolution, 658 (box)
Foreign aid, 659
Determinants of growth, 659–60

QUESTIONS

1. In what ways do you think underdeveloped countries are different from the American Colonies in the mid-1600s? Think of literacy, attitudes toward work and thrift, and other such factors. What about the relationship to more advanced nations in each case?

2. Why do you think it is so difficult to change social attitudes at the lowest levels of society? At the upper levels? Are there different reasons for social inertia at different stations in society?

3. Does the United States have a population problem? Will population growth here affect economic or social aspects of life more? Do you think we should adopt an American population control policy? What sort of policy?

4. Many economists have suggested that all advanced nations should give about 1 percent of their GNP for foreign aid. In the U.S., that would mean a foreign aid appropriation of $15 billion. Actually we appropriate about $3 billion. Do you think it would be practicable to suggest a 1 percent levy? How would the country feel about such a program?

5. What are the main variables in determining whether or not growth will be self-sustaining? If net investment were 8 percent of GNP and the capital output ratio were ¼, could a nation grow if its rate of population increase were 2¼ percent? What changes could initiate growth?

6. What do you think is the likelihood of the appearance of strong-arm governments and collectivist economies in the underdeveloped world? For the appearance of effective democratic governments? For capitalist economies? Socialist ones? Is it possible to make predictions or judgments in these matters that do not accord with your personal preferences?

7. If you had to plan the 50-year development of a nation like India, and if you knew that it would be essential to economize on the production and consumption of minerals, how would you suggest that patterns of consumption be changed to effect major resource savings? To what extent would such changes impose further changes in the pattern of social life?

Underdevelopment

It is difficult to compress the problem of underdevelopment into one chapter. It deserves book-length treatment, which we cannot give it in an introductory text. But here is a small array of charts and tables* that will give you more perspective on underdevelopment. We have presented them without comment, because they speak for themselves. They will repay a few minutes of your time now and many hours of reflection afterward:

Table 42 · 2 Populations having insufficient protein/energy supply, 1970

	Total population (millions)	Population with insufficient protein/energy supply	
		Millions	Percent
Developed countries*	1,072	28	3
Developing countries†	1,755	434	25
Latin America	284	36	13
Africa	279	67	24
Near East	171	30	18
Far East	1,021	301	30
World†	2,827	462	16

NOTE: The table is based on the daily per capita supply of grams of protein and kilocalories contained in the food locally available.
*Europe, North America, U.S.S.R., and Japan.
†Excluding Asian centrally planned economies.

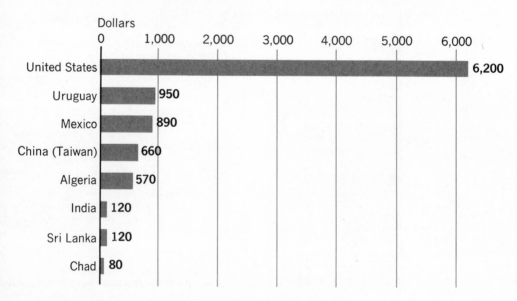

FIG. 42 · 1   Per capita GNP, 1973

*From Overseas Development Council, The U.S. and World Development (New York: Praeger, 1976).

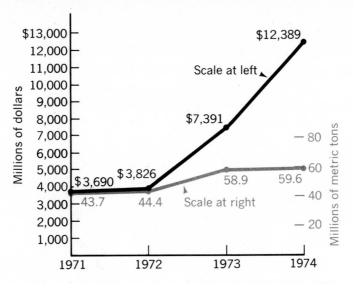

FIG. 42 · 2 Developing-country imports of grains, 1971–1974

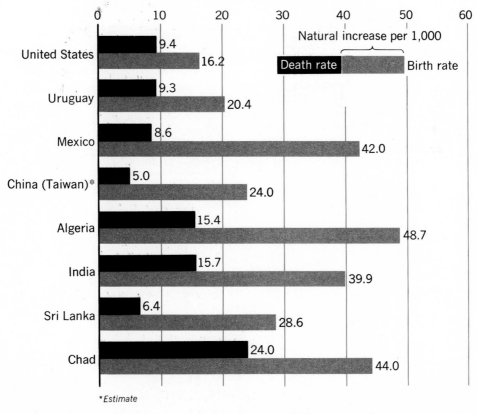

FIG. 42 · 3 Death and birth rates per 1,000 (1970–1975 average)

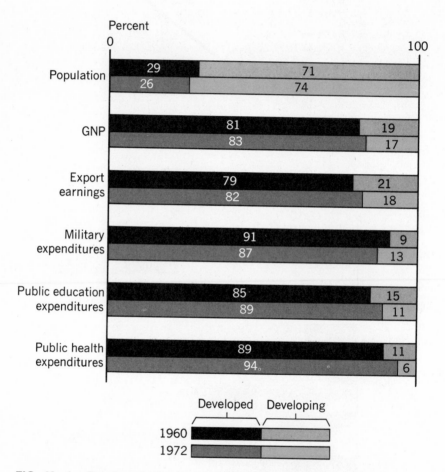

FIG. 42 · 4   Relative shares of selected resources and expenditures of developed and developing countries, 1972 (percentages)

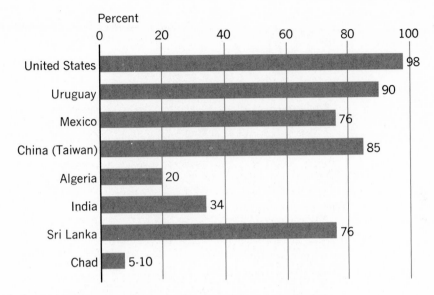

FIG. 42 · 5   Literacy (percentages)

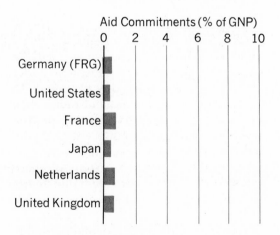

FIG. 42 · 6   Per capita aid commitments,
developed countries, 1974

From market to planning

The beginning of worldwide economic development is a genuine watershed in human history. An active and dynamic form of economic life, until recently the distinctive characteristic of the industrial West, is about to be generalized over the face of the globe. The process of diffusion will take generations, but it marks a profound, irreversible, and truly historic alteration in the economic condition of man.

Yet, if the process of economic growth is henceforth to be carried out on a global scale, it is also clear that there will be significant change in the auspices under which this process is likely to unfold. As we have seen, it is command rather than the market system which is in the ascendant as the driving force in the underdeveloped regions. And when we combine the geographic extent of these regions with those where communism has become firmly entrenched, it seems that command now bids fair to become *the* dominant means of organizing economic activity on this planet, as tradition was, not very long ago.

But again there is a difference. During the centuries when tradition held sway over most of the world, the economies run by the market system were the locus of

43

progress and motion. Today one cannot with assurance say the same; nor will we be able to, in the future, for a preeminent motive of the rising economies of command is to *displace* the market societies as the source of the world's economic vitality.

Does this mean that economic history now writes finis to the market system? Does it mean that the market, as a means of solving the economic problem, is about to be relegated to the museum of economic antiquities or at best limited to the confines of North America, Western Europe, and Japan? The question brings to a focus our continuing concern with the market system. Let us attempt in these last pages to appraise its prospects.

Stages of Economic Development

We might well begin an appraisal by taking a last survey of the array of economic systems that mark our times. It is, at first glance, an extraordinary assortment: we find, in this third quarter of the twentieth century, a spectrum of economic organization that represents virtually every stage in economic history, from the earliest and most primitive. But at second look, a significant pattern can be seen within this seemingly disordered assemblage. The few remaining wholly traditional economies, such as those of the South Seas or tribal Africa, have not yet begun to move into the mainstream of economic development. A much larger group of underdeveloped nations, in which institutions of economic command are now rising amid a still traditional environment, have just commenced their development efforts and are now coping with the initial problems preparatory to eventual all-out industrialization. Going yet further along we

find the economies of iron command, such as China and to a lesser extent Russia. Here we find national communities that are (or recently were) wrestling with the gigantic task of rapid massive modernization. Finally, we pass to the market economies of the West, to encounter societies with their developmental days behind them, now concerned with the operation of high-consumption economic systems.

The categorization suggests a very important general conclusion. **The economic structures of nations today bear an integral relation with their stage of economic development.** Acts of foreign intervention aside, the choice of command or market systems is not just the outcome of political considerations or ideologies and preferences. It is also, and perhaps primarily, the result of functional requirements that are very different at different levels of economic achievement.

Inception of growth
We have already noted this connection in our discussion of the underdeveloped areas. Now, however, we can place what we have learned into a wider frame of reference. For if we compare the trend of events in the underdeveloped economies with the "equivalent" stage of development in Western history, we see a significant point of resemblance between the two. The emergence of command in the development-minded countries today has a parallel in the mercantile era, when the Western nations also received a powerful impetus toward industrialization under the organizing influence of the "industry-minded" governments of the seventeenth and early eighteenth centuries.

Thereafter, to be sure, the resemblance ceases. In the West, following the first push of mercantilism, it was the market mechanism that provided the main directive force for growth; in the underdeveloped lands, as we have seen, this influence is likely to be preempted to a much larger extent by political and economic command.

Present vs. past   Three main reasons lie behind this divergence of paths. *First, the underdeveloped areas today start from a lower level of preparedness* than did the West in the seventeenth and eighteenth centuries. Not only have the actual institutions of the market not yet appeared in many backward lands, but the whole process of acculturation has failed to duplicate that of the West. In many ways—not all of them economic—the West was "ready" for economic development. A similar readiness is not in evidence in the majority of the backward lands today, with the result that development, far from evincing itself as a spontaneous process, comes about as the result of enforced and imposed change.

Second, the *West was able to mount its development effort in leisurely tempo.* This is not to say that its rate of growth was slow or that strong pressures did not weigh upon many Western countries, arousing within them feelings of dissatisfaction with their progress. Yet the situation was unlike that of the backward areas today. Here immense pressures, both of population growth and of political impatience, create an overwhelming need and desire for speed. As a result, the process of growth is not allowed to mature quietly in the background of history, as it did for much of the West, but has been placed at the very center of political and social attention.

Finally, the underdeveloped countries, who suffer from so many handicaps in comparison with the developmental days of the West, enjoy one not inconsiderable advantage. Because they are in the rear guard rather than the vanguard of history, they know where they are going. In a manner denied to the West, underdeveloped countries can see ahead of them the goal they seek to reach. They do not wish to reach this goal, however, by retreading the painful and laborious path marked out by the West. Rather, they intend to shortcut it, to move directly to their chosen destination by utilizing the mechanisms of command to bring about the great alterations that must be made.

Can economic command significantly compress and accelerate the growth process? The remarkable performance of the Soviet Union suggests that it can. In 1920 Russia was but a minor figure in the economic councils of the world. Today it is a country whose economic achievements bear comparison with those of the United States.

The case of China is less clearcut. Until the famine disaster of 1959–1960, Chinese economic growth was double or triple that of India; since then, perhaps because of the convulsions of the Cultural Revolution, its record is less easy to appraise. It has probably grown more rapidly than India in *quantitative terms;* but by the reports of all observers, its *qualitative* improvements in health, education, and welfare are strikingly better than those of India.

It is no doubt wise not to exaggerate the advantages of a command system. If it holds the potential for an all-out attack on backwardness, it also contains the possibilities of substantial failure, as in the disappointments of the planned Cuban economy. The mere existence of a will to plan is no guarantee that the plans will be well drawn or well carried out or reasonably well obeyed. Nonetheless, these caveats must be set against the dismal record of economies that continue to wallow in the doldrums of tradition or that undertake the arduous transition into modernity under the inadequate stimulus of half-hearted regimes and half-formed market systems.

Planning and Its Problems

What are the advantages, what are the problems of planning? The subject is large enough to fill many books, and this short chapter will not attempt to discuss the full economics of planning. But a few general remarks may serve as an introduction to the subject.

How is planning carried out? The question goes to the heart of the matter, for all planned economies have found their central difficulty in going from the vision of a general objective to the actual attainment of that objective in fact. It is one thing to plan for 6 percent growth, another to issue the directives to bring forth just the right amounts of (quite literally) hundreds of thousands of items, so that 6 percent growth will result.

Soviet planning In the Soviet Union this complicated planning mechanism is carried out in successive stages. The overall objectives are originally formulated by the Gosplan, the State Planning Agency. The long-term overall plan is then broken down into shorter one-year plans. These one-year plans, specifying the output of major sectors of industry, are then transmitted to various government ministries concerned with, for example, steel production, transportation, lumbering, and so forth. In turn, the ministries refer the one-year plans further down the line to the heads of large industrial plants, to experts and advisers, and so on. At each stage, the overall plan is thus unraveled into its subsidiary components, until finally the threads have been traced as far back as feasible along the productive process—typically, to the officials in charge of actual factory operations. The factory manager of, for instance, a coking operation is given a planned objective for the next year, specifying the output needed from his plant. He confers with his production engineers, considers the condition of his machinery, the availability of his labor force, and then transmits his requirements for meeting the objective back upward along the hierarchy. In this way, just as "demand" is transmitted downward along the chain of command, the exigencies of "supply" flow back upward, culminating ultimately in the top command of the planning authority (the Gosplan) itself.

Success indicators The coordination and integration of these plans is a tremendously complicated task. Recently the Soviets adopted techniques of input-output analysis (see pp. 378–79), which have considerably simplified the problem. Even with input-output, however, the process is bureaucratic, cumbersome, slow, and mistake-prone. A Russian factory manager has very little leeway in what he produces or the combination of factors that he uses for production. Both inputs and outputs are carefully specified for him in his plan. What the manager *is* supposed to do is to beat the plan, by "overproducing" the items that have been assigned to his plant. Indeed, from 30 to 50 percent of a manager's pay will depend on bonuses tied directly to his "overfulfillment" of the plan, so that he has a very great personal incentive to exceed the output "success indicators" set for him.

Official literature of the Communist movement gives little guidance for running a socialist society. Marx's *Das Kapital,* the seminal work of communism, was entirely devoted to a study of capitalism; and in those few essays in which Marx looked to the future, his gaze rarely traveled beyond the watershed of the revolutionary act itself. With the achievement of the revolution, Marx thought, a temporary regime known as "the dictatorship of the proletariat" would take over the transition from capitalism to socialism, and thereafter a "planned socialist economy" would emerge as the first step toward a still less specified "communism."

What is the difference between *socialism* and *communism*? In the West, *socialism* implies an adherence to democratic political mechanisms, whereas *communism* does not. But within the socialist bloc there is another interesting difference of definition. Socialism there represents a stage of development in which it is still necessary to use "bourgeois" incentives in order to make the economy function; that is, people must be paid in proportion to the "value" of their work. Under communism, a new form of human society will presumably have been achieved in which these selfish incentives will no longer be needed. Then will come the time when society will be able to put into effect Karl Marx's famous description of communism: "From each according to his ability; to each according to his need."

In a true communist economy—the final terminus of economic evolution according to Marx—there were hints that the necessary but humdrum tasks of production and distribution would take place by the voluntary cooperation of all citizens, and society would turn its serious attention to matters of cultural and humanistic importance. Indeed, in a famous passage in *State and Revolution,* Lenin described the activities of administering a socialist state as having been "*simplified* by capitalism to the utmost, till they have become the extraordinarily simple operations of watching, recording, and issuing receipts, within the reach of anybody who can read and who knows the first four rules of arithmetic."

Many of the problems of early So-

PLANNING UNDER LENIN AND STALIN

viet history sprang from the total absence, on the part of its rulers, of any comprehension of the staggering difficulties of planning in fact rather than in thought. The initial Soviet attempt to run the economy was a disastrous failure. Under inept management (and often cavalier disregard of "bourgeois" concerns with factory management), industrial output declined precipitously; by 1920 it had fallen to *14 percent* of prewar levels. As goods available to the peasants became scarcer, the peasants, themselves, were less and less willing to acquiesce in giving up food to the cities. The result was a wild inflation followed by a degeneration into an economy of semibarter. For a while, toward the end of 1920, the system threatened to break down completely.

To forestall the impending collapse, in 1921 Lenin instituted a New Economic Policy, the so-called NEP. This was a return toward a market system and a partial reconstitution of actual capitalism. Retail trade, for instance, was opened again to private ownership and operation. Small-scale industry also reverted to private direction. Most important, the farms were no longer requisitioned but operated as profit-making units. Only the "commanding heights" of industry and finance were retained in government hands.

There ensued for several years a bitter debate about the course of action to follow next. While the basic aim of the Soviet government was still to industrialize and to socialize (i.e., to replace the private ownership of the means of production by state ownership), the question was how fast to move ahead—and, indeed, *how* to move ahead. The pace of industrialization hinged critically on one highly uncertain factor: the willingness of the large, private peasant sector to deliver food for sustaining city workers. To what extent, therefore, should the need for additional capital goods be sacrificed in order to turn out the consumption goods that could be

used as an inducement for peasant cooperation?

The argument was never truly resolved. In 1927 Stalin moved into command and the difficult question of how much to appease the unwilling peasant disappeared. Stalin simply made the ruthless decision to appease him not at all, but to *coerce* him by collectivizing his holdings.

The collectivization process solved in one swoop the problem of securing the essential transfer of food from the farm to the city, but it did so at a frightful social (and economic) cost. Many peasants slaughtered their livestock rather than hand it over to the new collective farms; others waged outright war or practiced sabotage. In reprisal, the authorities acted with brutal force. An estimated five million "kulaks" (rich peasants) were executed or put in labor camps, while in the cities an equally relentless policy showed itself vis-à-vis labor. Workers were summarily ordered to the tasks required by the central authorities. The right to strike was forbidden, and the trade unions were reduced to impotence. Speedups were widely applied, and living conditions were allowed to deteriorate to very low levels.

The history of this period of forced industrialization has left abiding scars on Russian society. It is well for us, nonetheless, to attempt to view it with some objectivity. If the extremes to which the Stalinist authorities went were extraordinary, often unpardonable, and perhaps self-defeating, we must bear in mind that industrialization on the grand scale has always been wrenching, always accompanied by economic sacrifice, and always carried out by the more or less authoritarian use of power.

We might note in passing that universal male suffrage was not gained in England until the late 1860s and 1870s. Aneurin Bevan has written: "It is highly doubtful whether the achievements of the Industrial Revolution would have been permitted if the franchise had been universal. It is very doubtful because a great deal of the capital aggregations that we are at present enjoying are the results of the wages that our fathers went without." (From Gunnar Myrdal, *Rich Lands and Poor.* New York: Harper, 1957, p. 46.)

All this seems sensible enough. Trouble comes, however, because the manager's drive to exceed his factory's quota tends to distort the productive effort from the receivers' point of view. For example, if the target for a textile factory is set in terms of yards of cloth, there is every temptation to weave the cloth as loosely as possible, to get the maximum yardage out of a given amount of thread. Or if the plan merely calls for tonnages of output, there is every incentive to skimp on design or finish or quality, in order to concentrate on sheer weight. A cartoon in the Russian satirical magazine *Krokodil* shows a nail factory proudly displaying its record output: one gigantic nail suspended from an immense gantry crane. (On the other hand, if a nail factory has its output specified in terms of the *numbers* of nails it produces, its incentive to overfulfill this "success indicator" is apt to result in the production of very small or thin nails.)

Profit as a success indicator

What is the way out of this kind of dilemma? A few years ago, a widely held opinion among the Russian planners was that more detailed and better integrated planning performed on a battery of computers would solve the problem. Few still cling to this belief. The demands of planning have grown far faster than the ability to meet them: indeed, one Soviet mathematician has predicted that at the current rate of growth of the planning bureaucracy, planning alone would require the services of the entire Russian population by 1980. Even with the most complete computerization, it seems a hopeless task to attempt to beat the problem of efficiency by increasing the "fineness" of the planning mechanism.

Rather, the wind for reform in the Soviet Union is now blowing from quite another quarter. Led by economist E. G. Liberman, there is a growing demand that the misleading plan directives of weight, length, etc., be subordinated to a new "success indicator" independently capable of guiding the manager to results that will make sense from the overall point of view. And what is that overriding indicator? It is the *profit* that a factory manager can make for the enterprise!

We should note several things about this profit. To begin with, it is not supposed to arise from price manipulations. Factory managers must continue to operate with the prices established by planners; but they will now have to *sell* their output and *buy* their inputs, rather than merely deliver or accept them. This means that each factory will have to be responsive to the particular needs of its customers if it wishes to dispose of its output. In the same way, of course, its own suppliers will now have to be responsive to the factory's needs if the suppliers are to get the factory's business.

Second, the profit will belong not to the factory or its managers, but to the State. A portion of the profit will indeed be allocated for bonuses and other rewards, so that there is a direct incentive to run the plant efficiently, but the bulk of the earnings will be transferred to the State.

The market as a planning tool

Thus, profits are to be used as an efficiency-maximizing indicator, just as we saw them used in our study of microeconomics.

Indeed, to view the change even more broadly, we can see that the reintroduction of the use of profits implies a deliberate return to the use of the *market mechanism* as a means of achieving economic efficiency. Not only profits but also interest charges—a capitalist term that would have been heresy to mention in the days of

Stalin—are being introduced into the planning mechanism to allow factory managers to determine for themselves what is the most efficient thing to do, both for their enterprises and for the economy as a whole.

The drift toward the market mechanism is still new in the Soviet Union, and we do not know how far it will ultimately progress. The objectives of the 1971–1975 Plan called for a much greater emphasis on consumer goods, but spoke of "an extensive use of economic-mathematical methods," which implied something of a return to the computer rather than a rapid movement in the direction of freer trade. Nonetheless, there seems to be no doubt from which quarter the winds blow most steadily. As Soviet economist A. Birman has put it: "Only three years ago, no one would have thought that there would be anything but the direct physical allocation of goods. Now economists talk of *torgovat* (trading) instead of *snabzhat* (allocating)." Furthermore, the government has warmly endorsed the idea of "production associations,"—groups of geographically separate plants that coordinate their marketing, purchasing, research, and management, just like corporations. The market idea of economies of large-scale production has triumphed over the political idea of production organized by locality.

Market socialism   Meanwhile, the trend toward the market has proceeded much further in a large part of Eastern Europe; above all in Yugoslavia. There, the market rules very nearly as supreme as it does in Western capitalist countries. Yet the Yugoslavs certainly consider themselves a socialist economy. As in the U.S.S.R., enterprise profits do not go to the "owners" of the business but are distributed as incentive bonuses or used for investment or other purposes under the overall guidance of the State. And again as in the U.S.S.R., the market is used as a deliberate instrument of social control, rather than as an institution that is above question. Thus, the main determination of investment, the direction of development of consumers' goods, the basic distribution of income—all continue to be matters established at the center as part of a planned economy. More and more, however, this central plan is allowed to realize itself through the profit-seeking operations of highly autonomous firms, rather than through being imposed in full detail upon the economy.

Market vs. plan   The drift of planning toward markets raises a question of fundamental importance. Why plan at all? Why not let the market take over the task of coordination that has proved such a formidable hurdle for industrial planners, for is not the market itself a "planning mechanism"?

After all, in the market, the signal of profitability serves as the guide for allocation of resources and labor. Entrepreneurs, anticipating or following demand, risk private funds in the construction of the facilities that they hope the future will require. Meanwhile, as these industrial salients grow, smaller satellite industries grow along with them to cater to their needs.

The flow of materials is thus regulated in every sector by the forces of private demand, making themselves known by the signal of rising or falling prices. At every moment there emanates from the growing industries a magnetic pull of demand on secondary industries, while, in turn, the growth salients themselves are guided, spurred, or slowed down by the pressure of demand from the ultimate buying public. And all the while, counterposed to these pulls of demand, are the obduracies of supply—the cost schedules of the producers themselves. In the cross fire of demand and supply exists a marvelously sensitive social instrument for the integration of the overall economic effort of expansion.

Economies in mid-development

This extraordinary integrative capacity of market systems returns us to the consideration of the suitability of various economic control mechanisms to different stages of development. We have seen that central planning is likely to be necessary to move stagnant, traditional economies off dead center. Once the development process is well under way, however, the relative functional merits of the market and the command mechanisms begin to change. After planning has done its massive tasks—enforcing economic and social change, creating an industrial sector, rationalizing agriculture—another problem begins to assume ever more importance. This is *the problem of efficiency*, of dovetailing the innumerable productive efforts of society into a single coherent and smoothly functioning whole.

In the flush period of mid-development the market mechanism easily outperforms the command apparatus as a means of carrying out this complex coordinating task. Every profit-seeking entrepreneur, every industrial salesman, every cost-conscious purchasing agent becomes in effect part of a gigantic and continuously alert planning system within the market economy. Command systems do not easily duplicate their efforts. Bottlenecks, unusable output, shortages, waste, and a cumbersome hierarchy of bureaucratic forms and officials typically interfere with the maximum efficiency of the planned economy in midgrowth.

What we see here is not just a passing problem, easily ironed out. One of the critical lessons of the twentieth century is that the word *planning* is exceedingly easy to pronounce and exceedingly difficult to spell out. When targets are still relatively simple, and the priorities of action beyond dispute—as in the case of a nation wrenching itself from the stagnation of an ineffective regime—planning can produce miracles. But when the economy reaches a certain degree of complexity, in which the coordination of 10 activities gives way to the coordination of 10 thousand, innumerable problems arise, *because planned economies enjoy no "natural" congruence between private action and public necessity.*

Here is where the market comes into its own. As we know from our study of microtheory, each firm must combine its factors of production with one eye on their relative costs and the other on their respective productivities, finally bringing about a mix in which each factor is used as effectively as possible, given its cost. Thus in seeking only to maximize their own profits, the units in a market system inadvertently tend also to maximize the efficiency of the system as a whole.

Private aims, public goals

Even more remarkable: one operating rule alone suffices to bring about this extraordinary conjunction of private aims and public goals. *That single rule is to maximize profits.* By concentrating on that one criterion of success and not by trying to maximize output in physical terms or by trying to live by a complicated book of regulations, entrepreneurs in a competitive environment do in fact bring the system toward efficiency. In other words, *profits are not only a source of privileged income, but also an enormously versatile and useful "success indicator" for a system that is trying to squeeze as much output as possible from its given inputs.*

Furthermore, the market mechanism solves the economic problem *with a minimum of social and political controls.* Impelled by the drives inherent in a market society, the individual marketer fulfills his public economic function without constant attention from the authorities. In contradistinction to his counterpart in a centralized command society, who is often prodded, cajoled, or even threatened to act in ways that do not appeal to his self-interest, the classical marketer obeys the peremptory demands of the market as a voluntary exercise of his own economic "freedom."

Thus it is not surprising that we find many of the motivating principles of the market being introduced into command societies. For as these societies settle into more or less established routines, they, too, can utilize the pressure of want and the pull of pecuniary desire to facilitate the fulfillment of their basic plans.

Economic freedom, as we know it in the West, is not yet a reality or even an official objective in any of these countries. The right to strike, for example, is not recognized, and nothing like the fluid consumer-responsive market system is allowed to exert its unimpeded influence on the general direction of economic development. But the introduction of more and more discretion at the factory level argues strongly that the principles of the market society are apt to find their place in planned societies at an appropriate stage of economic development.

beyond the need for forced industrialization and now enter the stage of high consumption.

From our foregoing discussion, it is clear that the market mechanism finds its most natural application in this fortunate period of economic evolution. Insofar as the advanced Western societies have reached a stage in which the consumer is not only permitted but encouraged to impose personal wants on the direction of economic activity, there is little doubt that the market mechanism fulfills the prevailing social purpose more effectively than any other.

Public goods

Nonetheless, as we noted in Chapter 16 the market is not without its own grave problems, even in this regard. For one thing, *it is an inefficient instrument for provisioning societies*—even rich societies—*with those goods and services for which no "price tag" exists,* such as education or local government services or public health facilities.

A market society "buys" such public goods by allocating a certain amount of taxes for these purposes. Its citizens, however, tend to feel these taxes as an exaction in contrast with the items they voluntarily buy. Typically, therefore, a market society underallocates resources to education, city government, public health or recreation, since it has no means of "bidding" funds into these areas, in competition with the powerful means of bidding them into autos or clothes or personal insurance.

High consumption economies

Thus our survey of successive stages of development brings us to a consideration of Western economic society; that is, to the advanced economies that have progressed

Income distribution

A second and perhaps even deeper-seated failing of the market system is its application of a strictly economic calculus to the satisfaction of human wants and needs. As we said before, the market is an assiduous servant of the wealthy, but an indifferent servant of the poor. Thus it presents us with the anomaly of a surplus of luxury housing existing side-by-side with a shortage of inexpensive housing, although the social need for the latter is incontestably greater than the former. Or it pours energy and resources into the multiplication of luxuries for which the wealthier classes offer a market, while allowing more basic needs of the poor to go unheeded and unmet.

Externalities

These shortcomings are aggravated by the tendency of market systems to ignore externalities. *We have seen in Chapter 16 how the failure to capture social costs within the calculus of private benefits leads to patterns of production that are often freighted with serious consequences.* These externalities can be corrected within the market framework, but only by the imposition of an element of command—of political decision—over the workings of the market, whether by taxes, subsidies, or outright regulation.

In considering the side effects of market systems, we should not forget that elusive but very important externality we call "the quality of life." We count as gains the increases in GNP that result from the market system, but we do not give much heed to the commercialism, the trivialization, the psychological frustration and dissatisfaction that also accompany so much market activity.

Malfunctions

This recital of the failings of a market system ends with the micro and macro ills that spring up as a consequence of its operations. We know the severity and extent of these maladies, having just finished an examination of micro and macro economics. But it is well to remember that inflation and unemployment,

monopoly and the MNC, the urban plight and the threat to the environment are all to some degree the products of the hugely vital, but careless and even dangerous momentum that the market imports to the social process. We have already cautioned against linking every social ill with the economic system in which it appears (see "An extra word," pp. 66–69), but it would be equally foolish to absolve the market for all responsibility for the malfunctions that threaten our well-being.

The rise of planning

There is no need to dwell further on the deficiencies of the market system. In one way or another, all its difficulties are indicative of one central weakness. *This is the inability of the market system to formulate stimuli or restraints other than those that arise from the marketplace itself.*

So long as the public need roughly coincides with the sum of the private interests to which the market automatically attends, this failing of the market system is a minor one. But in an advanced economic society, it tends to become ever more important. As primary wants become satisfied, the public aim turns toward stability and security, objectives not attainable without a degree of public control. As technological organization becomes more complex and massive, again a public need arises to contain the new agglomerations of economic power. So, too, as wealth increases, pressure for education, urban improvement, welfare, and the like comes to the fore, not only as an indication of the public conscience, but as a functioning requirement of a mature society. And finally, the public stimulus and management of continued growth take on increased political urgency as the ecological problems of industrial societies multiply.

We have already paid much attention to the rise of planning in the advanced market societies as a corrective force to deal with just such problems. Now we can generalize the economic meaning of this trend. **Planning arises in the advanced market societies to offset their inherent goal-setting weaknesses, just as the market mechanism arises in advanced command societies to offset their inherent motivational weaknesses.** In other words, planning and market mechanisms, in those societies which have begun to enter the stage of high consumption, are not mutually incompatible. On the contrary, they powerfully supplement and support one another.

A convergence of systems?

What seems to impend at the moment, then, is a *convergence of economic mechanisms* for the more advanced societies. In the planned economies, the market is being introduced to facilitate the smoother achievement of established objectives; while in the market economies, a degree of planning is increasingly relied upon to give order, stability, and social direction to the outcome of private activity.

This does not imply that the two major systems today are about to become indistinguishable. The convergence of economic mechanisms may blur but not obliterate the basic distinctions between them. Nor does the convergence of mechanisms in itself portend profound changes in the larger social structures of socialism and capitalism. A gradual rapprochement of the economic mechanisms should not lead us to hasty conclusions about the rebirth of "capitalism" in the Soviet Union or the advent of "socialism" in the United States. Indeed, the crucial problem will be the degree of flexibility and adaptation that both systems can

evince, not the "subversion" of one by the other.

Common problems

There is another way in which the phenomenon of economic convergence reveals itself. *It is the appearance of similar problems in advanced industrial societies.*

When we examine capitalism and socialism, we usually pay special attention to the problems that separate and distinguish these two kinds of societies. Here it is important to realize that they are also bound together by certain common difficulties.

What is the nature of these overarching problems? As we would expect, they stem from the very technical capability and social organization that bring similar economic mechanisms into being. Three problems in particular seem of major importance.

1. Control over technology

One of the most important attributes of modern history is lodged in a striking difference between two kinds of knowledge: the knowledge we acquire in physics, chemistry, engineering, and other sciences, and that which we gain in the sphere of social or political or moral activity. The difference is that knowledge in some sciences is cumulative and builds on itself, whereas knowledge in the social sphere does not. The merest beginner in biology soon knows more than the greatest biologists of a century ago. By way of contrast, the veteran student (or practitioner) of government, of social relations, of moral philosophy is aware of his modest stature in comparison with the great social and moral philosophers of the past.

The result is that all modern societies tend to find that their technological capabilities are constantly increasing, while the social and political and moral institu-

All through Europe we see a reliance on planning that is both greater and more outspoken than anything we have encountered in the United States. In our own country, we have arrived at a consensus as to fiscal and monetary policy as the proper implements for achieving a stable and satisfactory rate of growth. But in most European nations, there is visible a further commitment to planning as a means of achieving publicly determined patterns of resource allocation as well as adequate rates of growth.

In France, for example, a central planning agency, working in consultation with Parliament and with representatives of industry, agriculture, labor, and other groups, sets a general plan for French growth—a plan that not only establishes a desired rate of expansion but determines whether or not, for example, the provincial cities should expand faster or slower than the nation as a whole, or where the bulk of new housing is to be located, or to what degree social services are to be increased. Once decided, the plan is then divided

CONSERVATIVE PLANNING

into the various production targets needed for its fulfillment, and their practicality is discussed with management and labor groups in each industry concerned.

From these discussions arise two results. First, the plan is often amended to conform with the wishes or advice of those who must carry it out. Second, the general targets of the plan become part of the business expectations of the industries that have helped to formulate them. To be sure, the government has substantial investment powers that can nudge the economy along whatever path has been finally determined. But in the main, French "indicative" planning works as a *self-fulfilling prophecy*—the very act of establishing its objectives sets into motion the behavior needed to realize them.

In England, Germany, the Netherlands, Italy, and Scandinavia, we see other forms of government planning, none so elaborately worked out as the

French system, but all also injecting a powerful element of public guidance into the growth and disposition of their resources.

The plans have not been wholly successful. Inflation has been the curse of Europe to an even greater degree than it has here; and nothing like a successful "incomes policy" has been worked out in any nation. But considerable success has been attained in the allocation of resources for public purposes through planning, and in the shaping of the general contours of national development.

What is beyond dispute is that a basic commitment to planning seems to have become an integral part of modern European capitalism. Note, *however, that all these planning systems utilize the mechanism of the market as a means for achieving their ends.* The act of planning itself is not, of course, a market activity; but the realization of the various desired production tasks for industry is entrusted largely to the pull of demand acting on independent enterprises. Thus the market has been utilized as an instrument of social policy.*

*Anyone who wishes to learn more about the important subject of European planning should read Andrew Shonfield, *Modern Capitalism: the Changing Balance of Public and Private Power* (New York: Oxford University Press, 1969).

tions by which those capabilities are controlled cannot match the challenges with which they are faced. Television, for example, is an immense force for cultural homogenization; medical technology changes the composition of society by altering its age groups and life expectancy; rapid transportation vastly increases mobility and social horizons; and the obliterative power of nuclear arms casts a pervasive anxiety over all of life. All these technologically-rooted developments fundamentally alter the conditions and problems of life, but we do not know what social, political, and moral responses are appropriate to them. *As a result, all modern societies—socialist and capitalist—experience the feeling of being at the mercy of a technological and scientific impetus that shapes the lives of their citizens in ways that cannot be accurately foreseen nor adequately controlled.*

2. The problem of participation

The second problem derives from the first. Because advanced societies are characterized by high levels of technology, they are necessarily marked by a high degree of organization. The technology of our era depends on the cooperation of vast masses of men, some at the levels of production, some at the levels of administration. The common undergirding of all advanced industrial or "post-industrial" societies lies not alone in their gigantic instrumentalities of production, but in their equally essential and vast instrumentalities of administration, whether these be called corporations, production ministries, or government agencies.

The problem is then how the citizen is to find a place for his individuality in the midst of so much organization; how he is to express his voice in the direction of affairs, when so much bureaucratic management is inescapable; how he is to "participate" in a world whose technological structure calls for ever more order and coordination. This is a matter which, like the sweeping imperative of technology, affects both capitalism and socialism. In both kinds of societies, individuals feel overwhelmed by the impersonality of the work process, impotent before the power of huge enterprises—above all, the state itself—and frustrated at an inability to participate in decisions that see more and more beyond any possibility of personal influence.

No doubt much can be done to increase the feeling of individual participation in the making of the future, especially in those nations that still deny elementary political freedoms. *But there remains a recalcitrant problem of how the quest for increased individual decision making and participation can be reconciled with the organizational demands imposed by the technology on which all advanced societies depend.* This is a problem that is likely to trouble societies—capitalist or socialist—as long as technology itself rests on integrated processes of production and requires centralized organs of administration and control.

3. The problem of the environment

As we saw in Chapter 4, all industrial nations face an era in which exponential growth is beginning to absorb resources at rates faster than we may be able to provide them with new technologies; and all industrialized societies—indeed, the whole world—may soon be entering an era in which environmental limitations on energy or the ability to absorb heat will impose a slowdown on rates of growth.

Moreover, we stand at a period in history when underdeveloped nations are belatedly making their own bid for a share in the rising output per capita that has until now mainly been confined to advanced nation-states.

In this period of long-run economic stringency, industrial socialist and capitalist nations again seem likely to share common problems—not alone in bringing about a controlled slowdown in output, but in achieving social harmony under conditions that no longer allow their citizens to look forward to ever-higher standards of material consumption. Here, too, similar social and political problems may override differences in economic institutions and ideologies.

Convergence and history   In a larger sense, then, "convergence" brings us beyond economics to the common human adventure in which economic systems are only alternate routes conducting humanity toward much the same general direction and destination. Perhaps it is well that we end our survey of economic history with the recognition that the long trajectory of the market system does not bring us to a terminus of social history, but only to a state in which some kinds of problems—the pitifully simple problems of producing and distributing goods—begin to be solved, only to reveal vastly larger problems in the very technology and organization that prepared the means for solving them.

FOCUS In this concluding chapter of our book, we back away from events to try to find a perspective in which to place the last chapters. It is, of course, a perspective of historic change, still unfinished; and our final effort is to find a line of sight that will give us a glimpse, however indistinct, of the history that lies ahead—the future.

This glimpse comes in the realization that market systems have their place in the evolution of economic societies. As we have seen in the chapter on underdeveloped countries, market systems are not to be found in tradition-bound societies. Nor are they prominent in most societies that are now making or have recently made the enormously difficult leap into "modernity." Here is where we find command economies whose main purpose is to reproduce the tasks performed by the market in the nineteenth century, to do it more quickly and with different social goals.

This leads us to reflect on the strengths and weaknesses of both planning and market systems, and to a recognition that the market *is* a planning system, albeit one of a very special kind. Planned systems do not manage high-level consumption well; market systems do not handle growth adequately. Thus we find market elements entering planned economies and elements of planning entering market systems.

Our speculations about this "convergence" of economic systems are only speculations. We do not yet know how far the command economies will move toward the increasing use of markets, and the market system toward increasing use of planning. But there is no doubt that the two kinds of systems face similar underlying problems of technology, bureaucracy, and environmental safety. Here perhaps are the overriding issues of our century, for which economics alone cannot bring a solution, but for which no solution can be found that will not use the best reasoning and investigation that economics can produce.

WORDS AND CONCEPTS YOU SHOULD KNOW

Stages of economic development, 671–73
Central planning and its problems, 673–75
Central planning and profits, 675
Market socialism, 676

Market vs. planning, 676–77
Market societies and their problems, 678–79
Convergence, 680–82

QUESTIONS

1. How do you account for the simultaneous existence in the world of such radically different economic systems?

2. Discuss the difference in social goals and priorities between a nation that is just beginning its development and one in mid-development. Between one in mid-development and one at a stage of high mass consumption. What is the relevance of planning techniques for each of these stages of development? Would you expect the techniques of planning to be similar in all stages? What differences would you look for?

3. What is meant by the congruence of self-interest and public requirement in a market system? Is this what we mean by the "invisible hand"? How can this congruence be reconciled with the fact that the market has no means of establishing public priorities.

4. What are the advantages of the market system for economic freedom? Do you think the market system is also productive of political freedom? Draw a scatter diagram showing on one axis the degree of planning and on the other axis your estimate of relative political freedoms for the following nations: Sweden, England, U.S., France, South Africa. Is there much, if any, relationship between the two variables?

5. Do you think there can be a convergence of economic systems without a convergence of social and political systems?

6. What specific technological processes seem to defy social control? How about the effect of television? Urbanization? The arms race? Can you think of others?

7. Why do you think that knowledge accumulates more easily in science than it does in the areas of morality or politics or social activities?

8. Do you think that bureaucracy is an avoidable aspect of industrial society? If so, how? If not, what problems does it pose?

QUANTITATIVE METHODS

PART

6

An introduction to statistics and econometrics

Statistics are central to the study of economics. Why? Because economics, more than any other social science, involves things that can be counted, concepts that can be quantified, activities that can be measured. Prices, wages, GNP itself, as we have learned, all express our ability to quantify certain aspects of social activity. This ability to quantify is often essential to our ability to analyze and control. The GNP accounts, invented in the 1930s, made it possible to develop macroeconomics. Without these accounts, only fuzzy impressionistic statements could be made about macroeconomic activity, just as only vague statements could be made about the velocity of money before we could actually measure output (see p. 31–32). If we could quantify "utility," we could measure welfare far better than we now do.

Hence an economist is constantly using statistics and *econometrics*, a branch of economics that combines statistical techniques with economic theory. To understand the techniques of statistics or econometrics you must learn much more than we are going to teach in this chapter. This is most emphatically not a mini-course that will substitute for a thorough study of both, but we hope that it will pave the way for further study by taking away some of the mystery surrounding the use and compilation of the numbers on which economics depends.

44

What this chapter is about

You will find this longish chapter divided into eight sections, really eight sub-chapters. The first of them has to do with some over-all *cautions and warnings*. It is easy to read and does not involve any "work," unless you call learning something useful "work." Everyone should take its message to heart. Statistics are indispensable for economics, but they are also the source of much trouble for the unwary amateur.

Section II is about *Distributions and Averages*. These are concepts we use every day, as economists or in everyday life. If ever there was a word loaded with problems, it is that deceptive word *average*. This is a section that will richly repay study, and it is basically easy to master.

Section III is about *Price Indexes*. This is a more specialized subject, into which we have already looked very briefly (p. 337). It takes a little calculation to work through the construction of a price index, but the results are worth the effort, especially if you are thinking of taking further courses in economics. Then you will really have to understand "weighting" and how to convert a price index in current dollars into one in constant dollars.

Section IV is about *Sampling*, a tremendously important subject for anyone interested in empirical research. We can give you only a general idea of the often complex considerations involved in sampling, but we hope you will emerge from these few pages with a much better understanding of the general problems of sampling than you probably had before you began.

Section V brings us to econometrics and specifically to *Functions*. We have already had an introduction to functional relationships in Chapter 8, but the subject is so useful that a careful review of the field is worthwhile, particularly since functions lie at the heart of econometrics.

This brings us to *Correlations and Regression*, section VI. Here is the core of econometrics. Part of the section, about regressions, introduces you to the general notion of the techniques of one very important branch of functional analysis. It does not try to teach you how to make an actual regression analysis, but it should make clear what you are trying to do when you sit down with a desk calculator or use a computer to work out the complex formulae of econometric analysis.

Section VII is perhaps even more important. It is a series of warnings about the meaning of *causation and correlation*. In particular, it alerts you against easy conclusions that such-and-such is the "cause" of so-and-so, just because the arithmetic "looks right." You ought to look at this section, even if you have only the haziest notion of how you go about finding a "least squares" coefficient.

From here we go to section VIII, *Forecasting*. As we said in Chapters 6 and 9, prediction is one of the most important— and troublesome—aims of economic analysis. Our brief review will serve to remind you of these problems before you find yourself forecasting on the basis of flimsy data or uncertain premises.

We don't suggest that you sit down to read this chapter as a single lesson. Use it as a reference source. Perhaps you have already looked into it, when the text suggested you look ahead into certain pages. Or read it in short takes, section by section, to get a feeling for the field of statistics and econometrics. If the chapter dispels some of the fog surrounding that field and tempts you to take a course in statistics, it will have amply served its purpose.

I. Some Initial Cautions

Quality vs. quantity

We should immediately clear up two misconceptions about statistics. The first might be called "statistics worship." It finds expression in the view that if you can't count something, it doesn't count. The second is just the opposite. It scoffs at statistics because all the important things in life are qualitative and therefore can't be measured.

Both of these *are* misconceptions, and it is important to understand why. The statistics worshipper must realize that before anyone can count anything, he must *define* it, and that definition is ultimately an act of judgment, not measurement. And the statistics scoffer must realize that before he can bring his reason to bear on social problems involving good and evil, he must have at least some notion of how *large* a good or evil he is concerned with. Some of these matters we have touched on in Chapter 9, but it will do no harm to look into them again a little more carefully.

Take as an illustration the problem of poverty. When Professor Galbraith wrote *The Affluent Society* in 1958, he said that one family in thirteen in America was poor. By current official statistics, one in seven is poor. Does that mean that a larger fraction of Americans are poor today? Of course not. The answer is that today the United States statistical authorities' *definition* of poverty is different from the definition used by Galbraith, so that the "growing" percentage of the poor reflects nothing more than a changing conception of what poverty means.

Thus, the extent of poverty in America is a quantitative measure founded on a qualitative definition, and the person who places a blind faith in the "facts" must re-member that many of these facts change as our definition of social problems changes. But isn't that just the point, asks the statistical skeptic. Since definition is everything, the problem of poverty boils down in the end to what we *think* poverty is. What is important is not what the numbers tell us, but our moral judgments from which the numbers emerge.

Of course it is true that definitions *do* come first, but they establish the unit or yardstick by which we measure the problem. Poverty may rise or fall in America if we use an unchanged yardstick. It can also rise or fall because we change its definition. But once we have made that choice of the yardstick, we use the definition to learn the magnitude of the problem *as we have defined it*. For until we know its magnitude as measured by the *same* yardstick, we cannot know how serious a problem it is, much less determine what action will be needed to remedy it.

Patterns of movement

Often, as with poverty, *the pattern of movement is as important as, or even more important than, the absolute value of the variable*. If poverty is rapidly diminishing, we may need a set of public programs very different from those needed if it seems to persist. So, too, with other measured magnitudes, such as GNP. Is GNP rising or falling, and how fast? It is no accident that most discussions of GNP in different countries tend to focus on comparative rates of growth. Changes in GNP (per capita) are probably a better measure of changes in economic welfare within a country than are efforts to measure the absolute level of GNP in one nation and to compare it with another.

Unemployment presents a similar problem. Different countries define unemployment in different ways, and the seriousness of any given level of unemployment can often be determined only by comparing the current level with its historical path. For this reason, any new statistical series should be used with caution. Its usefulness cannot be determined until we see how it moves over time and under different circumstances.

Sometimes definitions themselves are important in determining the pattern of movement of economic variables. Sometimes they are not. One of the techniques for investigating the importance of different definitions is to see if they imply that the economy is changing in different ways. If Professor Galbraith's definition of poverty yielded a pattern of movement different from the official definition (suppose poverty was growing on one definition and falling on the other) then the movement of poverty is *sensitive* to its definition. If this were true, one would want to be extremely careful when discussing poverty.

The problem of definitions

The second lesson follows from the first. Words are slippery, even when no arbitrary judgment is involved. Any maker or user of statistics must be exceedingly sure of the exact meaning of the terms being used. In Chapter 9, p. 117, we showed how tricky the words *family* or *household* could be, for, a household can be a single person! Another example of a treacherous definition is the one for—of all things—*motor vehicles*. If you look up the data in the *Statistical Abstract*, and read the footnotes, you will see that a "motor vehicle" includes a mobile trailer home. The result is that the motor vehicle statistics overstate the production of vehicles if you think of these as cars and trucks, and that correspondingly, the statistics for real housing investment (in which mobile

trailer homes are not included) understate the value of residential construction.

Updating series

Numbers, perhaps even more than words, have a magical authority inherent in them, but that does not mean that either are necessarily correct, even from the most impeccable sources. People make honest mistakes in gathering statistics, or mistakes creep in because of the difficulties in compiling statistics, some of which we will learn about later.

In Chapter 9, p. 117 (box), we also saw how official figures, such as those for GNP can change from one edition of the *Statistical Abstract* to the next.

The reason is that many statistical series are refined and corrected as more complete data are collected, so that virtually all figures change until the "final" returns are in. Most economic statistics are necessarily based on fragmentary data and are gradually improved as fuller information is obtained. The latest statistics are *always* subject to revision and are often marked *prelim.*, or *est.*, to warn the reader that they will be subject to change. The changes are usually not large, but occasionally large enough to alter precise calculations based on earlier data.

At regular intervals, the various government offices concerned with the collection of statistical information bring out revised—sometimes drastically revised—series of data. These revisions not only establish new "bases" and "weights" for many indices (we will come to the meaning of these terms), but involve recalculation of many past series based on new concepts, on more sophisticated data-handling techniques, and so on. (One recent controversy, for example, concerns the problem of whether or not we have accurately measured the value of the private capital stock in the United States.

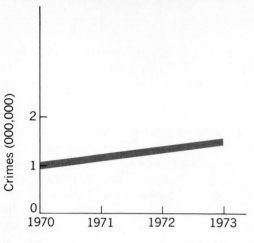
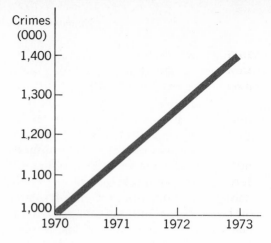

FIG. 44 · 1   Visual deceptions

Economist Robert Gordon has claimed that we have "mislaid" $45 billion of this stock by failing to make allowance for various government transactions, such as the very low prices at which some companies acquired plants built by the government during World War II and subsequently sold at nominal figures to private enterprise.*)

Of course no ordinary user of official statistics can be aware of all these pitfalls or can anticipate the revisions that may alter the numbers on which he is relying. An excess of wariness would only paralyze the research that we must carry on with the only data we have at hand. But a healthy pinch of caution, allowing for moderate changes in the magnitudes at hand, has saved many a researcher from trying to prove a point by relying on very *small differences in magnitudes that may later disappear.*

Mountains out of molehills   The best recent example of misusing small differences is in the handling of the monthly reports on the rate of inflation. Monthly changes are multiplied by 12 to get the annual rate of

*See *American Economic Review*, June 1969, and rejoinder, *ibid.*, September 1970.

inflation published in newspaper headlines. Let's assume that in one month the rate of inflation is 0.34 percent, and in the next month it is 0.36 percent. Since the Bureau of Labor and Statistics rounds its numbers to one place to the right of the decimal, these would be reported as a 0.3 percent increase and a 0.4 percent increase. When they are multiplied by 12, they yield a 3.6 percent rate of inflation versus a 4.8 percent rate of inflation.

In fact, the initial difference is probably well within sampling error (see below). This means that the two numbers 0.34 and 0.36 may be the same; they only appear different because of the errors inherent in any process of measurement and sampling. As a result, one should not place too much weight on month-to-month changes, but look at the pattern of movement over several months.

Visual deceptions   Often visual devices are used to display statistical data. These are particularly subject to misleading interpretations. Let's say we are trying to chart a crime wave over time. We have two graphs, displaying exactly the same numbers, but on different scales. In the first graph, it looks as if there were little or no change in crime; the second looks as if there were a horrendous acceleration. Can you see the reason for the difference?

Perspectives on data

Normally, the statistical "truth" about any phenomenon depends upon examining it from a number of different perspectives. Consider the much discussed question of the size of government in the U.S. economy. This is a matter we have already looked into in Chapter 30, but it is worth reconsidering here as a general problem in statistics. The size of government will depend largely on how we define *government*. Do we mean federal government or federal plus state and local? Do we mean purchases of goods and services or all expenditures, including transfer payments? Just as a review of the difference that these definitions make, consider the following "measures" of government size:

	Percent of GNP, 1973
Federal expenditures	20
Federal state and local expenditures	31
All federal purchases	8
All government purchases	21

All these statistics accurately indicate something about the relationship of "government" and the size of the economy. The important thing, therefore, is to use the figures that are appropriate to the problem you are investigating. Are you interested in federal or total government activity? In production, purchases, or in expenditure? In the *uses* of production or expenditure? (In the last case, you will need more data, since the figures above do not show, for example, welfare vs. warfare; subsidies or public investment, etc.)

Uses of statistics

These are very general warnings, but not to be taken lightly. More than one researcher has been in serious trouble because of overlooking the caption at the top of a table of figures or failing to check on the most recent compilations of data or being fooled by numbers that did not adequately reflect the changing nature of the problem to be measured.

Now, at the end, a word to redress the balance. We have stressed skepticism toward statistics because the general attitude of the beginning student is generally one of blind acceptance. But too much skepticism is perhaps worse than none at all. **Carefully defined and collected data, clearly labeled and competently used, are the only way we have of measuring very important facets of our social activity.** This book would be impossible to write without statistics, and economics would be severely crippled if we could not rely on numerical magnitudes. Statistics really are an integral part of economics. The thing is to be wary of their weaknesses while appreciating their great virtues and absolute necessity.

II. Distributions and Averages

Distributions and averages are essentially statistical devices for viewing aggregate phenomena from different perspectives. For example, GNP measures total output. Sweden had an aggregate output of $39 billion in 1972; Spain had a GNP of $42 billion; the U.S. one of $1,118 billion. These numbers indicate something about the potential economic power of each country—although not very much, since Spain's ability to wage war, for example, is probably less than that of a nation such as Sweden. But even less do the numbers tell us about the amounts of goods and services that are available to typical people in each nation. To learn about this, GNP needs further examination.

Means

The simplest procedure is to divide total GNP by the total population to obtain the "average" GNP per person. We call this arithmetical average the *mean:* in the U.S. in 1972 it was $1,118 billion divided by 209 million individuals, or $5,353 per capita. In Sweden the per capita (mean) GNP was $4,749; in Spain, $1,221. In common usage this is what we usually have in mind when we use the word *average*, but to the statistician it is only one of several ways to give meaning to that very important word.*

Medians

Means can be very misleading "averages." Suppose that one person or a very few people had virtually all the income, and the rest had very little (not so far from reality in a country like Pakistan). The mean income would then tell us very little about the income of an individual chosen at random. Hence, statisticians often use another definition of "average" called the *median.* As the word suggests, the median income is the income of the middle individual. If we lined up the population in order of income and selected the person who stood midpoint in the line, that person's income would be the median. Half the country would have smaller incomes; half larger.

*Here is a problem in perspectives on data. If we want "average" GNP to tell us something about welfare, we probably don't want to use GNP as the measuring rod, because too much GNP becomes corporate or government end-product. Better to use an aggregate such as personal income.

Another caution: choice of units

Here is a good place to interject cautions about data and definitions, once more. If we were to calculate the median income of *individuals* in the United States, the answer would be zero! This is because more than half of all individuals have zero incomes. They are children, nonworking females, older retirees, and others. (You can see that it makes a difference if we choose "income" or "income plus transfers.") But it obviously makes no sense to say that the median individual in the U.S. had no income. Therefore, we focus on *family* income, on the assumption that all members of a family share equitably in the income received by the family as a whole. Actually that assumption is not true: children have much less purchasing power than adults; but it serves our general purposes to make this assumption, as long as we know that we are using the data in a special way.

Means and medians

Is there a systematic difference between means and medians? There is: *medians are almost always smaller than means.* A moment's thought tells us that if the median income is $7,100, then the range of income in the poorer half of the population must be smaller than the range in the half that is richer; 50 percent of the population must receive between $1 and $7,100, and 50 percent between $7,100 and the income of the richest person in the country. *This asymmetry in the distribution of income is at the root of the difference between the two averages.*

A simple illustration

Perhaps the principle involved is clear to you by now. If not, an arithmetical example may help.

Assume that there are two towns, A and B, and that each consists of five families. The following table represents the distribution of income.

A	$4,000	$6,000	$7,000	$8,000	$10,000
B	$4,000	$6,000	$7,000	$8,000	$15,000

In each town, the median is $7,000, the income of the family in the middle. But notice that in town A, the distribution of income is symmetrical; that is, the median family is $1,000 away from the second and fourth families, and $3,000 away from the first and fifth families. Note, however, that this is not true of town B. The income of the top (fifth) family is much further away from the median than the income of the first family.

In town A, the median should be equal to the arithmetic mean. And, of course, it is: total income of $35,000 of town A divided by 5 equals $7,000. But in town B, because of the imbalance of income toward the wealthier side, the arithmetic mean is higher than the median: total income of $40,000 of town B divided by 5 equals $8,000. So the mean is $1,000 greater than the median in B.

In its way, town B is a highly simplified version of the country as a whole. If we lined up all the approximately 54 million families in the U.S., from poorest to richest, and picked the middle family—that is, the family with 27 million families on either side—our designated *median* household would have an income of $11,116. If instead, we added up the *incomes* of all families, in any order, and divided by 54 million, the resulting *mean* income would be $12,625.

Skewness

This asymmetry in distribution is called *skewness*, a term we shall make use of subsequently. A quick way of grasping skewness is to plot data on a graph. For example, in Fig. 44 • 2, A and B show two hypothetical distributions, one skewed and one not. In both graphs we measure income along the horizontal axis and the number of families along the vertical axis.

The nonskewed distribution is shown in A, where we can see that the distribution of income is just the same on one side of the median as on the other. For example, if the median income is $8,000, we note that 5 million families have an income of $6,000 and that 5 million families have an income of $10,000, each income

FIG. 44 • 2   Normal and skewed distributions

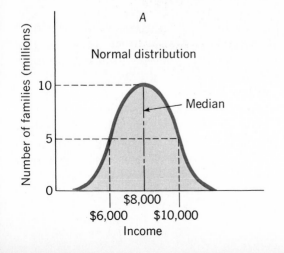

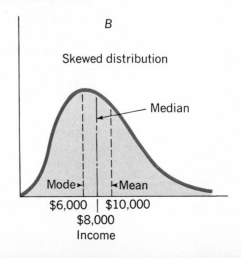

being the same $2,000 distance from the median figure.

This kind of unskewed frequency distribution is called a *bell-shaped curve* or a *normal* curve. Graph *B*, on the other hand, is skewed to the right. Suppose that $8,000 is the median income for this population. We can see from the shape of the curve that there is no longer an even pairing of families on either side of this median. The incomes of the families on the right "tail" of the curve are further from the median than the incomes of those on the left "tail," and so the mean (the "old-fashioned" average) must be above the median (middle) income.

Here the mean, as we know from our definition above, is higher than the median (we suppose it to be $10,000 on the graph).

Modes

Furthermore, we can now speak of *another* kind of average, called a *mode*, which shows the particular income level on which there is the *largest number* of families. In our graph, this is represented by the figure of $6,000. Notice that in a bell-shaped distribution, the mode is the same as the median and the arithmetic mean, but this is true for only a normal, bell-shaped distribution.

Which average to use?

If we want to express the average income in the United States, which average should we use? To know the complete truth, we would need to know the shape of the entire distribution of incomes, but we often need a summary measure. Ordinarily, we choose the median as the summary measure, because what we have in mind with the word *average* is indeed that income which is "middlemost." If we use the arithmetic mean, we distort the picture of the middle family, for we now show an amount of "average" income swollen by the presence of very large incomes at the upper end of the income register.

Sometimes, however, the mean is a better average than the median. This is the case when the distribution of income is approximately normal. Under these circumstances, the arithmetic mean has the advantage that it takes into account the *actual value* of the money incomes received by rich and poor families, whereas the median counts only the number of families on either side of the middle figure.

But bear in mind that in some kinds of distributions, the use of either average can be misleading. Say we had a country where 95 percent of the population received about $500, and the other 5 percent received more than $500, ranging up to $1 million. This is not unlike the situation in India. With such a violent skewness, we probably should use the *mode*, $500. It tells us more than either the mean or the median reveals about the distribution of income.

But suppose the upper 5 percent were all clustered around $10,000. Then we could separate the population into two main groups, one rich and one poor. Such a curve is likely to be *bimodal*, showing that a great many families cluster around one income level, and another group clusters around a wholly different level. We show such a bimodal distribution in Fig. 44 • 3.

Statisticians are well aware of the difficulties of accurately representing such bimodal frequencies with "averages." Thus when you see well-conceived data that present averages—whether for IQs, academic grades, incomes, or other phenomena—you can be pretty confident that the data have only one mode and represent the kind of frequency distribution shown in Fig. 44 • 2.

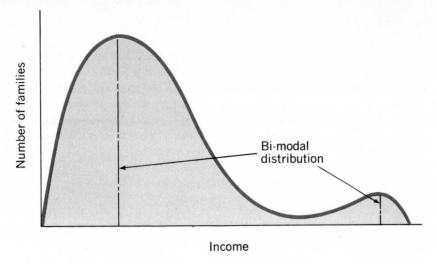

FIG. 44 · 3   Bi-modal distribution

III. Price Indexes

The problem of finding a useful way to represent "average" or typical incomes brings us to another problem when we want to reduce aggregate figures to their "real meaning." This has to do with price changes, a subject we are familiar with from our discussion in macroeconomics. In fact, in Chapter 23 we looked into the problem of how we change GNP in current dollars into GNP in constant dollars.

Here we want to investigate that problem a little more carefully. As we know, the device we use to discover changes in "real" purchasing power is a *price index*. There are many different kinds of price indexes, depending on what prices we want to measure: price indexes for wholesale commodities, for housing, for capital goods, for GNP.

Usually, when we try to discover changes in consumer well-being, we use the *Consumer Price Index*, constructed by the Department of Labor. It reflects the changing prices of a typical "market basket" of goods and services bought by an urban consumer over the period we want

to investigate. By taking the prices in an initial or *base year* and the prices for the same commodities in other years, we arrive at a consumer price series, or an index of consumer purchasing power over that period.

Building a price index   The idea of a price index is simple (although the actual statistical problems, such as collecting the data, are formidable). Let us quickly review the main steps.

Take an imaginary economy with only one consumer product, which we will call bread. Say that in the first year, which we will use as our base, bread sells for $2 per baker's dozen, and that in the second year its price is $4. What would the price index be for the second year? Elementary algebra gives us the answer:

$2 is to $4 as 100 is to X

$$\frac{2}{4} = \frac{100}{x}$$

Solving by cross-multiplying, we get:

$$2x = 400$$
$$x = 200$$

Note that a price index is a percentage: in the above example, an index of 200 means that prices in that year are double the index (100) in the base year.

With 200 as our price index, we are now ready to compute real income in the second year in terms of base-year prices, just as we did earlier. Suppose a worker in a one-product economy was paid $5,000 the first year and $11,000 the second. What has happened to his real income? To find out, we divide this money income by the price index for that year, and then multiply the quotient by 100.

$$\frac{\$5,000}{100} \times 100 = \$5,000$$

(real income in Year 1)

$$\frac{\$11,000}{200} \times 100 = \$5,500$$

(real income in Year 2)

Thus, his real income has risen, but not by nearly so much as the sheer dollar increase indicates.

Weights

Now let's drop the assumption of a one-product economy and see what happens when there is more than one product. Assume an economy that consists of two products, bread and shoes. How would we compute a price index in this case?

Here we face a new problem. Before we can calculate *one* index for *two* products, we have to impute a proportional importance to each. For example, if more than half of consumer expenditures went for bread, then a doubling in its price would count more heavily than if the price of shoes doubled. The way we customarily deal with such a problem is *to take the amount of each product that the "typical" consumer purchased in the base year, and then compute the rise in living costs,* *under the assumption that the consumer will buy each product in the same proportion in succeeding years.*

Let us say that the consumer spent $100 in the base year and allotted the money in this way, between bread at $2 per unit and shoes at $10 per pair.

Product	No. units bought	× Price	= Total
Bread	35 dozen	× $2	= $70
Shoes	3 pairs	× $10	= $30
			$100

In the second year, the price of bread doubles to $4 and the price of shoes is cut in half to $5. If the consumer plans to buy the same number of units of each, then his new budget must look like this:

Product	No. units bought	× Price	= Total
Bread	35 dozen	× $4	= 140
Shoes	3 pairs	× $5	= $15
			$155

This gives us an aggregate expenditure for each year, from which we can compute the price index. Since it cost $100 to buy a typical basket of goods in the base year and $155 to buy *the same basket of goods* in the succeeding year, then the relevant index numbers are, of course, 100 and 155.

A more common way to go about this computation is *to derive "weights" from the proportional number of dollars spent on each product in the base year.* Since 70 percent of the typical consumer's money was spent on bread and 30 percent on shoes in 1967, the weights are .7 and .3, respectively.

In order to use the weights, however, we must first compute a separate price index for each product. For bread, which doubled in price, the index is 200 for the second year; for shoes, which halved in price, the index is 50. Now we multiply the index for each product by its corresponding weight and add up the results. For the base year:

Product	Index	×	Weight	=	Total
Bread	100	×	.7	=	70
Shoes	100	×	.3	=	30
					100

For the succeeding year:

Product	Index	×	Weight	=	Total
Bread	200	×	.7	=	140
Shoes	50	×	.3	=	15
					155

Again, our index numbers are 100 and 155.

Generally speaking, we assign weights by the value of purchases of the base year.* But what is more important is that the *same* weights must be used in the computation of each index number (or weights that are at least approximately the same). The consequences of doing otherwise are that an index number for one year would have little or no relation to an index number for another. If we are going to talk about fluctuations in a price level, then it must be a price level for the *same* basket of goods, as in the two products of our example, or for a basket of goods that is *relatively unchanging* in composition.

New goods

What do you do about the price of goods that do not exist in the base year? They have no base-year price. What price should they be multiplied by? There is no easy answer.

Perhaps the good is a new product, such as a microwave oven, with an old function, cooking meals. In that case, government statisticians, in conjunction with an outside panel of experts, try to determine how much of the price of the new good reflects quality improvements and how much reflects price increases.

For example, suppose a conventional oven sold for $100 at the time the microwave oven was introduced at $150. Suppose further that the expert committee thought the microwave oven was 50 percent better than a conventional oven. Then the higher cost microwave oven would not show up as an increase in prices but as an increase in the quality of output. Each microwave oven produced would have the same effect on the real GNP as one and one-half conventional ovens; it would count as a $150 contribution to real GNP rather than a $100 contribution.

But suppose the committee thought that the microwave oven was *not* a quality improvement. Then each oven would show up as a $100 increase in the real GNP, just as conventional ovens. To the extent that people bought the higher price, but not higher quality microwave ovens, the prices of ovens in the GNP price indexes would go up, even though the price of conventional ovens did not change. In quality terms, you are being sold a conventional oven at a new higher price—$150.

New functions

But what can you do about products that serve completely new functions? Television sets were such an example. Since there was nothing to compare them with when they were introduced after World War II, these goods and services were evaluated at the prices for which they were first sold.

*For special purposes, there are also "chain indices," where weights are changed every year, as usage changes.

This creates a problem in measuring real growth. Most new goods are sold for very high prices when they are first introduced. Thereafter, their prices fall as they become mass produced and consumed. Let's assume that TV sets cost $500 when they were first sold in 1947. Each TV set produced would thus add $500 to the real GNP. If one million sets were produced in a year, this would add $500 million to the GNP. But let's now assume that the price of black-and-white sets fell to $100 and the government moved its base year forward to a year in which TVs cost only $100. Now the production of one million sets per year would add only $100 million to the real GNP, even though the same number had added $500 million when the government was using an earlier year as the base year.

This could be avoided by not moving the base year. But in that case the base year will rapidly become obsolete as new goods are introduced into the economy.

As a result, corrections for price changes can be only an approximation of the truth. They should never be relied on "down to the last dollar" to make comparisons in real standards of living, especially if the periods being compared are widely separated in time. They are absolutely necessary to rid ourselves of the "money illusion," but they offer no more than thoughtful estimates—not precise measures—of what is happening to real standards of living over time.

Applying the indexes

Constructing indexes is difficult; applying them is easy, and we have already given the basic rule on p. 32. But let us review it here, for completeness.

Suppose that the results of research give us the following data:

Year	Income in current $	Price index
1	$5,000	60
2	6,000	80
3	7,000	100
4	8,000	105

It now becomes very simple to compute the changes in real income. We divide the income in current dollars in each year by the price index and multiply by 100. The answers are:

Year	Real income
1	$5,000 ÷ 60 × 100 = $8,333
2	6,000 ÷ 80 × 100 = 7,500
3	7,000 ÷ 100 × 100 = 7,000
4	8,000 ÷ 105 × 100 = 7,619

Changing the base

Note that in this case the base year is year 3. Would it make a difference if the base year were 1 or 2? Obviously, the numbers would change. If year 1 were the base, then the "real income" in year 1 becomes $5,000 instead of $8,333. *But the relative changes over time would not be different.*

Suppose we graph the profile of real income, using each year in turn as a base. Figure 44 • 4 shows us that we have in fact only shifted the location of the series on the vertical scale. The *shape* of the real income series is not thereby affected.

Splicing

Changing the base suggests that we can "splice" one time series, with a certain "base," onto another. Indeed, we can and do. As the statistical agencies "update" their bases to prevent them from becoming obsolete, they usually splice the old series onto the new, by recomputing it on the new base. The only problem here is one of interpretation. By splicing one series to another we can get charts that extend far

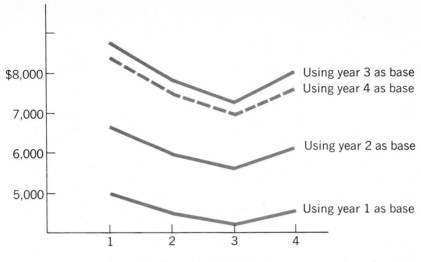

FIG. 44 · 4   Shifting the base

IV. Sampling

into the past. They tend to make us forget the difficulties of making "real" corrections with which we have been concerned. Remember when you see a long time series that it has probably been spliced many times and that its apparent unbroken continuity very likely masks many difficult problems of statistical definition. Use such series with care!

Most economic data, such as family income, is collected with sampling techniques rather than complete enumeration. Few things are more disconcerting to someone who begins to work with such data than to be told that most of the "facts" to be correlated or used are based on *samples*—that is, on figures derived from observing or counting not the entire set of objects in which one is interested, but only a fraction of that population, and often a very small fraction at that. How can the statistician presume to be telling us the exact story, knowing only a part of it?

The question is a very important one. We should understand the answer, for it is true that most economic data *are* derived from samples. And yet it is also true that sampling can provide extraordinarily accurate information about "populations" that are not counted—or even *countable!* For example, during World War II, American and British statisticians estimated the totals for German war production by applying sampling methods to the serial numbers on captured equipment. After the war, many of their figures turned out to be just as accurate as the figures that the Germans compiled from the actual records of production itself. Moreover, the Allied figures were available sooner, since their method of counting took much less time.

The logic of sampling

What is the logic of sampling? It is based on a kind of reasoning that we use all the time. For example, we may complain that the streets in a city are dirty. Yet it is very unlikely that our complaint is based on an inspection of *all* the streets in the city or even a majority of them. Does this render our conclusion untrustworthy? It all depends. If we have seen a "fair" number of streets in all parts of the city, and all those we saw were dirty, we are quite justified in concluding that those we haven't seen would look much the same. But what is a "fair" number? What are the other criteria for selecting a sample that will enable us to generalize with a high degree of reliability about data that we have not observed?

Sample size

The first and most obvious requirement for a "fair sample" is its size. Yet, surprisingly, in making accurate statements based on samples, size turns out to be much less of a stumbling block than we might think. The U.S. Census Bureau, for example, on the basis of a sample of only about 5 percent of all families, gives a detailed and reliable description of the United States population. And if we want to study collections of data less complicated than those for the U.S. population, a sample much smaller than 5 percent will yield surprisingly good results. The Gallup and other polls forecast election results—on the whole quite accurately—on the basis of a sample of less than 100th of 1 percent of all voters.

How big a sample do we need to arrive at accurate estimates? That depends on two things: (1) how much we know about the larger "universe" of data that we are sampling, and (2) how accurate we want to be.

Suppose, for example, that we had two barrels of marbles, one filled with marbles of only two colors, white and black, and the other filled with an unknown number of colors. Obviously, the proportion of black to white marbles can be found from a much smaller sample than we would need for the second barrel, where a whole spectrum of colors and their various proportions are involved. Hence, the simpler the problem and the more clear-cut the data, the smaller the sample can be: it takes many fewer cases to establish the proportion of male to female births than to establish the pattern of average weight-to-height relation of infants at birth.

But suppose we have a "universe" that is well understood, such as our first barrel. How many marbles will we have to draw until we can make some kind of reliable statement about the *actual* proportion of black to white in the whole barrel? Here the answer depends on how accurate we want to be. Statisticians speak of "confidence intervals" to describe the fact that we can establish our own limits of reliability by increasing the size of a sample.

The "correct" sample size then turns out to depend on our need for accuracy. If we want to be 100 percent accurate, after all, we will have to check each and every marble, thereby raising the sample to the size of the population itself, assuming we make no enumeration errors—no easy task.

Bias

Surprisingly, then, the problem of sample size is not so much of a difficulty as we might have thought, assuming that we know something about the characteristics of the population we are investigating. But suppose we do not. Suppose that we have traveled exclusively in the downtown streets of a city, not knowing there was a great slum just a few blocks away, and we based our judgments of the city as a whole on the cleanliness of the business district alone. Here we have encountered a much more serious problem. *Bias* has entered our calculations. **By *bias* we mean that we have not planned our sampling technique in such a way that each and every item in the population has an equal chance of being observed.**

Bias can enter sampling in the most unexpected ways. Suppose, for example, that the white marbles in our barrel were (unknown to us) slightly heavier than the black ones, so that when we shook up the barrel to be certain the marbles were fairly mixed, we were actually causing the white marbles to move toward the bottom. If our sample were taken from the top of the barrel, it would be biased in favor of black marbles. Or suppose that we chose our city streets absolutely by chance, but that we failed to take into account that the Sanitation Department visited different parts of the city on different days. Our sample could easily be biased in one direction or another.

Perhaps the most famous example of bias was the *Literary Digest* poll of the Roosevelt-Landon election in 1936. The magazine (long since defunct) sampled 2.3 million people, most of whom said they were going to vote for Alfred Landon. On this basis, the *Digest* predicted a landslide for the Republican candidate. In fact, as we all know, the election *was* a landslide—but for the other side.

What went wrong? Obviously, the problem was that the sample, although very large, was terribly biased. It was taken from subscription lists of magazines, telephone directories, and automobile registration lists. In 1936, people who subscribed to magazines, had phones, and owned autos were highly concentrated in the upper brackets of income distribution. Furthermore, in that year, income had a great deal to do with party choice. The result has been used in statistics texts ever since as the perfect example of bias.

Correcting for biases

How do we avoid biases? The answer is to strive to choose our sample as randomly as possible—that is, in such a way that every unit in the population has an equal chance of being in our sample. A purely random sample has the best chance to duplicate, in miniature, all the characteristics of the larger "universe" it represents. Clearly, the more complex

that universe, the larger the random sample will have to be to give us figures that fall within respectable confidence intervals. That is why the U.S. Bureau of the Census uses a sample *as large as* 5 percent to collect information about age, sex, race, income, place of residence and many more attributes of the population as a whole.

Getting a sample that is free of bias is by no means easy. Statisticians spend much time in devising ways to avoid the errors of bias and in detecting unsuspected errors in the work of others. Doesn't this mean, then, that sampling is a technique we should view with considerable suspicion? In fact, doesn't it more or less cast serious doubt on a good deal of what we think are "the facts"?

As we have said before, a healthy skepticism with regard to data is often very useful. But skepticism is not at all the same thing as a rejection of sampling as a statistical *technique*. Sampling is ultimately based on the laws of probability about which we know quite a bit. Hence, far from avoiding sampling, we should use our knowledge to perfect it.

Here are three reasons why sampling is both essential and reliable:

1. Samples may be the only way of obtaining information.

Suppose that you are in charge of planning the development program for a nation like India and that you need to know many facts about the birth rate, the average size of landholdings, or average incomes. *There may be no possible way of obtaining this information except by sampling.* Or suppose you are a historian interested in reconstructing the average length of life or the average family size of some period far in the past. There may be no possible method of gaining this information except by sampling (for example, using the data on gravestones), thereafter making the best adjustment you can for the inevitable biases that have crept into your sample (the poorest people didn't get gravestones). Or suppose your doctor wants to test your blood. Would you want him to test *all* of it?

2. Samples may be cheaper than counting.

Even when you can count all the items in a collection, it may not be worth your while to do so. It would take an enormous expenditure of time and effort to interview each and every householder in the U.S. about every set of facts in the decennial census. It would cost a fortune to test each and every light bulb that General Electric makes. Sampling gives us accurate enough data at a vast saving in cost and time.

3. Sampling may be more accurate than counting.

Because of human error, sampling is often more accurate than taking a full count. For example, a census survey of every household would require the services of an army of census takers, most of whom could not be trained in all the pitfalls of interviewing. It is quite likely that the inaccuracies of their mass survey would be greater than those in the much smaller number of reports prepared by expert census takers who are careful to follow instructions to the letter. In full counts, immense amounts of data must be handled and transcribed. Clerical errors are apt to be fewer in smaller but more easily manipulated samples.

Sampling, in short, has its inescapable problems. But it is an absolutely indispensable and astonishingly reliable technique with which to deal with the overwhelming mass of data in the real world.

V. Econometrics. The Use of Functions

Now that we have an idea how sampling and other statistical techniques generate different types of economic data, we want to learn something about how data are used to test economic theories. This brings us to a relatively new use for statistics called *econometrics, a use that applies statistics to test various hypotheses about how the economy works.*

Functional relationships   One of the central uses of econometrics is to discover functional relationships among the variables of the economic system. From Chapter 8 we are familiar with the general meaning of functional relationships, and we have again and again looked for, or applied, such relationships, as in the propensity to consume, a functional relationship between income and consumption.

Let us increase our basic knowledge by studying the consumption function further—not as a problem of empirical research, but as an exercise that will introduce us further to the vocabulary and techniques of econometrics.

For this purpose let us assume that the consumption function is this:

$$C = 2 + .8Y$$

This formula enables us to set up a table or schedule, relating C and Y, as follows:

If Y is equal to	then C is equal to		shown on graph as point
0	2 + .8(0)	= 2 + 0 = 2	A
10	2 + .8(10)	= 2 + 8 = 10	B
20	2 + .8(20)	= 2 + 16 = 18	C
40	2 + .8(40)	= 2 + 32 = 34	D
75	2 + .8(75)	= 2 + 60 = 62	E
100	2 + .8(100)	= 2 + 80 = 82	F

Let's now graph this relationship. Remember that each point in the two-dimensional graph represents *two* numbers; namely, C and Y.

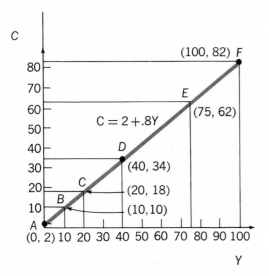

FIG. 44 • 5   Propensity to consume

All this, of course, is very familiar. But now consider: *how do we know that the consumption function is a straight line?*

The answer is that the word *straight* means that the line has an *unchanging slope*. If it were not a straight line, the slope would be increasing or decreasing from point to point, as Fig. 44 • 6 shows. By

FIG. 44 • 6   Nonlinear functions

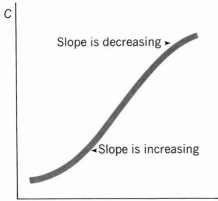

way of contrast, all lines of unchanging slope are always straight, although they need not all slope at the same angle. Figure 44 • 7 shows a variety of lines of *unchanging* slope, with very *different angles of slope*.

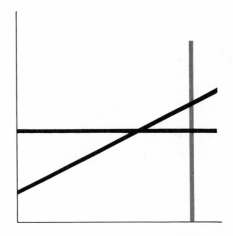

FIG. 44 • 7   Linear functions

What is it about our formula that tells us that the (hypothetical) consumption function of $C = 2 + .8Y$ is a straight line? It is not the number 2, which simply tells us the value of C when $Y = 0$. This so-called *intercept* tells us where our line "begins" on the vertical axis, but it says nothing about its slope. That is determined by the second term. In this term, the number .8 is called the *coefficient* of Y, and shows the slope of the line. The "linearity" (straight line) aspect of the equation depends on the fact that Y is of the "first order"—that is, it is not squared or of a higher power. $C = 2 + .8Y^2$ would *not* be a linear function, but a curvilinear one. A linear function is always of the form $Y = a \pm bx$.

Coefficients   The coefficient of the independent variable tells us how much the dependent variable will change for each unit of change of the independent variable. That is, .8 tells us that for each variation of $1 in income, consumption will change by 80¢. Given our unchanging coefficient, this relationship will remain the same, whether we are dealing with $1 or with $1 million. In each case, the change in C will be 80 percent the change in Y. If, in fact, the coefficient did change—if, e.g., we consumed a larger fraction of a small income than of a large one—the line would not be straight, and the equation that represented that line would not be an equation of the very simple form we have used.*

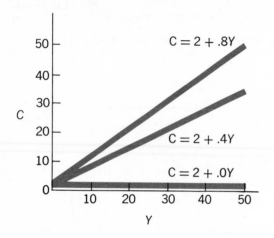

FIG. 44 · 8   Changing coefficients

Coefficients, even of the simplest kinds, can represent all kinds of slopes. In Fig. 44 • 8 we show three coefficients that give rise to three slopes. The lowest line has a coefficient of zero, giving rise to a straight horizontal line parallel to the income axis. (Such a line depicts a situation in which we would not consume any more than a fixed amount, no matter how high our incomes—a highly implausible state of affairs.) The middle line shows a consumption function of approximately .4—a state

*The two numbers 2 and .8 in our formula are called *parameters*. A change in either or both parameters indicates a *shift* in the consumption line.

of affairs in which we regularly consume 40¢ out of each additional $1 of income over the $2 intercept. The topmost line shows us our familiar coefficient of .8.

Note three final points.

1. The coefficient describes the slope of a line.
2. All lines described by unchanging coefficients are straight.
3. Econometrics commonly uses equations rather than graphs because equations can handle many more variables than we can conveniently show on a graph.

VI. Correlations and Regression

Up to this point we have spoken of functional relationships as if we knew the relationship among the variables in our equations. But one of the most difficult problems in actual economic research is to determine this relationship. In everyday language, we spend much time in econometric research trying to determine what affects what, and by how much. Once we have determined these relationships, it is relatively simple to put the results into formulas and to solve for the answers. Hence we are now going to turn to a fundamental technique of econometrics—correlation and regression—that will lead into the important problem of establishing reliable functional relationships.

Analysis of relationships   We have come into contact with this problem in our study of the propensity to consume. There we were interested in examining the association between two variables, income and consumption. Much of econometrics is concerned with the kinds of *problems* exemplified by the income-consumption relationship, although the kinds of *activities* that econometrics investigates runs a vast gamut that includes price-quantity relations, interest rate-investment relationships, and wage-employment relationships.

What is it that we want to discover when we look into the relationship of two variables, such as income and consumption, wages and employment, or whatever? Generally, we seek to establish three things: (1) whether a change in one of these variables—say, income—or wages—is usually associated with a change in the second variable; (2) if there *is* such an association, whether a given change in one variable usually results in large or small change in the associated variable; and (3) once two variables have been shown to be linked in some way, just how precisely the relationship between the two can be described.

Correlation and scatter diagrams

All of these problems use statistical techniques that we will not attempt to teach fully in this text. But for each of them there is also an intuitive representation that will make you familiar with the nature of these econometric questions.

The first such task, we have said, is to discover whether or not a relationship exists at all between two variables. The simplest way to test for the probable existence of such a relationship is to perform the operation we did in Chapter 27, where we made a *scatter diagram* of income and consumption. In Fig. 44•9, we show two such scatter diagrams, each a visual representation of the association between two variables. On the left, we show a diagram that depicts the relationship of the heights and weights of a group of male adults; on the right we show one that portrays the heights and IQs of a group of male adults (both diagrams are fictitious).

FIG. 44 • 9   Scatter diagrams

Male Adults

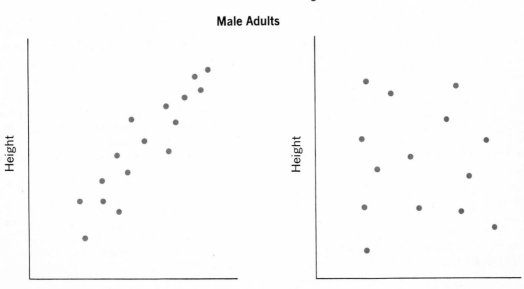

Height / Weight   Height / IQ

The difference between the two diagrams is obvious. There is a clear-cut relationship between height and weight—the taller the man, the heavier he tends to be (with exceptions, of course). But there is no clear-cut relation between height and IQ: tall men are neither brighter nor more stupid than short men. In the first case, there is prima facie evidence that a correlation exists; in the second case there is none.

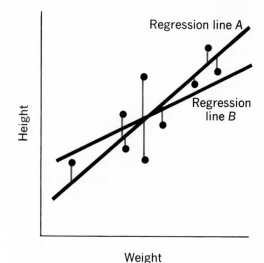

FIG. 44 • 10   Least squares

Regression

Once we have some evidence that a correlation exists, we would like to find a way of describing it. That is, we would like to discover the value of one variable, if we know the value of the other, or the rate of change in one variable, given a change in the other. For example, we would like to know the *average change* in weight associated with an additional inch of height, or the *average change* in consumption associated with an additional dollar of income. (The last is, of course, our familiar marginal propensity to consume.)

When econometricians seek to reduce this relationship to a numerical magnitude, they speak of "running a regression" of one variable (such as height or consumption) on the other (weight or income). How do you run such a regression? The first problem, to which we shall turn in Section VII, is to establish the direction of causality—that is, whether we are regressing X on Y, or Y on X. The second problem is the procedure by which we measure the association in which we are interested. The details of computation are better reserved for a statistics course. We will just ask you to take on faith that there is a fairly simple arithmetical technique for deriving a regression line that will tell us what variable A will tend to be, given Variable B.

In Fig. 44 • 10, we show a very simple height-weight scatter diagram (it could be, of course an income-consumption scatter diagram) with *two* regression lines. Each line was drawn visually in an attempt to show the form of the relationship which the dots exhibit. Forget the colored lines for a moment. How do we know which is the better of the two, line A or B?

Least squares

The answer is that we try to find the line that describes the relationship best; that is, the line that lies closest to the dots. But how do we define "closest"? Here is where the colored lines enter. (1) From each dot we draw a vertical line to a given regression line (line A in our example). (2) We measure each "colored-line" distance and *square* it.* (3) We add together the squared distances.

*Why do we square the distances? One answer is that this gives additional importance (weight) to any dots that lie considerably away from the regression line, thereby making our measure more sensitive to "exceptions" to what seems to be the rule. The mathematics of statistical theory is another, and more fundamental, reason.

In our diagram we have shown the distances of the dots from line *A*. Now we would have to do the same thing for line *B*, or for any other line we could draw. In the end, *we choose the line that has the smallest sum of squared distances as being the best fit.* We call this technique of finding such a line "fitting a regression by least squares." There are other ways of fitting lines, as well. We must leave these problems for a statistics course. But the basic idea of a "least squares" fit should now be plain.

What does the resulting line show? We know the answer from the propensity to consume (note the least squares line fitted on the diagram, Fig. 27 • 5). The regression coefficient, or the *slope* of the regression line, shows us the change in the dependent variable (*C*) associated with a change in the independent variable (*Y*). We know that this relationship can also be expressed (very roughly) in the formula on page 407, where the coefficient is .94*Y*. Thus once again we have shown that a diagram and an equation are only two ways of depicting the same thing—in this case, the relationship between consumption and income.*

Correlation coefficient   There remains one last problem. We know now what we mean by correlation and by a regression analysis. We even understand, in general, the criterion by which we fit a line to a group of "dots." But we do not know how

we distinguish between two correlations to determine which is better.

Once again, an example will help make the answer clear. In Fig. 44 • 11 we show two regression lines, *each one of which is the best fit we can get by the least squares criterion.* Yet, clearly, the line on the right shows a better correlation of *Y* on *X* than the line on the left, simply because the dots lie directly on, or just off, the regression line, whereas in the second case they lie at some distance from it.

There is a mathematical way of describing the difference in "closeness of fit" of the two lines; it is called a *correlation coefficient*. A correlation coefficient is a number that tells us how closely our regression line fits the actual data. This coefficient always has a value between +1 and −1. If the correspondence is perfect— that is, if the dots lie exactly *on* the line, the correlation coefficient is either +1 or −1 (depending on whether the two variables move in the same direction or in directions opposite to each other). If the correlation coefficient is 0, then no correlation exists, as in the case of our example of height and IQ. Once again, we leave the calculation of the coefficient itself to a statistics course. But you can now see that the closer a correlation coefficient (for which we use the symbol *r*) is to +1 or −1, the stronger is the relationship between the two variables, and the better is the correlation.

One further piece of information. Statisticians usually use the *square* of the correlation coefficient (r^2) to describe the degree of association between two variables. In other words, a high r^2 is evidence of a "significant" relationship between two variables, and a low r^2 is evidence of the *lack* of such a relationship. This raises two questions: (1) by a "significant" correlation, do we imply that changes in one variable *cause* changes in the other? and

*Note that we have been talking exclusively about *positive* coefficients; that is, about cases where an added inch of height is associated with an *added* amount of weight, or where an extra dollar of income is associated with *extra* consumption spending. We can also have negative regression coefficients, where the groups of "dots" would be downward sloping, and where the coefficient would have a minus sign in front of it. For example, if you graph weight on the vertical axis and life expectancy on the horizontal, you would find a downward sloping cluster of dots. Can you think of other such cases?

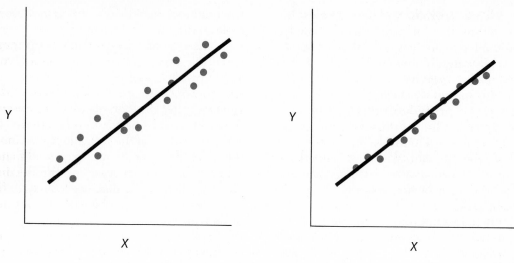

FIG. 44 · 11   Closeness of fit

(2) how high an r^2 is "significant"? The first of these questions we will examine in our next sections. The second is a technical matter that must be left for explanation in a course on statistics.

Multiple correlation   A last problem remains, to which we can only allude in passing in this introduction to correlation analysis. It is the question of how we deal with the problem of correlation when more than one variable is associated with changes in another. For instance, how do we figure out the relationship not merely between consumption and income, but between consumption and income *and* wealth *and* changes in prices *and* consumer expectations *and* still other variables that may influence consumption expenditures?

The answer is that we run what is called a *multiple regression analysis*. We do this by quantifying the relationship between the variable in which we are interested (the *dependent variable*) and the other variables (the *independent variables*), by techniques that enable us to discover the separate effect of each independent variable on the dependent variable. Once again, the techniques for doing this must be kept for a statistics course, but we should now be able to understand the meaning of the complicated formulas that emerge from multiple regression analysis.

Such a formula (purely imaginary in this case) might look like this:

$$C = .8Y + .3W - 2T$$

The purpose of such a multiple regression formula is to show us the different effects on our dependent variable, consumption (C), of various independent variables such as income (Y), wealth (W), taxes (T), and so on. What our particular formula tells us is that the net effect on consumption of $1 of added income is 80 cents, assuming that there is no change in wealth, taxes, etc.; that the net effect of an increase in wealth is 30 cents (again assuming that we have held the other variables constant); that the net effect of a rise in taxes is a *decline* in consumption (note the minus sign before the coefficient of .2), again with other variables held constant.

VII. Correlation and Causation

Regression techniques are widely used in econometric research, and we have been able only to indicate in very general terms the actual procedures that econometricians use. But the idea of correlation opens up for us a problem into which we must look very carefully. This is the connection between *correlation and causation.* When we say that there is a high correlation between two variables—let us say cigarette smoking and heart disease—do we mean that cigarette smoking *causes* heart disease?

The question is obviously of very great importance. All sorts of disputes rage over the degree of "causation" that can be attributed to correlations. Econometrics cannot solve these disputes, because the word "cause," as anyone knows who has ever looked into a book on philosophy, is a perplexing and elusive one. But econometrics can shed a strong light on some of the pitfalls associated with it. In particular, it makes us very cautious about declaring that such-and-such an event is the cause of another, simply because there is a high degree of correlation between them.

We have already covered the problem of spurious causation and *ceteris paribus* in Chapter 8. You might want to review Chapter 8 before going on.

What can correlation tell us? As we know, econometricians are extremely cautious about using correlations to "prove" causal hypotheses. *Even the closest correlation may not show in which direction the causal influences are working;* for instance, the high correlation between the number of corporate mergers and the level of stock prices in the 1960s does not show whether mergers caused stock prices to move up or whether booming prices encouraged companies to merge and float their new securities on a favorable market.

So, too, *the interconnectedness of the economic process often causes many series of data to move together.* In inflationary periods, for example, most prices tend to rise, or in depression many indexes tend to fall, without establishing that any of these series was directly responsible for a movement in another particular series.

And finally, econometricians are constantly on the lookout for factors that have not been held constant during a correlation, so that *ceteris paribus conditions were not in fact maintained.*

Is there an answer to these (and still other) very puzzling problems of correlation and causation? There is a partial answer which is important enough to warrant repeating what we said before. We cannot claim that a correlation is proof that a causal relationship exists. But a causal relationship is likely to exist when we can demonstrate a strong correlation, backed up by theoretical reasoning. That is, every valid economic hypothesis (or for that matter every valid hypothesis of any kind) *must* show a high and "significant" correlation coefficient between the "cause" and the "effect," provided that we are absolutely certain that our statistical test has rigorously excluded spurious correlations of various kinds and unsuspected "other things." Needless to say this is often very difficult and sometimes impossible to do with real data. A physicist can hold "other things equal" in his laboratory, but the world will not stand still just so an economist can test his theories. The net result is that correlations are a more powerful device for *disproving* hypotheses than for proving them.

VIII. Forecasting

In addition to their role in testing economic hypotheses, correlations and regressions are used to build forecasting models. Indeed, this is one of the most important functions of econometrics.

How does an econometrician attempt to forecast? We know part of the answer from our introduction to econometrics. The first step is to assemble all available statistical information concerning important economic relationships. Suppose, for example, it is known from multiple regression that the demand for automobiles can be represented by an equation in which the demand for cars is related to changes in disposable income, to changes in car prices, to credit conditions, etc. This long and complicated equation will then become one element in a model of the economy that will also contain the demand for many other final products, as well as the relationships (also econometrically derived) between or among elements such as the quantity of money and the level of prices, the level of employment and consumer disposable income, and so on.

Thus, the predictive tool of the econometrician consists of *a series of equations which depict the simultaneous interaction of those activities that the model-builder believes to be crucial in affecting the economy.* As can be imagined, this leads to extremely complex equations and systems of equations. The famous model of the Wharton School of Business of the University of Pennsylvania, for example, has some 150 equations, most of them with strings of multiple regression elements. To solve such a system of equations by pencil and paper would be impossible—or would take so long that the future would long ago have become history. Thus the computer with its lightning speeds is an integral part of the econometrician's equipment.

Exogenous and endogenous variables

When we examine forecasting models, we find that the many variables they contain can be classified into two kinds. Many of the variables *depend* on other variables for their values; for example, automobile purchases depend on disposable income, car prices, and other variables. These are *dependent* variables in the model; that is, elements whose values will be determined by the action of the independent variables in the system.

These *exogenous* ("outside") variables must be introduced into the system to determine the values of the dependent variables. Where does the econometrician get these exogenous variables? Some of them may be known facts from which various kinds of future economic activity may be inferred by econometric analysis. For instance, the model-builder may introduce the known level of population growth as an exogenous variable on which the future level of home-building or car-buying may depend. Or exogenous variables may be based on surveys or on expected policy decisions, such as surveys of intended corporate investment or policy statements of the Federal Reserve. These and other exogenous variables are arranged along with the endogenous variables in a set of simultaneous equations that make up the econometric model and reflect the complex mechanism of the economy. The econometrician then solves the model, thus deriving values for his endogenous variables, such as consumer disposable income, automobile purchases, or GNP itself.

Here, of course, lies a central problem for econometric forecasting. We can never be certain of the accuracy of our all-important exogenous variables. We cannot predict with certainty, for instance, what the money supply will be, because we cannot know whether Federal Reserve policy will change. We cannot predict with certainty what business investment will be, because business expectations may change. To the extent that our exogenous variables are wrongly estimated, the values we derive from them for dependent elements in our model will also be wrong. In 1966, for example, the Council of Economic Advisers predicted that the rate of inflation was about to slow down. Actually, it accelerated. The mistake did not lie with the reasoning of the Council or with its econometric model. It lay in the fact that the Council assumed, on the basis of the data at hand, that the budget for 1967 was going to be balanced. What happened in fact was that a budgetary deficit of $9 billion was incurred to finance an expansion of the Vietnam War—a deficit that had not been included in the original budget estimates.

One way to get around such problems is to assume several sets of values for key "policy variables" and to run the model for each one. For example, a forecast put out by the Federal Reserve Bank of St. Louis has made three different predictions based on three different postulated rates of growth in the money supply. Having such a spectrum of predictions seems at first to be weaseling on the job. But actually it serves a very useful purpose. Such alternative models show us the probable *range* of our results and can therefore tell us, for instance, if the consumption of autos will be much or little affected if the money supply grows fast or slowly.

Second, because many of the key policy variables *cannot* be accurately predicted (who can foretell with certainty what next year's federal budget will be?) a spectrum of forecasts enables individuals

or corporations to make their own guesstimates about these critical variables and then to examine what the probable configuration of *other* economic variables are apt to look like, given these key assumptions.

Every person or firm bases his economic decisions on some kind of implicit or explicit estimate of future economic conditions. To try to improve these decisions, econometric forecasting is increasingly used by large industrial corporations, by financial institutions, and by governments. The results of the big models at the Brookings Institution or the Wharton School are even featured in news articles. Hence it is important to ask how well the econometric predictions have fared.

Performance

Most econometricians would be the first to admit that their performance has been uneven. The models have worked very well—have predicted changes in the economy quite accurately—as long as things were moving along fairly steadily in one direction. But when things changed direction, *which is just when we want our models to work best*, they have not been too reliable. The influential Brookings Model, for example, did not forecast the recessions of 1957–58, or of 1960–1961. In 1968, most econometricians predicted a recession for 1969, but it did not actually take place until 1970.

What accounts for this disappointing performance? Part of the trouble lies in the problems of "specifying" the model correctly—that is, of overcoming the numerous problems of econometrics that we have touched on in this chapter. The fact that different econometric models use different multiple regression coefficients for the same variables attests in itself to the fact that there is more than one way to depict certain relationships.

Second is the problem that econometricians, as we have also made clear, ultimately rely on economics; and economists are by no means of one mind about the relative importance of certain key exogenous variables, such as the influence of fiscal or monetary policy on the price level or on GNP. Hence our models misperform because we are still in disagreement about economic theory itself.

And last, our models misperform because we cannot predict the course of certain critical exogenous variables that lie beyond the reach of economic reasoning itself. For example, no economic theory could have predicted the degree of escalation of the Vietnam War. Yet that event dominated macroeconomic behavior in the late Sixties.

Limits of prediction

Does this mean that econometric forecasting is doomed to failure? Not necessarily. The need is rather to understand better what our models can do for us and what they cannot. One thing they can certainly do is to clarify the nature of the interactions of many economic activities, so that important relationships within the economic system can be specified with much greater accuracy. A second very important purpose of models is to make clear the economic *requirements* to reach given targets, a task that is not quite the same as that of prediction, but that is no less important regarding the future.

Equally certainly, however, we cannot use our models to give us predictions about such things as the date of the next stock market crash or even the level of GNP ten years hence. When matters of volatile *behavior* are concerned, such as the psychology of the stock market, an econometric model has nothing to go by. By definition, such unforecastable psychological changes *alter* the very coefficients on which predictive equations are built.

In the same way, long-term predictions are made hazardous by events such as international crises, technological breakthroughs, or political upheavals, all of which also upset the parameters on which all prediction is ultimately based.

Here, in the realm of the exogenous, the *science* of econometric forecasting ends, and the art of forecasting begins. For it is here that the shrewd guess of the economist or the hunch of the econometrician will lead him—in the face of the established patterns of the past—to postulate that things have shifted or are about to shift and therefore to regard the results of his model with more than the usual degree of caution, or to recast the parameters on which his model is based. At this point the economist or the econometrician certainly does not claim access to the occult, but humbly confesses that scientific methods, powerful as they are, still cannot describe the shape of many things to come.

Focus

In all likelihood you will be using this chapter to fill yourself in on, not to "study," beginning statistics and econometrics. So we have simply added a review of words and concepts that may help you remember what you've read.

Definitions

I. SOME INITIAL CAUTIONS

Deceptions

Statistics are always best approached with caution. *Definitions* are often key to the interpretations we place on data. Data can be out-dated, misleading if not carefully identified, deceptive if "overin-terpreted" (be wary of making mountains out of molehills).

Means

Visual tricks using data to make a point or the failure to get a rounded perspective on facts are frequent sources of statistical error—or worse—statistical deception.

Medians

Skewness

II. DISTRIBUTIONS AND AVERAGES

Learn to distinguish between *means*—the arithmetic average—and *medians*—the middle value of a series. Mean values are usually different from medians, because data are often *skewed*.

Bell-shaped curve

Modes are "averages" in terms of that value which has the largest number of units. *In a normal, bell-shaped distribution, mode, mean, and median will all be the same.* This will not be the case in skewed distributions.

Bi-modal

We must be particularly careful to guard against *bi-modal* distribu-tions—distributions in which there are two (or more) modal clusters.

Real vs. money values

III. PRICE INDEXES

Price indexes are used to "correct" current dollar values, in order to establish "real" changes in economic magnitudes.

Consumer Price Index

Price indexes can be constructed from many kinds of data. The De-partment of Labor's *Consumer Price Index* is an index number that measures the changing cost of a "market basket" of typical consumer goods.

Market basket

Weights

It is simple to construct an index if only one good is involved. When more than one good is in the market basket, we must assign *weights* to the various items. Each is given the degree of importance propor-tional to its value in the "market basket."

New goods

New goods present many difficult problems for the construction of an index. To the extent that the good fulfills a new *function,* the problem is magnified because, typically, new goods fall in price.

Base

Price indexes, once constructed, are simple to apply: current dollar values are divided by the index and then multiplied by 100. The result-ing "real" series will differ in its dollar values according to which year is used as a *base,* but the relative changes from year to year will be the same. Thus *indexes can be spliced.* Be wary, however, of ignoring the statistical difficulties of long-term time series, just because they are spliced into one continuous series.

Splicing indexes

Probability

IV. SAMPLING

The logic of sampling is based on *probability.* There are well-established laws of probability that enable us to determine certain characteristics of large "universes" of data by sampling techniques.

Bias

Random selection

Econometrics

The most important objective of good sampling is to avoid *bias.* This is accomplished by aiming for a random sample. The size of the random sample will then depend on the size of the total "universe" and on the number of its characteristics that we wish to test for.

Sampling, surprisingly enough, may be more accurate than full enumeration, as well as cheaper and easier.

Functional relationships

V. ECONOMETRICS AND FUNCTIONAL RELATIONSHIPS

One main use of econometrics is the use of statistics to test economic hypotheses by statistical methods.

Linear graphs

Another principal use is to establish the existence or nonexistence of functional relationships.

Coefficients

Functional relationships are usually described by equations, rather than graphs, especially if the variables are numerous. *The slope of the line on all linear graphs will be determined by the coefficients* in the equation that describes the functional relationship.

Associations among variables

VI. CORRELATIONS AND REGRESSIONS

Correlations attempt to establish *associations among variables,* and regressions are the means by which we quantify these associations.

Scatter diagrams

Scatter diagrams give us a visual clue to whether correlations exist. But we test for such correlations by a method known as *least squares.* This method gives us a *regression line* that is mathematically defined as the closest possible fit to a scatter of paired variables. The regression equation describes the nature and direction of the association between the two variables.

Least squares

Regression line

Regressions do not tell us how closely the data cluster around a given line. To establish the "tightness" of fit, we need another measure called the *correlation coefficient.*

Correlation coefficient

A method known as *multiple correlation* enables us to quantify the relationship among more than two variables by holding all variables "fixed" while we test the correlation of the particular pair we wish to investigate.

VII. CORRELATION AND CAUSATION

Multiple correlation

We must be very careful about attributing causal relationships to correlated variables. There are many pitfalls: *wrong-way correlation, spurious correlation,* improper attention to *ceteris paribus.* All can deceive us as to the existence or nonexistence of a causal connection between variables.

Correlations, when carefully interpreted, can often be useful in disproving hypotheses. They are less dependable as "proofs" of hypotheses.

Causation

VIII. FORECASTING

Wrong-way correlation

Forecasting is essentially an effort to *predict the movement of dependent variables on the basis of assumptions regarding the independent variables.*

The independent variables are *exogenous,* introduced into the system from outside. They are treated as stated values that will determine or limit the values of the dependent variables.

Spurious correlation

Because exogenous variables are intrinsically unpredictable, the forecasting powers of econometrics are inherently limited.

Exogenous variables

Econometrics models are still invaluable as a means of examining the interrelationships among various parts of the economy and testing theories that seek to explain those relationships.

QUESTIONS

1. If someone told you that the unemployment rate was 4 percent in West Germany and 5 percent in the U.S., would you conclude that unemployment was therefore higher in the U.S.? What cautions would you advise before coming to that conclusion?

2. Draw a graph that is *calculated* to deceive someone. Example: an alarming depiction of stock price changes in the last month.

3. What is the best average to describe the "average" IQ of a population? What do you mean by "best"? What characteristics would be shown by a mean that would not be shown by a median? Would a mode be useful? Suppose instead of IQ, you wanted to show the "average" stockholdings of the same population. What answers do you now give to the questions?

4. Describe a series that is likely to be bi-modal. Try to think of one that isn't in the text. The trick is to find something that typically comes in two or more "sizes" instead of being more or less evenly spaced over the range of all sizes.

5. Write down four median incomes and four price index numbers; figure out real income for each year. Shift bases and compare your results.

6. How would you handle the problem of fitting new cars into the Consumer Price Index? How much of their price is improved quality, how much is just inflation? How would you go about making such a decision?

7. Take a market basket with two goods: bread and wine. Bread costs 50¢; wine $5.00. In year 1, you spend $10 for bread, $5 for wine. Now bread falls to 25¢, wine rises to $6.00. Can you make a weighted index from this data? Do you need to know how much you spend for bread and wine in year 2?

8. Describe some data that could be more accurately surveyed by sampling techniques than by complete enumeration. Numbers of grains of sand on a beach? Name some economic possibilities.

9. What is meant by regression? By correlation? How would you decide if a high correlation was a prima facie case for causation? Describe a highly correlated pair of variables in which causation is uncertain. Are cigarette smoking and ill-health one? How would you find out? *Could* you find out "beyond all possibility of error"?

10. Why is the forecaster's life a hard one?

Index

A

Abstraction, 5–7, 118–19, 131
Accelerator, 432–33, 571–72
Accessions tax, 304
Advertising, 169, 226–27, 560
Affirmative action programs, 278
Affluence, *see* Wealth
Age, 20, 260, 407–8
    unemployment linked to, 53, 555
    of workers, 18, 269, 273, 348, 350
Aggregation problems, 117–18, 342
Agriculture, 20, 225, 230, 247, 491
    agricultural exports, 586
    as competitive industry, 200
    employment in, 353
    foreign, investment in, 637
    as functional sector, 16
    Soviet, 674
    subsidized, 162–66, 447, 449
    technology of, 564, 565
    Third World, 648–50, 654–55, 658, 660–
        62, 667
    unemployment rate for, 553–54
Aid-in-kind, 411
Allocation, 134–45, 142–45
American Challenge, The (Servan-
        Schreiber), 633–34
American Telephone and Telegraph, 16, 28,
        433, 462–63
Analytical tools, 105–11
Antitrust legislation, 645
Arab "takeover" threat, 645
Arc elasticity, 153–54
Armaments, *see* Defense
Assets, private, 16, 243, 327–28, 498
    described, 497
    inflation's effect on, 540
    net foreign, 328
    public vs., 462–64, 470
    ranking by sales or, 38
Assets, reserve (SDRs), 613–14, 620, 625–
        26, 628
Atomic Energy Commission, 58
Automation-unemployment relationship,
        556, 559, 564–65
Automobiles and auto industry, 11, 117, 158,
        197, 338, 378–79, 558, 664, 689
    assembly of, 39, 355
    foreign, 619, 627; *see also* Volkswagen
    public transport vs., 240–41
    recession hitting, 40
Averages, statistical, 123–24, 687, 691–94
Averitt, Robert, 265

B

"Bads," economic, 229–31
Balance of payments, 608–13, 711
  "balances" in, 611–12, 620
  deficit in, 617–26, 638
  multinationals complicating, 638–39, 642
Ball, George, 641
Bankruptcy, 40, 168, 572
  limited liability for, 26–27
Banks and banking, 16, 328, 383, 413, 493–508
  bank deposits, 493–96, 498, 500–507, 512
  central, 495, 515, 532, 612–14
    foreign, 621–23, 629
  foreign-exchange, 605–7, 610, 612–13
  runs on, 496
Bases, statistical, 689, 695–99
  shifts in, 698–99
Bastiat, Frédéric, *Social Fallacies,* 596–99
Baumol, William, 51, 231
Behavioral relationships, 107
Bell-shaped curves, 356, 694
Berle, A. A., 60, 635
Bethlehem Steel, 544
Bevan, Aneurin, 674
Bias, econometric, 700–702
Bimodal distribution, 694–95
Birman, A., 676
Birth (population) control, 138, 652, 661
Black, Eugene, 650, 662
Black market, 137, 139, 165
Blacks, *see* Race problem
Boards of directors, 28, 413, 643
  public members of, 58–59
Bonds, 22, 328, 381*n*, 412–13, 450, 461–63, 465–66, 504–5
  defaulting on, 473
  foreign, 620–21
  indexing of, 550
  interest rate on, 27, 435, 505, 523
  as legal tender, 493
  newly issued, 383, 385, 413, 463
  on open market, 507–9
  ratings on, 472
  tax-exempt, 294
  yields on, 505, 524
Boom periods, 351, 418, 424*n*, 572
  absence of, 375
Bottlenecks, 534–35, 677
"Bottoming out," 479, 573
Boulding, Kenneth, 32, 64, 138, 340
Brannan Plan, 164
British economy, *see* Great Britain
Budget constraints, 144, 326
Business, 19, 37–40, 130–31
  as investor, 413
  organization of, 25–28
  size of, 15–17, 29, 38–40, 55–60, 196–97
    competitive business, 170
    predictability problem, 123
    public supervision, 42
    social responsibility, 55–56, 58–60
Business cycles, 40, 568–73, 577
Business debts, 462–65, 467

C

Canada, 360, 546, 561, 585, 649
  national interests of, 641
  U.S. investment in, 637

Capital, 33–34, 168–70, 270, 352–55, 653–56
  emergence of, 45–47
  hiring of, 169–70, 243
  human, 265–66, 352–53, 656
  under inflation, 538–39
  marginal efficiency of, 436
  as productive wealth, 327
  ratio of output to, 575–76, 660
  short-term flow of, 621, 638
  supply of, 247–49, 253, 352–55
    measurement, 689–90
    shortage, 394, 428
    Third World lack, 649
Capital accounts, 462, 464, 609–11, 617–22
  restraints on, 624
  trends in, 620–21
Capital-gains tax, 303–4
Capital goods, *see* Investment goods
Capitalism, 9–11, 13, 577, 579, 664, 674, 680–82
  as market system, 15, 66
  profile of, 66–69
  "state," 662
  stationary, 63–64
  unemployment inherent in, 560–62
Capitalization, 38, 262, 327
  theory of, 243, 252
Cash flow, defined, 368
Causation, 113–15, 687, 709
Census, 19, 36*n*, 551, 700–702
Ceteris paribus, 105–7, 120, 709
  problems inherent in, 114–15, 117
Chance (luck), 37, 195, 261–63
Chandler, Alfred, 635*n*
Checking accounts, 493–96, 498, 501, 503, 508–10, 605
Chinese economy, 9, 13, 67, 648, 671, 672
  economic revolution, 662–63
  hyperinflationary, 540
Circular causation, 275
Circular flow, 323, 325, 362, 477–78
  described, 13–14
  macro model of, 374–76
  microview of, 129–31, 270
  of profits, 391
  of savings, 381, 392
Claims, 383–85, 412, 495, 498
  types of, 328
"Classical medicine," 623, 626
"Closed" system, defined, 437
Cobwebs, 224–26
Coefficients, 703–4, 707–9, 712
Collectivism, 661–63, 674
Colt, Samuel, 635
Command, economies of, 45, 135, 137, 670–72, 677–78, 680
Commodity stabilization agreements, 657
Comparative advantage, 590–92, 595
Competition, foreign, 600, 603
Competitive activity, 147, 182–200, 520, 677–78
  control exercised over, 165
  entry into and exit from, 191–93
  marginal cost curves in, 186–89
  pure, 242–43
Competitive operation, 39, 167–81
  total costs and revenues of, 175–76
Complementarity, 158
Composition, fallacy of, 111
Concentration, theory of, 196
Congestion, 231

Construction, 54, 416, 428, 689
  investment in, 414, 416, 434
Consumer Price Index, 695
Consumer protection, 58–59, 226–27
Consumer units, defined, 396
Consumption, 19, 323–26, 334–35, 599, 708
  as economic aim, 324
  national, 488
  technical term for, 334
Consumption demand, 396–411, 414, 418, 475–76, 479–80, 557–58
  income related to, 397–98, 400, 402–9, 421–22, 479, 704–5, 708
  individual vs. aggregate, 407
  passive, 408–9
  planning and, 676, 678
  public, 398–400, 447, 664
Consumption function (propensity to consume), 402–4, 421–22, 479
Consumption goods, defined, 12
Contraction, 572–73
Control-ownership separation, 28
Convergence of systems, 680, 682
Correlation analysis, 113–15, 687, 704–10
  correlation coefficients, 707–9
  multiple correlations, 708, 710
Cost push, 535
Costs, 263, 346–47, 536–41, 636, 702
  antipollution, 230–32
  under competition, 174–91, 193–97
    average, 183–91, 193, 196–97
    fixed and variable, 182–86, 193
    long-run, 196–97
    unit, 183–87, 189–90
  demand and, 147, 363–76
  of family assistance, 280
  foreign-trade, 592–93, 596, 598
  Gross National, 340, 478
  income relative to, 267, 295
  increasing, 383
    law, 175, 346, 590*n*
  of inflation, 537–41
  reduction of, 39
  rental, 251, 297–98
  transport, 240–41
  of unemployment, 468, 536–37, 541, 554
  wage, 50, 535
Council of Economic Advisers, 453, 711
Credit, 169, 408, 572, 613
  collapse of, 54
  tax, 295–96
Credit cards, 493
Credit crunches (squeezes), 428, 472, 528, 532, 619
Currency, 328, 493–94, 510–11
  reserve, 613, 614*n*

D

Data, *see* Statistical data
Debt, 501
Defense (wartime), 58, 133, 300, 561, 573, 599, 642, 668, 681
  as economic drain, 619, 624, 626
  employment in, 23
  expenditure on, 40, 41, 446–48
  as national budget item, 609–10
  obsolete weapons, 338
  as public good, 227–29
  wartime inflation, 49–50
Deficit spending, *see* Public debt

Demand, monetary, 371, 522–24
Demand and supply, 120, 130–31, 146–60
  competitive, 147, 177–78, 187
  direct and derived, 243–44
  legal intervention in, 277
  macroview of, 474–80, 484–85, 574–75
    automation, 564–65
    GNP demand curve, 475–76
    profits and, 390–92
    restoring demand level, 554–57
  medical-care, 263–64
  planning vs., 676–77
  redistribution affecting, 270, 277
  supply of growth, 348–52
Demand gap, 382–84, 415, 450–51
  above equilibrium, 478–79
  two ways of closing, 386
Demand pull, 535
Demography, 651–52
Denison, Edward F., 340, 354
Dependent variables, 109, 708, 710–11
Depreciation, 382, 431, 607
  accrued, 413
  cost of, 182, 368–74
Depressions, 40, 64, 115, 709
  consumption rate during, 398–401, 409
  recession vs., 52
Devaluation, 624–28, 636
Diagrams, 4; see also Scatter diagrams
Diminishing returns, law of, 172, 175, 184
Discounting future returns, 434–36
Discount rates, described, 507
Discrimination, see Race problem; Slums;
    Women—working
Diseconomies of scale, 197
Disinvestment, 325
Distribution, 13–14, 34–35, 339
  first-come, first-serve, 165
  of income, see Income distribution
  individual, 129, 131
  statistical, 687, 691–95
  total, 129
Disutility, labor, 244–45, 247
Dividends, corporate, 27, 430

E

Easterlin, Richard, 578
Ecology (environment), 58, 664
Econometrics, 113–15, 442, 686–715
Economic behavior, 120–24, 712
Economic development stages, 671–73, 677
Economic fallacies, 110–11, 483n
Economic frontier, defined, 356
Economic institutions, 8–28, 119, 661
  history of, 9–11
Economic malfunction, 43, 679
Economic mystique, 1–2
Economic planning, 577, 641, 661, 670–84
  central, 673–78
  national, 578–80, 582–83, 681
Economic policy, 515, 521, 566, 711
  for balanced growth, 577
  based on behavior, 124
  deflationary, 544–46, 549–50
  monetary and fiscal, 527–28, 531–32, 573,
    712
  multinational problems in, 637–38
  recession-causing, 573
  wage policy, 560
Economic profit, 168–69, 194

Economic rents (quasi rents), 194–96, 250–
    53, 255, 261, 264–65
  land rent vs., 250–51
  sources of, 195–96
Economic revolution, 46–47
Economic sectors, described, 16
Economic segregation, 238–39, 264–65
Economic theory, 3, 55–56, 196, 576
  of cycles, 571
  microtheory, 168
  three uses of, 123–25
Economic vocabulary, 2, 4, 107
  definitions problem, 688–89, 691
Economies of scale, 39, 196–97
Education (training), 36, 228, 229, 238, 342,
    436
  benefits of, 34, 231, 261, 266
  income redistributed via, 275–76
  job retraining, 559–60
  on-the-job, 268–71
  public, 11, 23, 41, 43, 133
  spending on, 447, 448
  Third World, 662, 668, 672
    foreign aid, 660
    literacy rate, 656, 669
Efficiency, 255, 280–83, 600, 675
  marginal, of investment, 435–36
  as planning problem, 677–78
  of production, 137, 359–60
Efficiency frontiers, 345–48
Effluent charges, 233–34, 240
Elasticity, price, 150–60, 162–63, 248–49
  tax dependent on, 291–93
  unit, 152–55
Employment, see Full employment; Income;
    Labor; Unemployment
Employment Act of 1946, 521, 566
Employment multiplier, 425–26
Employment services (labor exchanges),
    560, 561
Endogenous variables, 710–11
Energy crisis, 61–63, 158–60, 428, 579, 599,
    682
  Arab embargo causing, 3
  importing due to, 586
England, see Great Britain
"Entitlement," philosophy of, 43, 267
Entrepreneurship, 168–69, 179, 195, 269
Environment, 58, 664
Equalities, designations of, 106–7
Equations, 109–10, 704, 710
  quantity, 516–17
Equilibrium, 190, 193–95, 524–25, 639
  point of, 110, 138, 479, 483
  stationary, 375
  as tautology, 119–20
  unemployment, 521
Equilibrium GNP, 477–86
Equimarginal rule, 143, 145, 178–79
Equipment, 490–91, 656
  investment in, 415–16, 441
Equity, 280–81, 286–88, 383, 466
  tax, 299–300
Eurodollars, 619
Exchange, voluntary, 281–83
Exchange rates, 593, 605–14, 619, 623
  appreciation of, 607, 627
  fixed, 612–14, 627–30
  flexible, 625–26
  floating, see Floating rates
Exogenous variables, 710–12

Expansion process, 479–80
Expectations, 121–22, 662, 711
  failure of, 223–27
  inflationary, 224, 543–44
  investment, 225, 430–31
  See also Prediction
Expenditures, 294–95, 338, 369–76
  elasticity affecting, 154–55
  investment, 413–15
  money and, 517, 522–28
  public, 451–56, 473, 531
    expenditure flow, 443–47
  replacement, see Replacement
    investment
  saving offset by, 383–84
  sector, 371
  three streams of, 369–70
  See also Consumption demand; Costs;
    Tax expenditures
Exploitation, 253–56, 652–53
Export mechanism, 606
Export sector (net exports), 334–35, 437–39,
    488
  defined, 334, 437–38
Ex-post and ex-ante economics, 482–83,
    576n
Externalities, 229–35, 679
  control over, 229, 231–35
Exxon Corporation, 16, 462–63, 634–35

F

Factor costs, 364–66, 369–70
  national income at (Y), 374–75, 406–7
Factor mix, 170, 174
Factors of production, 168–79, 242–55,
    269–70, 362
  bidding for, 177–79
  emergence of, 45–47
  factor incomes, 253, 269, 292–93
  hiring of, 169–70, 176–77, 179, 188, 243,
    269
  market price for, 253–55
  number of, 13, 168, 171
  quantity theory of, 517
  tax impact on, 291–93
Fairness, 274, 278, 283
Farming, see Agriculture
Federal Deposit Insurance Corporation, 54
Federal Reserve Bank (New York), 622
Federal Reserve System, 495–99, 504–11,
    528, 532, 543, 619, 710–11
  independence of, 515
  regulatory function of, 42, 506, 527
Final goods, 323–24, 333–35
Financial demand, 522–23
Financial intermediaries, 383, 528
Fiscal drag, 456
Fishbowl regulation, 58
Floating rates, 625–30, 636
  "dirty," 628–30
Food, see Agriculture; Nutrition
Food stamps, 411, 452
Ford Motor Company, 39, 123, 162
  as multinational, 632–35, 642–43
Forecasting, 62–63, 120–23, 168, 543, 600
Foreign aid, 620, 656
  to Third World nations, 624, 629, 656–57,
    659, 669
Foreign exchange, 326, 328, 619–21, 657

Foreign trade, *see* Export sector; International trade
Foreign travel, 609–11, 619, 628, 638
Fourth World nations, 657–58, 660
Fractional reserve system, 496–97, 502
France, 47, 58, 360, 586, 613, 624, 627, 640–42, 669
  inflation in, 540, 546
  1962 government protest by, 640, 641
  planning system of, 681
  "takeover" of French industry, 633
Free riding, 228
Free trade, 594–96, 600–601
Friedman, Milton, 55–56, 531, 532, 550
Full employment, 554–55, 566–67, 579
  budget based on, 453–54, 456
  equilibrium under, 485–86
  Marxist theory of, 561
  prices related to, 517, 519–21
  trade policy allied to, 598
Functional relationships, 106–9, 407, 687, 702–5
  analysis of relationships, 704–5

G

Galbraith, John Kenneth, 56–58, 688, 689
Gallup polls, 700
General Electric (G.E.), 640, 641
General Motors (GM), 10, 56, 123, 328
  executive salaries at, 265
  as multinational, 633–35, 639
George, Henry, 253
Germany, 45, 58, 60, 69, 360, 613, 624, 627–30, 633, 645, 654, 681
  employment rate of, 68, 561
  German mark's strength, 627–28, 630
  GNP of, 359, 669
  inflation in, 540, 546
  MNCs in, 639, 640, 642
  Nazi, 287, 699
  professional women in, 267
Ghettos, 37, 55, 237–41, 297
Gini coefficients, 276
Goal-oriented economics, 124–25, 168
Gold, 326, 328, 571, 620–28
  flows of, 613, 622
  gold cover (standard), 511–12, 614
  1967–68 gold rush, 622–23
Goldwater, Barry, 300
Goods and services, 12–13, 338–39, 697
  balance of, 610
  competitive, 169, 243
  durable and nondurable, 398
  "free" goods, 156n
  government purchase of, 334, 445–46
  luxury and inferior, 109
  service-industry increase, 50–51
Gordon, David, 662–63
Gordon, Robert, 690
Goshen, Sir Harry, 450
Government (politics), 8–9, 326, 521–22
  aid programs of, 411, 452
  currency issued by, 493–94, 510–11
  cycles caused by, 573
  deflationary policy of, 544–46
  as economic institution, 14, 19, 22–23, 447–57, 491
    intersectoral relationships, 469–70
    public markets, 130–31, 133
    public ownership, 11–12

economy planned by, 479, 582–83
as employer of last resort, 560, 566–67
growth affecting, 29–30, 40–43, 60
measuring the size of, 691
policy made by, 125, 283
political decision-making, 241
socialist, 67–68
unemployment remedied by, 54–55, 560, 566–67
Government demand, 362–63, 443–60, 475–76
  demand manager, 443, 453–57
  federal vs. state and local, 446, 448, 456–57, 459–60
  fiscal demand policy, 450–51
  expansionist influence of, 51
  private vs., 436, 447, 449
  purchase demand, 334–35, 398–99, 488
    transfers vs., 444–45
Grants-in-aid, 290, 446, 448–49, 456–57, 459
Great Britain (U.K.), 46, 58, 69, 360, 546, 549, 561, 640–42, 669, 681
  British imperialism, 654
  crisis triggered by, 626
  in history, 46, 122, 352, 635, 656, 664, 674, 699
  London gold market, 622–23
  pound sterling of, 608, 612, 627
  trade relations of, 585, 586
  U.S. skyscraper financed in, 642
Great Depression (1930s), 54, 162, 398, 400–401, 407, 430, 485
  effects of, 43, 368–69, 519, 521, 532
  negative investment during, 417–18
  profile of, 54
  reserves increased during, 509, 527
  unemployment rate during, 553
Green revolution, 648n, 658
Gross national income, 372, 374–75, 476–78
  accounting for, 488–89
  under inflation, 537
  supply curve of, 476–77, 480
Gross national product, 30–34, 333–44, 359–61, 372–74, 412, 537–39
  comparative, 359–60, 688
  consumption dynamics of, 398–99, 418
  critique of, 335–40
  definitions of, 333, 373–74
    GNI as, 372, 537
  demand for, 363–67, 369–76
  determination of, 474–91
    net vs. gross, 490–91
  forecast for, 428, 712
  foreign trade affecting, 437–39, 596
  invention of, 520, 686
  as measuring device, 691–92
  multinationals exceeding, 634–35
  potentials, 574, 577
  predictable function of, 451–52
  real and current, 31, 33, 336–37
  Third World, 659, 660, 666, 668
  two measures of, 373–74
  unemployment tied to, 52–54, 555
Growth, 29–34, 60–64, 659–60, 671–72
  exponential, 32, 60–61
  full-employment, 555, 579
  long-run, 343, 355–57, 568–69, 573–80
  means of analyzing, 106, 698
  per-capita, 32–33, 343–44
  planning for, *see* Economic planning
  potential, 574, 577

problems arising from, 568–83
  balanced growth, 576–77
  growth gap, 576
  saving, investment, and, 387, 392
  supply of, 348–56
  zero, 63, 138
"Guest workers," 561
Gunther, John, 648–49

H

Hansen, Alvin, 649
Happiness-growth relationship, 578
Heat pollution, 62–63
Highways (roadways), 34, 228
Hong Kong textiles, 594–96, 658
Households, 29–30, 36, 117, 491, 689
  consumer demands of, 396–99
  as decision makers, 130–31
  as economic institutions, 18–22
Housing, 238, 342, 413
  construction of, 54, 416, 428, 434, 689
  homelessness, 647
  shortage of, 138, 139
Humphrey-Hawkins bill (1977), 566–67
Hyperinflations, 224, 537–38, 540, 550

I

IBM, 610, 633–35, 640
ICC, 57–58
Ideal types, 66–67
Identities, 497, 516–17, 576n
  savings and investment as, 482–83
  uses of, 106–7
Imperialism, 636, 652–54
Import mechanism, 605
Imports, *see* International trade
Incentives, work, 279
Income, 339, 363–70, 372–73, 575–78
  consumption related to, 397–98, 400, 402–9, 421–22, 479, 704–5, 708
  factor, 253, 269, 292–93
  foreign-investment, 619–20
  household, 362, 365, 402
    disposable personal, 397–98, 400
  imputed, 339
  inflation's effect on, 537–40
  means of analyzing, 106, 109, 692–94, 701, 704–5
    multiple analysis, 708
    real income, 696, 698
  national, 364–65, 374, 480–81, 488–91
    foreign trade boosting, 596, 601
  output growing to match, 575–77
  psychic, 245–46
  respent, *see* Multipliers
  sharing out of, 14, 25
  unemployment and, 556–57
  "voting," 133
Income distribution, 19–23, 36, 52, 54, 139, 242–88, 692–94, 701
  inequality of, 19, 294, 678–79
  initial, 137
  in practice, 259–73, 455
    inequalities, 267, 276, 286–88
  redistribution, 274–88, 466, 578
    programs, 270, 275–80
  theoretical, 242–58
  "unearned" incomes, 251
Income elasticities, 153

Income support, 164, 166
Income tax, 278–80, 290, 367–69, 390
   corporate, 258, 296, 299, 367–68
   federal reliance on, 444–45, 448–49, 470
   personal, 265, 293–96, 299, 397–98
Incomes policies, 549–50, 681
Income transfers, *see* Subsidies
Independent variables, 109, 708
Indeterminacy of behavior, 122–23
Indexing, 550; *see also* Price indexes
India, 586, 647–50, 657, 666–67, 669
   Chinese development vs., 672
   livestock inventory of, 329
   population forecast for, 650
Individualism, 9–12, 43
Individual preferences, 282–83, 287
Individual supply curves, 245
Indivisibility, 170
Industrial construction, 416
Industrial sector, 16–17
Infant-industries argument, 599
Inflation, 48–54, 115, 533–50, 561–62, 569, 577, 674, 681, 709
   causes of, 50, 52, 425, 531, 711
   characteristics of, 533–36
   chronic, 49, 51–52, 546
   control of, 165, 528, 532, 544, 549
   fear of, 539–40
   under full employment, 520–22
   global, 546–47
   GNP influenced by, 31–32
   as national problem, 129
   planning option for, 583
   relative rate of, 630
   statistics on, 690
   trade deterioration due to, 618
Information, 121, 225–27, 263
   from samples, 701–2
   social, 680
   three types of, 356
Injections, 481–82, 484–86
Input-output analysis, 378–79, 582, 673
Inputs, 33–34, 183, 348
   defined, 171
   productive, 345, 346
Insurance, 22, 40, 554
Interest, tax-exempt, 294–95
Interest costs, 13, 434, 437, 467
Interest rates, 248, 428, 507, 510, 522–28, 532, 705
   on bonds, 27, 435, 505, 523
   in capitalization, 252
   to cure deficit, 623–24
   decline in, 522, 527
   determination of, 525
   economic profit as, 168–69
   foreign, 611
   to motivate investment, 434–37, 441–42
Intermediate goods, 323, 365–66
Internal labor markets, 268–71
International Monetary Fund, 625
International monetary system, 604–13, 636
   crises in, 617–30
      August 1971, 613, 626–28
   short-term capital flows in, 621, 638
   speculative "flights" in, 611
   speculative raids on, 626, 628–29
International trade, 3–4, 166, 585–603, 636
   deterioration of, 617–18
   frictional problems of, 600
   as leakage, 424–25
   Third World, 585, 656–57, 668

Interpolation, defined, 109n
Intersectoral offsets, 384–87
Interstate Commerce Commission (ICC), 57–58
Inventions, 262, 556–59, 571
Inventories (inventory investment), 324–27, 414–15, 489, 572
   increases in, 374
   intended and unintended, 419, 482
Investment, 54, 380–95, 462n, 479–81, 572–77, 705, 711
   banking, 496, 504–6
   cycles of, 572–73
   defined, 412
   discouragement of, 468–69
   dysfunctional, 225–27
   foreign, 609–11, 620–21, 645
      development via private, 658–60
      direct, 633, 636–37
   gross private domestic, 334–35, 413–14, 417–18, 488
   in human capital, 275–77
   intended and unintended, 419, 581–82
   inventories as, 374, 414–15, 419
   investor profile, 387
   rate of return on, 262
   real and financial, 412–13
   technological boost to, 433–34, 558–59
   See also Savings—investment interacting with
Investment demand, 401–2, 412–28, 475–76
   capacity-generating, 574–76
   categories of, 413–16
   continuation of, 419–21
   reversals in, 398–99
Investment goods (capital goods), 324–26, 329, 357
   defined, 12
   gross and net, 324–25
Investment motivation, 429–42
   autonomous, 433–34, 436, 479–80
   induced, 431–34, 442, 482
Iran, 657

J

Jánossy, Ferenc, 352–53
Japan, 51, 408, 546, 561, 586, 613, 624, 629, 669
   currency revaluation in, 627
   growth rate of, 32
   hypothetical exchange with, 604–7
   labor policy of, 641
   national planning in, 582
   productivity of, 359–60, 618–19, 648
Jawboning, 544
Jevons, W. S., 571
Job Corps program, 559
Justice, 255, 269–70, 280–81; *see also* Equity; Fairness

K

Keyfitz, Nathan, 660
Keynes, John Maynard, 403, 433, 450, 482

L

Labor, 50, 243, 253–55, 270, 276–77
   as economic institution, 10, 11, 16–20
   government employees, 22–23
   working class, 20, 22, 35

elastic labor force, 552
   "exporting" of jobs, 639, 645
   hiring of, 195, 243
      recruitment, 169–76
   history of, 45–46
   during inflation, 538–39
   input-output analysis of, 378–79
   job conditions, 245–47, 342, 360, 641
      discrimination, 265
      exploitation, 253
      fringe benefits, 226, 245
      numbers of work hours, 245, 247, 293, 350–52, 552
   labor-market growth, 31, 33
   on-the-job training, 268–71
   self-employed, 37
   specialized, 588–89
   strikes staged by, 52, 678
   supply of, 244–47, 249, 348–57
      monetization of work, 350–51
      service sector, 353–54, 564–65
   Third World, 647, 650, 653
      saved labor, 654–56
   See also Income; Internal labor markets; Occupations; Participation rate; Unemployment; Wages
Labor exchanges, 560, 561
Labor unions, 29–30, 246, 674
   size of, 19, 40, 243
      accountability and, 58, 60
   union rates, 264, 272–73, 560
Land, 169–72, 540, 649, 663
   distribution theory of, 243, 248–52, 255
   hiring of, 169–70, 177, 243
   in premarket economy, 45–46
   public, 11, 326
   utilization of, 33
   See also Property ownership
Lange, Oskar, 68
Leakage curves, 484, 486
Leakages, 423–25, 450, 481–82, 484–85
   leakage ratio, 576
Least squares, 706–7
Leisure, 339, 352
Leninism, 674
Leontieff, Wassily, 378
Liabilities, 497, 591, 629
Liberman, E. G., 675
Libya, 642, 647, 656
Linear equations, 703–4
Liquidity, 496, 522–26
   defined, 27
   international, 613–14, 622, 625, 628
Liquidity preference, 523, 526–28
Literary Digest poll (1936), 701
Liu Shao-chi, 662
Living standards, 329, 344, 355, 375, 398, 600, 630
   based on appliances, 664
   comparative, 359–60
   farmers', 166
   measurement of, 698
   Third World, 647, 661, 662
Loans, 226, 383, 496, 501–4, 506
   defaulting on, 509
   Mideastern source of, 657
   processing of, 498–99
   reduction of, 528
   "soft," 659; *see also* Foreign aid
   See also Credit
Loopholes, *see* Tax expenditures
Lorenz curve, 276

Loss, 195, 277, 462, 490
   adjustment to, 192–93
   liability for, 25–27
Luck, 37, 195, 261–63
Lumpy investment, 225–27
Luxuries, 109, 270, 293, 411, 663, 679
   substitutes for, 156–57

M

Machines Bull, 640
Macroeconomics, 3, 321–583, 686, 712
   economic models, 363, 374–76
   in history, 343–44, 351–52, 400–2, 417–
      18, 443–47, 564, 568–71
   important problem of, 371
   micro- vs., 128–29, 322–23, 474–75
   public vs. private spheres of, 325–26,
      331–32, 436, 447
Management (executives), 247, 264–65, 413,
      653
   appointment of, 28
   chief-executive profile, 59
   entrepreneurial, 168–69, 179, 195, 269
   of money, 527–28
   Soviet, 673–75
Marginal capital-output ratio, 575–76, 660
Marginal disutility, 244–45
Marginal private and social costs, 230–31
Marginal productivity, 171–74, 184, 244,
      264, 266–70
   changing the, 274–77
   defined, 171
   zero, 260, 655
Marginal productivity theory, 254–55, 269–
      70, 520
   limits of, 259–63
Marginal propensity
   to consume, 404, 421–22, 479
   to save (mps), 421–24
Marginal revenue and cost, 174–79
   average and, 185–94
Marginal utilities, 107, 143–45
   equalizing the, 144–45
   of substitutes, 156, 157
Margins, defined, 54
Market system, 12–15, 30, 579, 674–77
   alternatives to, 661, 670–72
   capitalism as, 15, 66
   defined, 12
   division-of-the-market, 639–40
   historic rise of, 45–47
   importance of, 119
   planning and, 674–82
      critique, 676–79
   strengths of, 235
   two-market model, 129–31
   See also Imperialism; Microeconomics;
      Stock exchanges
Marshall, Alfred, 150
Marxist theory, 120, 253, 674
   of unemployment, 561
Mass production, 39, 354–55
Materials costs, 365–67
Matrix algebra, 379
Maximization, 136–37, 167–68
   meaning of, 122–23
   See also Equimarginal rule
Means, statistical, 692–93
Medians, 692–93
Medical care, 36, 297, 411, 455
   shift in demand for, 263–64

Mergers, corporate, 39–40
MEW (Measure of Economic Welfare), 340
Mexico, 632, 657, 658, 666, 667, 669
   population of, 650
Microeconomics, 3, 127–323, 474–75
   major problem in, 290
   of market imperfections, 168, 223–41,
      261, 263–70
      remedies, 226–29, 231–34
   more-is-better economics, 282
   of a moving market, 146–66
      limits to adjustment, 159–60
   private vs. public economics, 133, 241
   self-enforcing, 137
   two-market model of, 129–31
Middle class, 16, 19, 539, 660
   dollar limits of, 35
   as economic institution, 21–22
   middle-income bracket, 262–63
Military budget, *see* Defense
Millionaires, 22, 261–62, 298
Minimum wages, 264, 272–73, 277
Mobility, 248, 596–97
   of labor, 246, 276
   See also Transportation
Modes, statistical, 693–94
Monetarism, 526, 531–32, 543
Money, 1–2, 371, 492–532, 625
   defined, 493
   issuance of, 493–94, 510–11, 540
   real, 387
   tight vs. easy, 507n, 528, 572
   See also Capital; Currency; Eurodollars;
      Exchange rates; International
      monetary system; Petrodollars
Money supply, 493–96, 498–510, 512, 522–
      28, 711
   changes in, 506–10, 524–25
   demand and, 522–26
   expansion of, 499–505, 532, 550
   management of, 527–28
   quantity theory of, 516–22, 526, 543
Monopolies, 5, 167, 200, 503
   dissolution of, 56–57
   as market imperfection, 264
Multinational corporations, 611, 632–45,
      653–54
   described, 632–33
   political economics of, 639–43, 645
   takeover by foreign, 645
Multiple regression analysis, 708, 710
Multiplier accelerator interaction, 571–72
Multipliers, 418–26, 483–86, 508
   basic formula for, 421–24, 502, 575
   defined, 418
   downward, 424–26
   export, 439

N

Nader, Ralph, 60
National income and product accounts,
      374, 488–91
Nationalistic bias, 586–87, 598–99, 625
Nationalization, 58, 642
Natural constraints, 174, 175
Natural resources, *see* Resources
Necessities, 156–57, 293, 411
Negative income tax, 279
Negroes, *see* Race problem
Neighborhood effect, 239
Nestlé Chocolate, 610, 634

Net Economic Welfare (NEW), 340
Net exports, *See* Export sector
Net national product (NNP), 374–75, 490–91
Nevins, Allan, 39, 355
New Deal economics, 163, 443
New Economic Policy (NEP), 674
New York City, 250–51, 649
   mass transport in, 157
   1976 debt crisis in, 472–73
New York Stock Exchange, 27, 108
Normal (bell-shaped) curves, 356, 694
Nutrition (diet), 54, 411, 662
   famine relief, 659
   underdevelopment allied to, 651, 654–55,
      666
   See also Agriculture

O

Occupations, 18–19, 353–54
   income related to, 247, 261
   See also Labor
Oil, 225, 360, 459, 549, 582, 628, 637
   depletion of, 62, 158–59, 294
   multinational oil companies, 633–35
   OPEC squeeze on, 3, 629–30
   quotas on, 691n
   Third World, 647, 653, 657, 660
Okun, Arthur, 395, 555
Oligopolies, 155, 196, 296, 639, 643
   causing market failure, 225
OPEC (Organization of Petroleum
      Exporting Countries), 628–30, 657,
      659
   1973 crisis (embargo) created by, 3, 629–
      30
Open-market operations, 507–9
Opportunity costs, 245, 346–47, 434, 468,
      522
   foreign-trade, 592–93
Organization of Petroleum Exporting
      Countries, *see* OPEC
Output, 322–32, 343–79, 564–65, 654–56
   average, 171, 173
   under competition, 169, 171–73, 183–86,
      194, 677–78
      average cost per unit, 183–85
      marginal output, 186
      optimum output, 189–91
      scale of output, 196
   demand for, 361–79
      new output, 364–66
   flow of, 323–24, 326, 333–35
   growth of, 574–77, 659–60
      capital ratio, 575–76
   money vis-à-vis, 518–21
   public, 23, 325–26; *see also* Public goods
   saving the, 655–56
   supply of, 343–60
      comparative statistics, 359–60
   total, 171–73, 322, 326; *see also* GNP
   See also Circular flow; Production;
      Productivity
Overhead, defined, 186
Ownership, *see* Production—means of;
      Property ownership; Share
      ownership

P

Pan-national enterprises, 640–41, 643
Parameters, 704n, 712

Pareto Optimality, 281–83, 603
Participation rate, 18, 552, 681–82
    trends in, 348–52
Partnerships, 15, 25–27, 169
Patent rights, 200
PepsiCo, 632
Perlmutter, Harold, 634
Perverse market reactions, 224
Petrodollars, 629
Philips Lamp Works, 634–35
Phillips curve, 535–36, 541–43
Point elasticity, 153–54
Policy variables, 711
Politics, see Government
Pollution control, 42, 58, 62–64, 229–34,
        338, 428
    growth vs., 578
    heat pollution, 62–63
    methods of, 231–34
Population control, 138, 652, 661
Population density (congestion, explosion),
        231, 650–52, 660, 667; see also
        Census
Portugal, 634–35, 654
Poverty, 35–37, 69, 117, 339, 539, 688
    antipoverty strategies, 279–80, 411
    color of, 266
    decrease in, 36–37, 276–77
    feeling of, 578
    institutionalized, 19–20
    Third World, 647–49, 658, 660
    the working poor, 260, 279–80
Power, 653
    control of corporate, 56–60; see also
        Regulation
    natural sources of, see Energy crisis
Prediction, 62–63, 120–23, 168, 543, 660
    background information for, 121, 122
    consumer, 403, 407
    function of, 227
    for 1980, 428, 675
    of population, 650
    quantitative, 687, 710–12
    See also Expectations
Preference, see Individual preferences;
        Liquidity preference
Price controls, 165–66, 544–46
    fixed prices, 138–39
    price ceilings, 138, 166
    price freezes, 165, 166, 545
Price deflator, 337
Price indexes, 337, 517, 519, 687, 695–99,
        709
    application of, 698
    construction of, 695–96
    inflationary, 49–51, 115
    stock, 108
Price supports, 163–64
Prices, 31, 120–22, 134–66
    competitive, 176–79, 195, 520
        price of goods, 191–93
    distribution theory of, 248–51, 253–55
    equilibrium, 120, 135–36, 138–39, 146–49,
        195, 224
    agricultural, 163, 165–66
        described, 146
    factor market, 263–64
    foreign-exchange, 607, 612, 629
    formation of, 150
    GNP in, 336–37
    of government bonds, 505

inflationary, 224, 533–36, 540, 541, 547
international, 607, 612, 623–26
    of gold, 623, 624
    price squeeze, 629–30
    trading, 593–94
means of analyzing, 106, 108–10, 705
money vis-à-vis, 516–18, 520
"price signals," 234, 579, 630
price-system advantages, 137
sticky, 509–10
target, 164
    See also Assets; Costs; Elasticity
Private ownership, see Production—means
        of; Property ownership; Share
        ownership
Producer's welfare, 599–600
Production, 10–13, 47, 64, 588–92
    efficient, 137, 359–60
    "indirect," 601
    individual, 129, 131; see also
        Microeconomics
    means of, ownership of, 10, 11, 66, 674
    overproduction, 163, 576, 673
    overseas, see Multinational corporations
    purpose of, 338
    total, 129; see also Macroeconomics
    zero, 193
    See also Externalities; Factors of
        production; GNP; Goods and
        services; Mass production; NNP;
        Output
"Production associations," 676
Production-possibility (p.p.) curves, 344–48,
        475, 590–92; see also Efficiency
        frontiers
Production-possibility surface, 345–46
Productivity, 275–77, 351–57, 560
    foreign, 359–60, 618–19
        Third World, 648–49, 655, 659–60
    group, 268
    increasing, 34, 564, 630
        productivity curve, 171, 176
    marginal, see Marginal productivity
    service, 51, 351–52
    total and average, 171–73
Profits, 388–92, 429–31, 639
    under competition, 168–69, 178–79, 190–
        92, 194–96
    zero, 190, 194–95
    critique of, 391–92, 561
    as factor cost, 364
    inflationary, 535
    intramarginal, see Economic rents
    as success indicator, 675, 677–78
Profit-sharing stocks, 27
Progressive taxes, 278, 293–300
    loss of, 295–96
Project Independence, 599
Property ownership, 9–12, 66, 261, 303
    history of, 45–46
    income from, 22, 261, 294
Property taxes, 290, 297–99, 303–4
    incidence of, 298–99
Proportional tax system, 278, 299–300
Proprietorships, 15, 16, 26, 37, 169, 413
    described, 25
    proprietor's income, 538–39
Public debt (deficit spending), 446, 454,
        461–70, 521, 531
    national, 388, 465–70
    perpetual, 466–68

private vs., 462–69, 670
    internal vs. external, 465–69
Public goods, 227–29, 331–32, 678
Public sector, see Government
Purchasing power, defined, 362

Q

Quality-improvement committees, 337
Quantitative analysis, see Econometrics;
        Statistical data
Quantity equation, 516–19
Quantity theory, 516–22, 526, 543
Quasi rents, see Economic rents

R

R&D (research and development), 62, 579,
        640
    need for, 159, 200
Race problem, 237–38, 246, 653
    antidiscrimination practices, 276–78
    income tied to, 260, 263–66, 402
    poverty linked to, 20, 36, 266
    unemployment perpetuating, 53, 537,
        553–54
Random samples, 226, 701
Ratchet tendency, defined, 51
Rationality, assumption of, 167–68
Rationing, 134–40, 165, 401
    nonprice, 137–40
Receipts, elasticity affecting, 154–55; see
        also Profits
Recession approach, 545
Recessions, 40, 277, 351, 418, 424n, 571–73,
        711
    absence of, 375
    equilibrium changes with, 479
    government-induced, 573
    1974–1975, 472, 528, 553–54, 569, 573
    prevention of, 51, 450
    profits during, 431
    unemployment related to, 52–53, 553–54
Reference cycles, 570–71
Reference groups, 267–68
Regression, statistical, 687–704, 706–10
    running a regression, 706
Regressive taxes, 278, 293, 296–300
Regulation, 41–42, 57–58, 227
    environmental, 231–34, 240; see also
        Pollution control
    See also Rationing
Rents, 13, 182, 243, 250–54, 538–39
    as discriminatory tool, 264–65, 297
    as measurement, 338–39
    quasi-, see Economic rents
    rent control, 545
Replacement investment (expenditures),
        324–25, 382, 432, 558
    cost of, 368–70, 372
    in equipment, 415–16, 491
Reproduction rates, 651
Research and development, see R&D
Reservation prices, 136, 142–43
"Reserve army of the unemployed," 561,
        566
Reserves, 494–96, 501–9, 657
    creation of new, 506, 625
    excess, 498, 501, 502, 505, 508, 527
    reserve assets (SDRs), 613–14, 620, 625–
        26, 628

Reserves (cont.)
  reserve ratio, 494–95, 503, 507, 509
  reserve requirements, 506–7
  See also Federal Reserve System; Gold;
    Liquidity
Residential construction, 54, 416, 428, 689
Residuals, 169, 324n
Resources (raw materials), 647, 656–57, 663
  exhaustion of, *see* Energy crisis
  exploitation of, 652–53
  idle, 425–26, 521
  See also Ecology; Oil
Revenue, 187
  system of sharing, 456–57, 459
  See also Income; Marginal revenue and
    costs; Taxes and taxation
Riches, *see* Millionaires; Wealth
Roads (highways), 34, 228
Royal Dutch/Shell, 634–35, 640
Russia, *see* Soviet Union

S

S and D (supply and demand) curves, 106–
    10, 131, 139, 150–58, 164, 244
  antipollution, 232
  downward-sloping, 121, 523
  elastic and inelastic, 151–58, 291, 657
  foreign-exchange, 606–8
  for GNP, 475–77, 480, 485
  horizontal, 187–88
  inflationary, 224, 533–35
  for money, 522–25
  shifts in, 147–48
  upward-sloping, 109
  See also Supply curves
Salaries, *see* Wages
Sales, 153, 194, 464–65, 517
  ranking by assets or, 38
Sales tax, 290–91, 293, 299, 367
Sampling, 226, 687, 699–702
Samuelson, Paul, 21, 340
Saving fraction (mps), 421–24
Savings, 54, 380–95, 400–405, 421, 450–
    51, 480–83
  corporate, 258, 423–24
  gross vs. net, 381–82
  income from, 22
  intended and unintended, 481–82
  investment interacting with, 258, 380, 387,
    413–15, 450
    equilibrium and, 480–81
  as leakages, 423–24
  rate of, 303, 394–95, 407–9, 428, 659
  ratio of, to income, 401–5, 423
  real and monetary, 387
  savings deposits, 493, 495
  supply and allocation of, 248–49, 254
  thrift paradox, 483
Scale, economies of, 39, 196–97
Scarcities, *see* Shortages
Scatter diagrams, 405–6, 705–6
Schedules, 107–8, 120, 480; *see also* S and
    D curves; Supply curves
Securities, *see* Bonds; Investment; Share
    ownership; Stocks
Segregation, *see* Race problem; Slums
Self-interest, individual, 9
Self-sufficiency, economic, 598–99
Serfdom, 10, 11, 46, 47

Servan-Schreiber, Jean-Jacques, 633–34,
    640
Services, *see* Goods and services
Share ownership (shareholders), 26–28, 55–
    56, 169, 328, 412–13, 463n
  change affecting, 35–36
  GNP vs. stocks, 335
  by income class, 395
  to offset savings, 383
  organizational advantages of, 26–27
  See also Investment
Shortages (scarcities), 138–39, 159, 401,
    572, 629, 677
  agricultural, 165, 166
  of capital, 394, 428
  material meaning of, 345
  of space, 251
Singer Sewing Machine Company, 635
Single tax, 253
Skewness, 693–94
Skills, 55, 326–27, 559
Slavery, 10–12, 288, 327
Slums, 37, 55, 237–41, 297
  fiscal causes of, 237–39
  inner-city, improvement of, 560
Smith, Adam, *The Wealth of Nations*, 47, 600
Snowball effect, 418–19
Social class, 650; *see also* Labor; Middle
    class; Poverty; Race problem
Social indicators, 342
Socialism, 468, 680–82
  capitalism vs., 10, 66–68, 447
  defined, 66
  market, 68, 674–76
  See also Marxist theory
Social Security, 348, 446–47, 455
  allocation of, 40, 41, 388
  cost-of-living increase in, 538
Social Security (insurance) taxes, 290, 296–
    97, 299–300, 444, 448
Social welfare, *see* Welfare
Soviet Union (USSR), 9, 13, 45, 67, 288, 447,
    662
  female work force of, 267
  planned economy of, 582, 655, 671–74,
    680
Spaceship economy, 64
Space vs. land, 249–51, 297–98
Spanish GNP, 691–92
Special Drawing Rights (SDRs), 613, 625,
    628
Specialization, 588–90, 599, 653
Speculators, 538
Splicing, 698–99
Stabilizers, automatic, 452–53
Stalinism, 674
Standard of living, *see* Living standards
Statics, comparative, 107
Statistical data, 117–18, 122, 686–702
  on population, 650–51, 700
  techniques of collecting, 695–702, 705,
    706
  updating series of, 689–90, 698
  warnings about, 117, 688–92
  See also Econometrics; Information
Stock exchanges, 27–28
Stock market, 108, 709, 712
  business-investment effects of, 433
  fall of, 2, 54, 540
Stocks, 335; *see also* Investment; Share
    ownership

Stop-go effect, 546
Subsidies (transfers), 124, 139, 331, 388–91,
    397, 447–52
  agricultural, 162–66, 447–49
  antipollution, 234
  income redistributed via, 277–80
  loss due to, 490
  purchases vs., 444–45
  trade-adjustment, 603
  unemployment offset by 554
  See also Grants-in-aid; Social Security;
    Welfare
Substitution, demand, 156–60
Success indicators, 673–75, 677–78
Supply, *see* Demand and supply; Labor—
    supply of; Output—supply of; S
    and D curves
Supply curves, 107, 189–90, 193
  backward-bending, 245, 247
  defined, 189
  of factors, 177–78, 244–50, 253–54
  short-run, 297, 476–77
Support prices, 163–64
Surpluses, 136–39, 163–64, 629
  consumer's and producer's, 136–37, 145;
    see also Economic rents
  demand, 478, 479
  public, 395, 521, 528, 628
  surplus value, 253
Swedish GNP, 691–92
Sweezy, Paul M., 66, 68n

T

T (economic transactions), 517–19
T accounts, 497–500, 504–5
Takeovers, described, 28
Tariffs, 595–601, 603, 636
Tautologies, 119–20, 145, 246
Taxes and taxation, 133, 138, 289–304, 389–
    91, 430, 450–56, 708
  as costs, 366–73
    direct vs. indirect, 367, 369–71, 375
  on foreign securities, 621, 624
  income redistributed via, 277–79
  as leakages, 423
  local, 459–60
    federal vs. state and, 237, 290, 299
    metropolitan, 237–39, 473
  on multinationals, 638
  on oil, 629
  sales vs., 464–65
  savings offset by, 383
  single, 253
  tax burden (incidence), 290–93, 298–99
  tax cuts, 395, 455–57, 571, 573
  tax reform, 300, 304, 663
  tax-returns disclosure, 58
  as transfer payments, 389–90
  See also Effluent charges; Income tax
Tax expenditures (loopholes, deductions),
    278–79, 293–95, 299–300, 304
Tax integration, 296
Teamwork, 268
Technology, 50–51, 106, 270, 555–59, 579,
    663
  agricultural, 163–64
  control over, 42, 680–82
  growth due to, 34, 39, 355–57
  investment due to, 433–34, 558–59
  lack of, 229

Technology (cont.)
  of multinationals, 636, 637, 640
  raw materials for, 61–62
  substitutes through, 159–60
  unemployment due to, 555–57, 564–65
Tennessee Valley Authority (TVA), 58, 490
  560
Terms of world trade, 657
Third World (underdeveloped nations), 63,
  64, 353, 578, 585, 624, 646–72
  background history of, 646–49, 652–54
  development of, 654–64
  investment shifted away from, 636–37
  nationalization within, 642
  OPEC aid to, 629, 659
  political (leadership) struggle within, 654,
  663–64
  social problems of, 649–50, 656, 660–61,
  663–64
Thrift, *see* Savings
Time, 107, 157, 165, 480
Time deposits, *see* Savings
Time lags, 263–64, 543, 573
  in adopting policy, 454–55
  in spending, 426, 527
Tobin, James, 543
Tourism, *see* Foreign travel
Trade, *see* Business; Free trade; International trade; Market system
Trade Adjustment Act (1974 modification),
  603
Trade-off dilemma, 536
Trade-off relationships, 395, 590–91
Trade unions, *see* Labor unions
Tradition, 14, 45, 647–49, 661
Transactions costs, 226–27, 263
Transactions demand, 522–26
Transfers, *see* Subsidies; Unilateral transfers
Transition costs, 598
Transportation, 16, 17, 43, 159, 353, 681
  monetary crisis due to, 619
  urban, 239–41
  See also Automobiles and auto industry;
  Foreign travel
Transportation costs, 596, 636

U

Underdeveloped nations, *see* Third World
Unemployment, 5, 52–55, 346, 349, 401, 418,
  479, 520–22, 551–67
  causes of, 554–60

costs of, 468, 536–37, 541, 554
defined, 551–52
as downward multiplier, 425–26
European levels of, 68, 561–62
frictional, 560–61
hidden, 552
idle unemployed, 260, 425–26, 521
impact of, 553–54
inflation vs., 521, 535–37, 541–43, 545,
  547, 561–62, 577, 583
Latin American, 660
outlays for, 452
protection from increased, 600
remedies for, 54–55, 559–60
statistics on, 688–89
structural, 559–61
technological, 555–56, 559, 564–65
Unemployment insurance, 40, 554
UNESCO (economic) reports, 650
Unilateral transfers, 610
United States Steel (U.S. Steel), 38, 39, 508
Urban conditions, *see* Slums
Urbanization, 42–43
U-shaped curve, 184
USSR, *see* Soviet Union
Utilities, 11, 16, 17, 353, 434
  marginal, *see* Marginal utilities
  maximization of, 119, 122
  profit vs. 429–30

V

V (Velocity of circulation), 517–18
Values, ethical, 280–84, 286–88, 299–300,
  411
  social value tests, 284
  valueless price system, 137
  See also Fairness; Justice
Variable proportions, law of, 170–74, 184
Vertical inequities, 295
Vietnam (Indochinese) War, 546, 569, 610,
  624
  escalation of, 711, 712
  as imperialistic policy defeat, 654
Volkswagen, 240, 586, 633, 645
Volume growth, 31
Voting (suffrage), 228, 674

W

Wage contours, 267–68, 544–45
Wage discrimination, 265–67
Wage-price guidelines, 544

Wages, 13, 54, 245–46, 364, 636, 645, 705
  of foreign workers, 594–95
  for hours worked, 245
  inflation's effect on, 50–51, 535, 538
    wage controls, 544–46
  low, 260
  management's, *see* Economic profit
  mean, 262
  wage cuts, 509–10
  wage policy, 560
  See also Income; Minimum wages
Wartime, *see* Defense; Vietnam War; World
  War II
Wealth, 37, 322–32, 578, 708
  distribution of, 260–62, 286–87; *see also*
  Income distribution
  inflationary, 52
  institutionalized, 11, 20–22
  national, 326–29; *see also* GNP
  prices geared to, 137
  taxes on, 298, 303–4
  See also Assets; Capital; Millionaires
Weber, Max, 66
Weights, statistical, 689, 696–97
Welfare, 40, 54, 332, 411, 452, 538, 672
  defense spending vs., 446–48
  measurement of, 340, 342, 686
  See also Living standards; Social Security
Welfare argument, 599–601
Wharton School of Business (Philadelphia),
  710, 711
Women, 20, 36, 53, 260, 338–39, 692
  unemployment rate for, 553–54
  working, 18, 245, 348–51
    discrimination, 262–63, 266–67, 277
Workers, *see* Labor
Work incentives, 279
World War II, 399, 401, 405, 469, 545, 571,
  690
  enemy weapons estimated in, 699
  unemployment ended by, 553

Y

Y (national income at factor cost), 374–75,
  406–7
Yield, 505, 524
Yugoslavia, 68, 447, 561, 676

Z

Zero Population Growth (ZPG), 138, 652
Zero-sum games, 537–38, 638
Zoning, economics of, 238–39

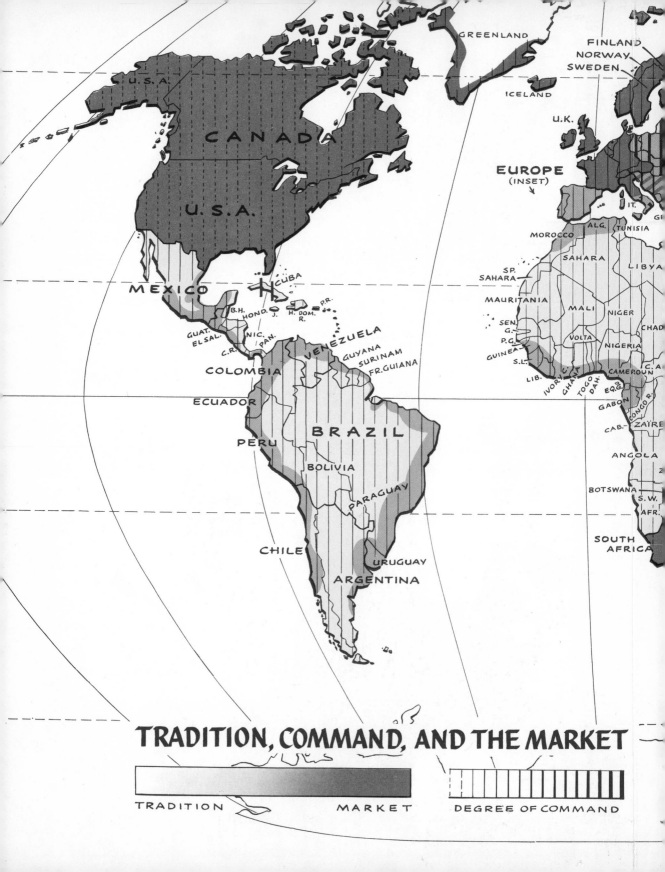

TRADITION, COMMAND, AND THE MARKET

TRADITION   MARKET   DEGREE OF COMMAND